KT-215-575

Around Unter den Linden
See pp56–71

North of the Centre
See pp100–115

East of the Centre
See pp88–99

North of the Centre

East of the Centre

Around Unter den Linden

Museum Island

Tiergarten

Kreuzberg

Kreuzberg
See pp140–149

Museum Island
See pp72–87

EYEWITNESS TRAVEL

BERLIN

Berlin Area by Area

Modern architecture by the former Checkpoint Charlie *(see p145)*

Greater Berlin

The Spree river passing by the Nikolaiviertel *(see pp90–91)*

Travellers' Needs

Survival Guide

Berliner Leber (veal or pork liver) *(see p229)*

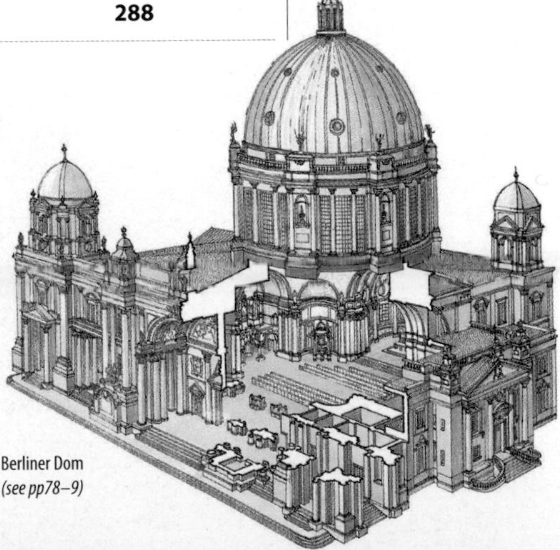

Berliner Dom *(see pp78–9)*

HOW TO USE THIS GUIDE

This Dorling Kindersley travel guide helps you to get the most from your visit to Berlin. It provides detailed practical information and expert recommendations. *Introducing Berlin* maps the city and the region, and sets it in its historical and cultural context, and describes events through the entire year. *Berlin at a Glance* is an overview of the city's main attractions. *Berlin Area by Area* starts on page 54. This is the main sightseeing section, which covers all of the important sights, with photographs, maps and illustrations. *Greater Berlin* covers the nearby historic city of Potsdam, as well as three walking tours. Information about hotels, restaurants, shops and markets, entertainment and sports is found in *Travellers' Needs*. The *Survival Guide* has advice on everything from using Berlin's medical services, telephones and post offices to the public transport system.

Berlin Area by Area

Each of eight sightseeing areas in Berlin is colour-coded for easy reference. Every chapter opens with an introduction to the area of the city it covers, describing its history and character, and has a *Street-by-Street* map illustrating typical parts of that area. Finding your way around the chapter is made simple by the numbering system used throughout. The most important sights are covered in detail in two or more full pages.

BERLIN AREA BY AREA | 57

AROUND UNTER DEN LINDEN

Colour-coding Each area has colour-coded tabs.

A locator map shows where you are in relation to other areas in the city centre.

Stars indicate the features that no visitor should miss.

1 Area map
For easy reference, the sights in each area are numbered and plotted on an area map. To help the visitor, this map also shows U- and S-Bahn stations, main bus and tram stops and parking areas. The area's key sights are listed by category, such as museums.

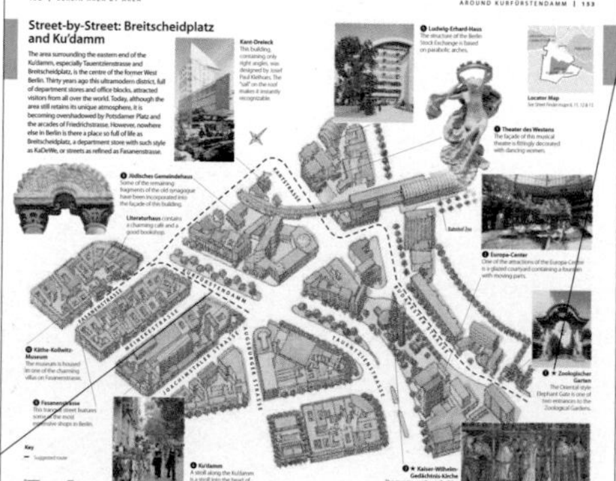

152 | BERLIN AREA BY AREA

AROUND KURFÜRSTENDAMM | 153

Street-by-Street: Breitscheidplatz and Ku'damm

A suggested route takes in some of the most interesting and attractive streets in the area.

2 Street-by-Street map
This gives a bird's-eye view of interesting and important parts of each sightseeing area. The numbering of the sights ties up with the area map and the fuller description of the entries on the pages that follow.

Berlin Area Map

The coloured areas shown on this map *(see inside front cover)* are the eight main sightseeing areas used in this guide. Each is covered in a full chapter in *Berlin Area by Area (see pp54–169)*. They are highlighted on other maps throughout the book. In *Berlin at a Glance*, for example, they help you locate the top sights. They are also used to help you find the position of three walks *(see pp209–215)*.

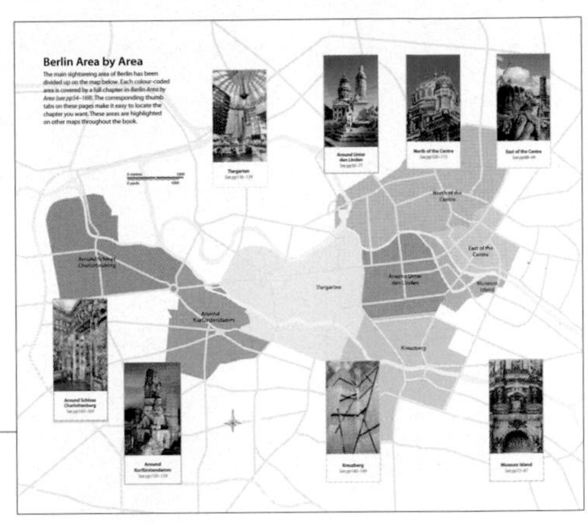

Practical information provides everything you need to know to visit each sight. Map references pinpoint the sight's location on the *Street Finder* map *(see pp300–323)*.

Numbers refer to each sight's position on the area map and its place in the chapter.

Story boxes provide information about historical or cultural topics relating to the sights.

3 Detailed information on each sight

All the important sights in Berlin are described individually. They are listed in order following the numbering on the area map at the start of the section. Practical information includes a map reference, opening hours and telephone numbers. The key to the symbols is on the back flap.

The Visitors' Checklist gives all the practical information needed to plan your visit.

The star sights recommend the places that no visitor should miss.

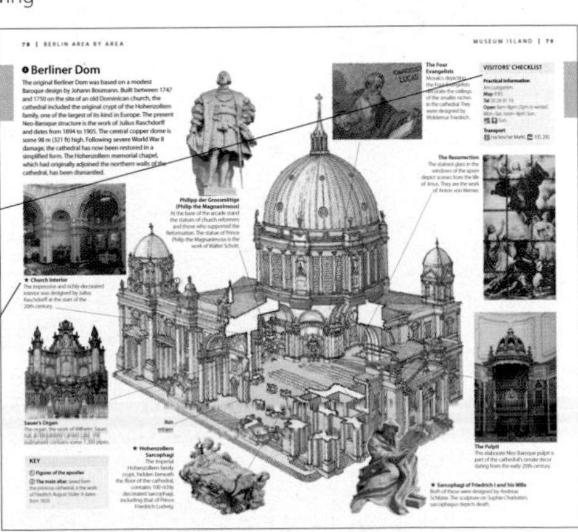

4 Berlin's major sights

Historic buildings are dissected to reveal their interiors; museums and galleries have colour-coded floorplans to help you find the most important exhibits.

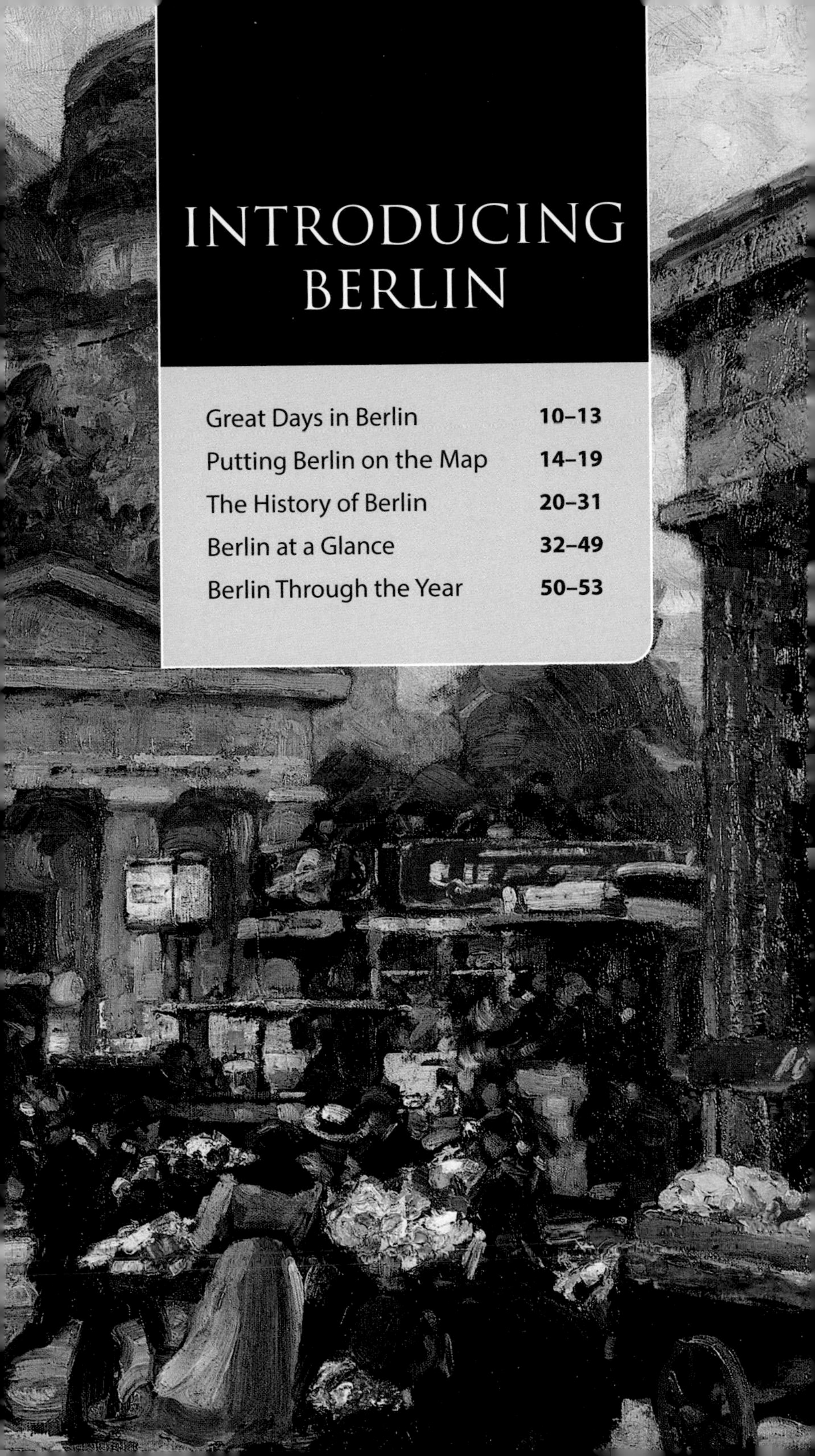

INTRODUCING BERLIN

GREAT DAYS IN BERLIN

Berlin is a city packed with treasures and wonderful things to see and do. Whether here for several days, or just wanting a flavour of this great city, you need to make the most of your time so that you can take in as much of the city as possible. Over the following pages, you'll find itineraries for some of the best of the city's attractions, arranged first by theme and then by length of stay. The price guides on pages 10–11 include travel, food and admission for two adults, while family prices are for two adults and two children.

History and Culture

Two adults
allow at least €95

- **See Brandenburger Tor**
- **Walk along Wilhelmstrasse**
- **Lunch at a brasserie**
- **Zeughaus/Museum Island**
- **Checkpoint Charlie**

People-watching from pavement tables, Kurfürstendamm

Morning

Start on the Unter den Linden at the city's most famous landmark, **Brandenburger Tor** *(see p69)*, one of the few remaining historic city gates. Walk south from the gate, past or across the Holocaust Memorial, to Wilhelmstrasse. The **Reich's Chancellery** and **Hitler's office** *(see p68)* were to your right at No. 77 Vossstrasse. Another grim reminder of Germany's Nazi past is round the corner. The **Topographie des Terrors** *(see p144)*, at the site of the former Gestapo and SS HQ, details crimes at the excavated torture cells. An original section of the Berlin Wall that used to run just behind the Neo-Renaissance **Martin-Gropius-Bau** building is nearby *(see p144)*. From here, walk back along Wilhelmstrasse to 39 Unter den Linden for lunch at the brasserie **Dressler** *(see p232)*.

The Rotunda gallery of the Altes Museum, Museum Island

Afternoon

Tour the German history exhibits at the **Zeughaus (Deutsches Historisches Museum)** *(see p60–61)*. Then head north along the canal to **Museum Island** *(see pp73–87)*, a world-class museum complex, and explore the **Neues Museum** or the **Pergamonmuseum** with its famous Isthar Gate from Babylon. Detour to Kreuzberg by walking south on Friedrich-strasse to **Checkpoint Charlie**, the former Allied border crossing, and visit the museum **Haus am Checkpoint Charlie** *(see p145)*.

A Family Day

Family of four
allow at least €220

- **Visit the zoo**
- **A quick self-service lunch**
- **Hands-on technology fun**
- **Studio tour at the Filmpark**

Morning

Start at the **Zoo Berlin** *(see p154)*, one of Germany's oldest and biggest zoos. Leave the zoo via the Hardenbergplatz exit and walk east towards the **Kaiser-Wilhelm-Gedächtnis-Kirche** on bustling Breitscheidplatz. Enjoy the jugglers and street artists on the square, then pop in to see the heavenly blue light in the church's modern section. Lunch at the Marché Mövenpick, set up like a street market on the elegant **Kurfürstendamm** *(see pp151–9)*

Afternoon

Catch a bus on Kurfürstendamm which will take you to the

◄ *Leipziger Platz* by Antoine Otto, c.1910

Deutsches Technikmuseum *(see p148)*, with its planes, vintage cars, trains, boats and hands-on experiments to try. Bus back to Zoologischer Garten and then take the S-Bahn to Potsdam-Babelsberg and its **Filmpark Babelsberg** for a tour of Germany's biggest studio complex *(see p207)*. Grab a simple dinner in Kreuzberg or Neukölln.

A Shopping Day

Two adults
allow at least €50 (cost of lunch and travel only)

- **Shop at KaDeWe**
- **Stroll to Savignyplatz**
- **Snack on the go**
- **Friedrichstadtpassagen chic**

Morning
Begin at **Kaufhaus des Westens**, called KaDeWe by Berliners, Europe's largest department store *(see p159)*. Then explore the Tauentzienstrasse, a popular, affordable shopping avenue, and continue on Kurfürstendamm – the further west you go, the more elegant the shops and boutiques. Take detours into even more chic side streets such as **Fasanen-**, **Meineke-**, **Uhland-**, **Bleibtreu-** and **Schlüterstrasse** as you head to **Savignyplatz** *(see p158)* with its many boutiques and eateries.

Afternoon
Take the S-Bahn from Savignyplatz towards the east and exit at

Gardens of Sanssouci palace, in Park Sanssouci

The impressive French department store, Galeries Lafayette

Friedrichstrasse. Walk north; once over Unter den Linden, you'll find the huge complexes of the **Friedrichstadtpassagen**, including the French **Galeries Lafayette** and the uber-luxurious **Quartier 206**, alongside top designers Gucci, Versace and Donna Karan. If not yet shopped out, walk back north on Friedrichstrasse and then east on Oranienburger Strasse to **Hackescher Markt**. This is a hip area of mostly alternative-style, young fashion, as well as clubs, bars and pubs.

Berlin Outdoors

Two adults
allow at least €90

- **A walk to Grunewald forest**
- **Boat trip to Pfaueninsel**
- **The Tiergarten**
- **Schloss Bellevue**

Morning
From the S-Bahn station Grunewald, walk south past interesting villas and museums (about 60 minutes) to **Jagdschloss Grunewald** *(see p214–15)*, a lovely hunting palace with an art gallery, past fine historic villas. Continue through the forest to **Wannsee lake** *(see p188)* for a swim and a sunbathe or walk back to the S-Bahn and get off at Wannsee station. Take a bus ride to the ferry for a walk on **Pfaueninsel**, a nature reserve *(see p210–11)*. After a walk around the island, take a break at the scenic Wirtshaus Zur Pfaueninsel beer garden at the ferry landing before taking the bus back to Wannsee S-Bahn station.

Afternoon
From Wannsee, take the S-Bahn to the green lung of Berlin, the vast **Tiergarten** *(see pp117–39)*. Follow the Strasse des 17. Juni east and climb the **Siegessäule** *(see p136–7)*, the victory column with a great view of the city. Follow Spreeweg to **Schloss Bellevue** *(see p137)*, the official Presidential seat. To finish, walk southwest to **Neuer See**, a pretty lake in the park. Rent a boat at the Café am Neuen See and return for supper.

2 Days in Berlin

- **Enjoy a bird's-eye view of the city from the Fernsehturm**
- **Stroll in leafy Tiergarten**
- **View a slice of history at Checkpoint Charlie**

Day 1

Morning Take a lift to the top of the **Fernsehturm** *(p95)* for panoramic views of Berlin. Then board bus 100 for a tour of the once-divided city; hop off at Lustgarten for the **Berliner Dom**, Berlin's most lavish church *(pp78–9)*, and **Museum Island** *(pp72–87)*, where you can see the stunning bust of Egyptian Queen Nefertiti in the **Neues Museum** *(p80)*.

Afternoon Continue by bus along **Unter den Linden** *(p62)* to Bundestag for the German parliament building, the **Reichstag** *(pp138–9)*, and iconic **Brandenburger Tor** *(p69)*, which once marked the city's western boundary. Nearby is **Tiergarten** *(p136)*, the city's largest central park, and **Kaiser-Wilhelm-Gedächtnis-Kirche** *(pp156–7)*, a monument to victims of World War II.

Day 2

Morning Begin at **Checkpoint Charlie** *(p145)*, the famous border crossing between former East and West Berlin. A section of the Berlin Wall survives on nearby Niederkirchnerstrasse, and a short walk away is the **Holocaust Denkmal** *(p69)*, a moving memorial to Berlin's Jews. End the morning with some shopping on **Friedrichstrasse** *(pp142–3)*.

Twin towers of the Gothic Marienkirche and futuristic Fernsehturm

Afternoon Cross the Spree over the Schleusenbrücke lock bridge to the **Nikolaiviertel** *(p92)* to discover the attractive **Nikolaikirche** *(p92)*, the Rococo **Ephraim-Palais** *(p93)* and the Gothic **Marienkirche** *(pp96–7)*. Round off the day at a bar in the old industrial courtyards of **Hackesche Höfe** *(p105)*.

3 Days in Berlin

- **Time travel through 750 years of Berlin history**
- **Explore the Kulturforum for some breathtaking art**

Day 1

Morning Take a stroll in the **Nikolaiviertel** *(p92)* on the banks of the Spree, stopping off to see exhibits on Berlin at the **Ephraim-Palais** *(p93)* and to visit the city's oldest parish church, the **Nikolaikirche** *(p92)*. Next, head north for **Marienkirche** *(pp96–7)*, with its impressive Neo-Gothic tower. Travel up to the top of the **Fernsehturm** *(p95)* for an impressive view of Berlin.

Afternoon After lunch, visit Berlin's Protestant cathedral, the **Berliner Dom** *(pp78–9)*, and continue on to **Museum Island** to see the **Pergamon-museum** *(pp82–5)* (note the Altar room is closed for renovations until 2019). Cross Schinkel's beautiful **Schlossbrücke** *(p76)* and walk the length of famous **Unter den Linden** *(p62)* to the **Brandenburger Tor** *(p69)*, the city's iconic gateway, and the **Reichstag** *(pp138–9)* – a potent symbol of reunified Germany. End the day at the **Holocaust Denkmal** *(p69)*, Germany's national Holocaust memorial.

Day 2

Morning Sample the city's two leading cultural centres. In lively **Potsdamer Platz** *(pp132–5)*, visit the entertaining **Filmmuseum Berlin** *(p132)*. There is so much on offer at the **Kulturforum** *(pp118–19)*; the superb **Gemäldegalerie** *(pp126–9)*, Berlin's largest art museum, boasts some of the finest European masterpieces. Have lunch at the café of the **Haus der Kulturen der Welt** *(p269)*.

Afternoon Explore the city's green lung, **Tiergarten** *(p136)*, and the nearby **Zoo Berlin** *(p154)*, which is great for both children and adults alike. End the day with a visit to the church-monument **Kaiser-Wilhelm-Gedächtnis-Kirche** *(pp156–7)* just south of the zoo.

Day 3

Morning Travel to Kochstrasse for Cold War nostalgia at **Haus am Checkpoint Charlie** *(p145)*. Visit the **Jüdisches Museum** *(pp144–5)* to learn about the history of Berlin's Jews, or visit the former nerve centre of the Nazi state, the **Topographie des Terrors** *(p144)*.

The exterior of the Neue Nationalgalerie in the Kulturforum

Afternoon Take a trip to **Schloss Charlottenburg** *(pp164–5)* and tour the state apartments. See decorative arts at the **Bröhan-Museum** *(p165)* and Picassos at the **Museum Berggruen** *(p168)* next door. Return to dine on the terraces around **Savignyplatz** *(p158)* in the evening.

5 Days in Berlin

- **Discover ancient treasures on Museum Island**
- **Tread In royalty's steps at Schloss Charlottenburg**
- **Escape the city on the waterfront at Wannsee**

Day 1

Morning Immerse yourself in art and history on **Museum Island** *(pp72– 87)*, selecting from the breathtaking array of galleries and museums here. Head on to **Bebelplatz** *(p64)*, an imposing architectural set piece celebrating Frederick the Great, whose statue stands guard outside. A little further south lies **Gendarmenmarkt** *(p66)*, Berlin's most beautiful square.

Afternoon Stroll down **Unter den Linden** *(p62)*, lined with restaurants and shops. Walk through the central arch of the **Brandenburger Tor** *(p69)*, and to Germany's restored parliament, the **Reichstag** *(pp138–9)*. Its dome was added by Sir Norman Foster in 1999. End with a visit to the **Holocaust Denkmal** *(p69)*, a memorial to Berlin's Jews.

Day 2

Morning Start at **Schloss Charlottenburg** *(pp164–5)*, to the west of the city, and tour the state rooms of King Frederick I and Queen Sophie Charlotte. Art lovers are spoiled for choice with the **Bröhan-Museum** *(p169)*, **Museum Berggruen** *(p168)* and **Museum Scharf-Gerstenberg** *(p168)* all nearby.

Afternoon While away a happy hour at the mouthwatering food hall of **KaDeWe** *(p159)*, and once sated visit the stunning Neo-Romanesque ruins of

The impressive architecture of the Sony Center, Potsdamer Platz

Kaiser-Wilhelm-Gedächtnis-Kirche *(pp156–7)*. Take a stroll down **Kurfürstendamm** *(pp152–9)*, the main artery through Berlin's west end, home to fashionable boutiques.

Day 3

Morning At **Bahnhof Friedrichstrasse** *(p71)*, take in the moving "Border Experiences" exhibition. Visit the famous **Checkpoint Charlie** *(p145)* border crossing, and watch docu-films on the Cold War era at **Haus am Checkpoint Charlie** *(p145)*. The nearby **Topographie des Terrors** *(p144)* and **Martin-Gropius-Bau** *(p144)* were both used by Nazi security services.

Afternoon Walk to the **Jüdisches Museum** *(pp146–7)*, which explores the history of Berlin's Jews, then take a break in the **Tiergarten** park *(p136)* and **Zoo Berlin** *(p154)*.

Day 4

Morning Take the S-Bahn to **Wannsee** *(pp188–9)* and stroll along the waterfront, or take a boat trip along the Havel. The more adventurous may fancy a dip in the lake. **Glienicker Brücke** *(p212)*, famous for featuring in the spy novels of John Le Carré, offers spectacular views.

Afternoon After lunch take a ferry to **Pfaueninsel's** *(p210)* ornamental gardens. In the evening head for **Prenzlauer Berg** *(p101)*, and enjoy lunch at one of the cafés on leafy **Kollwitzplatz** *(p107)*.

Day 5

Morning Head to the Gothic **Marienkirche** *(pp96–7)* to see the medieval fresco, *Dance of Death*. Be sure to view Berlin from above at the city's **Fernsehturm** TV tower *(p95)*, and wander the **Nikolaiviertel** area *(p92)*, stopping off to see the exhibition on Berlin's history in the city's oldest sacred building, the **Nikolaikirche** *(p92)*.

Afternoon Take the S-Bahn to **Potsdamer Platz** *(pp132–5)* to visit the **Filmmuseum Berlin** *(p132)* for the story of German cinema, and visit one of the museums at the **Kulturforum** *(pp118–19)*. The collection at the **Gemäldegalerie** *(pp126–9)* includes works by Titian, Vermeer, Holbein and Rubens, and is not to be missed. In the evening, relax in **Kreuzberg** *(pp140–49)*, Berlin's unofficial party quarter.

Statue of the poet Friedrich Schiller in front of the Deutscher Dom, Gendarmenmarkt

Putting Berlin on the Map

Berlin, the capital of the Federal Republic of Germany, has a population of approximately 3.4 million and covers 889 sq km (343 sq miles). Situated in the eastern part of the country, in the middle of the Brandenburg region, Berlin occupies the flatlands on the banks of the Havel and Spree rivers, which merge in the Spandau district. The whole city is criss-crossed with numerous canals.

For map symbols *see back flap*

Berlin and Environs
Oranienburg
Bernau
Hennigsdorf
Nauen
Falkensee
See next page
BERLIN
Potsdam
Berlin-Schönefeld
Werder
Königs Wusterhausen
Ludwigsfelde
DENMARK
Stralsund
Greifswald
Rostock
Lübeck
Wismar
Schwerin
Neubrandenburg
Neustrelitz
Lüneburg
Pritzwalk
Schwedt/Oder
Wittenberge
Uelzen
See inset map, right
Oranienburg
Stendal
BERLIN
Wolfsburg
Potsdam
Braunschweig
Magdeburg
Luckenwalde
Zielona Góra
Schönebeck
Lübbenau
Goslar
Lutherstadt Wittenberg
Cottbus
POLAND
Żary
Glogów
Nordhausen
Halle
Delitzsch
Hoyerswerda
Leipzig
Legnica
Mühlhausen
Naumburg
Döbeln
Bautzen
Görlitz
Wrocław
Erfurt
Weimar
Zeitz
Dresden
Gotha
Freiberg
Liberec
Wałbrzych
Gera
Chemnitz
Zwickau
Ústí nad Labem
Ilmenau
Annaberg-Buchholz
Hradec Králové
Coburg
Hof
Karlovy Vary
Kladno
Pardubice
Cheb
Prague
Kolín
Bayreuth
Bamberg
Plzeň
CZECH REPUBLIC
Erlangen
Weiden
Havlíčkův Brod
Nürnberg
Klatovy
Ansbach
Schwandorf
Jihlava
Tábor
Brno
Cham
České Budějovice
Regensburg
Straubing
Deggendorf
Ingolstadt
Passau
Landshut
Augsburg
Linz
Munich
Wels
Steyr
Gmunden
Kaufbeuren
Rosenheim
Salzburg
Kempten
AUSTRIA
Key
Berlin and environs
Ferry route
National border
Autobahn (motorway)
Dual carriageway
Major road
Railway
0 kilometres 100
0 miles 75

Greater Berlin

Berlin in its present form was created in 1920, through an amalgamation of several towns and villages surrounding the historic centre. It now consists of 12 administrative districts, some of which were formerly separate municipalities, such as Spandau. The city is surrounded by recreational areas, including lakes and woodlands. To the southwest lies the city of Potsdam, with its splendid palaces, which can be reached easily by public transport.

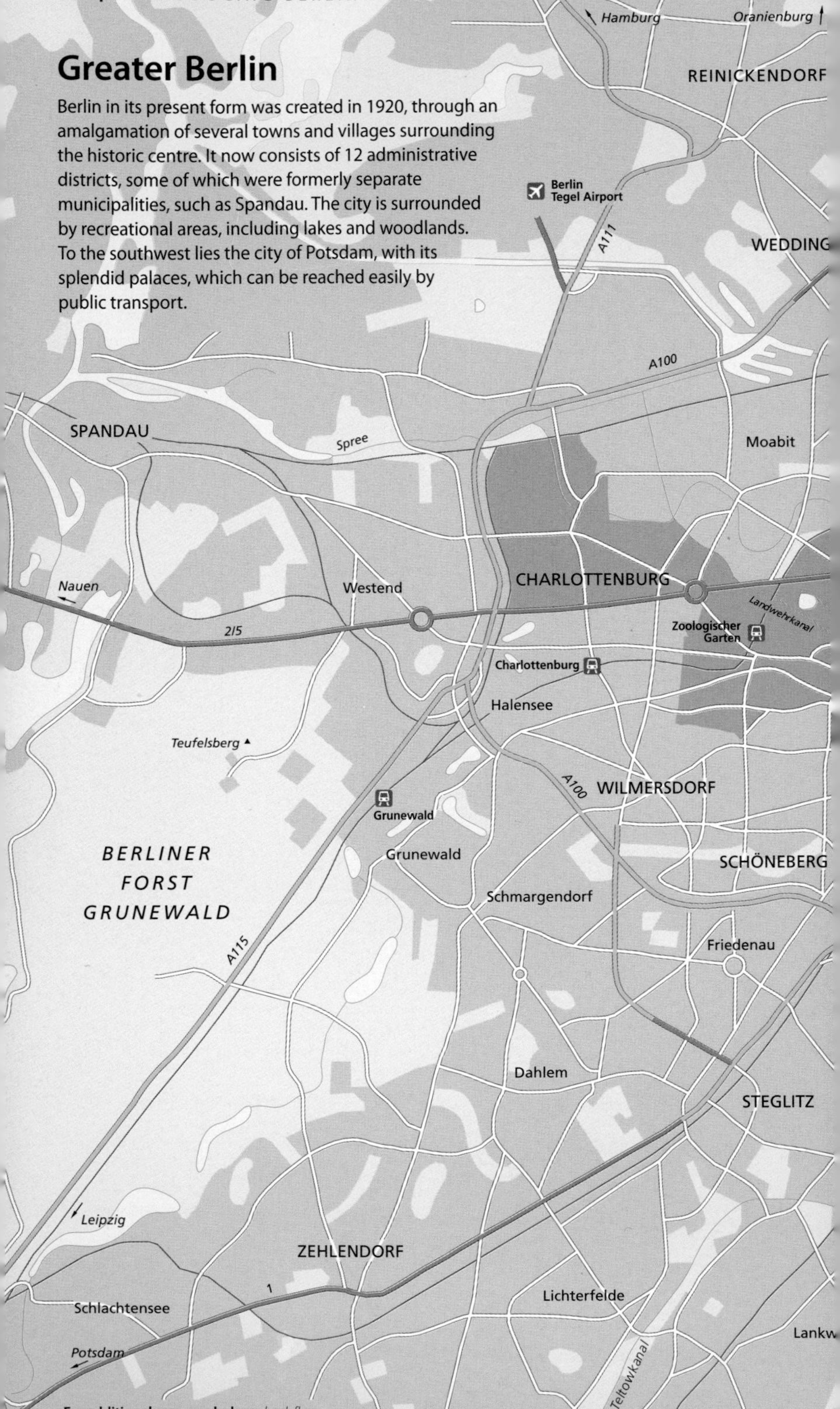

For additional map symbols *see back flap*

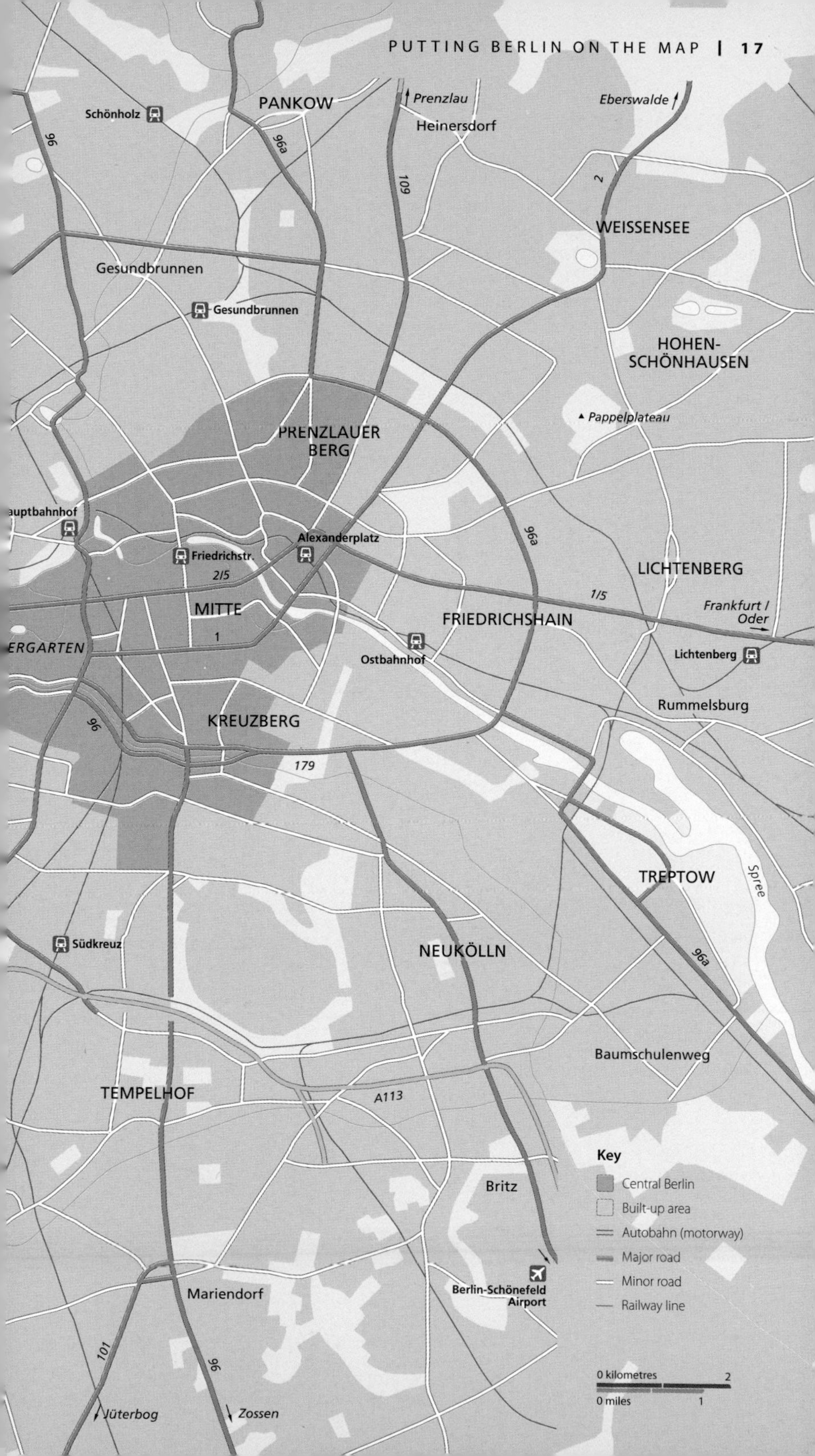

PANKOW
Schönholz
Prenzlau
Heinersdorf
Eberswalde
96
96a
109
2
WEISSENSEE
Gesundbrunnen
Gesundbrunnen
HOHEN-
SCHÖNHAUSEN
Pappelplateau
PRENZLAUER
BERG
auptbahnhof
Friedrichstr.
Alexanderplatz
96a
LICHTENBERG
2/5
1/5
Frankfurt /
Oder
MITTE
FRIEDRICHSHAIN
1
ERGARTEN
Ostbahnhof
Lichtenberg
Rummelsburg
96
KREUZBERG
179
TREPTOW
Spree
Südkreuz
NEUKÖLLN
96a
Baumschulenweg
TEMPELHOF
A113
Key
Central Berlin
Built-up area
Autobahn (motorway)
Major road
Minor road
Railway line
Britz
Berlin-Schönefeld
Airport
Mariendorf
101
96
0 kilometres
2
0 miles
1
Jüterbog
Zossen

Central Berlin

Central Berlin is divided here into eight colour-coded sightseeing areas. The historic core is located along the eastern and northern banks of the Spree river, around the grand boulevard Unter den Linden and on Museum Island. West of the centre is the sprawling green Tiergarten. To the south is Kreuzberg, an area renowned for its alternative lifestyle. Further west is Kurfürstendamm, the centre of former West Berlin. Finally, at the edge of the city centre is the summer residence of the Prussian kings, the Schloss Charlottenburg.

Around Schloss Charlottenburg

The Baroque Charlottenburg Palace, named after Sophie Charlotte (wife of Friedrich III), is one of Berlin's greatest tourist attractions. Its magnificent rooms contain many beautiful objects *(see pp160–69).*

Kulturforum, Tiergarten

The Kulturforum is a cluster of interesting museums and libraries. It is also the home of the Berlin Philharmonic *(see pp116–39).*

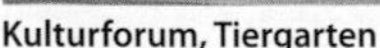

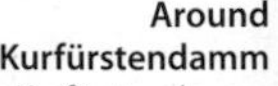

Around Kurfürstendamm

The Kurfürstendamm, or Ku'damm as it is often called, is the main thoroughfare of western Berlin. This area contains numerous shops, restaurants, bars and cinemas *(see pp150–59).*

Key

 Major sight

For keys to symbols *see back flap*

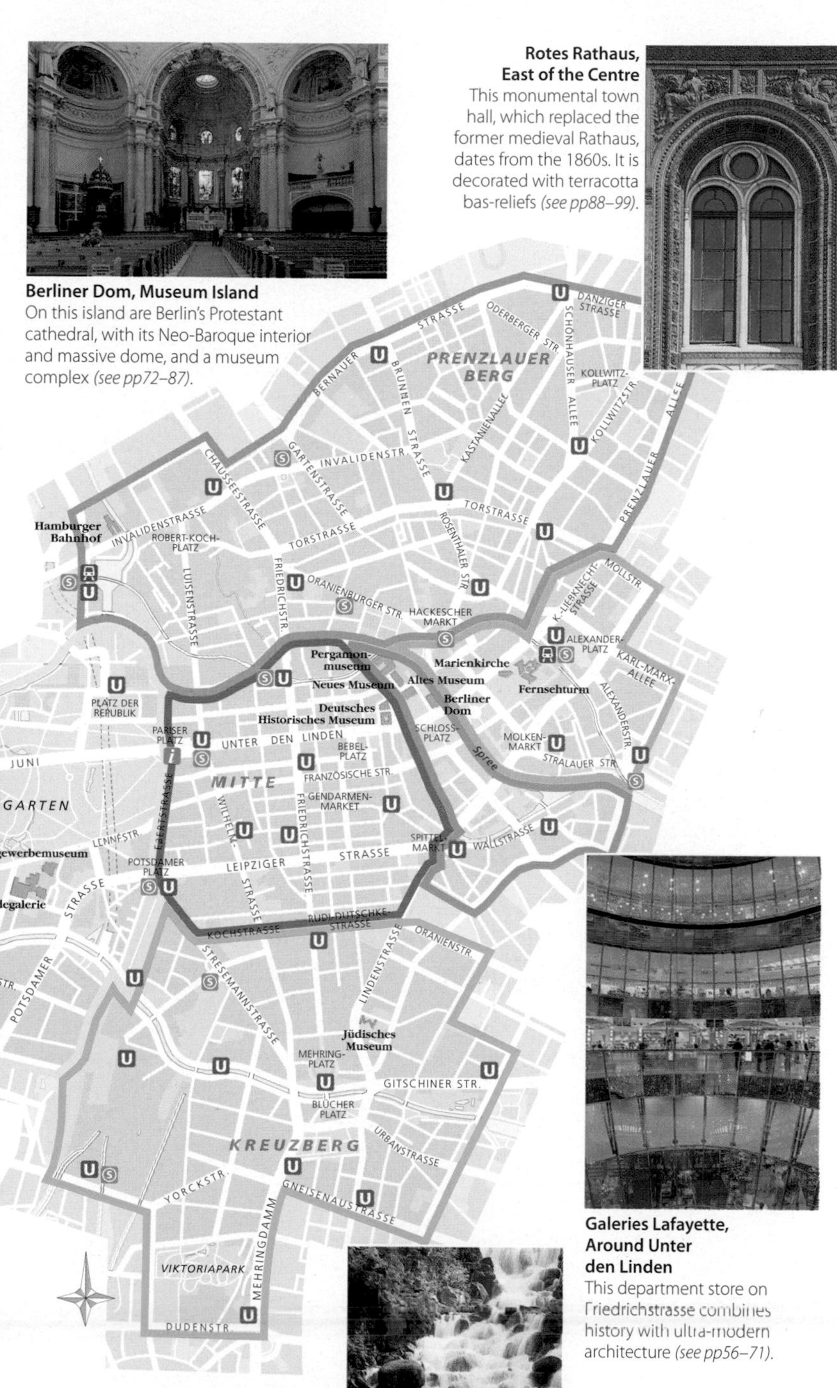

Berliner Dom, Museum Island
On this island are Berlin's Protestant cathedral, with its Neo-Baroque interior and massive dome, and a museum complex *(see pp72–87)*.

Rotes Rathaus, East of the Centre
This monumental town hall, which replaced the former medieval Rathaus, dates from the 1860s. It is decorated with terracotta bas-reliefs *(see pp88–99)*.

Galeries Lafayette, Around Unter den Linden
This department store on Friedrichstrasse combines history with ultra-modern architecture *(see pp56–71)*.

Viktoriapark, Kreuzberg
This park is situated on a hill in the Kreuzberg district, whose inhabitants include many Turks and eccentric artists *(see pp140–49)*.

0 metres 500
0 yards 500

THE HISTORY OF BERLIN

Berlin is one of the younger European capitals. The first written reference to the small fishing settlement of Cölln appeared in the year 1237. Together with the equally insignificant settlement of Berlin on the opposite bank of the Spree river, it was to become first a successful trading city under the control of the Margraves of Brandenburg, then capital of Prussia, and finally, the capital of Germany. Following World War II and the 1949 armistice, Berlin became a central arena for the Cold War. In 1991, after the fall of the Berlin Wall, the city became the capital of the newly united Federal Republic of Germany.

Early Settlements

During the first centuries AD the banks of the Spree and Havel rivers were inhabited by various tribes, most notably the Germanic Semnones. By the end of the 6th century the Semnones were competing for land with Slavic tribes, who built forts at what are now the Berlin suburbs of Köpenick *(see p183)* and Spandau *(see p177)*. Five hundred years later the Slavic tribes were finally defeated following the arrival of the warlike Saxon, Albrecht the Bear of the House of the Ascanians, who became the first *Markgraf* (Margrave, or Count) of Brandenburg. The banks of the Spree river were resettled with immigrants from areas to the west including the Harz mountains, the Rhine valley and Franconia.

Beginnings of the Modern City

Berlin's written history began in the early 13th century, when the twin settlements of Berlin and Cölln grew up on opposite banks of the Spree river, around what is now the Nikolaiviertel *(see p92)*. Trading in fish, rye and timber, the towns formed an alliance in 1307, becoming Berlin-Cölln, a deal celebrated by the construction of a joint town hall.

Following the death of the last Ascanian ruler in 1319, Brandenburg became the object of a long and bloody feud between the houses of Luxemburg and Wittelsbach, with devastating effects for the area's inhabitants. In 1411 the desperate townspeople appealed to the Holy Roman Emperor for help, receiving in response Friedrich von Hohenzollern as the town's special protector. In 1415, Rome duly rewarded Friedrich by naming him Elector of Brandenburg, a fateful appointment that marked the beginning of the 500-year rule of the House of Hohenzollern.

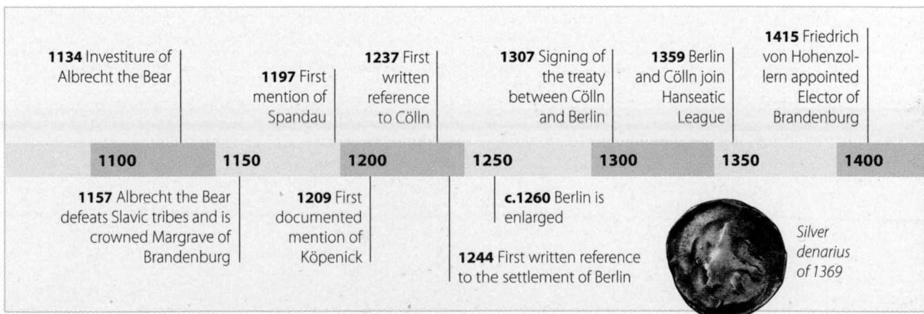
1134 Investiture of Albrecht the Bear
1197 First mention of Spandau
1237 First written reference to Cölln
1307 Signing of the treaty between Cölln and Berlin
1359 Berlin and Cölln join Hanseatic League
1415 Friedrich von Hohenzollern appointed Elector of Brandenburg
1100
1150
1200
1250
1300
1350
1400
1157 Albrecht the Bear defeats Slavic tribes and is crowned Margrave of Brandenburg
1209 First documented mention of Köpenick
1244 First written reference to the settlement of Berlin
c.1260 Berlin is enlarged

Silver denarius of 1369

◀ Adolf von Menzel's symbolic painting *Borussia*, or *Prussia* (1868), at the Ephraim-Palais

Deposition from the Cross (c.1520), a pane of a Gothic polyptych from the time of the Reformation

The Early Hohenzollerns

In 1432 Berlin and Cölln were formally unified. By 1443 Elector Friedrich II, son of Friedrich I, had begun construction of the town's first castle, the future Stadtschloss *(see p76)*. This was part of his plan to make Berlin-Cölln the capital of Brandenburg and to reduce the powers and privileges of its citizens. Despite fierce opposition from the local population, the castle was built. By 1448 all opposition had been violently crushed, and in 1451 the castle became the Elector's official residence. To symbolize the consolidation of Hohenzollern power, he added an iron chain and padlock around the neck of the city's heraldic bear. By the time Friedrich's nephew Johann Cicero became Elector in 1486, Berlin-Cölln was formally established as the capital of the March of Brandenburg.

Reformation and the Thirty Years' War

During the first half of the 16th century, the radical religious ideas of Martin Luther (1483–1546) spread quickly throughout the whole of Brandenburg. In 1539 the new Protestantism was adopted by the Elector, Joachim II Hector, and most of the town's aldermen.

For a time the city grew fast, boosted by the arrival of religious refugees from the Netherlands, as well as Italian artists invited by the subsequent elector, Joachim Georg. However, successive epidemics of the bubonic plague occurred in 1576, 1598 and 1600, checking the town's growth. The effect was compounded by the advent of the Thirty Years' War, which raged from 1618 to 1648, turning the whole of the Holy Roman Empire into a bloody battlefield. By 1627 the Elector of Brandenburg had fled, relocating his court to the less exposed town of Königsberg. By 1648 the population of Berlin-Cölln had fallen to just 6,000, its population being decimated by famine and disease.

Berlin Under the Great Elector

The fortunes of Berlin were turned by the arrival of Friedrich Wilhelm von Hohenzollern, who ascended the Brandenburg throne in 1640. Under the rule of this man, later known as the Great Elector, Berlin experienced a period of unprecedented growth. The city's population rose to 20,000 by 1688 at the end of Friedrich Wilhelm's

1415 · **1465** · **1515** · **1565**

1432 Unification of Cölln and Berlin

1442 Construction begins on the royal castle in Cölln

1447–8 Berlin rebellion against the Elector

1486 Elector Johann Cicero makes Berlin his permanent residence

1539 Elector Joachim II converts to the Protestant faith

1594 Building of the Spandau citadel completed

Tankard in the shape of Berlin's heraldic bear (1562)

The former Stadtschloss (Berlin Castle), with Lange Brücke in the foreground, c.1685

long reign. In 1648 work started on the modern fortification of the city. The Lustgarten *(see p76)* was established opposite the Stadtschloss, and the road later to become known as Unter den Linden *(see p62)* was planted with lime trees. The city's economic power increased following the building of the canal linking the Spree and Oder rivers, which turned Berlin into the hub of all Brandenburg trade.

Berlin began to expand in all directions with the creation of new satellite towns – first Friedrichswerder, then Dorotheenstadt and Friedrichstadt, all between 1650 and 1690. They would all be absorbed into a unified city of Berlin in 1709.

In 1671 several wealthy Jewish families expelled from Vienna settled in Berlin, while following the 1685 Edict of Potsdam, large numbers of French Huguenots flocked to Brandenburg, forced out of their homeland after Louis XIV repealed the Edict of Nantes. Both these events came to play a major role in the future development of the city.

The Capital of Prussia

The successor to the Great Elector, Friedrich III inherited the title in 1688. Thirteen years later he raised Brandenburg's status to that of a kingdom, and was crowned King Friedrich I of Prussia. Ambitious and with a taste for luxury, Friedrich became a powerful patron of the arts. Under his rule Berlin acquired its Academies of Fine Arts and Science. Artists transformed the castle into a Baroque palace. The Zeughaus *(see p60–61)* and the summer palace or Schloss in Lietzenburg, later renamed Charlottenburg *(seep164–5)*, were built at this time.

The next ruler of Prussia, Friedrich Wilhelm I (1713–40), was unlike his father and soon became known as the "Soldier-King". His initiatives were practical: Berlin was further expanded and encircled with a new wall, not for defence but as a measure against the desertion of conscripted citizens. Pariser Platz *(see p69)*, Leipziger Platz *(see p135)* and Mehringplatz *(see p148)* were all built at this time, and the population reached 90,000.

The next king was Friedrich II (1740–1786), otherwise known as Frederick the Great or "Alter Fritz" (Old Fritz). An educated man who appreciated art, he oversaw the city's transformation into a sophisticated cultural centre. He was also an aggressive empire builder, sparking the Seven Years' War of 1756–63 with his invasion of Silesia, during which Berlin was briefly occupied by Austrian and Russian troops. The city's development continued, however, and at the time of Friedrich II's death in 1786, its population numbered 150,000.

Friedrich II (1740–86)

1615 | **1665** | **1715** | **1765**

1618–48 Thirty Years' War

1668 Opening of the Spree-Oder canal

1685 Edict of Potsdam allows large numbers of French Huguenot refugees to settle in Berlin

1688 Establishment of the new town of Friedrichstadt

1696 Opening of the Academy of Fine Arts (Akademie der Künste)

1701 Coronation of Friedrich III as the first king of Prussia

1709 Unification of Berlin

1740 Coronation of Frederick the Great

1751–2 Friedrich II introduces conscription

1756–63 Seven Years' War

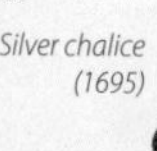

Silver chalice (1695)

The Baroque Period

Berlin's Baroque Period lasted from the second half of the 17th century to the end of the 18th, and saw the expansion of Berlin-Cölln from a small town, devastated by successive epidemics of bubonic plague and the ravages of the Thirty Years' War, into a rich and cosmopolitan metropolis. Population growth was rapid, aided by the official amalgamation of Berlin-Cölln with the previously independent communities of Dorotheenstadt, Friedrichstadt and Friedrichswerder. New city walls were built, as were many substantial buildings, including the Akademie der Künste, the Charité and Schloss Charlottenburg.

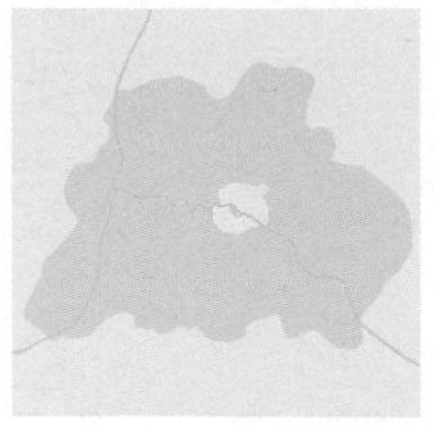

Extent of the City

1734 Today

Flute Concert

This painting by Adolf von Menzel shows the arts-loving King Friedrich II (1740–86) giving a flute recital for his guests in the music room of the Schloss Sanssouci.

Nikolaikirche

Frederick the Great

The famous French-born portrait painter, Antoine Pesne, created this portrait of Friedrich II of Prussia, heir to the Prussian throne, in 1739.

Rococo Tureen

This elaborate silver tureen, decorated with a gilded lemon, was made in the Berlin workshop of Georg Wilhelm Marggraf und Müller in 1765.

Stadtschloss (Royal Palace)

***Love in the Italian Theatre* (1714)**
French painter Jean-Antoine Watteau (1684–1721) was a favourite with King Friedrich II, and as a result many of his works can still be seen in Berlin.

Zeughaus (Former Arsenal)
The splendid Baroque Zeughaus was completed in 1730. Used to store weapons until 1875, it now houses the Deutsches Historisches Museum. This view of it was painted in 1786 by Carl Traugott Fechhelm.

King Friedrich I
This medallion bears the likeness of the first King of Prussia (1688–1713). The work of sculptor and architect Andreas Schlüter (1660–1714), it adorns the king's tomb.

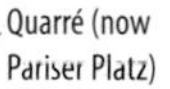

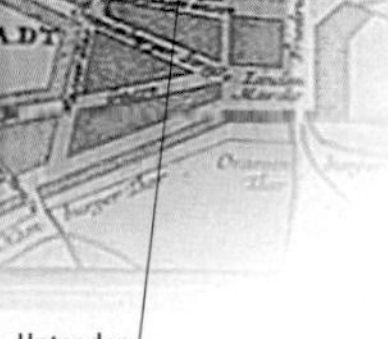

Berlin in 1740

This map shows the layout of the city's 18th-century fortifications, with various landmark buildings. Contrary to today's convention, this map was drawn with north pointing down, rather than up.

Baroque Architecture in Berlin

Many of Berlin's Baroque buildings have been destroyed, but in the city centre some fine examples still exist. Don't miss the Zeughaus *(see pp60–61)*, two fine churches in Gendarmenmarkt – the Deutscher Dom and the Französischer Dom *(see p66)* – the Parochialkirche *(see pp99)* and Sophienkirche *(see p106)*. Another Baroque highlight, even though it is largely a reconstruction, is Schloss Charlottenburg *(see pp164–5)* with its delightful park.

Schloss Charlottenburg

Antique scroll depicting the grand boulevard of Unter den Linden, 1821

Beginnings of the Modern Era

By the time Friedrich Wilhelm II (1786–97) ascended the throne of Prussia, the country's era of absolute rulers was nearing an end. New trends associated with Romanticism were gaining popularity, and there was an explosion of ideas from outstanding personalities such as writers Gotthold Ephraim Lessing (1729–81) and Friedrich and August-Wilhelm von Schlegel.

Throughout Europe, the French Emperor Napoleon Bonaparte (1769–1821) was waging war, defeating the Prussians in 1806 at the battles of Jena and Austerlitz. As French troops moved in to occupy Berlin, Friedrich Wilhelm took his court to Königsberg, while Berlin's pride, the horse-drawn chariot *(Quadriga)* crowning the Brandenburg Gate, was dismantled and taken to Paris.

By the end of 1809 the royal court had returned to Berlin and, having received huge reparations, Napoleon and his troops finally left the city. In 1814 the *Quadriga* was returned to Berlin, and a year later Napoleon was defeated at Waterloo. Granted the mineral-rich lands of the Rhineland and Westphalia at the subsequent Congress of Vienna, Prussia enjoyed rapid industrialization during the next 30 years, particularly in Berlin. By 1837 August Borsig had opened his locomotive factory in the city, and in 1838 the first train ran on the Berlin–Potsdam railway.

Many outstanding buildings were designed at this time by Karl Friedrich Schinkel *(see p181)*, including the Neue Wache *(see p62)* and the Schauspielhaus, renamed the Konzerthaus *(see p67)*. Berlin University (now Humboldt Universität) was established in 1810 and became a major seat of learning, attracting famous lecturers that included the philosophers Georg Hegel (1770–1831) and Arthur Schopenhauer (1788–1860).

In 1844, however, recession hit Europe, leaving a quarter of all Prussians in poverty. Hunger riots rocked the city in April 1847, and in 1848 Berlin saw a people's uprising in which over 250 demonstrators were shot dead by the Prussian army.

Portrait of Friedrich Wilhelm IV

Building an Empire

In 1861 Friedrich Wilhelm IV (1840–1861) was forced by madness to cede the throne to his brother Wilhelm (1861–1888).

1791 Building of the Brandenburg Gate completed

1799 Foundation of the Bauakademie

1810 Berlin University established

1831 Cholera epidemic breaks out

1844 Opening of the Berlin Zoo (Zoologischer Garten)

1785 | 1800 | 1815 | 1830 | 1845

Enamelled box, mid-18th century

1806 Beginning of the 2-year French occupation of Berlin

1830 Opening of the Altes Museum

1838 Opening of the Berlin–Potsdam railway line

Otto von Bismarck was soon appointed Chancellor, with a foreign policy to install Prussia in Austria's place at the head of all German-speaking states. In 1864 Prussia declared war on Denmark, and successfully acquired Schleswig-Holstein.

In 1866, following war with Austria, Prussia established dominance over the North German Confederation, an association of 22 states and free towns. In 1870 Prussia went to war with France, annexing the provinces of Alsace and Lorraine. Bismarck's next move was the proclamation of a German Empire on 18 January 1871, with Berlin as its capital and King Wilhelm I as Kaiser (Emperor). Thanks to the colossal reparations paid by France and the abolition of trade barriers, Berlin now entered another period of rapid industrial growth, accompanied by a population explosion. By 1877 Berlin's population had grown to one million; by 1905 it was two million.

II. KUNST-
AUSSTELLUNG
MAI-OCTOBER 1900.
BERLINER
SECESSION
KANTSTR. 12.
NEBEN DEM THEATER DES WESTENS
GEÖFFNET TÄGLICH v. 9-7 UHR
EINTRITTSPREIS 1 MK.

Poster advertising the Berlin Secession Exhibition of 1990, by Wilhelm Schulz

Triumph and Disaster

The late 19th century saw an explosion of scientific and cultural achievement, including the completion of a new sewage system in 1876, dramatically improving public health. By 1879 electric lamps lit the streets and in 1881 the first telephones were installed. A year later the first urban train line, the S-Bahn, was opened. Berlin's cultural and scientific life flourished, headed by such outstanding personalities as writer Theodor Fontane, painter Adolf von Menzel and bacteriologist Robert Koch. In 1898 Max Liebermann *(see p69)* founded the hugely influential Berlin Secessionist movement, with members including Käthe Kollwitz and Max Slevogt.

The Berlin Congress of 1878 by Anton von Werner

As the city prospered, political developments in Germany and throughout Europe were moving towards the stalemate of 1914. Initially, the outbreak of World War I had little effect on the life of Berlin, but the subsequent famine, strikes and total German defeat led to the November Revolution in 1918, and the abdication of Kaiser Wilhelm II.

1871 Berlin becomes the capital of the German Empire
1878 Berlin Congress takes place
1888 Year of three Kaisers
1902 Operation of the first underground train (U-Bahn)
1914 Outbreak of World War I
1860
1875
1890
1905
1920
1879 Technische Universität established
1882 Opening of the S-Bahn, the first urban train line
Mosaic by Martin-Gropius-Bau
1907 Completion of the Kaufhaus des Westens (KaDeWe)
1918 Abdication of Kaiser Wilhelm II

Capital of the German Empire

On 18 January 1871, Berlin became capital of the newly established German Empire, fulfilling the expansionist ambitions of the Prussian Chancellor Otto von Bismarck. Bringing together many previously independent German-speaking regions, the new Empire stretched beyond the borders of present-day Germany into what are now France, Poland, Russia and Denmark. Massive reparations paid by France after her defeat in the Franco-German war of 1870 stimulated the rapid growth of a fast-industrializing Berlin, accompanied by an explosion of scientific and artistic invention. Standing at just 300,000 in 1850, by 1900 the city's population had reached 1.9 million.

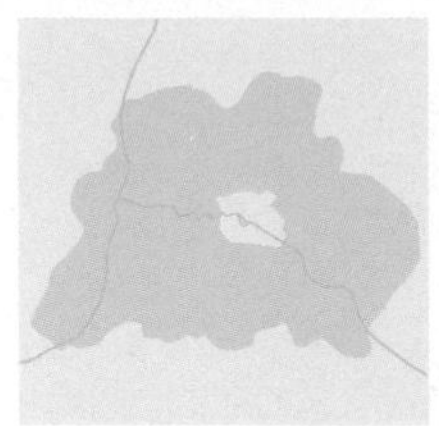

Extent of the City

1800 Today

The Stadtschloss
The Stadtschloss was the royal residence at the declaration of the Prussian Empire in 1871. Decorating the Rathausbrücke, in the foreground, was the magnificent statue of the Great Elector now in the courtyard of Schloss Charlottenburg *(see pp164–5)*.

House of Hohenzollern
Mosaics depicting the Hohenzollern rulers decorate the bombed remains of the Kaiser-Wilhelm-Gedächtnis-kirche *(see pp156–7)*, completed in 1895.

Prussian nobles

Members of Parliament

Riehmers Hofgarten
In the late 19th century a huge number of buildings were erected, from tenement blocks to grand buildings like this one.

Neptunbrunnen
This exuberant fountain *(see p94)*, created by sculptor Reinhold Begas in 1891, was a present to Wilhelm II from the Berlin town council.

Hackescher Markt Station
Formerly called Bahnhof Börse, this is one of Berlin's first S-Bahn stations, built to a design by Johannes Vollmer and opened in 1902.

Vase with Portrait of Wilhelm II
Designed by Alexander Kips and bearing a portrait of Kaiser Wilhelm II, this vase was mass-produced at the Berlin Königliche-Porzellan-Manufaktur. Pieces were often presented to visiting heads of state.

Empress Augusta Victoria

Heir to the throne, Wilhelm

Black mourning clothes for women and black armbands for men were obligatory after the deaths of the two Kaisers, Wilhelm I and Friedrich III, in 1888.

Diplomatic corps

Prussian Chancellor Otto von Bismarck

Kaiser Wilhelm II

Opening of the Reichstag

This enormous canvas, painted by Anton von Werner in 1893, portrays Kaiser Wilhelm II giving a speech to the Members of Parliament, nobles and other dignitaries at the official opening of the Reichstag. This important event took place only 11 days after the coronation of the new Kaiser.

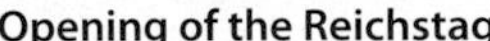

Portrait of Charlotte Berend in a White Dress
The arts flourished in the years before World War I. This 1902 portrait of an actress is by Berlin artist Lovis Corinth.

The burning of one of the thousands of buildings belonging to Jews on Kristallnacht, November 1938

The Weimar Republic

On 9 November 1918 two politicians simultaneously proclaimed the birth of two German Republics. Social democrat Philipp Scheidemann announced the founding of a Democratic Republic, while hours later Karl Liebknecht, founder of the German communist movement, declared the Free Socialist Republic of Germany. Rivalries between the two groups erupted in January 1919 in a week of rioting, crushed by the Freikorps army who also brutally murdered communist leaders Karl Liebknecht and Rosa Luxemburg.

In February 1919 the National Assembly elected Social Democrat Friedrich Ebert President of the German Republic. In 1920 urban reform dramatically increased the size of Berlin, causing the population to swell to 3.8 million. Berlin, like the rest of the country, fell on hard times, with rising unemployment and rampant hyperinflation.

At the same time, the city became the centre of a lively cultural life. Leading figures in theatre included Max Reinhardt and Bertolt Brecht, while from the UFA film studio came such classics as *The Cabinet of Dr Cagliari* and *Metropolis*. Jazz was popular, and the Berlin Philharmonic gained worldwide fame. Architecture flourished with Walter Gropius and Bruno Taut, while Berlin scientists Albert Einstein, Carl Bosch and Werner Heisenberg were all awarded the Nobel Prize.

The Third Reich

The world stock-market crash of October 1929 and the ensuing Depression put the fragile German democracy under great pressure, paving the way for extremist politicians. On 30 January 1933 Adolf Hitler was appointed Chancellor. The Reichstag fire in February was used as a pretext to arrest communist and liberal opponents, and by March 1933 Hitler's Nazi (National Socialist German Workers) Party was in control of the Reichstag. Books by "un-German" authors were burned, and works of art deemed as "degenerate" removed from museums. The 1936 Olympic Games in Berlin were meant as a showcase for Aryan supremacy. Although Germany won 33 gold medals, the real hero was the black US athlete Jesse Owens.

Ein Volk, ein Reich, ein Führer!

Nazi propaganda poster of Hitler, printed in 1938

The effects of the Nazi regime were felt particularly by Jews and intellectuals, many of whom were forced to emigrate. On the night of 9–10 November 1938, known as Kristallnacht (Night of the Broken Glass), thousands of

1919 Proclamation of the Weimar Republic

1920 Urban reform creates Greater Berlin

1926 The Funkturm (radio tower) is opened

1928 Premiere of *The Threepenny Opera* by Bertolt Brecht

1930 Opening of the Pergamonmuseum

1933 Hitler accedes to power

1938 Kristallnacht on the night of 9–10 November

1939 Outbreak of World War II on 1 September

1942 Wannsee Conference

Poster depicting the German race

1945 Germany surrenders on 8 May

24 June 1948–12 May 1949 Soviet blockade of Berlin

1961 Construction of the Berlin Wall on 13 August

1971 "Basic Treaty" allows travel from West to East Berlin

1920 | 1930 | 1940 | 1950 | 1960 | 1970

Historic buildings at the Gendarmenmarkt destroyed by British and American bombs, 1945–6

synagogues, cemeteries, Jewish homes and shops were looted and burned.

World War II

Hitler's invasion of Poland on 1 September 1939 signalled the start of World War II. For the citizens of Berlin, food shortages were followed in August 1940 by British air raids. By 1941 the government policy of the mass deportation of Jews to concentration camps had begun. Other groups targeted included homosexuals, priests and Romany gypsies. In January 1942, following a conference at Wannsee *(see p188)*, the systematic extermination of all European Jews began. The unsuccessful attempt to assassinate Hitler in 1944 led to Nazis murdering many members of the German resistance.

After nearly four years of bitter warfare, the tide began to turn against the Germans. In April 1945 more than 1.5 million Soviet soldiers invaded Berlin. On 30 April Hitler committed suicide, and Germany conceded defeat.

Berlin Divided

The Potsdam Conference of 1945 *(see p201)* divided Berlin into four sectors, occupied respectively by Soviet, US, British and French troops, putting the city at the centre of the Cold War. On 24 June 1948 the Soviet authorities, in their attempt to annex the whole city, introduced a blockade of its Western sectors. The Allies responded with the Berlin Airlift, which thwarted the Soviet plans. On 12 May 1949 the blockade was lifted. The same year saw the birth of the Federal Republic of Germany, with its capital in Bonn, and the German Democratic Republic (GDR), with the capital in East Berlin. West Berlin remained as a separate enclave. On 17 June 1953 workers' strikes in the GDR and East Berlin turned into an uprising which was bloodily crushed. In 1961, the GDR authorities surrounded West Berlin with a wall, and shot at any refugees attempting to cross it.

Reunification

The political changes which occurred all over Eastern Europe in 1989 led to the fall of the Berlin Wall. On 3 October 1990, Germany was officially reunified and Berlin once again became the capital. The government moved here in 1991. Today, Berlin's cutting-edge cultural scene in art, design, fashion, theatre, music and nightlife attracts visitors from all over the world to this buzzing capital city.

Celebrations as the Berlin Wall falls, 9 November 1989

1987 Celebration of Berlin's 750th anniversary
1990 Official reunification of Germany, 3 October
1991 Berlin becomes the German capital, 20 June
1994 Allies leave Berlin
2008 Opening of new US embassy on Pariser Platz marks complete restoration of the square
1980
1990
2000
2010
2020
1989 Fall of the Berlin Wall, 9 November
1999 The Federal German Parliament assembles at the rebuilt Reichstag in April
2004 Reopening of the Olympiastadion Berlin
2006 Berlin hosts the World Cup
2014 Germany wins the World Cup; celebration of the 25th anniversary of the fall of the Berlin Wall

Trabant – the most popular car in the GDR

BERLIN AT A GLANCE

More than 150 places of interest are described in the Area by Area section of this book. These include a range of sights from historic monuments, such as the Nikolaikirche *(see p92)*, to modern landmarks like the ambitious showcase architecture of the Potsdamer Platz district *(see pp132–5)*; from the peace of the Botanical Garden *(see p186)* to the noisier charms of Berlin's long-established zoo *(see p154)*. To help you make the most of your stay, the following 16 pages provide a time-saving guide to the very best that Berlin has to offer. Museums and galleries, historic buildings, parks and gardens, modern architecture, the legacy of the divided city and famous Berliners all feature in this section. Below is a selection of top ten attractions that no visitor should miss.

Berlin's Top Ten Attractions

Pergamonmuseum
See pp82–5.

Schloss Charlottenburg
See pp164–5.

Kunstgewerbemuseum
See pp122–5.

Gemäldegalerie
See pp126–9.

Nikolaiviertel
See pp90–91.

Zoo Berlin
See p154.

Fernsehturm
See p95.

Brandenburger Tor
See p69.

Reichstag
See pp138–9.

Kaiser-Wilhelm-Gedächtnis-Kirche
See pp156–7.

◀ Old master paintings at Gemaldegalerie at Kulturforum

Berlin's Best: Museums and Galleries

Berlin boasts some of the finest museum collections in the world. Since 1990 most of the collections previously split between East and West Berlin have been brought together in new venues. One example is the Gemäldegalerie collection, a magnificent collection of Old Master paintings. Berlin's major museum complexes are located on Museum Island, around Schloss Charlottenburg, at the Kulturforum and at Dahlem.

Kunstgewerbemuseum
The arts and crafts collection at the Kunstgewerbemuseum *(see pp122–5)* is among the most interesting in Europe. One of its many treasures is this 17th-century gold elephant-shaped vessel.

Gemäldegalerie
This world-famous collection illustrates the history of European painting from the 13th to the 18th centuries. Originally part of a triptych, *The Adoration of the Magi* (1470) was painted by Hugo van der Goes *(see pp126–9)*.

Museen Dahlem
This huge complex houses several museums devoted to ethnography, Asian art and European folk art and culture *(see p185)*.

Hamburger Bahnhof
Featuring artists such as Joseph Beuys and Andy Warhol, as well as the renowned Friedrich Christian Flick Collection, this art museum is housed in the former Hamburger railway station *(see pp114–15)*.

Pergamonmuseum
This museum owes its name to the reconstructed Pergamon Zeus Altar *(see pp82–5)*. Ongoing renovations mean the hall containing the Pergamon Altar will be closed until 2019.

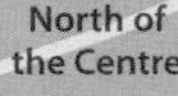

Altes Museum
The ground floor of Karl Friedrich Schinkel's Neo-Classical building has been used since 1998 to exhibit a collection of Greek and Roman antiquities *(see p77)*.

Deutsches Historisches Museum
The Baroque Zeughaus contains the Museum of German History. Everyday objects as well as works of art are used to illustrate historical events *(see pp60–61)*.

Jüdisches Museum
Berlin's Jewish museum was designed by Daniel Libeskind, an American architect of Jewish descent. The form of the building is based on the Star of David *(see pp146–7)*.

Deutsches Technikmuseum
The development of a range of industrial technologies, from locomotive-building to brewing, is illustrated in this entertaining museum *(see p148)*.

Exploring Berlin's Museums

Despite being damaged during World War II, Berlin's numerous museums are still among the finest, and the most heavily subsidized, in the world. Many collections were split up when the city was partitioned in 1946, and although the process of bringing them together again is almost complete, a few collections are still scattered around different sites, and many of the older museums are being refurbished.

Picasso's *Head of the Faun* (1937) in the Museum Berggruen

Ancient Art

The art of ancient Egypt is shown at the **Ägyptisches Museum** (Egyptian Museum). The jewel of this museum, which is housed in the **Neues Museum**, is the bust of Queen Nefertiti. The 19th-century **Altes Museum** contains a large Greek and Roman antiquities collection, as does the **Pergamonmuseum** – due to museum renovations there is no access to the Pergamon Zeus altar until 2019, but visitors can see several other reconstructed architectural wonders, including the Market Gate from Miletus and the huge Babylonian Ishtar Gate. There is also an impressive collection of Middle Eastern art.

The famous bust of Nefertiti, Neues Museum

Fine Art and Design

Berlin's largest collection of 13th- to 18th-century European painting is displayed in the **Gemäldegalerie** (Picture Gallery). Here are works by old masters including Dürer, Rembrandt, Titian, Botticelli and Caravaggio. In the same museum complex is the **Kupferstichkabinett**, with drawings and prints from the Middle Ages to the present.

Old masters can also be seen in the **Jagdschloss Grunewald**, a Renaissance palace home to German and Dutch paintings from the 14th to 19th centuries. A substantial collection of predominantly 17th-century paintings is housed in the **Bildergalerie** (Gallery of Paintings) in Potsdam. German and Italian sculpture is housed in the **Bode-Museum**, while the **Alte Nationalgalerie** (Old National Gallery) displays 18th- and 19th-century art, including paintings by the German Romantics, amongst which are famous landscapes by Caspar David Friedrich.

The **Neue Nationalgalerie**, closed for renovations until 2018, is filled with late 19th- and early 20th-century paintings and sculpture. Art Nouveau and Art Deco works are featured at the **Bröhan-Museum**, while works by modern greats, such as Pablo Picasso, Paul Klee and Georges Braque, are on show at the **Museum Berggruen** (Berggruen Museum).

The **Brücke-Museum** displays works from the German Expressionist movement by artists such as Ernst Ludwig Kirchner, Max Pechstein and Emil Nolde, and contemporary art is exhibited in the **Hamburger Bahnhof**.

Arts and crafts, from the Middle Ages to the present, are displayed at the **Kunstgewerbemuseum** (Museum of Applied Arts). The **Bauhaus-Archiv** displays applied arts from the influential interwar Bauhaus movement.

Other museums worthy of a visit include the **Newton-Sammlung**, which contains the life's work of the Berlin-born 20th-century photographer Helmut Newton, while the **Berlinische Galerie** showcases the city's collection of modern art and architecture.

Étienne Chevalier with St Stephen by Jean Fouquet, Gemäldegalerie

Non-European Art

Those interested in Asian art should visit the **Museen Dahlem**. This complex houses three large collections: the Museum für Asiatische Kunst (Museum of Asian Art), the **Ethnologisches Museum** (Museum of Ethnography), which explores the heritage of non-European nations, and the **Museum Europäischer Kulturen** (Museum for European Cultures). The **Museum für Islamische Kunst** (Museum of Islamic Art) is located in the same building as the Pergamonmuseum.

History

The collection housed at the **Deutsches Historisches Museum** (Museum of German History) traces German history from the Middle Ages to the present. The **Hugenottenmuseum** (Huguenot Museum), located in the tower of the Französischer Dom, charts the history of the city's Huguenots.

The **Centrum Judaicum** (Jewish Centre) in the Neue Synagogue (New Synagogue), and the **Jüdisches Museum** (Jewish Museum), in a striking building by Daniel Libeskind, are devoted to Jewish history and cultural heritage.

Berlin has several museums associated with World War II. The **Topographie des Terrors** (Topography of Terror) exhibition is displayed at the site of the former Gestapo and SS headquarters. A deeply shocking collection of documents concerning the Holocaust is kept at the **Haus der Wannsee-Konferenz**. The tools of terror used on the citizens of the German Democratic Republic can be seen at the **Stasi-Museum**, while the **Haus am Checkpoint Charlie** (House at Checkpoint Charlie) museum tells the stories of those who crossed the Berlin Wall. The **Alliiertenmuseum** focuses on life during the Cold War.

Technology and Natural History

The **Museum für Naturkunde** (Museum of Natural History) contains the world's biggest dinosaur skeleton. Also popular with visitors is the **Deutsches Technikmuseum** (German Technology Museum), which is situated in a large site around a former railway station. German movie history (including props, clips and original costumes worn by divas such as Marlene Dietrich) is presented at the **Filmmuseum Berlin**. Those interested in technology should also pay a visit to the **Museum für Kommunikation** (Museum of Communications).

Totem pole, Ethnologisches Museum

Specialist Subjects

Berlin is not short of specialist museums. There are museums devoted to laundry, sugar and even hemp. Lovers of theatre and literature can visit the one-time home of Bertolt Brecht (1898–1956), now the **Brecht-Weigel Gedenkstätte** (Brecht-Weigel Memorial). Worth a visit to marvel at the magnificent Wurlitzer organ alone is the **Musikinstrumenten-Museum** (Musical Instruments Museum). The outdoor **Domäne Dahlem** (Dahlem Farm Museum) displays three centuries of local farm life and exhibits old-fashioned tools.

Finding the Museums

A wide array of exhibits in the Musikinstrumenten-Museum

Berlin's Best: Historic Architecture

Berlin is a relatively new city. It expanded slowly until the first half of the 19th century, and then grew with increasing rapidity from around 1850 onwards. Although many of the city's finest architectural treasures were destroyed by World War II bombing, it is still possible to discover many interesting historic buildings (for more information, *see pp40–41*). In nearby Potsdam *(see pp192–207)* you can visit the splendid Schloss Sanssouci. Set in magnificent parkland, the palace was built for Friedrich II (1740–1786) and extended by subsequent rulers.

Schloss Charlottenburg
The construction of this Baroque royal palace at Charlottenburg was begun in 1695. Subsequent extension works took place throughout the 18th century *(see pp164–5)*.

Around Schloss Charlottenburg

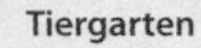

Around Kurfürstendamm

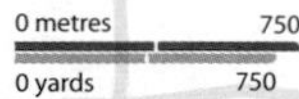

Schloss Bellevue
This Rococo palace by Michael Philipp Boumann is now the official residence of the President of the Federal Republic of Germany.

Schloss Sanssouci
This small palace was the favourite residence of Friedrich II.

Neues Palais
The Neues Palais combines elements of Baroque and Neo-Classical style.

Potsdam Palaces

The summer palace of Schloss Sanssouci gives its name to Potsdam's Park Sanssouci, a royal complex with highlights including the grand 18th-century Neues Palais and the small but charming Schloss Charlottenhof.

The Reichstag
This massive Neo-Renaissance building was designed in 1884 by Paul Wallot. Its elegant dome is the work of British architect Norman Foster *(see p138)*.

Zeughaus
This Baroque arsenal houses the Deutsches Historisches Museum *(see pp60–61)*. Its courtyard contains masks of dying warriors by sculptor Andreas Schlüter (1660–1714).

Marienkirche
This Gothic church, founded in the 13th century, contains a striking 15th-century mural. It is one of the city's oldest buildings *(see pp96–7)*.

Rotes Rathaus
Berlin's main Town Hall is named "red" after the colour of its brick exterior, not the political persuasion of the Mayor *(see p92)*.

Berliner Dom
This enormous cathedral, built between 1894 and 1905, is an example of the Neo-Renaissance style in Berlin *(see pp78–9)*.

Brandenburger Tor
This Neo-Classical gate stands at the end of Unter den Linden. Crowned by a *Quadriga* (chariot) driven by the Goddess of Victory, it is the symbol of Berlin *(see p69)*.

Konzerthaus
Built in 1820 to replace a theatre destroyed by fire, this beautiful building on the Gendarmenmarkt was designed by Karl Friedrich Schinkel *(see p67)*.

Exploring Berlin's Historic Architecture

Until the industrial revolution of the late 19th century, Berlin was little more than a small town surrounded by villages. As a result, the city's oldest buildings are concentrated in the central core around Unter den Linden and along the Spree river, an area which suffered heavy damage during World War II. Older country residences, however, as well as some important more recent buildings, can be seen in former villages such as Wedding and Charlottenburg, which now form part of Greater Berlin.

14th-century Gothic doorway of the Nikolaikirche in the Nikolaiviertel

Middle Ages and Renaissance

The **Nikolaikirche** is the oldest building in central Berlin. The base of its massive front tower is Romanesque and dates back to about 1230, although the church itself is Gothic and was built between 1380 and 1450. The second Gothic church in the city centre is the **Marienkirche**. Nearby are the ruins of a **Franciscan friary** and the **Heiliggeistkapelle**. Many medieval churches outside the city centre have survived the war. Among the most beautiful is the late Gothic **St-Nikolai-Kirche** in Spandau, dating from the early 15th century. A further ten village churches, most dating from the 13th century, can be found hidden among high-rise apartment buildings. **St Annen-Kirche** in Dahlem, however, still enjoys an almost rural setting.

The few surviving secular structures include fragments of the **city walls** in the city centre, and the **Juliusturm** in Spandau, a huge, early 13th-century tower which stands in the grounds of the Spandau Citadel. Berlin's only surviving Renaissance buildings are the **Ribbeckhaus** with its four picturesque gables, the **Jagdschloss-Grunewald**, a modest hunting lodge designed by Casper Theyss in 1542, and the **Spandau Citadel** (or fortress), a well-preserved example of Italian-style military defence architecture. Finished in 1592, the construction of the Citadel was begun in 1560 by Christoph Römer using plans by Italian architect Francesco Chiaramella da Gandino. It was brought to completion by Rochus Guerrini Graf zu Lynar (the Count of Lynar).

Detail of the Zeughaus

Renaissance-style defence, the Citadel building at Spandau

Baroque Expansion

The Thirty Years' War (1618–48) put a temporary stop to the town's development, and it was not until the Peace of 1648 that new building work in the Baroque style began. One of the first of the city's Baroque buildings is the late-17th-century **Schloss Köpenick**. More buildings followed, many of which survive today. They include the **Parochialkirche**, the **Deutscher Dom** and the **Französischer Dom**, as well as the magnificent **Zeughaus**, built between 1695 and 1730. During this period Andreas Schlüter (1664–1714) designed the now-demolished Stadtschloss (Royal Palace), while Johann Arnold Nering (1659–95) designed **Schloss Charlottenburg**. Other surviving Baroque palaces include **Palais Podewils** and **Schloss Schönhausen**.

One of the few buildings dating from the reign of Friedrich Wilhelm I (1713–40) is the **Kollegienhaus** at Lindenstrasse No. 14, designed by Philipp Gerlach and built in 1733. During the reign of Friedrich II (1740–86), many buildings were erected in the late Baroque and Rococo styles. These include **Schloss Sanssouci** in Potsdam and the **Alte Bibliothek** building on Unter den Linden, which completed the Forum Fridericianum project, now better known as Bebelplatz *(see pp58–9)*.

Neo-Classicism and Romanticism

The Neo-Classical architecture of the late 18th and early 19th centuries has given Berlin much of its basic form. One dominant figure of this period was Carl Gotthard Langhans (1732–1808), creator of the **Brandenburg Gate** and of **Schloss Bellevue**. Even more influential, however, was Karl Friedrich Schinkel *(see p181)*.

His work includes some of Berlin's most important public buildings, including the **Neue Wache**, the **Altes Museum** and the **Konzerthaus**. Many of Schinkel's residential commissions are also still standing, with some, such as **Schloss Klein Glienicke** and **Schloss Tegel**, open to the public. Schinkel's Neo-Gothic work includes **Schloss Babelsberg** and the **Friedrichswerdersche Kirche**.

Elegant Neo-Classicism at Karl Friedrich Schinkel's Schloss Klein Glienicke

Industrialization and the Modern Age

The second half of the 19th century was a time of rapid development for Berlin. After Schinkel's death, his work was continued by his students Ludwig Persius (1803–45) and Friedrich August Stüler (1800–65). Stüler designed the Neo-Classical **Alte Nationalgalerie** between 1866 and 1876.

Some splendid Neo-Romanesque and Neo-Gothic churches and several notable public buildings in various styles were also produced at this time. The spirit of the Italian Neo-Renaissance is seen in the **Rotes Rathaus** designed by Hermann Friedrich Waesemann, and in the **Martin-Gropius-Bau**, of 1877 by Martin Gropius. Late Neo-Renaissance features are used in Paul Wallot's **Reichstag** building and in Ernst von Ihne's **Staatsbibliothek** building. Julius Raschdorff's **Berliner Dom** shows Neo-Baroque influences. Much of the religious architecture of the period continued in the Neo-Gothic style, while Franz Schwechten designed the **Kaiser-Wilhelm-Gedächtnis-Kirche** in the Neo-Romanesque style. Many structures of this period are built in the Modernist style inspired by the Industrial Revolution, the textbook example being the huge power station, **AEG-Turbinenhalle**, designed by Peter Behrens in the 1890s.

Decorative frieze on the Martin-Gropius-Bau

20th-century Neo-Renaissance detail of the massive Berliner Dom

Between the Two World Wars

The greatest architectural achievements of this period include a number of splendid housing estates, such as the **Hufeisensiedlung** designed by Bruno Taut and Martin Wagner in 1924, and **Onkel-Toms-Hütte** in Zehlendorf. An interesting example of the Expressionist style is Erich Mendelsohn's **Einsteinturm** in Potsdam. Art Deco is represented by Hans Poelzig's **Haus des Rundfunks**, the country's first Broadcasting House. Hitler's rise to power in the 1930s marked a return to the classical forms that were to dominate German architecture of the Fascist period. Representatives of this period include the **Tempelhof Airport** Terminal building and the **Olympia-Stadion**, built for the 1936 Olympic Games.

Historic Buildings

Reminders of the Divided City

In 1945, as part of the post-war peace, Berlin was divided into four zones of occupation: Soviet, American, British and French. Hostilities erupted in June 1948, when the Soviets blockaded West Berlin in an attempt to bring the area under their control. The ensuing year-long standoff marked the start of the Cold War. By the 1950s, economic problems in the East had led to bloodily-suppressed riots and a mass exodus to the West. In 1961 the East German government constructed the infamous Berlin Wall *(die Mauer)* to contain its citizens. Between this time and reunification at the end of 1989, more than 180 people were shot trying to cross the Wall.

Berlin Wall
Protected to the east by land mines, the Wall, known by the East German authorities as the "Anti-Fascist Protection Wall", surrounded West Berlin and was 155 km (95 miles) long *(see p113)*.

Memorial to Soviet Soldiers
Part of West Berlin, the area around this monument to Red Army troops killed in the 1945 Battle of Berlin was closed for many years due to attacks on its Soviet guards *(see p139)*.

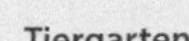

Berlin Before Reunification

The Wall cut the city in half, severing its main transport arteries, the S-Bahn and U-Bahn lines. West Berliners were excluded from the centre of the city. Running along the Wall was a no-man's-land.

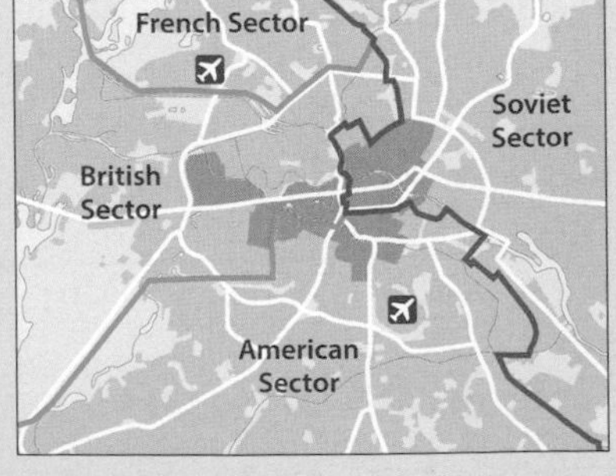

Key

- Berlin Wall
- Sector boundaries
- Airport

Tränenpalast (Palace of Tears)
Until 1989 the Tränenpalast, next to the final S-Bahn station in East Berlin, was a border checkpoint for S-Bahn passengers heading west.

Checkpoint Charlie
This border crossing between the American and Soviet sectors was used by foreign citizens and diplomats. It was the location of many dramatic events during the years of the Cold War *(see p145)*.

East Side Gallery
The longest remaining section of the Berlin Wall became an open-air gallery in 1990, covered with an eclectic mixture of paintings by 118 artists *(see p175)*.

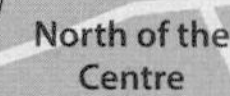

Luftbrücke
This striking memorial commemorates those who died during the Berlin Airlift of 1948–9. Allied planes delivered 2.3 million tons of supplies to West Berlin in the face of the year-long Soviet blockade *(see p149)*.

Haus am Checkpoint Charlie
This museum holds photos and other Wall memorabilia, including a selection of escape vehicles *(see p145)*.

Berlin's Best: Modern Architecture

Following Berlin's devastation in World War II, intense post-war reconstruction turned the city into a giant building site. With the help of architects from several countries the city acquired many modern structures and estates, ranked among the best in the world. The city's reunification in 1990 and the reinstatement of Berlin as the main seat of government gave rise to a second wave of building activity, carried out on a scale unprecedented in Europe. The architectural elite are participating in the design of the new Berlin, and the sites in the city centre that stood empty until 1990 are being filled with buildings at an incredible rate.

Bauhaus-Archiv
This cubist structure was completed in 1978 to house the Bauhaus museum. It was designed much earlier by Walter Gropius (1883–1969), director of the Bauhaus art school from 1919 to 1928.

Kammermusiksaal

Around Schloss Charlottenburg

Tiergarten

Around Kurfürstendamm

Gemäldegalerie

Kant-Dreieck
This building, with its pure forms and the eccentric sail-like structure mounted on the roof, is the work of Josef Paul Kleihues.

Nordische Botschaften
Built between 1997 and 1999, the five interconnected embassies of the Scandinavian countries are an example of daring architectural design. The building's green shutters adjust to the intensity and direction of available sunlight.

Kammermusiksaal
Both the Berliner Philharmonie building (1961) and the adjacent Kammermusiksaal, or chamber music hall (1987), were designed by Hans Scharoun. The latter was built posthumously by Edgar Wisniewski, Scharoun's pupil.

Galeries Lafayette
This elegant department store in Friedrichstrasse, designed by Jean Nouvel, brings Parisian chic to the heart of Berlin.

North of the Centre

East of the Centre

Around Unter den Linden

Museum Island

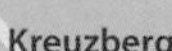

Quartier Schützenstrasse
This part of the city features the work of Italian architect Aldo Rossi. With high-rise blocks and bold colour schemes, the area shows modernity and classical forms standing side by side.

0 metres 750
0 yards 750

Gemäldegalerie
The Gemäldegalerie, designed by the Hilmer and Sattler Partnership, opened in June 1998. The main hall is particularly elegant.

Sony Center
This ultra-modern steel-and-glass building was designed by German-American architect Helmut Jahn. It houses offices, entertainment venues, the Kaisersaal and Sony's European headquarters.

Exploring Berlin's Modern Architecture

Around the world architects are forever designing buildings with innovative and interesting structures, but in Berlin this creative process is happening on an unprecedented scale. The city is a vast melting pot of trends and styles, where the world's greatest architects scramble for commissions and where buildings compete with each other in the originality of their form and in their use of the latest technology.

Haus der Kulturen der Welt in the Tiergarten

From 1945 to 1970

World War II exacted a heavy price from Berlin. The centre was reduced to rubble and the partitioning of the city made it impossible to carry out any coordinated reconstruction. In 1952, East Berlin decided to develop **Karl-Marx-Allee** in the Socialist-Realist style. In reply, West Berlin employed the world's greatest architects to create the **Hansaviertel** estate. Le Corbusier built one of his *unités d'habitation*, while the American architect, Hugh A Stubbins, built the Kongresshalle (now the **Haus der Kulturen der Welt**). The West's response to the cultural venues inherited by the East Berliners, including the opera, the library and the museums, was the **Kulturforum** complex. The complex included such magnificent buildings as the **Philharmonie**, designed by Hans Scharoun, and the **Neue Nationalgalerie**, designed by Mies van der Rohe. While West Berlin acquired its huge "trade temple"– the **Europa-Center**, constructed in 1965, East Berlin boasted its **Fernsehturm** (television tower), built in 1969.

From 1970 to 1990

The continuing rivalry, as each part of the city tried to outdo the other, resulted in the construction of East Berlin's now demolished Palast der Republic in 1976. The West replied with the ultra-modern **Internationales Congress Centrum** in 1979. The Kulturforum complex was further extended with designs by Scharoun, including the **Kammermusiksaal** and the **Staatsbibliothek** (library). The impressive **Bauhaus-Archiv** was developed from a design by Walter Gropius. In 1987 Berlin celebrated its 750th anniversary, which in the East saw the completion of the huge **Nikolaiviertel** development, with its pre-war allusions. In the West, the IBA's 1987 scheme gave the town its enormous Post-Modernist housing estates in Kreuzberg and also in the **Tegel** area.

Neue Nationalgalerie at Kulturforum designed by Mies van der Rohe

Post-Reunification Architecture

The government district was constructed within the bend of the Spree river. Its designers include Charlotte Frank and Axel Schultes. The **Reichstag** building has been famously remodelled by Norman Foster. **Pariser Platz** has been filled with designs by Günther Behnisch, Frank O Gehry, Josef Paul Kleihues and others. The magnificent **Friedrichstadt-passagen** complex became the scene of rivalry between Jean Nouvel and Oswald M Ungers. Many interesting office buildings have sprung up around town, including **Ludwig-Erhard-Haus** by Nicholas Grimshaw and the nearby **Kant-Dreieck** by Josef Paul Kleihues. Housing has also been transformed, with perhaps the most original example being Aldo Rossi's **Quartier Schützenstrasse**. The city has also acquired some fine museums, including the **Gemäldegalerie** designed by the Hilmer and Sattler Partnership, and the Deconstructivist style **Jüdisches Museum**, designed by Daniel Libeskind.

Modern Architecture

Bauhaus-Archiv *p131*
Europa-Center *p154*
Fernsehturm *p95*
Friedrichstadtpassagen *p67*
Gemäldegalerie *pp126–9*
Hansaviertel *p137*
Haus der Kulturen der Welt *p138*
Internationales Congress Centrum *p179*
Jüdisches Museum *pp146–7*
Kammermusiksaal *p120*
Kantdreieck *p152*
Karl-Marx-Allee *pp174–5*
Kulturforum *pp118–19*
Ludwig-Erhard-Haus *pp154–5*
Neue Nationalgalerie *p130*
Nikolaiviertel *p92*
Pariser Platz *p69*
Philharmonie *p120*
Quartier Schützenstrasse *p45*
Reichstag *pp138–9*
Staatsbibliothek *p120*
Tegel harbour site *p180*

Potsdamer Platz

Between 1993 and 1998, a financial, business and entertainment district was erected on the once vast and empty wasteland around Potsdamer Platz. It boasts splendid constructions designed by Renzo Piano, Arata Isozaki and Helmut Jahn. As well as office blocks, the area has many public buildings, including cinemas and a theatre, as well as a huge shopping centre – the Arkaden, plus luxury hotels, restaurants and several bars.

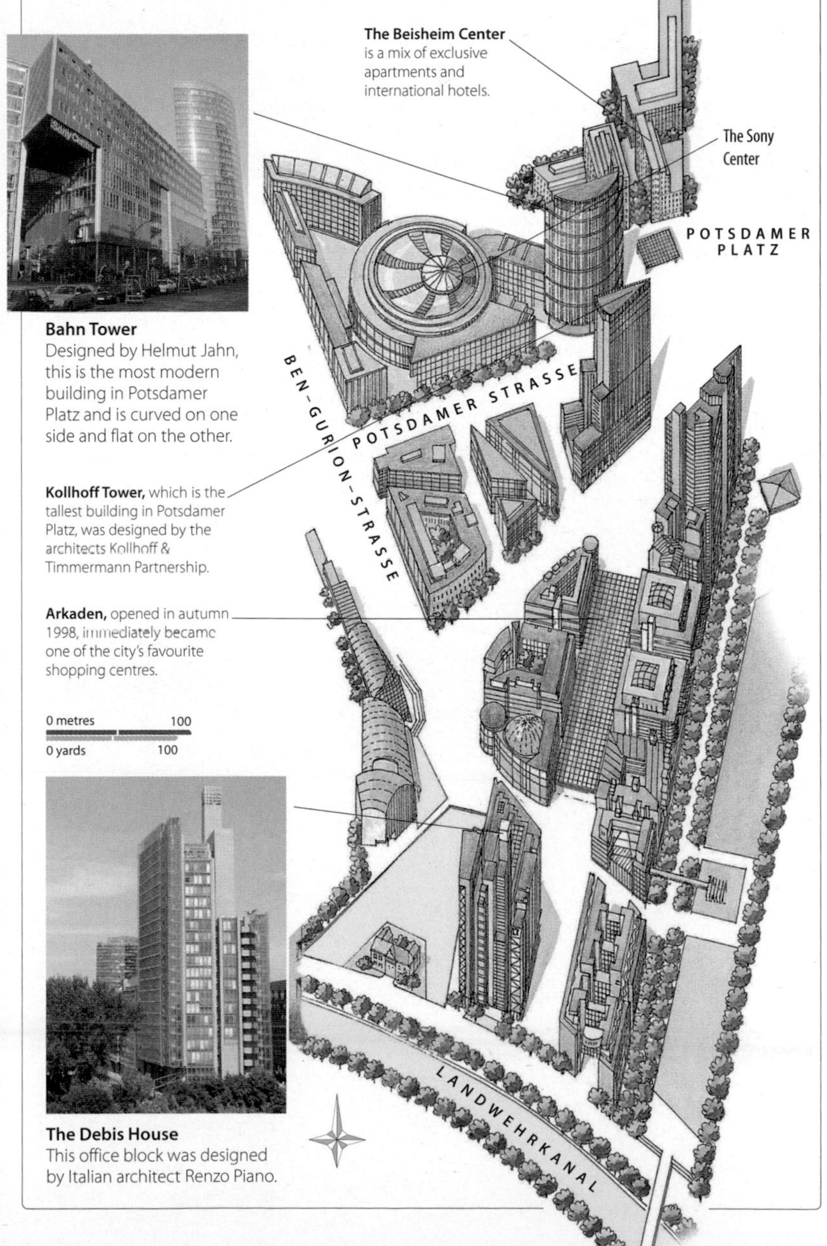

The Beisheim Center is a mix of exclusive apartments and international hotels.

Bahn Tower
Designed by Helmut Jahn, this is the most modern building in Potsdamer Platz and is curved on one side and flat on the other.

Kollhoff Tower, which is the tallest building in Potsdamer Platz, was designed by the architects Kollhoff & Timmermann Partnership.

Arkaden, opened in autumn 1998, immediately became one of the city's favourite shopping centres.

The Debis House
This office block was designed by Italian architect Renzo Piano.

Berlin's Best: Parks and Gardens

Berlin is undoubtedly one of Europe's greenest capital cities, with the sprawling Tiergarten at its centre. However, most of Berlin's districts have their own smaller parks and gardens, too, some of them with children's play areas and nature trails. To the west of the city is the vast Grunewald, a beautiful area of forest which contains mountain bike trails and scenic paths for walkers and cyclists. In summer, numerous lakes, rivers and canals provide excellent facilities for water sports.

Zoologischer Garten
Popular with children, Berlin's zoo has some 14,000 animals, representing 1,400 different species. It is the oldest zoo in Germany *(see p154)*.

Schloss Charlottenburg
The well-maintained grounds of this royal palace were designed in the French Baroque style *(see pp164–5)*.

Around Schloss Charlottenburg

0 metres 1000
0 yards 1000

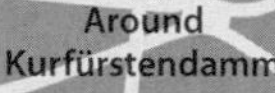

Botanischer Garten
Established from 1899 to 1910 in Dahlem, this botanical garden is one of the biggest in the world *(see p186)*.

Gutspark Britz
The landscaped park with its beautiful lime-tree avenue, surrounds the early 18th-century Schloss Britz *(see p183)*.

Park Babelsberg
This vast landscaped park was designed by Peter Joseph Lenné, and now lies within the Potsdam city limits. It surrounds the picturesque Schloss Babelsberg *(see pp212–13)*.

Tiergarten
Once a hunting reserve, this was converted into a park after 1818 by landscape designer Peter Joseph Lenné *(see p136)*.

Monbijoupark
The park once surrounded Monbijou Palace, which was destroyed during World War II *(see p105)*.

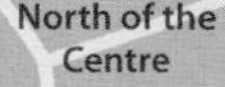

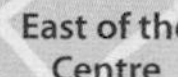

Around Unter den Linden

Museum Island

Tiergarten

Kreuzberg

Tierpark Friedrichsfelde
In 1954 the park at Schloss Friedrichsfelde was converted into the East Berlin Zoological Garden *(see p182–3)*.

Viktoriapark
This large park winds around a hill with good views of Kreuzberg. At its peak stands a memorial to the wars of liberation fought against Napoleon *(see p149)*.

BERLIN THROUGH THE YEAR

Like all major European capitals, Berlin offers a wide range of activities throughout the year. The best seasons for cultural and sporting events are spring and autumn, when the city hosts many spectacular fairs and exhibitions. During summer the city's population shrinks, as many locals head for their holiday destinations. But the weather is often pleasant, and rarely very hot, so this is a good time for serious sightseeing. In winter, although it can get quite cold, it is possible to spend time visiting museums or simply walking around the city. The streets teem with shoppers during the run-up to Christmas. A more detailed programme of events can be obtained from tourist information offices *(see p278)* or on the Internet at www.visitberlin.de.

The Karneval der Kulturen in the streets of Kreuzberg

Spring

In springtime, Berlin holds many interesting fairs and cultural events in its squares, parks and gardens, allowing the visitor to appreciate fully the beauty of the city as the trees and flowers burst into life. With the arrival of the warmer weather, another natural resource springs to life as cruise and rowing boats start operating on the Spree river and the city's canals.

March

ITB-Internationale Tourismus-Börse *(mid-Mar)*. The biggest European fair devoted to tourism where representatives from around the world try to attract visitors to their countries.
März Musik *(mid-Mar)* is a music festival featuring works by contemporary composers, including both German and world premieres.
Berlin Motorrad Tage *(end Mar)*. Motorcyclists from all over Germany converge on Berlin for this specialist event.

April

Festtage *(Apr)*. A series of popular concerts and operas performed by world-class musicians in the Philharmonie and at the Staatsoper.
Easter *(exact date varies)*. Markets open around the Kaiser-Wilhelm-Gedächtnis-kirche, Alexanderplatz and other central locations.
Britzer Baumblüte *(all of Apr)* is a month-long spring festival organized in Britz, a suburb in the south of the city famous for its gardens.
Neuköllner Maientage *(Apr–May)*, Hasenheide. Traditional springtime festival celebrating the new season.
Köpenicker Winzerfest *(end of Apr)*. Sample top wines and gourmet food in the charming old town square of Köpenick, a district in southeast Berlin.

May

1 Mai *(1 May)*. The traditional May Day celebrations are especially significant in Berlin. They have become a day of widespread demonstrations featuring activists, workers and curious tourists. Most of the daytime demonstrations are peaceful, but Kreuzberg should be avoided at night.
Theatertreffen Berlin *(May)*. This important Berlin theatre festival has been running since 1963, and provides a platform for theatre productions from German-speaking regions around the world.
Big 25 Berlin *(early May)*. A 25-km (15-mile) run that starts at the Olympiastadion and winds through the city.
Lange Nacht der Museen *(mid-May)*. Berlin's museums stay open until midnight or later.
Berliner Frauenlauf *(late May)*. is a popular 5-km (3-mile) fun-run through Tiergarten – but it is reserved for women only.

Street recitation of poetry during the Theatertreffen Berlin in May

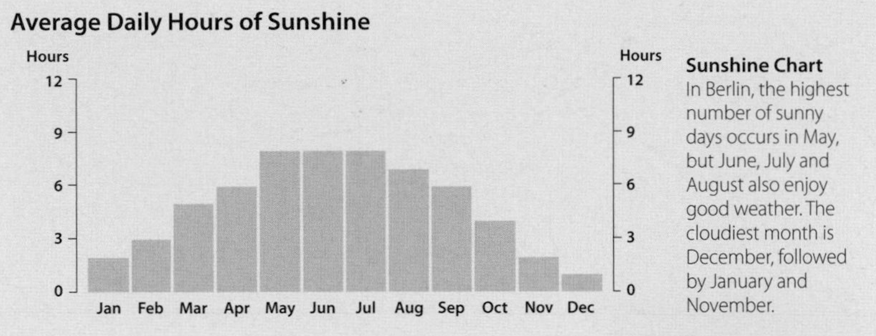

Sunshine Chart
In Berlin, the highest number of sunny days occurs in May, but June, July and August also enjoy good weather. The cloudiest month is December, followed by January and November.

Summer

Summertime in Berlin is marked by many open-air events. There are concerts of classical music and opera performances, jazz festivals and sports events, an annual air show, a series of open-air concerts and festivals for the young. It is also possible to take advantage of the good weather by taking a walk or bicycle ride in the Grunewald, or swimming in the lakes of Wannsee or Müggelsee.

An outdoor artist at work in the Potsdamer Platz

June

Deutsch-Französisches Volksfest *(early Jun–mid-Jul)*. German-French folk festival near Kurt-Schumacher-Damm.
Internationales Tango Festival Berlin *(mid-Jun)* brings a bit of South American culture to various venues.
Karneval der Kulturen *(mid-Jun)*. For three days, the streets of Kreuzberg district are brought to life by singing and dancing in this display celebrating multicultural Berlin.
Luft- und Raumfahrtausstellung Berlin-Brandenburg *(Jun/Sep, check in advance)*. This biannual festival and air show of civil, military and space craft fills the skies above Berlin Brandenburg airport.
Christopher Street Day *(end Jun)* features a gay and lesbian parade with revellers in extravagant outfits, held around Ku'damm. At night, the party continues until late in the city's many gay clubs and *Kneipen*.

July

Classic Open Air *(mid-Jul)*. Concerts and operas on Gendarmenmarkt, complemented by events in Waldbühne.
Konzertsommer im Englischen Garten *(early Jul–end Aug)*. Open-air concerts.
Berliner Gauklerfest *(late Jul–early Aug)*. Stalls on Unter den Linden sell speciality foods, while crowds are entertained by acrobats and musicians.

August

Deutsch-Amerikanisches Volksfest *(late Jul–mid-Aug)*. A programme of entertainment with an American theme that always draws the crowds.

Ku'damm full of revellers on Christopher Street Day

Kreuzberger Festliche Tage *(end Aug–early Sep)*. This is a large multi-event festival of art and music held in Kreuzberg.
Jüdische Kulturtage *(end Aug–early Sep)*. A festival devoted to Jewish arts and culture with films, plays, concerts and lectures.

Prokofiev's *The Love of Three Oranges* performed in the Komische Oper

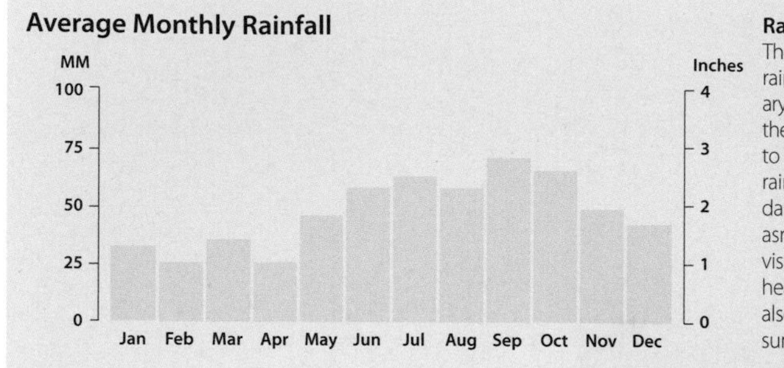

Rainfall Chart
The lowest amount of rainfall occurs in February and again in April, as the temperature begins to rise. The amount of rain in September can dampen the enthusiasm of the unprepared visitor. Unexpectedly heavy cloudbursts can also occur during the summer months.

Autumn

Autumn in Berlin is marked by major cultural events. In September the city's hotels fill with visitors arriving for the Berliner Festwochen, to hear concerts given by some of the world's top artists and to make the most of the wide range of culture on offer. Autumn is also a time for major sports events, including the Berlin-Marathon, the third biggest in the world after New York and London.

September

Internationale Funkausstellung *(early Sep, every two years)*. High-tech media and computer fair at the Internationales Congress Centrum *(see p179)*.

Bach Tage Potsdam *(early Sep)* features around 30 concerts of Johann Sebastian Bach's music, performed in concert halls in Potsdam. The festival lasts nine days.

Internationales Literaturfestival *(mid-Sep)*. Readings and events featuring old and new writing from around the world.

Popkomm *(mid-Sep)*. Europe's biggest pop music fair, with a very lively club and dance programme/festival too.

Berlin Art Week *(mid-Sep)*. Exhibitions and fairs organized by the city's art bodies offer insights into its busy gallery scene.

Musikfest Berlin *(mid-Sep)*. Orchestras and ensembles from across the world take part in this impressive classical music event, held mostly at the Philharmonie.

Berlin-Marathon *(3rd Sun in Sep)*. This international event attracts thousands of runners and brings the city's traffic to a halt for several hours.

Participants in the September Berlin-Marathon

October

Tag der Deutschen Einheit *(3 Oct)*. Berlin celebrates the reunification of Germany with street festivals.

International Salsa Festival *(early Oct)*. Salsa shows and more.

Festival of Lights *(mid-Oct)*. Dozens of modern and historical buildings are illuminated. There is a spectacular opening ceremony.

Haupstadt Turnier *(late Oct)*. International horse-jumping.

November

Jazzfest Berlin *(early Nov)*. Held annually since 1964, this respected jazz festival kicks off in the Haus der Kulturen der Welt *(see p138)*.

Treffen Junge Musik-Szene *(early Nov)*. Music for the younger generation.

Spielzeit Europa *(Oct–Dec)*. A festival of unusual and high-quality theatre and dance, held at the Haus der Berliner Festspiele.

Marching through the Brandenburg Gate on Tag der Deutschen Einheit

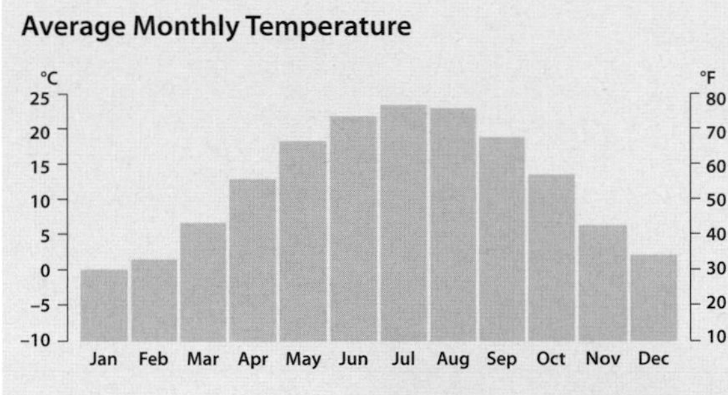

Temperature Chart
Average maximum and minimum temperatures are shown here. The warmest months are June, July and August, when the temperature exceeds 20ºC. Winters are cold and temperatures can drop below –5ºC in January, with the chance of heavy snowfalls or extreme frost.

Winter

Berlin's winters are usually cold and the temperature can sometimes drop to below zero, with a carpet of snow covering the streets. During December, the city prepares for Christmas with many traditional markets. January brings numerous Carnival balls, while the major event in February is a great cinema gala – the Berlin International Film Festival, Berlinale.

Berlinale – the grand festival of world cinema

December

Weihnachstmärkte *(throughout Dec)*. In the month before Christmas the city is dotted with picturesque fairs and festive stalls selling Christmas gifts and regional culinary specialities.
Christmas (Weihnachten) *(24–26 Dec)*. As in many other European cities, Berlin's traditional celebrations include Christmas trees, present-giving, family gatherings and communal feasts.
New Year's Eve (Silvester) *(31 Dec)* is celebrated across Berlin, in hotels, restaurants, clubs and in private homes; another traditional activity is the popping of champagne corks at the Brandenburg Gate while watching the fireworks.

January

Berliner Neujahrslauf *(1 Jan)*. For those unaffected by the previous night's revelry, this 4-km (2.4-mile) run along the city streets starts off at the Brandenburg Gate.
Internationale Grüne Woche *(last week of Jan)*. This giant agriculture and food fair provides an ideal opportunity to sample worldwide delicacies.
Transmediale *(Jan and Feb)* is a busy festival of experimental and electronic music.

February

Sechs-Tage-Rennen *(early Feb)*. This meeting in the Velodrome features a six-day bicycle race and other events.

Christmas shopping in the KaDeWe department store

Berlinale – Internationale Filmfestspiele *(2nd and 3rd week in Feb)*. This gala of cinematography brings international movie stars to Berlin and showcases the best films of the season. The festival is held in tandem with the **Internationales Forum des Jungen Films**, which is a platform for promoting and featuring low-budget movies and the best short films of the year.

Public Holidays

Neujahr New Year (1 Jan)
Karfreitag Good Friday
Ostermontag Easter Mon
Tag der Arbeit Labour Day (1 May)
Christi Himmelfahrt Ascension Day
Pfingsten Whitsun
Tag der Deutschen Einheit (3 Oct)
Weihnachten Christmas (25 & 26 Dec)

The Reichstag dome from the inside ▶

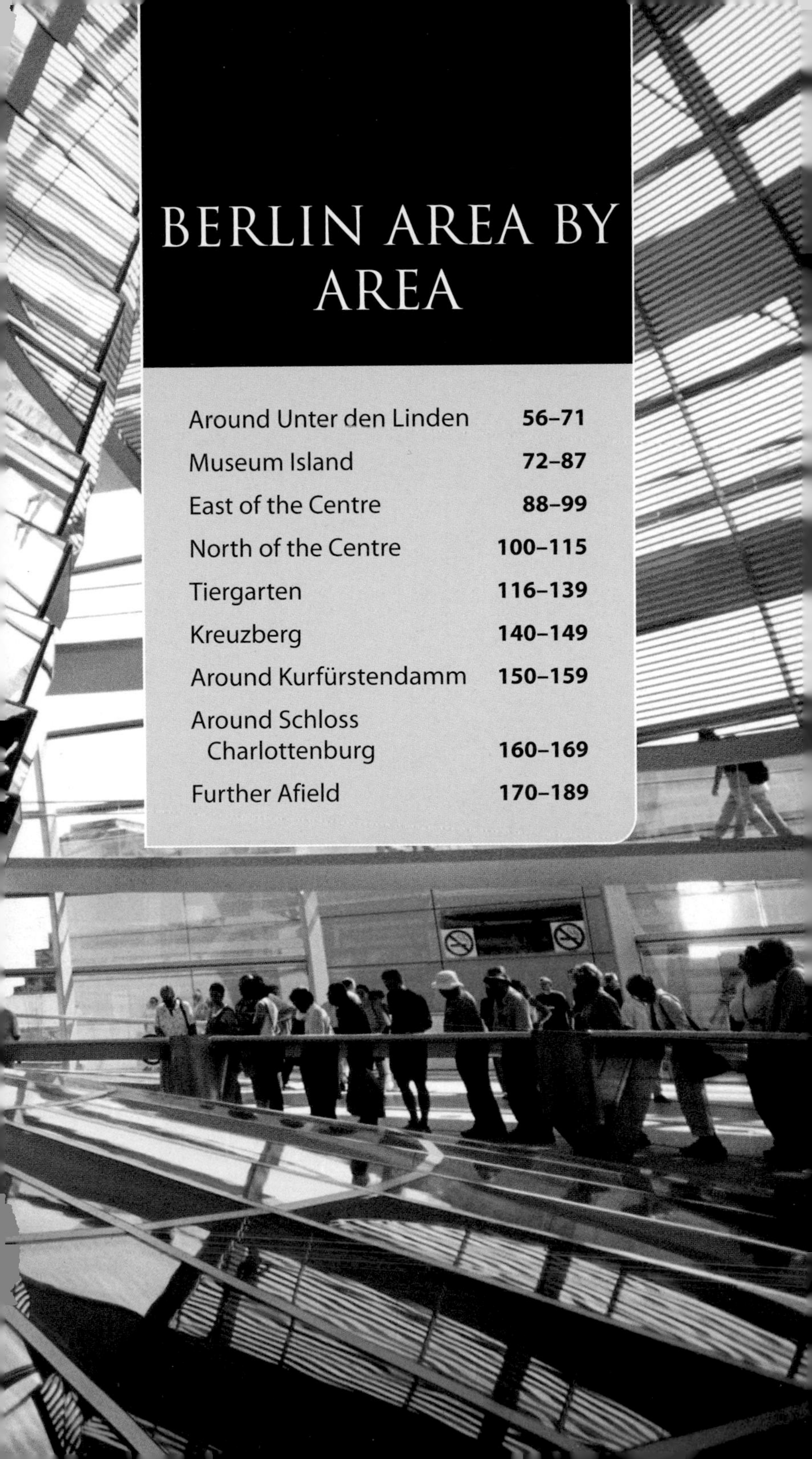

BERLIN AREA BY AREA

AROUND UNTER DEN LINDEN

The area around the grand avenue Unter den Linden is among the most attractive in Berlin. Its development began in the Baroque period with the establishment of Dorotheenstadt to the north and Friedrichstadt to the south. From the early 18th century, prestigious buildings began to appear here, and work started on the Forum Friedericianum (later Bebelplatz). Over the following two centuries Unter den Linden became one of the city's most imposing avenues. World War II bombing took a heavy toll, but despite only partial reconstruction by the East German government, the area is still home to the highest concentration of historic buildings in Berlin.

Sights at a Glance

Churches

- ⓫ St-Hedwigs-Kathedrale
- ⓮ Friedrichswerdersche Kirche
- ⓰ Französischer Dom
- ⓲ Deutscher Dom

Museums and Galleries

- ❶ *Zeughaus (Deutsches Historisches Museum) (pp60–61)*
- ❼ Deutsche Bank KunstHalle
- ㉒ Museum für Kommunikation

Streets and Squares

- ❷ Unter den Linden
- ❿ Bebelplatz
- ⓯ Gendarmenmarkt
- ㉔ Pariser Platz

Theatres

- ⓬ Staatsoper Unter den Linden
- ⓱ Konzerthaus
- ㉙ Komische Oper
- ㉛ Admiralspalast
- ㉜ Maxim Gorki Theater

Historic Buildings and Sites

- ❸ Neue Wache
- ❹ Humboldt Universität
- ❺ Reiterdenkmal Friedrichs des Grossen
- ❻ Staatsbibliothek
- ❽ Altes Palais
- ❾ Alte Bibliothek
- ⓭ Kronprinzenpalais
- ⑳ Mohrenkolonnaden
- ㉑ Spittelkolonnaden
- ㉕ Brandenburger Tor
- ㉖ Holocaust Denkmal
- ㉝ Palais am Festungsgraben

Others

- ⓳ Friedrichstadtpassagen
- ㉓ Ehemaliges Regierungsviertel
- ㉗ Hotel Adlon
- ㉘ Russische Botschaft
- ㉚ Bahnhof Friedrichstrasse

Restaurants

see pp232–3

1. Augustiner am Gendarmenmarkt
2. Bocca di Bacco
3. Borchardt
4. Cookies Cream
5. Chipps
6. Dressler
7. Fischers Fritz
8. Kaffeehaus Einstein
9. Lorenz Adlon Esszimmer
10. Das Meisterstück
11. Nante-Eck
12. Quarré
13. Samadhi
14. Vau
15. Zwölf Apostel

See also Street Finder maps 8, 9

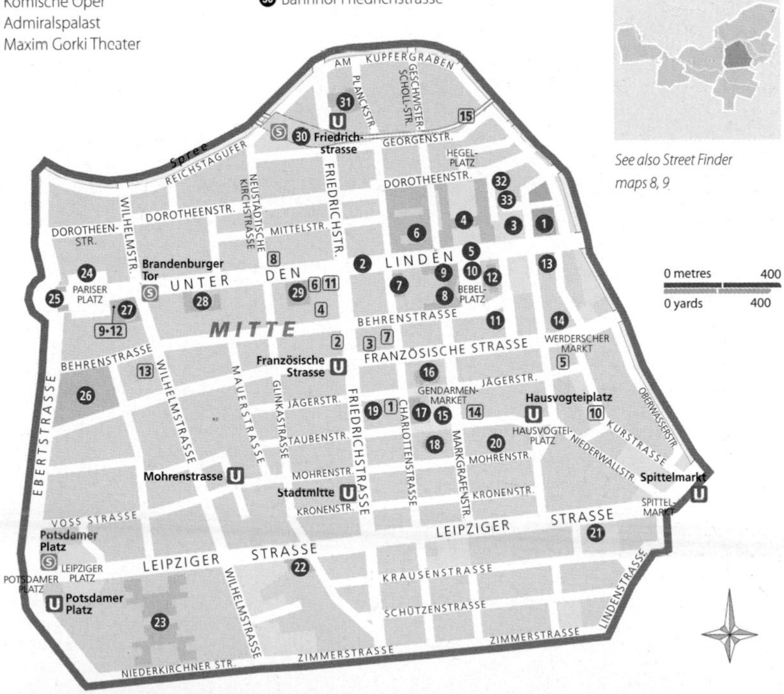

◀ Schiller's monument and Französischer Dom, Gendarmenmarkt

For map symbols *see back flap*

Street-by-Street: Around Bebelplatz

The section of Unter den Linden between Schlossbrücke and Friedrichstrasse is one of the most attractive places in central Berlin. There are some magnificent Baroque and Neo-Classical buildings, many of them designed by famous architects. There are also several restored palaces that are now used as public buildings. Of particular interest is the beautiful Baroque building of the Zeughaus (the former Arsenal), which now houses the German History Museum.

6 Staatsbibliothek
This Neo-Baroque building, designed by Ernst von Ihne, was built between 1903 and 1914. It houses a collection that dates from the 17th century.

4 Humboldt Universität
The entrance to the courtyard is framed by two guardroom pavilions and is crowned with the allegorical figures of Dawn and Dusk.

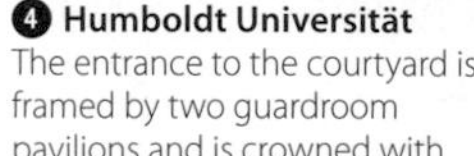

5 Equestrian Statue of Frederick the Great
This impressive statue dates from 1851 and is the work of Christian Daniel Rauch.

7 Deutsche Bank KunstHalle
Formerly known as Deutsche Guggenheim, this building provides a space for contemporary art exhibitions.

8 Altes Palais
This Neo-Classical palace was built between 1834 and 1837 for the future Kaiser Wilhelm I. It was reconstructed after World War II.

9 Alte Bibliothek
The west side of Bebelplatz features a Baroque building with an unusual concave façade. Locals have nicknamed it the "chest of drawers".

3 Neue Wache
Since 1993, this monument has served as a memorial to all victims of war and dictatorship.

1 ★ Zeughaus (Deutsches Historisches Museum)
A wing designed by I M Pei has been added to this beautiful Baroque building. The Zeughaus pediment shows the Roman goddess of wisdom.

Locator Map
See Street Finder maps 8, 9

0 metres 100
0 yards 100

Key
— Suggested route

2 Unter den Linden
This magnificent avenue was replanted with four rows of lime trees in 1946.

UNTER DEN LINDEN

HINTER DER KATH. KIRCHE

BEBELPLATZ

13 Kronprinzenpalais
The rear elevation of the palace pavilion features a magnificent portal from the dismantled Bauakademie building.

14 ★ Friedrichswerdersche Kirche
This Neo-Gothic church was designed by Karl Friedrich Schinkel, the architect of so many of Berlin's notable 19th-century buildings.

12 Staatsoper Unter den Linden
Unter den Linden's opera house is Germany's oldest theatre building not attached to a palace residence.

10 Bebelplatz
Designed in the 18th century as the Forum Friedericianum, this square was renamed in 1947 in honour of social activist August Bebel. The Nazis burned books here in 1933.

11 St-Hedwigs-Kathedrale
Bas-reliefs (1837) by Theodore Wilhelm Achtermann adorn the cathedral's supports.

❶ Zeughaus (Deutsches Historisches Museum)

This former arsenal was built in the Baroque style in 1706 under the guidance of Johann Arnold Nering, Martin Grünberg, Andreas Schlüter and Jean de Bodt. It is a magnificent structure; its wings surrounding an inner courtyard, its exterior decorated with Schlüter's sculptures, including masks of dying warriors in the courtyard. Since 1952 it has housed the German History Museum. Zeughaus is home to a permanent exhibition that contains more than 8,000 objects about German history in a European context. In the adjacent exhibition hall, designed by the famous architect I M Pei, are the museum's temporary exhibitions about significant historical events.

★ *Martin Luther*
This portrait, painted by Lucas Cranach the Elder in 1529, is the focal point of the exhibition devoted to the Reformation.

★ *Gloria Victis*
The death of a friend in the final days of the Franco-Prussian War (1870–71) inspired French artist Antonin Mercié to create this moving allegory.

Prisoner's Jacket
This jacket, which once belonged to a concentration camp prisoner, is used to illustrate the horrors of the Nazi regime.

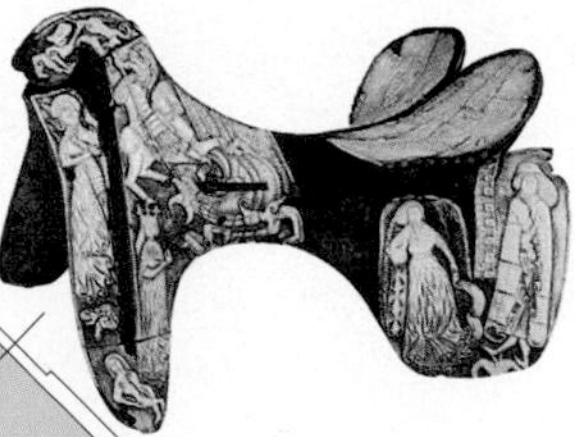

Saddle
This valuable mid-15th-century saddle is decorated with graphic carved plaques made of ivory.

VISITORS' CHECKLIST

Practical Information
Unter den Linden 2.
Map 9 A3.
Tel 20 30 40.
dhm.de
Open 10am–6pm daily.

Transport
S & U Friedrichstrasse. S Hackescher Markt. 100, 200.

First floor

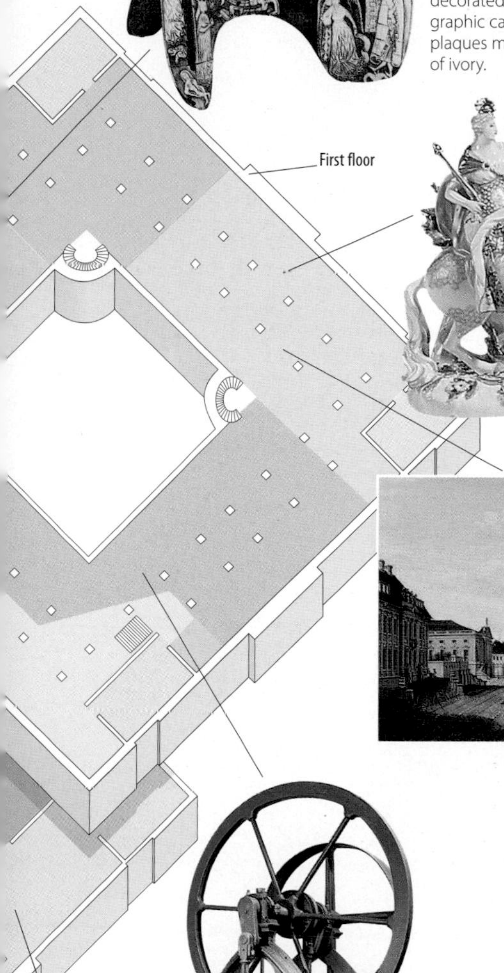

Europa
A group of Meissen porcelain figurines, depicting the continents, possibly designed by Johann Joachim Kändler.

Unter den Linden
Carl Traugott Fechhelm's painting shows Berlin's grandest avenue, Unter den Linden, at the end of the 18th century.

Key

- Early Civilizations and the Middle Ages
- 1500–1648
- 1648–1789
- 1789–1871
- 1871–1918
- 1918–1945
- 1945–1949
- 1949 to present day
- Non-exhibition rooms

Museum Cinema

Ground floor

Steam Engine
The history of the Industrial Revolution is illustrated with exhibits such as this 1847 steam-powered engine.

Gallery Guide

The ground floor houses exhibits from 1918 to the present. The first floor contains collections dating from early history to the beginning of the 20th century. A subterranean pathway links the Zeughaus to the temporary exhibitions in the exhibition hall by I M Pei.

Unter den Linden as depicted in Franz Krüger's *Opernplatz Parade* (1824–30)

❷ Unter den Linden

Map 8 E3, 8 F3. Ⓢ & Ⓤ Brandenburger Tor. 🚌 100, 200, TXL.

One of the most famous streets in Berlin, Unter den Linden starts at Schlossplatz and runs down to Pariser Platz and the Brandenburg Gate. It was once the route to the royal hunting grounds that were later transformed into the Tiergarten. In the 17th century the street was planted with lime trees, to which it owes its name. Although removed around 1658, they were replanted in four rows in 1820.

During the 18th century, Unter den Linden became the main street of the westward-growing city. It was gradually filled with prestigious buildings that were restored after World War II. Following the reunification of Germany, Unter den Linden has acquired several cafés and restaurants, as well as many smart new shops. This street is also the venue for many interesting outdoor events; it is usually crowded with tourists and students browsing the bookstalls around the Humboldt Universität and the Staatsbibliothek.

❸ Neue Wache

Unter den Linden 4. **Map** 9 A3. Ⓢ Hackescher Markt. 🚌 100, 200, TXL. **Open** 10am–6pm daily.

This war memorial, designed by Karl Friedrich Schinkel and built between 1816 and 1818, is considered to be one of the finest examples of Neo-Classical architecture in Berlin. The front of the monument is dominated by a huge Doric portico with a frieze made up of bas-reliefs depicting goddesses of victory. The triangular tympanum above the pediment shows allegorical representations of Battle, Victory, Flight and Defeat.

The building was originally used as a royal guardhouse, but during 1930 and 1931 it was turned it into a monument to the soldiers killed in World War I. In 1960, following its restoration, Neue Wache became the Memorial to the Victims of Fascism and Militarism. Then, in 1993 it was rededicated once again, this time to the memory of all victims of war and dictatorship.

Inside the building is a granite slab over the ashes of an unknown soldier, a resistance fighter and a concentration camp prisoner. Under the circular opening in the roof is a copy of the 20th-century sculpture *Mother with her Dead Son*, by Berlin artist Käthe Kollwitz, who lost her own son in World War I.

❹ Humboldt Universität

Humboldt University

Unter den Linden 6. **Map** 9 A3. **Tel** 20930. Ⓢ & Ⓤ Friedrichstrasse. 🚌 100, 200, TXL.

The university building was constructed in 1753 for Prince Heinrich of Prussia, the brother of Frederick the Great. The university was founded in 1810 on the initiative of Wilhelm von Humboldt. It became the Berlin University but was renamed in von Humboldt's honour in 1949.

The overall design of the palace, with its main block and the courtyard enclosed within a pair of wings, has been extended many times. Two marble statues (1883) by Paul Otto stand at the entrance gate and represent Wilhelm von Humboldt (holding a book) and his brother Alexander

Wilhelm and Alexander von Humboldt

The Humboldt brothers rank among the most distinguished Berlin citizens. Wilhelm (1767–1835) was a lawyer and politician, occupying various government posts. It was on his initiative that the Berlin University (later renamed Humboldt University) was founded, and he conducted studies in comparative and historical linguistics there. Alexander (1769–1859), a professor at the University, researched natural science, including meteorology, oceanography and agricultural science.

Statue of Alexander von Humboldt

(sitting on a globe), who was a famous explorer. The entrance gate leads to the courtyard, which was designed by Reinhold Begas.

Many famous scholars have worked at the University, including philosophers Fichte and Hegel, physicians Rudolf Virchow and Robert Koch and physicists Max Planck and Albert Einstein. Among its graduates are Heinrich Heine, Karl Marx and Friedrich Engels.

After World War II, the University was in the Russian sector of the divided city and the difficulties encountered by the students of the western zone led to the establishment of a new university in 1948 – the Freie Universität *(see p186)*.

Humboldt University courtyard with statue of Hermann von Helmholtz

❺ Reiterdenkmal Friedrichs des Grossen

Equestrian Statue of Frederick the Great

Unter den Linden. **Map** 9 A3. Ⓢ & Ⓤ Friedrichstrasse. 100, 200.

This is one of the most famous monuments in Berlin, featuring a massive bronze statue 5.6 m (18.5 ft) in height and standing on the centre lane of Unter den Linden. It was designed by Christian Daniel Rauch and created between 1839 and 1851. It depicts Frederick the Great on horseback, wearing a uniform and a royal cloak. The base of the high plinth is surrounded by statues of famous military leaders, politicians, scientists and artists. The top tier of the plinth is decorated with bas-reliefs depicting scenes from the life of Frederick the Great. Out of line with GDR ideology, the monument was removed to Potsdam, where until 1980 it stood by the Hippodrome in Park Sanssouci.

❻ Staatsbibliothek

State Library

Unter den Linden 8. **Map** 9 A3. **Tel** 2660. Ⓢ & Ⓤ Friedrichstrasse. 100, 200, TXL. **Open** 9am–9pm Mon–Fri, 9am–5pm Sat.

The nucleus of the State Library collection was the library belonging to the Great Elector – Friedrich Wilhelm – founded in 1661 and situated in the Stadtschloss. At the end of the 18th century it was moved to the Alte Bibliothek building. Its current home was designed by Ernst von Ihne and constructed between 1903 and 1914 on the site of the Academy of Science and the Academy of Fine Arts. This impressive building was severely damaged during World War II and underwent extensive restoration. The collection, numbering 3 million books and periodicals, was scattered during the war, including a collection of priceless music manuscripts, which ended up in the Jagiellonian Library in Cracow, Poland.

After the war only part of the collection was returned to the building in Unter den Linden, and the rest was held in West Berlin. Since reunification, both collections are once again under the same administration.

❼ Deutsche Bank KunstHalle

Unter den Linden 13–15. **Map** 9 A3. **Tel** 202 09 30. **Open** 10am– 8pm daily. Ⓢ & Ⓤ Friedrichstrasse. 100, 200, TXL. free on Mon.

After completing its successful collaboration with the Guggenheim Foundation, Deutsche Bank has opened its own gallery that showcases its private 56,000-piece collection, called "Art Works". The collection comprises valuable works of German Modernism.

The ivy-clad Staatsbibliothek building on Unter den Linden

A window with a heraldic shield on the Altes Palais

❽ Altes Palais

The Old Palace

Unter den Linden 9. **Map** 9 A3. Ⓢ & Ⓤ Friedrichstrasse. 🚌 100, 200, TXL. **Closed** to the public.

This Neo-Classical palace, near the former Opernplatz (Bebelplatz), was built for the heir to the throne – Prince Wilhelm (later Kaiser Wilhelm I). The Kaiser lived here all his life. He was able to watch the changing of the guards every day from the ground-floor window on the far left.

The palace, built from 1834 to 1837, was designed by Carl Ferdinand Langhans but its splendid furnishings were destroyed during World War II. The palace was subsequently restored and is now used by Humboldt Universität.

❾ Alte Bibliothek

The Old Library

Bebelplatz. **Map** 9 A3. **Tel** 20 93 0. Ⓢ & Ⓤ Friedrichstrasse. 🚌 100, 200, TXL.

The Old Library, known by locals as the *Kommode* or "chest of drawers" after its curved façade, is actually one of the city's most beautiful Baroque buildings. It was designed by Georg Christian Unger and built around 1775 to house the royal library collection. In fact, Unger based his design on an unrealized plan for an extension to the Hofburg complex in Vienna by Josef Emanuel Fischer von Erlach some 50 years earlier. The concave façade of the building is accentuated by the insertion of three breaks, surrounded at the top by a row of massive Corinthian pilasters. The building now houses the law faculty of Humboldt University.

❿ Bebelplatz

Map 9 A3. Ⓢ & Ⓤ Friedrichstrasse. 🚌 100, 200, TXL.

Once named Opernplatz (Opera Square), Bebelplatz was to be the focal point of the intended Forum Friedericianum, an area designed by Georg Wenzeslaus von Knobelsdorff to mirror the grandeur of ancient Rome. Although the initial plans were only partly implemented, many important buildings rose around the square with the passage of time.

On 10 May 1933 Opernplatz was the scene of the infamous book-burning act organized by the Nazi propaganda machine. Some 25,000 books written by authors considered to be enemies of the Third Reich were burned. These included works by Thomas and Heinrich Mann, Robert Musil and Lion Feuchtwanger.

Today, a monument at the centre of the square, designed by Micha Ullman, commemorates this dramatic event. A translucent panel inserted into the road surface provides a glimpse of a room filled with empty bookshelves. Next to it is a plaque bearing the tragically prophetic words of the poet Heinrich Heine, written in 1820: "Where books are burned, in the end people will burn."

⓫ St-Hedwigs-Kathedrale

St Hedwig's Cathedral

Bebelplatz. **Map** 9 A4. **Tel** 203 48 10. Ⓢ & Ⓤ Hausvogteiplatz. 🚌 100, 200, TXL. **Open** 10am–5pm Mon–Sat, 1–5pm Sun.

This huge church, set back from the road and crowned with a dome, is the Catholic Cathedral of the Roman Archdiocese of Berlin. It was built to serve the Catholics of Silesia (part of present-day Poland), which became part of the Kingdom of Prussia in 1742 following defeat in the Silesian Wars of 1740–63.

The initial design, by Georg Wenzeslaus von Knobelsdorff, was similar to the Roman Pantheon. Construction began in 1747 and the cathedral was consecrated in 1773, although work continued on and off until 1778. Its design was modified

The façade of St-Hedwigs-Kathedrale featuring beautiful bas-relief sculptures

repeatedly. Later, additional work was carried out from 1886 to 1887. The cathedral was damaged during World War II, and rebuilt between 1952 and 1963.

The crypt holds the tombs of many bishops of Berlin, a 16th-century Madonna and a Pietà dating from 1420. It is also the resting place of Bernhard Lichtenberg, a priest killed in a concentration camp and beatified as a martyr by Pope John Paul II.

Bas-relief of Apollo and Mars on the façade of the Staatsoper

⓬ Staatsoper Unter den Linden

State Opera House

Unter den Linden 7. **Map** 9 A3. **Tel** 20 35 40. S & U Friedrichstrasse. 100, 200, TXL. **Closed** for restoration until December 2015. Performances at Schiller Theater, Bismarckstrasse 110.

The early Neo-Classical façade of the State Opera House is one of the most beautiful sights along Unter den Linden. It was built by Georg Wenzeslaus von Knobelsdorff in 1741–3 as the first building of the intended Forum Friedericianum. After a fire, the opera house was restored from 1843 to 1844 under the direction of Carl Ferdinand Langhans, who altered only its interior.

Following wartime destruction, the opera house was rebuilt from 1952 to 1955 and is currently being restored. It has played host to famous singers, musicians and artists; one of its directors and conductors was Richard Strauss.

The imposing façade of the Kronprinzenpalais

⓭ Kronprinzenpalais

Crown Prince's Palace

Unter den Linden 3. **Map** 9 A3. S & U Friedrichstrasse. 100, 200, TXL. **Closed** to the public.

This striking late Neo-Classical palace takes its name from its original inhabitants – the heirs to the royal, and later to the imperial, throne. Its form is the outcome of numerous changes made to what was originally a modest house dating from 1663–9. The first extensions, designed in the late Baroque style, were conducted by Philipp Gerlach in 1732 and 1733. Between 1856 and 1857 Johann Heinrich Strack added the second floor. These extensions were rebuilt following World War II.

The palace served the royal family until the abolition of the monarchy. From 1919 to 1937, it was used by the Nationalgalerie. Under Communist rule it was renamed Palais Unter den Linden and reserved for official government guests. It was here, on 31 August 1990, that the pact was signed paving the way for reunification.

Next to the palace, with the prestigious address of Unter den Linden 1, is where the Kommandantur, the official quarters of the city's garrison commander, once stood. Totally destroyed in the last days of World War II, the original façade was rebuilt in 2003 by the German media company Bertelsmann, as part of their Berlin headquarters.

Joined to the main palace by an overhanging passageway is the smaller Prinzessinnenpalais (Princesses' Palace), built for the daughters of Friedrich Wilhelm III. The café is an excellent place for a coffee and pastry break.

⓮ Friedrichswerdersche Kirche

Werderscher Markt. **Map** 9 B4. **Tel** 266 42 42 42. S & U Friedrichstrasse. 100, 147, 200, TXL. **Closed** until further notice.

This picturesque church, designed by Karl Friedrich Schinkel and constructed between 1824 and 1830, was the first Neo-Gothic church to be built in Berlin. The small single-nave structure, with its twin-tower façade, resembles an English college chapel. Further Gothic details, including the zinc-tipped finials on the roof, were added by Schinkel's pupil Friedrich August Stüler.

Schinkel's original interior was largely destroyed in World War II, but in the 1980s a great deal of restoration work was done, including the recovery of coloured window-glass that had survived the war, forgotten in storage in the vaults of the Dom. The decommissioned church was used as an exhibition space for sculpture by the Nationalgalerie, but is currently closed for building work.

⓯ Gendarmenmarkt

This is one of Berlin's most beautiful squares, created at the end of the 17th century as a market square for the newly established Friedrichstadt. It is named after the Regiment Gens d'Armes who had their stables here. In 1950 it was renamed Platz der Akademie; after reunification the square reverted to its original name.

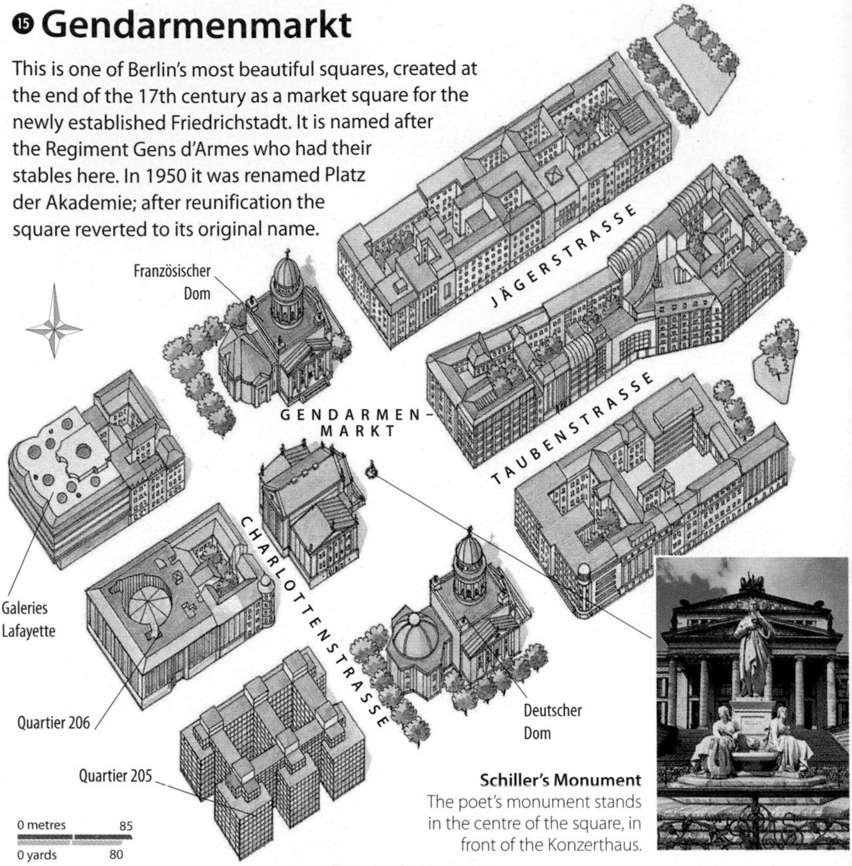

Französischer Dom

JÄGERSTRASSE

GENDARMEN-MARKT

TAUBENSTRASSE

CHARLOTTENSTRASSE

Galeries Lafayette

Quartier 206

Quartier 205

Deutscher Dom

0 metres 85

0 yards 80

Schiller's Monument
The poet's monument stands in the centre of the square, in front of the Konzerthaus.

⓰ Französischer Dom

French Cathedral

Gendarmenmarkt 6. **Map** 9 A4. **Tel** 20 30 60. U Stadtmitte or Französische Strasse. Museum: **Open** noon–5pm Tue–Sun. Church: **Open** 10am–6pm daily (to 7pm Nov–Mar). 9:30am & 11am Sun.

Although the two churches on the opposite sides of Schauspielhaus seem identical, they differ from each other quite considerably. Their only common feature is the front towers. The French cathedral was built for the Huguenot community, who found refuge in Protestant Berlin following their expulsion from France after the revocation of the Edict of Nantes. The modest church, built between 1701 and 1705 by Louis Cayart and Abraham

Side elevation of the Französischer Dom, built for Huguenot refugees

Quesnay, was modelled on the Huguenot church in Charenton, France, which was destroyed in 1688. The main entrance, on the west elevation (facing Charlottenstrasse), leads to an uncomplicated interior with a rectangular nave and semi-circular sections on both sides. It features a late Baroque organ from 1754.

The structure is dominated by a massive, cylindrical tower which is encircled by Corinthian porticoes at its base. The restored tower and porticoes were designed by Carl von Gontard and added around 1785, some 80 years after the church was built. It houses the Huguenot Museum, which details the history of the Huguenots in France and Brandenburg. Well-educated and highly skilled, they played a crucial part in Berlin's rise as a city of science, craft and commerce. The French language they brought with them survives to this day in many words used in the Berlin dialect.

The interior of the Konzerthaus, formerly the Schauspielhaus

17 Konzerthaus

Concert Hall

Gendarmenmarkt 2. **Map** 9 A4. **Tel** 20 30 92 33. U Stadtmitte or Französische Strasse.

A late Neo-Classical jewel, this magnificent theatre building, formerly known as the Schauspielhaus, is one of the greatest achievements of Berlin's best-known architect, Karl Friedrich Schinkel. It was built between 1818 and 1821 around the ruins of Langhan's National Theatre, destroyed by fire in 1817. The original portico columns were retained. Schinkel was responsible for the architectural structure and for the interior design, down to the door handles. Following bomb damage in World War II, it was reconstructed as a concert hall with a different interior layout. The exterior was restored to its former glory. The Konzerthaus is home to the Konzerthaus-orchester (formerly the Berlin Symphony Orchestra).

The theatre façade includes a huge Ionic portico with a set of stairs that was only used by the middle classes (the upper classes entered via a separate entrance where they could leave their horse-drawn carriages). The whole building is richly decorated with sculptures alluding to drama and music: statues of musical geniuses mounted on lions and panthers, as well as figures representing the Muses and a Bacchanal procession. The façade is crowned with the sculpture of Apollo riding a chariot pulled by griffins.

In front of the theatre stands a shining white marble statue of Friedrich Schiller. It was sculpted by Reinhold Begas, and erected in 1869. Removed by the Nazis during the 1930s, the monument was finally returned to its rightful place in 1988. Schiller's head was copied by the sculptor from a bust of the poet created in 1794 by Johann Heinrich Dannecker. The statue is mounted on a high pedestal surrounded by allegorical figures representing Lyric Poetry, Drama, Philosophy and History.

Sculpture from the Deutscher Dom

18 Deutscher Dom

German Cathedral

Gendarmenmarkt 1. **Map** 9 A4. U Stadtmitte or Französische Strasse. **Tel** 22 73 04 31. Exhibition: **Open** May–Sep: 10am–7pm Tue–Sun; Oct–Apr: 10am–6pm Tue–Sun.

The Cathedral at the southern end of the square, to the left of Konzerthaus, is an old German Protestant-Reformed church. It was designed by Martin Grünberg and built in 1708 by Giovanni Simonetti. The design was based on a five-petal shape, and in 1785 it acquired a dome-covered tower identical to that of the French cathedral. Burned down in 1945, the church was finally rebuilt in 1993. Its exterior was painstakingly reconstructed, including its sculpted decorations. The interior is now modern and has been adapted as an exhibition space. On display is *"Wege, Irrwege, Umwege"* ("Paths, Confusions, Detours"), an exhibition about Germany's parliamentary democracy.

19 Friedrichstadt-passagen

Friedrichstadt Passages

Friedrichstrasse Quartier 205, 206, 207. **Map** 8 F4. U Französische Strasse or Stadtmitte.

This group of passages is part of a huge development of luxury shops, offices, restaurants and apartments built along Friedrichstrasse.

Quartier 207 is the famous Galeries Lafayette, a branch of the French department store occupying a charming building designed by Jean Nouvel and constructed almost entirely of glass. The building's axis is formed by an inner courtyard, which is defined by two glass cones with their bases facing each other. The highly reflective glass panes, together with the multicoloured stands that are clustered around the structure, make an extraordinary impression on the visitor.

The next passage, Quartier 206, has offices and smart luxury boutiques, and is the work of the American design team Pei, Cobb, Freed & Partners. The building owes its alluring, but somewhat nouveau-riche appearance to the use of forms inspired by Art Deco architecture, including sophisticated details and expensive stone cladding.

The southernmost building in the complex, and the largest passage, is Quartier 205, now called "The Q", which is the work of Oswald Mathias Ungers.

The exterior and main entrance of Quartier 206

⑳ Mohrenkolonnaden

Mohrenstrasse 37b and 40/41. **Map** 8 F5. U Stadtmitte or Hausvogteiplatz.

Designed by Carl Gotthard Langhans, these Neo-Classical arcades resting on twin columns were constructed in 1787. They originally surrounded a bridge that spanned the moat around the city of Berlin. The bridge has since been demolished, and the arcades have been incorporated into buildings of a much later architectural style located on Mohrenstrasse.

One of the original arcades known as the Mohrenkolonnaden

㉑ Spittelkolonnaden

Leipziger Strasse. **Map** 9 B5. U Spittelmarkt.

In the vicinity of Spittelmarkt is a picturesque Baroque-Neo-Classical colonnade squeezed between several 20-storey tower blocks. These tower blocks were erected to obscure the view of the Axel Springer Publishers' building, which stood on the opposite side of the Berlin Wall.

A pair of such semicircular colonnades, designed by Carl von Gontard and built in 1776, originally surrounded Spittelmarkt. The southern one was demolished in 1929, and the northern one was destroyed during World War II. In 1979, a copy of one of the colonnades was erected in Leipziger Strasse, using elements from the original.

A copy of one of the original Spittelkolonnaden in Leipziger Strasse

㉒ Museum für Kommunikation

Museum of Telecommunications

Leipziger Strasse 16. **Map** 8 F5. **Tel** 20 29 40. U Stadtmitte or Mohrenstrasse. Bus 200, 265, M48. **Open** 9am–8pm Tue, 9am–5pm Wed–Fri, 10am–6pm Sat & Sun. **Closed** Mon, 24–25 & 31 Dec.

Founded in 1872 as the Post Office museum, this is the world's oldest establishment of its kind. A dozen or so years after it was founded, it moved into the corner of the huge building constructed for the main post office. The office wings, with their modest Neo-Renaissance elevations, contrast with the museum premises, which has a grand Neo-Baroque façade. The museum houses exhibits that illustrate the history of postal and telecommunication services, including contemporary digital communications.

㉓ Ehemaliges Regierungsviertel

Wilhelmstrasse, Leipziger Strasse, Voss Strasse. **Map** 8 E5. U Potsdamer Platz, Mohrenstrasse.

Wilhelmstrasse, and the area situated to the west of it up to Leipziger Platz, was the former German government district, where the main departments had offices from the mid-19th century until 1945. The building at Voss Strasse No. 77 was once the Reich's Chancellery and Otto von Bismarck's office. From 1933, it served as the office of Adolf Hitler, for whom the building was specially extended by Albert Speer.

In the spring of 1945 the square was the scene of fierce fighting, and after World War II most of the buildings had to be demolished. Among those that survived are the former Prussian Landtag offices – the huge complex occupying the site between Leipziger and Niederkirchner Strasse. This building in the Italian Renaissance-style was designed by Friedrich Schulz, and constructed from 1892 to 1904. It consists of two segments: the one on the side of Leipziger Strasse (No. 3–4) once housed the upper chamber of the National Assembly (the Herrenhaus) and is now used by the Bundesrat. The building on the side of Niederkirchner Strasse (No. 5) was once the seat of the Landtag's lower chamber, and is now the Berliner Abgeordnetenhaus (House of Representatives).

The second surviving complex is the former Ministry of Aviation (Reichsluftfahrtministerium), at Leipziger Strasse No. 5, built for Hermann Göring in 1936 by Ernst Sagebiel. This awesome building is typical of architecture of the Third Reich.

㉔ Pariser Platz

Map 8 E3. Ⓢ & Ⓤ Brandenburger Tor. 🚌 100, 200.

This square, at the end of Unter den Linden, was created in 1734. Originally called Quarrée, it was renamed Pariser Platz after 1814, when the *Quadriga* sculpture from the Brandenburg Gate was returned to Berlin from Paris.

The square, enclosed on the west by the Brandenburg Gate, saw most of its buildings, including the house of painter Max Liebermann, destroyed in 1945. Following reunification, the square was redeveloped.

Twin houses designed by Josef Paul Kleihues now flank the Brandenburg Gate. On the north side of the square are the Dresdner Bank building and the French Embassy. On the south are the US Embassy, the DZ Bank head office and the Akademie der Künste (Academy of Fine Arts). To the east is the Adlon Hotel.

Max Liebermann (1849–1935)

One of the greatest German painters, Max Liebermann was also one of the most interesting and controversial figures of Berlin's elite circles at the start of the 20th century. A sensitive observer as well as an outstanding portraitist, Liebermann was famously stubborn – he could stand up even to the Kaiser himself. From 1920 he was president of the Akademie der Künste (Academy of Fine Arts), but in view of his Jewish origin he was removed from office in 1933. He died just two years later, alone, and his wife committed suicide to escape being sent to a concentration camp.

A frieze from the Brandenburg Gate

㉕ Brandenburger Tor

Brandenburg Gate

Pariser Platz. **Map** 8 E3. Ⓢ & Ⓤ Brandenburger Tor. 🚌 100, 200.

The Brandenburg Gate is the quintessential symbol of Berlin. This magnificent Neo-Classical structure, completed in 1795, was designed by Carl Gotthard Langhans and modelled on the entrance to the Acropolis in Athens. A pair of pavilions, once used by guards and customs officers, frames its powerful Doric colonnade. The bas-reliefs depict scenes from Greek mythology, and the whole structure is crowned by the sculpture *Quadriga*, designed by Johann Gottfried Schadow. The *Quadriga* was originally regarded as a symbol of peace. In 1806, during the French occupation, it was dismantled on Napoleon's orders and taken to Paris. On its return in 1814, it was declared a symbol of victory, and the goddess received the staff bearing the Prussian eagle and the iron cross adorned with a laurel wreath. The Brandenburg Gate has borne witness to many of Berlin's important events, from military parades to celebrations marking the birth of the Third Reich and Hitler's ascent to power. It was here, too, that the Russian flag was raised in May 1945, and on 17 June 1953 that 25 workers demonstrating for better conditions were killed.

The gate, in East Berlin, was restored from 1956 to 1958, after it suffered extensive damage in World War II. Until 1989 it stood watch over the divided city. It was restored again between 2000 and 2002.

Oskar Kokoschka's *Pariser Platz in Berlin* (1925–6), Nationalgalerie

㉖ Holocaust Denkmal

Holocaust Memorial

Ebertstrasse. **Map** 8 E3. **Tel** 28 04 59 60. Ⓢ & Ⓤ Brandenburger Tor. 🚌 100, 200. **Open** Information Centre: Apr–Sep: 10am– 8pm; Oct–Mar: 10am–7pm.**Closed** Mon.

The memorial for the Jews killed by the Nazis between 1933 and 1945 was inaugurated in 2005. It covers 19,000 sq m (205,000 sq ft) next to the Brandenburg Gate. Above ground, visitors can walk through an undulating field of concrete slabs; beneath lies an information centre on the history of the genocide.

The luxurious interior of the Adlon Hotel

27 Hotel Adlon

Unter den Linden 77. **Map** 8 E3, 8 E4. **Tel** 226 10. S & U Brandenburger Tor. 100, 200.

Considered the most important society venue in Berlin, the original Hotel Adlon opened its doors in 1907. Its luxurious suites were once used by the world's celebrities, including Greta Garbo, Enrico Caruso and Charlie Chaplin. The hotel suffered bomb damage in World War II, and was demolished in 1945. A building bearing the same name opened in a blaze of publicity on 23 August 1997 and was later bought and branded Hotel Adlon Kempinski.

Today, it is once again the best address in town. Comfort, discretion and rich interiors featuring exotic timber, marble and heavy silk tempt visitors despite high prices. Those who cannot afford to stay should at least drop in for a cup of coffee: in the main hall stands the only authentic remnant of the former Adlon Hotel, an elegant black marble fountain decorated with elephants, which once stood in the orangery.

28 Russische Botschaft

Russian Embassy

Unter den Linden 63/65. **Map** 8 F3. S & U Brandenburger Tor. 100, 200.

The monumental white Russian Embassy building is an example of the Stalinist "wedding-cake" style, or *Zuckerbäckerstil*. Built between 1948 and 1953, it was the first postwar building erected on Unter den Linden. It is built on the site of a former palace that had housed the Russian (originally Tsarist) embassy from 1837.

The work of Russian architect Anatoli Strizhevsky, this structure, with its strictly symmetrical layout, resembles the old Berlin palaces of the Neo-Classical period. The sculptures that adorn it, however, belong to an altogether different era: the gods of ancient Greece and Rome have been replaced by working-class heroes.

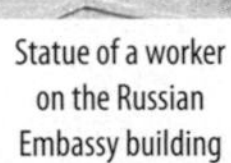

Statue of a worker on the Russian Embassy building

29 Komische Oper

Comic Opera

Behrenstrasse 55/57. **Map** 8 F4. **Tel** 47 99 74 00. U Französische Strasse. S & U Brandenburger Tor. 100, 147, 200.

Looking at the modern façade of this theatre, it is hard to believe that it hides one of Berlin's most impressive interiors. Originally called the Theater Unter den Linden, the theatre was built in 1892 by the internationally famous Viennese architectural practice of Ferdinand Fellner and Hermann Helmer. It has served as a variety theatre and as the German National Theatre in the past, and has only housed the Komische Oper since World War II. The postwar reconstruction deprived the building of its former façades but the beautiful Viennese Neo-Baroque interior remained, full of stuccoes and gilded ornaments. Particularly interesting are the expressive and dynamically posed statues on the pilasters of the top balcony – the work of Theodor Friedel. The Komische Oper is one of Berlin's three leading opera companies. Its repertoire consists mainly of light opera.

Crowded balconies and the plush interior of the Komische Oper

❸⓪ Bahnhof Friedrichstrasse

Map 8 F2, 8 F3.

One of the city's most famous urban railway stations, Bahnhof Friedrichstrasse used to be the border station between East and West Berlin. It was built in 1882 to a design by Johannes Vollmer. In 1925 a roof was added, covering the hall and the platforms.

The original labyrinth of passages, staircases and checkpoints no longer exists but it is possible to see a model of the station at the Stasi-Museum *(see p175)*. Now a museum itself, the only remaining structure from the original station is the special pavilion once used as a waiting room by those waiting for emigration clearance. It earned the nickname Tränenpalast, the "Palace of Tears", as it is here that Berliners from different sides of the city would say goodbye to each other after a visit.

❸① Admiralspalast

Friedrichstrasse 101–102. **Map** 8 F2. **Tel** 479 97 74 99. U & S Friedrichstrasse.

The Admiralspalast, built in 1911, was one of the Roaring Twenties' premier entertainment complexes in Berlin, and one of the many variety and vaudeville theatres once lining Friedrichstrasse. Originally designed as an indoor swimming pool above a natural hot spring, it was later transformed into an ice-skating rink and, after heavy damage in World War II, an Operettentheater that staged light musical entertainment.

In 2006, the theatre reopened with a much-discussed production of Bertolt Brecht's *Dreigroschenoper (The Threepenny Opera)*, and now once again serves as a vibrant entertainment complex, with a large stage, a café and a nightclub. Designed by Heinrich Schweitzer, the beautifully restored façade is punctuated by Doric half-columns and inlaid with slabs of Istrian marble. The restored façade on Planckstrasse, designed by Ernst Westphal, features exotic overlapping motifs.

A window of the Admiralspalast decorated with marble slabs

❸② Maxim Gorki Theater

Am Festungsgraben 2. **Map** 9 A3. **Tel** 20 22 11 15. U & S Friedrichstrasse. 100, 200. M1.

The Maxim Gorki theatre was once a singing school or *Sing-Akademie*. Berlin's oldest concert hall, it was built in 1827 by Karl Theodor Ottmer, who based his design on drawings by Karl Friedrich Schinkel. This modest Neo-Classical building, with its attractive façade resembling a Greco-Roman temple, was well known for the excellent acoustic qualities of its concert hall.

Many famous composer-musicians performed here, including violinist Niccolò Paganini and pianist Franz Liszt. In 1829, Felix Mendelssohn-Bartholdy conducted a performance of the *St Matthew Passion* by Johann Sebastian Bach here, the first since the composer's death in 1750. Following reconstruction after World War II, the building is now used as a theatre.

Maxim Gorki Theater, occupying the oldest concert hall in Berlin

❸③ Palais am Festungsgraben

Festungsgraben Palace

Am Festungsgraben 1. **Map** 9 A3. **Tel** 618 14 60. S Friedrichstrasse. 100, 200. M1.

The Palace in Festungsgraben is one of the few structures in this part of town that has maintained its original interior decor. Built as a small Baroque palace in 1753, it owes its present form to major extension work, carried out in 1864 in the style of Karl Friedrich Schinkel, by Heinrich Bürde and Hermann von der Hude.

The late Neo-Classical style of the building is reminiscent of Schinkel's later designs. The interior includes a magnificent double-height marble hall in the Neo-Renaissance style and modelled on the White Room in the former Stadtschloss *(see p76)*. In 1934 one of the ground-floor rooms was turned into a music salon, and many musical instruments were brought here from the 19th-century house (now demolished) of wealthy merchant and manufacturer Johann Weydinger (1773–1837).

Until 2009 the Palace in Festungsgraben housed the Museum Mitte. It is now used for private events.

SIEHE, ICH BIN BEI EUCH ALLE TAGE BIS AN DER WELT ENDE.
UNSER GLAUBE IST DER SIEG, DER DIE WELT UEBERWUNDEN HAT.
KOMMET HER ZU MIR ALLE DIE IHR MUEHSELIG UND BELADEN SEID ICH WILL EUCH ERQUICKEN

MUSEUM ISLAND

The long island that nestles in the tributaries of the Spree river is the cradle of Berlin's history. It was here that the first settlements appeared at the beginning of the 13th century – Cölln is mentioned in documents dating back to 1237 and its twin settlement, Berlin, is mentioned a few years later (1244). Not a trace of Gothic and Renaissance Cölln is left now: the island's character was transformed by the construction of the Brandenburg Electors' palace, which served as their residence from 1470. Over the following centuries, the palace was converted first into a royal and later into an imperial palace – the huge Stadtschloss. Although it was razed to the ground in 1950, some interesting buildings on the island's north side have survived, including the huge Berliner Dom (cathedral) and the impressive collection of museums that give the island its name – Museumsinsel.

Sights at a Glance

Museums and Galleries

6 *Altes Museum p77*
7 Alte Nationalgalerie
8 Neues Museum
9 *Pergamonmuseum pp82–5*
10 Bode-Museum
13 Historischer Hafen Berlin
14 Märkisches Museum
19 Galgenhaus

Streets, Squares and Parks

1 Schlossplatz
5 Lustgarten
15 Märkisches Ufer

Historic Buildings

3 Schlossbrücke
4 *Berliner Dom pp78–9*
11 Marstall
12 Ribbeckhaus
16 Ermeler-Haus
17 Gertraudenbrücke
18 Nicolai-Haus

Other Buildings

2 Staatsratsgebäude

Restaurants
see p233

1 Café im Bodemuseum
2 Rotisserie Weingrün

See also Street Finder maps 9, 10

◀ The elaborate façade of the Berliner Dom

For map symbols *see back flap*

Street-by-Street: Museum Island

On this island are the pretty Lustgarten and the Berliner Dom (Berlin Cathedral). It is also where you will find some of the most important museums in the east of the city. These include the Bode-Museum, the Altes Museum, the Alte Nationalgalerie and the splendid Pergamonmuseum, famous for its collection of antiquities and visited by crowds of art lovers from around the world.

⑩ Bode-Museum
The dome-covered rounded corner of the building provides a prominent landmark at the tip of the island.

Railway bridge, also used by the S-Bahn.

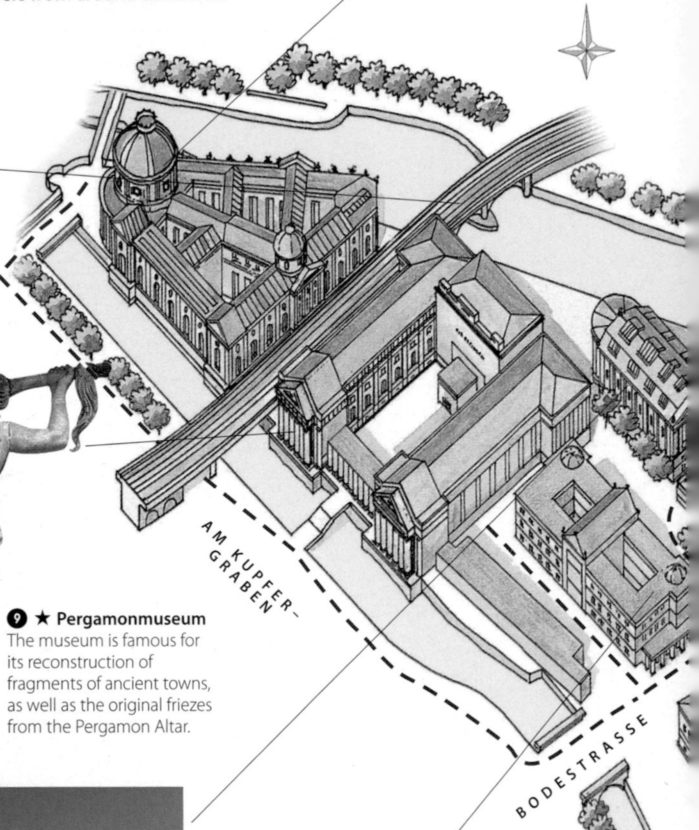

AM KUPFER-GRABEN

⑨ ★ Pergamonmuseum
The museum is famous for its reconstruction of fragments of ancient towns, as well as the original friezes from the Pergamon Altar.

BODESTRASSE

⑧ Neues Museum
This museum houses the Egyptian Museum plus parts of the Museum of Pre- and Early History, as well as items from the Collection of Classical Antiquities.

⑦ Alte Nationalgalerie
The equestrian statue of King Friedrich Wilhelm IV in front of the building is the work of Alexander Calandrelli.

0 metres 100

0 yards 100

Key

— Suggested route

6 ★ Altes Museum
The corners of the central building feature figures of Castor and Pollux, heroes of Greek myth also known as the Dioscuri.

Locator Map
See Street Finder map 9

5 Lustgarten
The 70-ton granite bowl was the biggest in the world when it was placed in the garden in 1828.

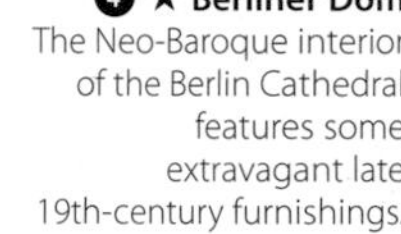

4 ★ Berliner Dom
The Neo-Baroque interior of the Berlin Cathedral features some extravagant late 19th-century furnishings.

3 Schlossbrücke
Under the GDR regime this unusual bridge was called Marx-Engels-Brücke. It features statues made of stunning white Carrara marble.

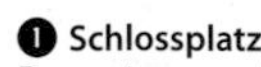

1 Schlossplatz
Excavations conducted here have unearthed the cellars of the demolished Stadtschloss.

BODESTRASSE
LUSTGARTEN
KARL-LIEBKNECHT
SSBRÜCKE
SCHLOSSPLATZ

❶ Schlossplatz

Map 9 B3. Ⓢ Hackescher Markt. 🚌 100, 200.

This square was once the site of a gigantic residential complex known as Stadtschloss (City Palace). Built in 1451, it served as the main residence of the Brandenburg Electors. It was transformed from a castle into a palace in the mid-16th century when Elector Friedrich III (later King Friedrich I) ordered its reconstruction in the Baroque style. The building works (1698–1716) were overseen initially by Andreas Schlüter and then by Johann von Göthe and Martin Heinrich Böhme.

The three-storey residence, designed around two court-yards, was the main seat of the Hohenzollern family *(see pp21–2)* for almost 500 years until the end of the monarchy. The palace was partly burned during World War II, but after 1945 it was provisionally restored and used as a museum. In 1950–51, despite protests, the palace was demolished and the square was renamed Marx-Engels-Platz under the GDR.

Now all that remains of the palace is the triumphal-arch portal that once adorned the façade on the Lustgarten side. This is now incorporated into the wall of the government building, the Staatsratsgebäude.

In 1989 the square reverted to its original name. In 1993 a full-scale model of the palace was built out of cloth stretched over scaffolding. After a lengthy debate and an architectural competition won by Franco Stella, it was decided to rebuild the palace as a museum complex that will have three reconstructed historical façades and a modern one. This Humboldt-Forum will house the Dahlem museums' overseas collections. Completion is due in 2018. Until then, the temporary Humboldt Box will serve as an information centre.

The surviving Stadtschloss portal fronting a government building

❷ Staatsrats-gebäude

Map 9 B3. Ⓢ & Ⓤ Alexanderplatz. 🚌 100, 147, 200, M48, TXL.

The former Staatsratsgebäude, once the seat of the highest state government council of East Germany, was built in 1964. It now stands alone on the southern side of the square, as all the other former Socialist state buildings that once formed the government centre in this area have long been demolished. The Staatsratsgebäude features the remaining original sculptures, including the magnificent atlantes by the famous Dresden sculptor Balthasar Permoser. Their inclusion, however, was not due to their artistic merit, but rather to their propaganda value: it was from the balcony of the portal that Karl Liebknecht proclaimed the birth of the Socialist Republic *(see p30)*.

❸ Schlossbrücke

Map 9 B3. Ⓢ Hackescher Markt. 🚌 100, 200.

This is one of the town's most beautiful bridges, connecting Schlossplatz with Unter den Linden. It was built in 1824 to a design by Karl Friedrich Schinkel, who was one of Germany's most influential architects *(see p181)*. Statues were added to the top of the bridge's sparkling granite pillars in 1853. These figures were also created by Schinkel and made of stunning white Carrara marble. The statues depict tableaux taken from Greek mythology, for instance Iris, Nike and Athena training and looking after their favourite young warriors. The wrought-iron balustrade is decorated with intertwined sea creatures.

Sculptures on the Schlossbrücke

❹ Berliner Dom

Berlin Cathedral

See pp78–9.

❺ Lustgarten

Map 9 B3. Ⓢ Hackescher Markt. 🚌 100, 200.

The enchanting garden in front of the Altes Museum looks as though it has always been here, but in its present form it was established from 1998 to 1999.

Used to grow vegetables and herbs for the Stadtschloss until the late 16th century, it became a real *Lustgarten* (pleasure garden) in the reign of the Great Elector (1620–88). However, its statues, grottoes, fountains and exotic vegetation were removed when Friedrich Wilhelm I (1688–1740), known for his love of military pursuits, turned the garden into an army drill ground.

Following the construction of the Altes Museum, the ground became a park, designed by Peter Joseph Lenné. In 1831 it was adorned with a monolithic granite bowl by Christian Gottlieb Cantian, to a design by Schinkel. The 70-ton bowl, measuring nearly 7 m (23 ft) in diameter, was intended for the museum rotunda, but was too heavy to carry inside.

After 1933, the Lustgarten was paved over and turned into a parade ground, remaining as such until 1989. Its current restoration is based on Lenné's original designs.

6 Altes Museum

The museum building, designed by Karl Friedrich Schinkel, is undoubtedly one of the world's most beautiful Neo-Classical structures, with an impressive 87-m- (285-ft-) high portico supported by 18 Ionic columns. Officially opened in 1830, it was built to house the royal collection of paintings and antiquities. It now houses part of Berlin's Collection of Classical Antiquities, with an exhibition focused on the art and culture of ancient Greece. The first floor houses a permanent exhibition of Roman and Etruscan art and sculptures and the second floor is used for temporary exhibitions.

VISITORS' CHECKLIST

Practical Information
Am Lustgarten (Bodestrasse 1–3).
Map 9 B3. **Tel** 266 42 42 42.
Open 10am–6pm Tue–Sun (to 8pm Thu).

Transport
S Hackescher Markt. 100, 200, TXL.

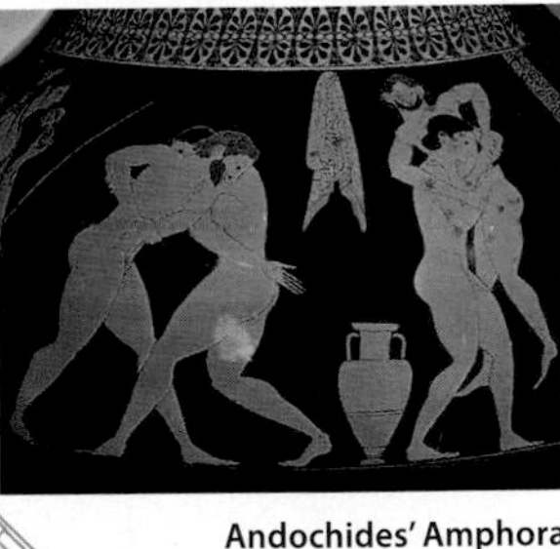

Andochides' Amphora
The amphora is decorated with the figures of wrestlers, a common motif.

Pericles' Head
This is a Roman copy of the sculpture by Kresilas that stood at the entrance to the Acropolis in Athens.

Staircase

The monumental colonnade at the front of the building dominates the façade.

Key

- Greek and Roman antiquities
- Temporary exhibitions

Main entrance

The stately rotunda is decorated with sculptures and ringed by a colonnade. Its design is based on the ancient Pantheon.

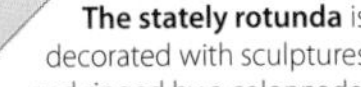

Mosaic from Hadrian's Villa
(c.117–138)
This colourful mosaic depicts a battle scene between centaurs and a tiger and lion. The mosaic comes from a floor of Hadrian's Villa, near Tivoli on the outskirts of Rome.

Gallery Guide

The ground-floor galleries house Greek and Roman antiquities; the first floor is used for temporary exhibitions.

❹ Berliner Dom

The original Berliner Dom was based on a modest Baroque design by Johann Boumann. Built between 1747 and 1750 on the site of an old Dominican church, the cathedral included the original crypt of the Hohenzollern family, one of the largest of its kind in Europe. The present Neo-Baroque structure is the work of Julius Raschdorff and dates from 1894 to 1905. The central copper dome is some 98 m (321 ft) high. Following severe World War II damage, the cathedral has now been restored in a simplified form. The Hohenzollern memorial chapel, which had originally adjoined the northern walls of the cathedral, has been dismantled.

Philipp der Grossmütige (Philip the Magnanimous)
At the base of the arcade stand the statues of church reformers and those who supported the Reformation. The statue of Prince Philip the Magnanimous is the work of Walter Schott.

★ Church Interior
The impressive and richly decorated interior was designed by Julius Raschdorff at the start of the 20th century.

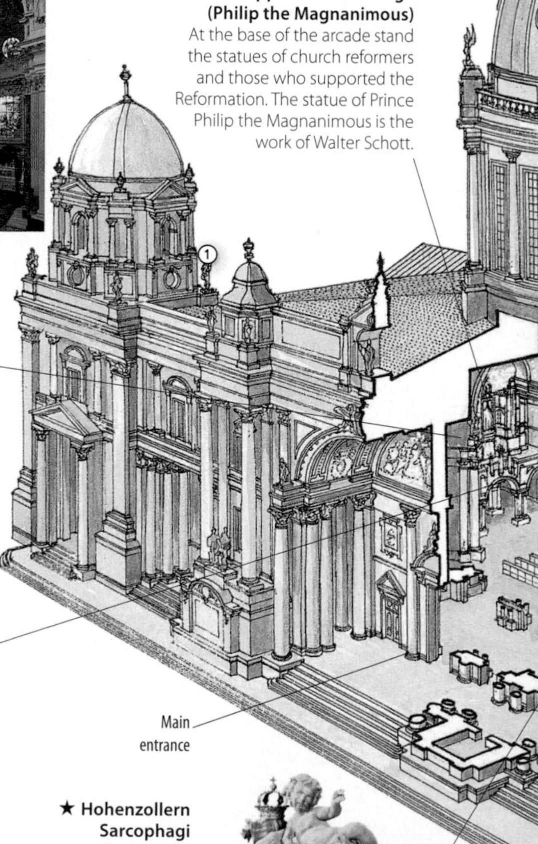

Sauer's Organ
The organ, the work of Wilhelm Sauer, has an exquisitely carved case. The instrument contains some 7,200 pipes.

★ Hohenzollern Sarcophagi
The Imperial Hohenzollern family crypt, hidden beneath the floor of the cathedral, contains 100 richly decorated sarcophagi, including that of Prince Friedrich Ludwig.

KEY

① **Figures of the apostles**

② **The main altar**, saved from the previous cathedral, is the work of Friedrich August Stüler. It dates from 1820.

The Four Evangelists
Mosaics depicting the Four Evangelists decorate the ceilings of the smaller niches in the cathedral. They were designed by Woldemar Friedrich.

VISITORS' CHECKLIST

Practical Information
Am Lustgarten.
Map 9 B3.
Tel 20 26 91 19.
Open 9am–8pm Mon–Sat (to 7pm in winter), noon–8pm Sun & public hols. Sun.

Transport
Hackescher Markt. 100, 200.

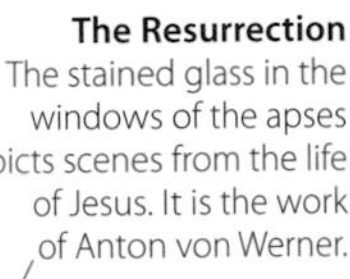

The Resurrection
The stained glass in the windows of the apses depicts scenes from the life of Jesus. It is the work of Anton von Werner.

The Pulpit
This elaborate Neo-Baroque pulpit is part of the cathedral's ornate decor dating from the early 20th century.

★ Sarcophagi of Friedrich I and his Wife
Both of these were designed by Andreas Schlüter. The sculpture on Sophie Charlotte's sarcophagus depicts Death.

Arnold Böcklin's *The Island of the Dead* (1883), Alte Nationalgalerie

7 Alte Nationalgalerie

Old National Gallery

Bodestrasse 1–3. **Map** 9 B2. **Tel** 266 42 42 42. Ⓢ Hackescher Markt, Friedrichstrasse. 100, 200. 12, M1, M4, M5. **Open** 10am–6pm Tue–Sun (to 8pm Thu).

The Nationalgalerie building was erected between 1866 and 1876 and designed by Friedrich August Stüler, who took into account the sketches made by Friedrich Wilhelm IV. The building is situated on a high platform reached via a double staircase. On the top stands an equestrian statue of Friedrich Wilhelm IV, the work of Alexander Calandrelli in 1886. The façade of the building is preceded by a magnificent colonnade, which becomes a row of half-columns higher up. The decorations are in keeping with the building's purpose – the tympanum features Germania as patroness of art, while the top is crowned with a personification of the arts.

The museum was originally meant to house the collection of modern art that had been on display since 1861 in the Akademie der Künste *(see p69)*. The current collection includes works of masters such as Adolph von Menzel, Wilhelm Leibl, Max Liebermann and Arnold Böcklin. Other works include paintings by the Nazarene Brotherhood and the French Impressionists. There is also no shortage of sculptures, including works by Christian Daniel Rauch, Johann Gottfried Schadow, Antonio Canova and Reinhold Begas. Two additional exhibition halls now present paintings (formerly shown at the Schloss Charlottenburg) from the German Romantic era, as well as works by Caspar David Friedrich, Karl Friedrich Schinkel and Karl Blechen.

8 Neues Museum

New Museum

Bodestrasse 1–3. **Map** 9 B2. **Tel** 26 64 24 242. Ⓢ Hackescher Markt or Friedrichstrasse. 100, 200. 12, M1, M4, M5. **Open** 10am–6pm daily (to 8pm Thu).

The Neues Museum was built on Museum Island in order to relieve the Altes Museum, which was already very crowded. The building was erected between 1841 and 1855 to a design by Friedrich August Stüler. Until World War II it housed a collection of antiquities, mainly ancient Egyptian art. The monumental building's beautiful rooms were decorated to complement the exhibitions they contained. Wall paintings by Wilhelm von Kaulbach depicted key events in world history.

In 1945 the building was badly damaged and it took a long time to decide if it would be feasible to rebuild it. But the reconstruction effort under British architect David Chipperfield, a skilful blend of conservation, restoration and creating new spaces, was highly successful.

Façade statue, Neues Museum

History remains palpable in every room. The resurrected museum again houses the collection of Egyptian art (with the bust of Queen Nefertiti as its star exhibit), the Collection of Classical Antiquities and the Museum for Pre- and Early History. The latter portrays the evolution of mankind from prehistoric to medieval times, including a magnificent collection from the ancient city of Troy and gold jewellery belonging to the "Treasure of Priam".

9 Pergamonmuseum

See pp82–3.

⑩ Bode-Museum

Monbijoubrücke (Bodestrasse 1–3). **Map** 9 A2. **Tel** 266 42 42 42. Ⓢ Hackescher Markt or Friedrichstrasse. 100, 147, 200. 12, M1, M4, M5, M6. **Open** 10am–6pm daily (to 8pm Thu).

The fourth museum building on the island was erected between 1897 and 1904. It was designed by Ernst von Ihne to fit the wedge-shaped end of the island. The interior was designed with the help of an art historian, Wilhelm von Bode, who was the director of the Berlin state museums at the time. The museum displayed a rather mixed collection that included some Old Masters. Its original name, Kaiser Friedrich Museum, was changed after World War II. Following the reassembling of the Berlin collections, all of the paintings were put in the Gemäldegalerie *(see pp126–7)*. The Egyptian art and the papyrus collection were moved to the Ägyptisches Museum (Egyptian Museum) at Charlottenburg. They are now housed at the Neues Museum *(see opposite)*.

All the collections are back on display following renovation work. Highlights include an outstanding coin collection of some of the world's oldest coins, from Athens in the 6th century BC, as well as Roman, medieval and 20th-century coins. There are also sculptures by Tilman Riemenschneider, Donatello, Gianlorenzo Bernini and Antonio Canova.

⑪ Marstall

The Royal Stables

Schlossplatz/Breite Strasse 36–37. **Map** 9 B3, C3, C4. Ⓤ Spittelmarkt. 147, 248, M48.

This huge complex, occupying the area between the Spree and Breitestrasse, south of Schlossplatz, is the old Royal Stables block. The wing on the side of Breite Strasse is a fragment of the old structure built in 1669. It was designed by Michael Matthias Smids and is the only surviving early Baroque building in Berlin. The wings running along Schlossplatz and the Spree river were built much later, between 1898 and 1901. Although they were designed by Ernst von Ihne, these buildings are reminiscent of the Berlin Baroque style – probably because von Ihne modelled them on designs by Jean de Bodt from 1700.

⑫ Ribbeckhaus

Ribbeck's House

Breite Strasse 35. **Map** 9 C4. Ⓤ Spittelmarkt. 147, 248, M48.

Four identical, picturesque gables crown central Berlin's only surviving Renaissance building. The house was built c.1624 for Hans Georg von Ribbeck, a court counsellor, who sold it shortly afterwards to Anna Sophie of Brunswick. The architect Balthasar Benzelt converted the house for her in 1629. After her death in 1659, the house passed to her nephew, Elector Friedrich Wilhelm. As crown property, the building later housed various state administrative offices. When another storey was added, the row of gables was retained by royal decree.

The Ribbeckhaus, central Berlin's only surviving Renaissance building

The house also has an interesting late Renaissance portal, ornamented with the date and coat of arms of the first owners – von Ribbeck and his wife, Katharina von Brösicke. This was replaced in 1960 with a copy. Original features of interest include the beautiful wrought-iron grilles on the ground-floor windows.

⑬ Historischer Hafen Berlin

Historic Port of Berlin

Märkisches Ufer. **Map** 10 D4. **Tel** 21 47 32 57. Ⓤ Märkisches Ufer. Ⓢ Jannowitzbrücke. 147, 248, 265. **Open** 1–6pm Sat & Sun.

Moored on the south shore of Museum Island in an area called Fischerinsel, and opposite the Märkisches Ufer, are several examples of boats, barges and tugboats which operated on the Spree river at the end of the 19th century. These craft constitute an open-air museum which was once located in the Humboldt Port. One of the boats is now used as a summer café, while another, the *Renate Angelika*, houses a small exhibition illustrating the history of inland waterway transport on the Spree and Havel.

The Bode-Museum, designed by Ernst von Ihne

9 Pergamonmuseum

Built between 1910 and 1930 to a design by Alfred Messels and Ludwig Hoffmann, this museum houses one of Europe's most famous collections of antiquities. It is named for the famous Pergamon Altar displayed in the main hall. The three independent collections – the Collection of Classical Antiquities (Greek and Roman), the Museum of the Ancient Near East and the Museum of Islamic Art – are the result of intensive archaeological excavations by late 19th- and early 20th-century German expeditions to the Near and Middle East. Due to renovations, the hall containing the Pergamon Altar will remain closed until 2019.

★ **Pergamon Altar** (170 BC)
This scene, featuring the goddess Athena, appears on the large frieze illustrating a battle between the gods and the giants.

Roman Mosaic
(3rd or 4th century AD)
This ancient mosaic was found at Jerash, Jordan. A second part of it was sold to an unknown collector.

First floor

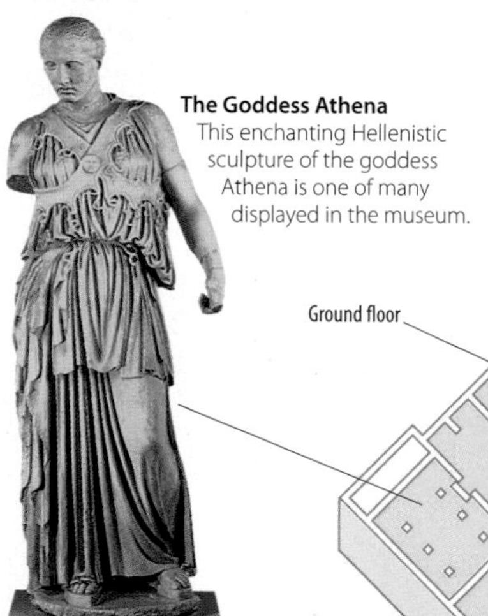

The Goddess Athena
This enchanting Hellenistic sculpture of the goddess Athena is one of many displayed in the museum.

Ground floor

Assyrian Palace
Parts of this beautifully reconstructed palace interior, from the ancient kingdom of Assyria, date from the 9th and 13th centuries BC.

Aleppo Zimmer (*c.*1601–3)
This magnificent panelled room comes from a merchant's house in the Syrian city of Aleppo.

VISITORS' CHECKLIST

Practical Information
Am Kupfergraben 5.
Map 9 A2, B2. **Tel** 266 42 42 42.
smb-spk-berlin.de
Open 10am–6pm daily (to 8pm Thu); call to check which sections are open.

Transport
Hackescher Markt or Friedrichstrasse. 100, 200. 12, M1.

Key

- Collection of Classical Antiquities
- Museum of the Ancient Near East (Vorderasiatisches Museum)
- Museum of Islamic Art (Museum für Islamische Kunst)
- Special exhibition rooms

Façade of the Mshatta Palace (AD 744)
This fragment is from the southern façade of the Jordanian Mshatta Palace, and was presented to Wilhelm II by Sultan Abdul Hamid of Ottoman in 1903.

★ Market Gate from Miletus (AD *c.* 120)
This gate, measuring over 16 m (52 ft) in height, opened onto the southern market of Miletus, a Roman town in Asia Minor.

★ Ishtar Gate from Babylon (6th century BC)
Original glazed bricks decorate both the huge Ishtar Gate and the impressive Processional Way that leads up to it.

Main entrance

Gallery Guide

The central section of the ground floor houses reconstructions of ancient monumental structures. The left wing is closed for renovation until 2019. The right wing houses the Museum of the Ancient Near East; the first floor of the right wing houses the Museum of Islamic Art.

Exploring the Pergamonmuseum

Opened in 1930, the Pergamonmuseum is the newest museum in the Museum Island complex and is one of Berlin's major attractions. The building was one of the first in Europe designed specifically to house big architectural exhibits. The richness of its collections is the result of large-scale excavations by German archaeologists at the beginning of the 20th century. Currently, the museum is at the heart of a significant redevelopment programme, due for completion in 2025, that will considerably increase the range of large-scale exhibits on display.

The Greek goddess Persephone, from Tarentum, 5th century BC

Restored entrance hall of the Athena temple from Pergamon, 2nd century BC

Collection of Classical Antiquities

Berlin's collection of Greek and Roman antiquities (Antikensammlung) came into existence during the 17th century. Growing steadily in size, the collection was opened for public viewing in 1830, initially in the Altes Museum *(see p77)*, and from 1930 in the new, purpose-built Pergamonmuseum. The highlight of the collection is the huge Pergamon Altar from the acropolis of the ancient city of Pergamon in Asia Minor (now Bergama, Turkey). It formed part of a larger architectural complex, a model of which is also on display in the museum. The magnificently restored altar is thought to have been built to celebrate victory in war and to have been commissioned by King Eumenes in 170 BC. Probably dedicated to the god Zeus and the goddess Athena, this artistic masterpiece was discovered in a decrepit state by German archaeologist Carl Humann, who, after long negotiations, was allowed to transport the surviving portions of the altar to Berlin. The front section of the building was restored at the museum, together with the so-called small frieze, which once adorned the inside of the building, and fragments of the large frieze, which originally encircled the base of the colonnade.

The large frieze has now been reconstructed around the interior walls of the museum and its theme is the Gigantomachy (the battle of the gods against the giants). The small frieze tells the story of Telephos, supposed founder of the city and son of the hero Heracles. The frieze is an attempt to claim an illustrious ancestry for Pergamon's rulers.

The collection also contains fragments of other Pergamon structures from the same period, including part of the Athena temple. Also featured here are some excellent examples of Greek sculpture, both originals and Roman copies, as well as many statues of the Greek gods unearthed at Miletus, Samos and Nakosos, and various examples of Greek ceramic art.

Roman architecture is represented by the striking market gate from the Roman city of Miletus, on the west coast of Asia Minor. The gate dates from the 2nd century AD, and shows strong Hellenistic influences. Discovered by a German archaeological expedition, it was transported to Berlin, where it was restored in 1903. Also on display are a number of magnificent Roman mosaics.

Roman marble sarcophagus depicting the story of Medea, 2nd century AD

A huge and impressive marble sarcophagus dates from the 2nd century AD and is decorated with delicate bas-relief carvings depicting the story of the Greek heroine Medea.

Glazed-brick wall cladding from the palace of Darius I in Susa, capital of the Persian Empire

Museum of the Ancient Near East

The collection now on display in the Museum of Near Eastern Antiquities (Vorderasiatisches Museum) was made up initially of donations from individual collectors. However, hugely successful excavations, begun during the 1880s, formed the basis of a royal collection that is one of the richest in the world. It features architecture, sculpture and jewellery from Babylon, Iran and Assyria.

One striking exhibit is the magnificent Ishtar Gate and the Processional Way that leads to it. They were built during the reign of Nebuchadnezzar II (604–562 BC) in the ancient city of Babylon. The original avenue was about 180 m (590 ft) long. Many of the bricks used in its reconstruction are new, but the lions – sacred animals of the goddess Ishtar (mistress of the sky, goddess of love and patron of the army) – are all originals. Although impressive in size, the Ishtar Gate has in fact not been reconstructed in full and a model of the whole structure shows the scale of the original complex. Only the inner gate is on display, framed by two towers. Dragons and bulls decorate the gate, emblems of the Babylonian gods Marduk, patron of the city, and Adad, god of storms.

The collection also includes pieces from the neighbouring regions of Persia, Syria and Palestine, including a gigantic basalt sculpture of a bird from Tell Halaf and a glazed wall relief of a spear-bearer from Darius I's palace in Susa. Other Mesopotamian peoples, including the Assyrians and the Cassians, are represented here too, as are the inhabitants of Sumer in the southern part of the Babylonian Empire with pieces dating from the 4th century BC.

Museum of Islamic Art

The history of the Museum of Islamic Art (Museum für Islamische Kunst) begins in 1904, when Wilhelm von Bode launched the collection by donating his own extensive selection of carpets. He also brought to Berlin a 45-m- (150-ft) long section of the façade of a Jordanian desert palace. The façade, covered with exquisitely carved limestone cladding, was presented to Kaiser Wilhelm II in 1903 by Sultan Abdul Hamid of Ottoman. The palace was part of a group of defence fortresses and residential buildings dating from the Omayyad period (AD 661–750), and probably built for the Caliph al-Walid II.

Another fascinating exhibit is a beautiful 13th-century *mihrab*, the niche in a mosque that shows the direction of Mecca.

Brilliantly glazed *mihrab* from a Kashan mosque built in 1226

Made in the Iranian town of Kashan, renowned for its ceramics, the *mihrab* is covered in lustrous metallic glazes that make it sparkle as if studded with sapphires and gold.

The collection's many vivid carpets come from as far afield as Iran, Asia Minor, Egypt and the Caucasus. Highlights include an early 15th-century carpet from Anatolia decorated with an unusual dragon and phoenix motif and, dating from the 14th century, one of the earliest Turkish carpets in existence.

Other rooms hold collections of miniature paintings and various objects for daily use. An interesting example of provincial Ottoman architecture is an exquisitely panelled early 17th-century reception room, known as the Aleppo Zimmer, which was once part of a Christian merchant's house in the Syrian city of Aleppo.

17th-century carpet with flower motif from western Anatolia

The exterior of the Märkisches Museum, echoing a medieval monastery

⓮ Märkisches Museum

Am Köllnischen Park 5. **Map** 10 D4. **Tel** 24 00 21 62. Ⓤ Jannowitzbrücke, Märkisches Museum. Ⓢ Jannowitzbrücke. 🚌 147, 248, 265, M48. **Open** 10am–6pm Tue–Sun. Presentation of mechanical musical instruments 3pm Sun.

This architectural pastiche is a complex of red-brick buildings that most resembles a medieval monastery. It was built between 1901 and 1908 to house a collection relating to the history of Berlin and the Brandenburg region, from the time of the earliest settlers to the present.

Inspired by the brick-Gothic style popular in the Brandenburg region, architect Ludwig Hoffmann included references to Wittstock Castle and to St Catherine's Church in the city of Brandenburg. In the entrance hall, a statue of the hero Roland stands guard, a copy of the 15th-century monument in the city of Brandenburg. The main hall features the original Gothic portal from the Berlin residence of the Margraves of Brandenburg *(see pp19–21)*, demolished in 1931. Also featured is a horse's head from the Schadow *Quadriga,* which once crowned the Brandenburg Gate *(see p69)*.

A further collection in the same building is devoted to the Berlin theatre during the period 1730 to 1933, including many posters, old programmes and stage sets. One of the galleries houses some charming old-time mechanical musical instruments, which can be heard playing during special shows.

The Märkisches Museum is a branch of the Stadtmuseum Berlin organization, and those who wish to find out more about the history of the city can visit other affiliated museums and monuments such as the Nikolaikirche *(see pp92–3)* and the Ephraim-Palais *(see p93)*. Surrounding the museum is the Köllnischer Park, which has a kennel built in 1928 to house brown bears kept as city mascots, and an unusual statue of Berlin artist Heinrich Zille.

⓯ Märkisches Ufer

Map 10 D4. Ⓤ Märkisches Museum. Ⓢ Jannowitzbrücke. 🚌 147, 248, 265, M48.

Once called Neukölln am Wasser, this street, which runs along the Spree river, is one of the few corners of Berlin where it is still possible to see the town much as it must have looked in the 18th and 19th centuries. Eight picturesque houses have been meticulously conserved here.

Two Neo-Baroque houses at No. 16 and No. 18, known as Otto-Nagel Haus, used to contain a small museum displaying paintings by Otto Nagel, a great favourite with the communist authorities. The building now houses the photographic archives for the state museums of Berlin. A number of picturesque garden cafés and fashionable restaurants make this attractive area very popular with tourists.

Barges moored alongside Märkisches Ufer

The Neo-Classical exterior of the Ermeler-Haus

⓰ Ermeler-Haus

Ermeler House

Märkisches Ufer 10. **Map** 9 C4. Ⓤ Märkisches Museum. Ⓢ Jannowitzbrücke. 🚌 147, 248, 265, M48.

With its harmonious Neo-Classical façade, Märkisches Ufer No. 10 stands out as one of the most handsome villas in Berlin. This house was once the town residence of Wilhelm Ferdinand Ermeler, a wealthy merchant and shopkeeper who made his money trading in tobacco. It originally stood on Fischerinsel on the opposite bank of the river, at Breite Strasse No. 11, but in 1968 the house was dismantled and reconstructed on this new site. The house was remodelled in 1825 to Ermeler's specifications, with a decor that includes a frieze alluding to aspects of the tobacco business. Restorers have recreated much of the original façade. The Rococo furniture dates from about 1760 and the notable 18th-century staircase has also been rebuilt.

A modern hotel has been built to the rear of the house facing Wallstrasse, using Ermeler-Haus as its kitchens, while the first-floor rooms are used for special events.

⑰ Gertraudenbrücke

St Gertrude's Bridge

Map 9 B4. U Spittelmarkt. 265, M48.

One of Berlin's more interesting bridges, this connects Fischer Island with Spittelmarkt at the point where St Gertrude's Hospital once stood. The Gertraudenbrücke was designed by Otto Stahn and built in 1894.

Standing in the middle of the bridge is a bronze statue of the hospital's patron saint, St Gertrude, by Rudolf Siemering. A 13th-century Christian mystic, St Gertrude is shown here as a Benedictine abbess. Leaning over a poor youth she hands him a lily (symbol of virginity), a distaff (care for the poor) and a vessel filled with wine (love). The pedestal is surrounded by mice, a reference to the fact that Gertrude is patron saint of farmland and graves – both popular environments for mice.

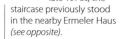

Statue of St Gertrude

⑱ Nicolai-Haus

Brüderstr. 13. **Map** 9 B4. **Tel** 20 45 81 63. U Spittelmarkt. 147, 265, M48. **Open** by appointment only.

Built around 1670, the Nicolai-Haus is a fine example of Baroque architecture, with its original, magnificent oak staircase still in place. The house owes its fame, however, to its time as the home and bookshop of the publisher, writer and critic Christoph Friedrich Nicolai (1733–1811). Nicolai acquired the house around 1788, when he had it rebuilt to a Neo-Classical design by Karl Friedrich Zelter to become a bookshop and major German cultural centre.

One of the outstanding personalities of the Berlin Enlightenment, Nicolai was a great supporter of such notable cultural figures as the Jewish philosopher Moses Mendelssohn *(see p104)* and the playwright Gotthold Ephraim Lessing (1729–81). Other regular literary visitors to the Nicolai-Haus at this period included Johann Gottfried Schadow, Karl Wilhelm Ramler and Daniel Chodowiecki, all commemorated with a wall plaque. Between 1905 and 1935 the building housed a museum devoted to Lessing. Today the rear wing features a fine staircase from the Weydinger-Haus, demolished in 1935. Installed in the Nicolai-Haus in the late 1970s, the staircase previously stood in the nearby Ermeler Haus *(see opposite)*.

East German fashion now on show in the Märkisches Museum *(see opposite)*

⑲ Galgenhaus

Gallows House

Brüderstrasse 10. **Map** 9 B4. **Tel** 206 13 29 13. U Spittelmarkt. 147, 265, M48. **Open** only during special events.

Local legend has it that an innocent girl was once hanged in front of this building, which dates from 1700. It was originally built as the presbytery of the now vanished church of St Peter. Redesigned in the Neo-Classical style around 1805, the front portal and one of the rooms on the ground floor are all that remain of the original Baroque structure.

Today the Galgenhaus houses an archive of historic photographs. These reveal the ways in which Berlin has developed over the years through changes in its buildings and monuments.

Cölln

An ancient settlement in the area called Fischerinsel at the southern end of Museum Island, the village of Cölln has now been razed almost to the ground. Not even a trace remains of the medieval St Peter's parish church. Until 1939, however, this working-class area with its tangle of narrow streets maintained a historic character and unique identity of its own. This vanished completely in the 1960s, when most of the buildings were demolished, to be replaced with prefabricated tower blocks. A few historic houses, including Ermeler-Haus *(see opposite)*, were reconstructed elsewhere, but the atmosphere of this part of town has changed forever.

An engraving of old Cölln

EAST OF THE CENTRE

This part of Berlin, belonging to the Mitte district, is the historic centre. A settlement called Berlin was first established on the eastern bank of the Spree river in the 13th century. Together with its twin settlement, Cölln, it grew into a town. This district contains traces of Berlin's earliest history, including the oldest surviving church (Marienkirche). In later centuries, it became a trade and residential district, but the old town (around today's Nikolaiviertel) survived until World War II. The GDR regime replaced the huge apartment buildings and department stores just to the north with a square, Marx-Engels-Forum, and built the Fernsehturm (television tower). Their redevelopment of the Nikolaiviertel was controversial – buildings were faithfully rebuilt but were grouped rather than being placed in their original locations. The area still offers cosy mews and alleys, which are surrounded by postwar high-rise blocks.

Sights at a Glance

Churches

3 Nikolaikirche
10 Heiliggeistkapelle
12 *Marienkirche pp96–7*
16 Franziskaner Klosterkirche
18 Parochialkirche

Historic Buildings

1 Rotes Rathaus
4 Knoblauchhaus
5 Palais Schwerin and Münze
6 Ephraim-Palais
7 Gerichtslaube
15 Stadtgericht
17 Palais Podewils
19 Gaststätte Zur letzten Instanz
20 Stadtmauer

Others

2 Nikolaiviertel
8 Marx-Engels-Forum
9 DDR Museum
11 Neptunbrunnen
13 *Fernsehturm p95*
14 Alexanderplatz

Restaurants

see p233

1 Domklause
2 Fernsehturm Sphere Restaurant
3 Reinhard's
4 Típica
5 Zur letzten Instanz
6 Zum Nussbaum

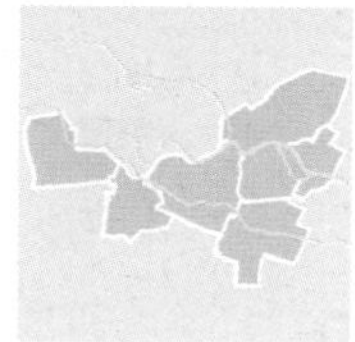

See also Street Finder maps 9, 10

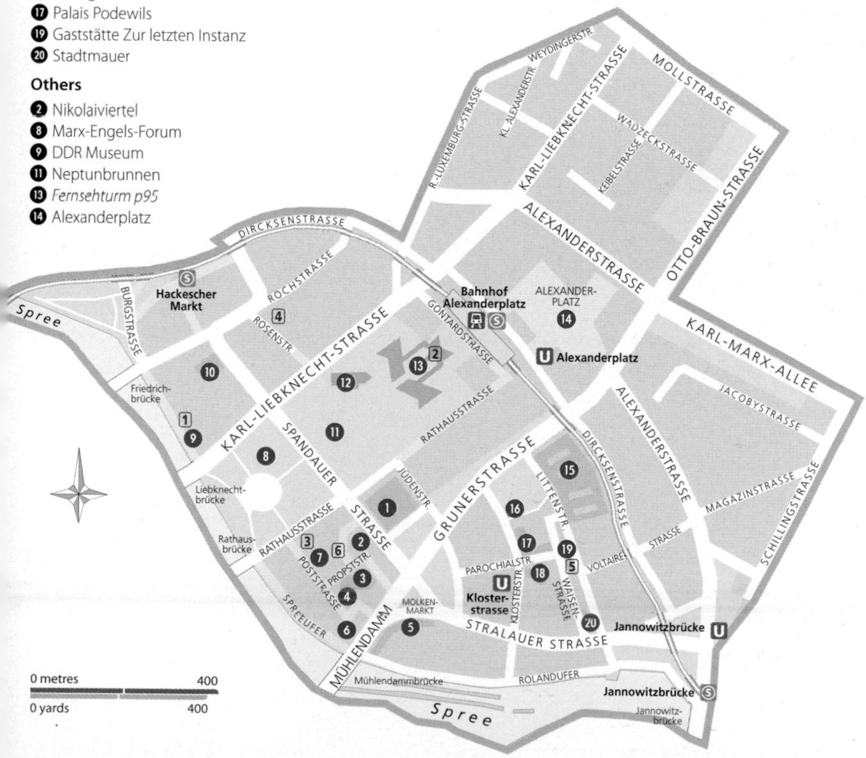

◀ Detail from the Neptunbrunnen (Neptune Fountain)

Street-by-Street: Nikolaiviertel

St Nicholas' Quarter, or the Nikolaiviertel, owes its name to the parish church whose spires rise above the small buildings in this part of town. The Nikolaiviertel is full of narrow alleys crammed with popular restaurants, tiny souvenir shops and small museums. The district retains the old features of long-destroyed Old Berlin and is usually filled with tourists looking for a place to rest after an exhausting day of sightseeing – particularly in the summer. Almost every other house is occupied by a restaurant, inn, pub or café, so the area is quite lively until late at night.

❸ Nikolaikirche
The church is now a museum, with its original furnishings incorporated into the exhibition.

❼ Gerichtslaube
The replica arcades and medieval courthouse now contain restaurants.

POSTSTRASSE

SPREEUFER

St George Slaying the Dragon
This statue once graced a courtyard of the Stadtschloss.

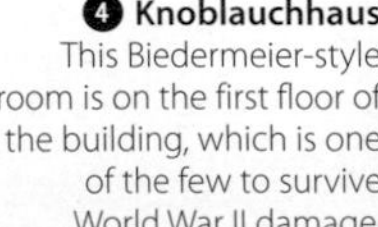

❹ Knoblauchhaus
This Biedermeier-style room is on the first floor of the building, which is one of the few to survive World War II damage.

❻ Ephraim-Palais
A feature of this palace is the elegant façade. Inside there is also an impressive spiral staircase and balustrade.

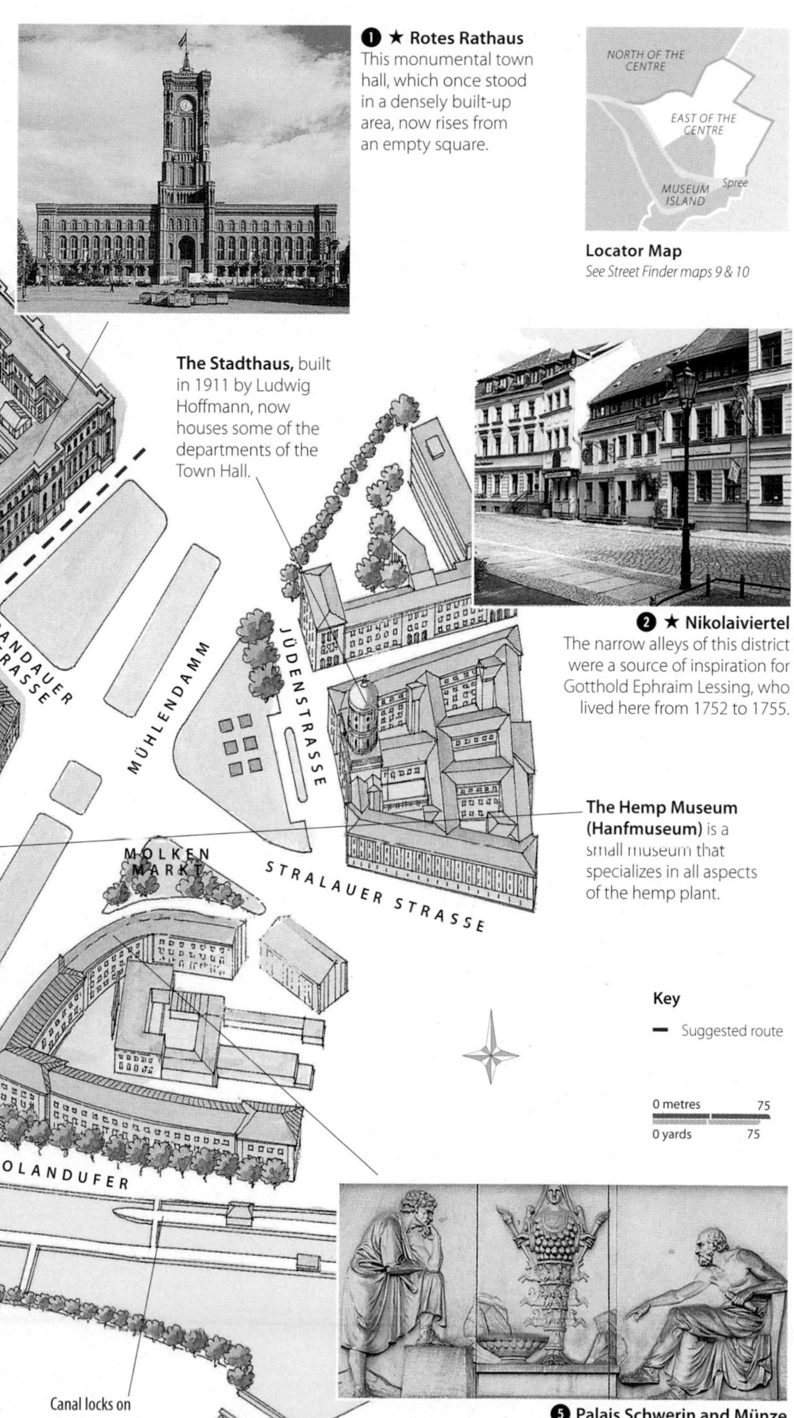

1 ★ Rotes Rathaus
This monumental town hall, which once stood in a densely built-up area, now rises from an empty square.

Locator Map
See Street Finder maps 9 & 10

The Stadthaus, built in 1911 by Ludwig Hoffmann, now houses some of the departments of the Town Hall.

2 ★ Nikolaiviertel
The narrow alleys of this district were a source of inspiration for Gotthold Ephraim Lessing, who lived here from 1752 to 1755.

The Hemp Museum (Hanfmuseum) is a small museum that specializes in all aspects of the hemp plant.

Key

– Suggested route

0 metres 75
0 yards 75

Canal locks on the Spree

5 Palais Schwerin and Münze
The palace façade is decorated with a Neo-Classical frieze by Johann Gottfried Schadow, depicting the development of metal-processing and coin-minting.

Red-brick walls giving the Red Town Hall its name

❶ Rotes Rathaus

Red Town Hall

Rathausstrasse 15. **Map** 9 C3. **Tel** 90 26 0. U & S Alexanderplatz. U Klosterstrasse. 🚌 100, 200, 248, M48, TXL. **Open** 9am–6pm Mon–Fri.

This impressive structure is Berlin's main town hall. Its predecessor was a much more modest structure and by the end of the 19th century it was insufficient to meet the needs of the growing metropolis.

The present building was designed by Hermann Friedrich Waesemann, and the construction went on from 1861 until 1869. The architect took his main inspiration from Italian Renaissance municipal buildings, but the tower is reminiscent of Laon cathedral in France. The walls are made from red brick and it was this, rather than the political orientation of the mayors, that gave the town hall its name. The building has a continuous frieze known as the "stone chronicle", which was added in 1879. It features scenes and figures from the city's history and the development of its economy and science.

The Rotes Rathaus was badly damaged during World War II and, following its reconstruction (1951–8), it became the seat of the East Berlin authorities. The West Berlin magistrate was housed in the Schöneberg town hall *(see p187)*. After the reunification of Germany, the Rotes Rathaus became the centre of authority, housing the offices of the mayor, the magistrates' offices and state rooms. The forecourt sculptures were added in 1958. These are by Fritz Cremer and depict Berliners helping to rebuild the city.

❷ Nikolaiviertel

Map 9 C3, C4. U & S Alexanderplatz. U Klosterstrasse. 🚌 100, 200, 248, M48, TXL.

This small area on the bank of the Spree, known as the Nikolaiviertel (St Nicholas Quarter), is a favourite place for strolling, for both Berliners and tourists. Some of Berlin's oldest houses stood here until they were destroyed in World War II. The redevelopment of the whole area, carried out by the GDR government between 1979 and 1987, was an interesting, if somewhat controversial, attempt at recreating a medieval village. With the exception of one or two restored buildings, the Nikolaiviertel consists of replicas of historic buildings.

The narrow streets of the Nikolaiviertel tempt the visitor with their small shops, as well as many cafés, bars and restaurants. One of the most popular is Zum Nussbaum, a historical inn that was once located on Fischer Island. The original building, dating from 1507, was destroyed but was subsequently reconstructed at the junction of Am Nussbaum and Propststrasse.

The interior of the Nikolaikirche, one of Berlin's oldest churches

❸ Nikolaikirche

Nikolaikirchplatz. **Map** 9 C3. **Tel** 24 00 21 62. U & S Alexanderplatz. U Klosterstrasse. 🚌 100, 147, 200, 248, M48, TXL. **Open** 10am–6pm daily. ♿

The Nikolaikirche is the oldest sacred building of historic Berlin. The original structure erected on this site was started probably around 1230, when the town was granted its municipal rights. What remains now of this stone building is the massive base of the two-tower façade of the present church, which dates from c.1300. The presbytery was completed around 1402, but the construction of the main building went on until the mid-15th century. The result was a magnificent Gothic brick hall-church, featuring a chancel with an ambulatory and a row of low chapels. In 1877 Hermann

Riverside buildings of the Nikolaiviertel

Blankenstein, who conducted the church restoration works, removed most of its Baroque modifications and reconstructed the front towers.

Destroyed by bombing in 1945, the Nikolaikirche was eventually rebuilt in 1987 and shows a permanent exhibit on Berlin's history. The west wall of the southern nave contains Andreas Schlüter's monument to the goldsmith Daniel Männlich and his wife, which features a gilded relief portrait of the couple above a mock doorway.

❹ Knoblauchhaus

Poststrasse 23. **Map** 9 C3. **Tel** 24 00 21 62. U & S Alexanderplatz. U Klosterstrasse. 248, M48. **Open** 10am–6pm Tue–Sun.

A small town house in Poststrasse, the Knoblauchhaus is the only Baroque building in Nikolaiviertel that escaped damage during World War II. It was built in 1759 for the Knoblauch family, which includes the famous architect, Eduard Knoblauch. His works include, among others, the Neue Synagoge *(see p104)*.

The current appearance of the building is the result of work carried out in 1835, when the façade was given a Neo-Classical look. The ground floor houses a popular wine bar, while the upper floors belong to a museum. On the first floor it is possible to see the interior of an early 19th-century middle-class home, including a beautiful Biedermeier-style room.

❺ Palais Schwerin and Münze

Molkenmarkt 1–3. **Map** 9 C4. U & S Alexanderplatz. U Klosterstrasse. 248, M48.

These two adjoining houses have quite different histories. The older one, at Molkenmarkt No. 2, is Palais Schwerin, which was built by Jean de Bodt in 1704 for a government minister, Otto von Schwerin. Despite subsequent remodelling, the palace kept its beautiful sculptured window cornices, the interior wooden staircase, and the magnificent cartouche featuring the von Schwerin family crest.

The adjoining house is the mint, which was built in 1936. Its façade is decorated with a copy of the frieze that once adorned the previous Neo-Classical mint building in Werderscher Markt. The antique style of the frieze was designed by Friedrich Gilly and produced in the workshop of JG Schadow.

A fine example of German Baroque architecture, the Ephraim-Palais

❻ Ephraim-Palais

Poststrasse 16. **Map** 9 C3. **Tel** 24 00 21 62. U & S Alexanderplatz. U Klosterstrasse. 248, M48. **Open** 10am–6pm Tue & Thu–Sun, noon–8pm Wed.

The corner entrance of the Ephraim-Palais, standing at the junction of Poststrasse and Mühlendamm, used to be called "die schönste Ecke Berlins", meaning "Berlin's most beautiful corner". This Baroque palace was built by Friedrich Wilhelm Diterichs in 1766 for Nathan Veitel Heinrich Ephraim, Frederick the Great's mint master and court jeweller.

During the widening of the Mühlendamm bridge in 1935 the palace was demolished, which may have been due in some part to the Jewish origin of its owner. Parts of the façade, saved from demolition, were stored in a warehouse in the western part of the city. In 1983 they were sent to East Berlin and used in the reconstruction of the palace, which was erected a few metres from its original site. One of the first-floor rooms features a restored Baroque ceiling, designed by Andreas Schlüter. The ceiling previously adorned Palais Wartenberg, which was dismantled in 1889.

Currently Ephraim-Palais houses a branch of the Stadtmuseum Berlin (Berlin City Museum). It shows a series of temporary exhibitions on Berlin's local artistic and cultural history.

Frieze from the façade of the Münze (the Mint)

7 Gerichtslaube

Poststrasse. 28. **Map** 9 C3. **Tel** 241 56 97. U & S Alexanderplatz. U Klosterstrasse. 100, 200, 248, M48, TXL.

This small building, with its sharply angled arcades, has had a turbulent history. It was built around 1280 as part of Berlin's old town hall in Spandauer Strasse. The original building was a single-storey arcaded construction with vaults supported by a central pillar. It was open on three sides and adjoined the shorter wall of the town hall. A further storey was added in 1485 to provide a hall, to which the magnificent lattice vaults were added a few decades later, in 1555.

In 1692, Johann Arnold Nering refurbished the town hall in a Baroque style but left the arcades unaltered. Then, in 1868, the whole structure was dismantled to provide space for the new town hall, the Rotes Rathaus *(see p92)*. The Baroque part was lost forever, but the Gothic arcades and the first-floor hall were moved to the palace gardens in Babelsberg, where they were reassembled as a building in their own right *(see pp212–13)*. When the Nikolaiviertel was undergoing restoration it was decided to restore the court of justice as well. The present building in Poststrasse is a copy of a part of the former town hall, erected on a different site from the original one. Inside it is a restaurant serving local cuisine.

8 Marx-Engels-Forum

Map 9 C3. S Hackescher Markt or Alexanderplatz. 100, 200, 248, M48, TXL.

This vast, eerily empty square, which stretches from the Neptune river to the Spree river in the west, was given the inappropriate name Marx-Engels-Forum (it is not really a forum). Devoid of any surroundings, the only features in this square are the statues of Karl Marx and Friedrich Engels.

Statues of Karl Marx and Friedrich Engels in Marx-Engels-Forum

The statues, added in 1986, are by Ludwig Engelhart. Due to the extension of an underground line which started in 2010, the statues were moved into a corner and the square will be inaccessible for several years. Berlin plans to build up the area after completing the underground works, rather than restore the uninspiring square.

9 DDR Museum

Karl-Liebknecht-Strasse 1. **Map** 9 B3. **Tel** 847 12 37 31. S Hackescher Markt. 100, 200. **Open** 10am–8pm daily (to 10pm Sat). **W ddr-museum.de**

This hands-on museum on the Spree embankment opposite the Berlin cathedral gives an insight into the daily lives of East Germans and demonstrates how the secret police kept a watchful eye on the city's people. Exhibits include a replica of a typical living room and a shiny Trabant car.

10 Heiliggeistkapelle

Chapel of the Holy Spirit

Spandauer Strasse 1. **Map** 9 B2. S Hackescher Markt. 100, 200, 248, M48, TXL. M4, M5, M6.

This modest Gothic structure is the only surviving hospital chapel in Berlin. It was built as part of a hospital complex in the second half of the 13th century, but was subsequently rebuilt in the 15th century. The hospital was demolished in 1825, but the chapel was retained. In 1906, it was made into a newly erected College of Trade, designed by Cremer and Wolffenstein.

The chapel is a fine example of Gothic brick construction. Its modest interior features a 15th-century star-shaped vault. The supports under the vault are decorated with half-statues of prophets and saints.

11 Neptunbrunnen

Neptune Fountain

Spandauer Strasse (Rathausvorplatz). **Map** 9 C3. S & U Alexanderplatz. S Hackescher Markt. 100, 200, 248, M48, TXL.

This magnificent, Neo-Baroque style fountain, sparkling with cascades of running water, provides a splendid feature on the main axis of the town hall building. It was created in 1886 by Reinhold Begas, to stand in front of the southern wall of the former Stadtschloss (Berlin Castle). It was moved to its present site in 1969.

The statue of Neptune in a dynamic pose at the centre of the fountain is surrounded by four figures representing Germany's greatest rivers of the time: the Rhine, the Vistula, the Oder and the Elbe. The naturalism of the composition and the attention to detail, such as the beautiful bronze fishes, crayfish, snails and fishing nets, are noteworthy.

Neptune surrounded by goddesses personifying Germany's rivers

12 Marienkirche

See pp96–7.

⓭ Fernsehturm

The television tower, called by the locals *Telespargel,* or toothpick, remains to this day the city's tallest structure, at 368 m (1,207 ft), and one of the tallest structures in Europe. The tower was built in 1969 to a design by a team of architects including Fritz Dieter and Günter Franke, with the help of Swedish engineering experts. However, the idea for such a colossal tower in Berlin originated much earlier from Hermann Henselmann (creator of the Karl-Marx-Allee development), in the Socialist-Realist style. The interior was given a face-lift in 2012.

VISITORS' CHECKLIST

Practical Information
Panoramastrasse.
Map 9 C2.
Tel 247 57 537.
Open Mar–Oct: 9am–midnight daily; Nov–Feb: 10am–midnight daily.

Transport
S & U Alexanderplatz. 100, 200, M48, TXL. M2, M4, M5, M6.

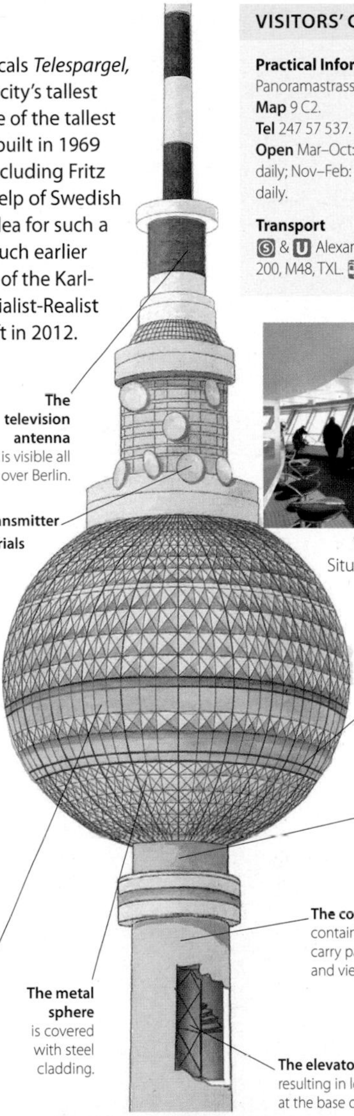

The television antenna is visible all over Berlin.

Transmitter aerials

Viewing Platform
Situated inside a steel-clad giant sphere, the viewing platform is 203 m (666 ft) above the ground.

Television Tower
The slim silhouette of the Fernsehturm is visible from almost any point in Berlin. The ticket office and elevator entrance are located at the base of the tower.

Concrete structure rising to 250 m (820 ft)

The concrete shaft contains two elevators that carry passengers to the café and viewing platform.

The metal sphere is covered with steel cladding.

The elevators are small, resulting in long queues at the base of the tower.

Sphere Restaurant
One of the attractions of the tower is the revolving restaurant. A full rotation takes about half an hour, so it is possible to get a bird's-eye view of the whole city while sipping a cup of coffee.

View from the Tower
On a clear day the viewing platform offers a full view of Berlin. Visibility can reach up to 40 km (25 miles).

⑫ Marienkirche

St Mary's Church, or the Marienkirche, was first established as a parish church in the second half of the 13th century. Construction started around 1280 and was completed early in the 14th century. During reconstruction works in 1380, following a fire, the church was altered slightly but its overall shape changed only in the 15th century, when it acquired the front tower. In 1790, the tower was crowned with a dome designed by Carl Gotthard Langhans. The church was once hemmed in by buildings, but today it stands alone in the shadow of the Fernsehturm (Television Tower). The early Gothic hall design and the lavish decorative touches make this church one of the most interesting in Berlin.

Crucifixion (1562)
This image of Christ, flanked by Moses and St John the Baptist, was painted in the Mannerist style by Michael Rihestein.

Retable
The central part of the Gothic altar, dating from 1510, features figures of three unknown monks.

KEY

① **Totentanz,** meaning "dance of death", is the name of a 22-m- (72-ft-) long Gothic wall fresco, dating from 1485.

② **The dome** that crowns the tower includes both Baroque and Neo-Gothic elements.

Main entrance

★ Pulpit
Carved from alabaster, this masterpiece by Andreas Schlüter, completed in 1703, is placed by the fourth pillar. The pulpit is decorated with bas-reliefs of St John the Baptist and the personifications of the Virtues.

VISITORS' CHECKLIST

Practical Information
Karl-Liebknecht-Str 8.
Map 9 C2.
Tel 24 75 95 10.
Open 10am–6pm daily.

Transport
S & U Alexanderplatz. 100, 200, 248, M48, TXL. M4, M5, M6.

Von Röbel Family Tomb
This richly decorated Mannerist-Baroque tomb of Ehrentreich and Anna von Röbel was probably built after 1630.

Main Altar
The Baroque altar was designed by Andreas Krüger c.1762. The paintings, including *Deposition from the Cross* in the centre and *Christ on the Mount of Olives* and *Doubting Thomas* on the sides, are the works of Christian Bernhard Rode.

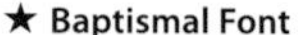

★ Baptismal Font
This Gothic font dating from 1437 is supported by three black dragons and decorated with the figures of Jesus Christ, Mary and the Apostles.

The magnificent interior of the Stadtgericht

⓮ Alexanderplatz

Map 10 D2. Ⓤ & Ⓢ Alexanderplatz. 100, 200, 248, M48, TXL. M5, M6, M8.

Alexanderplatz, or "Alex" as it is locally called, has a long history, although it would be difficult now to find any visible traces of the past. Once called Ochsenmarkt (oxen market), it was the site of a cattle and wool market. It was later renamed after Tsar Alexander I, who visited Berlin in 1805. At the time, the square boasted a magnificent monumental colonnade designed by Carl von Gontard *(see p187)*.

With the passage of time, many houses and shops sprang up around the square, and a market hall and an urban train line were built nearby. "Alex" had become one of the town's busiest spots. Its frenzied atmosphere was captured by Alfred Döblin (1878–1957) in his novel *Berlin Alexanderplatz*.

In 1929, attempts were made to develop the square, though only two office buildings were added – the Alexanderhaus and the Berolinahaus. These two, both by Peter Behrens, are still standing today. World War II erased most of the square's buildings. It is now surrounded by characterless 1960s edifices, including the Park Inn (formerly Hotel Stadt Berlin) and the Fernsehturm *(see p95)*.

Alexanderplatz awaits its next transformation, which might happen soon: a winning design has been chosen from a competition for the square's redevelopment.

⓯ Stadtgericht

Courts of Justice

Littenstrasse 13–17. **Map** 10 D3. Ⓤ & Ⓢ Alexanderplatz or Ⓤ Klosterstrasse. 248.

This gigantic building, situated on a long stretch of Littenstrasse, does not seem particularly inviting, but its interior hides a true masterpiece of the Viennese Secession style of architecture.

At the time of its construction, the building was the largest in Berlin after the Stadtschloss *(see p76)*. The Neo-Baroque structure, built between 1896 and 1905, was designed by Paul Thomer and Rudolf Mönnich, but its final shape is the work of Otto Schmalz. This maze-like complex, with its 11 inner courtyards, was partly demolished in 1969. What remains, however, is still worth seeing, especially the magnificent staircase in the form of overlying ellipses. The staircase is an example of Secession architecture at its boldest. The slim Neo-Gothic pillars and the Neo-Baroque balustrades further enhance the fairy-tale interior.

⓰ Franziskaner Klosterkirche

Franciscan Friary Church

Klosterstrasse 74. **Map** 10 D3. Ⓤ Klosterstrasse. 248.

These picturesque ruins surrounded by greenery are the remains of an early Gothic Franciscan church. The Franciscan friars settled in Berlin in the early 13th century. Between 1250 and 1265 they built a church and a friary, which survived almost unchanged until 1945. The church was a triple-nave basilica with an elongated presbytery, widening into a heptagonal section that was added to the structure in *c.*1300. Protestants took over the church after the Reformation and the friary became a famous grammar school, whose graduates included Otto von Bismarck.

The friary was so damaged in World War II that it was subsequently demolished, while the church was partially reconstructed in 2003–4 and is now a venue for concerts and exhibitions. The giant Corinthian capitals,

Ruins of the Franziskaner Klosterkirche (Franciscan Friary Church)

emerging from the grass near the church ruins, are from a portal from the Stadtschloss (Berlin Castle) *(see p76)*.

Façade of the twice-restored Palais Podewils

⑰ Palais Podewils

Podewils Palace

Klosterstrasse 68–70. **Map** 10 D3. Ⓤ Klosterstrasse. 🚌 248.

This charming Baroque palace, set back from the street, was built between 1701 and 1704 for the Royal Court's counsellor, Caspar Jean de Bodt. Its owes its present name to its subsequent owner, a minister of state called von Podewils, who bought the palace in 1732.

After World War II, the palace was restored twice: in 1954, and then again in 1966 after it had been damaged by fire. The carefully reconstructed building did not lose much of its austere beauty, but the interior completely changed to suit its current needs. It is now a performance space used by several arts companies and a number of dance groups, who conduct classes on the site.

⑱ Parochialkirche

Parish Church

Klosterstr. 67. **Map** 10 D3. **Tel** 24 75 95 10. Ⓤ Klosterstrasse. 🚌 248. **Open** 9am–5pm Mon–Fri.

This building was, at one time, one of the most beautiful Baroque churches in Berlin. Johann Arnold Nering prepared the initial design, with four chapels framing a central tower. Unfortunately, Nering died as construction started in 1695. The work was continued by Martin Grünberg, but the collapse of the nearly completed vaults forced a change in the design. Instead of the intended tower over the main structure, a vestibule with a front tower was built. The church was completed in 1703, but then, in 1714, its tower was enlarged by Jean de Bodt in order to accommodate a carillon.

World War II had a devastating effect on the Parochialkirche. The interior was completely destroyed, and the tower collapsed. Following stabilization of the main structure, the façade has been restored, with some reproduced historic elements set within a plain interior. During the summer, mass is held in the church.

Medallion from a headstone in the Parochialkirche

⑲ Gaststätte Zur letzten Instanz

Inn of the Last Instance

Waisenstrasse 14–16. **Map** 10 D3. Ⓤ Klosterstrasse. 🚌 248.

The small street at the rear of the Parochialkirche leads directly to one of the oldest inns in Berlin, Zur letzten Instanz, which translates as the Inn of the Last Instance. The inn occupies one of the four picturesque houses on Waisenstrasse – the only survivors of the whole row of houses that once adjoined the town wall. Their history goes back to medieval times, but their present form dates from the 18th century. The houses are actually the result of an almost total reconstruction carried out after World War II. This was when one of the houses acquired its spiral Rococo staircase, which came from a dismantled house on the Fischerinsel.

The Zur letzten Instanz was first established in 1621 and initially specialized in serving alcoholic beverages. Interestingly, it was frequently patronized by lawyers. Today, however, the Zur letzten Instanz is one of Berlin's finest historic pub-restaurants frequented by all types of people, not just lawyers *(see p233)*. Its interior is full of old memorabilia.

⑳ Stadtmauer

Town Wall

Waisenstrasse. **Map** 10 D3. Ⓤ & Ⓢ Alexanderplatz or Ⓤ Klosterstrasse. 🚌 248.

The town wall that once surrounded the settlements of Berlin and Cölln was erected in the second half of the 13th century. The ring of fortifications, built from brick and fieldstone, was made taller in the 14th century. Having finally lost its military significance by the 17th century, the wall was almost entirely dismantled. Today, some small sections survive around Waisenstrasse, because they were incorporated into other buildings.

Remains of the Berlin's Stadtmauer (old town wall)

NORTH OF THE CENTRE

The area northwest of Alexanderplatz, formerly called Spandauer Vorstadt, is a historic district that has developed into a lively neighbourhood, buzzing with bars, cafés and designer shops. The southeastern part of the area is known as Scheunenviertel (Barn Quarter). In 1672, the Great Elector moved the hay barns – a fire hazard – out of the city limits. From that time it became a refuge for Jews fleeing Russia and Eastern Europe. To the north is Prenzlauer Berg, a bohemian hub in the 1990s and now, after gentrification, a beautiful and pleasant place to live and visit.

Sights at a Glance

Streets and Parks

3 Oranienburger Strasse
4 Monbijoupark
9 Sophienstrasse
10 Alte and Neue Schönhauser Strasse
12 Torstrasse
13 Kollwitzplatz

Churches and Synagogues

1 Neue Synagoge
8 Sophienkirche
14 Synagogue Rykestrasse
19 Zionskirche

Theatres

11 Volksbühne
20 Friedrichstadtpalast
21 Berliner Ensemble
23 Deutsches Theater

Museums

2 Centrum Judaicum
26 Brecht-Weigel-Gedenkstätte
28 Museum für Naturkunde
29 *Hamburger Bahnhof pp114–15*

Cemeteries

7 Alter Jüdischer Friedhof
16 Jüdischer Friedhof
25 *Dorotheenstädtischer Friedhof pp110–11*

Others

5 Hackesche Höfe
6 Gedenkstätte Grosse Hamburger Strasse
15 Wasserturm
17 Kulturbrauerei
18 Prater
22 Sammlung Boros
24 Charité
27 Gedenkstätte Berliner Mauer

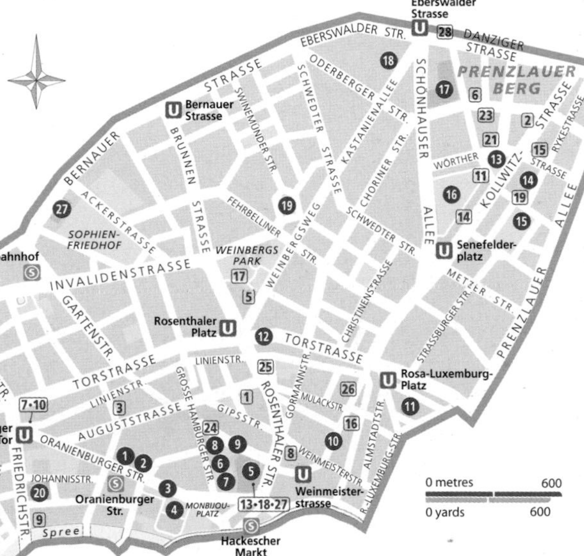

Restaurants

see pp233–5

1 Al Contadino sotto le Stelle
2 Anna Blumne
3 Beth Café
4 Brecht-Keller
5 Cafe Fleury
6 Cenacolo
7 Dada Falafel
8 Dos Palillos
9 Friedrichs 106
10 Gambrinus trifft Bacchus
11 Gugelhof
12 Habel Weinkultur and Brasserie
13 Hackescher Hof
14 Khushi
15 Mao Thai
16 Monsieur Vuong
17 Nola's am Weinberg
18 Oxymoron
19 Pasternak
20 Reinstoff
21 Restauration 1900
22 Sarah Wiener Café and Restaurant
23 Savanna
24 Sophieneck
25 Transit
26 Yam Yam
27 Yosoy
28 Zum Schusterjungen

See also Streetfinder maps 1, 2, 8 & 9

◀ The golden Neue Synagoge

Street-by-Street: Scheunenviertel

Until World War II Scheunenviertel lay at the heart of Berlin's large Jewish district. During the 19th century the community flourished, its prosperity reflected in grand buildings such as the Neue Synagoge, which opened in 1866 in the presence of Chancellor Otto von Bismarck. Left to crumble for nearly 50 years after the double devastations of the Nazis and Allied bombing, the district has enjoyed a huge revival since the fall of the Wall. Cafés and bars have opened and visitors can expect to find some of the liveliest nightlife in East Berlin.

1 ★ Neue Synagoge
Sparkling with gold, the restored New Synagogue is now used again for services.

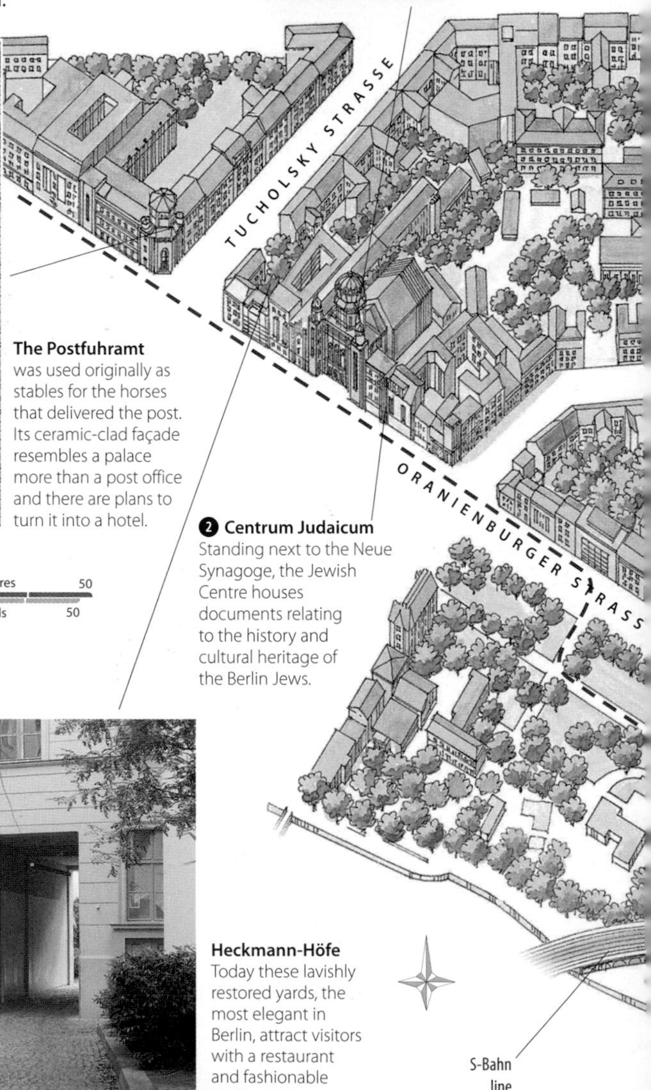

TUCHOLSKY STRASSE

ORANIENBURGER STRASSE

The Postfuhramt
was used originally as stables for the horses that delivered the post. Its ceramic-clad façade resembles a palace more than a post office and there are plans to turn it into a hotel.

2 Centrum Judaicum
Standing next to the Neue Synagoge, the Jewish Centre houses documents relating to the history and cultural heritage of the Berlin Jews.

0 metres 50
0 yards 50

Key

— Suggested route

Heckmann-Höfe
Today these lavishly restored yards, the most elegant in Berlin, attract visitors with a restaurant and fashionable clothes shops.

S-Bahn line

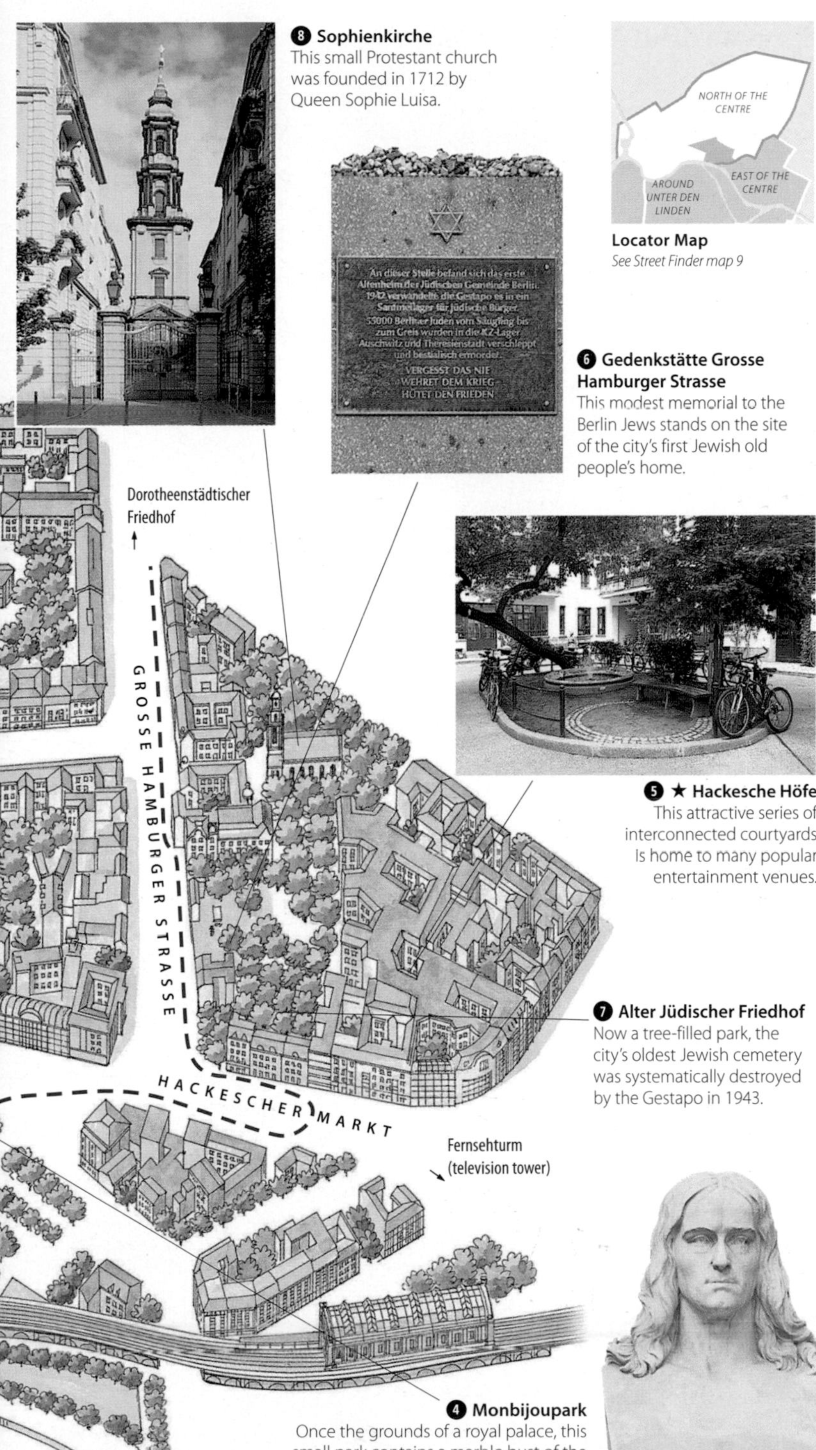

8 Sophienkirche
This small Protestant church was founded in 1712 by Queen Sophie Luisa.

Locator Map
See Street Finder map 9

6 Gedenkstätte Grosse Hamburger Strasse
This modest memorial to the Berlin Jews stands on the site of the city's first Jewish old people's home.

5 ★ Hackesche Höfe
This attractive series of interconnected courtyards is home to many popular entertainment venues.

7 Alter Jüdischer Friedhof
Now a tree-filled park, the city's oldest Jewish cemetery was systematically destroyed by the Gestapo in 1943.

4 Monbijoupark
Once the grounds of a royal palace, this small park contains a marble bust of the poet Adelbert von Chamisso.

❶ Neue Synagoge

New Synagogue

Oranienburger Strasse 30. **Map** 9 A1. **Tel** 880 28 300. Ⓢ Oranienburger Strasse. M1, M6. **Open** Mar–Oct: 10am–8pm Sun & Mon, 10am–6pm Tue–Thu, 10am–2pm Fri (to 5pm Fri from Apr–Sep); Nov–Feb: 10am–6pm daily (to 2pm Fri). **Closed** Jewish festivals.

The building of the New Synagogue was started in 1859 by architect Eduard Knoblauch, and completed in 1866. The design, a highly sophisticated response to the asymmetrical shape of the plot of land, used a narrow façade flanked by a pair of towers and crowned with a dome containing a round vestibule. Small rooms opened off the vestibule, including an anteroom and two prayer rooms – one large and one small. The two towers opened onto a staircase leading to the galleries, and the main hall had space for around 3,000 worshippers. An innovative use of iron in the construction of the roof and galleries put the synagogue at the forefront of 19th-century civil engineering.

This fascinating structure was Berlin's largest synagogue until 9 November 1938, when it was partially destroyed during the infamous *"Kristallnacht"* *(see pp30–31)*. The building was damaged further by Allied bombing in 1943 and was finally demolished in 1958 by government authorities.

Reconstruction began in 1988 and was completed with due ceremony in 1995. The building is used for public exhibitions by the Centrum Judaicum and includes a small prayer room.

The Centrum Judaicum, centre for research into Jewish heritage

❷ Centrum Judaicum

Jewish Centre

Oranienburger Strasse 28–30. **Map** 9 A1. **Tel** 880 28 300. Ⓢ Oranienburger Strasse. M1, M6. **Open** Mar–Oct: 10am–8pm Sun & Mon, 10am–6pm Tue–Thu, 10am–2pm Fri (to 5pm Fri from Apr–Sep); Nov–Feb: 10am–6pm daily (to 2pm Fri). **Closed** Jewish festivals.

The entrance to the Jewish Centre is easy to recognize thanks to the policemen permanently stationed here. All visitors must undergo a strict security check involving the use of a metal detector: the guards are polite but firm. The Centrum Judaicum occupies the former premises of the Jewish community council, and contains a library, archives and a research centre devoted to the history and cultural heritage of the Berlin Jews. Next door to the Centrum, the restored rooms of the Neue Synagoge are used to exhibit material relating to the local Jewish community, including one of the greatest of all Jewish thinkers and social activists, Moses Mendelssohn.

❸ Oranienburger Strasse

Map 8 F1, 9 A1, 9 B2. Ⓢ Oranienburger Strasse or Hackescher Markt. Ⓤ Oranienburger Tor. 12, M1, M4, M5, M6.

Oranienburger Strasse is home to many of Berlin's most popular nightspots. People of all ages flock here, spending pleasant hours in the area's numerous cafés, restaurants and bars. The district has traditionally been a centre for alternative culture, home to the famous state-sponsored Tacheles centre for the arts, previously occupied by artist squatters. The Tacheles centre has closed, but many good art galleries remain in this area. As you stroll around the district it is worth looking out for a number of interesting buildings, such as the one at Oranienburger Strasse No. 71–2, which was built by Christian

The Neue Synagoge with its splendidly reconstructed dome

Moses Mendelssohn (1729–1786)

One of the greatest German philosophers of the 18th century, Moses Mendelssohn arrived in Berlin in 1743 and was a central figure in the Jewish struggle for citizenship rights. About 50 years later the first Jewish family was granted full civic rights; however, it was not until the Emancipation Edict of 1812 that Jewish men finally became full citizens. The grandfather of composer Felix Mendelssohn-Bartholdy, he is immortalized in the drama *Nathan der Weise* (Nathan the Wise) by his friend Gotthold Ephraim Lessing.

Friedrich Becherer in 1789 for the Great National Masonic Lodge of Germany.

Note that there is a seedy red-light edge to the area at night.

❹ Monbijoupark

Monbijou Park

Oranienburger Strasse. **Map** 9 B2. Ⓢ Oranienburger Strasse or Hackescher Markt. M1, M4, M5, M6.

This small park, situated between Oranienburger Strasse and the Spree river, was once the grounds of the Monbijou Palace. Damaged by bombing during World War II, the ruined palace was dismantled in 1960. A rare green space in this part of the city, the well-kept park is a pleasant place to spend time relaxing. It features a marble bust of the poet Adelbert von Chamisso, and there is also an open-air swimming pool for children.

❺ Hackesche Höfe

Rosenthaler Strasse 40–41. **Map** 9 B1, 9 B2. Ⓢ Hackescher Markt. Ⓤ Weinmeisterstrasse M1, M4, M5, M6.

Running from Oranienburger Strasse and Rosenthaler up as far as Sophienstrasse, the Hackesche Höfe (*Höfe* means "yards") is a huge, early 20th-century complex. It is made up of an intricate series of nine interconnecting courtyards surrounded by tall and beautifully proportioned buildings. The development dates from 1906, and was designed by Kurt Berendt and August Endell, both of whom were outstanding exponents of the German Secession style.

One of the striking inner courtyards at the Hackesche Höfe

Damaged during World War II, Hackesche Höfe has been restored to its original splendour. The first courtyard is especially attractive, featuring glazed facings with geometric designs decorated in fabulous colours. A whole range of restaurants, bars, art galleries, shops and restaurants can be found here, as well as offices and apartments on the upper floors. The complex also has its own theatre, the Hackesche Hoftheater, specializing in mime. For many Berliners the Hackesche Höfe has become something of a cult spot, and for visitors it is definitely a sight not to be missed.

❻ Gedenkstätte Grosse Hamburger Strasse

Grosse Hamburger Strasse Memorial

Grosse Hamburger Strasse. **Map** 9 B1. Ⓢ Hackescher Markt. 12, M1, M4, M5, M6.

Until the years leading up to World War II, Grosse Hamburger Strasse was one of the main streets of Berlin's Jewish quarter. It was home to several Jewish schools, an old people's home and the city's oldest Jewish cemetery, established in 1672. The home was used during World War II as a detention centre for many thousands of Berlin Jews condemned to death in the camps at Auschwitz and Theresienstadt. The building was later destroyed, and in its place now stands a small monument representing a group of Jews being led to their deaths. A modest commemorative plaque is displayed nearby.

Nearby, at Grosse Hamburger Strasse No. 27, stands a Jewish school founded in 1778 by Moses Mendelssohn. Rebuilt in 1906, the building was reopened as a Jewish secondary school in 1993. The empty space once occupied by house No. 15–16, which was destroyed by World War II bombing, is now an installation, *The Missing House* by Christian Boltanski, with plaques recording the names and professions of the former inhabitants of the house.

The Gedenkstätte Grosse Hamburger Strasse, commemorating Berlin Jews murdered in the Holocaust

❼ Alter Jüdischer Friedhof

Old Jewish Cemetery

Grosse Hamburger Strasse. **Map** 9 B2. Ⓢ Hackescher Markt. M1.

The Old Jewish Cemetery was established in 1672 and, until 1827 when it was finally declared full, it provided the resting place for over 12,000 Berliners. After this date Jews were buried in cemeteries in Schönhauser Allee and in Herbert-Baum-Strasse. The Alter Jüdischer Friedhof was destroyed by the Nazis in 1943, and in 1945 the site was turned into a park. Embedded in the original cemetery wall, a handful of Baroque *masebas* (or tombstones) continue to provide a poignant reminder of the past. A *maseba* stands on the grave of the philosopher Moses Mendelssohn *(see p104)*, erected in 1990 by members of the Jewish community.

❽ Sophienkirche

Grosse Hamburger Str. 31. **Map** 9 B1. **Tel** 308 79 20. Ⓢ Hackescher Markt. Ⓤ Weinmeisterstrasse. M1, M4, M5, M6. **Open** May–Sep: 3–6pm Wed, 3–5pm Sat. 10am Sun.

A narrow passageway and a picturesque gate take you through to this small Baroque church. Founded in 1712 by Queen Sophie Luisa, this was the first parish church of the newly developed Spandauer Vorstadt area *(see p101)*. Johann Friedrich Grael designed the tower, which was built between 1729 and 1735.

Interior of the Sophienkirche with its original 18th-century pulpit

Eighteenth-century buildings along Sophienstrasse

In 1892 the building was extended to include a presbytery, though the church still retains its original Baroque character. A modest, rectangular structure, Sophienkirche is typical of its period, with the tower adjoining the narrower side elevation. The interior still contains a number of its original 18th-century furnishings, including the pulpit and the font.

Several gravestones, some from the 18th century, have survived in the small cemetery surrounding the church.

❾ Sophienstrasse

Map 9 B1. Sammlung Hoffmann Sophienstrasse 21. **Tel** 28 49 91 20. Ⓢ Hackescher Markt. Ⓤ Weinmeisterstrasse. M1, M4, M5, M6. **Open** 11am–4pm Sat, by appointment.

The area around Sophienstrasse and Gipsstrasse was first settled at the end of the 17th century. In fact, Sophienstrasse was once the main street of Spandauer Vorstadt. The area underwent extensive restoration during the 1980s that preserved its small-town character. Today, the narrow lanes and three-storey buildings are reminiscent of Prague's Old Town. It was one of the first parts of East Berlin in which renovation was chosen in favour of large-scale demolition and redevelopment. Now these modest but charming 18th-century Neo-Classical buildings are home to a number of different arts and crafts workshops, cosy bars, unusual boutiques, a puppet theatre and interesting art galleries.

One building with a particularly eventful history is Sophienstrasse No. 18. The house was erected in 1852, although its striking and picturesque terracotta double doorway dates from the time of its extensive restoration, undertaken in 1904 by Joseph Franckel and Theodor Kampfmeyer on behalf of the Crafts Society. Founded in 1844, the Crafts Society moved its headquarters to Sophienstrasse in 1905. On 14 November 1918 the very same house was used as the venue for the first meeting of the Spartacus League, which was later to become the Communist Party of Germany. Today, No. 18 houses a modern dance and theatre company.

The main door of the house at Sophienstrasse No. 21 leads into a long row of interior courtyards running up as far as Gipsstrasse. In one of these courtyards is a private modern art gallery, the **Sammlung Hoffmann**, which can be reached by passing through a brightly lit tunnel.

❿ Alte and Neue Schönhauser Strasse

Map 9 B1, 9 C1. Ⓢ Hackescher Markt. Ⓤ Weinmeisterstrasse. 🚋 M1.

Alte Schönhauser Strasse is one of the oldest streets in the Spandauer Vorstadt district, running from the centre of Berlin to Pankow and Schönhausen. In the 18th and 19th centuries this was a popular residential area among wealthy merchants. The proximity of the neighbouring slum area of the Scheunenviertel *(see pp102–3)* to the west, however, lowered the tone of the neighbourhood quite considerably.

For a long time, bars, small factories, workshops and retail shops were the hallmark of the neighbourhood around Alte Schönhauser Strasse. Small private shops survived longer here than in most other parts of Berlin, and the largely original houses maintained much of their pre-1939 atmosphere.

Much has changed, however, since the fall of the Berlin Wall. Some of the houses have been restored, and many old businesses have been replaced by fashionable new shops, restaurants and bars, making it one of the most expensive retail areas in the city. Throughout the district, the old and the new now stand side by side. One poignant example is at Neue Schönhauser Strasse No. 14. This interesting old house in the German Neo-Renaissance style was built in 1891 to a design by Alfred Messel. The first-floor rooms were home to the first public reading-room in Berlin, while on the ground floor was a *Volkskaffeehaus*, a soup-kitchen with separate rooms for men and women. Here the poor of the neighbourhood could get a free bowl of soup and a cup of ersatz (imitation) coffee.

Ironically, in the 1990s, the building became home to one of Berlin's most fashionable restaurants.

One of the Neo-Renaissance buildings on Neue Schönhauser Strasse

⓫ Volksbühne

People's Theatre

Rosa-Luxemburg-Platz. **Map** 10 D1. **Tel** 24 06 55. Ⓤ Rosa-Luxemburg-Platz. 🚌 100, 200. 🚋 M8.

Founded during the early years of the 20th century, this theatre owes its existence to the efforts of the 100,000 members of the Freie Volksbühne (Free People's Theatre Society). The original theatre was built to a design by Oskar Kaufmann in 1913, a time when the Scheunenviertel district was undergoing rapid redevelopment. During the 1920s the theatre became famous thanks to the director Erwin Piscator (1893–1966), who later achieved great acclaim at the Metropol-Theater on Nollendorfplatz.

Destroyed during World War II, the theatre was eventually rebuilt during the early 1950s to a design by Hans Richter.

⓬ Torstrasse

Torstrasse. **Map** 1 B8–9, 2 D5–E5. Ⓤ Oranienburger Tor, Rosenthaler Platz, Rosa-Luxemburg-Platz. 🚌 142. 🚋 M1, M8.

Formerly a customs road and Berlin's northern border around 1800, Torstrasse is now a main thoroughfare connecting Prenzlauer Allee and Friedrichstrasse. From 1949 to 1990, the street was given the name

Café in bustling Torstrasse

Wilhelm-Pieck-Strasse after East Germany's first president, and some old buildings were replaced by prefabs. Although it is a busy, noisy and sometimes polluted street, Torstrasse has its charms and is transforming from a largely working-class bohemian area into a more appealing location, particularly for young urbanites.

The 19th-century residential buildings lining the street have been gentrified to make way for happening bars, trendy cafés and gourmet restaurants, art galleries, and fashion shops with numerous bargains to be found. "Soto", the area south of Torstrasse has the highest concentration of independent designers and brand outfitters in the city.

⓭ Kollwitzplatz

Ⓤ Senefelderplatz.

This green square is named after the German artist Käthe Kollwitz (1867–1945), who once lived nearby. It was here that the socially engaged painter and sculptor observed and painted the daily hardships of the working-class people living in overcrowded tenements. One of her sculptures stands on the square, now the socializing hub of the district, with a Thursday organic farmers' market, cool bars, restaurants and shops that extend into the surrounding streets. Käthe Kollwitz's work can be seen at the Käthe-Kollwitz-Museum *(see p158)*.

⓮ Synagogue Rykestrasse

Rykestrasse 53. **Map** 2 F4. **Tel** 88 02 81 47. Ⓤ Senefelderplatz. **Open** for services only; times vary.

This synagogue is one of the few reminders of old Jewish life in Berlin, and one of the few in Germany left almost intact during the Nazi terror regime. Built in 1904, the red-brick synagogue has a basilica-like nave with three aisles and certain Moorish features. Due to its location inside a huge tenement area, Nazi SA troops did not set it on fire during the *Kristallnacht* pogrom on 9 November 1938, when hundreds of other synagogues were razed to the ground. The synagogue welcomes visitors to its public services; call ahead to check times.

⓯ Wasserturm

Knaackstrasse/Belforter Strasse. **Map** 2 F4. Ⓤ Senefelderplatz.

The unofficial symbol of the district is a 30-m- (100-ft-) high water tower, standing high on the former mill hill in the heart of Prenzlauer Berg. It was here that some of the windmills, once typical in Prenzlauer Berg, produced flour for the city's population. The distinctive brick water tower was built in 1874 by Wilhelm Vollhering and served as a water reservoir for the country's first running water system. In the 1930s, the basement served as a makeshift jail, where Nazi SA troops held and tortured Communist opponents. This dark period is marked by a plaque.

The giant Wasserturm looming high in Knaackstrasse

Gravestones in the peaceful Jüdischer Friedhof

⓰ Jüdischer Friedhof

Jewish Cemetery

Schönhauser Allee 22–25. **Map** 2 E4. **Tel** 441 98 24. Ⓤ Senefelderplatz. **Open** 8am–4pm Mon–Thu, 7:30am–2:30pm Fri. **Closed** Sat, Sun & public hols.

This small Jewish cemetery is hidden behind thick walls on Schönhauser Allee, but the serene atmosphere, with tall trees and thick undergrowth, is a welcome oasis. The cemetery was laid out in 1827, though the oldest gravestone dates back to the 14th century. It was Berlin's second-largest Jewish cemetery after the Jüdischer Friedhof Weissensee *(see p173)*. Among the many prominent Berliners resting here are the painter Max Liebermann (1847–1935); the composer and musical director of the Staatsoper Unter den Linden; and the author David Friedländer (1750–1834). The lapidarium displays historic gravestones from various Jewish cemeteries.

⓱ Kulturbrauerei

Schönhauser Allee 36–39. **Map** 2 E3. **Tel** 44 35 26 14. Museum Alltagsgeschichte der DDR: **Open** 10am–6pm Tue–Sun (to 8pm Thu). Ⓤ Eberswalder Strasse. 🚋 12, M1, M10.

This vast Neo-Gothic, industrial red-and-yellow-brick building was once Berlin's most famous brewery, Schultheiss, built by architect Franz Schwechten in 1889–92. Now housing the Kulturbrauerei, the huge complex with several courtyards has been revived as a cultural and entertainment centre, with concert venues, restaurants and cafés, and a cinema, as well as artists' ateliers. Inside the Kulturbrauerei, the **Museum Alltagsgeschichte der DDR** (Museum of Everyday Life in the GDR) features exhibitions on the former East Germany.

⓲ Prater

Kastanienallee 7–9. **Map** 2 E3. **Tel** 448 56 88. Ⓤ Eberswalder Strasse. 🚋 12, M1.

Prater has been one of Berlin's best-known entertainment institutions for more than a century. The building, along with its quiet courtyard, was constructed in the 1840s and later became the city's oldest and largest beer garden *(see p249)*. It now houses a restaurant, serving Berlin specialities, and stages a variety of pop, rock and folk concerts and theatre shows.

⓳ Zionskirche

Zionskirchplatz. **Map** 2 D4. **Tel** 449 21 91. Ⓤ Senefelderplatz, Rosenthaler Platz. 🚋 12, M1. **Open** irregular opening hours; call ahead.

Located in the square named after it, Zionskirchplatz, this Protestant church was built between 1866 and 1873 – a tranquil oasis in the middle of this lively district. Both the square and the church have always been centres of political opposition. During the Third Reich, resistance groups against the Nazi regime congregated at the church, and when the Communists were in power in East Germany the alternative "environment library" (an information and documentation centre) was established here. Church and other opposition groups active here played a decisive role in the transformation of East Germany in 1989–90.

⑳ Friedrichstadt-palast

Friedrichstadt Palace

Friedrichstrasse 107. **Map** 8 F2. **Tel** 23 26 23 26. U Oranienburger Tor. S Oranienburger Strasse or Friedrichstrasse. 147. 12, M1.

Multicoloured glass tiles and a pink, plume-shaped neon sign make up the gaudy but eye-catching façade of the Friedrichstadtpalast. Built in the early 1980s, this gigantic theatre complex specializes in revues and variety shows. Nearly 2,000 seats are arranged around a huge podium, used by turns as a circus arena, a swimming pool and an icerink. In addition, a further huge stage is equipped with every technical facility. There is also a small cabaret theatre with seats for 240 spectators.

The original and much-loved Friedrichstadtpalast suffered bomb damage during World War II and was later condemned and replaced with the existing version. Built as a market hall, the earlier building was later used as a circus ring. In 1918 it became the Grosse Schauspielhaus, or Grand Playhouse, opening on 28 November 1919 with a memorable production of Aeschylus's *The Oresteia,* directed by the extraordinary Max Reinhardt *(see p112).*

The building itself was legendary, its central dome supported by a forest of columns and topped with Expressionist, stalactite-like decoration. An equally fantastical interior provided seating for 5,000 spectators.

The eye-catching façade of the Friedrichstadtpalast theatre complex

㉑ Berliner Ensemble

Bertolt-Brecht-Platz 1. **Map** 8 F2. **Tel** 28 40 81 55. S & U Friedrichstrasse. 147. 12, M1.

Designed by Heinrich Seeling in the Neo-Baroque style and built from 1891 to 1892, this theatre has been witness to many changes in Berlin's cultural life. First known as the Neues Theater am Schiffbauerdamm, it soon became famous for staging important premieres. In 1893 it put on the first performance of *The Weavers,* by Gerhart Hauptmann. Later on, the theatre was acclaimed for its memorable productions by Max Reinhardt. These included Shakespeare's *A Midsummer Night's Dream* in 1905, which, for the first time, used a revolving stage and real trees as part of the set. In 1928 the theatre presented the world premiere of Bertolt Brecht's *The Threepenny Opera.* The building was destroyed during World War II and subsequently restored with a much simpler exterior, but its Neo-Baroque interior, including Ernst Westphal's decorations, survived intact. After 1954 the theatre returned to prominence with the arrival of the Berliner Ensemble under the directorship of Bertolt Brecht and his wife, the actress Helene Weigel. The move from its former home, the Deutsches Theater, to the new venue was celebrated in November 1954 by staging the world premiere of *The Caucasian Chalk Circle,* written by Brecht in 1944/5. After Brecht's death his wife took over the running of the theatre, maintaining its innovative tradition.

Bertolt Brecht's monument in front of the Berliner Ensemble

㉒ Sammlung Boros

Reinhardtstrasse 20. **Map** 8 E2. **Tel** 27 59 40 65. S & U Oranienburger Tor. 147. M1, M12. Thu–Sun; book in advance. W **sammlung-boros.de**

This former air-raid bunker, built by architect Albert Speer, is an intriguing gallery location. The bunker has a chequered history; once used as a POW prison by the Red Army, it later became a warehouse, then in the 1990s it was a popular club.

In 2003, art collector Christian Boros bought the building and converted it into a gallery space. It houses the Boros Collection, which features modern art. No more than 12 guests can visit at one time and advance online registration is required.

㉕ Dorotheenstädtischer Friedhof

This small cemetery, established in 1763, is the final resting place of many famous Berlin citizens. It was enlarged between 1814 and 1826, but in 1899, following the extension of Hannoversche Strasse, the southern section of the cemetery was sold and its graves moved. Many of the monuments are outstanding works of art, coming from the workshops of some of the most prominent Berlin architects, including Karl Friedrich Schinkel *(see p181)* and Johann Gottfried Schadow. A tranquil, tree-filled oasis, the cemetery is reached via a narrow path, leading from the street between the wall of the French Cemetery and the Brecht- Weigel-Gedenkstätte house *(see p112)*.

★ **Johann Gottfried Schadow** (1764–1850)
Schadow created the famous *Quadriga*, which adorns the Brandenburg Gate.

BIRKENALLEE

Friedrich August Stüler (1800–1865)
Damaged during World War II, the grave of this famous architect was rebuilt in a colourful, post-modernist style.

Heinrich Mann (1871–1950)
This famous German novelist died in California but was buried in Berlin. The portrait is the work of Gustav Seitz.

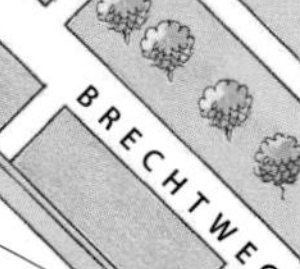

BRECHTWEG

Bertolt Brecht (1898–1956)
The grave of this famous playwright is marked with a rough stone. Beside him rests his wife, the actress Helene Weigel.

Hermann Heinrich Alexander Wentzel Königl. Baurath

Hermann Wentzel (1820–1889)
This architect designed his own tombstone; the bust was carved by Fritz Schaper.

Main entrance

KEY

① **Luther's statue** is a copy of the monument designed by JG Schadow.

② **Chapel**

Friedrich Hoffmann
(1818–1900)
The tomb of this engineer, best known as the inventor of the circular brick-firing kiln, takes the form of a colonnade faced with glazed bricks.

VISITORS' CHECKLIST

Practical Information
Chausseestrasse 126.
Map 8 F1.
Tel 461 72 79.
Open 8am–sunset daily.

Transport
U Naturkundemuseum or Oranienburger Tor.
Bus 142, 245, 247.
Tram M6, M8, 12.

★ Karl Friedrich Schinkel
(1781–1841)
Schinkel was the most prominent German architect of his time, and the creator of many of Berlin's best-loved buildings.

Johann Gottlieb Fichte (1762–1814)
A well-known philosopher of the Enlightenment era, Fichte was also the first Rector of Berlin University.

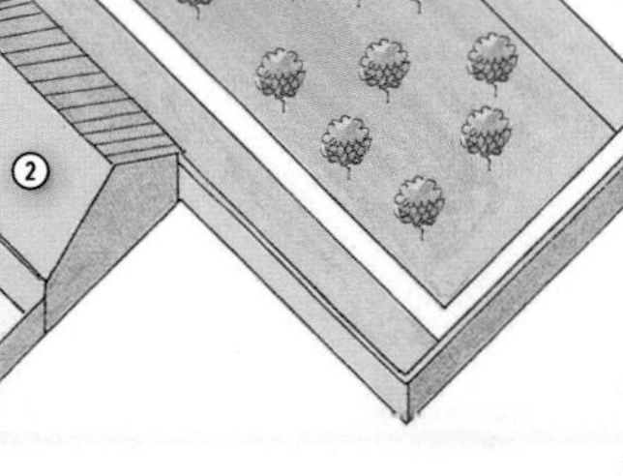

Georg Wilhelm Friedrich Hegel
(1770–1831)
Probably the greatest German philosopher of the Enlightenment era, Hegel worked for many years as a professor at Berlin University.

0 metres 20
0 yards 20

Elegant 19th-century façade of the Deutsches Theater

㉓ Deutsches Theater

Schumannstrasse 13A. **Map** 8 E2. **Tel** 28 44 10. Kammerspiele U Oranienburger Tor. 147. 12, M1.

This theatre building was designed by Eduard Titz and built between 1849 and 1850 to house the Friedrich-Wilhelm Städtisches Theater. In 1883, following substantial reconstruction, it was renamed Deutsches Theater and opened with Friedrich Schiller's *Intrigue and Love*. The theatre became famous under its next director, Otto Brahm, and it was here that Max Reinhardt began his career as an actor, before eventually becoming director from 1905 until 1933. On Reinhardt's initiative the theatre's façade was altered and in 1906 the adjacent casino was converted into a compact theatre – the Kammerspiele. At the time, the first-floor auditorium was decorated with a frieze by Edvard Munch (now in the Neue Nationalgalerie).

Another famous figure associated with the theatre was Bertolt Brecht who, until 1933, wrote plays for it; after World War II he became the director of the Berliner Ensemble, whose first venue was the Deutsches Theater. Brecht's debut as director was his play *Mother Courage and Her Children*.

Max Reinhardt (1873–1943)

This actor and director became famous as one of the 20th century's greatest theatre reformers. He worked in Berlin, first as an actor in the Deutsches Theater, and then from 1905 as its director. As well as setting up the Kammerspiele, he produced plays for the Neues Theater am Schiffbauerdamm (renamed the Berliner Ensemble) and the Schumann Circus (later to become the Friedrichstadtpalast), which was converted specially for him by Hans Poelzig. His experimental productions of classic and modern works brought him worldwide fame. Forced to emigrate because of his Jewish origins, he left Germany in 1933 and settled in the United States, where he died in 1943.

Huge 19th-century building complex housing the Charité hospital

㉔ Charité

Chariteplatz 1. **Map** 8 E1, E2. U Oranienburger Tor. 147. 12, M1. Berliner Medizinhistoriches Museum der Charité: **Tel** 450 53 61 56. **Open** 10am–5pm Tue, Thu, Fri & Sun; 10am–7pm Wed & Sat.

This huge building complex near Luisenstrasse contains the Charité hospital. Germany's oldest teaching hospital, it was first established in 1726 and has been attached to the Humboldt University *(see p62)* since its foundation in 1810. The oldest buildings of the current complex date back to the 1830s. Over the years, Charité has been associated with many famous German doctors and scientists who worked here, including Rudolf Virchow and Robert Koch.

In 1899 Virchow founded the Museum der Charité, next to the Institute of Pathology. Its collection consists of some 23,000 specimens, which are available for public viewing. Although many artifacts were destroyed in World War II, the museum itself has survived and reopened in 1999.

㉕ Dorotheenstädtischer Friedhof

See pp110–111.

㉖ Brecht-Weigel-Gedenkstätte

Brecht-Weigel Memorial

Chausseestrasse 125. **Tel** 200 57 18 44. **Map** 1 A5, 8 E1. U Naturkundemuseum or Oranienburger Tor. 147, 245. M6, 12. **Open** 10–11:30am & 2–3:30pm Tue, 10–11:30am Wed & Fri, 10–11:30am & 5–6:30pm Thu, 10am–3:30pm Sat, 11am–6pm Sun. compulsory. Every half-hour (every hour on Sun). **Closed** Mon & public hols.

Bertolt Brecht, one of the greatest playwrights of the 20th century, was associated with Berlin from 1920, but emigrated in 1933. After the war, his left-wing views made him an attractive potential resident of the newly created German socialist state. Lured by the promise of his own theatre he returned to Berlin in 1948, with his wife, the actress Helene Weigel. He directed the Berliner Ensemble until his death, concentrating mainly on the production of his own plays.

He lived in a first-floor apartment at Chausseestrasse 125 from 1953 until his death in 1956. He is buried in Dorotheenstädtischer Friedhof *(see pp110–11)*. His wife lived in the second-floor apartment, and after Brecht's death moved to the ground floor. She also founded an archive of Brecht's works which is located on the second floor of the building.

Remains of the Berlin Wall on Bernauer Strasse

㉗ Gedenkstätte Berliner Mauer

Berlin Wall Memorial

Bernauer Strasse 119. **Map** 1 B4. Ⓢ Nordbahnhof. Ⓤ Bernauer Strasse. M8, M10. 245, 247. Wall Documentation Center: **Tel** 467 98 66 66. **Open** Apr–Oct: 9:30am–7pm Tue–Sun; Nov–Mar: 9:30am–6pm Tue–Sun. call ahead.

On the night between 12 and 13 August 1961 the East German authorities decided to close the border around the western sectors of Berlin. Initially the Berlin Wall *(die Mauer)* consisted simply of rolls of barbed wire. However, these were soon replaced by a 4-m (13-ft) wall safeguarded by a second wall made from reinforced concrete. This second wall was topped with a thick pipe to prevent people from reaching the top of the Wall with their fingers. Along the Wall ran what was known as a "death zone", an area controlled by guards with dogs. Where the border passed close to houses, the inhabitants were relocated. Along the border with West Berlin there were 293 watchtowers, along with 57 bunkers and, later on, alarms.

On 9 November 1989, with the help of Soviet leader Mikhail Gorbachev, the Berlin Wall was finally breached. Dismantling it took much longer, however, with more than a million tons of rubble to be removed.

Only small fragments of the Wall have survived. One of these, along Bernauer Strasse between Acker- and Bergstrasse, is now an official place of remembrance. The location of the memorial is poignant, as the Wall was cut in two here at Bernauer Strasse. This resulted in people jumping to the West side from upper-floor buildings that stood right on the dividing line, while border guards were bricking up doors and windows facing west. Today, the memorial is a grim reminder of the hardship the division inflicted on the city. It includes a museum and various installations along a mile of the former border. The Chapel of Reconciliation replaces the original church, which was demolished in 1985.

During the Wall's 28-year existence, about 5,000 people managed to escape into West Berlin; a total of 192 people were killed by the Eastern border guards while attempting to do so.

㉘ Museum für Naturkunde

Natural History Museum

Invalidenstrasse 43. **Map** 8 E1. **Tel** 20 93 85 91. Ⓤ Naturkundemuseum. 147, 245. **Open** 9:30am–6pm Tue–Fri, 10am–6pm Sat, Sun & public hols.

One of the biggest natural history museums in the world, the collection here contains over 30 million exhibits. Occupying a purpose-built Neo-Renaissance building, constructed between 1883 and 1889, the museum has been operating for over a century, and despite several periods of renovation has maintained its old-fashioned atmosphere.

The highlight of the museum is the world's largest original dinosaur skeleton, which is housed in the glass-covered courtyard. This colossal 23-m- (75-ft-) long and 12-m- (39-ft-) high Brachiosaurus was discovered in Tanzania in 1909 by a German fossil-hunting expedition. Six other smaller reconstructed dinosaur skeletons and a replica of the fossilized remains of an Archaeopteryx, thought to be the prehistoric link between reptiles and birds, complete this fascinating display.

The adjacent rooms feature extensive collections of colourful shells and butterflies, as well as taxidermy, including birds and mammals. Particularly popular are the dioramas – scenes of mounted animals set against the background of their natural habitat. A favourite with children is Bobby the Gorilla, who was brought to Berlin Zoo in 1928 as a 2-year-old and lived there until 1935. The museum also boasts an impressive collection of minerals and meteorites.

Brachiosaurus skeleton in the Museum für Naturkunde

㉙ Hamburger Bahnhof

This art museum is situated in a specially adapted Neo-Classical building that was built in 1847 as a railway station. Following extensive refurbishment by Josef Paul Kleihues, it was opened to the public in 1996. At night, the façade is lit up by a neon installation by Dan Flavin. The museum has an ever-changing rotation of artworks, including pieces by Joseph Beuys and a selection from the world-renowned Friedrich Christian Flick Collection of Art from the second half of the 20th century, as well as from the Marx and Marzona collections. The result is one of the best modern and contemporary art museums in Europe, which features film, video, music and design alongside painting and sculpture.

Restaurant
This stylish restaurant, run by chef Sarah Wiener, provides a welcome respite for visitors.

Museum Façade
The museum's impressive Neo-Classical façade is flanked by two towers and has a grand entrance hall and inner courtyard.

Main entrance

First Time Painting (1961)
This work by American artist Robert Rauschenberg was created while he worked with John Cage at Black Mountain College.

★ ***Richtkräfte*** (1974–7)
Joseph Beuys' work – often a record of his thoughts – created an archive of the artist's vision.

VISITORS' CHECKLIST

Practical Information
Invalidenstrasse 50/51.
Map 8 D1.
Tel 39 78 34 11.
hamburgerbahnhof.de
Open 10am–6pm Tue–Sun (to 8pm Thu). **Closed** 24 & 31 Dec.

Transport
S & U Hauptbahnhof.
120, 123, 147, 240, 245, TXL, M41, M85.

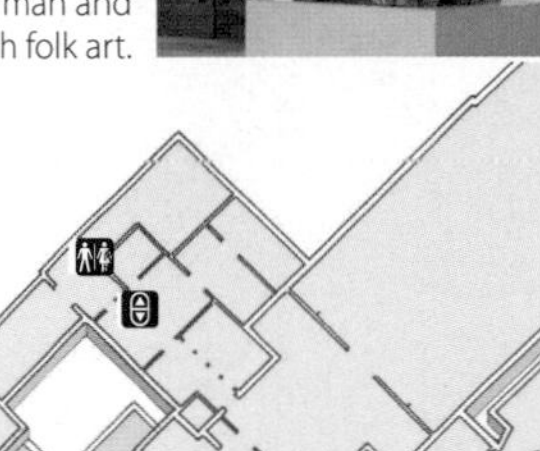

Volk Ding Zero (2009)
This 3-m (9-ft) high bronze sculpture by Georg Baselitz was inspired by African, German and Polish folk art.

★ ***Mao*** (1972)
This well-known portrait by Andy Warhol initially elevated the Chinese communist leader to the rank of pop icon.

Key

- Ground floor
- Rieckhallen
- First floor
- Second floor

Main Hall
The main hall is used for unusual installations and even fashion shows. Here, models are showcasing the collections at the 2010 BOSS Black Fashion Show.

Gallery Guide

The gallery has more than 10,000 sq m (108,000 sq ft) of exhibition space. All the works on display at the Hamburger Bahnhof are temporary and exhibits described here may not necessarily be on display. The Rieckhallen shows selected works from the Friedrich Christian Flick Collection in rotation.

RESTAURANT
Josty

TIERGARTEN

Once a royal hunting estate, the Tiergarten became a park in the 18th century. In the 19th century a series of buildings, mostly department stores and banks, was erected at Potsdamer Platz. During World War II many of these buildings were destroyed. The division of Berlin changed the character of the area. The Tiergarten area ended up on the west side of the Wall, and later regained its glory with the creation of the Kulturforum and the Hansaviertel. The area around Potsdamer Platz fell in East Berlin and became a wasteland. Since reunification, however, this area has witnessed exciting development. Together with the government offices near the Reichstag, this ensures that the Tiergarten area is at the centre of Berlin's political and financial district.

Sights at a Glance

Museums and Galleries

2 Musikinstrumenten-Museum
4 *Kunstgewerbemuseum pp122–5*
5 Kupferstichkabinett
6 Kunstbibliothek
8 *Gemäldegalerie pp126–9*
9 Neue Nationalgalerie
12 Bendlerblock (Gedenkstätte Deutscher Widerstand)
14 Bauhaus-Archiv

Districts, Squares and Parks

10 *Potsdamer Platz pp132–5*
15 Diplomatenviertel
16 Tiergarten
17 Grosser Stern
19 Hansaviertel
22 Regierungsviertel

Historic Buildings

1 Staatsbibliothek
3 Philharmonie und Kammermusiksaal
7 St-Matthäus-Kirche
11 Shell-Haus
13 Villa von der Heydt
20 Schloss Bellevue
21 Haus der Kulturen der Welt
23 Reichstag

Monuments

18 Siegessäule
24 Sowjetisches Ehrenmal

Restaurants
see pp235–6

1 Angkor Wat
2 Cafe am Neuen See
3 Cafe Mohring
4 Facil
5 Gaststatte Ambrosius
6 Kafers Dachgarten
7 Lanninger
8 Lindenbrau
9 Lutter & Wegner in Kaisersaal
10 OM
11 Rikes Gasthaus
12 Teehaus Tiergarten

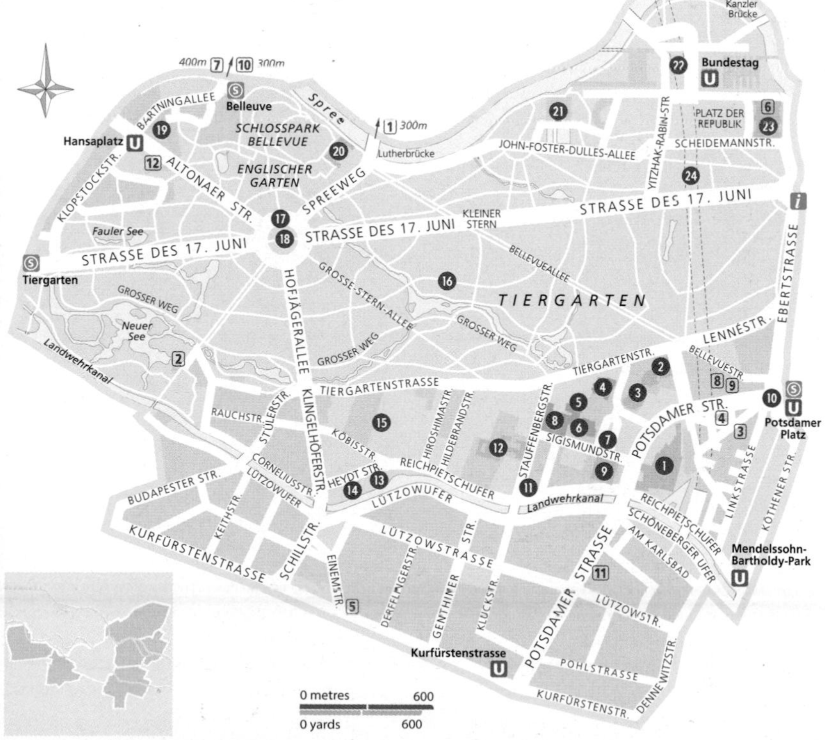

See also Street Finder maps 6, 7, 8, 13 & 14

◀ View of the Sony Centre, Potsdamer Platz

For map symbols *see back flap*

Street-by-Street: Around the Kulturforum

The idea of creating a new cultural centre in West Berlin was first mooted in 1956. The first building to go up was the Berlin Philharmonic concert hall, built to an innovative design by Hans Scharoun in 1961. Most of the plans for the various other components of the Kulturforum were realized between 1961 and 1987, and came from such famous architects as Ludwig Mies van der Rohe. The area is now a major cultural centre which attracts millions of visitors every year.

4 ★ Kunstgewerbemuseum
Among the collection at the Museum of Arts and Crafts you can see this intricately carved silver and ivory tankard, made in an Augsburg workshop in around 1640.

5 Kupferstichkabinett
The large collection of prints and drawings owned by this gallery includes this portrait of Albrecht Dürer's mother.

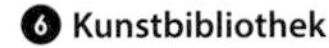

6 Kunstbibliothek
The Art Library boasts a rich collection of books, graphic art and drawings, many of which are displayed in its exhibition halls.

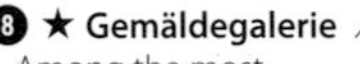

8 ★ Gemäldegalerie
Among the most important works of the Old Masters exhibited in this gallery of fine art is this *Madonna in Church* by Jan van Eyck (circa 1425).

9 Neue Nationalgalerie
Sculptures by Henry Moore and Alexander Calder stand outside this streamlined building, designed by Ludwig Mies van der Rohe.

Key

— Suggested route

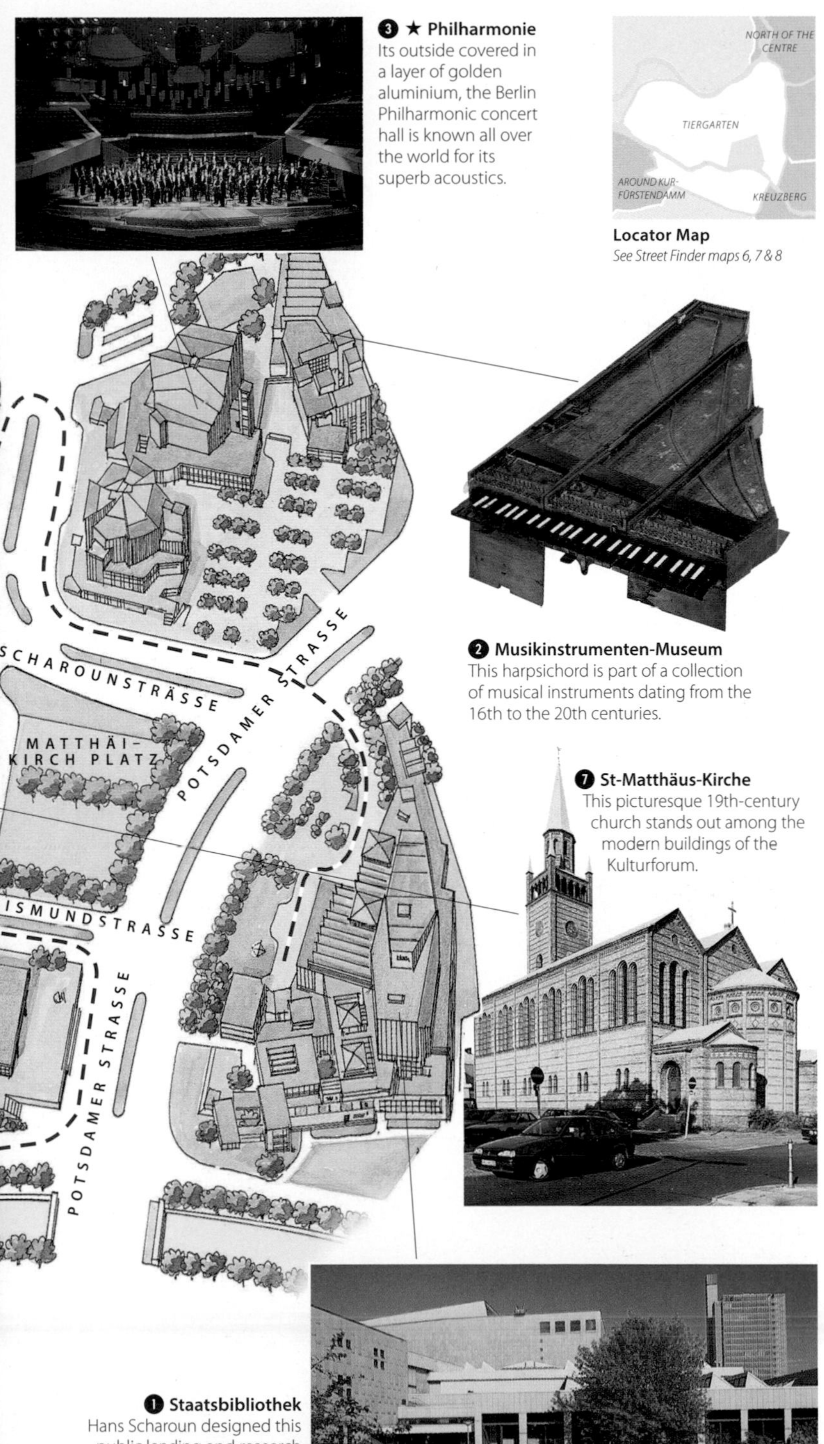

3 ★ Philharmonie
Its outside covered in a layer of golden aluminium, the Berlin Philharmonic concert hall is known all over the world for its superb acoustics.

Locator Map
See Street Finder maps 6, 7 & 8

2 Musikinstrumenten-Museum
This harpsichord is part of a collection of musical instruments dating from the 16th to the 20th centuries.

7 St-Matthäus-Kirche
This picturesque 19th-century church stands out among the modern buildings of the Kulturforum.

1 Staatsbibliothek
Hans Scharoun designed this public lending and research library built in 1978.

The main reading room in the Staatsbibliothek

❶ Staatsbibliothek

State Library

Potsdamer Strasse 33. **Map** 8 D5. **Tel** 266 0. Ⓢ & Ⓤ Potsdamer Platz. 🚌 200, M29, M48, M85. **Open** 9am–9pm Mon–Fri, 9am–7pm Sat.

An unusually shaped building with an east-facing gilded dome, the Staatsbibliothek is home to one of the largest collections of books and manuscripts in Europe and is fondly referred to by Berliners as the Stabi. After World War II, East and West Berlin each inherited part of the pre-war state library collection and the Staatsbibliothek was built to house the part belonging to West Berlin. The building itself was designed by Hans Scharoun and Edgar Wisniewski and constructed between 1967 and 1978.

It is a building where the disciplines of function and efficiency take precedence over that of form. The store rooms hold about five million volumes; the hall of the vast reading room is open-plan, with an irregular arrangement of partitions and floor levels; general noise and the sound of footsteps is muffled by fitted carpets, making the interior a very quiet and cosy place in which to work.

The library itself houses more than four million books, and an excellent collection of manuscripts. The Staatsbibliothek has been formally linked to the Staatsbibliothek on Unter den Linden *(see p63)*.

❷ Musikinstrumenten-Museum

Museum of Musical Instruments

Tiergartenstrasse 1. **Map** 8 D5. **Tel** 25 48 10. Ⓢ & Ⓤ Potsdamer Platz. 🚌 200, M48, M85. **Open** 9am–5pm Tue–Fri (to 10pm Thu), 10am–5pm Sat & Sun. Wurlitzer Organ demonstration: noon Sat.

Hidden behind the Philharmonie, in a small building designed by Edgar Wisniewski and Hans Scharoun between 1979 and 1984, the fascinating Museum of Musical Instruments houses over 750 exhibits in a collection dating from 1888. Intriguing displays enable you to trace each instrument's development from the 16th century to the present day. You can marvel at the harpsichord of Jean Marius, once owned by Frederick the Great, and the violins made by Amati and Stradivarius.

Most spectacular of all is the silent-film-era cinema organ, a working Wurlitzer dating from 1929. With a range of sounds that extends even to locomotive impressions, the Saturday demonstrations of its powers attract enthusiastic crowds. However, during the the week the sounds of exhibited instruments can be heard on tapes. The museum also has an excellent archive and library open to the public.

❸ Philharmonie und Kammermusiksaal

Philharmonic and Chamber Music Hall

Herbert-von-Karajan-Strasse 1. **Map** 8 D5. **Tel** 25 48 88 00. Ⓢ & Ⓤ Potsdamer Platz or Ⓤ Mendelssohn-Bartholdy-Park. 🚌 200, M48, M85.

Home to one of the most renowned orchestras in Europe, this unusual building is among the finest postwar architectural achievements in Europe. The Philharmonie, built between 1960 and 1963 to a design by Hans Scharoun, pioneered a new concept for concert hall interiors. The orchestra's podium occupies the central section of the pentagonal-shaped hall, around which are galleries for the public, designed to blend into the perspective of the five corners. The exterior reflects the interior and is

The tent-like gilded exterior of the Philharmonie and Kammermusiksaal

reminiscent of a circus tent. The gilded exterior was added between 1978 and 1981.

The Berlin orchestra was founded in 1882, and has been directed by such luminaries as Hans von Bülow, Wilhelm Furtwängler, the controversial Herbert von Karajan, who led the orchestra from 1954 until his death in 1989, and Claudio Abbado. The current director is Sir Simon Rattle. The orchestra attained renown not only for the quality of its concerts but also through its prolific symphony recordings.

Between the years 1984 to 1987 the Kammermusiksaal, which was designed by Edgar Wisniewski on the basis of sketches by Scharoun, was added to the Philharmonie. This building consolidates the aesthetics of the earlier structure by featuring a central multi-sided space covered by a fanciful tent-like roof.

❹ Kunstgewerbemuseum

Museum of Arts and Crafts

See pp122–5.

❺ Kupferstichkabinett

Print Gallery

Matthäikirchplatz 8. **Map** 7 C5. **Tel** 266 42 42 42. Ⓢ & Ⓤ Potsdamer Platz or Ⓤ Mendelssohn-Bartholdy-Park. 🚌 200, M29, M41, M48, M85. Exhibitions: 10am–6pm Tue–Fri, 11am–6pm Sat & Sun.

The print collections of galleries in the former East and West Berlin were united in 1994 in this building located in the Kulturforum. These displays originate from a collection started by the Great Elector in 1652, which has been open to the public since 1831. Despite wartime losses it has an imposing breadth and can boast around 2,000 engraver's plates, over 520,000 prints and around 110,000 drawings and watercolours. Unfortunately, only a small fraction of these delicate treasures can be even

Edvard Munch's *Girl on a Beach*, a coloured lithograph

briefly exposed to daylight; therefore the museum does not have a permanent exhibition, only galleries with temporary displays of selected works. For those with a special interest, items in storage can be viewed in the studio gallery by prior arrangement.

The collection includes work from every renowned artist from the Middle Ages to contemporary times. Well represented is the work of Botticelli (including illustrations for Dante's *Divine Comedy*), Dürer, Rembrandt and the Dutch Masters, Watteau, Goya, Daumier and painters of the Die Brücke art movement.

❻ Kunstbibliothek

Art Library

Matthäikirchplatz 6. **Map** 7 C5. **Tel** 266 42 41 41. Ⓢ & Ⓤ Potsdamer Platz or Ⓤ Mendelssohn-Bartoldy-Park. 🚌 200, M29, M41, M48, M85. **Open** 10am–6pm Tue–Fri, 11am–6pm Sat & Sun.

The Kunstbibliothek is not only a library with a vast range of books and periodicals about the arts, making it a tremendous resource for researchers; it is also a museum with a huge collection of posters, advertisements and an array of other forms of design. Worth seeing is a display on the history of fashion, as well as a vast collection of items of architectural interest. The latter includes around 30,000 original plans and drawings by architects such as Johann Balthasar Neumann, Erich Mendelsohn and Paul Wallot.

The exhibitions can be seen in the reading and studio rooms, and parts of the collection are also in the library's own galleries.

❼ St-Matthäus-Kirche

St Matthew's Church

Matthäikirchplatz. **Map** 7 C5. **Tel** 262 12 02. Ⓢ & Ⓤ Potsdamer Platz or Ⓤ Mendelssohn-Bartholdy-Park. 🚌 148, 200, M41, M48, M85. **Open** 11am–6pm Tue–Sun, and for services.

St Matthew's Church once stood in the centre of a small square surrounded by buildings. After bomb damage in World War II, the structure was restored, making it the focal point of the Kulturforum. The church was originally built between 1844 and 1846 to a design by Friedrich August Stüler and Hermann Wentzel, in a style based on Italian Romanesque temples.

Each of the three naves is covered by a separate two-tier roof, while the eastern end of the church is closed by a semi-circular apse. The exterior of the church is covered in a two-tone brick façade arranged in yellow and red lines. Ironically, this picturesque church with its slender tower now creates quite an exotic element among the many ultramodern and sometimes extravagant buildings of the Kulturforum complex.

The colourful exterior of the St-Matthäus-Kirche

❹ Kunstgewerbemuseum

The Museum of Decorative Arts embraces many genres of craft and decorative art, from the early Middle Ages to the modern day. Goldwork is especially well represented. Among the most valuable exhibits is a collection of medieval goldwork from the church treasuries of Enger near Herford, and the Guelph treasury from Brunswick. The museum also takes great pride in its collection of late Gothic and Renaissance silver from the town of Lüneberg's civic treasury. There are fine examples of Italian majolica, and 18th- and 19th-century German, French and Italian glass, porcelain and furniture. Exhibits also include fashion, Jugendstil and Art Deco glassware and furniture, and Bauhaus and contemporary design.

★ **Domed Reliquary** (1175–80)
From the Guelph treasury in Brunswick, the figures in this temple-shaped reliquary are made from walrus ivory.

Minneteppich (c.1430)
The theme of this famous tapestry is courtly love. Amorous couples, accompanied by mythical creatures, converse on topics such as infidelity, their words extending along the banners they hold.

★ **Goblet** (c.1480)
This glass goblet was made in Venice and is decorated with scenes from the lives of Adam and Eve.

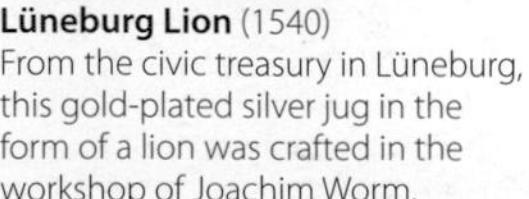

Lüneburg Lion (1540)
From the civic treasury in Lüneburg, this gold-plated silver jug in the form of a lion was crafted in the workshop of Joachim Worm.

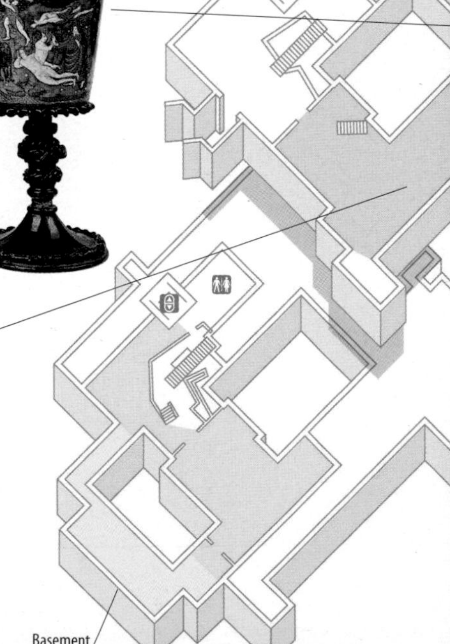

VISITORS' CHECKLIST

Practical Information
Matthäikirchplatz.
Map 7 C5.
Tel 266 42 42 42.
smb.museum/kgm
Open 10am–6pm Tue–Fri, 11am–6pm Sat & Sun.

Transport
Potsdamer Platz.
Potsdamer Platz or Mendelssohn-Bartholdy-Park.
200, 347, M29, M48, M85.

Candelabrum (1900)
This striking Art Nouveau candelabrum made from silver, ivory and onyx is the work of Belgian artists Egide Rombaux and Frans Hoosemans.

Wedding Dress (c.1780)
Made from brocade, with a lace collar and cuffs, this Rococo wedding dress is thought to have belonged to Eleonor Schuster from Breslau (now Wrocław).

★ **Harlequin Group** (c.1740)
These highly decorative, comic porcelain characters from Meissen are just one of the treasures from the cabinets of curiosities and Baroque collections to be found on the second floor.

Key

- Middle Ages
- Renaissance
- Baroque
- Neo-Classical, Art Nouveau
- 20th century
- Temporary exhibitions

Gallery Guide

The entrance to the museum is on the first floor, where there is also an information gallery. In the basement is an exhibition of contemporary design, on the ground floor are exhibits from the Middle Ages and the Renaissance, and on the second floor are handicrafts from the Renaissance through to Art Nouveau.

Exploring the Kunstgewerbemuseum

Opened in 1868, the Museum of Decorative Arts was the first of its kind in Germany. It was housed initially in the Martin-Gropius-Bau *(see p144)*, then from 1921 to 1939 occupied the Stadtschloss *(see p76)*. In 1940 it was moved to Schloss Charlottenburg *(see pp164–5)*. The current building, completed in 1985, underwent major renovations for several years and reopened in November 2014 with an extensive fashion gallery and expanded fashion, Jugendstil and Art Deco displays.

Middle Ages

A large part of this collection is devoted to sacred art, much of it originating from church treasuries. A fine 8th-century reliquary in the shape of a burse (the container used in the Roman Catholic mass to hold the white linen cloth on which the bread and the wine are placed) comes from the treasury of a church in Enger in Westphalia. More reliquaries, many in the form of crosses, date from the 11th and 12th centuries. Two of the most interesting are the Heinrichskreuz, a gift to the cathedral in Basel from the Roman Emperor Heinrich II, and the Welfenkreuz, which comes from the Guelph treasury in Brunswick. Also from the latter comes a beautiful domed reliquary taking the form of a small temple, and a portable altarpiece decorated with enamelwork, produced around 1150 by the craftsman Eilbertus of Cologne.

Exhibits from the Gothic period (12th to 16th centuries) include the stunning reliquary of St George of Elbing, made around 1480. Also fascinating are examples of secular art from this period, including caskets, vessels, a mirror, a knight's amulet and the renowned Minneteppich. This tapestry depicts a number of love scenes, and is designed to hang on the wall above a seat as a decorative means of keeping out draughts.

11th-century reliquary cross

Renaissance

The arts and crafts of the Renaissance period are well represented here. Especially valuable is a collection of Italian majolica, a type of pottery glazed in bright metallic oxides, imported into Tuscany from Majorca in the 15th century. Majolica workshops flourished during the 16th century, and many, including those of Faenza, Cafaggiolo and Urbino, are on show here.

Other interesting exhibits in this section are 15th- and 16th-century Venetian glass, porcelain decorated with enamelwork from Limoges in central France, and fine collections of furniture and tapestry.

The highlight of the collection is a set of 32 magnificent, richly decorated goblets, bowls and jugs from the civic treasury at Lüneburg in northern Germany, acquired by the museum in 1874. Made from gold-plated silver, the set is the work of the skilled metalworkers of the town; some vessels take the form of lions. Also notable are the works of the Nürnberg master craftsmen, above all the renowned Wenzel Jamnitzer and his nephew Christoph Jamnitzer.

As a result of the 16th-century fashion for *Kunstkammern*, or curiosity cabinets, the collection also includes rare examples of naturalistic and exotic creations from other cultures, as well as some unusual technical equipment. Look out for the pieces from the Pommersche Kunstschrank (curio cabinet) made for a 16th-century Pomeranian prince, Phillip II, as well as a display of 17th-century clocks and scientific instruments.

Baroque

Treasures from the Baroque period include an exquisite collection of German and Bohemian glass. A few of the pieces are made from so-called "ruby glass", a technique that was pioneered by Johann Kunckel in the second half of the 17th century.

A varied and rich collection of 18th-century ceramics includes some German faïence work, with amusingly decorated jugs and tankards. The porcelain display begins with a series of Böttger ceramics, the result of some of the very first European

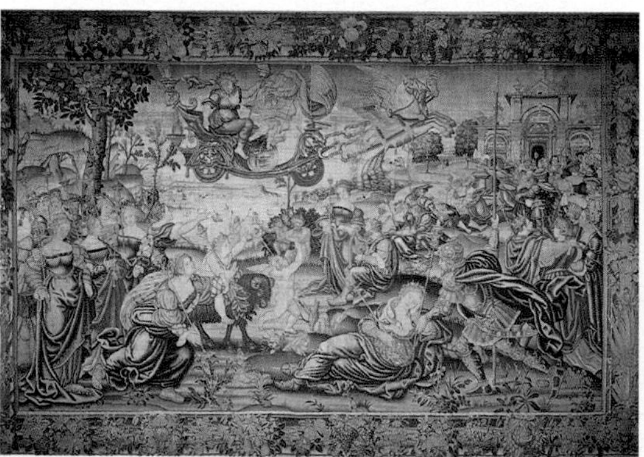

Sixteenth-century tapestry entitled *The Triumph of Love*

Desk-board (*c.*1610–17) from the Pommersche Kunstschrank

experiments in porcelain production, undertaken by Johann Friedrich Böttger with the assistance of Ehrenfried Walther von Tschirnhaus.

Among some of the finest works from a variety of European factories, the porcelain from the Meissen factory is particularly well represented, with several pieces by one of the most famous Meissen modellers and designers, Johann Joachim Kändler.

Also on show is a fascinating selection of artifacts from the Königliche Porzellan-Manufaktur (Royal Porcelain Factory) in Berlin *(see p137)*, which is well known for its porcelain pieces depicting views of the city.

The collection of porcelain is complemented by a display of silver dishes produced in European workshops at the same period, and some decorative tableware.

Neo-Classical Revival and Art Nouveau

A comprehensive collection of late 18th- and early 19th-century Neo-Classical artifacts includes porcelain from some of the most famous European and Russian factories, French and German silver, and comprehensive exhibitions of glassware and furniture.

The Revival movement in central European art and crafts took place during the second half of the 19th century and is well represented here. A high standard of craftsmanship is seen in the sophisticated Viennese glass and jewellery. The collection also includes furniture made from papier-mâché. This interesting technique was first applied to furniture in England around 1850 and involves a wooden or wire frame which is covered in layers of paste and paper. Decorative techniques include painting and inlaying with mother-of-pearl.

The Secessionist and Art Nouveau movements of the 1890s and 1900s are represented by various artists, including Henri van der Velde and Eugène Gaillard. Many pieces were acquired at the various World Fairs that occurred at this time. Of note are the frosted glass vases by French artist Emile Gallé, and pieces by the American Louis Comfort Tiffany, creator of the Favrile style of iridescent stained glass. Also displayed are pieces by the legendary René Lalique, including jewellery and glassware.

Baroque clock by Johann Gottlieb Graupner (1739)

An interesting diversion is offered by two entertaining pieces of furniture, both dating from 1885, by the Italian designer Carlo Bugatti. Taking inspiration from Native American, Islamic and Far Eastern art, Bugatti made unique and spectacular use of rare woods and delicate inlays.

The 20th Century

The years between the two World Wars were a time of mixed trends in the decorative arts. On the one hand the traditions of the 19th-century Historical movement were continued, while on the other many artists were developing a completely new perspective on both form and decoration.

Art Nouveau vase, Emile Gallé (1900)

This part of the museum includes pieces that embody both approaches, but the strongest emphasis is placed on the innovative Art Deco style. Notable examples include a small porcelain tea service by Gertrud Kant, and a silver coffee set decorated with inlaid ebony, designed by Jean Puiforcat.

The museum's unique 20th-century collection has been continually updated since 1945, aiming to document developments in 20th- and 21st-century decorative arts. On display are a wide range of ceramics, furniture by well-known designers, and a variety of items in daily use.

❽ Gemäldegalerie

The Gemäldegalerie collection is exceptional in the consistently high quality of its paintings. Unlike those in many other collections, they were chosen by specialists who, from the beginning of the 19th century, systematically acquired pictures to ensure that all the major European schools of painting were represented. Originally part of the Altes Museum collection *(see p77)*, the paintings achieved independent status in 1904 when they were moved to what is now the Bode-Museum *(see p81)*. After the division of Berlin in 1945, part of the collection was kept in the Bode-Museum, while the majority ended up in the Dahlem Museums *(see p185)*. Following reunification, with the building of a new home as part of the Kulturforum development, this unique set of paintings was united again.

★ ***Cupid Victorious*** (1602)
Inspired by Virgil's *Omnia vincit Amor*, Caravaggio depicted a playful god, trampling over the symbols of Culture, Fame, Knowledge and Power.

Madonna with Child (c.1477)
A frequent subject of Sandro Botticelli, the Madonna and Child depicted here are surrounded by singing angels holding lilies, symbolizing purity.

Circular lobby leading to the galleries

Birth of Christ (c.1480)
This beautiful religious painting is one of the few surviving paintings on panels by Martin Schongauer.

Portrait of Hieronymus Holzschuher (1529)
Albrecht Dürer painted this affectionate portrait of his friend, who was the mayor of Nürnberg.

The Glass of Wine (c.1658–61)
Jan Vermeer's carefully composed picture of a young woman drinking wine with a young man gently hints at the relationship developing between them.

VISITORS' CHECKLIST

Practical Information
Matthäikirchplatz 4–6.
Map 7 C5.
Tel 266 42 42 42.
Open 10am–6pm Tue–Sun (to 8pm Thu).
Closed 24 & 31 Dec.

Transport
S & U Potsdamer Platz.
U Mendelssohn-Bartholdy-Park.
200, M29, M41, M48, M85.

Love in the French Theatre
This picture has a companion piece called *Love in the Italian Theatre* *(see p25)*. Both are the work of French painter Jean-Antoine Watteau.

★ ***Portrait of Hendrickje Stoffels*** (1656–7)
This portrait of Rembrandt's lover, Hendrickje Stoffels, is typical in that the painter focuses on the subject and ignores the background.

Key

- 13th–16th-century German painting
- 14th–16th-century Dutch and French painting
- 17th century Flemish and Dutch painting
- 18th-century French, English and German painting
- 17th–18th-century Italian painting, 17th-century German, French and Spanish painting
- 13th–16th-century Italian painting
- 16th–18th-century miniatures
- Digital gallery
- Non-exhibition space

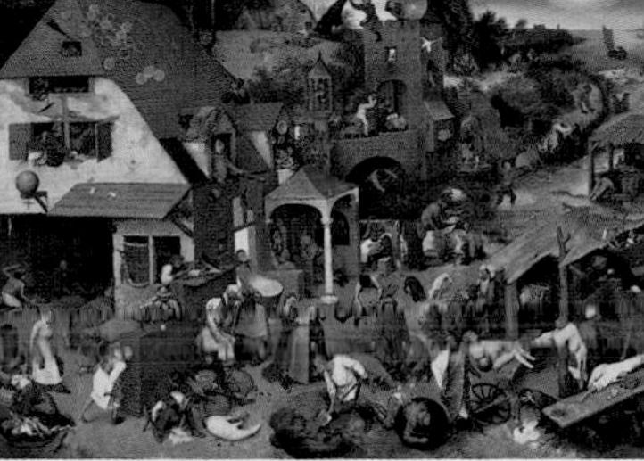

★ ***Dutch Proverbs*** (1559)
Pieter Bruegel managed to illustrate more than 100 proverbs in this painting.

Gallery Guide

The main gallery contains about 1,000 masterpieces grouped according to their country of origin and period. The educational gallery on the lower floor houses about 400 13th–18th-century European paintings and another digital gallery.

Visiting the Gemäldegalerie

The Gemäldegalerie's Modern building was designed by Heinz Hilmer and Christoph Sattler and its exhibition space offers a superb environment in which to view the paintings. The pictures are gently lit by the diffused daylight that streams in from above, while the walls are covered in light-absorbing fabric. The vast hall that occupies the centre of the building allows the visitor to take a break from sightseeing at any time. The hall, with a futuristic sculpture by Walter de Maria set in a water-filled pool, provides an ideal setting for a few moments of quiet contemplation and rest.

Frans Hals' portrait, *Malle Babbe* or *Crazy Babette* (c.1629–30)

Hans Holbein's *Portrait of Georg Gisze* (1532)

German Painting

German paintings are exhibited in several areas of the gallery. The first group comprises art from the 13th–16th centuries. A fine body of religious paintings and altarpieces contains a historic 13th-century rectangular altarpiece from Westphalia. Other notable religious artifacts include the side panels of the 15th-century *Wurzach Altar*, ascribed to Hans Multscher, which vividly depict the torment of Christ and the life of the Virgin Mary. A real rarity is the *Nativity* by Martin Schongauer. Often thought of primarily as an engraver, he was one of the most significant painters of the late 15th century but few of his paintings have survived.

Another artist known for his engravings as well as paintings, Albrecht Dürer was a major figure in Renaissance art in northern Europe. His works displayed here include *Madonna with the Siskin*, painted in 1506 while he was visiting Italy, and two later portraits of Nürnberg patriarchs. There are also exhibits by Hans Süss von Kulmbach, Hans Baldung Grien and Albrecht Altdorfer. Among the many works by Lucas Cranach the Elder is the delightful *Fountain of Youth*, from which old women emerge young and beautiful, while men regain their youth through amorous liaisons with the women. Another excellent painting in this collection is a portrait of the Danzig merchant Georg Gisze, painted by Hans Holbein the Younger at a time when both men were living in London. 17th- and 18th-century paintings, including the works of Adam Elsheimer and Johann Heinrich Tischbein, are on show elsewhere.

Dutch and Flemish Painting

The gallery with Dutch and Flemish paintings begins with the captivating canvases of Jan van Eyck. In addition to his precise portraits, you can see here the celebrated *Madonna in a Church*. The high quality of paintings is maintained with the works of Petrus Christus and Rogier van der Weyden. Among the pictures by Hugo van der Goes, the most prized is *The Adoration of the Magi*, once the centre panel of a triptych.

The collection has four paintings by Hans Memling, and also the small *Madonna with Child* painted by one of his pupils, Michel Sittow. There is a large group of paintings by Gerard David, Jan Gossaert and Joos van Cleve. Try to keep an eye out for a modest picture by Hieronymus Bosch called *St John on Patmos*. One of the most outstanding paintings of the collection is Pieter Bruegel the Elder's *Dutch Proverbs*. However, in order to fully appreciate the mastery and humour in this work, make sure you use the accompanying board which explains all the one hundred or so proverbs illustrated here.

Within the large collection of excellent Flemish paintings you can marvel at the Baroque vitality and texture evident in the canvases of friends and

Salomon van Ruysdael's *Dutch Landscape with a Raid* (1656)

sometime collaborators Pieter Paul Rubens, Jacob Jordaens, Jan Brueghel the Elder and Frans Snyders. The exceptional portraits of Anton van Dyck, who painted complex, psychologically revealing studies, are indicative of the artist at the height of his powers.

The gallery of 17th-century Dutch paintings probably holds the richest collection in the museum. Included among these are portraits by Frans Hals that perfectly illustrate his enormous artistic talents. Excellent examples of his varied work are the vigorous *Malle Babbe* (c.1629–30) – a portrait of the "crazy Babette" of Haarlem.

In fact, all the most famous Dutch painters are represented here but, of course, the works of Jan Vermeer and the master, Rembrandt, attract the greatest amount of interest. Rembrandt's works include the paintings *Samson and Delilah, Susanna and the Two Elders* and *Joseph and the Wife of Potiphar*. It is also worth taking time to view the *Man in the Golden Helmet*, a sad yet noble painting originally attributed to Rembrandt. Carbon-dating has shown it to be the work of members of his studio. It is a magnificent tribute to his skill as a teacher.

Jean Baptiste Siméon Chardin's *The Draughtsman* (1737)

French, English and Spanish Painting

The collection of French art can be found in various parts of the gallery. Paintings of the 15th and 16th century are exhibited alongside Dutch paintings of that era. The oldest works date from the beginning of the 15th century, and the *Madonna with Child*, dating from c.1410, is one of the oldest preserved works of art painted on a canvas. One of the most valuable French works is by Jean Fouquet, entitled *Étienne Chevalier with Saint Stephen*. Comprising half of the *Diptych of Melun,* this is one of Fouquet's few non-miniature paintings.

Titian's *Venus with the Organ Player* (1550–52)

Nicolas Poussin, the mainspring of the French Classical tradition, and Claude Lorrain, famous for his idealized landscapes, represent 17th-century French painting. Eighteenth-century painting is strongly represented by the canvases of Jean-Antoine Watteau, Jean Baptiste Siméon Chardin and François Boucher.

Two areas in which this collection is less complete are Spanish and English painting. Nevertheless, there is a portrait by Diego Velázquez which is worth seeing, while the English pictures include good portraits by rivals Sir Joshua Reynolds and Thomas Gainsborough.

Sir Joshua Reynolds' *Portrait of Lady Sunderlin* (1786)

Italian Painting

The collection of Italian paintings is fairly comprehensive. There are exemplary works by 14th-century masters, including *Laying the Body to Rest in the Grave* by Giotto and parts of *Scenes from the Life of St Humilitas* by Pietro Lorenzetti. Paintings by Piero della Francesca, Fra Angelico, Masaccio, Andrea del Verrocchio, Sandro Botticelli, and Antonio del Pollaiuolo all represent the 15th century. In this collection you will also find later works by Raphael, including the *Madonna di Casa Colonna*, and the *Madonna di Terranuova*, painted after Raphael's arrival in Florence around 1505. There is also a collection of works by the Venetian Renaissance painter Giovanni Bellini.

Indeed, the Venetian school in general is well represented: *Portrait of a Young Man* by Giorgione is a vibrant and colourful study; there is also Titian's *Venus and the Organ Player* and Tintoretto's *Virgin and the Child Adored by Saints Mark and Luke*. It is worth comparing Caravaggio's *Cupid Victorious*, whose provocative and distinctly human sexuality contrasts with the spiritual orthodoxy of *Heavenly and Earthly Love,* by Giovanni Baglione. Similar in style, the two paintings convey opposing ideologies. Cardinal Giustiani, whose brother owned Caravaggio's controversial canvas, commissioned the latter painting. Works by Giovanni Battista Tiepolo, Francesco Guardi and Antonio Canaletto represent the art of 18th-century Venice.

Karl Schmidt-Rottluff's *Farm in Daugart* (1910), Neue Nationalgalerie

❾ Neue Nationalgalerie

New National Gallery

Potsdamer Strasse 50. **Map** 7 C5. **Tel** 266 424 242. U & S Potsdamer Platz or U Mendelssohn-Bartholdy-Park. 200, M29, M41, M48, M85. **Closed** until 2018 for renovation.

The magnificent collection of modern art housed in the Neue Nationalgalerie has a troubled history. The core of the collection consisted of 262 paintings that belonged to banker JHW Wagener. In the late 1860s, when Wagener died, he bequeathed them to Crown Prince William, who housed them in the Nationalgalerie on Museum Island.

However, in 1937, a Nazi programme of cultural cleansing meant that over 400 of the works in the collection, which had grown to include paintings by Monet, Manet and Renoir, were confiscated.

After World War II the Berlin municipal authority decided to rebuild the collection and authorized the construction of a suitable building in West Berlin to house it. A commission was given to the elder statesman of modern architecture, the 75-year-old Mies van der Rohe. The result was the first museum in what would later become known as the Kulturforum. The national gallery is a striking, minimalist building with a flat steel roof over a glass hall, which appears to float in mid-air supported only by six slender interior struts. The permanent collection is in the basement of the museum, while the spacious ground-level glass hall plays host to temporary exhibitions.

The collection of the Neue Nationalgalerie comprises largely 20th-century art, but begins with artists of the late 19th century, such as Edvard Munch, Ferdinand Hodler and Oskar Kokoschka. German movements, such as Die Brücke, are well represented, with pieces by Ernst Ludwig Kirchner (notably his *Potsdamer Platz)* and Karl Schmidt-Rottluff.

As well as the Bauhaus movement, represented by Paul Klee and Wassily Kandinsky, the gallery shows works by exponents of a crass realism, such as Otto Dix and Georg Grosz. The most celebrated artists of other European countries are also included in the collection – Pablo Picasso, Ferdinand Léger, and the Surrealists Giorgio de Chirico, Salvador Dalí, René Magritte and Max Ernst. Post-World War II art is represented by the works of Barnett Newman and Frank Stella, among many others. The sculpture garden houses a variety of important works, both figurative and abstract.

Following reunification, a number of new works by artists from the former East Germany were added to the collection. Some of the art is sometimes on display at the Hamburger Bahnhof *(see pp114–15)*, as both museums draw on the same collection.

The impressive exterior of the Shell-Haus office building

❿ Potsdamer Platz

See pp132–5.

⓫ Shell-Haus

Reichpietschufer 60. **Map** 13 C1. U Mendelssohn-Bartholdy-Park. 200, M29, M48, M85.

This is undoubtedly a gem for lovers of the architecture developed during the period between World Wars I and II. This modernist office block was designed by Emil Fahrenkamp. Built from 1930 to 1932, it was one of the first buildings in Berlin to use a steel-frame construction.

The most eyecatching wing extends along Landwehrkanal with a zig-zag elevation; from a height of five storeys it climbs upwards in a series of steps, finishing up ten storeys high.

Damaged during World War II, Shell-Haus went through several stages of restoration and several incarnations, including as headquarters of the German navy and as a military hospital. Beautiful proportions and original design place the structure among the finest of Berlin's buildings of its era.

The German State Naval Office, now part of the Bendlerblock complex

⓬ Bendlerblock (Gedenkstätte Deutscher Widerstand)

Stauffenbergstrasse 13–14. **Map** 7 B5, 7 C5. **Tel** 26 99 50 00. Potsdamer Platz or Kürfurstenstrasse. M29, M48. **Open** 9am–6pm Mon–Fri (to 8pm Thu), 10am–6pm Sat & Sun. **Closed** 1 Jan, 24, 25 & 31 Dec.

The collection of buildings known as the Bendlerblock was originally built during the Third Reich as an extension to the German State Naval Offices. During World War II these buildings were the head-quarters of the Wehrmacht (German Army). It was here that a group of officers planned their famous and ultimately unsuccessful assassination attempt on Hitler on 20 July 1944. When the attempt led by Claus Schenk von Stauffenberg failed, he and his fellow conspirators were quickly rounded up and arrested. The death sentences on these men were passed at the Plötzensee prison *(see p180)*. General Ludwig Beck was forced to commit suicide, while Stauffenberg, Friedrich Olbricht, Werner von Haeften and Ritter Mertz von Quirnheim were shot in the Bendlerblock courtyard.

A monument commem-orating this event, designed by Richard Scheibe in 1953, stands where the executions were carried out. On the upper floor of the building there is an exhibition documenting the history of the German anti-Nazi movements.

⓭ Villa von der Heydt

Von-der-Heydt-Strasse 18. **Map** 13 B1. **Tel** 266 41 28 88. Nollendorfplatz. 100, 200, M29.

This fine villa, built in a late Neo-Classical style, is one of the few surviving reminders that the southern side of the Tiergarten was one of the most expensive and beautiful residential areas of Berlin.

Designed by Hermann Ende and GA Linke, the villa was built from 1860 to 1862. The neatly manicured gardens and railings around the villa are adorned with busts of Christian Daniel Rauch and Alexander von Humboldt. The statues, by Reinhold Begas, originally lined the Avenue of Triumph in the Tiergarten before being moved here. After restoration in 1980, the villa became the head-quarters of one of the most influential cultural bodies, the Stiftung Preussischer Kulturbesitz (Foundation of Prussian Cultural Heritage).

Neo-Classical façade of the elegant Villa von der Heydt

The captivating, streamlined buildings of the Bauhaus-Archiv

⓮ Bauhaus-Archiv

Klingelhöferstrasse 14. **Map** 13 A1. **Tel** 25 40 02 78. Nollendorfplatz. 100, 106, 187, M29. **Open** 10am–5pm Wed–Mon.

The Bauhaus school of art, started by Walter Gropius in 1919, was one of the most influential art institutions of the 20th century. The belief of the Bauhaus group was that art and technology should combine in harmonious unity.

Originally based in Weimar, and from 1925 in Dessau, this school provided inspiration for numerous artists and architects. Staff and students included Mies van der Rohe, Paul Klee, Wassily Kandinsky, Theo van Doesburg and László Moholy-Nagy. The school moved to Berlin in 1932, but was closed down by the Nazis in 1933.

After the war, the Bauhaus-Archiv was relocated to Darmstadt. In 1964 Walter Gropius designed a building to house the collection, but it was never realized. The archive was moved to Berlin in 1971 and the design had to be adapted to the new site. Because the maestro was no longer alive, the project was taken over by Alexander Cvijanovic. The gleaming white building with its distinctive glass-panelled gables was built between 1976 and 1979 and houses the archive, library and exhibition halls for temporary displays.

⑩ Potsdamer Platz

To experience the vibrant energy of the new Berlin, there is no better place to visit than Potsdamer Platz. During the Roaring Twenties it was Europe's busiest plaza and a bustling entertainment centre, but during World War II it was bombed into a mountain of rubble. After the war, the square was left as a derelict, wide-open space, a no-man's-land beside the Berlin Wall. With reunification, the square was redeveloped by various international business concerns, such as DaimlerChrysler and Sony, who subsequently sold the properties. This building project is Berlin's largest to date. Berlin's old hub is once again a dynamic centre, a jewel of modern architecture created by architects such as Renzo Piano, Helmut Jahn and Arata Isozaki.

View of modern-day Potsdamer Platz

Beisheim Center
Lenné-, Bellevue- and Ebertstrasse.
W beisheim-center.de

Otto Beisheim, the founder and owner of the Metro retail chain, and one of Europe's wealthiest entrepreneurs, has created a glass and steel monument on Potsdamer Platz – the Beisheim Center. The two elegant high-rise towers on the northern edge of the square encompass several de luxe apartments. The largest was sold for around \$5 million, to an American émigrée returning to her home city, and is probably Berlin's most expensive apartment. The center also incorporates a luxurious Ritz-Carlton and an elegant Marriott hotel.

The building was designed by the Berlin architectural team Hilmer, Sattler & Albrecht, although parts of the building were also created by architect David Chipperfield. The sandstone appearance of the small 19-floor skyscrapers, with receding façades on the upper levels, is meant to be a modern reinterpretation of New York's Rockefeller Center.

Filmmuseum Berlin
Potsdamer Strasse 2 (at Sony Center).
Tel 30 09 03 54. **Open** 10am–6pm Tue–Sun, 10am–8pm Thu.
W filmmuseum-berlin.de

In a city once famous for its world-class film industry, the film museum takes visitors backstage to Hollywood and the historic UFA (Universal Film AG) film studios.

Located in the Sony Center and run by the Freunde der Deutschen Kinemathek, a non-profit-making association for film-lovers, the museum chronicles the development of cinema from the first silent movie hits to the latest science-fiction productions. However, the main focus is on German films from the glorious UFA days in the 1920s, when Germany's leading film company produced one smash hit after another at the Babelsberg studios *(see p207)*. Films such as *The Cabinet of Dr Caligari*, directed by Friedrich Wilhelm Murnau (1888–1931), or *M* and *Metropolis* by Fritz Lang (1890–1976), are presented with costumes, set sketches, original scripts, models and photos. The Nazi era, when film-making became a propaganda machine, is particularly interesting, and the museum documents the life and work of the actor Kurt Gerron, who died in Auschwitz, as well as other exhibits relating to the uses of propaganda in film.

One of the treasure troves of the museum is the collection of personal effects of the Berlin-born diva Marlene Dietrich (1901–1992). The exhibition presents her gowns, personal correspondence and complete luggage set. A unique item is a minute cigarette case, given to her as a gift by the director Josef von Sternberg (1894–1969), bearing the inscription: "To Marlene Dietrich, woman, mother and actress as there never was one before". Also on display are personal possessions from German film and TV stars such as Heinz Rühmann (1902–1994) and Hans Albers (1891–1960).

The museum features a range of exhibitions with changing themes and special film programmes.

Façade of the Filmmuseum Berlin

Arkaden, one of Berlin's favourite shopping centres

Potsdamer Platz Arkaden
Alte Potsdamer Strasse 7. **Tel** 25 59 270. **Open** 10am–9pm Mon–Sat. CinemaxX: Potsdamer Strasse 5. **Tel** (040) 8080 69 69.

This entertainment and shopping complex is hugely popular with visitors. Spread over three floors, the building includes around 140 shops, restaurants and boutiques. The basement houses a food court with many budget eateries offering regional specialities from all over Germany, as well as several grocery shops. Berlin's largest cinema, the **CinemaxX**, is nearby. With 19 screens, it can accommodate up to 3,500 filmgoers.

Theater am Potsdamer Platz
Marlene-Dietrich-Platz 1. **Tel** (0180) 544 44. **Open** 8am–8pm daily. Spielbank Berlin: Marlene-Dietrich-Platz 1. **Tel** 25 59 90. **Open** 11am–5am daily.

Situated in a square dedicated to the famous actress Marlene Dietrich, Berlin's largest musical stage is housed in the modern Theater am Potsdamer Platz, designed by Renzo Piano as part of the Daimler Quartier *(see pp134–5)*. It stages German versions of Broadway hit musicals and shows such as *Beauty and the Beast*.

The exclusive Adagio nightclub is located in the basement of this building and Berlin's most popular casino, **Spielbank Berlin**, can be found here too.

The theatre complex is also the main forum for the **Berlin Filmfestspiele**, known as the Berlinale. One of the film industry's most important festivals, it is held throughout the city each February *(see p53)*. Over the course of the 10-day event, around 400 films are shown, most of which are world and European premieres. Perhaps the most important part of the festival are the Golden and Silver Bears awards, which are awarded to noteworthy major international films. Tickets for screenings can be hard to come by, so plan well ahead if you wish to attend.

Bluemax Theater, the Blue Man Group's Berlin location, is found on the opposite side of Marlene-Dietrich-Platz. The famous mute performers hold seven shows a week.

Historic Potsdamer Platz

Potsdamer Platz first evolved from a green park in 1831 and was named after one of the city's gates, the Potsdamer Tor, located to the east of today's square. Thanks to a new railway station of the same name, where the city's first ever train made its maiden journey in 1838, the square developed into a major traffic hub at the intersection of Potsdamer Strasse and other thoroughfares. Later an underground train line, along with a total of 31 tram and bus lines, added to the traffic chaos here. At the beginning of the 20th century it became the centre of Berlin's celebrated nightlife, with legendary, huge entertainment venues such as Haus Vaterland and the Café Josty (a meeting place for famous artists including author Theodor Fontane and painter Adolph von Menzel), as well as several luxury hotels. Germany's first radio transmission was broadcast in 1923 at the Vox Haus. The square was almost destroyed by Allied bombardments during the final Battle of Berlin in April 1945. It became a vast open space in the shadow of the Berlin Wall, where Western tourists, standing on high observation platforms, could peek over the wall. The empty square featured in Wim Wenders' 1987 hit film *Wings of Desire*.

Development commenced in 1992, and Potsdamer Platz rose to become Europe's largest construction site where a total of $25 billion has been invested.

Bustling Potsdamer Platz in the 1930s

Sony Center

Potsdamer Strasse 2. **Open** 24 hrs.

The Sony Center, designed by the German-American architect Helmut Jahn, is one of Berlin's most exciting architectural complexes. Built between 1996 and 2000, the glitzy steel-and-glass construction covers a breathtaking 4,013 sq m (43,195 sq ft).

The piazza at the heart of the Center has become one of Berlin's most popular attractions. Set under a soaring tent-like roof, it is dominated by a pool with constantly changing fountains where the water sprays high into the air, then falls back to rise again in a different location. The light and airy piazza is surrounded by the offices of Sony's European headquarters, as well as apartment complexes, several restaurants, cafés and shops including the Sony style store. There is also the Cinestar *(see pp264–5)*, a huge multiplex cinema with eight different screens, in addition to the Filmmuseum Berlin *(see p132)*. The integrated IMAX cinema shows nature and science films on imposing 360-degree screens.

Inside the Sony Center is the small but magnificent **Kaisersaal**, a historic architectural gem that is set behind a glass façade. This dining hall, one of the city's finest, but private, function locations, was once part of the Grand Hotel Esplanade. The epitome of luxury in pre-war Berlin, it was almost destroyed during World War II. When the site was sold to Sony by the City of Berlin in the early 1990s, the Berlin magistrate stipulated that the Kaisersaal, stairways, bathrooms and several other smaller rooms should be restored and integrated into the Sony Center.

The historic ensemble originally stood some 46 m (150 ft) away and was carefully moved on air cushions to its present location in 1996. The fully restored Kaisersaal is dominated by a portrait of Kaiser Wilhelm II, the last German emperor, whose frequent visits to the original hotel gave this hall its name, although he never actually dined in this particular room.

Interior of the cupola of the Sony Center, designed by Helmut Jahn

The glass façade of the Kaisersaal, part of the Sony Center

Daimler Quartier

Around Alte Potsdamer Strasse. Panorama Punkt observation platform: Potsdamer Platz 1. **Tel** 25 93 70 80. **Open** 10am–8pm daily.

This vast complex was built between 1993 and 1998 and comprises 19 modern buildings, all designed in different styles according to an overall plan by architects Renzo Piano and Christoph Kohlbecker. The buildings form a long, narrow column of modern architectural jewels leading south from Potsdamer Platz all the way down to the Landwehr Canal.

Standing on either side of Alte Potsdamer Strasse, the red-brick high-rise block and its sister building opposite mark the entrance to this city quarter, and were designed by Berlin architect Werner Kollhoff. The western skyscraper is topped by a 96-m- (315-ft-) high observation platform called **Panorama Punkt** (Panorama Point). It offers a breathtaking view, which can be reached via Europe's fastest elevator.

The green traffic-light tower in front of the Daimler Quartier is a replica of the first automatic traffic light in Berlin (and Europe), which was erected on the same spot in 1924. In pre-war days, Potsdamer Platz was an intricate crossing of several major streets and avenues, making it Europe's busiest traffic junction at the time.

At the southern end of this complex is yet another high-rise tower block, the **Debis-Haus** (formerly the DaimlerChrysler software subsidiary). This 90-m- (295-ft-) high, 22-floor, yellow and green skyscraper is topped by a striking green cube and was designed by Renzo Piano and Hans Kollhoff *(see p47)*. A captivating sculpture by Jean Tinguely, entitled *Meta-Maxi*, adorns its soaring atrium. The sculpture is powered by 16 engines and symbolizes the constant movement of time.

Various works of art were commissioned especially for this complex and these can be seen throughout the public areas.

The red-brick office block of Daimler House

Leipziger Platz

Leipziger Platz, a small square just east of Potsdamer Platz, is being regenerated and a huge new shopping complex now occupies the site of the former Wertheim department store, once the largest in Europe. At the southern end of the square lies the Dali Museum. The original octagonal but rather bland square was created between 1732 and 1734 and later renamed Leipziger Platz in commemoration of the Battle of Leipzig in 1813 (the first decisive defeat of Napoleon). In the 19th century, the architects Karl-Friedrich Schinkel (1781–1841) and Peter Joseph Lenné (1789–1866) transformed the square into an architectural gem with landscaped gardens, surrounded by some of the most elegant city palaces and mansions in the whole of Berlin.

At the beginning of the 20th century the modern buildings, most notably the Kaufhaus Wertheim by Alfred Messel (1853–1909) built 1897–1905, made Leipziger Platz one of the major, and more fashionable, shopping districts in pre-war Berlin.

Unfortunately, there are no historic remnants left. The current buildings have a modern look but are restricted to a maximum height of only 35 m (115 ft), the same height as the original buildings. They house various shops and restaurants, the Canadian Embassy and further international company headquarters.

Rauschenberg's sculpture *Riding Bikes*, with Haus Huth in the background

Haus Huth

Alte Potsdamer Strasse 5.
Tel 25 94 14 20.
Daimler Contemporary:
Open 11am–6pm daily.
6pm daily.

The only historic building on Potsdamer Platz to escape destruction in World War II was the grey limestone building of the Haus Huth. Originally a restaurant and wine shop and still widely known as the Weinhaus, it was one of the first buildings in Berlin to be erected with a steel frame, intended to support the weight of the wine. It was designed by architects Conrad Heidenreich and Paul Michel in 1912. After the war, it stood alone on the vast eroded square. Today, however, the offices of the famous car manufacturers Daimler are located here, along with the Diekmann im Haus Huth restaurant, a small café and Hardy's, an upmarket wine shop.

Haus Huth is also home to **Daimler Contemporary**, a small exhibition featuring key works and new additions to the corporation's collection of 20th-century art, which mostly consists of abstract and geometric paintings by German and international artists.

The best view of the building is from its south side where a jubilant, bright light installation by Robert Rauschenberg called *Riding Bikes* can be found.

The historic Haus Huth on Leipziger Platz

⑮ Diplomatenviertel

Diplomatic Quarter

Map 6 F5, 7 A5, B5, C5. Ⓤ Nollendorfplatz or Potsdamer Platz. 🚌 100, 106, 187, 200.

Although a number of consulates existed in the Tiergarten area as early as 1918, the establishment of a diplomatic district along the southern edge of the Tiergarten, between Stauffenbergstrasse and Lichtensteinallee, did not take place until the period of Hitler's Third Reich, between 1933 and 1945. During 1938–43 large embassies representing the Axis Powers, Italy and Japan, were built here.

Despite the fact that these monumental buildings were designed by a number of different architects, the Fascist interpretation of Neo-Classicism and the influence of Albert Speer as head architect meant that the group was homogenous, if bleak. Many of the buildings did not survive World War II bombing.

A diplomatic area has now emerged along Tiergartenstrasse. The Austrian embassy, designed by Hans Hollein, stands at the junction of Stauffenbergstrasse, next door to the embassies of India and the Republic of South Africa. At Tiergartenstrasse Nos. 21–3 the pre-World War II Italian embassy still stands, while next door is a copy of the first Japanese embassy. Between Klingelhöferstrasse and Rauchstrasse stands an imposing complex of five embassies. Completed in 1999, these represent Norway, Sweden, Denmark, Finland and Iceland. The complex has an art gallery and café which are open to the public.

⑯ Tiergarten

Map 6 E4, 7 A3, 8 D3. Ⓢ Tiergarten or Bellevue. 🚌 100, 106, 187, 200.

This is the largest park in Berlin. Situated at the geographical centre of the city it occupies a surface area of more than 200 ha (495 acres). Once a forest used as the Elector's hunting reserve, it was transformed into a landscaped park by Peter Joseph Lenné in the 1830s. A half-kilometre Triumphal Avenue was built in the eastern section of the park at the end of the 19th century, lined with statues of the country's rulers and statesmen.

One of many tranquil areas within the Tiergarten

World War II inflicted huge damage on the Tiergarten, including the destruction of the Triumphal Avenue, many of whose surviving monuments can now be seen in the Lapidarium *(see p148)*. Replanting, however, has now restored the Tiergarten which is a favourite meeting place for Berliners. Its avenues are now lined with statues of figures such as Johann Wolfgang von Goethe and Richard Wagner.

By the lake known as Neuer See and the Landwehrkanal are memorials to the murdered leaders of the Spartacus movement, Karl Liebknecht and Rosa Luxemburg *(see p30)*. Also worth finding is a collection of gas lamps, displayed near the Tiergarten S-Bahn station.

⑰ Grosser Stern

Great Star

Map 7 A4. Ⓢ Bellevue. Ⓤ Hansaplatz. 🚌 100, 106, 187.

This vast roundabout at the centre of the Tiergarten has five large roads leading off it in the shape of a star. At its centre is the enormous Siegessäule (Triumphal Column). Surrounding it are various monuments brought over from the nearby Reichstag building *(see pp138–9)* during the late 1930s. At the same period the Strasse des 17 Juni was widened to twice its size, the square surrounding the roundabout was enlarged and much of the existing statuary removed.

In the northern section of the square stands a vast bronze monument to the first German Chancellor, Otto von Bismarck (1815–98). Around it stand allegorical figures, the work of late 19th-century sculptor Reinhold Begas. Other statues represent various national heroes including Field Marshal Helmuth von Moltke (1800–91), chief of the Prussian general staff between the years 1858 and 1888, who won the Franco-German war.

Monument to Otto von Bismarck at the Grosser Stern

⑱ Siegessäule

Triumphal Column

Grosser Stern. **Map** 7 A4. **Tel** 391 29 61. Ⓢ Bellevue. Ⓤ Hansaplatz. 🚌 100, 106, 187. **Open** Apr–Oct: 9:30am–6:30pm daily; Nov–Mar: 10am–5pm daily.

The triumphal column is based on a design by Johann Heinrich Strack, and was built to commemorate victory in the Prusso-Danish war of 1864. After further Prussian victories in wars against Austria (1866) and France (1871), "Goldelse", a gilded figure by Friedrich Drake representing Victory, was added to the top. The monument stood in front of the Reichstag building until the Nazi government moved it to its present location in 1938. The base is decorated with bas-reliefs commemorating battles. Higher up the column a mosaic frieze by Anton von Werner depicts the 1871 founding of the German Empire. An observation terrace at the top offers magnificent vistas over Berlin.

Königliche Porzellan-Manufaktur

Established in 1763, the Königliche Porzellan-Manufaktur (Royal Porcelain Factory) was soon producing items of the highest artistic quality, competing with the products of the older Meissen factory in Saxony. The Berlin factory is particularly renowned for its Neo-Classical urns and plates decorated with views of the city. Large collections of porcelain with the markings KPM can be seen at the Ephraim-Palais *(see p93)*, in the Kunstgewerbemuseum *(see pp122–5)* and at the Belvedere within the grounds of Schloss Charlottenburg *(see pp164–5)*. It is also worth visiting the factory, located at Wegelystrasse 1, which is still producing porcelain, and includes a sales gallery and exhibition hall.

Neo-Classical vase with a view of the Gendarmenmarkt

Siegessäule (Triumphal Column)

⓳ Hansaviertel

Map 6 E3, E4, F3. Bellevue. Hansaplatz. 100, 106, 187. Akademie der Künste: Hanseatenweg 10. **Tel** 20 05 72 00 0. **Open** 11am–8pm Tue–Sun.

This area to the west of Schloss Bellevue is home to some of the most interesting modern architecture in Berlin, built for the 1957 Internationale Bauausstellung (International Architectural Exhibition). Taking on a World War II bomb site, prominent architects from around the world designed 45 projects, of which 36 were realized, to create a varied residential development set in an environment of lush greenery. The list of distinguished architects involved in the project included Walter Gropius (Händelallee Nos. 3–9), Alvar Aalto (Klopstockstrasse Nos. 30–32) and Oskar Niemeyer (Altonaer Strasse Nos. 4–14). The development also includes a school, a commercial services building and two churches.

In 1960, a new headquarters for the **Akademie der Künste** (Academy of Arts) was built at Hanseatenweg No. 10. Designed by Werner Düttmann, the academy has a concert hall, an exhibition area, archives and a library. In front of the main entrance is a magnificent piece, *Reclining Figure*, by eminent British sculptor Henry Moore.

⓴ Schloss Bellevue

Bellevue Palace

Spreeweg 1. **Map** 7 A3. Bellevue. 100, 187. **Closed** to the public.

This captivating palace with its dazzlingly white Neo-Classical façade is now the official residence of the German Federal President. Built in 1786 to a design by Michael Philipp Boumann for the Prussian Prince August Ferdinand, the palace served as a royal residence until 1861. In 1935 it was refurbished to house a Museum of German Ethnology. Refurbished again in 1938, it became a hotel for guests of the Nazi government.

Following bomb damage during World War II, the palace was carefully restored to its former glory, with the oval ballroom rebuilt to a design by Carl Gotthard Langhans. The palace is set within an attractive park laid out to the original late 18th-century design, though unfortunately the picturesque garden pavilions did not survive World War II.

Imposing façade of Schloss Bellevue, now the official Berlin residence of the German President

Haus der Kulturen der Welt or "pregnant oyster" as it is also known

㉑ Haus der Kulturen der Welt

House of World Culture

John-Foster-Dulles-Allee 10.
Map 7 C3. **Tel** 39 78 70. S & U Hauptbahnhof & Bundestag. 100. **Open** 10am–7pm daily. Exhibitions 11am–7pm Wed–Mon.

This former congress hall's squat structure and parabolic roof has given rise to its affectionate nickname "the pregnant oyster". Built between 1956 and 1957 to a design by the American architect Hugh Stubbins, it was intended as the American entry in the international architecture competition "Interbau 1957" (from which the Hansaviertel apartment blocks originated). It soon became a symbol of freedom and modernity in West Berlin during the Cold War, particularly when compared to the GDR-era monumental buildings of Karl-Marx-Allee in East Berlin *(see pp174–5)*. However, its roof failed to withstand the test of time and the building partially collapsed in 1980.

After reconstruction it was re-opened in 1989, with a change of purpose. It is now used to bring world cultures to a wider German audience, and stages various events and performances to this effect. It is known for its jazz festivals in particular *(see pp50–53)*.

Standing nearby is the black tower of the Carillon, built in 1987 to commemorate the 750th anniversary of Berlin. Suspended in the tower is the largest carillon in Europe, comprising 67 bells. Daily at noon and 6pm, the bells give a brief computer-controlled concert.

㉒ Regierungsviertel

Government District

Map 8 D2, E2. S Brandenburger Tor. U Bundestag. 100, 248.

This bold concept for a government district in keeping with a 21st-century capital was the winning design in a competition held in 1992. Construction of the complex began in 1997 and was completed in 2003. Axel Schultes and Charlotte Frank's grand design proposed a rectangular site cutting across the meander of the Spree river just north of the Reichstag.

While many of the buildings have been designed by other architects, their plans fitting within the overall concept, Schultes and Frank designed the Bundeskanzleramt, situated opposite the Reichstag, which is the official residence of the German Chancellor. The offices – Alsenblock and Luisenblock – are the work of Stephan Braunfels, as is the office Dorotheenblöcke, built by a consortium of five architects. The whole project is complemented by the neighbouring Hauptbahnhof railway station, an impressive glass-and-steel construction with several levels above and underground. In 2009 the city's newest U-Bahn line, the U55, was completed, connecting Hauptbahnhof to the Bundestag and Brandenburger Tor. This will eventually be extended to Alexanderplatz to meet with the U5 line.

㉓ Reichstag

Platz der Republik. **Map** 8 D3, E3. U Bundestag. 100, 248. **Tel** 227 32 152. Dome: **Open** by appointment only via W **bundestag.de**. Assembly Hall: **Open** by appointment only. 10:30am, 1:30, 3:30 & 6:30pm daily when parliament is not sitting. **Closed** 1 Jan, 24–26 & 31 Dec.

Built to house the German Parliament, the Reichstag was intended to symbolise national unity and the aspirations of the new German Empire, declared in 1871. The Neo-Renaissance design by Paul Wallot captured the prevailing spirit of German optimism. Constructed between the years 1884 and 1894, it was funded by money paid by the French as wartime reparations.

On 23 December 1916, the inscription *"Dem Deutschen Volke"* ("To the German People") was added to the façade. The Reichstag became a potent symbol that would be exploited in the years to come.

In 1918 Philipp Scheidemann declared the formation of the Weimar Republic from the building. The next time the world heard about the

The Bundeskanzleramt, the official residence of the Federal Chancellor

The Reichstag crowned by a dome designed by Sir Norman Foster

Reichstag was on the night of 28 February 1933, when a fire destroyed the main hall. The Communists were blamed, accelerating a political witch-hunt driven by the Nazis, who subsequently came to power.

With the onset of World War II, the building was not rebuilt. Yet its significance resonated beyond Germany, as shown by the photograph of the Soviet flag flying from the Reichstag in May 1945, which became a symbol of the German defeat.

Between 1957 and 1972, the dome and most of the ornamentation was removed. As well as providing a meeting-place for the lower house of the German Bundestag (Parliament), the Reichstag also made a spectacular backdrop for huge festivals and rock concerts, much to the annoyance of the East German authorities.

On 2 December 1990, the Reichstag was the first meeting-place of a newly elected Bundestag following German reunification. On 23 June 1995, the artist Christo and his wife Jeanne-Claude wrapped the Reichstag in glistening fabric – an artistic statement that lasted for two weeks.

The latest phase of rebuilding, between 1995 and 1999 to a design by Sir Norman Foster, transformed the Reichstag into a modern meeting hall beneath an elliptical dome. Visits to the cupola's viewing gallery are free and the views are breathtaking. Advance registration is required, either online or at least two hours in advance at the service centre on Scheidemannstrasse.

㉔ Sowjetisches Ehrenmal

Monument to Soviet Soldiers

Strasse des 17 Juni. **Map** 8 D3. Ⓢ & Ⓤ Brandenburger Tor. 🚌 100, 248.

This huge monument near the Brandenburg Gate was unveiled on 7 November 1945, on the anniversary of the start of the October Revolution in Russia. Flanked by the first two tanks into the city, the monument commemorates over 300,000 Soviet soldiers who perished in the battle for Berlin at the end of World War II. The vast column was made from marble taken from the headquarters of the Chancellor of the Third Reich, when it was being dismantled. The column was designed by Nicolai Sergievski, while the imposing figure on top, a soldier cast in bronze, is the work of Lew Kerbel. This monument is also a cemetery for around 2,500 Soviet casualties.

Following the partition of Berlin, the site ended up in the British sector, but formed a kind of non-territorial enclave to which Soviet soldiers posted to East Berlin had access.

The sculpture of a Soviet soldier atop the Sowjetisches Ehrenmal

Berlin's Bridges

Despite wartime damage, Berlin's bridges are still well worth seeing. The Spree river and the city's canals have some exemplary architecture on their banks, while many of the bridges were designed and decorated by famous architects and sculptors. Probably the most renowned bridge is the Schlossbrücke designed by Karl Friedrich Schinkel *(see p76)*. Further south along the Kupfergrabenkanal, the Schleusenbrücke dates from around 1914, and is decorated with reliefs of the early history of the city's bridges and sluices. The next bridge, heading south, is the Jungfernbrücke dating from 1798, which is the last drawbridge in Berlin. The next bridge along is the Gertraudenbrücke *(see p87)*. Where Friedrichstrasse crosses the Spree river is the Weidendammer Brücke, originally built in 1695–7 and subsequently rebuilt in 1923, with an eagle motif decorating its balustrade. On the Spree near the Regierungsviertel is the magnificent Moltkebrücke (1886–91). The bridge is guarded by a huge griffin wielding a shield adorned with the Prussian eagle, while cherubs dressed in a military fashion hold up lamps. On the arches of the bridges are portraits of leaders designed by Karl Begas.

Ornamental feature of a bear on the Liebknechtbrücke

KREUZBERG

The area covered in this chapter is only a part of the district of the same name. The evolution of Kreuzberg began in the late 19th century, when it was a working-class area. After World War II, unrepaired buildings were abandoned by those who could afford to move, leaving a population of artists, foreigners, the unemployed and members of a variety of subcultures.

Kreuzberg is now an area of contrasts, with luxury apartments next to dilapidated buildings. Some parts of Kreuzberg are mainly Turkish, while others are inhabited by affluent young professionals. The district's attractions are its wealth of restaurants and Turkish bazaars, as well as an interesting selection of nightclubs, cinemas, theatres and galleries.

Sights at a Glance

Museums

2 Martin-Gropius-Bau
3 Topographie des Terrors
4 Checkpoint Charlie
5 Berlinische Galerie
6 *Jüdisches Museum Berlin pp146–7*
8 Lapidarium
9 Deutsches Technikmuseum Berlin

Historic Buildings

1 Anhalter Bahnhof
11 Riehmers Hofgarten
13 Flughafen Tempelhof

Squares, Parks and Cemeteries

7 Mehringplatz
10 Friedhöfe vor dem Halleschen Tor
12 Viktoriapark

Restaurants

see pp236–7

1 Ø
2 Altes Zollhaus
3 Bar Centrale
4 Cafe do Brasil
5 e.t.a. hoffmann
6 Golgotha
7 Gropius
8 Seerose
9 Tim Raue
10 Tomasa
11 Yorckschlosschen

See also Street Finder maps 8, 9, 14, 15

Street-by-Street: Mehringplatz and Friedrichstrasse

The areas north of Mehringplatz are the oldest sections of Kreuzberg. Mehringplatz, initially called Rondell, together with the Oktogon (Leipziger Platz) and the Quarré (Pariser Platz) were laid out in 1734 as part of the enlargement of Friedrichstadt. World War II totally changed the character of this area. It is now full of modern developments such as the Friedrichstadt Passagen – a huge complex of shops, apartments, offices, galleries and restaurants. Only a few buildings recall the earlier splendour of this district.

4 ★ Checkpoint Charlie
This small hut marks the place of the notorious border crossing between East and West Berlin.

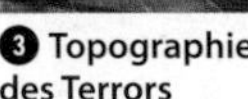

3 Topographie des Terrors
A shocking exhibition detailing Nazi crimes occupies the site of the former Gestapo and SS headquarters.

KOCHSTRASSE
WILHELMSTRASSE
FRIEDRICHSTR
PUTTKAMERSTRASSE
HEDEMANNSTRASS

Key

— Suggested route

2 Martin-Gropius-Bau
This interesting, multi-coloured Neo-Renaissance building is now the main temporary art exhibition space in the city.

Haus am Checkpoint Charlie
Butterflies on a piece of the Berlin Wall mark the entrance to this museum.

Deutsches Technikmuseum

Springer-Hochhaus
This shopping and restaurant complex is located inside the Axel-Springer-Hochhaus, a 1960s high-rise built adjacent to the Berlin Wall as a highly visible political statement.

Locator Map
See Street Finder maps 14 & 15

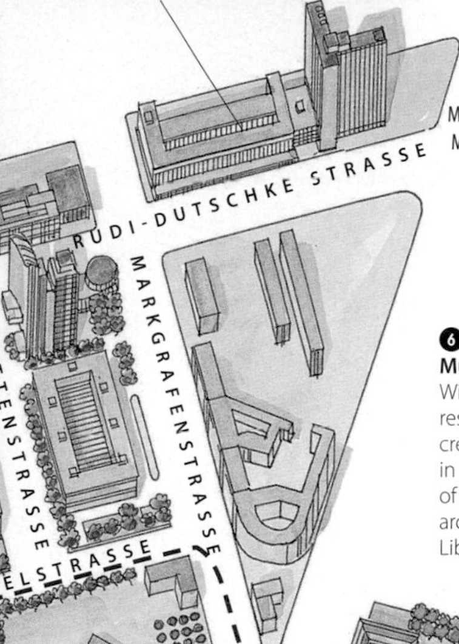

❻ ★ Jüdisches Museum Berlin
Windows made to resemble cracks create a striking effect in the metallic facing of this building by architect Daniel Libeskind.

0 metres 150
0 yards 150

❼ Mehringplatz
The former Rondell was known for many years as Belle-Alliance-Platz. Completely destroyed during World War II, it was rebuilt by Hans Scharoun, who followed the original design.

❶ Anhalter Bahnhof

Askanischer Platz 6–7. **Map** 14 E1. Ⓢ Anhalter Bahnhof. Ⓤ Potsdamer Platz. Ⓤ Mendelssohn-Bartholdy-Park. 🚌 M29, M41.

Only a tiny fragment now remains of Anhalter Bahnhof, which was named after the Saxon royal family. It was once Berlin's largest and Europe's second-largest railway station.

The hugely ambitious structure was designed by Franz Schwechten and constructed in 1880. The station was intended to be the biggest and most elegant in Europe in order to impress official visitors to the capital of the German Empire. Some of the most famous people to alight at Anhalter Bahnhof were the Italian king Umberto, who was welcomed by Kaiser Wilhelm II himself, and the Russian Tsar Nicholas. The station was taken out of public use in 1943 after its roof was destroyed by Allied bombing. Only the front portico remains, crowned by still-damaged sculptures and the hole that housed a large electric clock, as well as fragments of its once glorious façade. On the vast grounds behind it is the tent-like entertainment venue, Tempodrom *(see p269)*.

❷ Martin-Gropius-Bau

Niederkirchnerstrasse 7 (corner of Stresemannstrasse). **Map** 14 E1. **Tel** 25 48 60. **Open** 10am–7pm Wed–Mon. Ⓢ & Ⓤ Potsdamer Platz. 🚌 200, M29, M41.

The innovative Martin-Gropius-Bau was originally built to fulfil the requirements of an arts and crafts museum. It was designed by Martin Gropius with the participation of Heino Schmieden and constructed in 1881. The building is in a style reminiscent of an Italian Renaissance palace, with a magnificent glazed interior courtyard, an impressive atrium and unusual, richly decorated elevations. Located between the windows are the crests of German cities, and within the friezes are reliefs illustrating the different arts and crafts. In the plaques between the windows of the top storey are beautiful mosaics containing allegorical figures representing the cultures of different eras and countries.

From 1922 Martin-Gropius-Bau accommodated the Museum of Ethnology, but after World War II the building was abandoned and left in ruins. Although plans for an inner-city motorway threatened it until the 1970s, a reconstruction programme eventually commenced in 1981, led by architects Winnetou Kampmann and Ute Westroem. This was followed in 1999 by a further refurbishment, and since then the building has housed a changing series of exhibitions on art, photography and architecture.

Exhibition hall of Topographie des Terrors, documenting Nazi crimes

Allegorical mosaic on display in the Martin-Gropius-Bau

❸ Topographie des Terrors

Stresemannstrasse 110 (entrance on Niederkirchnerstrasse 8). **Map** 8 F5, 14 F1. **Tel** 254 50 90. Ⓢ & Ⓤ Potsdamer Platz, Kochstrasse. Ⓢ Anhalter Bahnhof. 🚌 M29, M41.
Open 10am–8pm daily.
W topographie.de

During the Third Reich Prinz-Albrecht-Strasse was probably the most frightening address in Berlin. In 1934 three of the most terrifying Nazi political departments had their headquarters in a block between Stresemann-, Wilhelm-, Anhalter- and Prinz-Albrecht-Strasse (now Niederkirchner Strasse), making this area the government district of National Socialist Germany.

The Neo-Classical Prinz-Albrecht palace at Wilhelm-strasse No. 102 became the headquarters of Reinhard Heydrich and the Third Reich's security service (SD). The arts and crafts school at Prinz-Albrecht-Strasse No. 8 was occupied by the head of the Gestapo, Heinrich Müller, while the Hotel Prinz Albrecht at No. 9 became the headquarters of the Schutzstaffel, or SS, with Heinrich Himmler in command. It was from the buildings in this area of the city that decisions about the Germanization of the occupied territories were made, as well as plans for the genocide of European Jews. After World War II, the ruins of the heavily bombed buildings were pulled down. In 1987, however, an exhibition documenting Nazi crimes was installed in former cellars here by committed citizens of Berlin. An exhibition building was added in 2010. A preserved section of the Berlin wall runs alongside the building, on Niederkirchner Strasse.

❹ Checkpoint Charlie

Friedrichstrasse 43–45. **Map** 9 A5. **Tel** 253 72 50. U Kochstrasse. M29. Haus am Checkpoint Charlie: **Open** 9am–10pm daily.

A Alpha, B Bravo, C Charlie. Not many people remember that the name of this notorious border crossing between the American and Soviet sectors stemmed from the word that signifies the letter C in the international phonetic alphabet.

Between 1961 and 1990, Checkpoint Charlie was the only crossing point for foreigners between East and West Berlin. During that time, it represented a symbol of both freedom and separation for the many East Germans trying to escape from the DDR's Communist regime.

Little remains of the former crossing point, which was witness to a number of dramatic events during the Cold War, including a tense two-day standoff between Russian and American tanks in 1961.

In 1990, the checkpoint was formally closed with an official ceremony attended by the foreign ministers of the four occupying powers: the US, Great Britain, France and the Soviet Union.

Today, there are no longer any gates, barriers or barbed wire to be seen; instead there is a replica checkpoint booth, complete with sandbags and the famous huge sign on the old Western side that reads "You are leaving the American Sector". There is also an exhibition space called the BlackBox, housing the Zentrum Kalter Krieg (Cold War Centre), which documents and explores the period after World War II up until 1989.

The replica booth at the former Checkpoint Charlie

Also on Friedrichstrasse are two large photographs of an American and a Russian soldier that form part of a well-known series by the Berlin photographer Frank Thiel. His portraits commemorate the departure of the Allies.

One of the original watchtowers is worth visiting at the museum nearby – **Haus am Checkpoint Charlie**. The museum's rich collection details Cold War border conflicts, and the construction of the Berlin Wall. Of special interest are the exhibits connected with the escape attempts of East Germans to the West. The ingenuity and bravery of these escapees is astonishing, using devices such as secret compartments built into cars, and specially constructed suitcases.

A separate exhibition illustrates the peaceful campaigns carried out in the name of democracy in many totalitarian countries.

❺ Berlinische Galerie

Alte Jakobstrasse 124–28. **Map** 9 C5. **Tel** 78 90 26 00. U Kochstrasse. 248, M29. **Open** 10am–6pm Wed–Mon.

The city's museum for modern art, design and architecture is one of the finest regional museums in the country. Themed exhibitions, which are regularly changed, draw upon its huge collection of German, East European and Russian paintings, photographs, graphics and architectural artifacts.

One of the highlights is the 5,000-strong paintings collection, which covers all the major art movements from the late 19th century until today. It includes works by Max Liebermann, Otto Dix, Georg Baselitz, Alexander Rodtschenko, Iwan Puni and Via Lewandowsky.

The museum's collection of sketches, prints and posters encompasses the Berlin Dadaists George Grosz, Hannah Höch and Werner Heldt, as well as works by Ernst Ludwig Kirchner and Hanns Schimansky.

Amongst the architectural items held by the Galerie are drawings and models for buildings that were never built, offering fascinating glimpses into how the city might have looked. A fine example is the shell-like Expressionist Sternkirche (Star Church), designed by Otto Bartning in 1922.

Kühn Malvessi's *Letter Field* in front of the Berlinische Galerie

❻ Jüdisches Museum Berlin

The Jewish Museum, designed by Daniel Libeskind, a Polish-Jewish architect based in the United States, is an exciting and imaginative example of late 20th-century architecture. The plan, shape, style, and interior and exterior arrangement of the building are part of a complicated philosophical programme to illustrate the history and culture of Germany's Jewish community, and the repercussions of the Holocaust. The exhibition has gathered together many artifacts, such as books and photographs, to bring the memories and stories of Jewish life alive. The long, narrow galleries with slanting floors and sharp zig-zagging turns are designed to evoke the feeling of loss and dislocation. These are interspersed by "voids" that represent the vacuum left behind by the destruction of Jewish life.

★ Moses Mendelssohn's Glasses
These glasses are on show in the section entitled "Moses Mendelssohn and the Enlightenment", which details the philosopher's fight for religious tolerance in a time when Jews possessed no civil rights.

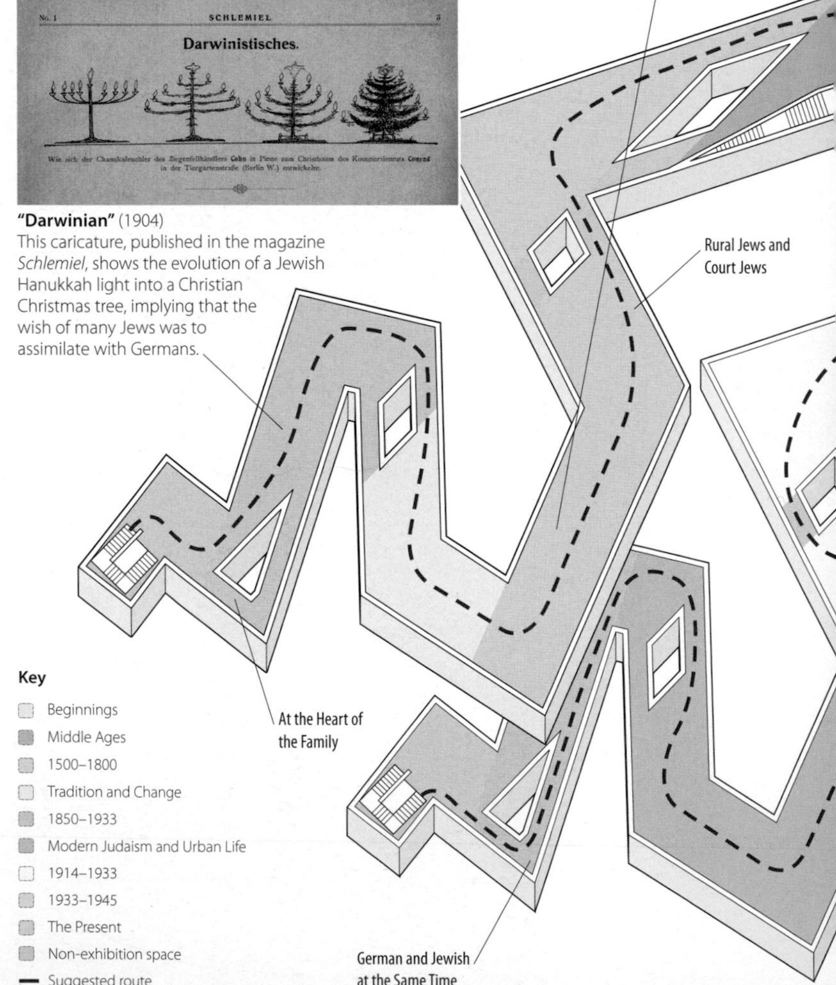

"Darwinian" (1904)
This caricature, published in the magazine *Schlemiel*, shows the evolution of a Jewish Hanukkah light into a Christian Christmas tree, implying that the wish of many Jews was to assimilate with Germans.

Key

- Beginnings
- Middle Ages
- 1500–1800
- Tradition and Change
- 1850–1933
- Modern Judaism and Urban Life
- 1914–1933
- 1933–1945
- The Present
- Non-exhibition space
- — Suggested route

Museum Guide

Entrance to the museum is via an underground path from the former Berlin Museum next door. Stairs lead up to the start of the exhibition, which is divided into 14 sections, taking visitors through German Jewish history and culture from early history, through the Middle Ages and up to the present day.

Entrance to exhibition via underground tunnel

World War I and Weimar Republic

Exit

Persecution Resistance–Extermination

East and West

VISITORS' CHECKLIST

Practical Information
Lindenstrasse 9–14.
Map 15 A2.
Tel 25 99 33 00.
jmberlin.de
Open 10am–10pm Mon, 10am–8pm Tue–Sun.
Closed Jewish hols and 24 Dec.

Transport
Hallesches Tor or Kochstrasse.
M29, M41, 248.

★ Daniel Libeskind's Design
The extraordinary zinc-clad, jagged structure of the museum is likened to a deconstructed Star of David, and attracted over 350,000 visitors to the museum in the two years before the exhibitions were installed.

Electric Iron AEG
An iron made by one of Germany's largest electrical companies, founded by Emil Rathenau, forms part of the collection celebrating the dominant position of Jews in trade and industry in Berlin throughout the late 19th and early 20th centuries.

★ Garden of Exile
Comprising 49 tilted pillars to represent the foundation of the state of Israel in 1948, plus one for Berlin, the garden also symbolizes the forced exile of Germany's Jews.

A representation of Peace, by Albert Wolff, in Mehringplatz

7 Mehringplatz

Map 15 A2. U Hallesches Tor. 248, M41.

Mehringplatz was planned in the 1730s, when the boundaries of the city were extended. Its original name was Rondell, meaning "circus", an appropriate name, as Wilhelmstrasse, Friedrichstrasse and Lindenstrasse all converged here.

Rondell was originally the work of Philipp Gerlach; then, in the 1840s, Peter Joseph Lenné designed the decoration of the square. At the centre is the Column of Peace, commemorating the Wars of Liberation in 1815. The column is crowned by the figure of Victory by Christian Daniel Rauch. Two sculptures were added in the 1870s: *Peace* by Albert Wolff; and *Clio* (the Muse of History) by Ferdinand Hartzer.

In the 19th and early 20th centuries the area was populated with politicians, diplomats and aristocrats, and in 1947 the square was named after the writer Franz Mehring. The current buildings date from the 1970s.

8 Lapidarium

Hallesches Ufer 78. **Map** 14 E2. U Mendelssohn-Bartholdy-Park.

This interesting building, decorated with an enchanting Oriental-style chimney, was once Berlin's pumping station. It was built from 1873 to 1876 and designed by Hermann Blankenstein. The original steam pumps have survived to this day. The Lapidarium once contained numerous sculptures, including virtually all the sculptures that once decorated the Avenue of Victory in the Tiergarten, known as "Puppenallee". These majestic statues of celebrated warriors and rulers stood side by side in their robes and weapons, only slightly diminished by the loss of many heads, arms and other body parts. In 2009 the Lapidarium was sold, and all the statues were transferred to the Zittadelle Spandau.

9 Deutsches Technikmuseum Berlin

Trebbiner Strasse 9. **Map** 14 E2. **Tel** 90 25 40. U Gleisdreieck. M29, M41. **Open** 9am–5:30pm Tue–Fri, 10am–6pm Sat & Sun.

The Technical Museum was first established in 1982 with the intention of grouping more than 100 smaller, specialized collections under one roof. The current collection is arranged on the site of the former trade hall, the size of which allows many of the museum's exhibits, such as locomotives, aircraft, boats, water towers and storerooms, to be displayed full-size and in their original condition.

Of particular interest in the collection are the dozens of locomotives and railway carriages from different eras as well as the vintage cars. There are also exhibitions dedicated to flying, the history of paper manufacture, printing, weaving, electro-technology and computer technology. There are also two windmills, a brewery and an old forge. The section called Spectrum is especially popular with children as it allows them to conduct "hands-on" experiments.

10 Friedhöfe vor dem Halleschen Tor

Mehringdamm, Blücher-, Baruther & Zossener Strasse. **Map** 15 A3. **Tel** 691 61 38. U Hallesches Tor. 140, 248, M41. **Open** Dec & Jan: 8am–4pm daily; Feb & Nov: 8am–5pm daily; Mar & Oct: 8am–6pm; Apr & Sep: 8am–7pm; May–Aug: 8am–8pm.

Beyond the city walls, next to the Hallesches Tor, are four cemeteries established in 1735. Among the beautiful gravestones are great Berlin artists including the composer Felix Mendelssohn-Bartholdy, architects Georg Wenzeslaus von Knobelsdorff, David Gilly and Carl Ferdinand Langhans, and the writer, artist and composer ETA Hoffmann.

11 Riehmers Hofgarten

Yorckstrasse 83–86, Grossbeerenstrasse 56–57 & Hagelberger Strasse 9–12. **Map** 14 F4. U Mehringdamm. 140, 248, M19.

Riehmers Hofgarten is the name given to the 20 or so exquisite houses arranged around a

Headstone in the picturesque Friedhöfe vor dem Halleschen Tor

Renaissance-style façade in Riehmers Hofgarten

picturesque garden in the area bordered by the streets Yorckstrasse, Hagelberger Strasse and Grossbeerenstrasse. These houses were built between 1881 and 1899 to the detailed designs of Wilhelm Riehmer and Otto Mrosk, respected architects who not only designed intricate, Renaissance-style and Neo-Baroque façades but also gave equal splendour to the elevations overlooking the courtyard garden. The streets of Riehmers Hofgarten have been carefully restored and Yorckstrasse also has quite a few cafés. Next to Riehmers Hofgarten is the church of St Bonifaz, which was designed by Max Hasak. Adjacent to the church is a similar complex of houses built in an impressive Neo-Gothic style.

To experience the authentic atmosphere of old Kreuzberg, you need to go no further than Bergmannstrasse. Here, entire districts of 19th-century houses have been restored to their original state. The atmosphere is further enhanced by antique streetlamps, a pedestrianized street, and bars and galleries. This is also true for Marheinekeplatz, where there is a lively covered market.

⓬ Viktoriapark

Map 14 E4, E5, F5. U Platz der Luftbrücke. 104, 140, M19.

This rambling park, with several artificial waterfalls, short trails and a small hill, was designed by Hermann Machtig and built between 1884 and 1894. The Neo-Gothic Memorial to the Wars of Liberation at the summit of the hill is the work of Karl Friedrich Schinkel, created between 1817 and 1821. The monument commemorates the Prussian victory against Napoleon's army in the Wars of Liberation. The cast-iron tower is well ornamented. In the niches of the lower section are 12 allegorical figures by Christian Daniel Rauch, Friedrich Tieck and Ludwig Wichmann. Each figure symbolizes a battle and is linked to a historic figure – either a military leader or a member of the royal family.

⓭ Flughafen Tempelhof

Platz der Luftbrücke. **Map** 14 F5. **Tel** 200 03 74 41. U Platz der Luftbrücke. 104, 248. **Open** tours 3pm Sat & 2pm Sun.

Tempelhof airport was once Germany's largest. Built in 1923, it was enlarged during the Third Reich. The building is typical of Third Reich architecture, even though the eagles that decorate the buildings predate the Nazis. The additions to the original structure were designed by Ernst Sagebiel in 1939.

In 1951, a monument was added in front of the airport. Designed by Eduard Ludwig, it commemorates the airlifts of the Berlin Blockade. The three spikes on the top symbolize the air corridors used by Allied planes. The airport was permanently closed in 2008.

The Berlin Blockade (1948–9)

On 24 June 1948, as a result of rising tensions between East Germany and West Berlin, Soviet authorities blockaded all the roads leading to West Berlin. In order to ensure food and fuel for the residents, US General Lucius Clay ordered that provisions be flown into the city. British and American planes made a total of 212,612 flights, transporting almost 2.3 million tons of goods, among which were parts of a power station. In April 1949, at the height of the airlifts, planes were landing every 63 seconds. The blockade ended in May 1949. Although the airlifts were successful, there were casualties: 70 airmen and 8 ground crew lost their lives.

Allied plane bringing supplies during the Berlin Airlift

AROUND KURFÜRSTENDAMM

The eastern area of the Charlottenburg region, around the boulevard known as Kurfürstendamm, was developed in the 19th century. Luxurious buildings were constructed along Kurfürstendamm (the Ku'damm), while the areas of Breitscheidplatz and Wittenbergplatz became replete with hotels and department stores. After World War II, with the old centre (Mitte) situated in East Berlin, Charlottenburg became the centre of West Berlin. Traces of wartime destruction were removed very quickly and this area was transformed into the heart of West Berlin, and dozens of new company headquarters and trade centres were built. The situation changed after the reunification of Berlin and, although many tourists concentrate on the Mitte district, the heart of the city continues to beat around Kurfürstendamm.

Sights at a Glance

Museums

5 C/O Berlin
7 Newton-Sammlung
11 Käthe-Kollwitz-Museum

Streets and Squares

4 Kurfürstendamm
10 Fasanenstrasse
12 Savignyplatz
15 Tauentzienstrasse

Parks

1 Zoologischer Garten

Historic Buildings

2 Europa-Center
3 *Kaiser-Wilhelm-Gedächtnis-Kirche pp156–7*
6 Ludwig-Erhard-Haus
8 Theater des Westens
9 Jüdisches Gemeindehaus
13 Universität der Künste
14 Technische Universität
16 KaDeWe

Restaurants
see pp237–8

1 Baba Angora
2 Belmondo
3 Bleiburg's
4 El Borriquito
5 Brasserie Le Faubourg
6 Brenner
7 Cafe-Restaurant Wintergarten im Literhaus
8 Calcutta
9 Dickie Wirtin
10 Esswein am Fasanenplatz
11 Florian
12 Grüne Lampe
13 Marjellchen
14 Namaskar
15 Die Quadriga
16 Restaurant 44
17 Sachico Sushi
18 Satyam
19 Tastees
20 Trattoria Totó
21 Wilson's

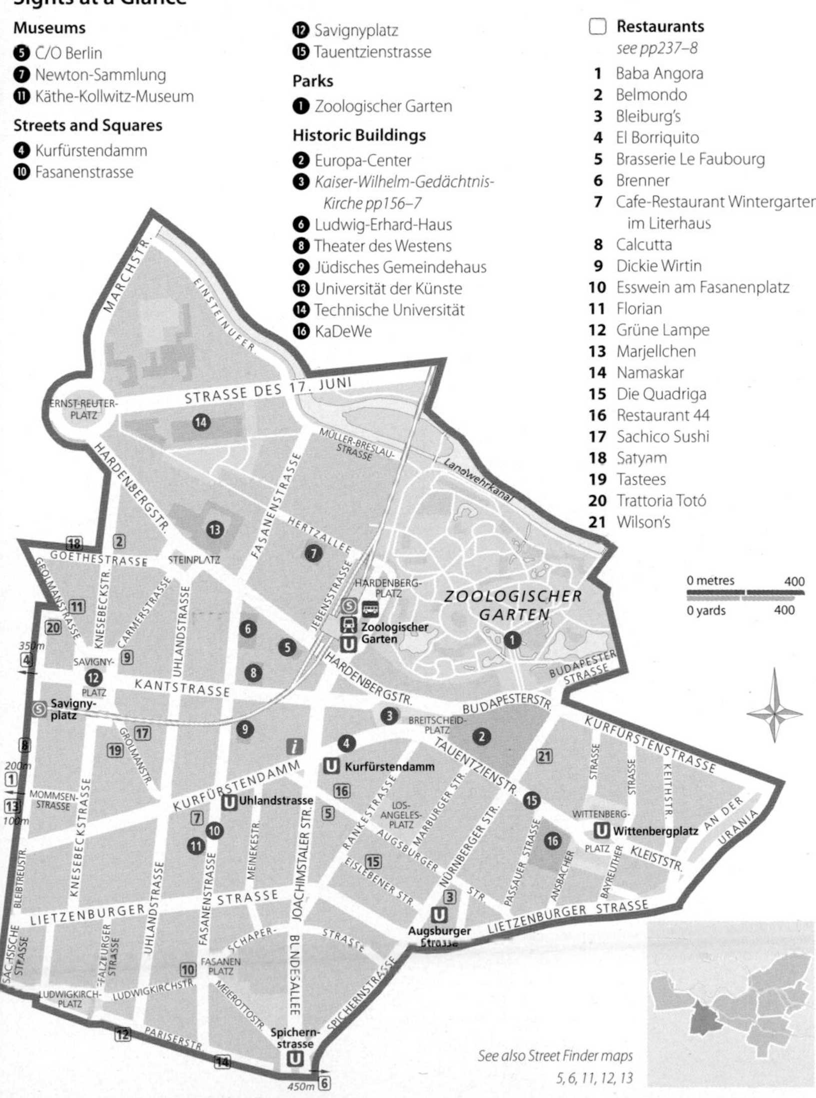

See also Street Finder maps 5, 6, 11, 12, 13

◀ The magnificent Kaiser-Wilhelm-Gedächtnis-Kirche

For map symbols *see back flap*

Street-by-Street: Breitscheidplatz and Ku'damm

The area surrounding the eastern end of the Ku'damm, especially Tauentzienstrasse and Breitscheidplatz, is the centre of the former West Berlin. Thirty years ago this ultra-modern district, full of department stores and office blocks, attracted visitors from all over the world. Today, although the area still retains its unique atmosphere, it is becoming overshadowed by Potsdamer Platz and the arcades of Friedrichstrasse. However, nowhere else in Berlin is there a place so full of life as Breitscheidplatz, a department store with such style as KaDeWe, or streets as refined as Fasanenstrasse.

Kant-Dreieck
This building, containing only right angles, was designed by Josef Paul Kleihues. The "sail" on the roof makes it instantly recognizable.

9 Jüdisches Gemeindehaus
Some of the remaining fragments of the old synagogue have been incorporated into the façade of this building.

Literaturhaus contains a charming café and a good bookshop.

11 Käthe-Kollwitz-Museum
The museum is housed in one of the charming villas on Fasanenstrasse.

10 Fasanenstrasse
This tranquil street features some of the most expensive shops in Berlin.

Key

— Suggested route

0 metres 400
0 yards 400

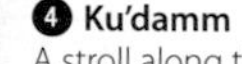

4 Ku'damm
A stroll along the Ku'damm is a stroll into the heart of Berlin, and an essential part of any visit to the city.

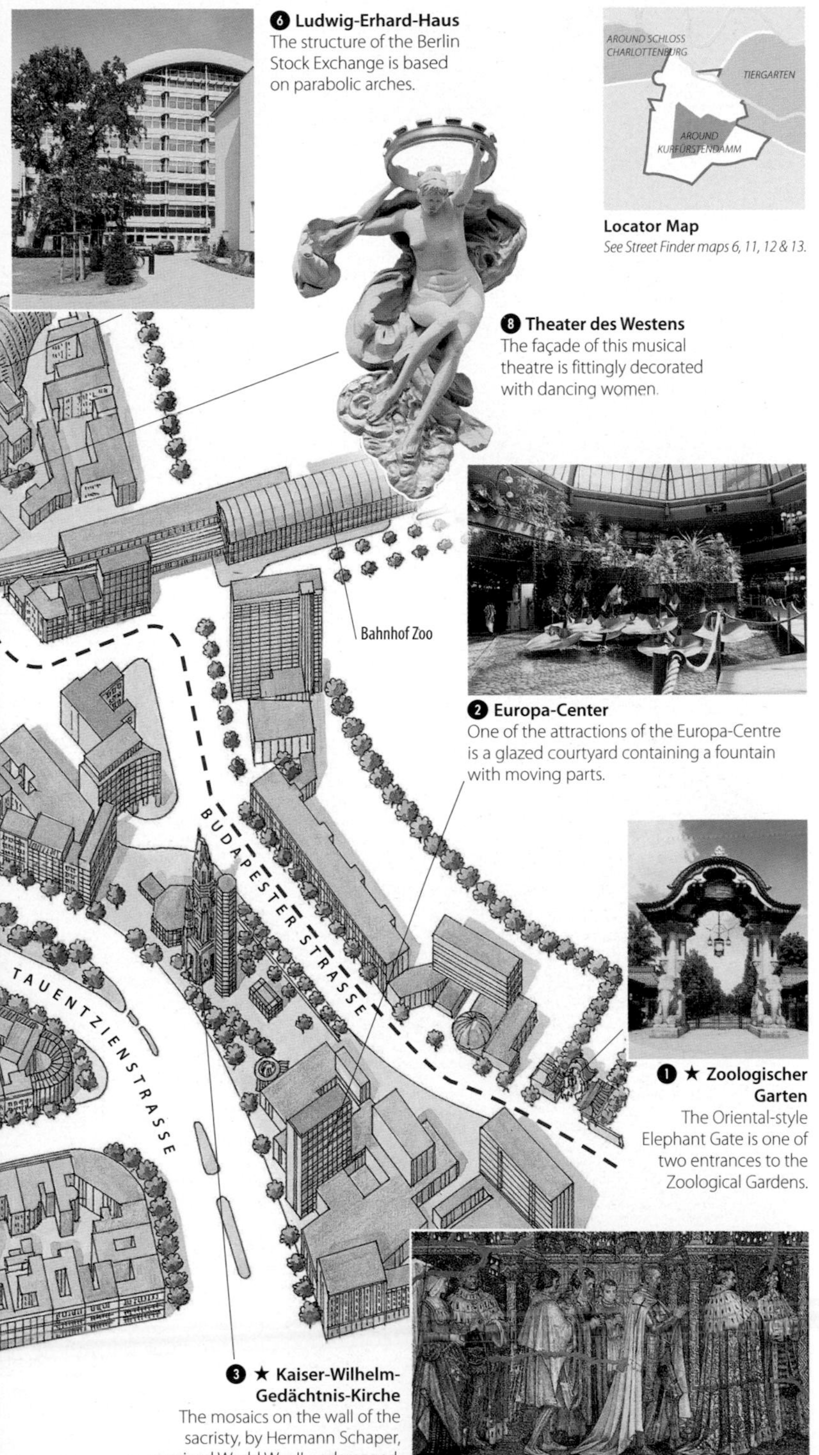

6 Ludwig-Erhard-Haus
The structure of the Berlin Stock Exchange is based on parabolic arches.

Locator Map
See Street Finder maps 6, 11, 12 & 13.

8 Theater des Westens
The façade of this musical theatre is fittingly decorated with dancing women.

2 Europa-Center
One of the attractions of the Europa-Centre is a glazed courtyard containing a fountain with moving parts.

1 ★ Zoologischer Garten
The Oriental-style Elephant Gate is one of two entrances to the Zoological Gardens.

3 ★ Kaiser-Wilhelm-Gedächtnis-Kirche
The mosaics on the wall of the sacristy, by Hermann Schaper, survived World War II undamaged.

Hippopotamus House is spanned by fine-meshed glass domes

❶ Zoo Berlin

Zoological Garden

Hardenbergplatz 8 or Budapester Strasse 34. **Map** 6 E5, 12 E1. **Tel** 25 40 10. Ⓢ & Ⓤ Zoologischer Garten. 🚌 100, 109, 110, 200, 204, 245, 249, M45, M46, M49, X9, X10, X34. **Open** 21 Mar–3 Oct: 9am–7pm daily; 4 Oct–20 Mar: 9am–5pm daily. 🍴 **W zoo-berlin.de**

Zoo Berlin is one of Berlin's greatest attractions and many animal "stars" are to be found here. It is part of the Tiergarten and dates from 1844, which makes this zoo the oldest in Germany. You can enter from Hardenbergplatz through the Lion's Gate, and from Budapester Strasse through the decorative Oriental-style Elephant Gate.

The zoo offers a number of attractions, including the monkey house, which contains a family of gorillas, and a darkened pavilion for nocturnal animals. The hippopotamus pool has a glazed wall that enables visitors to observe these enormous animals underwater. The aquarium, one of the largest in Europe, contains sharks, piranhas and unusual animals from coral reefs. There is also a huge terrarium with an overgrown jungle that is home to a group of crocodiles.

❷ Europa-Center

Breitscheidplatz. **Map** 12 E1. Ⓢ & Ⓤ Zoologischer Garten. 🚌 100, 109, 200, X9.

The Europa-Center stands on the site of the legendary Romanisches Café, a famous meeting place for Dada artists in the 1920s. The current building was established in 1965, and since that time it has been one of the largest complexes of its type in the whole of Germany. Designed by Helmut Hentrich and Hubert Petschnigg, the Europa-Center is a group of low-rise buildings housing a trade centre, numerous restaurants and pubs. The deluxe Hotel Palace Berlin has also been incorporated into the Center.

Around the Center are some fountains, including the "Flow of Time Clock", designed by Bernard Gitton. Seconds, minutes and hours are measured in vials and spheres of green liquid. The Europa-Center also houses the political cabaret *Die Stachelschweine.*

❸ Kaiser-Wilhelm-Gedächtnis-Kirche

See pp156–7.

❹ Kurfürstendamm

Map 11 A2, B2, C3, 12 D1. Ⓤ Kurfürstendamm or Uhlandstrasse or Zoologischer Garten. 🚌 109, 110, M19, M29.

One of the most elegant streets in Berlin, this wide avenue was established in the 1880s on the site of a former track that led to the Grunewald forest. It was quickly populated with imposing buildings and grand hotels. In the 20 years between World Wars I and II, the Ku'damm was renowned for its great cafés, visited by famous writers, directors and painters.

After World War II, the damaged houses were replaced with modern buildings, but the street's essential character remained. During the Cold War years it became the main shopping street in West Berlin. Today, elegant shops and cafés continue to attract a chic crowd.

❺ C/O Berlin

Hardenbergstr 22–24. **Map** 12 D1. **Tel** 284 44 160. Ⓤ Zoologischer Garten. 🚌 245, M49, X10, X34, 100, 200. **W co-berlin.org**

This photography exhibition centre showcases work by renowned photographers as well as young talent, and holds artist talks, lectures and guided tours. It is housed in Amerika Haus, the former American culture and information centre, built during the international building exhibition in 1956–7 to a light and airy design by Bruno Grimmek.

The Europa-Center, flanked by Bikini Berlin mall and Kaiser Wilhelm Gedächtnis-Kirche

❻ Ludwig-Erhard-Haus

Fasanenstrasse 85. **Map** 6 D5. Ⓢ & Ⓤ Zoologischer Garten. 🚌 245, M45, M49, X9, X34.

The distinctive curve of this innovative building houses the headquarters of the Berlin stock exchange as well as a trade and industry centre. Completed in 1998, it is the creation of British architect Nicholas Grimshaw and has been compared to the skin of an armadillo, a giant skeleton and the ribbing of a shell.

❼ Newton-Sammlung

Jebensstrasse 2. **Map** 6 D5. **Tel** 31 86 48 56. Ⓢ & Ⓤ Zoologischer Garten. **Open** 10am–6pm Tue, Wed & Fri–Sun, 10am–8pm Thu.

After his death in 2004, the society and art photographer Helmut Newton (1931–2004) bequeathed his life's work to the city of Berlin. Newton, who was born and received his first training as a photographer in Berlin, became one of the 20th century's most well-known photographers with his images of nudes and portraits of the rich and famous.

The museum is constantly extending its collections so as to serve as the city's museum of photography. It exhibits selections of Newton's work, including his early fashion and nude images as well as self-portraits and landscapes. There is also a collection of Newton's cameras.

The façade of the Theater des Westens on Kantstrasse

❽ Theater des Westens

Kantstrasse 9–12. **Map** 12 D1. **Tel** (0180) 544 44. Ⓢ & Ⓤ Zoologischer Garten. 🚌 M49, X9, X10, X34, 100, 109, 110, 200.

The Theater des Westens, one of the most picturesque of all Berlin's theatres, was built in 1896 to a design by Bernhard Sehring. The composition of its façade links Neo-Classical elements with Palladian and Art Nouveau details. The interior of the theatre has been designed in a splendid Neo-Baroque style, while the back and the section that houses the stage have been rebuilt within a Neo-Gothic structure, incorporating the decorative elements of a chess set.

From its very beginning the theatre catered for lighter forms of musical entertainment. Operettas and vaudeville were staged here, followed by musicals such as *Les Misérables*. Some of the world's greatest stars have appeared on the stage here, including Josephine Baker, who performed her famous banana dance in 1926. Near the theatre is the renowned Delphi cinema and popular jazz club Quasimodo.

❾ Jüdisches Gemeindehaus

Jewish Community House

Fasanenstrasse 79/80. **Map** 12 D1. **Tel** 88 02 80. Ⓢ & Ⓤ Zoologischer Garten. Ⓤ Uhlandstrasse or Kurfürstendamm. 🚌 245, M49, X10, X34.

The Jewish community has its headquarters in this building, constructed on the site of a synagogue that was burned down during *Kristallnacht* on 9 November 1938 *(see p31)*. The original synagogue was designed by Ehenfried Hessel in a Romanesque-Byzantine style and built in 1912. The ruins of the synagogue were removed only in the mid-1950s.

The entrance of the Jüdisches Gemeindehaus

The new building, designed by Dieter Knoblauch and Heinz Heise, was constructed in 1959. The only reminders of the splendour of the former synagogue are the portal at the entrance to the building and some decorative fragments on the façade.

Inside there are offices, a school, a kosher restaurant called Arche Noah and a prayer room covered by three glazed domes. At the rear there is a courtyard with a place of remembrance. There is also an emotive statue at the front of the building, depicting a broken scroll of the Torah (the holy book of Jewish law).

German Cinema

The 1920s were a boom time for the arts, and German cinema gained prominence throughout the world with the rise of Expressionism. The opening of the UFA film studios in 1919 in Babelsberg *(see p207)* was a milestone in the development of German cinema. The studios became the heart of the film industry and rivalled Hollywood as a centre for innovation. Many famous films were produced here, including the Expressionist masterpiece *The Cabinet of Dr Caligari* (1920) by Robert Wiene, Ernst Lubitsch's *Madame Dubarry* (1919) with Pola Negri, and *Nosferatu* (1922) by Friedrich Murnau. Other films released by the studios were Fritz Lang's *Doctor Mahuse* (1922) and his futuristic film *Metropolis* (1927). In April 1930, the studios premiered Josef von Sternberg's *The Blue Angel*, featuring the young Marlene Dietrich in the lead role. After Hitler came to power, many directors and actors left Germany.

Marlene Dietrich in the well-known film *The Blue Angel*

❸ Kaiser-Wilhelm-Gedächtnis-Kirche

This church-monument is one of Berlin's most famous landmarks, surrounded by a lively crowd of street traders, buskers and beggars. The vast Neo-Romanesque church was designed by Franz Schwechten. It was consecrated in 1895 but was destroyed by bombs in 1943. After World War II the ruins were removed, leaving only the massive front tower at the base of which the Gedenkhalle (Memorial Hall) is situated. This hall documents the history of the church and contains some of the original ceiling mosaics, marble reliefs and liturgical objects from the church. In 1961, Egon Eiermann designed an octagonal church in blue glass and a new free-standing bell tower.

Kaiser's Mosaic
Kaiser Heinrich I is depicted here in this elaborate mosaic, sitting on his throne.

Mosaic Decoration
Original mosaics remain on the arches and the walls near the staircase. These feature the Dukes of Prussia among the other decorative elements.

Main Altar
The vast figure of Christ on the Cross is the work of Karl Hemmeter.

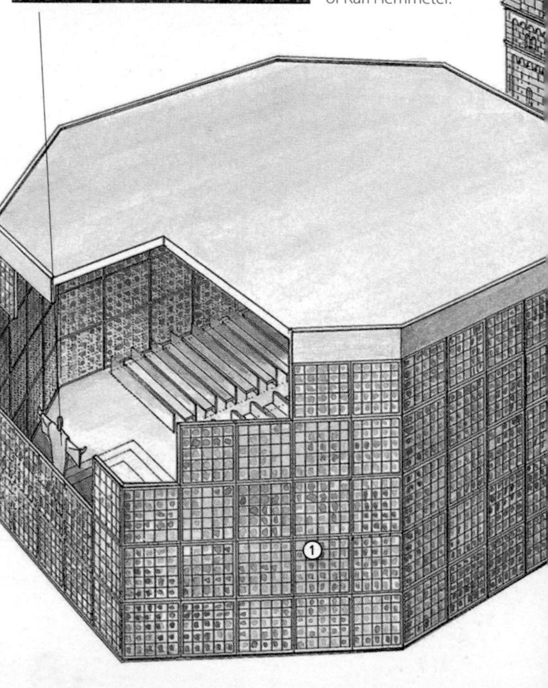

KEY

① **Walls** of reinforced concrete and blue-coloured glass form a dense grid.

② **Rose window**

③ **The damaged tower** roof of the former church is one of the best-known symbols of Berlin.

④ **The figure of Christ** is a vast sculpture by Hermann Schaper and once decorated the church altar. It survived World War II damage.

⑤ **Kaiser's Mosaic**

Bell Tower
The new hexagonal bell tower stands on the site of the former main nave of the destroyed church.

VISITORS' CHECKLIST

Practical Information
Breitscheidplatz.
Map 12 D1.
Tel 218 50 23.
Church: **Open** 9am–7pm daily. Gedenkhalle: 10am–6pm Mon–Sat, noon–6pm Sun. 10am & 6pm Sun.

Transport
S & U Zoologischer Garten or U Kurfürstendamm. 100, 109, 110, 200, 204, 245, M19, M29, M46, X9, X10, X34.

Tower Clock
The tower is decorated with a clock based on a Classical design.

★ Mosaic of the Hohenzollerns
The mosaic of the Hohenzollerns is in the vestibule. The family is led by Queen Luise and the centre is dominated by Kaiser Wilhelm I.

Orthodox Cross
This cross was a gift from the Russian Orthodox bishops from Volokolamsk and Yuryev, given in memory of the victims of Nazism.

★ Coventry Crucifix
This modest cross was fashioned from nails found in the ashes of Coventry Cathedral, England. The Cathedral was destroyed during German bombing raids in 1940.

Main entrance

Fasanenstrasse – one of the most elegant streets in Berlin

⑩ Fasanenstrasse

Map 11 C2, 12 D1, 12 D3. Ⓤ Uhlandstrasse. 🚌 109, 110, M49, X10, X34.

The discreet charm of Fasanenstrasse, particularly between Lietzenburger Strasse and Kurfürstendamm, has attracted the most exclusive designer shops in the world. Well-maintained buildings, *fin-de-siècle* villas set in tranquil gardens, and elegant shop windows of jewellers, art galleries and fashion shops will all entice you to take an afternoon stroll along this street.

It is worth seeing the villas at No. 23–25, which are called the Wintergarten-Ensemble. The first one, No. 23, dates from 1889. Tucked away in a garden, the villa is home to the Literaturhaus, which organizes interesting exhibitions and readings. It has an excellent café that extends into a conservatory. At No. 24 is the Käthe-Kollwitz museum, and No. 25, built in 1892 by Hans Grisebach, accommodates an auction house and art gallery.

⑪ Käthe-Kollwitz-Museum

Fasanenstrasse 24. **Map** 11 C2. **Tel** 882 52 10. Ⓤ Uhlandstrasse or Kurfürstendamm. 🚌 109, 110, 204, 249, X10. **Open** 11am–6pm daily. **kaethe-kollwitz.de**

This small private museum provides a unique opportunity to become acquainted with the work of Käthe Kollwitz (1867–1945). Born in Königsberg, the artist settled in Berlin, where she married a doctor who worked in Prenzlauer Berg, a working-class district *(see p101)*. Her drawings and sculptures portrayed the social problems of the poor, as well as human tragedy and suffering. She frequently took up the theme of motherhood and war after losing a son and grandson in World Wars I and II.

The museum exhibits her work, including sculptures, posters and drawings, as well as letters and photographs.

Mother and Child, from the Käthe-Kollwitz-Museum

⑫ Savignyplatz

Map 11 C1. Ⓢ Savignyplatz. 🚌 M49, X34.

Savignyplatz is enclosed on the south side by the arcade of a railway viaduct, which appears in the film *Cabaret* by Bob Fosse. During the day the square does not look interesting – there are no remarkable buildings, only carefully tended greenery and flowerbeds. However, the area around the square truly comes alive at night. The dozens of cafés and restaurants fill up, while in summer the entire edge of the square and neighbouring streets turn into one big garden filled with tables and umbrellas. People come from outlying districts to visit popular restaurants and cafés such as Esswein am Fasanenplatz, or Dicke Wirtin *(see p237)*. The arcades in the viaduct contain many cafés and bars, and one section has been taken up by the Bücherbogen bookshop *(see p254)*.

⑬ Universität der Künste

University of the Arts

Hardenbergstrasse 32–33 and Fasanenstrasse 1b. **Map** 6 D5. Ⓢ Zoologischer Garten or Ⓤ Ernst-Reuter-Platz. 🚌 245, M45, X9. **udk-berlin.de**

The Universität der Künste was originally called Preussische Akademie der Künste, and was established in 1696. It continued a long tradition of teaching artists in Berlin and has been headed by well-known figures including Johann Gottfried Schadow and Anton von Werner. As a result of a number of reforms between 1875 and 1882, the Academy was divided into two separate colleges. A complex of buildings was erected for them on Hardenbergstrasse and Fasanenstrasse. The Neo-Baroque buildings were built between 1897 and 1902 to a design by Heinrich Keyser and Karl von Grossheim.

After World War II, only two large buildings, both with decorative façades, survived. On the Hardenbergstrasse side was the Hochschule für Bildende Künste (College for Fine Art), while on the Fasanenstrasse side was the Hochschule für Musik und Darstellende Kunst (College for Music and Performing Arts). Unfortunately, the concert hall did not survive. A new one was built in 1955, designed by Paul Baumgarten.

Bas-relief sculpture on the façade of the Universität der Künste

A small *fin-de-siècle* building that looks like a castle, at Hardenbergstrasse No. 36, is a college for religious music which belongs to this group of college buildings.

⓮ Technische Universität

Technical University

Strasse des 17 Juni 135. **Map** 5 C4. Ⓤ Ernst-Reuter-Platz. 245, M45, X9.

The vast area that lies to the east of Ernst-Reuter-Platz along the Strasse des 17 Juni is occupied by the buildings of the Technische Universität. Officially called Technische Universität Berlin (TUB), it was established in 1879 after the unification of the School of Crafts and the renowned Bauakademie. From its inception the Technische Universität had five different departments, which were all housed, from 1884, in a Neo-Renaissance building designed by Richard Lucae, Friedrich Hitzig and Julius Raschdorff. After World War II, the ruined front wing was rebuilt as a flat block without any divisions, while the rear wings and three internal courtyards retained their original appearance.

It is worth continuing along Strasse des 17 Juni towards the colonnade of the Charlottenburger Tor (or gate), dating from 1908. The colonnade is ornamented with the figures of Friedrich and Sophie Charlotte holding a model of Schloss Charlottenburg *(see pp164–5)* in their hands. Beyond the gate and to the right, on the island, is an unusual green building with a gigantic pink pipe. This is the centre that monitors water currents and caters to the needs of seagoing vessels.

⓯ Tauentzienstrasse

Map 12 E1. Ⓤ Wittenbergplatz. M19, M29, M46.

This is one of the most important streets for trade and commerce in this part of Berlin. Some shops here are not as expensive or as elegant as on Kurfürstendamm – but they attract more visitors for this reason. One of the highlights of the street is the unusual façade of the department store Peek & Clopenburg. Designed by Gottfried Böhm, the walls of the building are covered with transparent, gently slanting and undulating "aprons".

Other highlights include the central bed of colourful flowers, as well as an interesting sculpture entitled *Berlin*. Created by Brigitte and Martin Matschinsky-Denninghoff, the sculpture was erected near Marburger Strasse in 1987 on the occasion of the 750th anniversary of Berlin.

⓰ KaDeWe

Tauentzienstrasse 21–24. **Map** 12 E2. **Tel** 21 21 0. Ⓤ Wittenbergplatz. M19, M29, M46. **Open** 10am–8pm Mon–Thu, 10am–9pm Fri, 9:30am–8pm Sat. **kadewe.de**

Kaufhaus des Westens, or KaDeWe, as it is popularly known, is the largest department store in Europe. It was built in 1907 to a design by Emil Schaudt, but it has been extended several times from the original building. From the very beginning KaDeWe was Berlin's most exclusive department store, with a comprehensive collection of goods for sale and with a slogan that ran "In our shop a customer is a king, and the King is a customer".

After World War II, KaDeWe effectively became the symbol of the economic success of West Berlin. You can buy everything here; however, the main attraction must be the Food Hall, a gourmet's paradise, with the largest collection of foodstuffs in the whole of Europe. Here there are exotic fruits and vegetables, live fish and seafood, 100 varieties of tea, more than 2,400 wines and a host of other gastronomic delights. KaDeWe also has a restaurant, the Wintergarten.

The sculpture *Berlin*, symbolizing the formerly divided city

AROUND SCHLOSS CHARLOTTENBURG

The area surrounding Schloss Charlottenburg is one of the most enchanting regions of the city, full of greenery and attractive buildings dating from the end of the 19th century. Originally a small settlement called Lützow, it was only when Elector Friedrich III (later King Friedrich I) built his wife's summer retreat here at the end of the 17th century *(see p23)* that this town attained significance. Initially called Schloss Lietzenburg, the palace was renamed Schloss Charlottenburg after the death of Queen Sophie Charlotte. By the 18th century Charlottenburg had become a town, and was for many years an independent administration, inhabited by wealthy people living in elegant villas. It became officially part of Berlin in 1920, and despite World War II and the ensuing division of the city, the central section of this area has kept its historic character.

Sights at a Glance

Museums

3 Neuer Flügel
6 Gipsformerei Berlin
9 Museum Scharf-Gerstenberg
10 Museum Berggruen
11 Bröhan-Museum

Historic Buildings

1 *Schloss Charlottenburg pp164–5*
4 Neuer Pavillon (Schinkel-Pavillon)
7 Mausoleum
8 Belvedere
12 Schlossstrasse Villas
13 Luisenkirche

Parks and Gardens

5 Schlosspark

Monuments

2 Reiterdenkmal des Grossen Kurfürsten

Restaurants
see pp238–9

1 Ana e Bruno
2 Brauhaus Lemke
3 Chenab
4 Don Giovanni
5 Engelbecken
6 Eosander
7 Genazvale
8 Le Piaf
9 Natural'mente
10 Restaurant Kien-Du
11 Taverna Ambrosios

0 metres 600
0 yards 600

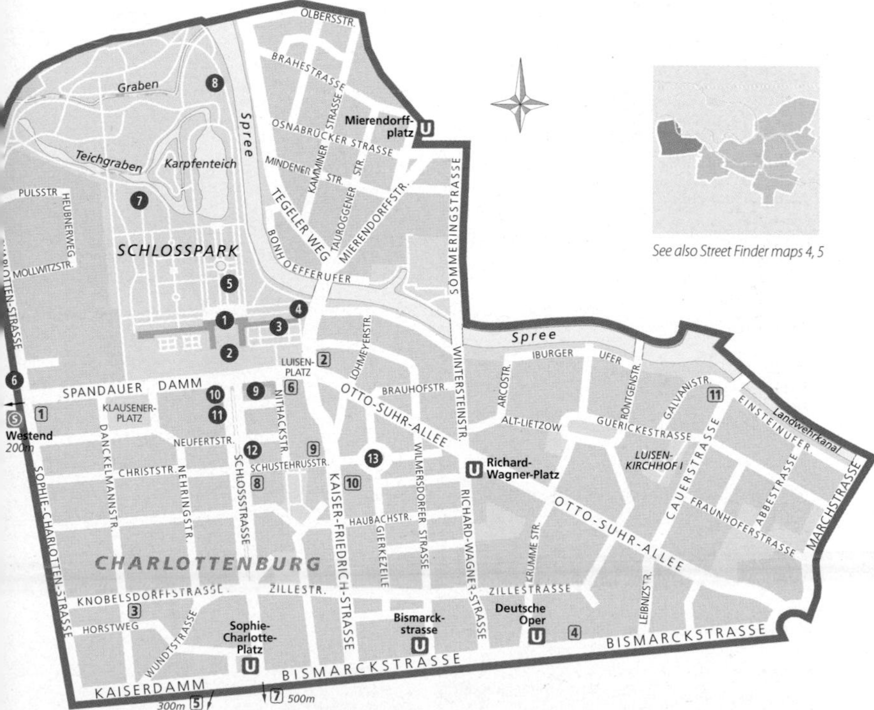

See also Street Finder maps 4, 5

◀ Porzellankabinett, the porcelain gallery inside Schloss Charlottenburg

Street-by Street: Around the Schloss

The park surrounding the former royal summer residence in Charlottenburg is one of the most picturesque places in Berlin. Visitors are drawn here by the meticulous post-war rebuilding of this luxury Baroque complex and outlying structures, whose marvellous interiors were once home to Prussian nobles. The wings of the palace and its pavilions house interesting exhibitions. After a stroll in the beautiful park, you can take refreshment in the Kleine Orangerie.

1 ★ Schloss Charlottenburg
The central section of the palace is called Nering-Eosanderbau, in honour of the architects who designed the building.

2 Reiterdenkmal des Grossen Kurfürsten
The monument to the Great Elector was funded by his son King Friedrich I and designed by Andreas Schlüter.

0 metres 150
0 yards 150

Kleine Orangerie

3 Neuer Flügel
The palace's new wing was once home to the royal art collection. Today the building houses changing art and history exhibits.

Key

— Suggested route

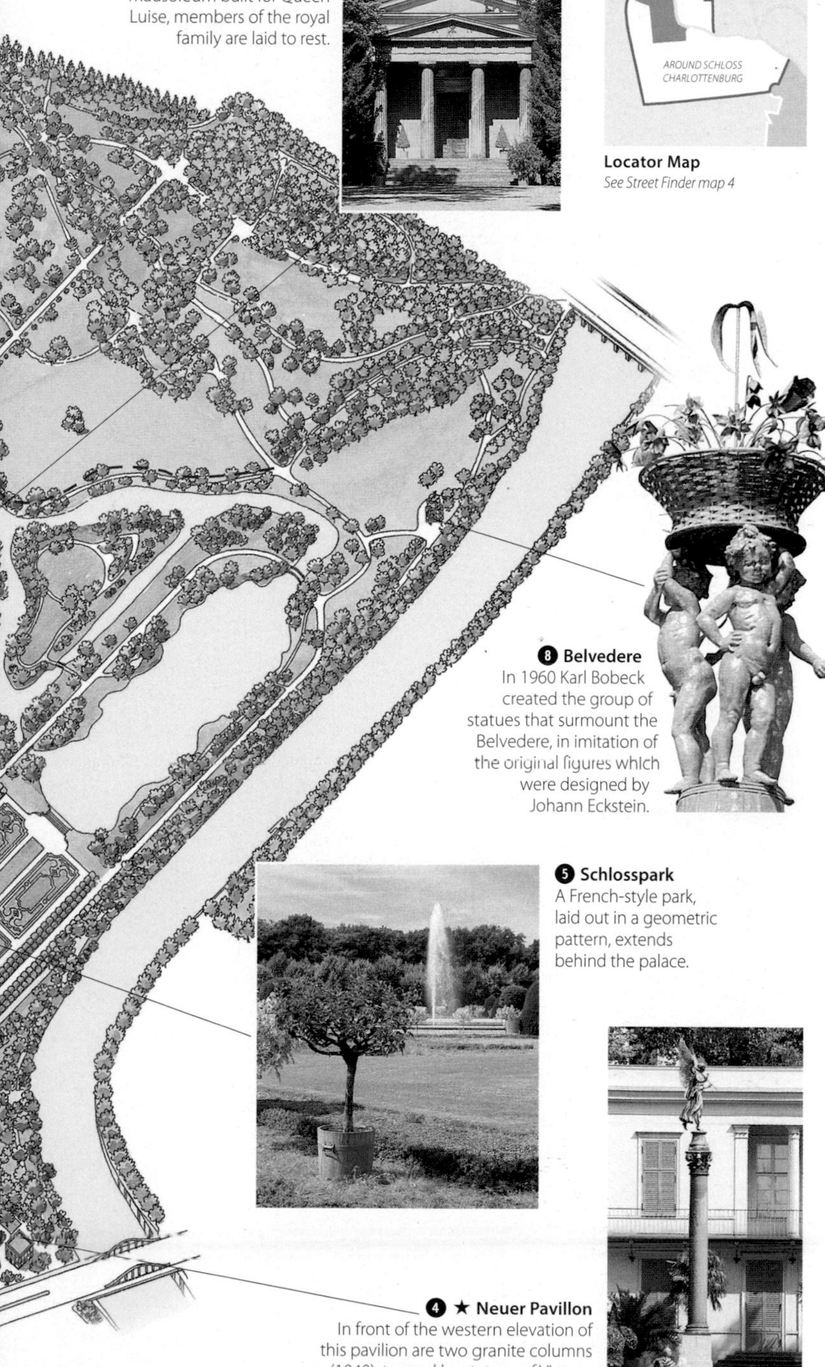

7 Mausoleum
In the Neo-Classical mausoleum built for Queen Luise, members of the royal family are laid to rest.

Locator Map
See Street Finder map 4

8 Belvedere
In 1960 Karl Bobeck created the group of statues that surmount the Belvedere, in imitation of the original figures which were designed by Johann Eckstein.

5 Schlosspark
A French-style park, laid out in a geometric pattern, extends behind the palace.

4 ★ Neuer Pavillon
In front of the western elevation of this pavilion are two granite columns (1840), topped by statues of Victory, the work of Christian Daniel Rauch.

❶ Schloss Charlottenburg

The palace in Charlottenburg was intended as a summer home for Sophie Charlotte, Elector Friedrich III's wife. Construction began in 1695 to a design by Johann Arnold Nering. Between 1701 and 1713 Johann Friedrich Eosander enlarged the palace, crowning it with a cupola and adding the orangery wing. Subsequent extensions were undertaken by Frederick the Great (Friedrich II), who added the Neuer Flügel, designed by Georg Wenzeslaus von Knobelsdorff, between 1740 and 1746. Restored to its former elegance following World War II, its collection of richly decorated interiors is unequalled in Berlin.

Gallery Guide

The ground floor of Altes Schloss houses the opulent Baroque chambers of Frederick I, a Portrait Gallery and the Porcelain Cabinet. The upper floors include the apartment of Friedrich Wilhelm IV and a silver and tableware collection.

First floor

Ground floor

★ Porzellankabinett
This exquisite mirrored gallery has walls lined from top to bottom with a fine display of Japanese and Chinese porcelain.

Schlosskapelle
Only parts of the pulpit in the court chapel are original to the palace. All the other furniture and fittings, including the royal box, are reconstructions.

Main entrance

Façade
The central section of the palace is the oldest part of the building, and is the work of Johann Arnold Nering.

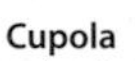

Cupola
The palace's tall, Baroque cupola completes the perspective from Schlossstrasse.

Fortuna
A sculpture by Richard Scheibe crowns the palace, replacing the original statue destroyed during World War II.

Key

- Official reception rooms
- Apartments of Sophie-Charlotte
- Neuer Flügel or Knobelsdorff-Flügel exhibition space
- Friedrich Wilhelm II's summer apartments
- Mecklenburg apartments
- Apartments of Friedrich Wilhelm IV
- Friedrich Wilhelm II's winter apartments
- Frederick the Great's apartments

VISITORS' CHECKLIST

Practical Information
Spandauer Damm 20–24.
Map 4 E2. Altes Schloss (Nering-Eosanderbau):
Tel (030) 32 09 11.
spsg.de
Open 10am–6pm Tue–Sun (to 5pm Nov–Mar). compulsory on ground floor only.
Neuer Flügel (Knobelsdorff-Flügel):
Tel (030) 32 09 10.
Open 10am–6pm Wed–Mon (to 5pm Nov–Mar).

Transport
Richard-Wagner-Platz & Sophie-Charlotte-Platz. Westend. 109, 145, 210, X21.

Goldene Galerie
This garden ballroom dating from 1746 is one of the most creative examples of Prussian Rococo interior design.

Weisser Saal

Neuer Flügel
The new wing holds the elegant apartments and exquisite furniture of Friedrich Wilhelm II.

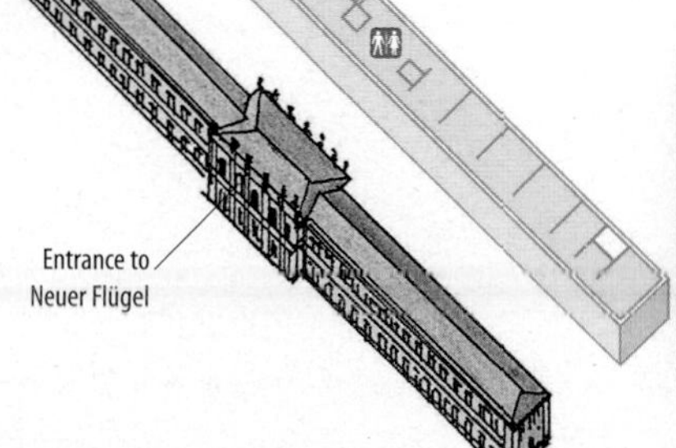

★ ***Gersaint's Shop Sign*** (1720)
An avid collector of French paintings, Frederick the Great bought this and other fine canvases by Antoine Watteau for his collection.

The Monument to the Great Elector standing in front of Schloss Charlottenburg

❷ Reiterdenkmal des Grossen Kurfürsten

Monument to the Great Elector

Luisenplatz. **Map** 4 E2. Ⓤ Richard-Wagner-Platz & Sophie-Charlotte-Platz. Ⓢ Westend. 🚌 109, 309, M45.

The statue of the Great Elector (Friedrich Wilhelm) is the finest in Berlin and was paid for by his son, Elector Friedrich III (later King Friedrich I). Designed by Andreas Schlüter to be cast in one piece, the statue was started in 1696 but not finished until 1703. It was initially erected near the former Berlin palace, by Lange Brücke (now called Rathausbrücke). The statue was moved to safety during World War II, but ironically, on the return journey, the barge transporting the monument sank in the port of Tegel.

In 1949 the statue was retrieved intact from the water and erected in the courtyard of Schloss Charlottenburg. However, it lacked the original base, which was left behind in East Berlin, so a copy was commissioned. The original base finally ended up in the Bode-Museum topped with a replica of the statue. The statue portrays the Great Elector as a warrior in ancient armour (albeit wearing a 17th-century wig) mounted on horseback, triumphant over the figures of prisoners of war around the base. The base itself is decorated with patriotic reliefs of allegorical scenes. One scene depicts the kingdom surrounded by figures representing History, Peace and the Spree river; another shows the kingdom protected by embodiments of Faith, Bravery (in the form of Mucius Scaevola) and Strength (represented by the figure of Hercules).

❸ Neuer Flügel

Luisenplatz (Schloss Charlottenburg–Neuer Flügel). **Map** 4 E2. **Tel** 30 32 09 11. Ⓤ Richard-Wagner-Platz & Sophie-Charlotte-Platz. Ⓢ Westend. 🚌 109, 309, M45. **Open** Apr–Oct: 10am–6pm Tue–Sun; Nov–Mar: 10am–5pm Tue–Sun.

Built between 1740 and 1747, the new wing of Schloss Charlottenburg used to house the popular Galerie der Romantik. The main part of this collection of Romantic paintings has now been returned to the Alte Nationalgalerie *(see p80)*. The rest have been moved to the Neuer Pavillon. In its place, the new wing houses Frederick the Great's private quarters. Items on display include paintings he acquired and curiosities such as his collection of snuff boxes. The wing also hosts temporary art and history exhibitions.

❹ Neuer Pavillon (Schinkel-Pavillon)

Luisenplatz (Schlosspark Charlottenburg). **Map** 4 F2. **Tel** 30 32 09 11. Ⓤ Richard-Wagner-Platz & Sophie-Charlotte-Platz. Ⓢ Westend. 🚌 109, 309, M45. **Open** Apr–Oct: 10am–6pm Tue–Sun; Nov–Mar: 10am–5pm Tue–Sun.

This charming Neo-Classical pavilion, with its clean lines and first-floor balcony, was built for Friedrich Wilhelm III and his second wife, Princess Auguste von Liegnitz. During a visit to Naples, the king stayed in the Villa Reale del Chiamonte and was so impressed that he commissioned Karl Friedrich Schinkel to build him something similar. The pavilion was finished for the king's birthday on 3 August 1825. Schinkel designed a two-storey structure with a central staircase and ranged the rooms around it in perfect symmetry. Pillared galleries on the first floor added variety to the eastern and western elevations. A cast-iron balcony runs around the entire

The Neuer Pavillon, which was modelled on a Neapolitan villa

French-style garden in the Schloss Charlottenburg park

structure. Like many other Schloss Charlottenburg buildings, the pavilion burned down completely in World War II and was rebuilt in 1960. It re-opened after renovations in 2011.

The display inside the pavilion reveals the original splendour and atmosphere of the aristocratic interiors, enhanced with pictures and sculptures of the period. The prize picture is a renowned panorama of Berlin dated 1834, painted by Eduard Gärtner from the roof of the Friedrichswerdersche Kirche *(see p65)*. You can also admire paintings by Karl Friedrich Schinkel, who was not only a great architect but also a fine painter of fabulous architectural fantasies.

❺ Schlosspark

Palace Park

Luisenplatz (Schloss Charlottenburg). **Map** 4 D1. Ⓤ Richard-Wagner-Platz & Sophie-Charlotte-Platz. Ⓢ Westend. 🚌 109, 309, M45.

This extensive royal park that surrounds Schloss Charlottenburg *(see pp164–5)*, criss-crossed with tidy gravel paths, is a favourite place for Berliners to stroll at the weekend. The park is largely the result of reconstruction work carried out after World War II, when 18th-century prints were used to help reconstruct the varied layout of the original grounds. Immediately behind Schloss Charlottenburg is a French-style Baroque garden, made to a strict geometrical design with a vibrant patchwork of flowerbeds, carefully trimmed shrubs and ornate fountains adorned with replicas of antique sculptures. Further away from the palace, beyond the curved carp lake, is a less formal English-style landscaped park, the original layout of which was created between 1819 and 1828 under the direction of the renowned royal gardener, Peter Joseph Lenné. The lakes and waterways of the park are the habitat of various waterfowl, including herons. A bike path stretches along the Spree river from the palace park to the Grosses Tiergarten and beyond.

❻ Gipsformerei Berlin

Replica Workshop

Sophie-Charlotten-Strasse 17–18. **Map** 4 D3. **Tel** 32 67 69 11. Ⓤ Sophie-Charlotte-Platz. Ⓢ Westend. 🚌 309, M45. **Open** times vary depending on exhibition; call ahead.

Founded by Friedrich Wilhelm III in 1819, the Gipsformerei produces original-sized replicas from items in Berlin museums and other collections. The first head of the workshop, which also repairs damaged sculptures, was renowned sculptor Christian Daniel Rauch.

Visitors are welcome to this modest brick building west of Schloss Charlottenburg and can purchase items on the spot or choose from catalogues to have them made to order and shipped home. Sculptures are generally copied in white plaster or painted true to the original. Most moulds originate from the Middle Ages, the Renaissance and the 19th century.

❼ Mausoleum

Luisenplatz (Schlosspark Charlottenburg). **Map** 4 D2. **Tel** 32 09 14 46. Ⓤ Richard-Wagner-Platz & Sophie-Charlotte-Platz. Ⓢ Westend. 🚌 109, 309, M45. **Open** Apr–Oct: 10am–6pm Tue–Sun. **Closed** Nov–Mar.

Queen Luise, the beloved wife of Friedrich Wilhelm III, was laid to rest in this modest, dignified building, set among the trees in Schlosspark. The mausoleum was designed by Karl Friedrich Schinkel, in the style of a Doric portico-fronted temple.

In the original design, the queen's sarcophagus was housed in the crypt while the tombstone (actually a cenotaph sculpted by Christian Daniel Rauch) stood in the centre of the mausoleum. After the death of Friedrich Wilhelm in 1840, the mausoleum was refurbished, an apse added and the queen's tomb moved to one side, leaving room for her husband's tomb, also designed by Rauch. The second wife of the king, Princess Auguste von Liegnitz, was also buried in the crypt of the mausoleum, but without a tombstone.

Between the years 1890 and 1894, the tombs of Kaiser Wilhelm I and his wife, Auguste von Sachsen-Weimar, were added to the crypt. Both monuments are the work of Erdmann Encke.

The Schinkel-designed Mausoleum, final resting place of German royalty

The Belvedere's Baroque flourishes and clean Neo-Classical lines

❽ Belvedere

Spandauer Damm 20–24 (Schlosspark Charlottenburg). **Map** 4 E1. **Tel** 32 09 10. Ⓤ Richard-Wagner-Platz & Sophie-Charlotte-Platz. Ⓢ Westend. 🚌 109, 309, M45. **Open** Apr–Oct: 10am–6pm Tue–Sun; closed in winter.

The Belvedere is a summer house in the Schlosspark which served as a tea pavilion for Friedrich Wilhelm II and, in times of war, as a watchtower. It dates from 1788 and was designed by Carl Gotthard Langhans. The architect mixed Baroque and Neo-Classical elements, giving the building an oval central structure with four straight-sided annexes. The building is crowned by a low dome topped with a sculpture of three cherubs supporting a basket of flowers.

Though the Belvedere was ruined during World War II, the summer house was reconstructed between 1956 and 1960 and adapted to serve as an exhibition space. The exhibition is a large collection of porcelain from the Berlin Königliche Porzellan-Manufaktur (Royal Porcelain Workshop), which has pieces from the Rococo period up to late Biedermeier, including some outstanding individual items.

❾ Museum Scharf-Gerstenberg

Schlossstrasse 70. **Map** 4 E3. **Tel** 266 42 42 42. Ⓤ Richard-Wagner-Platz & Sophie-Charlotte-Platz. Ⓢ Westend. 🚌 309, M45. **Open** 10am–6pm Tue–Fri, 11am–6pm Sat & Sun.

The two pavilions on either side of Schlossstrasse were intended as officers' barracks for the King's Guard du Corps. Built between the years 1851 and 1859 by Friedrich August Stüler, they were inspired by a design by King Friedrich Wilhelm IV. The eastern pavilion joins the stable block and once housed the Ägyptisches Museum (Egyptian Museum), which has now moved to its original location, the Neues Museum, on Museum Island.

Odilon Redon's work in pastel, Museum Scharf-Gerstenberg

Since the departure of the Egyptian Museum, the Marstall (stable block) has housed the Museum Scharf-Gerstenberg. Titled "Surreal World", the museum presents paintings, sculptures and works on paper by Surrealist and associated artists such as Dalí, Magritte, Max Ernst, Paul Klee and Jean Dubuffet, and also older works by Goya, Piranesi and Redon. More than 250 objects are presented over three floors, explaining the history of surreal art, with pieces from almost all the leading Surrealists. A film programme features classic Surrealist films by Luis Buñuel and Salvador Dalí.

❿ Museum Berggruen

Schlossstrasse 1. **Map** 4 E3. **Tel** 266 42 42 42. Ⓤ Richard-Wagner-Platz & Sophie-Charlotte-Platz. Ⓢ Westend. 🚌 109, 309, M45. **Open** 10am–6pm Tue–Fri, 11am–6pm Sat & Sun.

Heinz Berggruen assembled this tasteful collection of art dating from the late 19th and first half of the 20th century. Born and educated in Berlin, he emigrated to the US in 1936, spent most of his later life in Paris, but finally entrusted his collection to the city of his birth. The museum opened in what was once the west pavilion of the barracks using space freed up by moving the Antiken-sammlung to Museum Island *(see p77)*. The exhibition halls were modified according to the designs of Hilmer and Sattler, who also designed the layout of the Gemäldegalerie. The Museum Berggruen is particularly well known for its large collection of quality paintings, drawings and gouaches by Pablo Picasso.

Pablo Picasso's *Woman in a Hat* (1939), Museum Berggruen

The Great Elector (1620–88)

The Elector Friedrich Wilhelm was one of the most famous rulers of the Hohenzollern dynasty. He inherited the position of Elector of Brandenburg in 1640. Brandenburg-Prussia, founded in 1618, was subject to the Polish crown. One of his first duties was to rebuild the region after the devastation of the 30 Years' War *(see p23)* and in 1660 he wrested the territory from Poland. During the course of his reign, Berlin became a powerful city. Rich families from all over Europe, fleeing persecution in their own land, chose to settle in Berlin – wealthy Dutch merchants, Huguenots from France and Jews from Vienna following the Edict of Potsdam (1685).

The collection begins with a drawing from his student days in 1897 and ends with works he painted in 1972, one year before his death. In addition to these, the museum displays more than 60 works by Swiss artist Paul Klee and more than 20 works by Henri Matisse. The museum also houses paintings by other major artists, such as Van Gogh, Braque and Cézanne. The collection is supplemented by some excellent sculptures, particularly those of Henri Laurens and Alberto Giacometti.

⓫ Bröhan-Museum

Schlossstrasse 1a. **Map** 4 E3. **Tel** 32 69 06 00. Ⓤ Richard-Wagner-Platz & Sophie-Charlotte-Platz. Ⓢ Westend. 🚌 109, 309, M45. **Open** 10am–6pm Tue–Sun. **Closed** 24 & 31 Dec. **W broehan-museum.de**

Located in a late Neo-Classical building which, like the Museum Berggruen, was formerly used as an army barracks, is this small but interesting museum. The collection of decorative arts was amassed by Karl H Bröhan, who from 1966 collected works of art from the Art Nouveau (Jugendstil or Secessionist) and Art Deco styles. The paintings of the artists particularly connected with the Berlin Secessionist movement, such as Karl Hagermeister and Hans Baluschek, are especially well represented. Alongside the paintings there are fine examples of arts and crafts in other media: furniture, ceramics, glassware, silverwork and textiles. Each of the main halls features an individual artist, but often using an array of artistic media. There is also a display of furniture by Hector Guimard, Eugène Gaillard, Henri van de Velde and Joseph Hoffmann, glasswork by Emile Gallé, and porcelain from the best European manufacturers.

Art Deco vase, Bröhan-Museum

⓬ Schlossstrasse Villas

Schlossstrasse 65–67. **Map** 4 E3. Ⓤ Sophie-Charlotte-Platz. 🚌 309.

Most of the historic villas and buildings that once graced Schlossstrasse no longer exist.

However, careful restoration of a few villas enables the visitor to get a feel for what the atmosphere must have been like at the end of the 19th century. It is worth taking a stroll down Schlossstrasse to look at three of the renovated villas – No. 65, No. 66 and especially No. 67. This last villa was built in 1873, in a Neo-Classical style to a design by G Töbelmann. After World War II, the building was refurbished to return it to its former splendour. The front garden, however, a characteristic of the area, was only returned to its original state in 1986, when several villas had their gardens restored. If you continue the walk down the nearby Schustehrusstrasse, there is an interesting school building at No. 39–43 linked to the Villa Oppenheim since the end of the 19th century.

⓭ Luisenkirche

Luise Church

Giekerplatz 4. **Map** 4 F3. **Tel** 341 90 61. Ⓤ Richard Wagner Platz & Sophie-Charlotte-Platz. 🚌 109, M45. **Open** 9am–1pm Mon, Tue, Thu & Fri, 2–6pm Wed & during Sunday service (10am).

This small church has undergone a series of redesigns and refurbishments in its lifetime. The original plans by Philipp Gerlach were first adapted by Martin Böhme, before the church was built (1713–16). Its Baroque styling was removed in the next course of rebuilding, undertaken by Karl Friedrich Schinkel from 1823 to 1826, when the church was renamed in memory of Queen Luise, who died in 1810. The last refurbishment took place after the church suffered major damage during World War II.

The shape of the church is based on a traditional Greek cross, with a tower at the front. The interior fixtures and fittings are not the originals, and the elegant stained-glass windows were only made in 1956.

FURTHER AFIELD

Berlin is an extensive city with a totally unique character, shaped by its history. Up until 1920 the actual city of Berlin consisted only of the present districts Mitte, Tiergarten, Wedding, Prenzlauer Berg, Friedrichshain and Kreuzberg. It was surrounded by satellite towns and villages, which for many years had been evolving independently. Each of these had its own administrative centre, parish church and individual architecture. Some of these town's residents still speak of "going to Berlin" when ultimately they are simply hopping on a bus for a few stops.

In 1920, as part of great administrative reforms, seven towns were incorporated into Berlin, along with 59 communes and 27 country estates. This reform effected the creation of an entirely new city occupying around 900 sq km (348 sq miles), with a population that had expanded to 3.8 million.

In this way the range of the metropolis extended and Berlin now had leafy suburbs and boroughs of medieval origins, such as Spandau. Villages, private estates and palaces, such as Schloss Britz and Schloss Schoenhausen, were absorbed into Berlin. (Even Schloss Charlottenburg was outside the city limits until 1920.) Industrialization called for workers and means of transporting and housing them. Both residential and commercial construction boomed following the city enlargement.

Over the following decades the faces of many of these boroughs changed. Modern housing developments have arisen together with industrial centres, although some places have kept their small-town or rural character. Thanks to this diversity, a stay in Berlin can equal visiting several cities simultaneously. A short journey by S-Bahn enables you to travel from the cosmopolitan city centre of the 21st century to the vast forests of the Grunewald, Peacock Island or the beach at Wannsee. You can explore everything from Dahlem's tranquil streets lined with villas, to Spandau's Renaissance citadel, cobbled lanes and vast Gothic church of St Nicholas – all just half an hour away from the centre and well worth a visit.

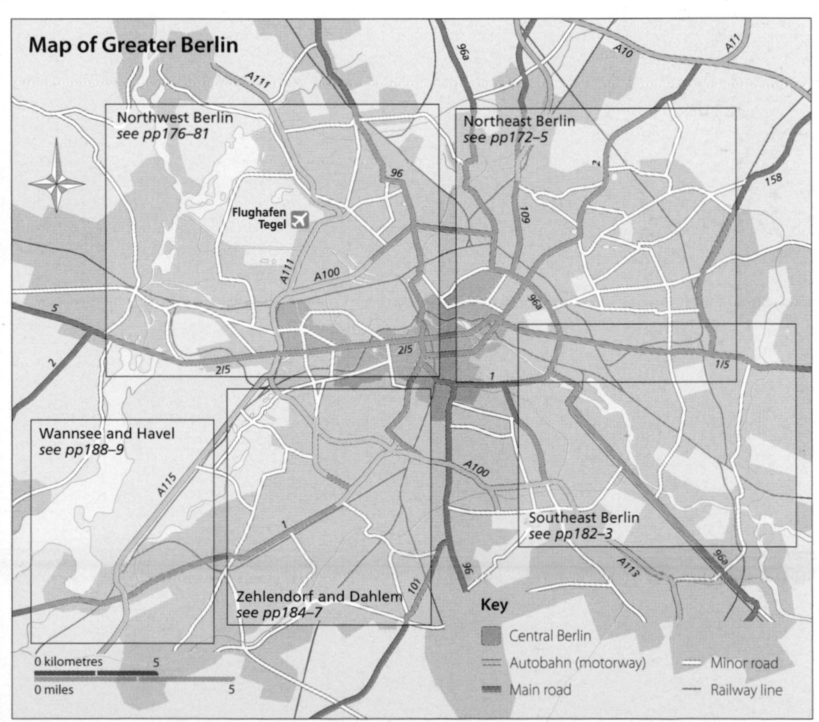

◀ Statue of Kaiser Wilhelm inside Grunewaldturm *(see p189)*

For map symbols *see back flap*

Northeast Berlin

To the north, the Baroque palace of Schönhausen is a real attraction in the middle of Pankow's Schlosspark gardens. From here it is worth visiting the Weissensee district, which has one of the largest Jewish cemeteries in Europe. Walking the partly neglected grounds is a haunting experience. Hohenschönhausen, in the very east of the district, is home to the Stasi-Museum, a memorial and museum on the grounds of East Germany's main secret service prison.

A section of the garden elevation of Schloss Schönhausen

1 Schloss Schönhausen

Tschaikowskistrasse 1. **Tel** (0331) 96 94 200. S & U Pankow. 150, 250. M1. **Open** Apr–Oct: 10am–6pm Thu–Sun; Nov–Mar: 10am–5pm Sat, Sun & hols.

This palace, located in an extensive and picturesque park, belonged to the von Dohna family during the 17th century. Ownership of the estate passed to the Elector Friedrich III in 1691, for whom Johann Arnold Nering designed the palace. In 1704 it was extended to a design by Johann Friedrich Eosander von Göthe, who added side wings. The palace was home to Queen Christine, estranged wife of Frederick the Great, between 1740 and 1797. In 1763 further extensive refurbishment was undertaken by architect Johann Boumann. The property remained in the hands of the Prussian royal family for the next hundred years. Among those who resided here were Princess Auguste von Liegnitz, following the death of her husband, King Friedrich Wilhelm III.

After World War II the rebuilt palace was occupied by the president of the German Democratic Republic, Wilhelm Pieck. In 1990 Round Table discussions were held here and the treaty to reunify Germany was signed here on 3 October that year.

Make time for a stroll through the vast park, which has kept the character bestowed by Peter Joseph Lenné in the 1820s.

2 Gethsemanekirche

Stargader Strasse 77. **Tel** 44 57 745. U & S Schönhauser Allee. 11am Sun.

This Neo-Gothic red-brick building is the most famous church in the area, playing as it did a crucial role in East Germany's peaceful revolution. The neighbourhood is dominated by the Protestant Gethsemanekirche, which dates back to 1890. The church was

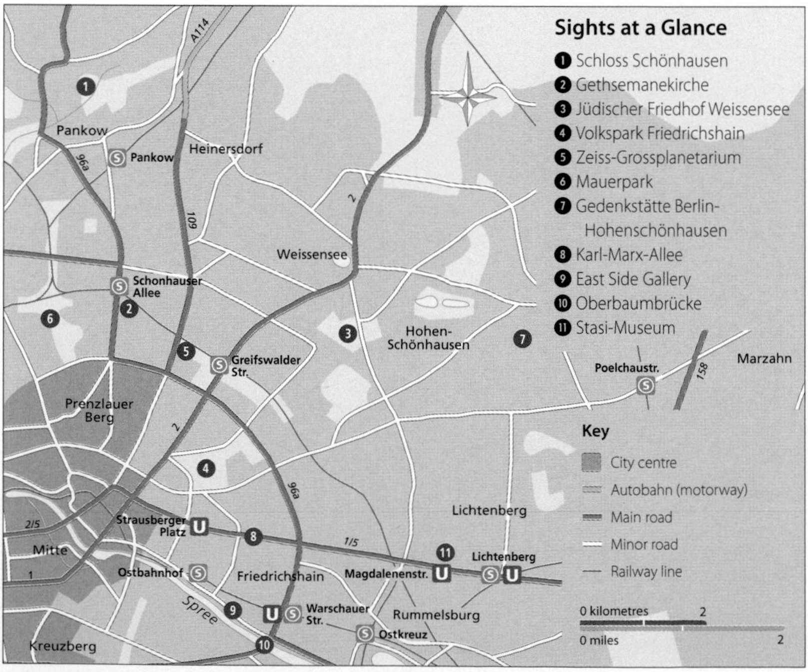

Sights at a Glance

1. Schloss Schönhausen
2. Gethsemanekirche
3. Jüdischer Friedhof Weissensee
4. Volkspark Friedrichshain
5. Zeiss-Grossplanetarium
6. Mauerpark
7. Gedenkstätte Berlin-Hohenschönhausen
8. Karl-Marx-Allee
9. East Side Gallery
10. Oberbaumbrücke
11. Stasi-Museum

Key

- City centre
- Autobahn (motorway)
- Main road
- Minor road
- Railway line

0 kilometres 2

0 miles 2

For map symbols *see back flap*

one of several built on the order of Emperor Wilhelm II, who wanted to increase religious worship among the mostly Social Democratic working-classes living in Prenzlauer Berg and other areas. The building was designed by August Orth (1828–1911), one of the period's most important architects of churches and railway stations.

The Protestant community here is proud to have pioneered civil rights movements, and hosted political anti-Nazi rallies from 1933 to 1945. The congregation also questioned the Socialist regime after World War II, while the church itself served as an assembly hall for peaceful opponents in October 1989. On 2 October that year, the praying crowd was brutally attacked by the East German secret service police, marking the start of the Communist regime's demise. Today, the square is surrounded by beautiful restored buildings, housing many sidewalk restaurants, cafés and quaint little shops. Only a few steps away is Kollwitzplatz *(see p107)*, a welcoming, leafy square with an atmosphere reminiscent of Paris. Nearby Kollwitzstrasse is home to an organic farmers' market on Saturdays.

Entrance to the red-brick Gethsemanekirche

❸ Jüdischer Friedhof Weissensee

Herbert-Baum-Strasse 45. **Tel** 925 33 30. Ⓢ Greifswalder Strasse, then 🚋 12, M4, M13. 🚌 156, 200.
Open Apr–Sep: 7:30am–5pm Mon–Thu, 7:30am–2:30pm Fri, 8am–5pm Sun; Oct–Mar: 7:30am–4pm Mon–Thu, 7:30am–2:30pm Fri, 8am–4pm Sun.
Closed Sat & public hols.

This extensive Jewish cemetery, established in 1880 according to a design by Hugo Licht, is the final resting place for more than 115,000 Berliners, many of whom were victims of Nazi persecution. It is chilling to note that many surnames listed on gravestones simply no longer exist in Germany, due to whole familes being eradicated or driven out of the country.

By the main entrance is a place of remembrance for the victims of the Holocaust, with plaques bearing the names of the concentration camps. Buried here are renowned figures from Berlin's Jewish cultural and commercial past. Among others here rest the publisher Samuel Fischer and the restaurateur Berthold Kempinski.

Some tombstones are outstanding works of art, such as that of the Panowsky family, designed by Ludwig Hoffmann, or the Cubist tombstone of Albert Mendel, designed by Walter Gropius. Some family graves are adorned with temple-like structures. The Nazis left this burial ground largely unharmed.

In 1999 the cemetery was desecrated in an act of anti-Semitic vandalism. Over 100 headstones were kicked over and some were smeared with swastikas.

Still in use today, most of the new graves belong to Jewish immigrants from the former Soviet Union, who outnumber the German-born Jews in Berlin.

Neo-Baroque Märchenbrunnen in Volkspark Friedrichshain

❹ Volkspark Friedrichshain

Am Friedrichshain/Friedenstrasse.
Map 10 F1. 🚌 142, 200. 🚋 M5, M6, M8, M10.

The extensive park complex of Friedrichshain, with its picturesque nooks and crannies, was one of Berlin's first public parks. It was laid out in the 1840s on the basis of a design by landscape architect Peter Joseph Lenné, with the idea of creating an alternative Tiergarten for the inhabitants of the eastern districts of the city. The greatest attraction of the park is the Fountain of Fairy Tales – Märchenbrunnen by Ludwig Hoffmann, built in 1902–1913. It is a spectacular feature, in a Neo-Baroque style with fountain pools made from Tivoli stone, decorated with small statues of turtles and other animals. The fountain is surrounded by well-known characters from the fairy tales by the Brothers Grimm. The park's frequent redesigns included, during World War II, the construction of two large bunkers. After the war the site was covered with a mound of earth.

Between the years 1969 and 1973, a sports and games area was established in the park, although there is still plenty of room for leisurely strolls. For the adventurous, there is a challenging outdoor climbing wall.

In the background, the silvery dome of the Zeiss-Grossplanetarium

❺ Zeiss-Grossplanetarium

Prenzlauer Allee 80 (Ernst-Thälmann-Park). **Tel** 42 18 450 (reservations). Ⓢ Prenzlauer Allee, then 🚌 156. 🚋 M2. **Closed** for restoration, due to reopen in 2016.

The silvery dome visible from afar is the huge planetarium, built in the grounds of a park dedicated to the memory of the inter-war communist leader Ernst Thälmann, who died at Buchenwald concentration camp. The foyer houses an exhibition of optical equipment and various accessories produced by the renowned factory of Carl-Zeiss-Jena.

❻ Mauerpark

Mauerpark, Gleimstrasse. Ⓤ Bernauer Strasse, Eberswalder Strasse. 🚋 M10. Flea market: **Open** 10am-6pm Sun, Bernauer Strasse.

Mauerpark is a largely treeless expanse of lawn, one of the very few extended green spaces in Prenzlauer Berg and a magnet for young locals and tourists alike. Although a little claustrophobic on warm days, it is a great spot for people-watching. On Sundays, aspiring pop stars can attempt karaoke at the amphitheatre and perform to a packed audience. Children love the park and an artificial rock can be climbed under professional supervision. The giant eclectic flea market held at weekends next to the park attracts huge crowds of mostly 20-somethings looking for a special bargain from Berlin, be it junk or vintage. Vegan burgers and cold beers complete the experience, which can be a welcome treat after seeing the haunting Wall Memorial nearby *(see p113)*. The Mauerweg, a shared walking and bicycle path, follows the path of the old Wall right across Mauerpark.

❼ Gedenkstätte Berlin-Hohenschönhausen

Genslerstrasse 13a. **Tel** 9860 82 30. Ⓤ & Ⓢ Lichtenberg, then 🚌 256 to Liebenwalderstrasse/Genslerstrasse. 🚋 16 to Genslerstrasse, M5 to Freienwalder, M6. **Open** 9am–6pm daily. (in German) 11am, 1pm & 3pm Mon–Fri, every hour 10am–4pm Sat, Sun & hols. In English: 2:30pm daily.

This museum was established in 1995 in the former custody building of the Stasi – the dreaded security service of the GDR. The custody building was part of a huge complex built in 1938. In May 1945 the occupying Russian authorities created a special transit camp here, in which they interned war criminals subsequently transported to Siberia. Shortly thereafter they started to bring anyone under political suspicion to the camp. During this time more than 20,000 people passed through here.

From 1946 this group of buildings was refashioned into the custody area for the KGB (Soviet secret service), and in 1951 it was given over for the use of the Stasi.

During a visit you can see prisoners' cells and interrogation rooms. Housed in the cellars was the "submarine" – a series of cells for the most "dangerous" suspects.

❽ Karl-Marx-Allee

Map 10 F3. Ⓤ Strausberger Platz, Frankfurter Tor or Weberwiese. 🚋 M10.

The section of Karl-Marx-Allee between Strausberger Platz and Frankfurter Tor is effectively a huge open-air museum of Socialist Realist architecture. The route leading east to Poland and Moscow, was named Stalinallee in 1949 and chosen as the site for the construction showpiece of the new German Democratic Republic. The avenue was widened to 90 m (300 ft) and, in the course of the next 10 years, huge residential

Façade of Gedenkstätte Berlin-Hohenschönhausen

tower blocks and a row of shops were built on it. The designers, led by architect Hermann Henselmann, succeeded in combining three sets of architectural guidelines. They used the style known in the Soviet Union as "pastry chef", according to the precept "nationalistic in form but socialist in content", and linked the whole work to Berlin's own traditions. Hence there are motifs taken from famous Berlin architects Schinkel and Gontard, as well as from the renowned Meissen porcelain.

The buildings on this street, renamed Karl-Marx-Allee in 1961, are now considered historic monuments. The buildings have been cleaned up and the crumbling details are gradually being restored.

The Eastern end of Karl-Marx-Allee continues as Frankfurter Allee. Its shabby sidestreets have yet to be gentrified, unlike the Prenzlauer Berg or Kreuzberg districts. Street art is everywhere and many buildings are former squats, but the atmosphere here is vibrant and relaxed. There is a young feel to the area, as most residents are in their mid-twenties, drawn to the alternative cafés and happening subculture bars.

Fragment of Socialist Realist decoration from Karl-Marx-Allee

❾ East Side Gallery

Mühlenstrasse. (S) & (U) Warschauer Strasse. (S) Ostbahnhof. 140, 240. M10.

Since 1990, this 1,300-m (1-mile) section of the Berlin Wall along Mühlenstrasse between Hauptbahnhof and Oberbaumbrücke has been known as the East Side Gallery. A huge collection of graffiti on display here, the work of 118 different artists hailing from 21 countries, organized by the Scottish artist Chris MacLean, was restored in 2009 to mark the 20th anniversary of the fall of the Wall.

Exterior of the Stasi-Museum – headquarters of the secret service

❿ Oberbaumbrücke

(S) & (U) Warschauer Strasse. (U) Schlesisches Tor. 347. M10.

This pretty bridge crossing the Spree river was built from 1894 to 1896 to a design by Otto Stahn. It is made from reinforced concrete, but the arches are covered with red brick. The central arch is marked by a pair of crenellated Neo-Gothic towers. The most decorative element of the bridge, a Neo-Gothic arcade, supports a line of the U-Bahn.

The bridge was not open to traffic for 12 or so years prior to reunification, as it linked districts from opposing sides of the Berlin Wall. Only pedestrians with the relevant documents were able to use this bridge. After reunification and renovation, it was returned to full working order.

The picturesque Neo-Gothic archway of Oberbaumbrücke

⓫ Forschungs- und Gedenkstätte Normannenstrasse (Stasi-Museum)

Ruschestrasse 103 (Haus 1). **Tel** 553 68 54. (U) Magdalenenstrasse. **Open** 10am–6pm Mon–Fri, noon–6pm Sat & Sun. (W) **stasimusem.de**

Under the German Democratic Republic, this huge complex of buildings at Ruschestrasse housed the Ministry of the Interior and the infamous Stasi (GDR secret service) headquarters. The Stasi's "achievements" in infiltrating its own community were without equal in the Eastern bloc.

Since 1990 one of the buildings has housed a museum that describes the organizational structure, history and ideology of the Stasi. It includes photographs and documents depicting the Stasi's activities. The breakup of the Stasi is covered, as well as an overview of subsequent events leading up to the reunion of Germany.

A model of the headquarters is on display, as well as equipment used for bugging and spying on citizens. You can also walk around the office of the infamous Stasi chief Erich Mielke, the commander of Ministry for State Security. A Big Brother -like figure, Mielke's legacy of suffering still lives on in the memory of millions of German citizens. The interior is just as it was when the Stasi used the complex.

Northwest Berlin

A visit to this part of the city provides a chance to see the grandeur of the Olympiastadion, which was inspired by the monumental architecture of ancient Rome. Nearby stands the monolithic Le Corbusier Haus, once regarded as the model for future housing. The historic town of Spandau has some pretty medieval streets and a well-preserved Renaissance citadel. Another attraction is the Messegelände, home of renowned trade fairs, and crowned by the Funkturm radio tower.

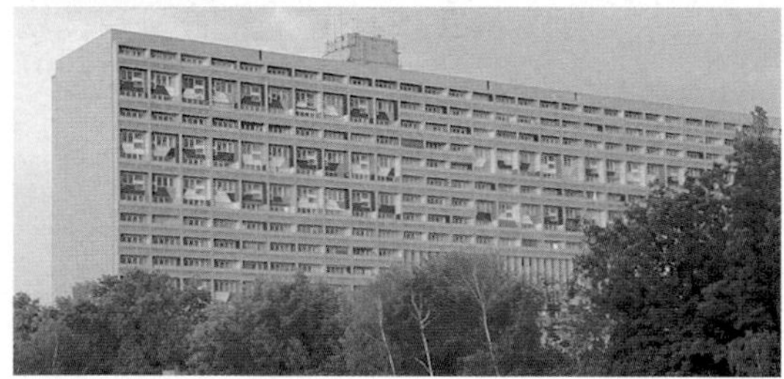

Le Corbusier Haus, by the renowned French architect

❶ Le Corbusier Haus

Flatowallee 16. Ⓢ Olympiastadion. 149, 218. 1st Sat of month in summer, register online.
corbusierhaus-berlin.de

This apartment building by Le Corbusier, on a hill near the site of the Olympiastadion, was the architect's entry to the 1957 Internationale Bauaustellung *(see p137)*. Following World War II, there was a housing shortage all over Europe. Le Corbusier's innovative design for what he called a *Unité d'Habitation* was his attempt to create fully self-sufficient housing estates in answer to this problem. He built three of these complexes, the most famous being in Marseilles. For his Berlin design, Le Corbusier wanted to build over 500 two-storey apartments with integral services, such as a post office, shops, a sports hall and nursery school. The structure fell short of Le Corbusier's aspirations as financial pressure meant the estate lacked some service elements; in addition, structural alterations changed the building's proportions from the original plans. Nevertheless, the monolithic building was a milestone for West Berlin's post-war architecture. For some, it has always remained the "Wohnmaschine" (dwelling machine) and they criticize the jail-like hallways, called "streets" by the architect. Others praise the Bauhaus-inspired clear lines, airy, light-filled apartments and the architectural departure from ornamental features.

Functionality triumphs in this "vertical city" and the view over the Grunewald and to the TV tower in the east is spectacular. Most of the 1,000 residents own apartments in the building.

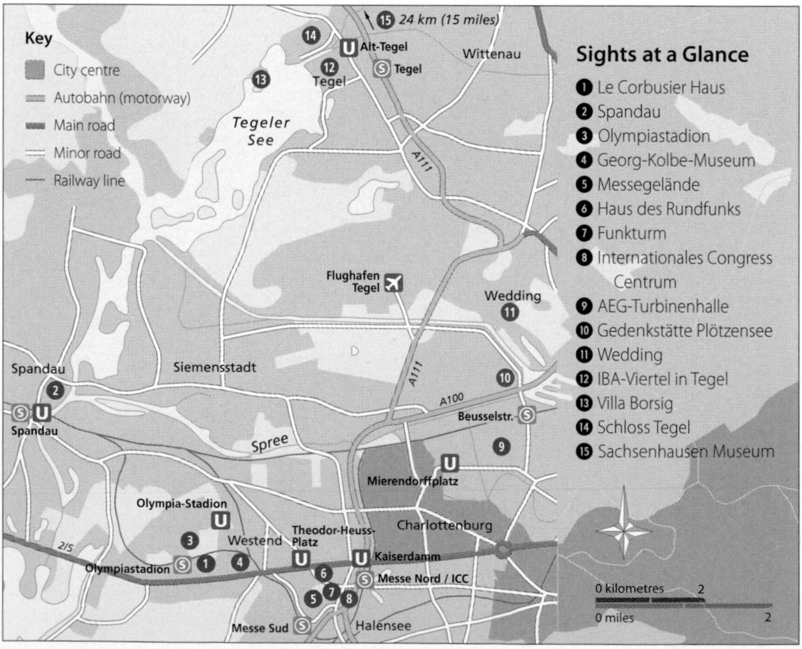

Key
City centre
Autobahn (motorway)
Main road
Minor road
Railway line
15 24 km (15 miles)
Alt-Tegel
Tegel
Wittenau
Tegel
Tegeler See
A111
Flughafen Tegel
Wedding
Spandau
Siemensstadt
A100
Beusselstr.
Spandau
Spree
Mierendorffplatz
Olympia-Stadion
Charlottenburg
Theodor-Heuss-Platz
Westend
Kaiserdamm
Olympiastadion
Messe Nord / ICC
Messe Sud
Halensee
2/5
Sights at a Glance
1 Le Corbusier Haus
2 Spandau
3 Olympiastadion
4 Georg-Kolbe-Museum
5 Messegelände
6 Haus des Rundfunks
7 Funkturm
8 Internationales Congress Centrum
9 AEG-Turbinenhalle
10 Gedenkstätte Plötzensee
11 Wedding
12 IBA-Viertel in Tegel
13 Villa Borsig
14 Schloss Tegel
15 Sachsenhausen Museum
0 kilometres 2
0 miles 2

❷ Spandau

Zitadelle Spandau Am Juliusturm 64.
Tel 354 94 40. U Zitadelle.
X33. **Open** 10am–5pm daily.
zitadelle-spandau.de

Spandau is one of the oldest towns within the area of greater Berlin, and it has managed to retain a distinctive character for itself. Evidence of the earliest settlement dates back to the 8th century, although the town of Spandau was only granted a charter in 1232. The area was spared the worst of the World War II bombing, so there are still some interesting sights to visit. The heart of the town is a network of medieval streets with a picturesque market square and a number of original timber-framed houses; in the north of Spandau sections of town wall still stand, dating from the 15th century. In the centre of town is the magnificent Gothic St-Nikolai-Kirche, dating from the 15th century. The church holds many valuable ecclesiastical furnishings, such as a splendid Renaissance stone altar from the end of the 16th century, a Baroque pulpit from around 1700 which came from a royal palace in Potsdam, a Gothic baptismal font and many plaques bearing epitaphs. A castle was first built on the site of the Zitadelle Spandau (citadel) in the 12th century, but today only the 36-m (120-ft) Juliusturm (tower) remains. In 1560 the building of a fort was begun here, to a design by Francesco Chiaramella da Gandino. It took 30 years to bring to completion, however, and most of the work was supervised by architect Rochus Guerrini, Graf zu Lynar. Though the citadel had a jail, Rudolf Hess, Spandau's most infamous resident, was incarcerated a short distance away in a military prison after the 1946 Nuremberg trials. In 1987 the former deputy leader of the Nazi party died, and the prison was torn down.

The Hohenzollern coat of arms above the main gate of the Spandau citadel

Interior of the Gothic St-Nikolai-Kirche in Spandau

Crowned black Prussian eagle

Zitadelle Spandau

This magnificent and perfectly proportioned 16th-century citadel stands at the confluence of the Spree and Havel rivers. Both the main citadel and its various 19th-century additions are still in excellent condition. The "Iron Chancellor", Otto von Bismarck *(see p26)*, moved the gold treasure of the Reichkriegsschatz (Imperial War Fund) here in 1874, where it remained until 1919. The citadel now holds museums of local history, and an observation terrace on the crenellated Juliusturm (tower).

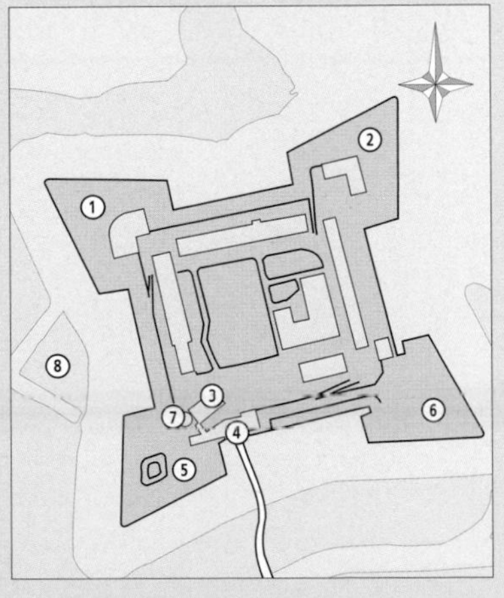

Key

① Bastion Kronprinz
② Bastion Brandenburg
③ Palace
④ Main gate
⑤ Bastion König
⑥ Bastion Königin
⑦ Juliusturm
⑧ Ravelin Schweinekopf

❸ Olympiastadion

Olympischer Platz. **Tel** 30 68 81 00. Ⓢ & Ⓤ Olympiastadion. 🚌 218, M49. **Open** 20 Mar–31 May: 9am–7pm daily; 1 Jun–15 Sep: 9am–8pm daily; 16 Sep–31 Oct: 9am–7pm daily; 1 Nov–19 Mar: 9am–4pm daily.

The Olympiastadion, or Reichssportfeld, as it was originally known, was built for the 1936 Olympic Games in Berlin. It was designed by Werner March in the Nazi architectural style and was inspired by the architecture of ancient Rome. The Olympiastadion was immortalized in the final scenes of István Szabó's classic film *Mephisto*. To the west lie the Maifeld and the Waldbühne. The former is an enormous assembly ground surrounded by grandstands and fronted by the Glockenturm, a 77-m (250-ft) tower, while the latter is an open-air amphitheatre. To the north are swimming pools and sports grounds.

Following a €236-million refurbishment, including a seemingly free-floating roof, the stadium was reopened in 2004 as a high-tech arena. The Deutsches Sportmuseum next to the stadium hosts concerts and shows.

Two sculptures of athletes decorating the Olympiastadion

Fountain in the garden of the sculptor Georg Kolbe's villa

❹ Georg-Kolbe-Museum

Sensburger Allee 25. **Tel** 304 21 44. Ⓢ Heerstrasse. 🚌 218, X34, X49. **Open** 10am–6pm Tue–Sun. **W georg-kolbe-museum.de**

One of the most renowned German sculptors, Georg Kolbe (1877–1947) bequeathed the house in which he lived and worked for almost his entire life to the city of Berlin. The villa was built by the Swiss architect Ernst Reutsch between 1928 and 1929 in a Functionalist style. Extended a few years later by the architect Paul Lindner, it was given an old-fashioned styling with rooms that open onto a large hall. Kolbe also left the city 180 of his sculptures and his art collection, which includes works by the Expressionist painter Ernst Ludwig Kirchner and the sculptor Wilhelm Lehmbruck. Visiting here is not only a rare chance to get to know Kolbe's works but also an opportunity to see his house and workshop, which display the tools and various devices for lifting a heavy or large sculpture.

Workshops with sculptors are held here regularly and controversial exhibitions on challenging and topical subjects, for example contemporary body image, draw large audiences.

❺ Messegelände

Hammarskjöldplatz. Ⓢ Messe Nord/ICC. Ⓤ Kaiserdamm. 🚌 104, 139, 349, X49.

The pavilions of the vast exhibition and trade halls which lie south of Hammarskjöldplatz cover more than 160,000 sq m (1,700,000 sq ft). Many of the international events organized here, including the food and agricultural fair Grüne Woche, are among the largest events of their kind in Europe. Even so, the exhibition areas are constantly enlarged and updated.
The original exhibition halls on this site were built before World War I, but nothing of these buildings remains. The oldest part is the Funkturm and the group of pavilions which surround it. The huge building at the front – Ehrenhalle – was built in 1936 to a design by Richard Ermisch, and is one of the few surviving buildings in Berlin designed in a Fascist architectural style.

The straight motorway that lies at the rear of the halls, in the direction of Nikolassee, is the famous Avus, the first German Autobahn, built in 1921. It was adapted for motor racing and became Germany's first car-racing track. It was here that the world speed record was broken before World War II. Now it forms part of the Autobahn system.

Monumental façade of the Ehrenhalle, part of the Messegelände

Clean, geometric shapes in the Art Deco lobby, Haus des Rundfunks

❻ Haus des Rundfunks

Masurenallee 8–14. Ⓢ Messe Nord/ICC. Ⓤ Theodor-Heuss-Platz. 🚌 104, 218, X34, X49.

This building's depressing, flat, brick-covered façade hides an interior of startling beauty. The huge edifice was constructed as a radio station between 1929 and 1931 to a design by Hans Poelzig. The building has a triangular shape, with three studio wings radiating from the central five-storey hall. The impressive Art Deco interiors, which are spectacularly lit from above, are enhanced by geometrically patterned rows of balconies and large, pendulous, octagonal lamps. They represent one of the finest architectural achievements of this era in Berlin.

From the studio concert hall, concerts are often broadcast on radio RBB (Rundfunk Berlin-Brandenburg).

❼ Funkturm

Hammarskjöldplatz. **Tel** 30 38 19 05. Ⓢ Messe Nord/ICC. Ⓤ Kaiserdamm. 🚌 104, 218, 349, X34. Observation Terrace: **Open** 10am– 8pm Mon, 10am–11pm Tue–Sun (may vary due to weather).

This radio tower, which resembles Paris's Eiffel tower, has become one of Berlin's most recognizable landmarks. Built in 1924 to a design by Heinrich Straumer, it rises 150 m (500 ft) into the air. It now operates as both an air-traffic control tower and a radio mast. Visitors can enjoy views on the observation terrace at 125 m (400 ft), or dine at the Funkturm's lofty restaurant at 55 m (180 ft).

❽ Internationales Congress Centrum

Messedamm 19. Ⓢ Messe Nord/ICC. Ⓤ Kaiserdamm. 🚌 104, 218, 349, X34, X49. Ⓦ **icc-berlin.de**

This silver futuristic structure stands on a peninsula of land, surrounded on two sides by a continuous stream of fast-moving cars. The Internationales Congress Centrum (ICC) marked yet another stage in the rivalry between East and West Berlin – it was built in reply to the East's Palast der Republik.

Constructed between 1973 and 1979, to a design by Ralf Schüler and Ursulina Schüler-Witte, the building is a mass of angular aluminium shapes that disguise its well-thought-out construction. The conference area is separate from the concert halls, for good soundproofing. One of the most modern buildings of its type in the world, it has a state-of-the-art electronic security system and an advanced means of co-ordinating and directing the several thousand people who come here to attend various meetings and conferences. More than 80 rooms and halls enable the venue to host a variety of events, from rock concerts for up to 5,000 spectators to a small artistic workshop or seminar.

The building also has a roof garden, where visitors can relax during intervals. In front of the main entrance stands *Alexander the Great in Front of Ekhatana*, by French sculptor Jean Ipoustéguy (born 1920).

Night-time view of the Funkturm, Berlin's radio tower

The impressive and modern AEG-Turbinenhalle

❾ AEG-Turbinenhalle

Huttenstrasse 12–19. Ⓤ Turmstrasse, then 🚌 M27.

This building is one of the most important textbook examples of modern architecture dating from the beginning of the 20th century. It was commissioned by the electronics company AEG in 1909 and designed by Peter Behrens in conjunction with Karl Bernhardt. While former Berlin's industrial buildings were mostly red-brick and fortress-like, the Turbinenhalle was among the earliest structures not to incorporate any element, decorative or otherwise, that reflected previous architectural styles. A huge hangar of a building, it has enormous windows and stretches 123 m (400 ft) down Berlichingenstrasse. The principal design imperative for this structure was to maintain a streamlined profile, while making no effort to disguise the materials used in its construction.

⑩ Gedenkstätte Plötzensee

Plotzensee Memorial

Hüttigpfad. **Tel** 344 32 26. Ⓢ Beuselstrasse, then 🚌 123. **Open** Mar–Oct: 9am–5pm; Nov–Feb: 9am–4pm. Ⓦ **gedenkstaette-ploetzensee.de**

A narrow street leads from Saatwinkler Damm to the site where nearly 2,500 people convicted of crimes against the Third Reich were hanged. The Gedenkstätte Plötzensee is a simple memorial in a brick hut, which still has the iron hooks from which the victims were suspended. The main figures in the unsuccessful assassination attempt against Hitler, on 20 July 1944, were executed in Bendlerblock *(see p131)*, although the remainder of the conspirators were killed here. Count Helmut James von Moltke, one of the leaders of the German resistance movement, was also executed here. The count organized the Kreisauer Kreis – a political movement which gathered together and united German opposition to Hitler and the Third Reich.

⑪ Wedding

Wedding. Ⓤ & Ⓢ Wedding, Gesundbrunnen. Ⓤ Seestrasse, Osloer Strasse. 🚌 133, 222, 224, then a 15-minute walk.

Wedding, part of the Mitte district, is an interesting, up-and-coming area. Artists are taking over abandoned industrial buildings, a lively theatre and gallery scene is developing, and the area is becoming more attractive to renters and buyers. Volkspark Rehberge, a beautiful park, is a hidden gem.

⑫ IBA-Viertel in Tegel

Karolinenstrasse & Am Tegeler Hafen. Ⓤ Alt Tegel.

The development around the southern edge of the port of Tegel is an essential stop for lovers of modern, and particularly Post-Modern, architecture. This complex developed out of the IBA (Internationale Baustellung) building exhibition in 1987. Over 30 architects were involved in the project, although the main designers were Charles Moore, John Ruble and Buzz Yudell. Within this complex stands the Humboldt-Bibliothek, which draws on Neo-Classical themes. In 1997 a monument was established to the eminent scientists Wilhelm and Alexander von Humboldt in front of this library.

Running the length of Am Tegeler Hafen street is a large housing estate where each unit has been designed by a different architect. For instance, at No. 8, the house by Stanley Tigerman recalls a style popular in Hanseatic architecture, while the red house at No. 10, designed by Paolo Portoghesi, looks as though it has been cracked lengthwise in two.

To the north, the IBA-Viertel estate borders another modern building, the Hotel Sorat, carefully built around the remaining section of an old windmill that was once part of the Humboldt estate.

The Villa Borsig façade viewed from the garden

⑬ Villa Borsig

Reiherwerder. Ⓤ Alt Tegel. 🚌 133, 222, 224, then a 15-minute walk.

This villa sits on a peninsula which cuts into the Tegeler See and is reminiscent of Schloss Sanssouci in Potsdam. It was built much later, however, between 1911 and 1913. It was designed by Alfred Salinger and Eugen Schmohl for the Borsig family, one of the wealthiest industrialist families in Berlin. This villa is particularly picturesque when observed from the lake, so it is worth looking out for it while cruising in a boat.

⑭ Schloss Tegel

Adelheidallee 19–21. **Tel** 886 71 50. Ⓤ Alt Tegel. 🚌 133, 222. **Open** (tours only) May–Sep: 10am, 11am, 3pm & 4pm Mon.

Schloss Tegel is one of the most interesting palace complexes in Berlin. In the 16th century there was already a manor house on this site, which in the second half of the 17th century was rebuilt into a hunting lodge for the Elector Friedrich Wilhelm. In 1766 the ownership of the

The elegant Neo-Classical façade of Schloss Tegel

property passed to the Humboldt family, and, between the years 1820 and 1824, Karl Friedrich Schinkel thoroughly rebuilt the palace, giving it its current style.

There are tiled bas-reliefs decorating the elevations on the top floor of the towers. These were designed by Christian Daniel Rauch and depict the ancient wind gods. Some of Schinkel's marvellous interiors have survived, along with several items from what was once a large collection of antique sculptures. The palace is still privately owned by descendants of the Humboldt family, but guided tours are offered when the palace is open. It is also worth visiting the park. On its western limits lies the Humboldt family tomb, designed by Schinkel and decorated with a copy of a splendid sculpture by Bertel Thorwaldsen; the original piece stands inside the palace.

⓯ Sachsenhausen Museum

Strasse der Nationen 22, Oranienburg. **Tel** 03301/2000. Ⓢ Oranienburg, then 804, 821. **Open** mid-Mar–mid-Oct: 8:30am–6pm daily; mid-Oct–mid-Mar: 8:30am–4:30pm daily; museum closed Mon.
W **stiftung-bg.de**

Built by the Nazis in 1936, the concentration camp at Sachsenhausen was liberated in 1945 by the Russians. Up to 200,000 people were incarcerated in this camp during its nine-year existence. However, when the Soviet Army entered Sachsenhausen, there were only 3,000 inmates in the camp, mostly women and sick people.

The iron gate at the entrance bears a sign that reads *"Arbeit macht frei"* ("Work will set you free"), and indeed many early prisoners were released on demonstrating that they had learned how to be "good German citizens". By 1939, however, fewer prisoners were being released. It is estimated that over 30,000 people died in the camp, killed by hunger, disease or mass extermination.

Sachsenhausen is now a memorial and museum. Each area of the camp hosts an exhibit – for example, the one in the former infirmary focuses on medicine and racism under the Nazi regime. Other exhibits illustrate the daily life of the prisoners, or the way Sachsenhausen worked as a Soviet Special Camp between 1945 and 1950, when it housed Nazi functionaries and political undesirables.

Former entrance to the Sachsenhausen prison camp

Karl Friedrich Schinkel (1781–1841)

Schinkel was one of the most renowned German architects; even today his work forms an essential element of the architectural landscape of Berlin. He graduated from the Berlin Bauakademie, and for many years held a high-profile position in the Prussian Building Ministry. He was equally skilled in producing both Neo-Classical and Neo-Gothic designs. In Berlin and Potsdam he designed several dozen buildings – palaces, civic buildings and churches, many of which still stand today. He also excelled at painting and even designed scenery for the opera house on Unter den Linden, among others. You can admire his paintings in the Galerie der Romantik in Schloss Charlottenburg. Schinkel's creativity had a truly enormous influence on the next generation of architects working in Prussia.

Southeast Berlin

An expedition to Berlin's furthest corners provides an opportunity to visit the building from which Germany surrendered in World War II, now home to the Deutsche-Russisches Museum. However, you can just as easily stroll through the zoological garden in the park at the Baroque Schloss Friedrichsfelde or enjoy a leisurely break in Köpenick, which has retained the atmosphere of a small town.

❶ Treptower Park

Archenhold-Sternwarte, Alt-Treptow 1. Ⓢ Treptower Park. 🚌 166, 265. Archenhold Sternwarte: **Tel** 536 06 37 19. **Open** 2–4:30pm Wed–Sun. 8pm Thu, 3pm Sat & Sun.

The vast park in Treptow was laid out in the 1860s on the initiative and design of Johann Gustav Meyer. In 1919 it was where revolutionaries Karl Liebknecht, Wilhelm Pieck and Rosa Luxemburg assembled a 150,000-strong group of striking workers.

The park, however, is best known for the colossal monument to the Red Army. Built between 1946 and 1949, it stands on the grave of 5,000 Soviet soldiers killed in the battle for Berlin in 1945. The gateway is marked by a vast granite sculpture of a grieving Russian Motherland surrounded by statues of Red Army soldiers. This leads to the mausoleum, topped by an 11-m- (35-ft-) high figure of a soldier rescuing a child and resting his mighty sword on a smashed swastika. The whole scheme was the work of architect Jakow Biełopolski and sculptor Jewgien Wuczeticz.

In the furthest section of the park it is worth going to see the astronomical observatory, **Archenhold Sternwarte**, built for a decorative arts exhibition held here in 1896. Given a permanent site here in 1909, the observatory was used by Albert Einstein for a lecture on the Theory of Relativity in 1915. It is also home to the longest refracting telescope in the world (21 m, or 70 ft) and a small planetarium.

Beyond Treptower Park lies another park, Plänterwald, while the Spree river provides an ideal place for a stroll or boat ride.

Gigantic wreath commemorating the Red Army in Treptower Park

❷ Tierpark & Schloss Friedrichsfelde

Am Tierpark 125. Ⓤ Tierpark. 🚌 194, 296, 396. 🚋 27, 37, M17. Schloss: **Tel** 51 53 10. **Open** Tue, Thu, Sat, Sun & hols. Tierpark: **Tel** 51 53 10. **Open** 1 Jan–16 Mar: 9am–5pm; 17 Mar–24 May: 9am–6pm; 25 May–9 Sep: 9am– 7pm; 10 Sep–21 Oct: 9am–6pm; 22 Oct–31 Dec: 9am–5pm.

This charming Baroque palace was built for the Dutchman Benjamin von Raule around 1695, to a design by Johann Arnold Nering. Under successive owners, it underwent major renovations. It was redesigned in 1719 by Martin Heinrich Böhme, and again in 1786, by Peter Biron.

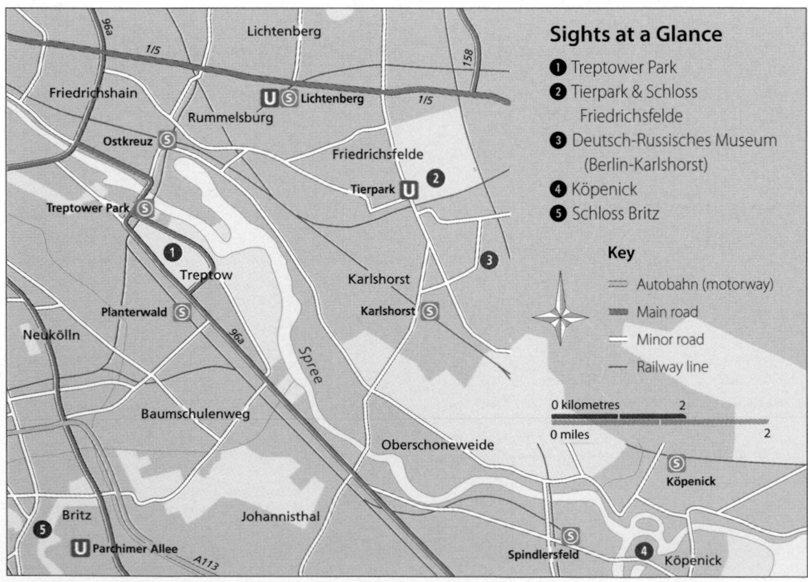

For map symbols *see back flap*

It was this renovation which gave the residence its current appearance.

The well-balanced structure, typical of the style during the transition from Baroque to Neo-Classical, was extensively restored in the 1970s. It now houses a museum of interiors, and is chiefly furnished with 18th- and 19th-century pieces. The palace's park was remodelled to become the zoological garden of East Berlin in 1957.

❸ Deutsch-Russisches Museum (Berlin-Karlshorst)

Zwieseler Strasse 4/Rheinsteinstrasse **Tel** 50 15 08 10. Ⓢ Karlshorst. 27, 37, M17. 296. **Open** 10am–6pm Tue–Sun.

This building was erected in the 1930s as the casino of the Wehrmacht (armed services of the Third Reich). It was here on the night of 8 May 1945 that Hitler's successor Grossadmiral Karl Dönitz, Field Marshal Wilhelm Keitel, Admiral Hans Georg von Friedeburg and General Hans-Jürgen Stumpff signed the unconditional surrender of Germany's armed forces. You can visit the renowned hall in which the surrender was signed, the office of Marshal Zhukov, and see an exhibition documenting the history of World War II.

❹ Köpenick

Kunstgewerbemuseum: Schlossinsel 1. **Tel** 266 42 42 42. Ⓢ Spindlersfeld, then 167, or Ⓢ Köpenick, then 164. 60, 61, 62, 67, 68. **Open** 11am–6pm Tue–Sun.

Köpenick is much older than Berlin. Already in the 9th century AD this island contained a fortified settlement called Kopanica. It was inhabited by Slavs from the Łaba river region, which in the 12th century was ruled by Duke Jaksa, who was waging a war against the Ascanian Albrecht the Bear over Brandenburg *(see p21)*. From the late 12th century Köpenick belonged to the Margrave of Brandenburg, also an Ascanian. In about 1240 a castle was built, around which a town began to evolve, though over the years it lost out in importance to Berlin. Craftsmen settled here, and after 1685 a large colony of Huguenots also settled here.

The façade of Schloss Friedrichsfelde

In the 19th century Köpenick recreated itself as an industrial town. Despite wartime devastation, it has retained its historic character. There are no longer any 13th-century churches; nevertheless, it is worth strolling around the old town. By the old market square and in nearby streets, such as Alt Köpenick and Grünstrasse, modest houses have survived which recall the 18th century, next to buildings from the end of the 19th century.

At Alt Köpenick No. 21 is a vast brick town hall built in the style of the Brandenburg Neo-Renaissance between the years 1901 and 1904 by Hans Schütte and Hugo Kinzer. It was here on 16 October 1906 that a famous swindle took place. Wilhelm Voigt dressed himself in a Prussian officer's uniform and proceeded to arrest the mayor and then fraudulently empty everything from the city treasury. This incident inspired a comedy, *The Captain from Köpenick* by Carl Zuckmayer, which is still popular.

Köpenick's greatest attraction is a magnificent palace on the island in the southern part of town. It was built between 1677 and 1681 for the heir to the throne Friedrich (later King Friedrich I), to a design by the Dutch architect Rutger van Langfeld. The three-storey Baroque building that resulted was extended to a design by Johann Arnold Nering, but until 1693 only part of the extension was completed: the chapel, entrance gate and a small gallery wing.

In 2004 the **Kunstgewerbemuseum** *(see pp122–25)* opened a series of Renaissance and Baroque rooms in the Köpenick palace. This collection also includes some examples of magnificent furniture.

❺ Schloss Britz

Alt-Britz 73. **Tel** 60 97 92 30. Ⓤ Parchimer Allee. 181, M44, M46. **Open** 11am–6pm Tue–Sun. **W schlossbritz.de**

Originally a small manor house built in 1706 for Sigismund von Erlach, Schloss Britz was extended to its current size between 1880 and 1883 to a design by Carl Busse. It is a one-storey palace with a modest Neo-Classical aspect adorned with Baroque statues at the front and a tower on the garden side. As well as housing a museum, the building is often used as a venue for concerts and exhibitions. The palace displays furnishings from the *Gründerzeit* – the years after the founding of the German Empire in 1871. The 19th-century interiors are excellent, but it is also worth strolling through the park, where there is a bust of one of the former owners, Rüdiger von Ilgen, which once stood in the Tiergarten.

Next to the palace is a housing estate called Hufeisensiedlung (Horseshoe Colony), built in the late 1920s to a design by Bruno Taut and Bruno Schneidereit. The architects' aim was to create spacious and affordable housing for Berliners.

Zehlendorf and Dahlem

With nearly half of Zehlendorf covered by forests, lakes and rivers, the region has a rustic, quiet atmosphere. One of the more interesting suburbs here is Dahlem, a settlement first mentioned in 1275. Retaining its Gothic parish church and its manor house, Dahlem was transformed into an affluent, tranquil city suburb with grand villas and museums, designed by Bruno Paul, at the beginning of the 20th century. The district was confirmed as a major cultural and educational centre after World War II with the establishment of the Freie Universität and the completion of the museum complex.

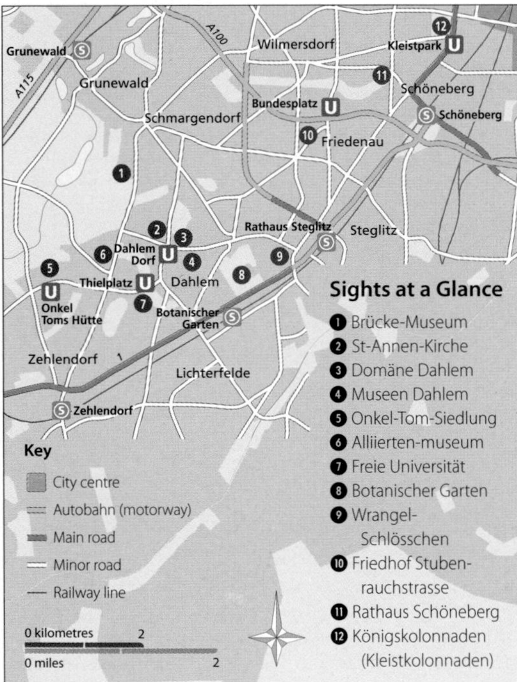

❶ Brücke-Museum

Bussardsteig 9. **Tel** 831 20 29. 🚌 115. **Open** 11am–5pm Wed–Mon.

One of the more interesting museums dedicated to 20th-century art is hidden away on a leafy, tranquil street lined with picturesque villas. The elegant Functionalist building was built by Werner Düttmann in 1966–7. The museum houses a collection of German Expressionist painting linked to the artistic group known as Die Brücke, which originated in Dresden in 1905 and was based in Berlin from 1910. The members of this group included Karl Schmidt-Rottluff, Emil Nolde, Max Pechstein, Ernst Ludwig Kirchner and Erich Heckel. The collection is based on almost 80 works by Schmidt-Rottluff bequeathed to the town in 1964. The collection quickly grew, thanks to donations and acquisitions. In addition to displaying other works of art contemporary to Die Brücke (which was disbanded in 1913), there are also some paintings from the later creative periods of these artists, as well as works of other closely associated artists. Nearby, at Käuzchensteig No. 8, lie the foundation's headquarters, established in the former studio of the sculptor Bernhard Heiliger. The garden, which borders the Brücke-Museum, has a display of his metal sculptures.

❷ St-Annen-Kirche

Königin-Luise-Strasse 55. **Tel** 841 70 50. Ⓤ Dahlem Dorf. 🚌 110, X11, X83. **Open** 11am–1pm Sat & Sun.

At the centre of a small leafy cemetery stands the Gothic 14th-century St-Annen-Kirche. The church was built initially with a plain roof. The chancel was completed in the 15th century, the vaulting in the 17th century and the tower was added in the 18th century.

Inside the church, 14th-century wall paintings depict scenes from the life of St Anna, alongside items of ecclesiastical furnishings. These include a 15th-century painting called *The Crucifixion* and 11 late Gothic figures of saints.

The cemetery, which dates back to the 13th century, is also worth exploring. It has a 1996 monument dedicated to the victims of Nazi tyranny. During the war, the congregation's pastor was Martin Niemöller, a founder of the Confessing Church, a Protestant movement that resisted the Nazification of churches. Activist Martin Niemöller was sent to a concentration camp in 1938 and survived imprisonment.

Gothic St-Annen-Kirche, dating back to the 14th century

For map symbols *see back flap*

The combined museum and working farm of Domäne Dahlem

❸ Domäne Dahlem

Dahlem City Farm

Königin-Luise-Str. 49. **Tel** 66 63 000. U Dahlem Dorf. 110, X11, X83. **Open** 10am–6pm Wed–Mon (museum: Sat & Sun only due to restoration). (museum only).
w domaene-dahlem.de

Domäne Dahlem, a manor house and farming estate, is a rare oasis of country life in the Berlin suburbs. The Baroque house was built for Cuno Johann von Wilmersdorff around 1680 and still retains its original character. Part of the Stadtmuseum Berlin (Museum of the City of Berlin), the manor house boasts period interiors, while the 19th-century farm buildings hold a collection of agricultural tools and a large and varied collection of beehives.

Domäne Dahlem is a farm and a museum with a garden, workshops and farm animals. Festivals and markets held here demonstrate rural crafts and skills – you can learn how to shoe a horse or milk a cow, or, if you prefer, you can just relax with a glass of cold beer. There is an organic food market on Saturday mornings.

❹ Museen Dahlem

Museum für Asiatische Kunst, Ethnologisches Museum (formerly Museum für Völkerkunde), Museum Europäischer Kulturen: Lansstrasse 8/ Arnimallee 25. **Tel** 266 42 42 42. U Dahlem Dorf. 110, X11, X83. **Open** 10am–5pm Tue–Fri, 11am–6pm Sat & Sun. **Closed** Mon, 24 & 31 Dec.

Dahlem's first museums were built between 1914 and 1923. After World War II, with many of Berlin's collections fragmented, a large miscellany of art and artifacts was put on display here. In the 1960s the museums were extended considerably: the Museen was created to rival East Berlin's Museum Island. Reunification in 1990 meant the collections could be reunited and reorganized. Paintings were moved to the Gemäldegalerie *(see pp126–9)*, and sculptures to the Bode-Museum *(see p81)*.

Three museums are now housed at Dahlem: Museum für Asiatische Kunst (Museum of Asian Art); Ethnologisches Museum (Museum of Ethnology); and Museum Europäischer Kulturen (Museum of European Culture).

The Museum für Asiatische Kunst shows the world's most important East Asian and Indian art collections from 4000 BC onwards and pays special homage to the art along the Silk Route and early Indian sculptures. Among the many exquisite pieces is a collection of Japanese paintings and East Asian lacquered art. The Ethnologisches Museum displays about 500,000 objects from pre-industrial societies around the world with a focus on non-European cultures. A highlight is the gold Inca jewellery. There are plans to move the Asian and non-European ethnological collections from Museen Dahlem to the Humboldt-Forum *(see p76)*, a project roughly estimated to take place in 2016.

Japanese woodcut from the Museum für Asiatische Kunst

The Museum Europäischer Kulturen is an ethnographic museum that specializes in European folk art and culture, and documents the daily life of its inhabitants. It hosts long-running but temporary exhibitions, often in conjunction with museums from other European countries. Among the exhibits on display are earthenware items, costumes, jewellery, toys and tools.

East Prussian carpet from the Museum Europäischer Kulturen

Country Churches

The establishment of Greater Berlin in 1920 swallowed up nearly 60 villages, some of which were older than the city itself. Now they have evolved into large residential estates, and many of the parish churches (more than 50) have survived. The most treasured, dating from the 13th century, can be seen in the south of Berlin, for instance in Britz by Backbergstrasse, Buckow (Alt-Buckow) or in Mariendorf (Alt Mariendorf). The oldest of the churches, dating from the 13th century, has survived in Marienfelde (Alt Marienfelde).

St Anna's in Dahlem   Wittenau

Marienfelde

Henry-Ford-Bau, the rector's office and library at the Freie Universität

5 Onkel-Tom-Siedlung

Riemeister Strasse/Argentinische Allee. U Onkel-Toms-Hütte.

This housing estate, known as "Uncle Tom's Estate", represents one of the most interesting urban architectural achievements of the Weimar Republic. It was built from 1926 to 1932, to a design by Bruno Taut, Hugo Häring and Otto Rudolf Salvisberg. Their primary intention was to solve the city's housing shortage by building large developments that were both pleasant to live in and fairly inexpensive. This project in Zehlendorf was the realization of the English concept of garden cities. The result is an enormous housing estate comprising single- and multiple-family houses. It is set in lush greenery on the borders of Grunewald and accommodates nearly 15,000 people.

6 Alliierten-museum

Clayallee 135. **Tel** 818 19 90. S Zehlendorf, then bus 115. U Oskar-Helene-Heim. **Open** 10am–6pm Thu–Tue. Tours by appointment.

In the heart of the former US military sector of Berlin is the Allied Museum, which combines exhibition space with open-air grounds.

A fascinating exhibition of everyday objects, military memorabilia, photographs and films explains life during the Cold War and the story of Berlin and its inhabitants between 1945 and 1994.

7 Freie Universität

Henry-Ford-Bau Garystrasse 35–39. **Tel** 83 85 11 11. U Thielplatz. bus 110. W **fu-berlin.de**

The Free University was established on 4 December 1948 on the initiative of a group of academics and activists, led by Ernst Reuter. This was a reaction to the restrictions introduced at the Humboldt-Universität in the Soviet sector and further evidence of the competition between the two halves of the city. The university was initially located in rented buildings. It was only thanks to the American Ford Foundation that the Henry-Ford-Bau, housing the rector's office, the auditorium and the library, was built. Designed by Franz Heinrich Sobotka and Gustav Müller, and built from 1951 to 1954, the building is distinguished by its fine proportions.

Another architectural highlight can be found at the Humanities and Social Science building, designed by Norman Foster and finished in 2005. It has a glass-domed centrepiece, housing the Philological Library, which is nicknamed the "Berlin Brain" due to its cranial shape.

8 Botanischer Garten

Botanical Garden

Unter den Eichen 5–10 & Königin-Luise-Strasse 6–8. **Tel** 83 85 01 00. U Dahlem-Dorf. S Botanischer Garten. bus M48, X83. **Open** daily; Nov–Jan: 9am–4pm; Feb: 9am–5pm; Mar & Oct: 9am–6pm; Apr & Aug: 9am–8pm; May–Jul: 9am–9pm; Sep: 9am–7pm. Museum: **Open** 10am–6pm daily. W **botanischer-garten-berlin.de**

This park is one of the most beautiful places in Berlin. It was created towards the end of the 19th century and has a romantic character with gentle hills and picturesque lakes. Of particular interest is the 19th-century palm house, designed by Alfred Koerner. The greenhouses were built between 1984 and 1987 to a design by Engelbert Kremser. The most popular plants are the exotic species such as the orchids and cacti.

By the entrance on the Königin-Luise-Platz side is the Botanisches Museum, home to an excellent collection of plant specimens.

The pleasantly cultivated spaces of the Botanischer Garten

❾ Wrangel-Schlösschen

Schlossstrasse 48. **Tel** 902 99 39 24. U Rathaus Steglitz. Bus M2, M48, M85.

This compact Neo-Classical palace derives its name from Field Marshal Wrangel, the building's mid-19th-century owner. However, the house was built much earlier, in 1804, following a design by Heinrich Gentz. The simplicity and clarity of its details make it a prime example of early Neo-Classical architecture. It currently houses the cultural centre for the district of Steglitz.

Wrangel-Schlösschen, a fine example of Neo-Classical architecture

❿ Friedhof Stubenrauchstrasse

Stuberauchstrasse Cemetery

Stubenrauchstrasse 43–45/Südwestkorso. S & U Bundesplatz. Bus 248.

This small cemetery in the shadow of a motorway achieved renown in 1993 as the burial place of Marlene Dietrich, who died on 6 May. Born Maria Magdalena von Losch in 1901, she grew up at Leberstrasse No. 65 in Schöneberg. For a few years she struggled to make a career as an actress, playing small parts. In 1929 she was discovered in Berlin by Hollywood director Josef von Sternberg, who was filming *The Blue Angel*, based on Heinrich Mann's novel *Professor Unrat*. The ensuing role of Lola took Marlene to the height of fame. She sang only once more in Berlin, giving a concert at the Titania-Palast in 1960. Although she died in Paris, she was laid to rest in the city of her birth.

Rathaus Schöneberg – the site of President Kennedy's speech

⓫ Rathaus Schöneberg

Schöneberg Town Hall

John F Kennedy Platz 1. U Rathaus Schöneberg. Bus 104, M46.

The gigantic building with a tower is the Schöneberg town hall, built between 1911 and 1914. From 1948 to 1990 it was used as the main town hall of West Berlin. It was here, on 26 June 1963, that US President John F Kennedy gave his famous speech. More than 300,000 Berliners assembled to hear the young president say, *"Ich bin ein Berliner"* – "I am a Berliner" – intended as an expression of solidarity from the democratic world to a city defending its right to freedom.

While Kennedy's meaning was undoubtedly clear, pedants were quick to point out that, strictly speaking, he actually said, "I am a small doughnut".

⓬ Königskolonnaden (Kleistkolonnaden)

Potsdamer Strasse **Map** 13 B4. U Kleistpark. Bus 106, 204, M46.

A short walk north of U-Bahn Kleistpark, the unremarkable architecture of Potsdamer Strasse suddenly transforms dramatically. Leading to the park, the elegant sandstone Königskolonnaden captivates the passer-by with its Baroque ornamental sculptures. The royal colonnade, designed by Carl von Gontard and built between 1777 and 1780, once graced the route from Königsstrasse to Alexanderplatz. In 1910, to protect it from traffic, it was moved to this new site.

The huge Kammergericht at the far boundary of the park was built between 1909 and 1913 to a design by Carl Vohl, Rudolf Mönnich and Paul Thömer. The site of the notorious Nazi Volksgericht or "People's Court", it was also used to try members of the failed July 1944 bomb plot against Hitler *(see p131)*.

Elegant façade of Königskolonnaden

Wannsee & Havel

Some of Berlin's most affluent neighbourhoods are scattered along the Wannsee lakeside and Havel shores, but above all it is the natural beauty of the area that attracts Berliners and visitors alike and makes it the city's most popular recreation spot. It is worth cycling or walking here *(see pp210–13)* to enjoy the views of sailing boats on Havel and Wannsee, and to see stunning summerhouses and royal parks. The museum in the Haus der Wannsee-Konferenz is poignant; the building was originally where the Nazis made their most shocking decisions.

Sights at a Glance

1. Strandbad Wannsee
2. Haus der Wannsee-Konferenz
3. Villenkolonie Alsen
4. Grabstätte von Heinrich von Kleist
5. Museumsdorf Düppel
6. Grunewaldturm

BERLINER FORST GRUNEWALD
Havel
A115
Krumme Lanke
Mexikoplatz
Schlachtensee
Nikolassee
Nikolassee
Grosser Wannsee
Wannsee
Wannsee
Pohlesee

Key

Autobahn (motorway)
Main road
Minor road
Railway line

0 kilometres 2
0 miles 2

❶ Strandbad Wannsee

Wannseebadweg 2s. Ⓢ Nikolassee. 🚌 218.

The vast picturesque lake of Wannsee, situated on the edge of Grunewald, is a principal destination for Berliners who are looking for some kind of recreation. Here you can take part in water sports, enjoy a lake cruise, bathe or simply enjoy relaxing on the shore. The most developed part is the south-eastern corner of the lake. Here, near S-Bahn Wannsee, there are yachting marinas and harbours, while further north is one of the largest inland beaches in Europe – Strandbad Wannsee. It has been in use since the beginning of the 20th century, and was developed between 1929 and 1930 with the construction of a complex of changing rooms, shops and cafés on top of man-made terraces.

On sunny summer days, sun-worshippers completely cover the sandy shore, while the lake is filled with yachts and windsurfers. It is also quite pleasant to take a walk around Schwanenwerder island. It has many elegant villas, one of which, Inselstrasse No. 24/26, was built for Axel Springer, the German newspaper publisher.

❷ Haus der Wannsee-Konferenz

Am Grossen Wannsee 56/58.
Tel 805 00 10. Ⓢ Wannsee, then 🚌 114. **Open** 10am–6pm daily.

This is one of the most beautiful of the luxury Alsen holiday villas, and yet the most abhorrent. Designed by Paul Baumgarten between 1914 and 1915, it is in the style of a small Neo-Baroque palace with an elegant portico. In 1940 the villa was sold to the Nazi SS. On 20 January 1942, a meeting took place between Richard Heydrich and 14 other officers from the secret service and the SS, among them Adolf Eichmann. It was then that the decision was taken about "the final solution on the question of Jews". Their plans for the outright extermination of 11 million Jews embraced the whole of Europe, including Great Britain and neutral countries.

Since 1992 this has been a museum and place of remembrance. An exhibition depicts the history of the

Boarding point for lake cruises on the Wannsee

The exterior of Haus der Wannsee-Konferenz

Holocaust with some shocking documents and photographs from the ghettos and extermination camps. For security reasons, the gate to the villa is always locked, and to enter the park you have to announce yourself through the intercom.

❸ Villenkolonie Alsen

Am Grossen Wannsee. Ⓢ Wannsee, then 🚌 114. Max-Liebermann Villa: **Closed** Tue. **W liebermann-villa.de**

This clutch of villas forms a delightful holiday resort – the oldest of its kind in Berlin. The villas are thought to be the most beautiful in the district, not just because of their picturesque lakeside location, but also because of the quality of their architecture.

Strolling along Am Grossen Wannsee, it is worth looking at the villa at No. 39/41, known as Haus Springer. It was designed by the architect Alfred Messel in 1901 and is covered with shingles, a reflection of contemporary American designs.

Another must-see villa stands at No. 42, designed by Paul Baumgarten in 1909 for the painter Max Liebermann (1845–1935). Liebermann spent many summers here painting in the garden on the shores of Wannsee. The villa is now a museum and houses around 40 of Liebermann's paintings.

❹ Grabstätte von Heinrich von Kleist

Grave of Heinrich von Kleist

Bismarckstrasse (near No. 3). Ⓢ Wannsee. 🚌 114, 316, 318.

A narrow street running from Königstrasse at the viaduct of the S-Bahn Wannsee leads to the spot where the playwright Heinrich von Kleist committed suicide. On 21 November 1811 he shot his companion Henriette Vogel and then turned the pistol on himself. They are both buried here. A stone marks their grave, on which flowers are left by well-wishers.

Reconstructed medieval settlement at the Museumsdorf Düppel

❺ Museumsdorf Düppel

Clauertstrasse 11. **Tel** 802 66 71. Ⓢ Mexikoplatz or Ⓤ Krumme Lanke, then 🚌 118, 622. **Open** late Mar–early Oct: 3–7pm Thu, 10am–5pm Sat & Sun. **W dueppel.de**

A visit here is like a trip back in time. A reconstruction of a medieval village has been made on the site of a 13th-century settlement, discovered in the 1940s. It is a living village surrounded by still-cultivated gardens and fields, where traditional breeds of pigs and sheep are raised in the sheds and pigsties.

On Sundays the village puts on displays of traditional crafts. Here you can see how primitive saucepans and tools were fashioned; how wool was spun, dyed and woven; and how baskets were made.

❻ Grunewaldturm

Havelchaussee 61. 🚌 218.

The Neo-Gothic tower built on a hill at the edge of the Havel river is one of the most prominent features of the area. This type of tower became popular in Germany during the 19th century as a way of commemorating important events or people. The Grunewaldturm was built in 1899 on the centenary of the birth of Wilhelm I. After 1871 he was the first Emperor of the Second Reich and the tower was initially named "Kaiser-Wilhelm-Turm". The 56-m (185-ft) tower was designed by Franz Schwechten and is made of red brick with plaster details. The tower is made all the more striking by the green background provided by the surrounding leafy trees.

Currently used as an observation tower, the view from the top of this structure is well worth climbing the 204 steps for. There is a popular restaurant in the base of the tower.

The impressive red-brick Neo-Gothic Grunewaldturm

GREATER BERLIN

SANS SOUCI

POTSDAM

Potsdam is an independent city bordering Berlin. It is also the capital of Brandenburg, with almost 140,000 inhabitants. The first historical reference to Potsdam dates from AD 993. The town blossomed in the 1600s, during the era of the Great Elector *(see p22)*, and then again during the 18th century.

Potsdam suffered very badly during World War II, particularly during the nights of 14 and 15 April 1945, when the Allies bombed the town's centre. Today, despite its wartime losses, Potsdam is one of the most interesting cities in Germany. Tourists flock to see the royal Park Sanssouci and palaces such as the Marmorpalais and Schloss Cecilienhof. It is also worth strolling around Neuer Garten and the historic area around the Rathaus. The Russian colony of Alexandrowka, the Holländisches Viertel, the film studios of Babelsberg and Babelsberg park *(see pp212–13)* also rate among the attractions of Potsdam.

Sights at a Glance

Historic Buildings

1 *Neues Palais pp196–7*
3 Communs
4 Schloss Charlottenhof
5 Römische Bäder
6 Chinesisches Haus
7 Orangerie
9 Neue Kammern
10 *Schloss Sanssouci pp202–203*
11 Bildergalerie
12 Historische Mühle
15 Schloss Cecilienhof
16 Marmorpalais
21 Altes Rathaus
24 Wasserwerk Sanssouci

Historic Areas

13 Alexandrowka
17 Holländisches Viertel

Churches

8 Friedenskirche
18 Peter und Paul Kirche
19 Französische Kirche
20 Nikolaikirche

Parks and Theme Parks

2 Park Sanssouci
14 Neuer Garten
25 Telegrafenberg
26 *Filmpark Babelsberg p207*

Museums

22 Potsdam-Museum
23 Marstall (Filmmuseum)

Restaurants

see p243

1 Alexandrowka
2 Juliette
3 Krongut Bornstedt
4 Maison Charlotte
5 Speckers Landhaus

◀ Terraced vineyard leading to the Sanssouci Palace, Park Sanssouci

Street-by-Street: Park Sanssouci

The enormous Park Sanssouci, covering an area of 287 hectares, is among the most beautiful palace complexes in Europe. The first building to be constructed was Schloss Sanssouci, the summer palace of Frederick the Great. It was built between 1744 and 1747 on the site of an orchard. Over the years, Park Sanssouci was expanded and enriched by the addition of other palaces and pavilions. Allow at least a whole day to enjoy the park fully.

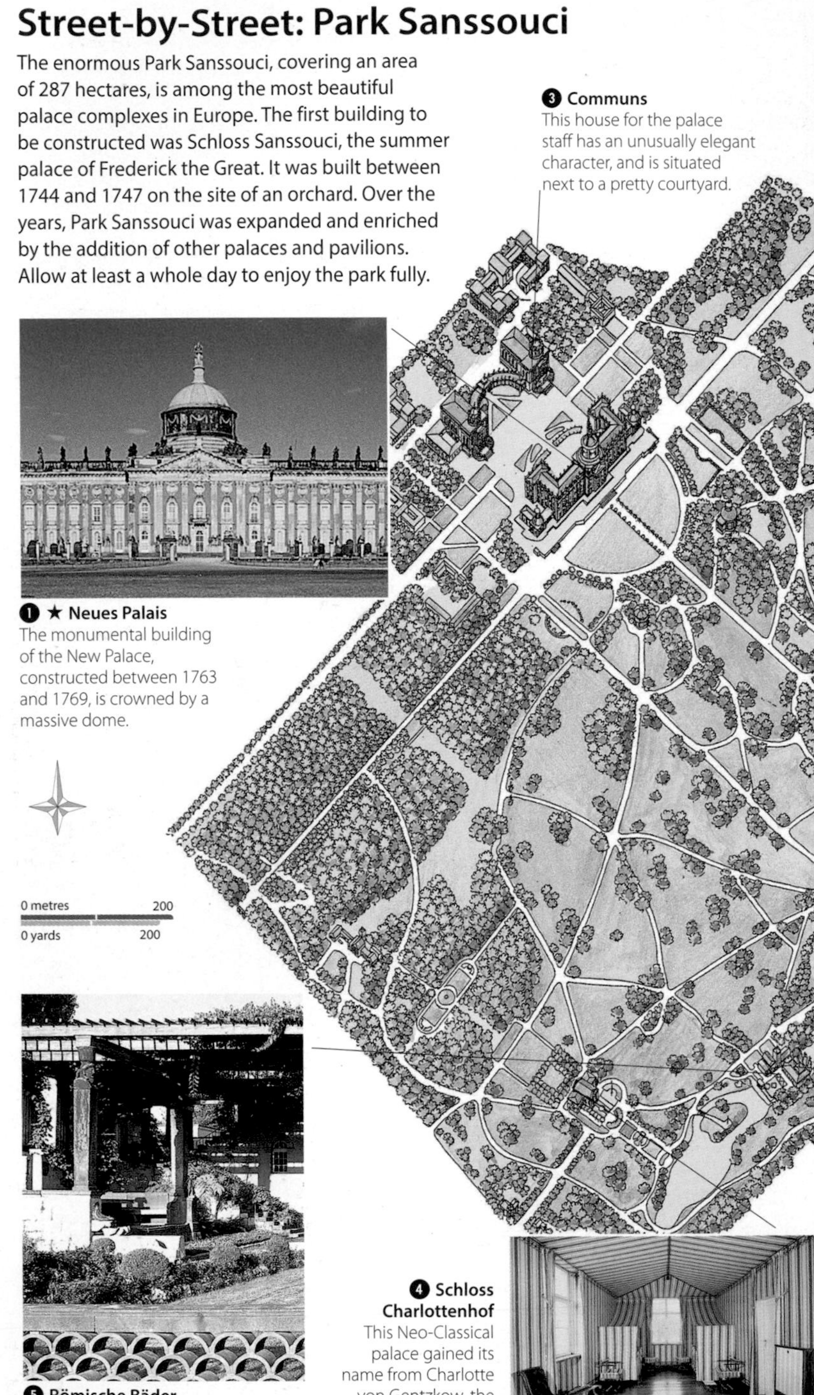

3 Communs
This house for the palace staff has an unusually elegant character, and is situated next to a pretty courtyard.

1 ★ Neues Palais
The monumental building of the New Palace, constructed between 1763 and 1769, is crowned by a massive dome.

5 Römische Bäder
The Roman Baths include a mock-Renaissance villa and a suite of Roman-style rooms.

4 Schloss Charlottenhof
This Neo-Classical palace gained its name from Charlotte von Gentzkow, the former owner of the land on which the palace was built.

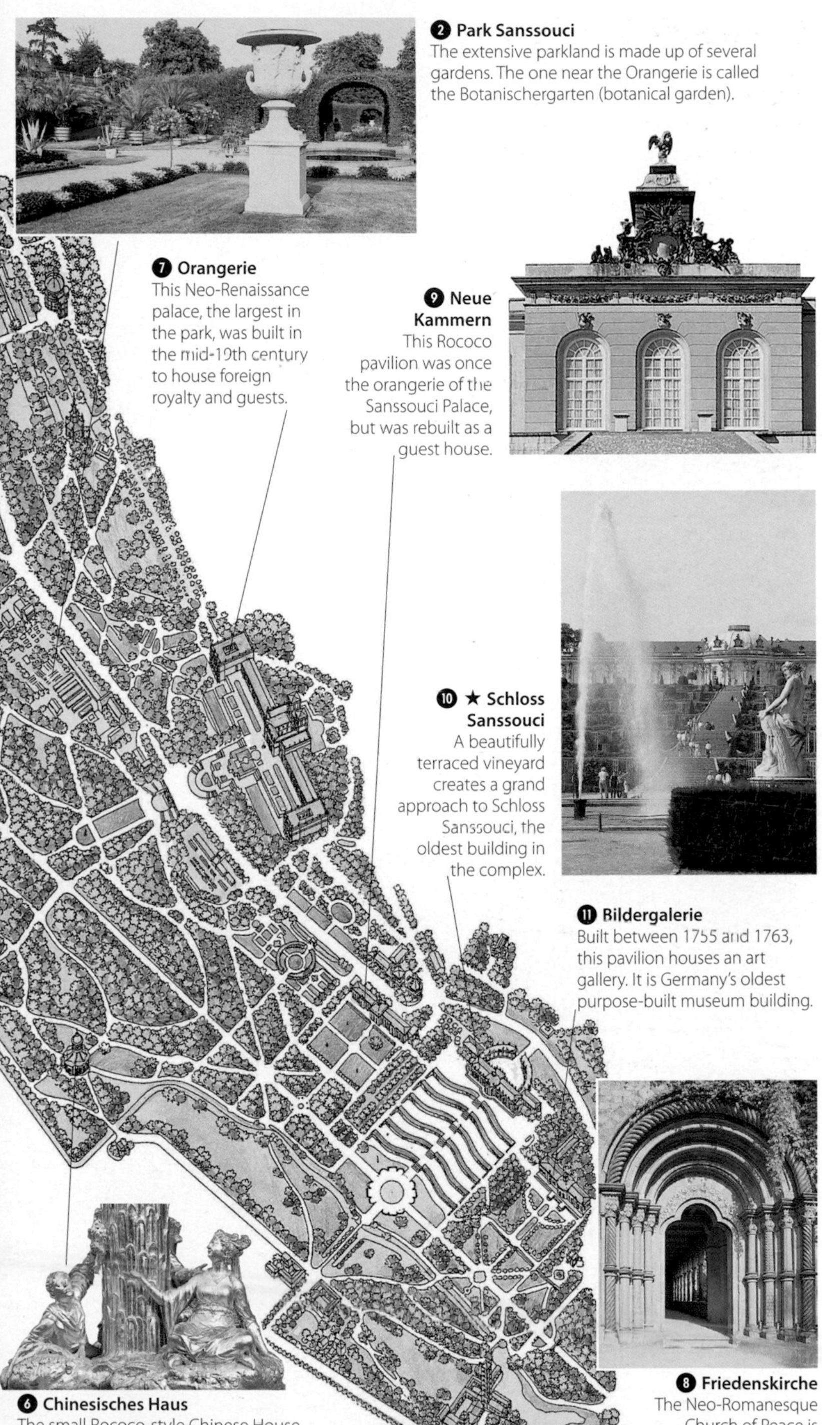

2 Park Sanssouci
The extensive parkland is made up of several gardens. The one near the Orangerie is called the Botanischergarten (botanical garden).

7 Orangerie
This Neo-Renaissance palace, the largest in the park, was built in the mid-19th century to house foreign royalty and guests.

9 Neue Kammern
This Rococo pavilion was once the orangerie of the Sanssouci Palace, but was rebuilt as a guest house.

10 ★ Schloss Sanssouci
A beautifully terraced vineyard creates a grand approach to Schloss Sanssouci, the oldest building in the complex.

11 Bildergalerie
Built between 1755 and 1763, this pavilion houses an art gallery. It is Germany's oldest purpose-built museum building.

6 Chinesisches Haus
The small Rococo-style Chinese House features an exhibition of exquisite Oriental porcelain.

8 Friedenskirche
The Neo-Romanesque Church of Peace is modelled on the Basilica of San Clemente in Rome.

❶ Neues Palais

This imposing Baroque palace, on the main avenue in Park Sanssouci, was built at the request of Frederick the Great. The initial plans were prepared in 1750 by Georg Wenzeslaus von Knobelsdorff. However, construction only began in 1763, after the Seven Years' War (*see p23*), to a design by Johann Gottfried Büring, Jean Laurent Le Geay and Carl von Gontard. The result was a vast two-storey building, decorated with hundreds of sculptures and more than 200 richly adorned rooms, which together make up one of Germany's most beautiful palaces.

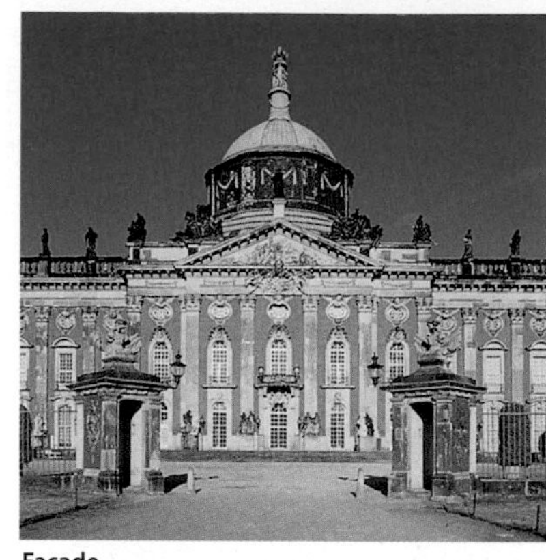

Façade
The entrance to the Neues Palais is through the gate on the western façade. The imposing gate is flanked by stone sentry boxes.

Study
This Rococo-style study was part of Frederick the Great's personal apartment.

Upper Gallery
The Rococo interior, with a beautiful inlaid floor, is decorated with Italian paintings.

KEY

① **The Schlosstheater** was completed in 1768, and designed by JC Hoppenhaupt.

② **Bas-reliefs** on the triangular tympanum depict figures from Greek mythology, including Minerva, the Muses and Pegasus.

Figures on the Dome
The Neues Palais is crowned by a dome with a gilded royal crown. The crown is carried by a sculpture of three nymphs.

VISITORS' CHECKLIST

Practical Information
Am Neuen Palais.
Tel (0331) 969 42 00.
spsg.de
Open Apr–Oct: 10am–6pm Wed–Mon; Nov–Mar: 10am–5pm Wed–Mon. only.

Transport
605, 606, 695.

★ Marmorsaal
This vast ballroom features walls inlaid with marble and a beautiful painting on the ceiling. The gallery was used by the orchestra.

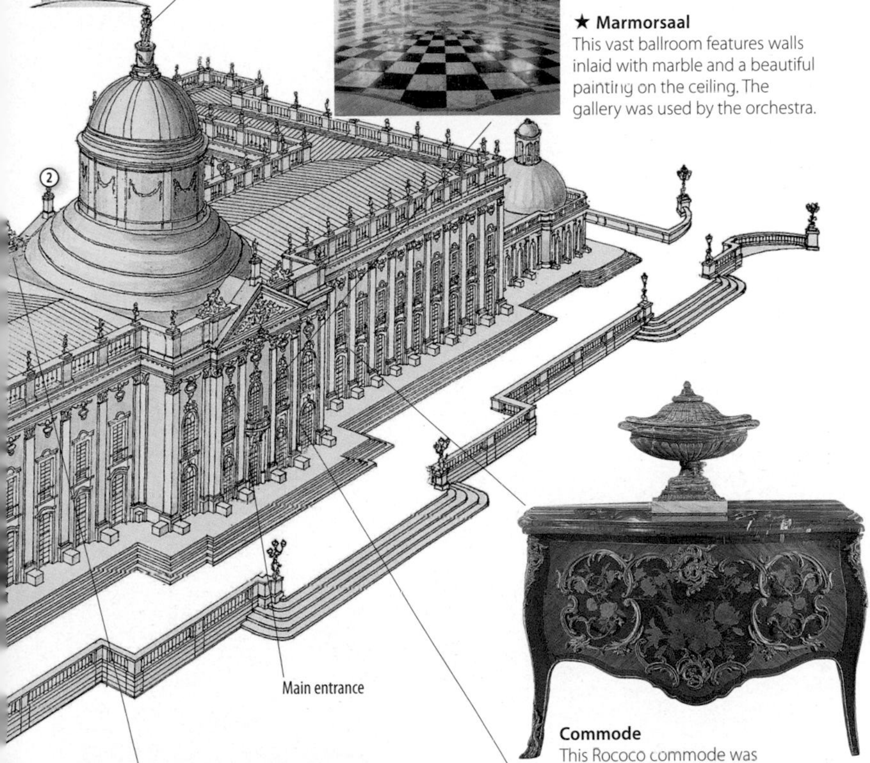

Main entrance

Commode
This Rococo commode was designed by JF Spindler in c.1765. It is located in the Red Room in the Duke's Apartments.

Upper Vestibule
This elegant room was designed by Carl von Gontard. The walls are covered with Silesian marble and the ceiling depicts Venus and the Graces.

★ Grottensaal
The walls of this unusual grotto-style room are lined with semi-precious stones, coral and shells as well as man-made stalactites.

❷ Park Sanssouci

Schopenhauerstrasse/Zur Historischen Mühle. 🚌 612, 614, 695.

This vast park, covering some 3 sq km (1 sq mile), was established in 1725 on the site of an orchard. However, it was only transformed into an enormous landscaped park when construction work began on Schloss Sanssouci *(see pp202–203)*. Today, the park is made up of smaller gardens dating from different eras, each of which has been maintained in the original style. At the foot of Schloss Sanssouci is the oldest section of the park, containing the Dutch garden, a number of fountains and the French-style Lustgarten (pleasure garden), with a symmetrical layout and lovely rose beds. Surrounding Friedenskirche is the Marlygarten, created in the mid-19th century by Ludwig Persius.

The eastern part of the park is called the Rehgarten, a beautifully landscaped park in the English style designed by Peter Joseph Lenné and established on the site of former hunting grounds. This park extends right up to the Neues Palais. To the south, surrounding the small palace, extends the Charlottenhof Park, also designed by Lenné. In the northern section of the park, next to the Orangerie, is the Nordischer Garten and the Paradiesgarten.

The range of different garden styles makes a simple stroll through this park particularly pleasant. There are also a large number of sculptures, columns, obelisks and grottoes for the visitor to explore. The vistas and perspectives that suddenly open up across the park and the picturesque groupings of trees are also beautiful.

❸ Communs

Am Neuen Palais. 🚌 605, 695.

This area of the park consists of a pair of two-storey pavilions linked by a semi-circular colonnade. They are unusually elegant buildings considering they were used for servants' quarters and the palace kitchens. However, they also served to screen from view the cultivated fields that extended past the park from the palace.

The Communs were built between 1766 and 1769 by Carl von Gontard, to a design by Jean Laurent Le Geay. The buildings are enclosed by an elegant courtyard reflected in the style of the buildings. The kitchen was in the south pavilion, linked to the palace by an underground passageway, and the north pavilion accommodated the servants of the king's guests. Today, the rectors' offices of the University of Potsdam are located here in the Communs.

Elegant façade of the Communs, the servants' quarters

One of the many sculptures on display in Park Sanssouci

❹ Schloss Charlottenhof

Charlottenhof Palace

Geschwister-Scholl-Strasse 34a (Park Charlottenhof). **Tel** (0331) 969 42 28. 🚌 605, 606. 🚋 91, 94. **Open** 1 May–31 Oct: 10am–5pm Tue–Sun.

This small Neo-Classical palace is located in the southern extension of Park Sanssouci, Park Charlottenhof. It was designed by Karl Friedrich Schinkel in 1829 for the heir to the throne, later King Friedrich Wilhelm IV. This small one-storey building was built in the style of a Roman villa. The rear of the palace has a portico that opens out onto the garden terrace.

Some of the wall paintings designed by Schinkel, which were made in the so-called Pompeiian style, are still in place. The most interesting part of the interior is the blue-and-white-striped Humboldt Room, also called the Tent Room due to its resemblance to a tent. The palace is surrounded by a picturesque landscaped park designed by Peter Joseph Lenné.

5 Römische Bäder

Roman Baths

Lenné-Strasse (Park Charlottenhof). **Tel** (0331) 969 42 00. 605, 606. 91, 94, 98. **Open** May–Oct: 10am–6pm Tue–Sun.

This picturesque group of pavilions, situated by the edge of a lake, forms the "Roman Baths", which actually served as accommodation for the king's guests. It was designed by Karl Friedrich Schinkel, with the involvement of Ludwig Persius, between 1829 and 1840. At the front is the gardener's house, which is adjacent to an asymmetrical low tower in the style of an Italian Renaissance villa. In the background, to the left, extends the former bathing pavilion, which is currently used for temporary exhibitions. All of the pavilions are arranged around an internal garden planted with a multicoloured carpet of shrubs. A closer look will reveal that many of these colourful plants are actually vegetables.

6 Chinesisches Haus

Chinese House

Ökonomieweg (Rehgarten). **Tel** (0331) 969 42 00. 606, 695. 91, 94. **Open** May–Oct: 10am–6pm Tue–Sun.

The lustrous, gilded pavilion that can be seen glistening from a distance is the Chinese House. Chinese art was popular during the Rococo period – people wore Chinese silk, rooms were wallpapered with Chinese designs, furniture was lacquered, drinks were served in Chinese porcelain, and Chinese pavilions were built in gardens.

The Chinesisches Haus was built in Park Sanssouci between 1754 and 1756 to a design by Johann Gottfried Büring. It is circular in shape, with a centrally located main hall surrounded by three studies. Between each of these are pretty *trompe l'oeil* porticoes. Ornaments, together with gilded figures of Chinese gentlemen and ladies, surround the pavilion. Originally the Chinesisches Haus served as a tearoom and a summer dining room. Today, it houses a collection of porcelain.

The Chinesisches Haus, now housing a collection of porcelain

7 Orangerie

Maulbeerallee (Nordischer Garten). **Tel** (0331) 969 42 80. 695. **Open** Apr: 10am–6pm Sat, Sun & hols; May–Oct: 10am–6pm Tue–Sun. Observation terrace: **Open** Apr: 10am–6pm Sat, Sun & hols; May–Oct: 10am–6pm Tue–Sun.

Towering above the park is the Orangerie, designed in the Italian Renaissance style and crowned by a colonnade. The Orangerie was built to house guests, not plants. It was constructed between 1851 and 1860 by Friedrich August Stüler on the initiative and direction of Friedrich Wilhelm IV. The final design was partly based on the plans of Ludwig Persius. It served as a guest residence for the king's sister and her husband, Tsar Nicholas I. The rooms were grouped around the Raphael Hall, which was based on the Regia Hall in the Vatican and decorated with copies of the works of Italian artist Raphael. It is also worth climbing up to the observation terrace, from where the view extends over Potsdam.

Long flight of stairs leading to the Renaissance-style Orangerie

8 Friedenskirche

Am Grünen Gitter. **Tel** (0331) 97 40 09. 695. 91, 94. **Open** late Apr: 11am–5pm Mon–Sat, noon–5pm Sun; May–1 Oct: 10am–6pm Mon–Sat, noon–6pm Sun; 2–16 Oct: 11am–5pm Mon–Sat, noon–5pm Sun; 17 Oct–late Apr: 11am–4pm Sat, 11:30am–5pm Sun.

Close to Schloss Sanssouci is Friedenskirche, or the Church of Peace. The foundation stone was laid by King Friedrich Wilhelm IV in 1845 and the church was completed in 1848. Designed by Ludwig Persius, Friedrich August Stüler and Ludwig Hesse, the church is based on San Clemente in Rome.

Inside, the vaulted ceiling of the apse is covered by a 12th-century mosaic depicting the figure of Christ as a judge. This Byzantine mosaic was originally located in the church of San Capriano on the island of Murano in Venice. Next to the church is a mausoleum containing the tombs of Friedrich Wilhelm I, Friedrich Wilhelm IV and Kaiser Friedrich III.

❾ Neue Kammern

New Chambers

Zur Historischen Mühle (Lustgarten). **Tel** (0331) 969 42 00. 695. **Open** Apr–Oct: 10am–6pm Wed–Mon; Nov–Mar: 10am–5pm Wed–Mon.

The Neue Kammern contains residential apartments. It is the mirror image of the Bildergalerie and was originally built as an orangery in 1747 to a design by Georg Wenzeslaus von Knobelsdorff. In 1777 Frederick the Great (Friedrich II) ordered the building to be remodelled as guest accommodation. The architect, Georg Christian Unger, left the elegant Baroque exterior of the orangery largely untouched and instead concentrated on converting the interior. As well as the sumptuous guest suites, the new design included four elegant halls. The best of these is the Ovidsaal, with its rich reliefs and marble floors. The interior decor has been maintained in Frederick's Rococo style. The building also houses a collection of Meissen figurines.

❿ Schloss Sanssouci

See pp202–203.

Detail of Caravaggio's *Doubting Thomas*, in the Bildergalerie

⓫ Bildergalerie

Zur Historischen Mühle. **Tel** (0331) 969 42 00. 695. **Open** May–Oct: 10am–6pm Tue–Sun.

The picture gallery housed in the building adjacent to Schloss Sanssouci was the first purpose-built gallery in Germany. It was constructed between 1755 and 1764 to a design by JG Büring. The garden elevation reveals an allegorical tableau representing Art, Education and Crafts, while busts of renowned artists have been placed in the windows.

The gallery contains an exhibition of Baroque paintings once owned by Frederick the Great, although part of the collection can be found in the Gemäldegalerie *(see pp126–9)*. Highlights include Caravaggio's *Doubting Thomas* and Guido Reni's *Cleopatra's Death*, as well as a number of canvases by Rubens and van Dyck.

⓬ Historische Mühle

Historic Windmill

Mauelbeerallee 5. **Tel** (0331) 550 68 51. 695. **Open** Apr–Oct: 10am–6pm daily; Nov, Jan–Mar: 10am–4pm Sat & Sun.

A mill has been located here since the early 18th century, although this is actually a reconstruction, dating from 1993. According to local legend, the original windmill was so noisy that Frederick the Great ordered it to be dismantled. However, a court upheld the miller's cause and the mill stayed. In 1790 a new windmill was built in its place, which lasted until 1945. The mill currently houses a museum of mechanical windmills.

⓭ Alexandrowka

Russische Kolonie Allee/ Puschkinallee. 92, 96. 604, 609, 692, 697.

A trip to Alexandrowka takes the visitor into the world of Pushkin's stories. Wooden houses made

A Russian-style wooden house in the settlement of Alexandrowka

from logs, decorated with carved motifs and set in their own gardens, create a very pretty residential estate. Although they appear to be picture-book traditional Russian houses, they were constructed in 1826 under the direction of a German military architect called Captain Snethlage. What is interesting is that the estate was created for the singers of a Russian choir. The choir was set up in 1812 to entertain the troops and was recruited from over 500 Russian prisoners of war, who had fought with Napoleon. In 1815, when the Prussians and the Russians joined forces, the choir was retained by Friedrich Wilhelm III.

Peter Joseph Lenné was responsible for the overall appearance of the estate, and it was named Alexandrowka after the Tsarina, the Prussian Princess Charlotte. It is based on the shape of the cross of St Andrew inscribed within an oval. In all, 12 houses were built here, as well as an outhouse which now contains a small museum. Some of the dwellings are still owned by the descendants of the choir. To the north of this estate stands the Russian Orthodox church of Alexander Nevski (1829).

Orange growing in the Neuer Garten's Marmorpalais

⓮ Neuer Garten

New Garden

Am Neuen Garten. 🚌 692.

Running along the edge of Heiliger See, on what was once the site of palace vineyards, is a park laid out between 1787 and 1791. It was landscaped originally by Johann August Eyserbeck on the instructions of Friedrich Wilhelm II, while the current layout was created by Peter Joseph Lenné in 1816. It is a Romantic park ornamented with numerous pavilions and sculptures. The charming Marmorpalais *(see p204)* stands beside the lake, while the northern section contains the early 20th-century Schloss Cecilienhof. Elsewhere you can see the red and green gardeners' houses, the pyramid-shaped ice house and a Neo-Gothic library pavilion completed in 1794.

Schloss Cecilienhof, summer residence of the Hohenzollern family

⓯ Schloss Cecilienhof

Am Neuen Garten. **Tel** (0331) 969 42 00. 🚌 692. **Open** Apr–Oct: 10am–6pm Tue–Sun; Nov–Mar: 10am–5pm Tue–Sun.

The Cecilienhof residence played a brief but important part in history because the 1945 Potsdam Conference took place here. Built between 1914 and 1917, the palace is the most recent of the Hohenzollern dynasty buildings and was designed by Paul Schultze-Naumburg in the style of an English country manor. It is a sprawling, asymmetrical building with wooden beams making a pretty herringbone pattern on its walls. The gatehouse passageways leading to the courtyards are decorated with Baroque reliefs.

The palace was the Hohenzollern family residence after they lost the crown; the family remained in Potsdam until February 1945. It now functions as a first-class hotel and restaurant, where history-lovers can relax amid carefully tended shrubbery. Most of the historic furnishings used during the famous Potsdam conference are on display.

The Potsdam Conference of 1945

On 17 July 1945 the heads of government of Great Britain (Winston Churchill, later represented by Clement Attlee), the United States (Harry Truman) and the Soviet Union (Joseph Stalin) met in Schloss Cecilienhof to confirm the decisions made earlier that year at Yalta. The aim of both conferences was to resolve the problems arising at the end of World War II. They decided to abolish the Nazi Party, to limit the size of the German militia and monitor it indefinitely, and also to punish war criminals and establish reparations. They also revised the German borders and arranged the resettlement of Germans from Poland. The conference played a major part in establishing the political balance of power in Europe, which continued for the next 45 years.

Attlee, Truman and Stalin at Cecilienhof

⑩ Schloss Sanssouci

The name Sanssouci is French for "without a care" and gives a good indication of the flamboyant character of this enchanting Rococo palace, built in 1745. The original sketches, made by Friedrich II (Frederick the Great) himself, were finalized by Georg Wenzeslaus von Knobelsdorff. The glorious interiors were designed by Knobelsdorff and Johann August Nahl. The king clearly loved this palace, as his final wishes were that he should be buried here, near the tomb of his Italian greyhounds. He was actually interred in the Garnisonkirche, Potsdam, but his final wishes were carried out in 1991.

Bacchanalian Figures
The carved male and female Bacchanalian figures on the pilasters are the work of Friedrich Christian Glume.

Voltaire Room
This room is decorated with naturalistic carvings of birds, flowers and fruit.

Domed Roof
The oxidized green dome covers the Marmorsaal. It is decorated with Baroque sculptures.

Marmorsaal
The imposing marble hall is decorated with pairs of columns made from Carrara marble. Frederick the Great wanted this room to be loosely based on the Pantheon in Rome.

KEY

① **The wings** were added to the building between 1841 and 1842.

② **The colonnade** frames the view of the artificial ruins on the hill.

Arbour
The palace design is completed by picturesque arbours and pergolas decorated with sun motifs.

VISITORS' CHECKLIST

Practical Information
Park Sanssouci.
Tel (0331) 969 42 00.
spsg.de
Open Apr–Oct: 10am–6pm Tue–Sun; Nov–Mar: 10am–5pm Tue–Sun.
Damenflügel: May–Oct: 10am–6pm Sat & Sun.
compulsory.

Transport
612, 614, 650, 695.
91, 94, X98.

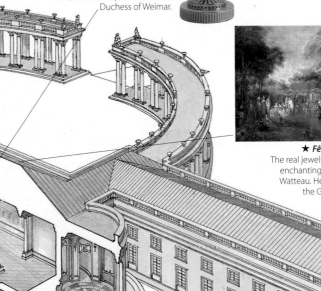

Weimar Urn (1785)
This Neo-Classical urn from the Berlin company KPM *(see p137)* is a copy of the original urn, which was presented to the Duchess of Weimar.

★ ***Fêtes Galantes*** (c.1715)
The real jewels in the palace are the enchanting paintings by Antoine Watteau. He was one of Frederick the Great's favourite artists.

★ **Konzertzimmer**
The walls of the salon are decorated with paintings by Antoine Pesne, based on Greek mythology.

Bibliothek
The library of Frederick the Great contains about 2,100 books. The walls are lined with cedar panelling to create a contemplative atmosphere.

⑯ Marmorpalais

Marble Palace

Am Ufer des Heiligen Sees (Neuer Garten). **Tel** (0331) 969 42 00. 692, 695. **Open** Apr: 10am–6pm Sat, Sun & hols; May–Oct: 10am– 6pm Tue–Sun; Nov–Mar: 10am–4pm Sat, Sun & hols.

The Marmorpalais is situated on the edge of the lake in Neuer Garten *(see p201)*, a park northeast of the centre of Potsdam. This small palace is a beautiful example of early Neo-Classical architecture and owes its name to its façade, which is lined with Silesian marble.

The square main body of the palace was the initiative of King Friedrich Wilhelm II. The original building was completed in 1791 to a design by Carl von Gontard, under the direction of Carl Gotthard Langhans. The single-storey building had small rooms around a central staircase, but it turned out to be too small, and in 1797 it was extended. An extra floor and two projecting wings were added. This gave the Marmorpalais the character of a Palladian villa.

The main part of the palace contains Neo-Classical furnishings from the late 1700s, including furniture from the workshops of Roentgen and porcelain from the English firm Wedgwood. The interiors of the wings date from slightly later, from the 1840s. The concert hall in the right-hand wing is particularly beautiful. King Friedrich Wilhelm II died in this palace in 1797.

The Neo-Classical Marmorpalais, with its inlaid marble façade

The historic Dutch district known as the Holländisches Viertel

⑰ Holländisches Viertel

Dutch Quarter

Friedrich-Ebert-/Kurfürsten-/Hebbel-/Gutenbergstrasse. 604, 609, 692. 91, 92, 94, 96.

Just as amazing as the Russian district of Alexandrowka *(see pp200–201)* is this Dutch district. The area is popular with tourists, with numerous shops, galleries, cafés and beer cellars, especially along the central Mittelstrasse.

Dutch workers, invited by Friedrich Wilhelm I, arrived in Potsdam at the beginning of the 18th century. Between 1733 and 1742 a settlement was built for them, comprising 134 gabled houses arranged in four groups, according to plans by Johann Boumann the Elder. They were built from small red bricks and finished with stone and plaster details. These houses are typically three-storey, with picturesque roofs and gables.

⑱ Peter und Paul Kirche

Bassinplatz. **Tel** (0331) 230 79 90. 604, 609, 612. 91, 92, 94, 96. **Open** Mon–Sat; opening hours vary, so call ahead. 10am Sun.

This 19th-century church was the first large Catholic church built in Potsdam, at the initiative of Friedrich Wilhelm IV. The first designs came from Friedrich August Stüler, but the final version is the work of Wilhelm Salzenberg. The church was built in 1870, in the shape of a Neo-Romanesque cross. Its slender tower is a copy of the campanile of San Zeno Maggiore in Verona, Italy. Inside are three beautiful paintings by Antoine Pesne.

The colonnaded portico of the Französische Kirche

⑲ Französische Kirche

French Church

Bassinplatz. **Tel** (0331) 29 12 19. 604, 609, 612. 93, 94, 99. **Open** late Mar–Oct: 1:30–5pm daily.

This church, reminiscent of the Pantheon in Rome, was built especially for the Huguenots in 1752. Following their expulsion from France, they were given the option of settling in Prussia in 1685 *(see p23)*. Those who settled in Potsdam initially benefited from the hospitality of other churches, then eventually the Französische Kirche was built for them. It was designed by Johann Boumann the Elder in the shape of an ellipse. The front elevation is supported by a grand columned portico. The side niches, which are the entrances of the church, are decorated with the allegorical figures of Faith and Knowledge.

The interior dates from the 1830s and is based on designs by Karl Friedrich Schinkel.

⑳ Nikolaikirche

Am Alten Markt. **Tel** (0331) 270 86 02. 🚌 604, 605, 609, 610, 695. 🚋 91, 92, 93, 94, 96, 99, X98. **Open** noon–2pm Mon, 10am–5pm Wed.

This imposing church, built in a late Neo-Classical style, is the most beautiful church in Potsdam. It was designed in 1830 by Karl Friedrich Schinkel and the building work was overseen by Ludwig Persius. The main body of the church is based on a square cross, with a semi-circular presbytery.

It was decided only in the 1840s to crown the church with a vast dome, supported on a colonnaded tambour (wall supporting a dome). Schinkel had envisaged this from the beginning of the project, but it was not included in the orders of the king. Initially it was thought that the dome would be supported by a wooden structure, though ultimately it was built using iron, between 1843 and 1848, according to a design by Persius and Friedrich August Stüler. The interior decoration and the furnishings of the church date back to the 1850s, and in the main area of the church they were based on the earlier interior designs by Schinkel.

In front of the church stands an obelisk built between 1753 and 1755 to a design by Prussian architect Georg Wenzeslaus von Knobelsdorff. Initially it was decorated by medallions bearing the portraits of Prussian rulers, but during the post-World War II restorations, they were replaced with portraits of renowned Prussian architects.

Nikolaikirche's imposing exterior, with its green, weathered dome

㉑ Altes Rathaus

Old Town Hall

Am Alten Markt. 🚌 604, 609, 692, 694. 🚋 90, 92, 93, 96, 98.

This elegant, colonnaded building, located on the eastern side of Alter Markt, is the old town hall. Designed by Johann Boumann the Elder, it was built in 1753 on the site of an earlier building that served a similar purpose. The uppermost storey, which features an ornamental attic roof, is decorated with the crest of Potsdam and allegorical sculptures. At the summit of the small tower are two gilded figures of Atlas, each carrying a globe of the Earth. The Altes Rathaus is currently used as a cultural centre. The interior of the neighbouring mid-18th-century building has also been refurbished, and a glassed-in passageway built, linking the two buildings.

Atlas at Altes Rathaus

The Potsdam Royal Palace was located at one time on the west side of Alter Markt. It was a massive two-storey building with three wings. There was also an elegant courtyard and a superb gateway crowned by a tower. The palace was built in 1662 on the site of a former castle, on the initiative of the Great Elector. Over the following years the palace was greatly enlarged and modernized for members of the royal family, including Frederick the Great (Friedrich II). After a bombing raid in 1945, the palace remained in ruins for many years, but the East German Government decided finally to pull down the remains in 1960. It is now the home of the Potsdam-Museum *(see p206)*.

Potsdam Town Gates

The city of Potsdam was enclosed by a wall in 1722. This wall did not serve a defensive purpose – it was supposed to contain criminals and stop soldiers deserting. When the borders of the town were extended in 1733, new districts were also enclosed by the wall. There was a total of five city gates, of which three have survived. Jägertor has survived in its original condition and dates from 1733. Featuring solid, wide pillars, the gate is crowned with a group of sculptures depicting hunting dogs attacking a deer. Nauener Tor was redesigned in 1755 by Johann Gottfried Büring and, interestingly, it is one of the earliest examples of Neo-Gothic design occurring outside Great Britain. The most imposing of the gates is the Brandenburger Tor. It was rebuilt in 1770 in a Neo-Classical style to commemorate victory in the Seven Years' War *(see p23)*. The designers, Gontard and Unger, gave it the appearance of an ancient triumphal arch. At the very top are a number of different groups of sculptures. These include figures from Greek mythology, such as Hercules and Mars.

Nauener Tor

Jägertor

Brandenburger Tor

㉒ Potsdam-Museum

In the Altes Rathaus, Am Alten Markt. **Tel** (0331) 289 68 00. 609, 692. 92, 96, 98. **Open** 10am–6pm Tue–Sun.

The Potsdam-Museum was founded in 1909 by the citizens of the city, and has been bequeathed a sizeable collection of art and artifacts. Its changing collection is a reflection of local history and tells the story of Potsdam's development, from the earliest historical reference to the present day. A nearby branch of the museum, Memorial Linde 54/55, is a former prison and interrogation centre used by both the Nazi and East German regimes.

The impressive façade of the Potsdam-Museum

㉓ Marstall (Filmmuseum)

Breite Strasse 1A. **Tel** (0331) 27 18 10. 605, 695. 91, 92, 96, 98. **Open** 10am–6pm Tue–Sun.

This Baroque pavilion, once used as a royal stables – hence the name Marstall – is the only remaining building of a former royal residence. It was first established in 1714 by refashioning the orangery built by Johann Nering in 1685. In 1746 it was extended and refashioned once more, according to a design by the architect GW von Knobelsdorff. It suffered extensive damage in World War II and in 1977, after major restoration, it was converted into a film museum.

Stately building of the Marstall (Filmmuseum)

As well as mounting temporary exhibitions, the museum documents the history and work of the Babelsberg studios, Germany's earliest film studios. Exhibits include old projectors, cameras and other equipment as well as props used in some of the most famous German films.

㉔ Wasserwerk Sanssouci

Breite Strasse 28. **Tel** (0331) 969 42 25. 605, 606. 91, 94, X98. **Open** May–Oct: 10am–6pm Sat, Sun & hols.

Although Potsdam once boasted a Russian and a Dutch community, the remarkable mosque (also called Dampfmaschinenhaus) was not built to serve the needs of an Islamic community, but to hide the special steam pump that serviced the fountains in Park Sanssouci. This Moorish-style building, with its minaret and Oriental dome, was designed by Ludwig Persius in 1842. The dome does not serve any useful purpose, although within the minaret there is a huge chimney. While visiting you can see the preserved steam-powered machinery made by the Borsig company.

Moorish Wasserwerk Sanssouci, complete with minaret

㉕ Telegrafenberg

Albert-Einstein-Strasse. Ⓢ Potsdam Hauptbahnhof. Einsteinturm: **Tel** (0331) 749 94 69. **Open** May–Oct, by appointment only. compulsory.

The buildings on the Telegrafenberg are considered to be some of the best 20th-century structures in the world and attract many admirers of modern architecture. The hill received its current name in 1832, when an optical telegraph station linking Berlin and Koblenz was built here. In the late 19th century, various educational institutes were located here, including the Institute of Astrophysics, for which the complex of buildings in yellow brick was built.

The meandering avenues lead to a picturesque clearing where the small Einsteinturm (Einstein's Tower) breaks through the surrounding trees. Specially designed to observe the solar system, the tower was intended to provide information that would support Einstein's Theory of Relativity. It was built in 1920 by Erich Mendelsohn and is regarded as one of the finest architectural examples of German Expressionism. Its fantastical appearance was intended to show what could be achieved with reinforced concrete. However, the costs of the complicated form limited the use of concrete, and above the first storey the building is made from brickwork covered in plaster.

26 Filmpark Babelsberg

This amazing theme park was laid out on the site of the film studios where Germany's first films were produced in 1912. From 1917 the studio belonged to Universum-Film-AG (UFA), which produced some of the most renowned films of the silent era, such as *Metropolis* *(see p155)*. Nazi propaganda films were also made here. The studio is still operational today, although part of the complex is open to visitors. Expect to see the sets from old films, special effects at work and stuntmen in action.

VISITORS' CHECKLIST

Practical Information
August-Bebel Strasse 26–53 (enter at Grossbeeren Strasse).
Tel (0331) 721 27 50.
filmpark-babelsberg.de
Open Apr–Nov: 10am–6pm daily.
Closed Mon in Sep.

Transport
601, 619, 690. Griebnitzsee.

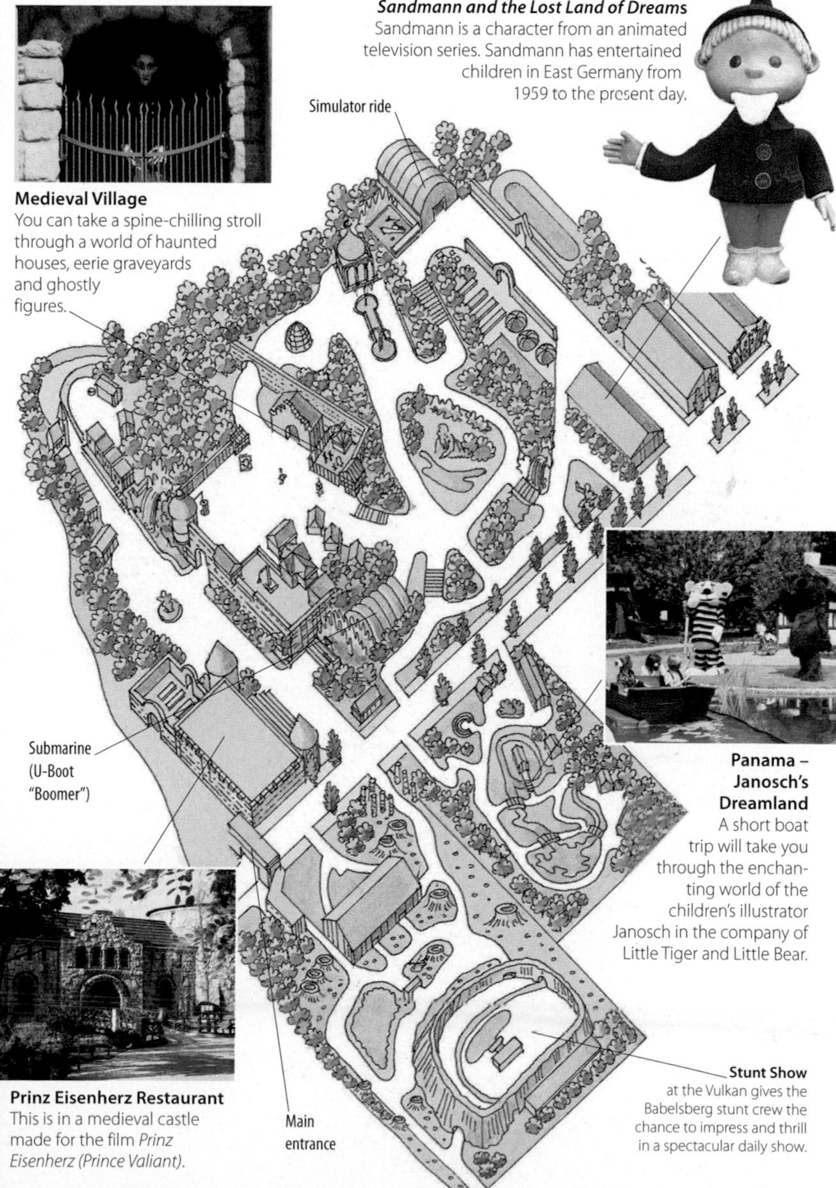

Sandmann and the Lost Land of Dreams
Sandmann is a character from an animated television series. Sandmann has entertained children in East Germany from 1959 to the present day.

Medieval Village
You can take a spine-chilling stroll through a world of haunted houses, eerie graveyards and ghostly figures.

Panama – Janosch's Dreamland
A short boat trip will take you through the enchanting world of the children's illustrator Janosch in the company of Little Tiger and Little Bear.

Prinz Eisenherz Restaurant
This is in a medieval castle made for the film *Prinz Eisenherz (Prince Valiant)*.

Stunt Show
at the Vulkan gives the Babelsberg stunt crew the chance to impress and thrill in a spectacular daily show.

THREE GUIDED WALKS

Berlin is full of enchanting parks, gardens, lakes and interesting monuments, and one of the best ways to enjoy them is by going on a guided walk. The three walks suggested in this chapter provide for relaxation far from the hustle and bustle of the city centre. The first takes you onto the picturesque Pfaueninsel (Peacock Island), which at the end of the 18th century was refashioned into a romantic English-style park with garden pavilions and an enchanting little palace. After visiting the island you can pay a short visit to Nikolskoe – a Russian-style *dacha* (country house) built for the future Tsar Nicholas I and his wife, the daughter of King Friedrich Wilhelm III. The second walk begins in Berlin and takes you first through the grounds of the Glienicke Park, which was laid out in the 1820s for Prince Karl of Prussia. This route continues across the former border between East and West Germany, in an area which is now part of Potsdam. There you can visit the Romantic-era park of Babelsberg, and the Neo-Gothic palace designed for Prince Wilhelm by Karl Friedrich Schinkel. The third walk, around the forest called Grunewald, takes you initially through a deluxe villa resort of the late 19th century, and then along forest paths to the Grunewaldsee. On the shores of this lake stands an enchanting hunting lodge. From there you can continue walking to the Brücke-Museum. Because each of these three walks leads you across unpaved paths, remember to wear comfortable shoes.

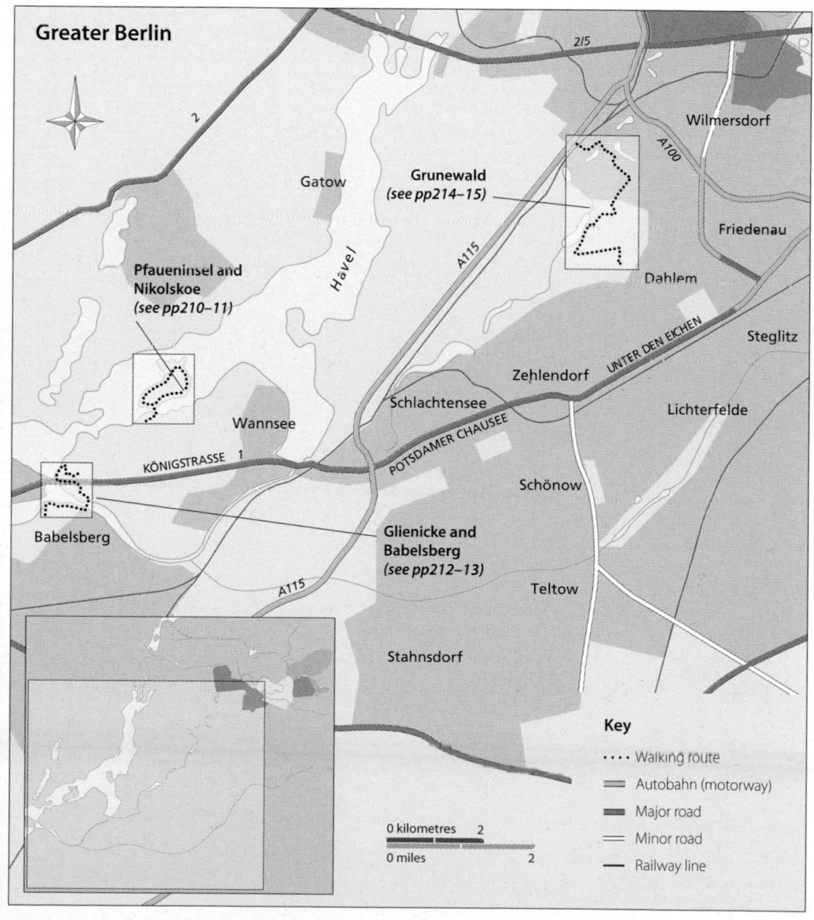

◀ The picturesque Neo-Gothic Babelsberg palace

Pfaueninsel and Nikolskoe

This walk takes you around Pfaueninsel (Peacock Island). This picturesque park, now a nature reserve, was laid out in 1795 according to a design by Johann August Eyserbeck. Its final form, which you see today, is the work of the renowned landscape architect Peter Joseph Lenné. This pleasant, relaxing walk allows you to explore several interesting sights, and to encounter the peacocks for which the island is named. Afterwards you can have refreshments at the lakeside, or head straight to Nikolskoe, the location of one of Berlin's finest restaurants.

One of the colourful peacocks on Pfaueninsel (Peacock Island)

Around Pfaueninsel

At the jetty ① you board a small passenger ferry, which takes you to the island in a few minutes. After disembarking, follow the path which leads to the left. It continues along the edge of the island, gently uphill to the Castellan's House ② and further on to the Swiss House, dating from 1830, in which the gardener lived. Continue along the path to the extensive clearing with a picturesque flower garden, beyond which is the small romantic palace of Schloss Pfaueninsel ③. Dating from 1794, it was designed by Johann Gottlieb Brendel for Friedrich Wilhelm II and his mistress Wilhelmine Encke (the future Countess Lichtenau). The palace was built of wood, with a façade (hidden away) fashioned in the form of a ruined medieval castle. The façade was visible from Neuer Garten in Potsdam. The cast-iron bridge which links the towers was built in 1807. During the summer months you can go inside the palace to see its furnishings from the 18th and 19th centuries.

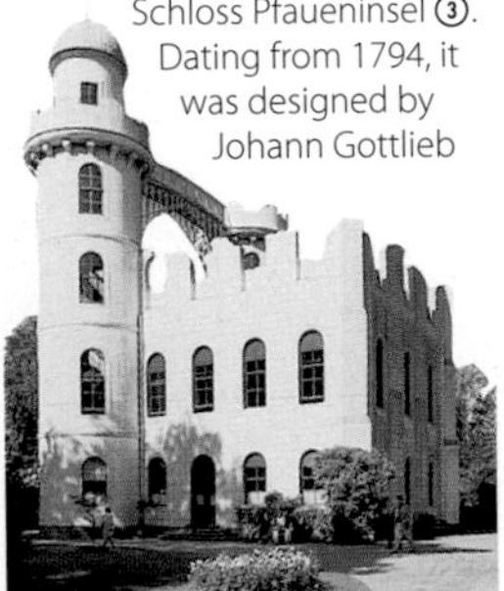

The Neo-Gothic Schloss Pfaueninsel designed by Johann Brendel

After leaving the palace, follow the path that leads along the edge, passing by the kitchen pavilion ④ on the left, which is set amid greenery. At the next junction turn gently right into the depths of the island. You will pass by James's Well ⑤ which was built to resemble an ancient ruin, and cross a meadow heading towards a small wood which contains the Kavalierhaus ⑥. This building was used to provide the royal household with accommodation. At the front of the house, Karl Friedrich Schinkel installed an authentic façade from a late Gothic house brought over from Danzig (now Gdansk) in Poland. From here you proceed further in the same direction, and

James's Well, deliberately built to resemble a picturesque ruin

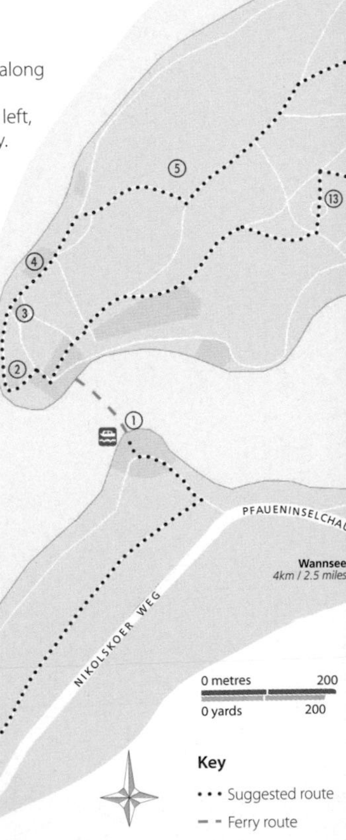

emerge again in a large clearing. To the left you can marvel at the Parschenkessel bay ⑦ in the distance, surrounded by dead trees on which cormorants nest. Take the path on the left to the Neo-Gothic Dairy ⑧ and the Dutch House ⑨. This was a cow shed and dates from 1802, while

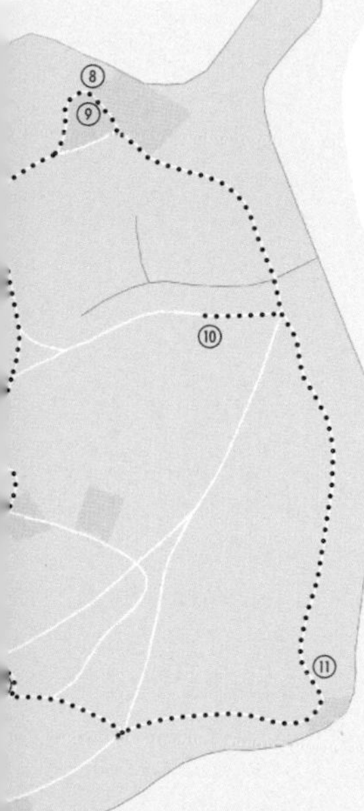

the Dairy is an artificial ruin of a medieval abbey dating from 1795. From here take the path along the edge of the lake heading south; you can marvel at the wonderful views. To the right by the edge of the forest you can see Luisentempel ⑩ in the form of a Greek temple. Its sandstone portico at the front was moved to the island from the mausoleum in Schlosspark Charlottenburg *(see p167)* in 1829. The path leads

Guests on the terrace of the Blockhaus Nikolskoe in summer

further along the edge of the lake, while on the right side among the trees you pass the stone commemorating Johannes Kunckel, an alchemist who lived on Pfaueninsel in the 17th century. In his quest to discover how to make gold, he in fact discovered a method of producing ruby-coloured glass. Carry on further through the forest, passing the Gothic Bridge ⑪, and then take the path to the right up towards the hill of the Aviary ⑫, home to multi-coloured parrots and pheasants. From here you continue towards the tall column of a Fountain ⑬ designed by Martin Friedrich Rabe in 1824. Next, walk onward to the jetty, passing the market gardens with their hothouses on the way.

From the Jetty to Nikolskoe

Once you've taken the little ferry back to the mainland, head off to the left, going south. When you come to the fork, take the right-hand path leading gently uphill. This leads to the church of Saints Peter and Paul ⑭, which rises above a large terrace from where there are pretty views of Pfaueninsel. The church was built between the years 1834 and 1837, according to a design by Friedrich August Stüler. The small, orderly, body of the church is fronted by a tower crowned by an onion-shaped dome, which reflects Russian Orthodox sacral architecture. This links to the adjacent Blockhaus Nikolskoe ⑮, a Russian-style wooden *dacha* (country house), built in 1819 by the architect Snethlage, who created the Alexandrowka estate in Potsdam. The *dacha* was a present from King Friedrich Wilhelm III to his daughter and son-in-law, the future Tsar Nicholas I. Following a fire in 1985 the *dacha* was reconstructed, and it currently houses an excellent restaurant. Nearby you will find a bus stop where you can catch buses back to the S-Bahn Wannsee.

Tips for Walkers

Beginning of the walk: the jetty for the ferry to Pfaueninsel.
Length: 4.4 km (2.7 miles).
Duration: 2.5–3 hours.
Getting there: bus 218 or 316 from S-Bahn Wannsee; or ferry from Wannsee or Potsdam.
Stops: Pfaueninsel has no restaurants. "Wirtshaus zur Pfaueninsel" is by the jetty; "Blockhaus Nikolskoe" is in Nikolskoe. Schloss Pfaueninsel: **Open** Apr–Oct: 10am–5:30pm Tue–Sun. **Tel** 80 58 68 30.
W spsg.de

The little ferry on the Havel river which takes passengers to Pfaueninsel

Glienicke and Babelsberg

This guided walk takes you through an area covered by two interesting palace-park complexes – Glienicke and Babelsberg. They were built originally for members of the royal family during the mid-19th century. The buildings of Glienicke were designed by Schinkel, Persius and von Arnim in a Neo-Classical style. Peter Joseph Lenné created the charming park in which they are located. Babelsberg has a more romantic park, which was completed by Hermann von Pückler-Muskau. It is maintained in a completely different style, with regal Neo-Gothic pavilions.

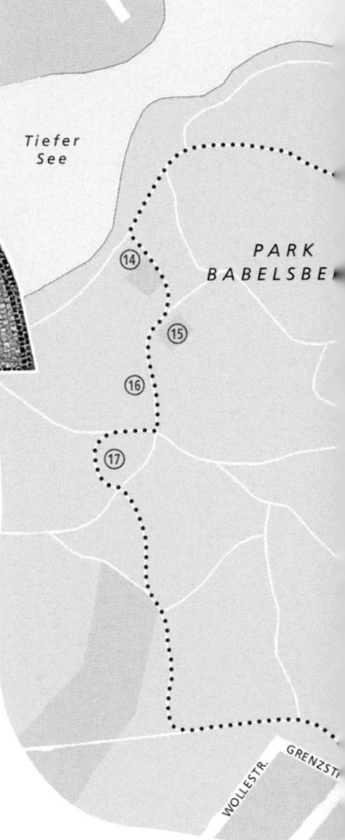

Mosaic from the Klosterhof in the gardens of Klein Glienicke

Around Glienicke

The walk begins by the main gate leading into the park. The southern section of the park has the feel of an Italianate Arcadian garden. Soon on the left you will see the Stibadium ①, a roofed pavilion designed by Ludwig Persius. Nearby you can marvel at the imposing Fountain of Lions ②, decorated with gilded figures of these royal beasts. The fountain stands on the axis of the palace ③, which was built in 1825, according to a design by Karl Friedrich Schinkel for Prince Karl of Prussia. During the summer, you can visit the palace between 10am and 6pm. Beyond the symmetrical, Neo-Classical building extends an irregular cluster of buildings, grouped around a courtyard with a veranda, which include a pergola and staff cottages. You pass by the palace and approach the Coach House ④, designed by Schinkel but refurbished several times. This now houses the Coach House restaurant.

The reconstructed Gothic Gerichtslaube (arcaded courthouse)

Beyond the Coach House you can see the orangery and greenhouses built by Persius ⑤. A path leads in the direction of the lake, but on the way it is worth diverting to the right to the Klosterhof ⑥, a mock monastery with pavilions, also by Persius. In the walls of these buildings are numerous Byzantine and Romanesque architectural elements from Italy. Further to the north extends a second "wild" section of the park created to resemble an alpine and Carpathian landscape, with man-made waterfalls, planks for crossing the water, and hunting lodges. You can return in the direction of the lake and go up to the Casino ⑦, which once contained guest apartments. From here a path extending along the lake takes you to the Grosse Neugierde ⑧, a circular pavilion with a roof supported by Doric columns, based on the Athenian monument to Lysikrates from the 4th century BC. From here there are beautiful views across the Havel river and Glienicker Brücke ⑨, known

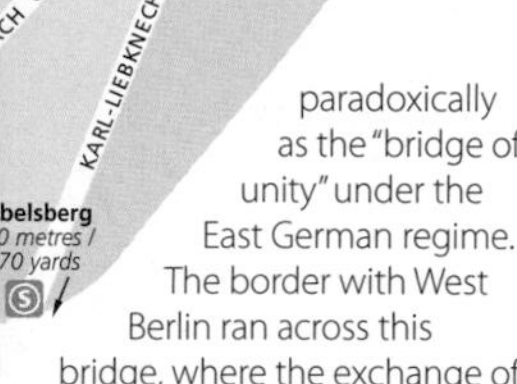

paradoxically as the "bridge of unity" under the East German regime. The border with West Berlin ran across this bridge, where the exchange of spies was conducted during the Cold War. You return via a path along the wall of the main gate, passing the Kleine Neugierde ⑩, a pavilion serving as a tearoom. This was built in the form of an ancient temple, and its walls contain original Roman and Byzantine fragments.

0 metres 300

0 yards 300

Key

• • • Suggested route

For map symbols *see back flap*

From Glienicke to Babelsberg

On leaving the park you cross to the other side of Potsdamer Chaussee and proceed along Mövenstrasse, passing the massive building of the Jagdschloss Glienicke ⑪ on the right. Located on the site of an earlier hunting lodge, its Neo-Mannerist appearance is the result of a massive rebuilding process undertaken in 1889 by Albert Geyer, on behalf of Prince Friedrich Leopold. It now houses an international meeting centre as well as an academy of folk art. Passing the Jagdschloss you turn right into Waldmüllerstrasse, then right again into Lankestrasse, which leads you to the bridge linking Glienicke with Babelsberg.

Around Schloss Babelsberg

From the bridge you head right towards the engine house ⑫, designed by Persius to look like a medieval castle with a tall tower covering the chimney. From here you head towards Schloss Babelsberg ⑬, designed by Karl Friedrich Schinkel for the future Kaiser Wilhelm I of Germany. The palace was built between 1833 and 1835 in a Neo-Gothic style and shows the influence of English architecture on Schinkel. This beautiful, irregular building with many towers and bay windows is one of Schinkel's greatest works. The

The Neo-Gothic Schloss Babelsberg, designed by KF Schinkel

Babelsberg's Neo-Gothic Flatowturm dating from 1853 to 1856

interior is currently closed for renovation.

From here, take the path leading along the edge of the Havel to the so-called Kleines Schloss ⑭. Another Neo-Gothic palace, although much smaller in scale, this was where ladies of the court once resided. It now houses a café.

From here you proceed further to the edge of the lake, taking the left branch to the Neo-Gothic stable ⑮, and further to the Gerichtslaube (Gothic arcaded courthouse) ⑯ which was moved here from Berlin. The final sight on this walk is the Flatowturm ⑰, a Neo-Gothic tower dating from 1853 to 1856, from which there are marvellous views of the surrounding area. From here follow the path to the park exit at Grenzstrasse. Turning left, you reach the bus stop for the No. 694, which goes to S-Bahn Babelsberg station.

Tips for Walkers

Beginning of the walk: bus stop at Glienicker Brücke.
Length: 4.2 km (2.6 miles).
Duration: 3 hours.
Getting there: bus 316 from S-Bahn station Wannsee or ferry from Wannsee or from Potsdam.
Stops: Café at Park Babelsberg; Coach House at Glienicke. Schloss Babelsberg: **Tel** (0331) 969 42 50 for latest information.
W spsg.de

Grunewald

This walk leads initially through one of Berlin's most elegant residential areas, established in 1889. Once the haunt of politicians, wealthy industrialists, renowned artists and academics, some villas now serve as the headquarters of academic institutes. This walk continues through the forest to a small hunting lodge with an interesting art collection, and ends at the edge of the Grunewald in a residential estate of elegant villas, home of the Brücke-Museum.

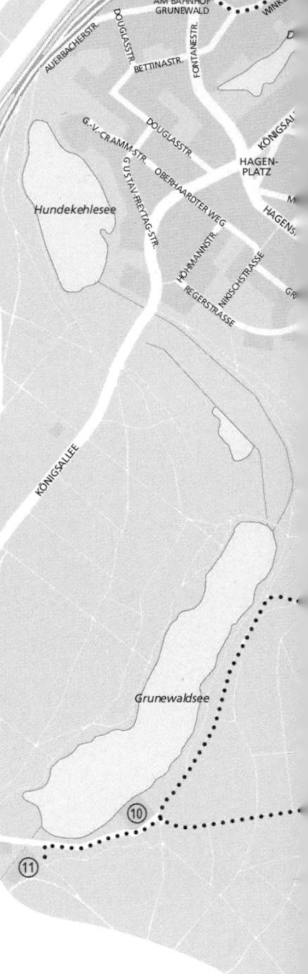

The elegant villa at Winklerstrasse No. 11

From Bahnhof Grunewald to Hagenstrasse

From the S-Bahn Grunewald station follow the signs to "Grunewald (Ort)". Be sure to take a close look at the station itself ① – this picturesque wooden-framed building was built in 1899. The station has a dark past, though, as Berlin's Jews were transported from here to the concentration camps. From the square in front of the station, go along Winklerstrasse, which turns left. Along the way you will pass stunningly beautiful villas. The Neo-Classical house at No. 15, dating from 1899, was home to architect Ewald Becher ②. Not much further on the same side of the road, at No. 11, is a villa dating from 1906 ③. It was designed by Hermann Muthesius, who transplanted onto German soil the style of English rustic building. On the right at No. 12 is Villa Maren, dating from 1897, an example of a Neo-Renaissance building in the style of an Italian palazzo with *sgraffito* decorations ④. The villa at No. 8–10, dating from 1902, boasts costly stone elevations, which fan out richly with decorations in the German Renaissance style ⑤. By this villa turn right into Hasensprung, which leads across the bridge decorated with running hares, dividing Dianasee from Königssee. You reach Königsallee and turn left before immediately turning right into Lassenstrasse, and then right again into Bismarckstrasse, which leads to a small square where you can marvel at the picturesque Neo-Gothic Grunewald-Kirche ⑥. From here go left into Furtwänglerstrasse, where it is worth looking at the villa at No. 15, a beautiful example of a southern German country house ⑦. Next turn right into Hubertusbader Strasse, where at No. 25 an interesting villa with Neo-Classical motifs has survived ⑧, which is the work of Arnold Hartmann, dating from 1896. He is also responsible for the villa at No. 23 Seebergsteig, featuring fantastic elevations decorated with Secessionist motifs ⑨. From here, continue along Hubertusbader Strasse to Hagenstrasse.

Rose window, Grunewald-Kirche

From Hagenstrasse to the Brücke-Museum

Cut through Hagenstrasse and continue further, straight into Wildpfad, where you turn left in Waldmeisterstrasse, which leads along the fence of the grounds of private clubs. Turn right into Eichhörnchensteig,

0 metres 400

0 yards 400

Key

• • • Suggested route

For map symbols *see back flap*

which gradually becomes surrounded by forest and changes from being a road into a forest path. Once past the grounds of the private clubs, follow a road which goes gently to the right, and down to the edge of the picturesque Grunewaldsee.

Turn left and continue along its edge to Jagdschloss Grunewald ⑩. This is one of the oldest civic buildings to survive in Berlin. It was built for the Elector Joachim II in 1542, and around 1700 it was rebuilt in a Baroque style. Through the gate you enter a courtyard enclosed on three sides with household buildings. In the small palace is Berlin's only surviving Renaissance hall. It houses a collection of paintings, with canvases by Rubens and van Dyck among others. In the east wing is the small Waldmuseum, with illustrations that depict forest life. Following a fire, which destroyed the roof and other parts of the building, the Jagdschloss underwent extensive renovation work and reopened in 2009.

From the palace you proceed further along the edge to Forsthaus Paulsborn ⑪ *(see p242)*. This picturesque building was constructed in 1905, according to a design by Friedrich Wilhelm Göhre. The entire building is maintained in the style of a hunting lodge with decorations that reflect hunting themes. During the

Restaurant in the Forsthaus Paulsborn near Jagdschloss Grunewald

The household buildings in the hunting lodge in Grunewald

summer the garden is filled with tables, where you can enjoy a tasty meal and have a rest, following the walk. From Paulsborn you return to Jagdschloss Grunewald; at the crossroads you should take the central avenue signposted "Wilmersdorf". This leads through the forest and emerges on Pücklerstrasse. Passing modern de luxe villas you continue straight on, and then turn right into Fohlenweg, then turn right again into Bussardsteig, at the end of which is the Brücke-Museum *(see p184)* ⑫. It is also worth looking at the exhibition of sculptures by Bernhard Heiliger arranged in the garden surrounding the villa at Käuzchensteig No. 8. From here you continue to Clayallee, where buses on the No. 115 route operate.

Tips for Walkers

Beginning of the walk: Grunewald S-Bahn station.
Distance: 3 km (1.8 miles).
Duration: 2.5–3 hours.
Getting there: S-Bahn line 3 or 7; U-Bahn Oskar-Helene-Heim; Bus 115.
Museum: Jagdschloss Grunewald. **Tel** 813 35 97.
Open Apr–Oct: 10am–6pm Thu–Sun; Nov–Mar: guided tours only, 11am, 1pm & 3pm Sat, Sun & hols.
Stops: The Grunewald area has numerous cafés and restaurants, including Forsthaus Paulsborn near Jagdschloss Grunewald.

TRAVELLERS' NEEDS

WHERE TO STAY

Berlin has a good selection of hotels to suit any budget. Many of the expensive hotels belong to well-known international chains, but you can also find reasonably priced rooms in and around the centre. There are good-quality mid-range hotels in eastern Berlin, where many new hotels have been built recently. There is no lack of luxurious hotels in eastern Berlin, either, particularly around Unter den Linden. Many of the more affordable hotels in the western part of Berlin require urgent repairs. The area around Grunewald is an oasis of peace that will guarantee a good rest. From the numerous hotels in Berlin, this section highlights some of the best; these have been categorized according to themes, location and price. Details about each of the hotels can be found on pages 222–5. Information about alternative ways of spending a night can be found on pages 220–21.

The elegant lobby of the Hotel Adlon Kempinski *(see p225)*

Where to Look

There are a few areas in Berlin with large concentrations of hotels. In each area there is usually at least one luxury hotel as well as several more affordable places. In Charlottenburg, around Kurfürstendamm and Tauentzienstrasse, are well-known hotels, such as the Kempinski Hotel Bristol Berlin, Savoy, Palace Berlin and the Steigenberger. Bear in mind that this part of Berlin was severely damaged during World War II and the majority of these hotels occupy modern buildings; hotels in old buildings, like the Brandenburger Hof, are a rarity. Inexpensive hotels and pensions can be found in the side streets off the main road, but ask to see the rooms before you decide. Good hotels are also situated in the east part of Tiergarten, around Lützowufer.

The most luxurious hotels can be found in eastern Berlin, where many first-class hotels occupy lavishly restored historic landmark buildings. The Adlon (now called Hotel Adlon Kempinski), Regent and Hotel de Rome, situated in the western part of Mitte around Unter den Linden, are the most luxurious. In the eastern part of this area, around Alexanderplatz, the hotels are more reasonably priced but still offer good-quality rooms.

Grunewald is an oasis of peace far from the bustle of Berlin. There is the luxurious Schlosshotel Berlin, as well as cosy pensions and little hotels, some set in 19th-century villas and palaces.

If you don't mind staying outside the centre of Berlin, you should head for Neukölln. Here, close to Treptower Park, is the enormous Estrel – the largest hotel in Germany.

Hotel Prices

Hotel prices in Berlin do not alter much with the season. However, major events and trade fairs do push up prices. Many more luxurious hotels offer weekend discounts and often, if you just turn up without a reservation, you can find yourself a good deal. If you intend to stay for an extended period of time, try to negotiate a better rate. Many hotels offer discounts if you book ahead via their website.

Hidden Extras

In Germany, taxes are included in hotel room rates, but you are expected to tip for any additional services, such as bringing luggage to the room or booking a theatre ticket. Hotels from the Dorint chain are an exception: they provide a range of services (such as free bicycle hire) at no additional cost.

There is also no hard-and-fast rule about breakfast: it is best to ask if it is included in the price when making a reservation.

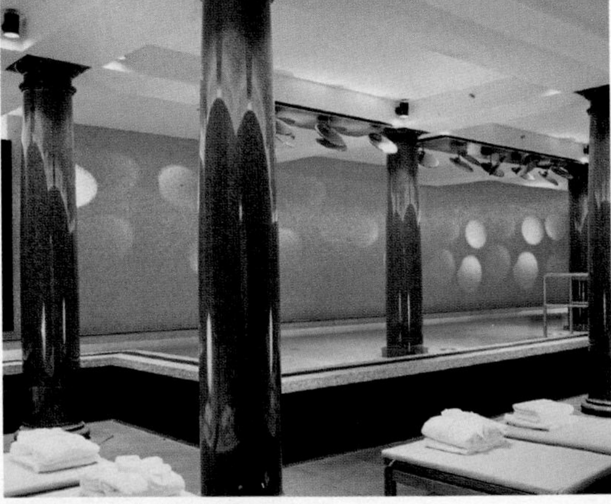

Swimming pool at the Hotel de Rome *(see p225)*

◀ Galeries Lafayette, Friedrichstrasse

One of the artist-decorated rooms In the Arte Luise Kunsthotel *(see p224)*

Most Berlin hotels have their own parking spaces, but rates are sometimes exorbitant. Ask about telephone charges before using the phone in your room and check the exchange rates before using this service. Items from the minibar and paid-television channels can also turn out to be surprisingly costly. Wi-Fi is available at most hotels; however, you may be charged for using the Internet.

Facilities

There is no standardized system of categorizing hotels by stars in Germany, although the price of a room usually reflects the quality. Small hotels usually include breakfast – typically rolls, jam, chocolate spread, cereal, cold meats, cheese and coffee. They will probably not have a restaurant and their services are limited. Larger hotels tend to provide a full American buffet on top of the traditional German fare.

If you are staying for a longer period, consider an Aparthotel (an apartment, complete with a full kitchen), or a private apartment (see www.craigslist.org/berlin or www.airbnb.com). This is a good idea if travelling with a small group.

Saunas and Spas

Many of the more expensive hotels are equipped with spa and sauna facilities. These are usually unisex (though some spas have women's days) and it is very unusual for either sex to wear a swimsuit. Guests should be prepared to only wear towels and for other sauna users to be in the nude. In fact, wearing swimsuits in sauna areas is often considered rude and unhygienic, particularly in Finnish or steam saunas, as well as in whirlpools. Spa etiquette usually also calls for silence in the room. In dry Finnish saunas, an "Aufguss", the repeated infusion of fresh herbs and heat, is usually announced.

When entering a steam sauna, clean the seat before you sit down. There is usually a water hose at the entrance for this purpose. After 8–15 minutes in the sauna, shower or rinse off with ice-cold water (the cold-water bath is only suitable for the physically fit). Rest and then continue the cycle once or twice. Do not drink alcohol when visiting a sauna, and make sure you take in fluids and vitamins (usually offered in the form of water and lemon slices).

Conference room in the Hotel Villa Kastania *(see p225)*

Hotel spas, such as those at the Grand Hyatt, Hotel de Rome and Hotel Intercontinental, are exceptional. In winter, try the Badeschiff Arena, a sauna and swimming pool complex built on pontoons on the Spree river *(see p272)*.

How to Book

You can book a room in Berlin by telephone, email or online. If you prefer, you can use the city's tourist service **Berlin Tourismus Marketing** *(see p221)*, www.visitberlin.de. This company can make your booking in hotels throughout Berlin. When making a reservation be prepared to give your credit card details

If you are already in Berlin and would like to find a comfortable room, your best option is to go to one of the large tourist information bureaux. Some of the best of these are situated in the **Neues Kranzler-Eck**, at the **Brandenburg Gate**, and at **Hauptbahnhof** *(see p221)*.

Private Rooms

Bed-and-Breakfast-style accommodation is not particularly popular in Berlin, although this kind of service can be found in some of the residential districts far from the city centre. You can obtain information about them from tourist information bureaux and the other organizations whose numbers are listed in the Directory *(see p221)*.

Travelling with Children

Travelling with children in Berlin should not present a problem. A cot can be requested in most hotels, and there is usually no extra charge for having a small child in the room, although an extra bed for an older child may sometimes incur a cost. In better hotels, a reliable babysitter can be obtained at a few hours' notice. In hotel restaurants, high-chairs for children are standard.

Modern lounge area in Motel One Berlin Alexanderplatz *(see p222)*

Disabled Travellers

Nearly all top-quality and luxury hotels are able to accommodate disabled travellers – at least one entrance will have wheelchair access and some rooms will have specially adapted bathrooms. Unfortunately, the situation in mid-range and lower standard hotels is not as promising; special equipment is a rarity. In very old buildings, there may not be an elevator. The **Hotel Mondial** *(see p223)*, located near Kurfürstendamm, is recommended for disabled travellers. It has many facilities for wheelchair users in all its public rooms and has as many as 22 bedrooms equipped for people with special needs.

Deposits

In many Berlin hotels, a deposit may be requested either when reserving the room or upon checking in at the hotel. A credit card is the most common way to secure a room over the telephone. Otherwise, be prepared to use cash to pay about 20 to 40 per cent of the price for one night's stay. The amount you pay as a deposit should always be credited to the final bill. In some smaller hotels or pensions, don't be surprised if you are asked to pay for your first night's accommodation in full on arrival.

Youth Hostels

It is easy to find inexpensive accommodation in Berlin at a youth hostel. The **DJH (Landesverband Berlin-Brandenburg)**, an organization that belongs to the International Youth Hostels Association, gives discounts to all its members. Membership is usually inexpensive and you will have to join to stay at a hostel. The DJH has hostels in different locations throughout Berlin. There are also many independent youth hostels and hotels for students in Berlin that do not belong to any organization. You can find them at www.hostelworld.com.

The type of accommodation usually consists of dormitory-style rooms with bunk beds. There is often a communal bathroom on each floor and a kitchen is usually available for cooking your own meals. Most youth hostels have a dining room where breakfast and a hot evening meal are served. Some youth hostels are closed during the day, allowing no access to the rooms; confirm this in advance.

Camping

Camping is a popular pastime throughout Germany, and the **Deutscher Camping Club** has a lot of information about campsites in and around Berlin. This organisation also provides information about independently run campsites in Berlin.

Campsites in Berlin are mostly not very close to the city centre. They are usually open all year. **DCC-Gatow** offers a quiet setting, **DCC-Kladow** is located on the edge of a wood with access to a lake and **Campingplatz Krossinsee** has an adventure playground, making it especially popular with families with children.

The majority of people staying at campsites are young, particularly during the Oktoberfest *(see p52)* and in June, when the Christopher Street Day Parade takes place *(see p51)*. During these times some campsites can be very busy and noisy.

Entrance to Aletto Kudamm *(see p222)*

Organized Youth Groups

Berlin has a large base of accommodation for organized youth groups. Most of these are hostel-style accommodation, situated on the outskirts of the city. They were established not only for the purpose of school trips but also for children from West Berlin; until the unification of Germany in 1990, it was difficult for youth groups to organize trips to the countryside so they had to opt for trips to the Grunewald instead. Information about availability and bookings is offered by **Berlin Tourismus Marketing** and by larger tourist information centres, such as at Neues Kranzler Eck.

Room with period furnishings in Pension Funk *(see p223)*

Recommended Hotels

The hotels on pages 222–5 are a selection of the best budget, business, charming, boutique and luxury hotels in Berlin. They are first listed according to theme, and then alphabetically by area. Most are spread across the main tourist areas, although some that are further afield are included if they offer particularly good value for money, facilities, service or charm. B&Bs, guesthouses and apartments are also listed. What they all have in common is that, regardless of category and price, they have something special to offer.

Where a hotel has an exceptional feature, such as great-value rates or spectacular views, it has been highlighted as a DK Choice.

DIRECTORY

Information and Booking

Berlin Tourismus Marketing
Am Karlsbad 11, Berlin.
Map 14 D1.
Tel 25 00 25.
W visitberlin.de

Brandenburg Gate
Pariser Platz, southern building.
Map 8 E3.
Open 9:30am–6pm daily (to 7pm in summer).

Hauptbahnhof
Europaplatz 1, level 0, northern entrance.
Map 8 D1.
Open 8am–10pm daily.

Potsdam Tourismus Service
Am Neuen Markt 1.
Tel (0331) 27 55 88 99.
W potsdamtourismus de

Tourist Information
Neues Kranzler-Eck, Kurfürstendamm 22.
Map 12 D1.
Open 10am–9:30pm Mon–Sat.

Private Rooms

Bed & Breakfast in Berlin
Tel 44 05 05 82.
W bed-and-breakfast-berlin.de

Coming Home
Tel 21 79 800.
W coming-home.org

Erste Mitwohn-zentrale
Sybelstrasse 53, 10629 Berlin-Charlottenburg.
Map 11 A2.
Tel 324 30 31.
W mitwohn.com

Fine and mine
Neue Schönhauser Str. 20, 10178 Berlin.
Map 9 C2.
Tel 23 55 120.
W fineandmine.com

Wohnwitz
Holsteinische Strasse 55, 10717 Berlin-Wilmersdorf.
Map 11 C4, C5.
Tel 861 82 22.
W wohnwitz.com

Disabled Travellers

Berliner Behinderten-verband
Jägerstrasse 63d, 10117 Berlin-Mitte.
Tel 204 38 47.
W bbv-ev.de

Der Landes-beauftragte für Menschen mit Behinderung
Oranienstrasse 106, 10997 Berlin. **Tel** 90 28 29 17.

Youth Hostels

DJH (Landesverband Berlin-Brandenburg)
Service centre: Kluckstrasse 3, 10785 Berlin.
Tel 264 95 20.
Open 8am–6pm Mon–Fri.

Hostelworld
W Hostelworld.com

Jugendherberge Berlin am Wannsee
Badeweg 1, 14129 Berlin.
Tel 803 20 34

Jugendherberge Berlin International
Kluckstrasse 3, 10785 Berlin. **Map** 13 C1.
Tel 747 68 79 10.

Jugendherberge Ernst Reuter
Hermsdorfer Damm 48, 13467 Berlin.
Tel 404 16 10.

Camping

Campingplatz Krossinsee
Wernsdorfer Str. 38, 12527 Berlin. **Tel** 675 86 87.**Open** Nov–Mar: 9am–5pm; Apr–Oct: 8am–8pm; Jul–Aug: 8am–9pm

DCC-Campingplatz Berlin-Gatow
Kladower Damm 213–17, 14089 Berlin. **Tel** 365 43 40.**Open** Apr–Sep: 6am–1pm, 3–10pm; Oct–Mar: 8am–1pm & 3–9pm.

DCC-Campingplatz Berlin-Kladow
Krampnitzer Weg 111, 14089 Berlin. **Tel** 365 27 97. **Open** Apr–Sep: 6am–1pm & 3–10pm; Oct–Mar: 8am–1pm & 3–9pm.

Deutscher Camping Club
Kladower Damm 207–213, 14089 Berlin. **Tel** 218 60 71.
W dccberlin.de

Where to Stay

Budget

Around Unter den Linden

City Hostel Berlin €
Glinkastrasse 5, 10117
Tel *238 866 850* **Map** 8 F5
W cityhostel-berlin.com
A hostel with modern rooms with en-suite baths. Breakfast and Wi-Fi are included. Great terrace bar.

East of the Centre

City Stay €
Rosenstrasse 16, 10178
Tel *236 240 31* **Map** 9 C2
W citystay.de
Loft-style rooms, a lobby bar, a cobbled courtyard and free Wi-Fi. Elaborate breakfast spread.

Motel One Berlin Alexanderplatz €
Dircksenstrasse 36, 10179
Tel *200 540 80* **Map** 9 C2
W motel-one.com
Centrally located, modern hotel. Relaxed and gay-friendly.

North of the Centre

A&O Berlin Hauptbahnhof €
Lehrter Strasse 11, 10557
Tel *809 47 51 09* **Map** 7 C1
W aohostels.com
Dorms, singles and doubles (with private showers available). Comfortable lounge area. Pet-friendly.

Generator Mitte €
Oranienburger Strasse 65, 10117
Tel *921 037 680*
W generatorhostels.com
Brand-new hostel with dorms, single rooms and doubles with private bathrooms.

Hotel Albrechtshof €
Albrechtstrasse 8, 10117
Tel *30 88 60* **Map** 8 F2
W hotel-albrechtshof.de
A reasonably priced hotel with simple and tasteful rooms, a garden and rooftop views.

Meininger City Hotel €
Ella-Trebe-Strasse 9, 10557
Tel *983 210 73* **Map** 8 D1
W meiningerhotels.com
Modern and functional rooms with free Wi-Fi. There is a games room. Excellent transport links.

Transit Loft €
Immanuelkirchstrasse 14a, 10405
Tel *484 937 73* **Map** 2 F4
W transit-loft.de
Medium-sized, family-friendly hotel in a converted factory. Clean, well-maintained rooms.

DK Choice

Circus €€
Rosenthaler Strasse 1, 10119
Tel *200 039 39* **Map** 9 B1
W circus-berlin.de
This fun hotel often wins accolades for its high standards of service and unbeatable value for money. The location on Rosenthaler Platz is another big plus for those drawn to the city's nightlife. Circus also offers guests numerous extras, from bike rentals to rickshaw tours and baby-sitting. Enjoy the elaborate breakfast spread, or a coffee at the Circus Cafe.

Tiergarten

Hotel am Schloss Bellevue €
Paulstrasse 3, 10557
Tel *391 12 27* **Map** 7 B2
W hotelamschlossbellevue.de
Small, cosy hotel with innovative rooms decorated by a young local graffiti artist.

Familie Herfort €€
Flensburger Strasse 27, 10557
Tel *399 043 33* **Map** 6 F2
W fewobe-berlin.de
Choose from nine spacious, well-equipped apartments with impeccable service.

Kreuzberg

Three Little Pigs Hostel Berlin €
Stresemannstrasse 66, 10963
Tel *263 958 80* **Map** 14 F1
W three-little-pigs.de
Old convent building in a vibrant, multicultural area. Free parking.

Price Guide
Prices are based on one night's stay in high season for a standard double room, inclusive of service charges and taxes.

€	up to €80
€€	€80–€180
€€€	over €180

Around Kurfürstendamm

Air in Berlin Hotel €
Ansbacher Strasse 6, 10787
Tel *212 99 20* **Map** 12 F1
W hotelairinberlin.de
This three-star hotel has modern comfortable rooms, many with a balcony or terrace.

Aletto Kudamm €
Hardenbergstrasse 21, 10623
Tel *233 21 41 00* **Map** 6 D5
W aletto.de
This simple hotel offers a multitude of leisure activities and opportunities to socialize.

ArtHotel Connection €–€€
Fuggerstrasse 33, 10777
Tel *210 21 88 00* **Map** 12 F2
W arthotel-connection.de
Gay-friendly hotel in an Art Nouveau building. Great service.

Berolina an der Gedächtniskirche €
Rankestrasse 35, 10789
Tel *236 396 82* **Map** 12 E1
W berolinahotels.de
No-frills hotel with cosy rooms. Close to West End restaurants and bars, and the Berlin Zoo.

City Pension €
Stuttgarter Platz 9, 10627
Tel *327 74 10* **Map** 11 A1
W city-pension.de
Small, friendly hotel with spacious, well-appointed rooms. Some have en-suite showers.

Bold interior design in Circus

Hotel Pension Kürfurst €–€€
Bleibtreustrasse 34/35, 10707
Tel *885 68 20* **Map** 11 B2
W kurfuerst.com
Beautiful Art Nouveau mansion with generously sized rooms that are tastefully furnished.

Pension Funk €
Fasanenstrasse 69, 10719
Tel *882 71 93* **Map** 12 D2
W hotel-pensionfunk.de
Early 20th-century town house with period features. Decent-sized rooms.

Further Afield

East Side Hotel €
Mühlenstrasse 6, 10243
Tel *29 38 33*
W eastsidecityhotel.de
Single, double and twin rooms in a historic building. Excellent on-site restaurant.

Econtel Hotel €
Sömmeringstrasse 24–26, 10589
Tel *34 68 10* **Map** 5 A2
W amber-hotels.de
Practical, well-run hotel in a quiet residential district; the X9 bus to Tegel airport stops right outside.

Michelberger Hotel €–€€
Warschauer Strasse 39/40, 10243
Tel *297 785 90*
W michelbergerhotel.com
Quirky but comfortable rooms, and a friendly vibe. Enjoy live music in the bar.

Pension Rotdorn €
Heerstrasse 36, 14055
Tel *300 992 92* **Map** 3 A5
W pension-rotdorn.de
Family-run pension set in a grand old mansion. Decent-sized rooms. Free parking and Wi-Fi.

Business

Around Unter den Linden

Arcotel John F €€
Werderscher Markt 11, 10117
Tel *405 04 60* **Map** 9 B4
W arcotelhotels.com
Modern hotel with large rooms and an unbeatable location. Great restaurant. Excellent service

Meliá Hotel €€
Friedrichstrasse 103, 10117
Tel *206 079 00* **Map** 8 F3
W meliaberlin.com
Spanish chain hotel perfectly located for major sights. Plush, comfortable rooms and a fully equipped gym.

The plush and inviting lobby of Derag Livinghotel Henriette

East of the Centre

Derag Livinghotel Henriette €€
Neue Rossstrasse 13, 10179
Tel *246 009 00* **Map** 9 C4
W deraghotels.de
Reputable chain hotel with comfortable, cosy rooms. Classy decor and great service.

North of the Centre

Mercure Hotel Berlin City €–€€
Invalidenstrasse 38, 10115
Tel *30 82 60* **Map** 1 A5
W accorhotels.com
Modern, centrally located hotel offering luxurious three-star rooms.

Adina Apartment Hotels €€
Platz vor dem Neuen Tor 6, 10115
Tel *200 03 20* **Map** 8 F1
W adina.eu
Well-furnished studios and apartments equipped with all modern amenities.

Kastanienhof €€
Kastanienallee 65, 10119
Tel *44 30 50* **Map** 2 D4
W kastanienhof.biz
Friendly hotel with modern, tastefully decorated rooms.

Maritim proArte Hotel €€
Friedrichstrasse 151, 10117
Tel *30 203 35* **Map** 8 F3
W maritim.de
Large, contemporary hotel with clean and generous sized rooms.

Tiergarten

Novotel am Tiergarten €–€€
Strassse des 17 Juni 106, 10623
Tel *60 03 50* **Map** 6 E4
W accorhotels.com
Comfortable large hotel with every possible four star amenity.

Hotel Abion Spreebogen €€
Alt Moabit 99, 10559
Tel *39 92 00* **Map** 6 F2
W abion-hotel.de
Slick hotel, great for corporate travellers. Spa service available.

Hotel Tiergarten €€
Alt-Moabit 89, 10559
Tel *39 98 96* **Map** 6 F1
W hotel-tiergarten.de
Bright, spacious rooms set in a 19th-century apartment block. Great breakfast buffet.

Around Kurfürstendamm

Mondial €–€€
Kurfürstendamm 47, 10707
Tel *88 41 10* **Map** 11 B2
W hotel-mondial.com
Rooms are spacious and pleasantly decorated at this hotel with disabled facilities.

Ellington Hotel €€
Nürnberger Strasse 50–5, 10789
Tel *68 31 50* **Map** 12 E2
W ellington-hotel.com
Historic 19th-century building with superior double rooms..

H10 Kudamm €€
Joachimstaler Strasse 31, 10719
Tel *322 92 23 00* **Map** 12 D2
W hotelh10berlinkudamm.com
Modern hotel in a converted 19th-century school building. Beauty and fitness centre on site.

Further Afield

Andel's €€
Landsberger Allee 106, 10369
Tel *153 05 30* **Map** 10 F2
W vi-hotels.com
Award-winning, British-designed hotel with great views over Berlin. Chic and spacious rooms.

Charming Hotels

North of the Centre

Honigmond Garden Hotel €€
Invalidenstrasse 122, 10115
Tel *284 455 77* **Map** 1 A5
W honigmond-berlin.de
Individually decorated rooms and a secluded courtyard garden.

Jurine €€
Schwedter Strasse 15, 10119
Tel *443 29 90* **Map** 2 D4
W hotel-jurine.de
Family-run hotel in a quiet location. Enjoy the healthy breakfast spread. Free Wi-Fi.

Myer's Hotel €€
Metzer Strasse 26, 10405
Tel *44 01 41 04* **Map** 2 E5
W myershotels.de
Classy hotel with a touch of elegance. Unwind in the tea room or on the outdoor terrace.

For more information on types of hotels *see pp218–21*

Tiergarten

Hansablick €–€€
Flotowstrasse 6, 10555
Tel *390 48 00* **Map** 6 E3
W hansablick.de
It's worth paying a little extra here for one of the de luxe double rooms. Free Internet in the lounge, plus a fitness room.

DK Choice

Altberlin €€
Potsdamer Strasse 67, 10785
Tel *26 06 70* **Map** 13 C1
W altberlin-hotel.de
All 50 rooms at this cosy hotel converted from a town house, are furnished in authentic period style. The excellent on-site restaurant offers traditional cuisine. Great modern amenities in an enviable location.

Kreuzberg

Hotel Johann €€
Johanniterstrasse 8, 10961
Tel *225 07 40* **Map** 15 B3
W hotel-johann-berlin.de
The bright, sunny rooms here have barrel-vaulted ceilings. Breakfast is served in the garden in summer.

Riehmers Hofgarten €€
Yorckstrasse 83, 10965
Tel *780 988 00* **Map** 14 F4
W riehmers-hofgarten.de
A grand mansion with elegant decor set in 19th-century courtyards. All modern amenities.

Around Kurfürstendamm

Art Nouveau €–€€
Leibnizstrrasse 59, 10629
Tel *327 74 40* **Map** 11 A1
W hotelartnouveau.de
Spacious, tastefully furnished rooms and suites with stucco ceilings and wooden floors.

25Hours Hotel €€
Budapester Strasse 40, 10629
Tel *0800 374 683 57* **Map** 12 E1
W designhotels.com
This stylish hotel is in the listed Bikinihaus building. The rooftop restaurant boasts great views of Zoo Berlin and of the city.

Axel €€
Lietzenburger Strasse 13/15, 10789
Tel *210 028 93* **Map** 12 F2
W axelhotels.com
Oriented towards the gay community but open to everyone. Great views from the skybar.

DK Choice

Louisa's Place €€
Ku'damm 160, 10709
Tel *63 10 30* **Map** 11 A2
W louisas-place.net
This modernized and well-furnished 1900s apartment building preserves all its original architectural features. The suites are lavish and vary in size. Relax in the hotel spa and heated indoor pool or enjoy the massage services on offer.

Mark Hotel Meineke €€
Meinekestrasse 10, 10719
Tel *0800 101 08 80* **Map** 12 D2
W berlinmarkhotels.de
Charming 19th-century town house, minutes from Ku'damm.

Further Afield

Hotel Pension Enzian €
Hortensienstrasse 28, 12203
Tel *832 50 75*
W hotel-pension-enzian.de
A charming hotel with spacious rooms near the Botanical Garden. Excellent on-site restaurant.

Ostel Hostel €
Wriezener Karree 5, 10243
Tel *257 686 60*
W ostel.eu
Set in a 1980s apartment block, this fun hotel recreates East Berlin decor of the 1970s and 1980s.

Schloss Hotel im Grunewald €€
Brahmsstrasse 10, 14193
Tel *89 58 40*
W schlosshotelberlin.com
Luxurious mansion with opulent rooms, restaurant, bar, cigar lounge and impeccable service.

Entrance to the luxurious Brandenburger Hof hotel

Design/Boutique

Around Unter den Linden

Cosmo €€
Spittelmarkt 13, 10117
Tel *585 822 22* **Map** 9 B5
W designhotels.com
A haven of tranquillity amid the bustle of the Mitte. Sleek rooms.

Hotel Gendarm Nouveau €€
Charlottenstrasse 61, 10117
Tel *206 06 60* **Map** 9 A4
W hotel-gendarm-berlin.de
Small hotel with tastefully furnished rooms and great service.

East of the Centre

Arte-Luise Kunsthotel €€
Luisenstrasse 19, 10117
Tel *28 44 80* **Map** 8 E2
W luise-berlin.com
Rooms here are individually decorated by local artists. Excellent on-site restaurant.

Lux 11 €€
Rosa-Luxemburg-Strasse 9–13, 10178
Tel *936 28 00* **Map** 10 C2
W lux-eleven.com
A minimalist hotel with clean, bright and spacious rooms and apartments. Fantastic service.

North of the Centre

DK Choice

Ackselhaus €€
Belforter Strasse 21, 10405
Tel *443 376 33* **Map** 2 E4
W ackselhaus.de
A beautifully restored 19th-century property with lots of charm and a lovely breakfast garden. The rooms and suites are individually designed and decorated with flair. There is also a special honeymoon suite. Relax in the lovely Thai garden.

Casa Camper €€€
Weinmeisterstrasse 1, 10178
Tel *200 034 10* **Map** 9 C1
W casacamper.com
A hotel with sleek design and spacious rooms, an excellent on-site restaurant and free Wi-Fi.

Tiergarten

Mandala €€–€€€
Potsdamer Strasse 3, 10785
Tel *590 05 00 00* **Map** 8 D5
W themandala.de
Luxurious living in studio rooms, suites or penthouses with views.

For key to prices *see p222*

Nhow Berlin's striking and quirky interior design

Around Kurfürstendamm

Artemisia Frauen Hotel €
Brandenburgische Strasse 18, 10707
Tel *860 93 20* **Map** 11 A3
W frauenhotel-berlin.de
A women-only hotel with a pleasant roof terrace. Great breakfast spread.

Bleibtreu €–€€
Bleibtreustrasse 31, 10707
Tel *88 47 40* **Map** 11 B2
W bleibtreu.com
Well-equipped rooms with pine-wood furnishings. Deli-restaurant, fitness centre and on-site spa.

Askanischer Hof €€
Kurfürstendamm 53, 10707
Tel *881 80 33* **Map** 11 B2
W askanischer-hof.de
Art Deco features and glitzy interiors. Rooms vary in size but all are decorated with antiques.

Q Hotel €€
Knesebeckstrasse 67, 10623
Tel *810 06 60* **Map** 11 C1
W hotel-q.com
Surprisingly affordable designer hotel aimed mainly at corporate travellers. Futuristic decor.

Brandenburger Hof €€€
Eislebener Strasse 14, 10789
Tel *21 40 50* **Map** 12 D2
W brandenburger-hof.com
A charming luxury hotel with lavish rooms and elegant decor. Soothing Japanese winter garden.

Further Afield

DK Choice

Nhow Berlin €€
Stralauer Allee 3, 10245
Tel *290 29 90*
W nhow-hotels.com
An amazing cantilevered structure jutting out over the Spree, this offbeat hotel will delight all lovers of design and music, which are the dominant themes. Nhow offers guitar and keyboard loans to rooms. There's also a rooftop sound studio.

Propeller Island City Lodge €€
Albrecht-Achilles-Strasse 58, 10709
Tel *891 90 16*
W propeller-island.com
Themed rooms, whimsically designed and furnished in a rather offbeat manner. Good service.

Villa Kastania €€
Kastanienallee 20, 14052
Tel *300 00 20* **Map** 3 A5
W villakastania.com
Rooms are decorated with great attention to detail. Spa services available. Impeccable service.

Luxury Hotels

Around Unter den Linden

DK Choice

Adlon Kempinski €€€
Unter den Linden 77, 10117
Tel *226 110* **Map** 8 F3
W kempinski.com
The Adlon has won numerous plaudits, both for its impeccable standards of service and for being the final word in luxury. It offers exquisitely decorated bedrooms, Michelin-starred gourmet dining and a huge spa in which to be pampered.

Hotel de Rome €€€
Behrenstrasse 37, 10117 **Map** 8 F4
Tel *460 60 90*
W roccofortecollection.com
Classy furnishings and alfresco dining on a rooftop terrace.

Regent €€€
Charlottenstrasse 49, 10117
Tel *203 38* **Map** 9 A4
W regenthotels.com
A celebrity magnet, this hotel boasts a Michelin two-star restaurant and other luxurious amenities. Work out in the state-of-the-art health club.

North of the Centre

Soho House €€€
Torstrasse 1, 10119
Tel *405 04 40* **Map** 10 E1
W sohohouseberlin.de
Rooms of various sizes in a prestigious private members club.

Tiergarten

Grand Hotel Esplanade €€
Lützowufer 15, 10785
Tel *25 47 80* **Map** 13 A1
W esplanade.de
Excellent amenities at this plush hotel. Convenient location.

Grand Hyatt €€–€€€
Marlene-Dietrich-Platz 2, 10785
Tel *255 312 34* **Map** 8 D5
W berlin.grand.hyatt.de
Large business hotel with comfortable rooms and a charming sun-bathing terrace.

Around Kurfürstendamm

Savoy €€
Fasanenstrasse 9–10, 10623
Tel *31 10 30* **Map** 12 D1
W hotel-savoy.com
Historic hotel famous for its refined decor. Well-stocked bar.

Swissôtel €€
Augsburger Strasse 44, 10789
Tel *22 01 00* **Map** 12 D1
W swissotel.de
Geared mainly towards business travellers. Large, well-lit rooms and warm service.

Waldorf Astoria €€
Hardenbergstrasse 28, 10623
Tel *814 00 00* **Map** 12 D1
W placeshilton.com
Located in the Zoofenster Tower. Rooms have panoramic views and marble bathrooms.

Sofitel Berlin Kurfürstendamm €€€
Augsburger Strasse 41, 10789
Tel *800 99 90* **Map** 12 D1
W sofitel.com
Sleek high-rise in a great location. Unwind in the wellness centre's sauna and solariums.

Das Stue €€€
Drakestrasse 1, 10787
Tel *311 72 20* **Map** 6 F5
W das-stue.com
Sophisticated Nordic design in a former embassy building by the Tiergarten.

For more information on types of hotels *see pp218–21*

WHERE TO EAT AND DRINK

Given that Berlin is so cosmopolitan, you will find a wider range of restaurants here than in any other city in Germany. International cuisines represented include Indian, Greek, Chinese, Thai and Turkish, as well as Alsatian and Cambodian. Recently, new places have been opened by famous chefs that maintain high European standards of international-style cuisine. There are also plenty of restaurants specializing in local dishes: the food can be a little heavy, but it is usually very tasty and served in large portions. Wherever you are in Berlin, you won't have to travel far to find somewhere to eat – every area has its own cluster of restaurants, cafés and bars, covering a range of styles and prices. Some of the best places are listed on pages 232–43. These have been chosen for their delicious food and/or good value. The listings on pages 244–9 should help those who would like a bite to eat but want the more relaxed setting of a café or bar.

Quarré, at the Adlon hotel *(see p233)*

Where to Go

Although good restaurants and cafés can be found all over Berlin, some of the best gourmet restaurants tend to be located in exclusive hotels, including **Facil** in the Mandala *(see p236)* or **Fischer's Fritz** in the Regent *(see p232)*. Alternatively, some good restaurants, such as the rustic **Zum Nussbaum** *(see p233)*, can also be found on quiet streets.

The largest concentrations of restaurants are in a number of well-known districts. In the former West Berlin, for example, the most famous restaurants are clustered around Savignyplatz. Good places to eat in the centre can be found in and around Oranienburger Strasse. One of the top spots in Berlin, popular with a younger crowd, is Prenzlauer Berg, near Kollwitzplatz. In the eastern part of Berlin, restaurants in Kreuzberg (particularly along Oranienstrasse) are among the busiest in the city. The places in these areas are all consistently good and offer a wide choice in style and price.

What to Eat

In the morning, nearly all eateries, including those in most hotels, will offer a substantial breakfast. This usually consists of eggs, ham or cold cuts and different kinds of cheese. On Sundays, some places also serve a German buffet-style brunch (breakfast combined with lunch) until 2pm. At lunchtime, it's easy to find an elaborate salad or a bowl of steaming soup almost anywhere. In addition, many restaurants may also offer their standard menus with slightly reduced prices.

The options for an evening meal are practically unlimited. In a restaurant serving local food options may be a tasty pork knuckle or potato soup *(see pp228–9)*. Lovers of Italian cuisine can easily find a good pizzeria or a restaurant serving regional Italian dishes. Fans of Oriental food can choose between many Asian national cuisines, a great variety of which are situated along Prenzlauer Berg and around Savignyplatz. Berlin also has very good Mexican restaurants, particularly around Oranienburger Strasse and in Kreuzberg, and the food served at Greek restaurants is usually quite good and very inexpensive. Vegetarians can easily find something suitable at most restaurants; vegetarian restaurants are marked in the listings *(see pp232–43)*.

Prices and Tipping

Menus, showing meals and their prices, are usually on display outside restaurants and cafés. Prices can vary a great deal. It is possible to eat a three-course meal, without alcohol, for €20, but in the centre of Berlin the price rises to €25–€30. In a top-notch establishment the cost of a meal can be over €150.

Outside Oxymoron *(see p235)*, in the Hackesche Höfe

Outside Dressler, Unter den Linden *(see p232)*

The price of alcohol varies as well, but the cheapest drink is beer. Although prices include service and tax, many Germans will round up the bill. In more expensive restaurants a 10 per cent tip is customary. Some restaurants add "service not included" to their menus and bills. Although it is not legal to demand a tip, it is polite to leave some extra for the waiting staff.

Eating Hours

In general, cafés open at 10am and restaurants at noon; the latter sometimes also close between 3 and 6pm. However, there are a lot of places that stay open late, sometimes until 2 or 3am. Some of the most expensive and best restaurants are only open in the evening and may be closed on one day during the week as well.

Booking

In the most upmarket restaurants, reservations are usually required – in popular places it is advisable to book well in advance. For the majority of good restaurants it is necessary to book only for Friday or Saturday evenings.

Disabled Diners

In order to avoid any problems in advance, you should discuss wheelchair access when booking. Bear in mind, however, that even though a dining room may be accessible on the ground floor, the toilets may be up or down stairs or through a narrow corridor.

Children

Casual restaurants usually welcome children, though this may not be the case in more upmarket establishments. Those that do cater for children may provide highchairs as well as light dishes, particularly during lunchtime. Some places will offer a separate children's menu with small portions. Children are also allowed in pubs and bars.

Reading the Menu

Menus are often written out in German and English, and some restaurants will provide menus in French as well. If you find yourself in a restaurant or bar where the menu is hand-written, ask a waiter for help. Many restaurants offer a menu of the day with seasonal dishes or the chef's specials, which are always worth considering.

Smoking

Smoking is banned in all public places, including restaurants, bars, pubs and clubs, but a handful of restaurants have a separate smoking area or room. In some parts of Berlin, such as Kreuzberg and Friedrichshain, the ban appears to have been ignored.

The stylish Bocca di Bacco *(see p232)*

Recommended Restaurants

The restaurants on pages 232–43 of this guide cover a range of cuisine styles and prices, and are the best of their kind. They are listed by area, mostly in the main tourist districts, although there are a number that merit a special trip further afield. Within these areas, they are listed alphabetically in each of three price categories.

Berlin's restaurant scene offers a huge variety of cuisine types *(see What to Eat, opposite)*.

Where a restaurant is in some way exceptional – perhaps for its cooking, its good-value menus, or family-friendly facilities – it has been highlighted as a DK Choice.

The elegant interior of Facil *(see p236)*

The Flavours of Berlin

To treat your senses in Berlin, you need do nothing more than stroll through the street markets, historic market halls and speciality food shops. Spicy, hot sausages such as *Currywurst* or *Thüringer* will lure you into the traditional German butcheries. The scent of freshly baked rolls and breads wafts from the corner bakeries. Fresh herbs, typical German garden vegetables such as red or green cabbage, and wild mushrooms are spectacularly displayed. Freshwater fish from the region's many lakes and rivers glisten on their beds of ice; particularly popular are pike-perch, eel, trout and even sweet river crabs.

Harzer Roller and *Emmenthaler* cheeses

Wild mushrooms, one of the region's most famous products

Berlin's Hearty Heritage

Historically, Berlin has never been a gourmet capital, and neither has the surrounding, rural Brandenburg region. The Hohenzollern court focused more on its army than on culture and cuisine. But the Great Electors were formidable hunters, and game such as wild boar, rabbit and duck, as well as goose and birds of prey were (and remain) an integral part of Berlin's cuisine. Later, in the 19th century, both the evolving Prussian well-to-do and the working class preferred hearty and simple food over fine dining – not only because Berlin was then a comparatively poor city, but also because of the long and hard winters and generally inclement weather.

Bread and Potatoes

There is an enormous variety of breads and rolls to be found on today's menus. Many are unique to Berlin, such as the wholewheat and rye, dark, crusty *Schusterjungen*

Mehrkornbrötchen (mixed grain roll)
Berliner Landbrot (mild rye bread)
Laugenbrötchen (salty sourdough rolls)
Graubrot (sourdough rye bread)
Semmel (milk-dough roll)

Selection of typical German loaves and bread rolls

Local Dishes and Specialities

Berliners have many ways of preparing pork, making it the most popular main dish. As *Kasseler*, created by Berlin butcher Cassel in the late 19th century, the meat is salted and then dried before being served with sauerkraut, mashed potatoes and very spicy mustard. Berlin's traditional pork knuckle, also accompanied by sauerkraut and potatoes, isn't complete without a portion of split pea purée (called *Erbspuree* in Berlin). Pork sausages include *Currywurst* – a post-World War II invention by Berlin *Imbiss* (food stall) owner Hedwig Mueller – which are served with a spicy sauce of curry, tomatoes and chili along with a roll or French fries. You can find this filling snack at *Imbisse* throughout the city.

Zanderfilet, or *Havel-Zander*, is pan-fried pike-perch with a vegetable sauce and onions, served with mashed potatoes.

Display of traditional German sausages in a Berlin butcher's shop

("shoemaker's boy") or *schrippen*, the cheap roll eaten daily at every meal.

Potatoes were introduced by Frederick the Great. They appear at most German meals, alongside fish or meat or cooked in a broth for dishes such as *Kartoffelsuppe*.

The Brandenburg Influence

Berlin's restaurants only rediscovered the region's true heritage after the fall of the Wall, absorbing culinary traditions from the Mark Brandenburg, the suddenly re-accessible rural countryside surrounding Berlin with its thick forests, rivers and lakes. Today, the fresh produce provided by the region's farms are an integral part of Berlin's cuisine. Old recipes have returned to modern kitchens. Freshwater fish like pike-perch, or game such as wild boar or duck, are flavoured with fresh herbs such as dill and parsley, and the famous *Brandenburger Landente* (Brandenburg country duck), stuffed with apples, onions and herbs, slowly roasted and coated with a honey-oil to make it perfectly crusty, is once again a favourite on Berlin menus.

Fresh vegetables from the Mark Brandenberg region

Berlin's Fine Dining Revolution

With the city's reunification came a new international influence, which gave birth to many Michelin-starred and other gourmet restaurants. Restaurants often prepare Berlin signature dishes with a more healthy or an exotic twist, giving traditional dishes a modern flavour. One of the Mark Brandenburg's most important products, fresh wild mushrooms, such as *Pfifferlinge* or *Steinpilze*, figure prominently, and classic ingredients like sauerkraut, cabbage and beet may be paired with Mediterranean fish or Asian spices.

Best Local Food

Restaurants: Altes Zollhaus *(p236)*; Nante-Eck *(p232)*; Lorenz Adlon Esszimmer *(p232)*; Zur letzten Instanz *(p233)*; Dressler *(p232)*.

Shops and markets: Marheineke-Markthalle; Turkish Market, Maybachufer, Markthalle Neun; KaDeWe gourmet food floor *(p258)*; Rogacki Gourmet Centre *(p258)*; Butter Lindner delicatessen chain.

***Imbisse* (food stalls):** Konnopke (below train tracks, Eberswalder Strasse subway, Prenzlauer Berg); Ku'damm 195 Imbiss, Kurfürstendamm; Currywurstbude, Wittenbergplatz, Charlottenburg.

Kasseler Nacken is salted and dried pork served with sauerkraut or green cabbage and mashed potatoes.

Berliner Leber is veal or pork liver on a bed of mashed potatoes, with fried onions and pan-fried apple slices.

Brandenburger Landente is stuffed duck served with red cabbage and potato dumplings or mashed potatoes.

What to Drink in Berlin

In Berlin, as throughout the rest of Germany, beer is the most widely drunk alcoholic beverage. There are no productive vineyards around Berlin, but wines from the Rhine and Mosel regions are always popular. As an *apéritif*, or with pork dishes, Berliners often enjoy a shot of rye vodka *(Korn)*, sometimes flavoured with herbs. With dessert, a glass of herbal liqueur often fits the bill.

A typical bar in Berlin

Pilsner beers from Berlin breweries

Lager (Pilsner)

Berliners drink beer on every occasion, and Germany's many beers are some of the best and purest in the world. Some of the best-known Berlin breweries are Schultheiss, Berliner Kindl, Berliner Pils and Engelhardt, but beers brewed in other parts of Germany are just as popular. Although beer is available in all sorts of venues and *"Ein Bier, bitte"* can be heard in pubs, cafés and restaurants, it is worth experiencing the atmosphere of an old-fashioned beerhouse, or *Kneipe*. The most highly esteemed beer is draught beer, drawn from the cask *(vom Fass)* and poured slowly into tall glasses. Pouring in a thin trickle is essential to achieve a thick head of foam, and a good barman will take a few minutes to fill your glass. Berliners drink mostly lager *(Pils)*, but other beers are also popular.

Strong, dark Bock beer

Other Beers

A *Brezel* makes a good snack with beer

In addition to the usual light, Pilsner-type beers, Berlin's breweries, many of them small and independent, also make a number of more adventurous brews. Dark, sweetish beer, known as *Schwarzbier* or black beer, is becoming more and more popular and has rather more than the standard four per cent alcohol. *Weizenbier* is made from wheat rather than barley, and is usually served in half-litre (one pint) glasses wth a slice of lemon. Another unusual drink is *Bock*, an especially strong beer made with barley. *Maibock* is a special version, available only in May.

Berliner Weisse, a light malted-wheat beer

Berliner Weisse with raspberry and woodruff cordials

Berliner Weisse mit Schuss

A Berlin speciality, called *Berliner Weisse mit Schuss*, is a light, newly fermented wheat beer that continues fermenting in the bottle. On its own, it is not very palatable as it is rather watery and sour, but when mixed with raspberry cordial it becomes fruity and delicious. Mixing with sweet woodruff syrup gives it a vivid green colour and a slightly medicinal flavour. *Berliner Weisse mit Schuss* is served in large wine glasses with a straw, and makes a very refreshing drink, particularly popular during the hot summer months.

Wine

No wine is produced around Berlin, as the climate here is too cold for vines, but a variety of wines from Germany's southern and western regions are available in Berlin. The most famous are the white wines, particularly those made from Riesling grapes. Most expensive are those from the Rheingau region. The northern climate dictates that most German wines are white, but lovers of red wine can try the Rhine Assmanshausen Spätburgunder, made from Pinot Noir grapes. Although there is no regional system of classification like the French *Appellation d'Origine Contrôlée,* a national quality control system divides German wines into three categories: *Tafelwein* or table wine is the most basic; next comes *Qualitätswein*, and the highest is *Qualitätswein mit Prädikat*, which includes wines made from specially selected grapes. *Trocken* means dry, *halbtrocken* means medium dry and *süss* means sweet. You can also find some very good sparkling wines known as *Sekt*.

A prize-winning bottle of German red wine

Riesling from Schloss Vollrads

Weizendoppelkorn rye vodka

Herbal digestive liqueur

Bitter-sweet Jägermeister liqueur

Other Alcoholic Beverages

Vodka is often drunk with more substantial meals, particularly those based on pork. Especially recommended is one of the rye vodkas, such as *Weizendoppelkorn*, that are popular in Berlin. Many establishments also serve brandies, known generically as *Weinbrand*. In addition, various digestive liqueurs and vodkas flavoured with plant extracts are quite popular, particularly *Kümmerling*, *Jägermeister* and, a Berlin favourite, *Kaulzzdorferkräuter Likör*. In many restaurants you will come across a speciality honey liqueur from east Prussia known as *Bärenfang*. More of an acquired taste is *Goldwasser* from Danzig, a traditional herbal liqueur containing flakes of gold leaf. It is made according to a secret 16th-century German recipe.

Non-Alcoholic Cold Drinks

Although Berlin tap water is safe to drink, it is not usually served with restaurant meals. If you want water you should order a bottle of mineral water *(Mineralwasser)* adding *"ohne Kohlensäure"* if you prefer still water. A wide variety of canned sparkling soft drinks, ubiquitous across Europe and the US, are popular in Berlin. Fruit juices are also widely drunk and a wide selection is available in every restaurant and café. Another popular soft drink is *Apfelschorle*, apple juice mixed in equal proportions with sparkling mineral water.

Apfelschorle

Coffee and Tea

Coffee is very popular in Berlin and is served in a variety of ways. The most usual is filter coffee, served by the cup or the pot, generally with condensed milk and sugar. If you prefer something stronger and more aromatic you should go for an espresso. It is also easy to enjoy a good cup of tea in Berlin, herbal or otherwise. Germans drink a lot of herbal teas, two of the most common being peppermint *(Pfefferminztee)* and camomile *(Kamillentee)*. If you want a cup of non-herbal tea, you can make a point of ordering *Schwarzen Tee*. If you want milk with your tea, then ask for *Tee mit Milch*.

Peppermint and camomile, two widely available herbal teas

Where to Eat and Drink

Around Unter den Linden

Das Meisterstück €
Traditional German **Map** 9 A5
Hausvogteiplatz 3–4, 10117
Tel *558 725 62*
A cosy bar and restaurant with tables grouped around an open fire, Das Meisterstück prides itself on its locally sourced, high-quality meats and sausages and well-kept craft beers.

Nante-Eck €
Traditional German **Map** 8 F3
Unter den Linden 35, 10117
Tel *22 48 72 57*
Berlin-style cheap eats are on offer in this homely pub on Unter den Linden. Fill up on Berlin calf's liver with port sauce or meatballs with mustard, washed down with local beer.

Augustiner am Gendarmenmarkt €€
Regional German **Map** 9 A4
Charlottenstrasse 55, 10117
Tel *204 540 20*
This Bavarian pub with wooden panelling and oak barrels overlooks Berlin's most beautiful square. It serves hearty German fare such as baked knuckle of pork with Bavarian sauerkraut and beef goulash in a beer sauce.

Chipps €€
German **Map** 9 B4
Jägerstrasse 35, 10117
Tel *364 445 88*
The serious breakfasts at this eatery include waffles and pancakes, but above all eggs. Try Dancing Queen – poached egg with spinach and fresh chives in a Hollandaise sauce, on wholemeal bread. Weekend brunch.

Cookies Cream €€
Vegetarian **Map** 8 F4
Behrenstrasse 55, 10117
Tel *274 929 40*
The chef at this unpretentious yet hip veggie hangout uses only the freshest locally grown ingredients to create inventive dishes that change seasonally. Free entry to on-site nightclub on Tuesdays and Thursdays.

Kaffeehaus Einstein €€
German **Map** 8 F3
Unter den Linden 42, 10117
Tel *204 36 32*
Rub shoulders with German politicians and other movers and shakers while admiring the changing photo and art exhibitions in the atrium. Try the house speciality, *Apfelstrudel*, for breakfast or elevenses.

Samâdhi €€
South Asian Vegetarian **Map** 8 E4
Wilhelmstrasse 77, 10117
Tel *224 888 50*
A short walk from the Brandenburger Tor, this vegetarian restaurant is very convenient for sightseers. Gluten-free dishes on request.

Zwölf Apostel €€
Italian **Map** 9 A3
Georgenstrasse 2, 10117
Tel *201 02 22*
This rambling restaurant beneath the railway arches near Friedrichstrasse station serves 12 pizza flavours, named for the 12 apostles, cooked to perfection in a stone oven.

Bocca di Bacco €€€
Italian **Map** 8 F4
Friedrichstrasse 167, 10117
Tel *206 728 28*
Master chef Loriano Mura directs the kitchen of this classy Italian restaurant with an elegant ambience that attracts the glitterati. Superb wine list.

Borchardt €€€
French-German **Map** 9 A4
Französische Strasse 47, 10117
Tel *81 88 62 62*
German politicians and celebrities flock to this Gendarmenmarkt restaurant with retro decor from the early 1900s. Schnitzel is the mainstay of an ever-changing menu. Reservations advised.

Price Guide
Prices are based on a three-course meal per person, including tax and service.

€	**under €30**
€€	**€30–60**
€€€	**over €60**

Dressler €€€
French-International **Map** 8 F4
Unter den Linden 39, 10117
Tel *204 44 22*
The Art Deco Dressler's signature dish is the Parisian Secret – a melt-in-the-mouth rump steak cooked in a mystery sauce.

DK Choice

Fischers Fritz €€€
Modern French **Map** 9 A4
Charlottenstrasse 49, 10117
Tel *203 363 63*
Fischers Fritz was awarded two Michelin stars in 2012 for the fifth year running, due to the creative flair of chef Christian Lohse. The meat dishes are tempting, but it is the fish and seafood dishes that receive most of the accolades. Try the Breton lobster roasted with salt, chilli and coriander, or the fillet of Mediterranean red mullet with mashed potatoes, Nyons olives and tomatoes. The two-course lunch menu is more accessibly priced.

Lorenz Adlon Esszimmer €€€
German fine dining **Map** 8 E4
Unter den Linden 77, 10117
Tel *226 119 60*
Dine at Berlin's gourmet temple *par excellence*, with views of the

Sophisticated interior of the Michelin-starred Fischers Fritz restaurant

Brandenburger Tor while enjoying the delicious creations of Michelin-starred chef Hendrik Otto

Quarré €€€
French-German **Map** 8 E4
Unter den Linden 77
Tel *226 119 59*
This brasserie has great views of Pariser Platz and the Brandenburg Tor. The Berliner Klassiker menu offers an alternative gourmet take on regional Brandenburg cuisine.

Vau €€€
Modern French **Map** 9 A4
Jägerstrasse 54–55, 10117
Tel *202 97 30*
Celebrity TV chef Kolja Kleeberg won this classy restaurant a Michelin star with his inspired take on French cooking. The striking interior is best described as modern meets Art Nouveau.

Museum Island

Café im Bode-Museum €
German **Map** 9 A2
Geschwister-Scholl-Straße 6, 10117
Tel *202 143 30*
Break for lunch or coffee in the surroundings of the Bode-Museum's Neo-Classical building while gazing down on Andreas Schlüter's magnificent equestrian statue of the Great Elector. No museum ticket required.

Rotisserie Weingrün €€
German **Map** 9 B4
Gertraudenstrasse 10, 10178
Tel *206 219 00* **Closed** *Sun*
Natural woods and gleaming glassware create a modern yet warm atmosphere. Great grilled meats and an excellent wine list.

East of the Centre

Domklause €
Traditional German **Map** 9 E2
Karl-Liebknecht-Strasse 1, 10178
Tel *847 12 37 37*
The chef in the DDR Museum restaurant once cooked for East German politicians. Down-to-earth meat dishes such as Mock Hare and Hunter's Schnitzel.

Típica €
Mexican **Map** 9 C2
Rosenstrasse 19, 10178
Tel *250 994 40*
Authentic Mexican dishes in a traditional *taqueria* (roadside café) specializing in meat or vegetable tortillas served with black beans, salad and sauces.

Enjoy stunning city views from Fernsehtum Sphere Restaurant in the TV tower

Fernsehturm Sphere Restaurant €€
German-International **Map** 9 C2
Panoramastrasse 1A, 10178
Tel *242 59 22*
This revolving restaurant in the TV tower serves typical Berlin-Brandenburg specialities including *kabeljau* (cod with beetroot and potato puree).

Zum Nussbaum €€
Traditional German **Map** 9 C3
Am Nussbaum 3, 10178
Tel *242 30 95*
In a Nikolaiviertel side street, this reconstructed country inn serves traditional Berlin cuisine including rollmop, *Bouletten* (spicy meatballs), fish and vegetable pancakes, as well as local beers.

DK Choice

Zur letzten Instanz €€
Traditional German **Map** 10 D3
Waisenstrasse 14–16, 10179
Tel *242 55 28* **Closed** *Sun*
Berlin's oldest pub, Zur letzten Instanz dates from 1621. Beethoven and Napoleon are thought to have eaten here and Charlie Chaplin, Mikhail Gorbachev and Angela Merkel certainly did. The classic German fare, including *Eisbein* (pork knuckle) and *Rinderroulade* (beef olive), is served in a cosy wood-panelled room with a majolica tiled stove. There is a shady courtyard garden.

Reinhard's €€€
International **Map** 9 C3
Poststrasse 28, 10178
Tel *242 52 95*
This stylish Nikolaiviertel restaurant is decorated with photographs of German artists and film stars of yesteryear. The house speciality is Secret of the Kaiser's Court – steak served in a sauce created for Max Liebermann.

North of the Centre

Anna Blume €
International **Map** 2 F3
Kollwitzstrasse 83, 10435
Tel *440 487 49*
This classy café-restaurant has a lovely terrace and lustre-lit interior. While some customers rave about the breakfast, others enthuse about brunch, while most crave the lime cheesecake dessert.

Beth Café €
Jewish **Map** 9 A1
Tucholskystrasse 40, 10117
Tel *281 31 35* **Closed** *Fri eve & Sat*
A kosher café in the New Synagogue area with a limited menu. Sample the speciality *kolbo platte* (salad with tahina, falafel and humus).

Brecht-Keller €
Austrian **Map** 8 F1
Chausseestrasse 125, 10115
Tel *282 38 43*
Convivial cellar restaurant in the Brecht Museum where the simple Austrian cooking is inspired by recipes invented by Brecht's wife, Helene Weigel.

Cafe Fleury €
French **Map** 1 C5
Weinbergsweg 20, 10119
Tel *440 341 44*
Lovely French-owned café with distinctive flowery wallpaper and an outdoor terrace. Wonderful smell of freshly brewed coffee, croissants, brioches and other breakfast delicacies greets guests.

For more information on types of restaurants *see pp226–7*

Dada Falafel €
Middle Eastern **Map** 8 F1
Linienstrasse 132, 10115
Tel *0171 359 7392*
Dada Falafel offers fast food worth lingering over, including arguably the best falafels this side of Damascus, as well as *grat shawarmas* and fresh salads.

Gambrinus trifft Bacchus €
Traditional German **Map** 8 F1
Krausnickstrasse 1, 10115
Tel *282 60 43*
Traditional *Kneipe* (pub) with old-fashioned tiles, dark wood furnishings, framed photos and posters of Old Berlin. Massive portions of German pub grub.

Gugelhof €
Alsatian **Map** 2 E4
Knaackstrasse 37, 10435
Tel *442 92 29*
Former US president Bill Clinton visited this lively restaurant near Kollwitzplatz with Alsatian specialities such as *tarte flambée* and lamb cassoulet.

Khushi €
Indian **Map** 2 E4
Kollwitzstrasse 37, 10405
Tel *484 937 90*
Delicious Indian food to eat in or take out, prepared with fresh ingredients. Moderately spicy.

Sophieneck €
Regional German **Map** 9 B1
Große Hamburger Strasse 37, 10115
Tel *282 21 09*
A warm pub-restaurant serving regional cooking with fresh ingredients and an international twist including vegetarian options and a kids' menu.

Transit €
Southeast Asian **Map** 9 B1
Rosenthaler Strasse 68, 10119
Tel *247 816 45*
Food here is served in tapas-sized portions – three bowls should suffice. All dishes are MSG-free, and have playful names including Duck in Pyjamas (crispy duck and plum sauce rolled in a pancake).

DK Choice

Yam Yam €
Korean **Map** 9 C1
Alte Schönhauser Strasse 6, 10119
Tel *246 324 85*
Popular with local fashionistas, this canteen-style restaurant run by Sumi Ha uses organic Korean vegetables and hot spices and flavouring typical of the region's cooking. Try *cha chang myun* (noodles with pork and black beans, served with pickled cabbage) or rise to the challenge of a *bibimbap* (beef, vegetables and fried egg mixed with a fiery red pepper paste.)

Zum Schusterjungen €
Traditional German **Map** 2 E2
Danziger Strasse 9, 10435
Tel *442 76 54*
Typical Berlin corner pub with quirky rustic touches. The home-cooked food includes large portions of liver and onions, knuckle of pork, and bacon wraps. Serves draught beer.

Al Contadino sotto le Stelle €€
Italian **Map** 9 B1
Auguststrasse 36, 10119
Tel *281 90 23* **Closed** *Tue*
Stylish, upmarket *trattoria* with friendly service and the flavours of southern Italy. Home-made pasta and good fish and meat dishes. Try the grilled swordfish marinated in white wine vinegar, honey and oregano.

Cenacolo €€
Italian **Map** 2 E3
Sredzkistrasse 23, 10435
Tel *440 447 43*
The aroma of fresh herbs and pizzas cooked in a traditional stone oven greets diners at this popular Prenzlauer Berg restaurant. Book ahead.

Friedrichs106 €€
Austrian **Map** 8 F2
Friedrichstrasse 106, 10117
Tel *405 205 94*
This modern coffee house with a lovely terrace overlooks the Spree. The Austrian menu offers breakfasts, savoury and fruit strudels, steaks and classic Austrian dishes including *tafelspitz* (boiled beef).

Habel Weinkultur and Brasserie €€
Modern German **Map** 8 E2
Luisenstrasse 19, 10117
Tel *280 984 84*
Upmarket brasserie inspired by Prussian culinary traditions, but with a Mediterranean twist. Impressive wine list.

Hackescher Hof €€
Modern German-International **Map** 9 B2
Rosenthaler Strasse 40–41, 10178
Tel *283 52 93*
Café-restaurant-patisserie with an interior reminiscent of a Viennese coffee house. Popular with office workers for its attractively priced two-course lunch menu. Stays open until 2am.

Mao Thai €€
Thai **Map** 2 F3
Wörther Strasse 30, 10405
Tel *441 92 61*
Popular with locals and visitors alike for its excellent, mildly spiced Thai food and alfresco seating in summer.

Monsieur Vuong €€
Vietnamese **Map** 9 C1
Alte Schönhauser Str. 46, 10119
Tel *99 29 69 24*
Oriental bistro with a two-course menu and specials up on the blackboard. Generous portions, efficient service and a tempting selection of scented teas.

Nola's am Weinberg €€
Swiss **Map** 1 C4
Veteranen Strasse 9, 10119
Tel *440 407 66*
Swiss cantonal cuisine featuring fondue, noodle and risotto dishes. Lovely summer terrace. Sunday brunch from 10am.

Casual outdoor seating on the tree-shaded pavement at Gugelhof

For key to prices *see p232*

Oxymoron €€
Italian-French **Map** 9 B2
Rosenthaler Strasse 40-41, 10178
Tel *283 918 86*
This fashionable Hackescher Markt dining space and night club attracts a young crowd. Art Deco interior with glittering lustres and wood-framed mirrors.

DK Choice

Pasternak €€
Russian-Jewish **Map** 2 F4
Knaackstrasse 22/24, 10405
Tel *441 33 99*
A long-time favourite with Berlin's sizeable Russian community, Pasternak prides itself on its authentic cuisine. Focus on the rich assortment of *zakuski* (starters), but do not overlook the *blini* (buckwheat pancakes filled with spinach and cheese, salmon and horseradish, or caviar). The warm dining space is adorned with traditional wallpaper, lamps and candles.

Restauration 1900 €€
Traditional **Map** 2 E3
Husemannstrasse 1, 10435
Tel *442 24 94*
The granny's kitchen menu at this Art Nouveau restaurant features old Prussian favourites such as *königsberger Klops* (meatballs in creamy caper sauce). Weekend brunch buffet from 10am; booking essential.

Sarah Wiener Cafe and Restaurant €€
Austrian-Mediterranean **Map** 8 D1
Invalidenstrasse 50–51, 10557
Tel *707 136 50* **Closed** *Mon*
Refined dining in the Hamburger Bahnhof museum. Tino Speer's cuisine uses fresh organic ingredients and serves some of Berlin's best schnitzels.

Savanna €€
African **Map** 2 E3
Sredzkistrasse 26, 10435
Tel *443 186 21*
The wide-ranging menu here features exotic antelope and zebra steaks as well as vegetable platters – fried yams, okra, lentils, bananas and spinach served with rice, couscous or *injera* (Eritrean flat bread).

Yosoy €€
Spanish **Map** 9 B2
Rosenthaler Strasse 37, 10178
Tel *283 912 13*
Commendably affordable, authentic tapas bar with Spanish regional wines to pair with the appetizing fish and meat main courses.

Range of Russian and Jewish goodies on offer at Pasternak

DK Choice

Dos Palillos €€€
International-Asian **Map** 9 B1
Casa Camper Hotel, Weinmeisterstrasse 1, 10178
Tel *200 034 13*
Sit facing the open kitchen of this cutting-edge restaurant and watch Catalan master chef Albert Raurich have his creative way with Asian-style tapas. The oysters cooked in sake are delicious. The 12-course menu costing €45 is good value. The steely interior was designed by the Parisian Bouroullec brothers. Book ahead.

Reinstoff €€€
Fine dining **Map** 1 A5
Schlegelstrasse 26c/Edison Höfe, 10115
Tel *308 812 14* **Closed** *Sun & Mon*
Daniel Achilles' sensational Michelin-starred inventions delight in unusual pairings – river trout and rowanberry, Norway lobster and rhubarb, carrot and lemon ice cream.

Tiergarten

Angkor Wat €
Cambodian **Map** 7 B2
Paulstrasse 22, 10557
Tel *393 39 22*
This well-established restaurant draws diners with its exotic decor and aromatic curries.

Cafe am Neuen See €
German-Mediterranean **Map** 6 F5
Lichtensteinallee 2, 10787
Tel *254 493 00*
In the heart of Tiergarten Park, this café has lakeside terrace views and a menu comprising Bavarian snacks and draught beers, as well as Italian mains including fresh pizzas. Cosy seating in winter, plus boat rental and a sandpit for kids.

Café Möhring €
Traditional German **Map** 8 D5
Weinhaus Huth, Alte Potsdamer Strasse 5, 10785
Tel *259 270 07* **Closed** *Mon*
Relocated to the Huth-Haus, the only surviving building from the old Potsdamer Platz, Möhring is one of the few remaining traditional Berlin cafés. Pasta, salads and tempting *Torten* (cream cakes).

Gaststätte Ambrosius €
Traditional German **Map** 13 A1
Einemstrasse 14, 10785
Tel *264 05 26*
Enjoy nourishing home cooking, with specialities such as Berlin-style liver, served with onions and apple sauce, and tasty potato soup, at this cosy restaurant .

Lindenbräu €
Traditional German **Map** 8 D5
Bellevuestrasse 3-5, 10785
Tel *257 512 80*
Popular watering hole on Potsdamer Platz. Bavarian specialities and home-brewed fruit-flavoured wheat beer are served on a large roof terrace.

OM €
Nepalese-Indian **Map** 7 A2
Kirchstrasse 16, 10557
Tel *39749554*
Family-friendly restaurant close to the Spree. Try the hot and spicy lamb kebabs or opt for milder dishes such as the crispy duck in coconut sauce.

For more information on types of restaurants *see pp226–7*

Teehaus Tiergarten €
International **Map** 5 A5
Altonaer Strasse 2/2a, 10557
Tel *394 804 00*
Lovely setting in the English garden next to Schloss Bellevue. Snacks, cakes and main courses served in the teahouse or on the terrace. Summer concerts Jul–Sep.

Lanninger €€
Modern German **Map** 6 F1
Alt-Moabit 99, 10559
Tel *399 207 98*
Smart modern restaurant and cocktail lounge with terrace views across a lovely, tree-fringed stretch of the Spree.

Lutter & Wegner im Kaisersaal €€
German-Austrian **Map** 8 D5
Bellevuestrasse 1, 10785
Tel *263 903 72*
This illustrious restaurant, founded over two centuries ago, is located in the former Kaisersaal dining room – a relic of Imperial Germany. Sample refined cooking and fine wines here.

Rikes Gasthaus €€
Traditional German **Map** 13 C1
Hotel Alt-Berlin, Potsdamer Strasse 67, 10785
Tel *26 06 70*
Old-world restaurant with menus based on original recipes from Frau Rike's grandmother's cookbook including Coachman's Goulash, beef cooked in beer.

Facil €€€
Modern Fusion **Map** 8 D5
Potsdamer Strasse 3, 10785
Tel *590 05 12 34*
Michelin-starred gourmet food in the Mandala Hotel *(see p224)* restaurant. A glass-roofed pavilion is the backdrop for master chef Michael Kempf's inspired culinary cuisine, which draws on the freshest market produce and subtly exotic spices.

DK Choice

Käfers Dachgarten €€€
Modern German **Map** 8 D3
Platz der Republik, 11011
Tel *226 29 90*
Overlooked by many visitors to Berlin, this lovely roof garden restaurant in the Reichstag building has a terrace with spectacular views across the city. Sample sophisticated German dishes made with the freshest regional produce and accompanied by choice wines. Book at least 3 hours in advance and remember to bring your passport.

Käfers Dachgarten restaurant, on the rooftop of the Reichstag building

Kreuzberg

Cafe do Brasil €
Brazilian **Map** 14 F4
Mehringdamm 72, 10961
Tel *780 068 87*
The party atmosphere at this popular Kreuzberg restaurant draws a lively international crowd. Specialities include Brazilian beach BBQ cooking, seafood stews (*moquecas*) and caipirinha cocktails. Sunday brunch.

Golgatha €
International **Map** 14 E5
Dudenstrasse 40-64, 10965
Tel *785 24 53*
Lively 1920s beer garden on the edge of picturesque Viktoria Park. Offers grills as well as ample vegetarian options. Adventure playground for children.

Gropius €
International **Map** 14 E1
Niederkirchnerstrasse 7, 10963
Tel *254 864 06* **Closed** *Tue*
Restaurant in the Martin-Gropius-Bau with a summer terrace and a seasonal menu that reflects the temporary art exhibitions.

Seerose €
Vegetarian **Map** 14 F4
Mehringdamm 47, 10961
Tel *698 159 27*
Dine buffet-style on spinach lasagne, pasta and rice dishes with pick-and-mix side salads. Delicious bio-wines, helpful staff and outdoor seating available.

DK Choice

Tomasa €
International **Map** 14 E4
Kreuzbergstrasse 62, 10965
Tel *810 098 85*
Great for families, this friendly restaurant in a red-brick villa has a well-stocked playroom and a great kids' menu. For the grown-ups, Tomasa caters for every possible taste and is especially strong on breakfast and brunch choices. It is spread out over two floors and has a courtyard garden.

DK Choice

Yorckschlösschen €
International **Map** 14 F3
Yorckstrasse 15, 10965
Tel *215 80 70*
A Kreuzberg haunt with a bohemian interior featuring velvet sofas, old wooden furnishings and a beer garden. The extensive menu offers 14 breakfast choices and includes lighter meals and hearty German favourites, such as *Leberkäse* (meat loaf) served with fried egg and salad. This spot has been popular for more than 20 years with jazz musicians, who regularly perform here.

Ø €€
Modern German **Map** 14 F4
Mehringdamm 80, 10965
Tel *773 262 13*
Describing itself as "the island in Kreuzberg", Ø – island in Danish – is pronounced something like the German letter "ö". The look is urban-chic and the menu likes to surprise with traditional German dishes and ingredients given a modern, sophisticated twist.

Altes Zollhaus €€
Modern German **Map** 15 B3
Carl-Herz-Ufer 30, 10961
Tel *692 33 00*
Charming half-timbered house and garden. Classic rustic cooking features the famous Beelitzer asparagus in season.

For key to prices *see p232*

Bar Centrale €€
Italian **Map** 14 F4
Yorckstrasse 82, 10965
Tel *786 29 89*
This bar-restaurant, offering fine Italian cuisine in the heart of Kreuzberg, has a loyal following.

e.t.a. Hoffmann €€€
Modern Austrian **Map** 14 F4
Yorckstrasse 83, 10965
Tel *780 988 09*
Tyrolean chef Thomas Kurt has his creative way with traditional Austrian and German recipes. Try the cushion of Brandenburg venison with Gatow radish and potato noodles.

Tim Raue €€€
Modern Asian fusion **Map** 9 A5
Rudi-Dutschke Strasse 26, 10969
Tel *259 379 30*
The Michelin-starred Tim Raue offers authentic Japanese, Thai and Chinese cooking. Minimalist interior with gallery lighting and American walnut furniture.

Around Kurfürstendamm

Baba Angora €
Turkish **Map** 11 B1
Schlüterstrasse 29, 10629
Tel *323 70 96*
Classic Anatolian cuisine such as spicy *Adana sis kebab* with yoghurt and herbs is served here. There are vegetarian and fish options as well. The unusual decor comprises ancient Hittite art. Large outdoor terrace.

Bleiberg's €
Jewish **Map** 12 E2
Nürnberger Strasse 45A, 10789
Tel *219 136 24* **Closed** *Fri eve & Sat*
Kosher café with a relaxed vibe and a menu that includes vegetarian and vegan dishes as well as Russian *blinis.*

Dicke Wirtin €
Traditional German **Map** 11 C1
Carmerstrasse 9, 10623
Tel *312 49 52*
This authentic Berlin *Kneipe* is a short walk from Savigny Platz. Try the *Eintopf,* a steaming hotpot, and the *Berliner Kindl,* one of the nine draught beers available.

Sachico Sushi €
Japanese **Map** 11 C1
Grolmanstrasse 47, Jeanne-Mammen-Bogen 584, 10623
Tel *313 22 82* **Closed** *Mon*
Handy refuelling stop after Ku'damm shopping, with a tempting business lunch of *kaitan* (conveyor belt) sushi; pay extra for sashimi and grills.

Satyam €
Indian Vegetarian **Map** 5 C5
Goethestrasse 5, 10623
Tel *318 061 11*
Vegetarian restaurant with specialities such as aubergine in lightly spiced tomato sauce with ginger and garlic. Some vegetables come directly from India.

Tastees €
Jamaican **Map** 11 C1
Grolmannstrasse 27, 10623
Tel *889 220 28* **Closed** *Sun*
Spicy Caribbean fare with specialities including patties, jerk chicken and curried shrimps with fried banana.

El Borriquito €€
Spanish **Map** 11 B1
Wielandstrasse 6, 10625
Tel *312 99 29*
Guests are entertained by Spanish guitarists and Flamenco dancers in this crowded Iberian-themed dining room that serves tapas, seafood and lamb specialities.

Brenner €€
German-International **Map** 12 E3
Regensburger Strasse 7, 10777
Tel *236 244 70*
A choice of Austrian, Italian and German dishes reflecting Tyrolean culinary influences is served in this restaurant with a wood-panelled interior and congenial atmosphere.

Sleek and minimalist decor at Tim Raue, serving Oriental cuisine

Cafe-Restaurant Wintergarten im Literaturhaus €€
German-International **Map** 12 D2
Fasanenstrasse 23, 10719
Tel *882 54 14*
Break from shopping on Ku'damm and visit this bolthole favoured by artists and intellectuals. Breakfast and international dishes are served in an Art Nouveau interior. Shady garden.

Calcutta €€
Indian **Map** 11 B1
Bleibtreustrasse 17, 10623
Tel *883 62 93*
Oldest Indian restaurant in Berlin reputated for its sophisticated dishes from all parts of the subcontinent. *Tandoori* dishes cooked in traditional wood-fired oven.

DK Choice

Esswein am Fasanenplatz €€
Modern German **Map** 11 C2
Fasanenstrasse 40, 10719
Tel *887 140 99*
Esswein is making waves within Berlin's culinary scene, thanks to its modern German cooking. The menu is seasonal but might feature *pfälzer Wurstsalat* (Rhineland sausage with cheese and bread), with *Ochsenfetzen* (ox slices baked in a râgout of grapes, mushrooms and chestnuts) to follow. Choose from a selection of more than 40 Mosel wines to accompany your meal for the makings of a memorable evening.

Warm interiors of e.t.a. Hoffmann, specializing in Austrian cuisine

The bright and grand interior at Die Quadriga

Florian €€
Swabian **Map** 5 C5
Grolmanstrasse 52, 10623
Tel *313 91 84*
Small, pristine restaurant with an understated charm that attracts celebrities. Excellent Swabian cuisine with a modern twist; uses organic produce.

Grüne Lampe €€
Russian **Map** 11 C3
Uhlandstrasse 51, 10719
Tel *887 193 93*
Popular with Russian expats, the authentic home cooking sees a large selection of *zakuski* and *blini*. Some vegetarian options.

Marjellchen €€
Regional German **Map** 11 B1
Mommsenstrasse 9
Tel *883 26 76*
Regional German cooking traditions survive here thanks to the original recipes of the owner's grandmother.

Namaskar €€
Indian **Map** 12 D3
Pariser Strasse. 56/57, 10719
Tel *886 806 48*
Rated as one of the city's best Indian restaurants. The menu celebrates the rich diversity of cooking on the subcontinent. Great choice of dishes.

Trattoria Totó €€
Italian
Bleibtreustrasse 55, 10623
Tel *312 54 49* **Map** 5 C5
This long-standing family-run restaurant serves Italian staples in a traditional setting.

Belmondo €€€
French **Map** 11 C3
Knesebeckstrasse 93, 10623
Tel *362 872 61*
Red leather banquettes and photos of the famous actor Jean-Paul Belmondo bring a touch of French elegance to this Charlottenburg bistro. Excellent fish and seafood dishes, and a sensational *bouillabaisse* (fish soup).

Brasserie Le Faubourg €€€
French **Map** 12 D1
Augsburger Strasse 41, 10789
Tel *800 999 77 00*
Inside the iSofitel Hotel, this brasserie offers refined French cooking at its best. Friendly and efficient staff add to a pleasurable dining experience. Outdoor terrace seating.

Die Quadriga €€€
European **Map** 12 D2
Eislebener Strasse 14, 10789
Tel *214 056 51* **Closed** *Sun*
French and European creations are served in the restaurant of the Hotel Brandenburger Hof.

Restaurant 44 €€€
International **Map** 12 D1
Augsburger Strasse 44, 10789
Tel *22 01 022 88*
Enjoy upmarket gourmet dining in the terrace restaurant of the Swissôtel with fine views of the Ku'damm.

Wilson's €€€
American **Map** 12 E1
Hotel Crowne Plaza, Nürnberger Strasse 65, 10787
Tel *210 070 00*
The focus here is on succulent prime ribs and steaks, using beef imported from the US. Save room for the home-made ice cream. Romantic terrace.

Around Schloss Charlottenburg

Chenab €
Indian **Map** 4 D4
Knobelsdorffstrasse 35, 14059
Tel *364 347 99*
Go for the tasty, mildly spiced vegetarian dishes at this neighbourhood eatery. The banana curry takes some beating. Great value for money.

Natural'mente €
Vegetarian and vegan **Map** 4 F3
Schustehrusstrasse 26, 10585
Tel *341 41 66* **Closed** *Sat, Sun, dinner daily*
This bio-restaurant uses only whole foods and organic produce. The menu features vegetable platters, soups, and desserts. Drinks include organic beers and wines.

Taverna Ambrosios €
Greek **Map** 5 B3
Galvanistrasse 12A, 10587
Tel *341 55 54*
Laid-back Greek taverna with ochre walls, blue check tablecloths and wonderful food. The weekday lunch menu offered here is especially good value.

Brauhaus Lemke €€
Traditional German **Map** 4 F3
Luisenplatz 1, 10585
Tel *308 789 79*
The micro-brewery adjacent to Schloss Charlottenburg enjoys views of the park from the pub terrace. There's hearty German fare on offer, and a good choice of stout, ale and Pilsner beers to wash it all down.

Don Giovanni €€
Italian **Map** 4 A4
Bismarckstrasse 28, 10625
Tel *341 76 53*
Don Giovanni serves huge thin-crusted pizzas, as well as an assortment of Tuscan meat and fish specialities. An excellent selection of German red wines is available.

Engelbecken €€
Regional German **Map** 4 E5
Witzlebenstrasse 31, 14057
Tel *615 28 10*
Sample delectable Bavarian white veal and pork sausages with sweet mustard, or the saddle of organic pork with fried mushroom, carrots and pureed nettle leaves. Bavarian lager or dark beers can be enjoyed outside on the pavement terrace.

Eosander €€
International **Map** 4 E3
Spandauer Damm 3, 14059
Tel *437 296 01*
This restfully sedate café-restaurant is situated just across the road from Schloss Charlottenburg. The Art Nouveau decor gives it a touch of sophistication and a nostalgic air. Open for breakfast.

Genazvale €€
Georgian **Map** 4 E5
Windscheidstrasse 14, 10627
Tel *450 860 26*
Friendly restaurant featuring dishes and flavours from the Black Sea. Must-tastes on the Georgian menu include *chatschapuri* (cheese bread), *saziwi* (chicken in walnut sauce) and the delicious Georgian regional wines.

For key to prices *see p232*

DK Choice

Le Piaf €€
French **Map** 4 E3
Schlossstrasse 60, 14059
Tel *342 20 40* **Closed** *Sun, Mon, lunch daily*
A classy bistro with a menu based on Alsatian and French recipes, including classics such as *confit de canard*, as well as frog legs and snails for the more adventurous. The wines are imported from the owner's favourite wineries. The cosy interiors, attentive French staff and a terrace make dining at Le Piaf a memorable experience.

Restaurant Kien-Du €€
Thai **Map** 4 F4
Kaiser-Friedrich-Strasse 89, 10585
Tel *341 14 47*
The oldest Thai restaurant in Berlin is known for its red and green curries and its garlanded Buddha shrine. Native draught beer is available.

Ana e Bruno €€€
Italian **Map** 4 D3
Sophie-Charlottenstrasse 101, 14059
Tel *325 71 10*
Bruno Pellegrini's inspired gourmet cooking at a reasonable price. Excellent wine list.

Further Afield

Amrit €
South Asian **Map** 16 E2
Oranienstrasse 202-3, 10999
Tel *612 55 50*
Popular Kreuzberg restaurant offering generous portions inspired by Indian, Thai and Malaysian flavours.

Baraka €
North African **Map** 16 F2
Lausitzer Platz 6, 10997
Tel *612 63 30*
Serves Moroccan and Egyptian specialities including tajine, couscous and vegetarian dishes in a cavernous ambience with seating on banquettes and cushions.

Britzer Mühle €
Traditional German
Buckower Damm 130, Neukölln, 12349
Tel *604 18 19*
Bucolic views of a mill from the large beer garden and the cosy dining room. Huge portions of attractively priced German pub grub. Live music on Mondays.

Il Casolare €
Italian **Map** 16 D3
Grimmstrasse 30, 10967
Tel *695 066 10*
Some of the best pizzas in Berlin, with wafer-thin crusts and delicious toppings. Bohemian ambience, tables overlooking the Landwehr Canal and famously brusque waiters. Book ahead.

Crêperie Bretonne €
French **Map** 16 E3
Reichenberger Strasse 30, 10999
Tel *600 311 92* **Closed** *Mon*
Savoury galettes filled with ham, Roquefort and pear. Follow with sweet pancakes, and Breton cider from the Val de Rance served in porcelain cups.

Da Baffi €
Italian
Nazarethkirchstrasse 41, 13347 Wedding
Tel *0176 692 6545*
This restaurant has a tempting menu of impeccable dishes that attracts diners from all over town.

Darjiling €
Indian
Alt-Tegel 25, 13507
Tel *430 045 65*
Exotic aromas of cardamom and coriander greet visitors at Darjiling. Chicken, mutton and fish standards come with a smile, and at low prices.

Golden Buddha €
Thai **Map** 1 C1
Gleimstrasse 26, Prenzlauer Berg, 10437
Tel *448 55 56*
Locals flock to this neighbourhood restaurant with a real buzz for its soft Thai flavours, vegetarian specials and friendly service.

Hasir Ocakbasi €
Turkish **Map** 16 E2
Adalbertstrasse 12, 10999
Tel *615 070 80*
Berlin's love affair with the doner kebab began here in 1971. Large selection of chargrilled meat and fish dishes, delicious mezes and homemade desserts.

Henne €
Traditional German **Map** 16 D1
Leuschnerdamm 25, 10999
Tel *614 77 30*
Ample chicken dishes on the menu at this wonderfully atmospheric Kreuzberg pub, now more than a century old.

Kurhaus Korsakow €
Traditional German
Grünberger Straße 81, 10245
Tel *547 377 86*
Hearty home cooking and draught beers in a cosy atmosphere. Place your orders for Berliner *Leber* (liver) or *Bouletten* with cabbage roulade.

Candlelit dining in a rustic and cosy setting at Kurhaus Korsakow

For more information on types of restaurants *see pp226–7*

Well-stocked bar at the popular Max und Moritz pub

Loretta am Wannsee €
Regional German
Kronprinzessinnenweg 260, 14109
Tel *801 053 33*
Traditional beer garden, grill and restaurant overlooking the Wannsee with lovely lake views. The house speciality is Hax'n: knuckle of pork cooked in dark beer.

Lotus Lounge €
Vegetarian **Map** 3 C3
Soorstrasse 85, 14050
Tel *232 550 65* **Closed** *Sun & dinner daily*
Restaurant in the Tibetan-Buddhist Centre offering mains such as spinach and potato gratin flavoured with garlic and tomato.

Matreschka €
Russian
Boxhagener Strasse 60
Tel *0163 987 0767*
This small restaurant offers simple Russian dishes like borscht and meat-stuffed dumplings, all accompanied by wines from Georgia and vodka.

Max und Moritz €
Traditional German **Map** 16 D1
Oranienstrasse 162, 10969
Tel *695 159 11*
Rustic-style pub grub with generous helpings of Berlin-style food. Try the meatballs with caper sauce or beef goulash with noodle dumplings.

Merhaba €
Turkish
Greifswalder Strasse 4, 10405
Tel *488 279 40*
Traditional Turkish restaurant with typical Anatolian meze and grilled specialities. Very boisterous at weekends, with live music and belly dancing.

Miss Saigon €
Vietnamese **Map** 16 F2
Skalitzer Strasse 38, 10999
Tel *695 333 77*
Small no-frills restaurant that surprises with the quality of its South Vietnamese seafood and vegetable dishes, seasoned and spiced with refinement.

Nirwana €
Indian **Map** E4
Schlossstrasse 49, 12165
Tel *793 16 59*
Excellent regional cooking and huge portions. The menu ranges from mild *korma* or *biryani* dishes to spicier *masalas* and *vindaloos*.

Old Shanghai €
Chinese **Map** 8 F1
Chausseestrasse 32, Prenzlauer Berg, 10115
Tel *288 794 66*
The chef is from Shanghai and his wife can advise on the traditional Chinese menu. Try the oven-baked ocean perch, cooked Shanghai-style in sweet and sour sauce.

Shaan €
Indian
Richardplatz 20, Neukölln, 12055
Tel *680 893 82*
Friendly restaurant with a typical range of regional dishes. Try chicken marinated in more than 20 spices and cooked in an earthenware *tandoori* oven.

Sufissimo €
Middle Eastern-Persian **Map** 16 D4
Fichtestrasse 1, 10967
Tel *616 208 33*
Try the yoghurt soup with herbs, followed by turkey breast with almonds and raisins in an apricot and cardamom sauce. The decor features blue banquettes and Oriental silverware.

Tandir €
Turkish **Map** 16 E5
Hermannstrasse 157, 12051
Tel *625 67 05*
Neighbourhood *Imbissbude* (takeaway) and small restaurant with outdoor seating. Serves grilled meat, falafel, soup and casseroles.

Taverna To Koutouki €
Greek **Map** 16 E3
Kottbusser Damm 9, 10967
Tel *692 52 17*
There's a welcoming glass of ouzo on arriving at this popular Greek restaurant with a candlelit interior and typical dishes including *bifteki* (cheese-filled meatballs) and a mixed grill platter.

Thüringer Stuben €
Regional German **Map** 2 F1
Stargarder Strasse 28, Prenzlauer Berg, 10437
Tel *446 33 39*
Stag heads adorn the wood-panelled walls in this mock-traditional Thuringian inn. Home-made potato dumplings, sausages and regional specialities.

Volta €
International
Brunnenstrasse 73, Pankow
Tel *0178 396 5490*
This trendy gastro-pub is best known for its large burger, which comes with bacon, cheese and rocket salad.

Vux €
Vegan
Wipperstrasse 14, Neukölln, 12055
Closed *Mon & Tue*
Cosy Neukölln café with a nice selection of home-made bagels. Also serves soups, quiches and delicious biscuits and waffles.

Weltrestaurant Markthalle €
Traditional German **Map** 16 F2
Pücklerstrasse 34, 10997
Tel *617 55 02*
Wood-panelled dining room near Görlitzer U-bahn station serving generous helpings of Berlin pub grub and draught beers.

Wirtshaus zur Pfaueninsel €
German-International
Pfaueninselchaussee 100, 14109
Tel *805 22 25*
Beer garden-restaurant with great views of the Havel. Ideally situated for a riverside stroll to work off the meal, or for the ferry hop to Peacock Island. Asparagus, mushroom and pumpkin dishes in season.

For key to prices *see p232*

Yellow Sunshine €
Vegetarian **Map** 16 F3
Wiener Strasse 19, 10999
Tel *695 987 20*
Vegan *Currywurst* is on the menu at this roomy Kreuzberg bistro, along with organic fries, soya burgers and a large choice of topping and sauces.

Yogi-Haus €
Indian **Map** 13 A5
Belziger Strasse 42, 10823
Tel *782 92 23*
Popular Schöneberg restaurant specializing in North Indian cuisine, mainly chicken and mutton dishes. Large dining space with an open kitchen.

Zum Bayernmichel €
Traditional German
Bornholmer Strasse 87, Prenzlauer Berg, 10439
Tel *444 30 44*
Traditional Bavarian-style inn with a beer garden serving Paulaner on draught. The *Bauerngrillpfanne* is a combo of Nuremberg sausages, pork medallions, chicken breast and bacon-wrapped runner beans – simply mouthwatering.

Austria €€
Austrian **Map** 15 A5
Bergmannstraße 30, 10961
Tel *694 44 40*
Famous with Berliners long before Pulitzer-prize-winning author Jeffrey Eugenides gave it a plug in *Middlesex*. Wiener schnitzel is the house speciality, served in mammoth portions.

DK Choice

Blockhaus Nikolskoe €€
German
Nikolskoerweg 15, 14109
Tel *805 29 14*
This restaurant is idyllically located, with the Grunewald forest as its backdrop and the broad expanse of Havel and Peacock Island ahead. The restaurant occupies a wooden *dacha* (country house) built for the heir to the Russian throne in 1819. The food, especially the fresh fish and local game, suit the spectacular views and waterside setting.

Brauhaus in Rixdorf €€
Traditional German
Glasower Straße 27, Neukölln, 12051
Tel *626 88 80*
Beer garden and restaurant in a converted 19th-century villa. Serves locally brewed beer and traditional dishes such as *Eisbein* (knuckle of pork) served with sauerkraut and boiled potatoes.

Cape Town €€
South African
Schönfliesser Strasse 15, Prenzlauer Berg, 10439
Tel *400 576 58*
A meat-eater's paradise a short walk from Schönhauser Allee S-Bahn. Generous portions of springbok and wildebeast. South African wines also available.

Fischerhütte €€
Regional German
Fischerhüttenstraße 136, 14163
Tel *804 903 10*
Picturesque views of the Schlachtensee from this lakeside beer garden and restaurant. There is a bio-grill and a kids' play area.

Fisherman's €€
Fish
Eisenhammerweg 20, 13507
Tel *437 464 70*
Fish and scallops come in inspired variations, accompanied by Rieslings. The view of the lake is priceless.

Freischwimmer €€
German
Vor dem Schlesischen Tor 2a, 10997
Tel *610 743 09*
Lively waterside café-bar set on floating stages overlooking the Spree and the Landwehrkanal. A young crowd gathers for Sunday brunch, and on summer evenings for the electronic and techno music on the opposite bank.

Funkturm Restaurant €€
German-Continental **Map** 3 B5
Hammarskjöldplatz 1, 14055
Tel *303 829 00*
Set in a 52-m- (171-ft-) high radio tower dating from the 1920s, with original Art Deco interiors. Panoramic views over West Berlin from the champagne bar.

Large glasses of frothy beer on offer in the popular Austria restaurant

Haus Sanssouci €€
German
Am Grossen Wannsee 60, 14109
Tel *805 30 34*
Smart, elegant restaurant with mouthwatering fish, seafood and game specialities. Located in the world's first pre-fabricated wooden villa. Large summer garden with fabulous views over Wannsee.

Hax'nhaus €€
Regional German
Alt-Tegel 2, 13507
Tel *433 90 34*
Decked out as a traditional Bavarian inn, with dark-wood furnishings and beamed ceilings. Hearty helpings of regional meat and fish specialities. There is a buffet as well.

Hugo €€
International **Map** 12 D4
Bundesallee 161, 10715
Tel *544 671 11*
A neighbourhood restaurant that is popular locally for its reasonably priced prime cuts of Argentine and Black Angus beef.

DK Choice

Jolesch €€
Austrian **Map** 16 F2
Muskauer Strasse 1, 10997
Tel *612 35 81*
Tobias Janzen shows a deft touch in his subtle reinterpretation of traditional Austrian cooking in this gourmet temple. The menu is seasonal but Austrian specialities are recommended. Try Emperor Franz-Josef's favourite *Tafelspitz* (boiled beef), served here with creamed spinach, apple-horseradish, chive sauce and fried potatoes. Wash it down with excellent Grüner Veltliner. The pine-green walls and plum-coloured banquettes create a calming ambience.

Juleps New York Bar & Restaurant €€
American **Map** 11 A1
Giesebrechtstrasse 3, 10629
Tel *881 88 23*
Experience shades of an American speakeasy in this brick-walled diner-style restaurant and cocktail bar. The burgers are made with imported American beef.

For more information on types of restaurants *see pp226–7*

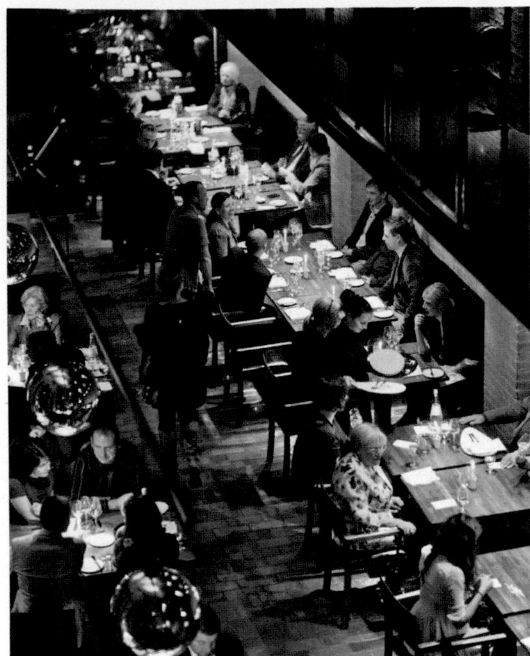

Diners at the elegant Restaurant Volt, popular for its regional cuisine

Lucky Leek €€
Vegan **Map** 2 E4
Kollwitzstrasse 54, Prenzlauer Berg
Tel *664 087 10*
Totally vegan, this top-notch gourmet spot plays with all kinds of vegetables to create dishes even carnivores will love.

La Mano Verde €€
Vegan **Map** 5 C5
Kempinski Plaza, Uhlandstrasse 181, 10623
Tel *827 031 20* **Closed** *Sun*
A wide choice of creative vegan options, with an emphasis on raw food, all of organic origin. In a very central yet slightly hidden location.

Milo €€
Jewish **Map** 11 A3
Münstersche Strasse 6, 10709
Tel *492 053 59* **Closed** *Sat*
Fine dining in this rabbi-certificated kosher restaurant in the Wilmersdor Lubawitsch Chabad Jewish centre. Traditional Jewish meat-based dishes, salmon latkes and kosher sushi!

Mio €€
Mediterranean
Samariterstrasse 36, Friedrichshain, 10247
Tel *486 241 73*
Small neighbourhood bistro with red-and-white check tablecloths and candlelit dining. An eclectic menu with healthy, flavoursome food from all parts of the Mediterranean.

Osmanya €€
Turkish
Birkenstrasse 17, 10559
Tel *488 299 99*
A cut above the average, this restaurant with opulent decor offers excellent traditional Ottoman cooking. Try the sea bass fillet, cooked in a butter and lime-flavoured sauce and served on a bed of blanched celery. Live music on weekends.

Restaurant Grunewaldturm €€
German-International
Havelchaussee 61, 14193
Tel *417 200 01*
A not too formal restaurant in a picturesque woodland setting. The terrace and beer garden offer sublime views.

Restaurant Vitruv €€
German-Mediterranean **Map** 10 E1
Hotel Leonardo Royal, Otto-Braun-Strasse 90, 10249
Tel *755 43 09 10*
Spacious hotel restaurant near Alexanderplatz offering classic German dishes and an enterprising Mediterranean-inspired menu with Asian touches.

Restaurant Z €€
Greek-Mediterranean **Map** 15 A5
Friesenstrasse 12, 10965
Tel *692 27 16*
Friendly Greek taverna best known for its lamb and fish specialities, but also well suited to vegetarians. Greek regional wines.

Schoenbrunn €€
Austrian-Mediterranean **Map** 10 F1
Am Friedrichshain 8, Friedrichshain 10407
Tel *453 05 65 10*
Enjoy a delicious Wiener schnitzel on the sun terrace of this restaurant-beer garden in Volkspark Friedrichshain.

Tugra €€
Turkish Map 11 A2
Kurfürstendamm 96, 10709
Tel *323 40 27*
Smart Turkish restaurant at the far end of Ku'damm offering Ottoman recipes from the Sultan's Golden Book. Sample the saddle of lamb in pepper cream sauce, with dates wrapped in turkey ham.

Zum Hax'nwirt €€
Regional German **Map** 11 B4
Hohenzollerndamm 185, 10713
Tel *822 51 33* **Closed** *Sun & lunch daily*
Hearty Bavarian home cooking, mainly pork dishes, is the stock-in-trade of this restaurant. Chintzy dining room and a large, leafy terrace.

Fortshaus Paulsborn €€€
Traditional German
Hüttenweg 90, 14193
Tel *818 19 10* **Closed** *Mon*
Set in a former hunting lodge and picturesquely situated near Grunewaldsee, Fortshaus Paulsborn offers game specialities, cakes and delicious pastries.

Hartmanns €€€
German **Map** 16 D4
Fichtestrasse 31, 10967
Tel *612 010 03*
Stefan Hartmann's Michelin-starred cellar restaurant is perfect for a romantic dinner à deux, Choose from the taster menu or dine à la carte. Judiciously selected and carefully curated wine list.

Horváth €€€
Modern German **Map** 16 E3
Paul Lincke Ufer 44a, 10999
Tel *612 899 92* **Closed** *Mon & Tue*
The Austrian roots of the young chef, Sebastian Frank, are

For key to prices *see p232*

reflected in the sophisticated regional German cuisine at this Michelin-starred restaurant.

Restaurant Volt €€€
Regional German **Map** 16 F4
Paul-Lincke-Ufer 21, 10999
Tel *338 402 320*
An original take on Brandenburg regional cooking from rising star chef Matthias Gleiss. Impressive setting in a 1920s electric power station.

Spindler & Klatt €€€
European-Asian **Map** 16 F1
Köpenicker Strasse 16-17, 10997
Tel *319 88 18 60*
Restaurant and nightclub overlooking the Spree. Seating indoors or on the pontoon terrace. The dance floor is in a converted warehouse building. Reservations advised.

Greater Berlin

Feine Dahme €
German-International
Gutenbergstraße 7, Kopenick, 12557
Tel *516486 47* **Closed** *Mon*
Views of Köpenick old town from this scenic spot at the confluence of the Spree and the Dahme rivers. Light meals, including breakfast and Sunday brunch, served on the sun terrace. Beer, wine and coffee also available.

Alexandrowka €€
Russian
Russische Kolonie Haus1, Puschkinallee, Potsdam, 14469
Tel *0331 200 64 78* **Closed** *Mon*
This two-storey log cabin with carved gables is located in Potsdam's delightful Russian Colony. Relax in the homely interior, complete with icon corner, while sampling beautifully prepared *zakuski* with beef stroganoff and chicken Kiev to follow.

Juliette €€
French
Jagerstr. 39, Potsdam, 14467
Tel *0331 270 17 91*
Savoir vivre in Potsdam – this elegant restaurant pleases with refined French cuisine and unobtrusive service.

Kid Creole €€
American
Bölschestrasse 10, Friedrichshagen, 12587
Tel *650 766 80*
Berlin meets New Orleans in this laid-back restaurant a short walk from Friedrichshagen S-Bahn. Mellow candelit interior and mouthwatering Cajun food. The menu features everything from gumbo and catfish to *jambalaya* (Creole stew) and ribs.

Krongut Bornstedt €€
Traditional German
Ribbeckstrasse 6, Potsdam, 14469
Tel *0331 550 65 10*
Formerly crown property, these splendid UNESCO-protected buildings have been converted into a home for a number of cafés and restaurants. The beer hall serves rustic cuisine and an original *Büffelbier* (buffalo beer) from 1689.

Maison Charlotte €€
French **Map** 8 F3
Mittelstrasse 20, Potsdam, 14467
Tel *0331 280 54 50*
This refined bistro with rustic decor and a charming back garden is in Potsdam's Dutch Quarter. It specializes in savoury pancakes as well as French classics such as *coq au vin* and Breton fish soup.

Speckers Landhaus €€–€€€
German-International
Jägerallee 13, Potsdam, 14469
Tel *0331 280 43 11* **Closed** *Sun & Mon*
Sophisticated German cooking in a restored country house dating from 1645. The menu includes rack of lamb with rosemary and Wiener schnitzel.

Spree-Arche €€
Modern German
Müggelschlösschenweg, Friedrichshagen, 12559
Tel *0172 304 21 11*
A boatman ferries guests to a floating blockhouse on the Spree. Alfresco dining on the terrace overlooking the attractive Muggelsee. The fish specialities are delicious.

Strandlust Grünau €€
Modern German
Seddinpromenade 3A, 12527
Tel *675 86 26* **Closed** *Nov–Feb, Mon*
A scenic tram ride from Köpenick Town Hall brings guests directly to the Müggelsee and this lakeside restaurant with terrace. Fish specialities and local draught beers on offer.

Weisse Villa €€
Modern German
Josef-Nawrocki-Strasse 10, 12587
Tel *640 956 47*
Wonderful views of the Müggelsee from the terrace of a 130-year-old villa, once part of the Friedrichshagen brewery. Well worth the trip out of town.

Outdoor seating on the pontoon terrace of Spindler & Klatt, located by the Spree

For more information on types of restaurants *see pp226–7*

Light Meals and Snacks

There are many popular fast-food bars and restaurants in Berlin that serve the all-pervading burgers, French fries and pizzas, some of them run by well-known international chains. By way of contrast, many of the self-service places specialize in local foods. The city's cafés are ideal stopping places for a quick meal and always offer something on the menu that will fill you up. Even more convenient are the many bars on wheels or small kiosks – *Imbissbuden* – that serve the traditional Berlin *Currywurst* *(see p228)*.

Imbissbuden and Snack Bars

The classic *Imbissbude* is a simple little kiosk selling drinks and a few light snacks, such as *Currywurst* or French fries *(Pommes)* served with mayonnaise or ketchup (or both). The former is a genuine Berlin speciality consisting of grilled, sliced sausage *(Bratwurst)*, topped with a spicy sauce and served on a paper plate with a plastic fork. These kiosks are usually located in convenient sites near the S-Bahn or U-Bahn stations, or on busy streets and junctions. **Ku'damm 195**, **Curry36** and **Konnopke** are considered the best places to experience traditional *Currywurst*, served with a home-made sauce instead of the now more usual tomato ketchup sprinkled with curry powder and fiery paprika.

Other popular snacks sold on the streets include other grilled sausages, collectively referred to as *Bratwurst*. The most common types are frankfurters *(Wienerwurst)* and a thicker kind of sausage known as *Bockwurst*. These are heated in hot water. The German variation on the hamburger theme is called *Boulette*.

Unfortunately there are few places similar to the *Imbissbuden* that offer food from other regions of Germany. One of the exceptions is **Spätzleexpress**, which also offers southern German dishes such as *Spätzle*, *Knödel* and *Maultaschen*.

Specialities from around the World

Traditional Berlin specialities are facing stiff competition from further afield. Turkish restaurants serving excellent *Döner kebabs* are on every corner. Typically a kebab is a piece of warmed flat pitta bread stuffed with hot sliced meat, lettuce, cucumber and tomatoes, and covered with a thick, aromatic, yoghurt-based sauce. Obviously the best kebabs are made by the Turks living around Kreuzberg, but you can also have an excellent version of this dish in most of the other Berlin districts. The restaurants worth trying are **Hasir**, **Maroush** or indeed any of the places around Kottbuser Tor or Oranienstrasse.

Vegetarians should opt for *falafel*, a Middle Eastern speciality widely available in Berlin. Balls of chickpeas and coriander or parsley are rolled in breadcrumbs and deep-fried, then served stuffed inside flat bread with salad and yoghurt sauce. The best places to try this excellent snack are around Winterfeldtplatz, for example **Habibi**, **Dada Falafel** and **Baharat Falafel**, or **Baraka** in the eastern part of the city. The grilled fresh vegetable kebabs at **Mustafa's Gemüsekebap** stall on Mehringdamm are also a delicious vegetarian option.

Fragrant Asian dishes are offered by **Hamy Cafe** in Hasenheide, while those with a passion for Chinese food should eat at **Pagode** in Kreuzberg on Bergmannstrasse. If you wish to try Korean cuisine, then pay a visit to **Korea-Haus** on Danziger Strasse, which serves a good-value "all you can eat" Korean buffet. A visit to **Chay Village** is a good opportunity to try out some Vietnamese specialities.

There are also many restaurants offering Indian food, mainly along Grolmanstrasse. Nearby, **Moon Thai** on Knesebeckstrasse serves delicious Thai curries and papaya salads.

Berlin's Japanese restaurants tend to be of the more exclusive type but still offer excellent soups and sushi. The best are **Sushi Bar Ishin**, **Sushi Izumi**, **Tao**, **FUKU Sushi** and **Musashi**.

Langano in Kreuzberg serves deliciously spiced Ethiopian platters; it is customary to eat here with your hands. **Taquiera Ta'Cabron** offers Mexican street food such as tacos and burritos.

Light Snacks

Those with an appetite for more traditional snacks are catered for in the establishments around S- and U-Bahn stations and on the main streets offering fresh baguettes with ham or cheese.

For an instant solution to hunger pangs, try one of the bakeries that offer delicious, freshly baked croissants or excellent *Brezeln* (pretzels) covered with coarse salt. At lunchtime, the popular **Nordsee** chain of restaurants offers fish sandwiches to take away, as does the stylish **Let's Go Sylt**. Some sandwich bars offer a selection of quiches and tarts alongside baguettes and rolls.

If a traditional American-Jewish bagel bar is what you fancy, then **Bagels & Bialys** in Rosenthaler Strasse is the place to go; the variety of fillings on offer is quite staggering.

Some places also specialize in one particular kind of dish or food. For example, **Soup-Kultur** and **Intersoup** serve only soup, but in a multitude of varieties – hot, cold, exotic, spicy or mild. Garlic-lovers should visit **Knofel** in Prenzlauer Berg. Also worth mentioning are **Deli 31** and **Deli Street**.

Another way to obtain a quick and inexpensive fill-up are self-service pizzerias such as **Piccola Italia**. Another authentic pizza restaurant is **Mr Pizz** on Kantstrasse, owned by Italians who pay special attention to the ingredients used.

Eating in Shopping Centres

One of the problems for the dedicated shopper is that eating can seriously cut down on shopping time. Fortunately, many snack bars in shopping centres have put the emphasis on fast service. Some, however, such as **KaDeWe**, manage this in stylish surroundings. A visit to this enormous shop features on most tourists' list of things to do, and its self-service café is therefore very popular. Lunch at one of the tables with a view of Wittenbergplatz is a very pleasant adjunct to a Berlin shopping trip. **The Duke** is another good choice and is just around the corner from both the KaDeWe and Peek & Cloppenburg stores, off Taventzienstrasse. This stylish restaurant serves light German and American fare, making it a popular lunch spot. Other equally busy venues are the self-service café situated in the basement of the chic **Galeries Lafayette** in Friedrichstrasse and the café in **Karstadt**.

For those reluctant shoppers who prefer to keep more emphasis on the food, there is an oasis of bars and cafés near Potsdamer Platz, in the **Arkaden** shopping centre. As well as a branch of Salomon Bagels, this centre provides a taste of the Orient in the Asia Pavillon, while fans of potatoes should pay a visit to Pomme de Terre. Here, the humble vegetable becomes the star of the meal and is served in a myriad of guises and with just as many different fillings.

For short stops in Arkaden, both the dedicated and the reluctant shopper should visit the classic Wiener Café for coffee and cakes, or Caffé e Gelato for delicious ice cream.

Eating in Museums

As a city offering a wealth of culture, many of Berlin's museums have established excellent cafés and bistros. **Café im Zeughaus** at the Deutsches Historisches Museum offers a great breakfast with views of the river Spree, while **Café im Jüdischen Museum** is a café/restaurant serving Jewish specialities at the Jüdisches Museum. **Sarah Wiener im Hamburger Bahnhof**, in the modern art museum, has some great German cakes, and the café inside the **Café im Haus am Waldsee** serves small snacks and drinks in the lush garden.

Cafés

Berlin is well served by cafés that provide a wide range of light snacks or cakes to suit everyone's budget and tastes. They are normally open from 9 or 10am in the morning until late at night. In the mornings they serve breakfast, either à la carte or as a buffet. After that the regular café menu comes into force, although breakfast items are often still available. Main meals on the menu might include a choice of salads, several hearty soup-type stews *(Eintöpfe)* and a few simple hot dishes. Prices are quite reasonable, not greater than €10. Invariably, every café has a great choice of desserts, ice creams and cakes, as well as a range of alcoholic drinks.

Around the Technical University, **Café Hardenberg** is popular with students, and near Kantstrasse you can visit **Schwarzes Café**, which is open 24 hours a day. If you are on Savignyplatz you might want to try **Café Brel**. **Café am Neuen See** is situated near the lake in the Tiergarten Park. **Buchwald**, a patisserie in Hansaviertel, offers a wide range of *Baumkuchen* (so-called "tree cakes", which resemble tree stumps).

Kreuzberg's Oranienstrasse has an array of good cafés, including **Milch und Zucker** and **Pfeiffers**. You can also explore Graefestrasse, where you'll find the delightful **Café Matilda**.

Other renowned cafés include the charming **Café Wintergarten**, located in the Literaturhaus on Fasanenstrasse, and the Viennese-style **Café Einstein**. Here you can enjoy coffee made with beans fresh from their own roasting room. The original café, in Kurfürstenstrasse, has been joined by another branch in Mitte, on Unter den Linden, whose cakes are almost as refined as those at the **Caffeehaus am Roseneck** *(see p259)*. **St. Oberholz** in Mitte is popular with freelance workers who need wireless Internet access and good coffee.

While taking a walk around Checkpoint Charlie, you could drop into **Sale e Tabacchi**, an excellent Italian restaurant.

There are many places that offer light lunches and coffee around Oranienburger Strasse and Alte and Neue Schönhauser Allees. In the evening they attract livelier crowds in search of decent music and good beer. Recommended is **Die Eins**, an atmospheric café.

An enjoyable evening can be spent investigating the options in Prenzlauer Berg. Join the in-crowd at **Anita Wronski**, a friendly café on two levels with menus in English and excellent people-watching from the tables outside. If you prefer somewhere cosy, try **Anna Blume**, with tables spilling out directly on Kollwitzplatz. On hot days a good spot to enjoy the sun is on the terrace of **November** or at **Seeblick**, which is a good place to eat.

Other reliable cafés that are well worth looking out for include **Atlantic** and **Keyser Soze**.

Coffee Bars and Tearooms

There are not many coffee bars in Berlin, but they are easily spotted, as they tend to be run by well-known coffee producers such as Eduscho or Tschibo.

Barcomi's is a real treat, an American-style coffee bar with its own roasting room and a large selection of coffees. If you need more sustenance than coffee and muffins, try **Barcomi's Deli**, where you can build your own sandwiches.

If you want a good cup of tea, then you should head for **Tadschikische Teestube**, or **TTT (Tee, Tea, Thé)**, where the choice is quite amazing.

DIRECTORY

Imbissbuden and Snack Bars

Curry36
Mehringdamm 36.
Map 14 F4.
Tel 251 73 68.
Open 9am–5pm daily.

Konnopke
Schönhauser Allee 44a (U-Bahnhof Eberswalder Str).
Tel 442 77 65.
Open 10am–8pm Mon–Fri, noon–8pm Sat.

Ku'damm 195
Kurfürstendamm 195.
Map 11 B2.
Tel 881 89 42.
Open 11am–5am Mon–Thu, 11am–6am Fri & Sat, noon–5am Sun.

Spätzleexpress
Wiener Strasse 11, Kreuzberg. **Map** 16 F2.
Tel 69 53 44 63.
Open noon–10pm daily.

Specialities from around the World

Baharat Falafel
Winterfeldstrasse 37.
Map 13 B3.
Tel 216 83 01.
Open 11am–2am daily.

Baraka
Lausitzer Platz 6.
Map 16 F2.
Tel 612 63 30.
Open noon–midnight Sun–Thu, noon–1am Fri, Sat & Sun.

Chay Village
Eisenacherstrasse 40.
Tel 89 20 45 54. **Open** 11:30am–10pm daily.

Dada Falafel
Linienstrasse 132.
Map 8 F1.
Tel 27 59 69 27.
Open 10am–3am daily.

FUKU Sushi
Husemannstrasse 14.
Tel 44 04 90 77.
Open noon–11pm Mon–Fri, 4–11pm Sat & Sun.

Habibi
Goltzstrasse 24.
Map 13 A3.
Tel 215 33 32.
Open 11am–3am Sun–Thu, 11am–5am Fri & Sat.

Hamy Cafe
Hasenheide 10.
Map 16 E5.
Tel 61 62 59 59.

Hasir
Oranienburger Strasse 4.
Map 9 B2.
Tel 28 04 16 16.
Open 11:30am–1am daily.

Korea-Haus
Danziger Strasse 195.
Tel 423 34 41.
Open noon–midnight Tue–Sun.

Langano
Kohlfurter Strasse 44.
Map 16 D3.
Tel 0151 166 723 65.
Open 4pm–midnight daily.

Maroush
Adalbertstrasse 93.
Map 16 E2.
Tel 69 53 61 71.
Open 11am–2am daily.

Moon Thai
Knesebeckstrasse 15.
Tel 312 90 42.
Open 11am–7pm Tue–Fri, 10am–4pm Sat.

Musashi
Kottbusser Damm 102.
Map 16 E3.
Tel 693 20 42.
Open noon–10:30pm Mon–Sat, 2–10pm Sun.

Mustafa's Gemüsekebap
Mehringdamm 32.
Tel 394 20 57.
Open 10am–midnight daily.

Pagode
Bergmannstrasse 88.
Map 15 A4.
Tel 691 26 40.
Open noon–11pm Mon–Thu, noon–midnight Fri–Sun.

Sushi Bar Ishin
Schlossstrasse 101.
Map 4 E4.
Tel 797 10 49.
Open 11am–7:30pm Mon–Sat.

Sushi Izumi
Kronenstrasse 66.
Tel 206 499 38.
Open 11am–11pm Mon–Fri, noon–11pm Sat, 1–11pm Sun.

Taqueria Ta'Cabron
Skalitzer Strasse 60.
Tel 32 66 24 39.
Open 1–11pm Tue–Sun.

Tao
Wilmersdorferstrasse 94.
Map 11 A2.
Tel 88 77 38 87.
Open noon–11pm daily.

Light Snacks

Bagels & Bialys
Rosenthaler Strasse 46–48.
Map 9 B2.
Tel 283 65 46.
Open 8am–11pm Mon–Sat, 9am–10pm Sun.

Deli 31
Bleibtreustrasse 31.
Map 11 B2.
Tel 88 47 41 01.
Open 11am–9pm Mon–Sat.

Deli Street
Chauseestrasse 4.
Map 8 F1.
Tel 28 09 28 33.
Open 8:30am–4:30pm Mon–Thu, 8:30am–4pm Fri.

Intersoup
Schliemannstrasse 31.
Map 8 F1.
Tel 0176 186 829 21.
Open 5pm–midnight daily.

Knofel
Wichertstrasse 33.
Tel 447 67 17.
Open Nov–Apr: 6pm–late Mon–Thu, 2pm–late Fri, 1pm–late Sat & Sun; May–Oct: 6pm–late daily.

Let's Go Sylt
Kurfürstendamm 212.
Map 11 C2.
Tel 88 68 28 00.
Open 11am–midnight Mon–Sat, noon–midnight Sun.

Mr Pizz
Kantstrasse 56a.
Tel 31 01 63 34.
Open 11am–9:30pm daily.

Nordsee
Wilmersdorfer Strasse 46.
Map 9 C3, 16 F2.
Tel 31 80 14 70.
Open 10am–8pm daily.

Piccola Italia
Oranienburger Strasse 6.
Map 9 B2. **Tel** 283 58 43.
Open noon–1am daily.

Soup-Kultur
Kurfürstendamm 224.
Map 12 D1.
Tel 88 62 92 82. **Open** noon–6:30pm Mon–Sat.

Tao
Dunckerstr. 18. **Map** 2 F2.
Tel 915 16049.

Eating in Shopping Centres

The Duke
Nürnbergerstrasse 50–55.
Map 12 A2.
Tel 68 31 54 00. **Open** 11:30am–11pm daily.

Galeries Lafayette
Französische Strasse 23.
Map 8 F4, 15 C3. **Tel** 20 94 80. **Open** 10am–8pm Mon–Sat.

KaDeWe
Tauentzienstrasse 21–24.
Map 12 E1. **Tel** 21 21 0.
Open 10am–8pm Mon–Thu, 10am–9pm Fri, 9:30am–8pm Sat.

Karstadt
Kurfürstendamm 231.
Map 12 D1. **Tel** 880 030.
Open 10am–8pm Mon–Sat.

Potsdamer Platz Arkaden
Alte Potsdamer Strasse 7.
Map 8 D5. **Open** 10am–9pm Mon–Sat.

Eating in Museums

Café im Haus am Waldsee
Argentinische Allee 30.
Tel 801 89 35.
Open noon–6pm Tue–Sun.

Café im Jüdischen Museum
Jüdisches Museum, Lindenstrasse 9–14. **Map** 15 A2. **Open** 10am–10pm Mon, 10am–8pm Tue–Sun.

Café im Zeughaus
Deutsches Historisches Museum, Unter den Linden 2. **Map** 9 A3.
Open 10am–6pm daily.

Sarah Wiener im Hamburger Bahnhof
Invaliden Strasse 50–51.
Map 8 D1.
Tel 707 136 50.
Open 10am–6pm Tue–Fri, 11am–8pm Sat, 11am–6pm Sun.

Cafés

Anita Wronski
Knaackstrasse 26–28.
Tel 442 84 83.
Open 9am–late daily.

Anna Blume
Kollwitzstrasse 2.
Tel 441 58 81.
Open 8am–midnight daily.

Atlantic
Bergmannstrasse 100.
Map 14 F4.
Tel 691 92 92.
Open 9:30am–1pm daily.

Buchwald
Bartningallee 29.
Map 6 F2. **Tel** 391 59 31.
Open 8am–8pm Mon–Sat, 9am–8pm Sun.

Café am Neuen See
Lichtensteinallee 2.
Map 6 F5. **Tel** 254 49 30.
Open 8am–late Mon–Fri, 9am–late Sat & Sun.

Café Bilderbuch
Akazienstrasse 28.
Tel 78 70 60 57.
Open 9am–midnight Mon–Sat, from 10am Sun.

Café Brel
Savignyplatz 1. **Map** 11 C1. **Tel** 318 00 20.
Open 9am–2am daily.

Café Cinema
Rosenthaler Strasse 39.
Map 9 B2. **Tel** 280 64 15.
Open noon–2am daily.

Café Einstein
Kurfürstenstrasse 58.
Map 13 A2. **Tel** 26 39 19 18. **Open** 8am–1am daily (closed in summer).
Unter den Linden 42.
Map 8 F3, 15 C3.
Tel 204 36 32.
Open 7am–10pm daily.

Café Hardenberg
Hardenbergstrasse 10.
Map 5 C5. **Tel** 312 26 44.
Open 9am–1am daily.

Café Lebensart
Unter den Linden 69–73.
Map 8 E3, 15 B3.
Tel 447 21 930.
Open 9am–11pm Sun–Thu, 9am–midnight Fri & Sat.

Café Matilda
Graefestrasse 12.
Map 16 D4.
Tel 81 79 72 88.
Open 9am–2am daily.

Café Morgenrot
Kanstanienallee 85.
Tel 44 31 78 44.
Open noon–1am Tue–Thu, 11am–3am Fri & Sat, 11am–midnight Sun.

Café Oliv
Münzstrasse 8.
Map 9 C2.
Tel 89 20 65 40.
Open 8:30am–7pm Mon–Fri, 9:30am–7pm Sat, 10am–6pm Sun.

Café Rix
Karl-Marx-Strasse 141.
Tel 686 9020.
Open 9am–midnight Mon–Thu, 9am–1am Fri & Sat, 10am–midnight Sun.

Café Ständige Vertretung
Schiffbauerdamm 8.
Tel 282 39 65.
Open 11am–late daily.

Café Wintergarten im Literaturhaus
Fasanenstrasse 23.
Map 12 D1.
Tel 882 54 14.
Open 9:30am–1am daily.

Caffeehaus am Roseneck
Hohenzollerndamm 92.
Tel 895 96 90.
Open 7:30am–10pm Mon–Fri, 8am–7pm Sat, 9am–7pm Sun.

Die Eins
Wilhelmstrasse 67A (entrance Reichstagsufer).
Map 8 E3.
Tel 22 48 98 88.
Open 9am–midnight Mon–Sat, 10am–midnight Sun.

Dolores
Rosa-Luxemburg-Strasse 7. **Map** 9 C2.
Tel 28 09 95 97.
Open 11:30am–10pm Mon–Sat, 1–10pm Sun.

Filmbühne am Steinplatz
Hardenbergstrasse 12.
Map 6 D5. **Tel** 312 65 89.
Open 9am–midnight daily.

Gorky Park
Weinbergsweg 25.
Tel 44 87 286. **Open** 9:30am–2am daily.

Kaffeestube im Nikolaiviertel
Poststrasse 19. **Map** 9 C3.
Tel 24 63 06 41. **Open** 9am–midnight daily.

Keyser Soze
Tucholskystrasse 33. **Map** 9 A1. **Tel** 28 59 94 89.
Open 7:30am–3am daily.

Kleine Orangerie
Spandauer Damm 20.
Map 4 E3. **Tel** 322 20 21.
Open 9am–midnight daily.

Milch und Zucker
Oranienstrasse 37.
Map 16 D2.
Tel 61 67 14 97.
Open 7am–8pm Mon–Fri, 8am–8pm Sat & Sun.

November
Husemannstrasse 15.
Tel 442 84 25.
Open 10am–2am Mon–Fri, 9am–2am Sat & Sun.

Pfeiffers
Oranienstr. 17 – am Heinrichplatz.
Map 16 E2. **Tel** 616 586 09. .**Open** 9am–11pm (from 10am Sun).

Potemkin
Viktoria-Luise-Platz 5.
Map 16 E2.
Tel 21 96 81 81.
Open 9am–midnight daily.

St. Oberholz
Rosenthaler Strasse 72a.
Map 9 B1. **Tel** 214 61 311.
Open 8am–midnight Mon–Fri, 9am–3am Sat & Sun.

Sale e Tabacchi
Rudi-Dutschke-Strasse 23.
Tel 252 11 55. **Open** 10am–11:30pm daily.

Schwarzes Café
Kantstrasse 148.
Map 11 C1.
Tel 313 80 38.
Open 24 hours daily.

Seeblick
Rykestrasse 14.
Tel 442 92 26.
Open 10am–2am Mon–Fri, 10am–noon Sat & Sun.

Coffee Bars and Tearooms

Balzac Coffee
Knesebeckstrasse 1.
Map 5 C5.
Friedrichstrasse 125.
Map 15 C4, 6 F4.
Open 7:30am–7:30pm Mon–Fri, 8:30am–7:30pm Sat, 8:30am–6:30pm Sun

Barcomi's
Bergmannstrasse 21.
Map 15 A5.
Tel 694 81 38.
Open 8am–9pm Mon–Sat, 9am–9pm Sun.

Barcomi's Deli
Sophienstrasse 21 (second courtyard).
Map 9 B1.
Tel 28 59 83 63.
Open 9am–9pm Mon–Sat, 10am–9pm Sun.

Einstein Coffeeshop
Friedrichstrasse 206.
Map 8 F4.
Open 7am–8pm Mon–Fri, 7:30am–8pm Sat, 9am–6pm Sun.
Friedrichstrasse 185.
Map 8 F4.
Open 8am–8pm Mon–Sat, 9am–6:30pm Sun.
Savignyplatz 11.
Map 11 C1.
Open 8:30am–7pm Mon–Sat, 9am–6pm Sun.

Tadschikische Teestube
Oranienburger Strasse 27 (in the Kunsthof arts centre). **Map** 9 A2.
Tel 204 11 12.
Open 4pm–midnight Mon–Fri, noon–midnight Sat & Sun.

TTT – Tee, Tea, Thé
Goltzstrasse 2. **Map** 13 A4. **Tel** 21 75 22 40.
Open 9am–7pm Mon–Sat, 10am–7pm Sun.

Bars and Wine Bars

Trying to make a clear distinction between wine bars, bars, pubs and *Bierstuben* or giving a precise definition for the word *Kneipe* is practically impossible. However, regardless of the nuances behind all these names, they do share some basic characteristics: they are places where drinking is the primary activity, although eating is sometimes possible; they are usually open from late afternoon or early evening but do not close till late at night or even till morning, if the atmosphere is lively.

Kneipen

In general terms, a *Kneipe* means a cosy sort of place which serves beer (although other drinks are available, too) and where you can have something to eat. The typical *Alberliner Kneipe* is a dark room with panelled oak walls, a big bar and buffet with snacks such as *Buletten* (made from pork), *Soleier* (pickled eggs), *Rollmöpse* (marinated herring) and a selection of cold meats, black pudding (blood sausage) and patés. This kind of traditional pub can still be found in the less affluent districts of Berlin – in Moabit, Kreuzberg and in Neukölln, for example – but they are not as common in the city centre. Among the most popular are **Zur Kneipe** and **Ranke 2**, as well as several *Kneipen* in Mitte around the Nikolaiviertel, including **Zum Nussbaum**.

Each *Kneipe* has its own character. More and more of them are choosing modern and inventive interiors, often specializing in less traditional kinds of food: Italian, French or Oriental. Whatever the blend, however, a relaxed atmosphere and a big choice of alcoholic beverages seem to be common features. Many *Kneipen* are evolving into a fashionable mix of *Kneipe*, bar, lounge and beer garden. One such is **Reingold** in Mitte. In Savignyplatz, you might want to visit **Dicke Wirtin**, where you can try a hearty *Eintopf* (a rich soup-type stew). The majority of these fashionable places are situated in Kreuzberg and in Prenzlauer Berg – especially around Kollwitzplatz, which is dotted with all sorts of bars and pubs. At **Ankerklause** students and political activists come together to drink, dance and put the world to rights.

Biergärten

A *Biergarten* is an outdoor venue only open during the summer months, and usually located somewhere scenic, maybe in a park or by a lake. In addition to the usual food and drinks, it completes the outdoor experience with a barbecue. **Golgatha** and **Schleusenkrug** provide a much welcome breath of fresh air in the centre of Berlin; or if you are exploring Prenzlauer Berg, try the **Prater**. After enjoying the views in Tiergarten, the **Café am Neuen See** is a pleasant place to end the day.

A Berlin trend is the open-air beach bar situated on one of the city's waterways. A popular and attractive one is **Strandbar Mitte**.

Wine Bars

Berlin wine bars tend to have a Mediterranean feel to them. Interiors are often quite rustic in style, but there are exceptions. They open from early evening and stay open late. As for food, menus feature predominantly Italian, Spanish and French cuisine, while the bar serves a huge selection of wines by the glass, bottle or carafe. **Wiener Beisl**, a wine bar with an established reputation, features French food and wine. If you are visiting Prenzlauer Berg, you might want to try **Weinstein**, which offers French and Spanish food and wine. By way of contrast, at **Lutter & Wegner** in Mitte you can match German-Austrian food with appropriate, native wines, or sample a selection of American snacks and cocktails at **Billy Wilder's**.

Bars

A Berlin bar is a good place to finish your evening, and the dedicated barfly is spoiled for choice. You should not count on food but you can drink till late, as most bars do not open until 8pm or later. Although there is no strict dress code, scruffy clothes are not really appropriate. The **Riva Bar**, one of the city's most elegant and hip bars, is tucked away under the S-Bahn viaduct, and serves some of the best cocktails in town. A Latin American atmosphere is created at **Roter Salon** by tango, salsa and all the fantastic dancers. You might step in to **Vox Bar** to try one of its huge range of cocktails in a pre-war movie setting. Don't forget to visit some of the hotel bars, which are among the best late-night venues in the city. Two worthy of mention are **Harry's New York Bar** (the later the better), in the Hotel Esplanade and the **Newton Bar**.

Gay and Lesbian Bars

Berlin has a unique tradition of nightlife for homosexuals, dating back to the 1920s, when its cabarets and bars, especially around Nollendorfplatz, were the most outrageous in Europe. Today that hardcore legacy remains, but there are also bars to suit every taste. Some, like **Café Seidenfaden**, are for women only, while **Roses** is exclusively for men. Many, like **Die Busche**, are frequented by both gays and lesbians. For a more mixed ambience, the friendly attitude of bars such as **Heile Welt** or **SO36** means they are popular with both gay and straight visitors alike.

DIRECTORY

Kneipen

Ankerklause
Maybachufer 1.
Map 16 E3.
Tel 693 56 49.

Dicke Wirtin
Carmerstrasse 9.
Map 5 C5.
Tel 312 49 52.

Diener Tattersall
Grolmanstrasse 47.
Map 11 C1.
Tel 881 53 29.

Gasthaus L.e.n.t.z
Stuttgarter Platz 20.
Tel 324 16 19.

Meilenstein
Oranienburger Strasse 7.
Map 9 B2.
Tel 282 89 95.

Ranke 2
Rankestrasse 2.
Map 12 E1.
Tel 883 88 82.

Reingold
Novalisstrasse 11.
Map 8 F1.
Tel 28 38 76 76.

Restaurant Zur Gerichtslaube
Poststrasse 28.
Map 9 C3.
Tel 241 56 97.

Slumberland
Goltzstrasse 24.
Map 13 A3.
Tel 216 53 49.

Zum Nussbaum
Am Nussbaum 3.
Map 9 C3.
Tel 242 30 95.

Zum Patzenhofer
Meinekestrasse 26.
Map 12 D1.
Tel 882 11 35.

Zur Kneipe
Rankestrasse 9.
Map 12 D2.
Tel 883 82 55.

Biergärten

Café am Neuen See
Lichtensteinallee 2.
Map 6 F5.
Tel 25 44 930.

Golgatha
Dudenstrasse 40, in Viktoriapark.
Map 14 E5.
Tel 78 52 453.

Prater
Kastanienallee 7–9.
Map 3 A5, 3 B3.
Tel 448 56 88.

Schleusenkrug
Müller-Breslau-Strasse at Tiergartenschleuse.
Map 6 E4.
Tel 313 99 09.

Strandbar Mitte
Am Monbijoupark.
Map 9 C1.
Tel 28 38 55 88.

Wine Bars

Billy Wilder's
Potsdamer Strasse 2.
Map 8 D5.
Tel 26 55 48 60.

Lutter & Wegner
Charlottenstrasse 56.
Map 9 A4.
Tel 202 95 40.

Weinstein
Lychener Strasse 33.
Tel 441 18 42.

Wiener Beisl
Kantstrasse 152.
Map 12 D1.
Tel 31 01 50 90.

Bars

Altes Europa
Gipsstrasse 11.
Map 9 B1.
Tel 28 09 38 40.

Ballhaus Berlin
Chausseestrasse 102.
Map 8 F1.
Tel 282 75 75.

Bar am Lützowplatz
Lützowplatz 7.
Map 13 A1.
Tel 262 68 07.

b-flat
Rosenthaler Strasse 13.
Map 9 B1.
Tel 283 31 23.

Gainsbourg – Bar Americain
Savignyplatz 5.
Map 11 B1, C1.
Tel 313 74 64.

Green Door
Winterfeldtstrasse 50.
Tel 215 25 15.

Haifischbar
Arndtstrasse 25.
Map 15 A5.
Tel 691 13 52.

Harry's New York Bar
Lützowufer 15 (in Hotel Esplanade).
Map 13 A1.
Tel 25 47 80.

Kumpelnest 3000
Lützowstrasse 23
Map 13 B1.
Tel 26 16 918.

Newton Bar
Charlottenstrasse 57.
Map 9 A4.
Tel 20 29 54 21.

Riva Bar
Dircksenstrasse, S-Bahnbogen 142.
Map 9 C2.
Tel 24 72 26 88.

Roter Salon
Rosa-Luxemburg-Platz 2.
Map 9 C1.
Tel 41 71 75 12.

Times Bar (cigar bar)
Fasanenstrasse 9–10.
Map 12 D1.
Tel 31 10 30.

Trompete
Lützowplatz 9. **Map** 13 A1.
Tel 22 35 75 59.

Vox Bar at the Grand Hyatt
Marlene-Dietrich-Platz 2.
Map 8 D5.
Tel 030 2553 1234.

Zur Fetten Ecke
Schlesische Strasse 16.
Tel 44 65 16 99.

Gay and Lesbian Bars

Café Seidenfaden
Dircksenstrasse 47.
Map 9 C3.
Tel 283 27 83.

Die Busche
Warschauer Platz 18.
Tel 296 08 00.

Heile Welt
Motzstrasse 5.
Map 13 A2.
Tel 21 91 75 07.

Möbel Olfe
Reichenbergerstrasse 177.
Map 16 D2.
Tel 23 27 46 90.

Roses
Oranienstrasse 187.
Map 16 E2.
Tel 615 65 70.

The Sharon Stonewall Bar
Kleine Präsidentenstrasse 3.
Map 9 C1.
Tel 24 08 55 02.

SO36
Oranienstrasse 190.
Map 15 B1, 16 D1.
Tel 61 40 13 06.

SHOPPING IN BERLIN

With a shopping centre in every district, each selling a wide variety of merchandise, Berlin is a place where almost anything can be bought, so long as you know where to look. The most popular places are Kurfürstendamm and Friedrichstrasse, but the smaller shops in Prenzlauer Berg, Friedrichshain, Schöneberg and the Tiergarten are also worth a visit. Small boutiques selling flamboyant Berlin-style clothes crop up in unexpected courtyards, while the top fashion houses offer the latest in European elegance. Early on Saturday morning is often the best time to visit the city's various markets, the most popular of which – with their colourful stalls full of hats, bags and belts – can be found on Museum Island and at the Tiergarten. The Galeries Lafayette, KaDeWe and any of the city's numerous bookshops all make ideal venues for a pleasant afternoon's window shopping.

Inside the modern, multi-level Europa-Center *(see p154)*

Opening Hours

The majority of shops are open Monday to Friday from 10am to 8pm (10am to 6pm or 8pm on Saturday), but some department stores open as early as 9am. The larger stores may open until 10pm or midnight on Friday and Saturday.

Generally, there are no lunch breaks unless the shop is a one-person business. During the six weeks before Christmas, shops stay open until late on Saturdays. Most shops close on Sundays. If you are in need of groceries or food, try one of the main train stations. You'll find supermarkets open at Hauptbahnhof, Friedrichstrasse and Ostbahnhof.

Department Stores

Kaufhaus Des Westens, better known as **KaDeWe** at Wittenbergplatz *(see p159)*, is undoubtedly the biggest and the best department store in Germany. Only products of the highest quality are sold in these luxurious halls, where virtually everything you need is on sale – from unusual perfumes and elegant underwear to *haute couture*, all sold in a system of shops-within-shops. The food hall on the sixth floor is legendary for its restaurant overlooking Tauentzienstrasse.

Galeries Lafayette on Friedrichstrasse is nothing less than a slice of Paris placed in the heart of Berlin. Perfumes, domestic accessories and clothing attract an enormous clientele, many of whom also visit the food counter, which offers a wide range of French specialities. An extraordinary glass cone rises through the middle of the store, reflecting the interiors of the shops.

Another very popular store is **Karstadt** on the Ku'damm. Although its range of goods is not as broad as the range at Galeries Lafayette, there is still an enormous choice and the top-floor restaurant offers excellent views over the city.

A typical street-side stall, brimming with souvenirs for visitors

Shopping Centres

In addition to the two biggest shopping districts in town – the Ku'damm and Friedrichstrasse – shopping centres are constantly being built, usually conveniently situated

The spacious interior of the Hugendubel department store

Milano tie shop on Kurfürstendamm

close to S-Bahn stations. These huge arcaded passageways contain an enormous number of shops. Two of the newest shopping centres are the **Bikini Berlin** concept mall near Zoo Station and the massive **Mall of Berlin** on Leipziger Platz. Like most of the shops in Berlin, they stay open until 8pm during the week. One of the newest shopping centres is the **Potsdamer Platz Arkaden**. It is very popular both as a shopping mall and a meeting place. It is visited by thousands of tourists and Berliners every day.

Of a similar character, although smaller yet still upmarket, are the glitzy shopping malls **Das Schloss**, Boulevard Steglitz and the budget-oriented Forum Steglitz, all on Schlossstrasse in the southern district of Steglitz. **Alexa** on Alexanderplatz is a huge shopping centre with some 180 stores spread over five levels, a large food court and extensive underground parking. Major international clothing retailers, bookshops, electronics outlets and toy shops are all represented.

Seasonal Sales

All shops in Berlin empty their racks and shelves in the sale, or *Schlussverkauf*, which takes place twice a year. At the end of January, before the new year's collections are displayed in shop windows, you can buy winter clothes for as little as 50 per cent of their original price. During the summer sales *(Sommerschlussverkauf)*, which take place at the end of July, you can find similarly reduced summer outfits. Goods bought in a sale are often non-returnable, but if you are really keen to take an item back, there is no harm in trying to negotiate with the shop assistant. It usually works.

A number of shops sell a variety of articles marketed as "second season" items. These are always new articles, albeit stocked for the previous season, and they are offered at often generously reduced prices. You will also find that various shops specialize in top-brand jeans, selling them at much reduced rates owing to what are often very minor defects.

How to Pay

When it comes to paying for goods, you may find that some small shops still insist on cash. In the centre of Berlin there should be a suitable cash machine not too far away *(see p284)*. Larger shops and department stores will also accept most major credit cards.

DIRECTORY

Department Stores

Galeries Lafayette
Friedrichstrasse 76–78.
Map 9 A4. **Tel** 20 94 80.

KaDeWe
Tauentzienstrasse 21–24.
Map 12 F2. **Tel** 21 21 0.

Karstadt
Kurfürstendamm 231.
Map 12 D1. **Tel** 88 00 30.

Shopping Centres

Alexa
Grunerstrasse 20.
Map 10 D3. **Tel** 269 340 121.

Bikini Berlin
Budapester Strasse 42–50.
Map 12 E1. **Tel** 55 49 64 52.

Das Schloss
Schlossstrasse 34. **Tel** 66 69 120.

Mall of Berlin
Leipziger Platz 12.
W mallofberlin.de

Potsdamer Platz Arkaden
Alte Potsdamer Strasse 7.
Map 8 E5. **Tel** 255 92 70.

Shopping Guide
W berlin-shopper.com

Shopping Guide

If you are planning to do some serious shopping in Berlin, and fear getting lost among the many possibilities, you may want to use the services of a "shopping guide". These are specialists in the know as to what's on offer in the department stores and boutiques.

A shop-floor display in the lobby of KaDeWe *(see p159)*

Clothes and Accessories

There are many shopping centres in Berlin, and nearly every district has its own high street where residents do their shopping. If it's luxury, elegance and a wide variety of goods you are after, however, then head for the shops on Kurfürstendamm, Friedrichstrasse and Potsdamer Platz. This is where all the major fashion houses and perfume makers have their shops, right in the heart of the city. Alternatively, if you want to explore the smaller boutiques of some lesser-known designers, make your way to Hackescher Markt in the Mitte district, or to Prenzlauer Berg.

Women's Fashions

The most famous fashion houses are on the Ku'damm (Kurfürstendamm) and its side streets, particularly in the area around the quietly elegant Fasanenstrasse. Among the many famous names doing business here are **Yves Saint Laurent**, **Max Mara**, **Bogner**, **Louis Vuitton**, **Chanel** and **Gucci**. Simplicity is the order of the day in the **Designer Depot** shop, making it the ideal place to buy a straightforward dress with exquisite accessories. Gucci has two shops in the area, one in Fasanenstrasse and another in the fashionable Quartier 206 on Friedrichstrasse. The latter shares the street with many other fashion houses that specialize in women's clothes: **Evelin Brandt**, **Department Store Quartier 206**, **Strenesse, Strenesse Blue** and **ETRO**, to name a few. The city's first international fashion concept store, **The Corner Berlin**, offers a mix of rare designer clothes by stars such as Roland Mouret and John Galliano, accessories, beauty products and even art in a minimalist, ultra-stylish setting.

Men's Fashions

For the full range of the latest in fashion for men, on or near Kurfürstendamm is the place to go shopping, for this is where various retailers sell clothing straight from Europe's best-known fashion houses. **Patrick Hellmann** is certainly worth a visit, with its wide choice of the best designer labels around. Clothes by Giorgio Armani, Helmut Lang, Christian Dior and Dolce e Gabbana can all be found here. Also very popular are **Anson's** and the more upmarket **Mientus**, which has a second outlet on Wilmersdorfer Strasse. **Peek & Cloppenburg**, Germany's second-largest speciality store, sells its own budget labels as well as designer clothes by Boss, Armani and Joop. **Zegna** on Kurfürstendamm is a flagship store for men. This Italian company sells some of the finest-quality suits in Germany.

Children's Clothing

Shops selling children's clothes can generally satisfy any taste, depending on how much you are willing to spend. **I Pinco Pallino** offers *haute couture* for all ages. Alternatively, the Prenzlauer Berg district, which has the highest birth rate in the whole of Germany, is dotted with small children's boutiques offering both brand names and handmade clothes. **H&M Kinder** has good-value clothes.

Young Designers

A number of galleries, studios and boutiques specialize in the so-called Berlin style, the collections on sale usually consisting of short-series items that are produced in strictly limited numbers. At one time it was possible to find shops like this across the whole of the city, but now they are concentrated mainly in the northern part of the Mitte area, where a unique fashion centre is firmly established. **NIX** offers timeless clothes made from heavy, dark fabrics and cut in classical fashion.

Among the other shops in Mitte, **Kaviar Gauche** is famous for its gorgeous cocktail dresses and bridal wear. **Made in Berlin**, on Neue Schönhauserstrasse, sells stylish vintage items. Berlin brand **MYKITA** makes high-quality eyewear that is now conquering the world. Another very popular place to buy clothes is **Chapeaux**, in Charlottenburg, while **Lisa D** offers classic and elegant dresses by one of Berlin's top female designers. Young fashion hunters looking for the latest underground trends should head to **Esther Perbandt** and **Temporary Showroom**, both located in the trendy fashion district Mitte.

Shoes and Accessories

One of the largest shoe shops in Berlin is **Schuhtick**, though the highest quality shoes can be found in the **Budapester Schuhe** chain. A good selection can also be found at the **Görtz** outlets around Kufürstendamm. The latest Italian designs are available at **Riccardo Cartillone**.

Penthesileia, on Tucholsky-strasse, offers an amusing range of handbags, which come in all kinds of shapes and sizes. If it's a hat you are after, then you need go no further than **Hut Up,** in the Heckmannhöfen. All kinds of headgear are available here, from typical Russian *shlapas* to party hats with Rastafarian dreadlocks.

Perfumes

All of the large department stores, including **KaDeWe** and **Galeries Lafayette**, offer a sizeable selection of the best-known perfumes, but there are also a number of specialist shops dotted around the city. The **Douglas** chain, which has numerous outlets, has a wide range of perfumes available at very reasonable prices.

Quartier 206 has a good selection of the better-known perfumes, but if you are looking for something unusual, then **Harry Lehmann** is the place to visit. This unique store is a perfume-lover's paradise, where Mr Lehmann himself continues an 80-year-long family tradition of mixing your very own perfume from a variety of 50 scents. He also stocks long-forgotten brands. The **Body Shop** group is popular in Berlin. Natural perfumes of all kinds can be bought here, and its policy of no animal testing is popular with customers. The Body Shop also encourages the return of its containers for recycling.

DIRECTORY

Women's Fashions

Bogner
Kurfürstendamm 42.
Map 11 C2.
Tel 88 71 77 80.

Chanel
Kurfürstendamm 188.
Map 11 C3.
Tel 885 14 24.

The Corner Berlin
Französische Strasse 40.
Map 9 A4.
Tel 94 60 30.

Department Store Quartier 206
Friedrichstrasse 71.
Map 8 F4.
Tel 20 94 65 00.

Designer Depot
Rochstrasse 2.
Map 9 C2.
Tel 28 04 67 00.

ETRO
Friedrichstrasse 71.
Map 8 F3.
Tel 20 94 61 20.

Evelin Brandt
Savignyplatz 6.
Map 11 C1.
Tel 313 80 80.

Gucci
Kurfürstendamm 190–192.
Map 11 C2.
Tel 885 63 00.
Friedrichstrasse 71.
Map 8 F3.
Tel 201 70 20.

Louis Vuitton
Friedrichstrasse 71.
Map 8 F4.
Tel 20 94 68 68.

Max Mara
Kurfürstendamm 178.
Map 12 D1.
Tel 885 25 45.

Strenesse & Strenesse Blue
Friedrichstrasse 71. **Map** 8 F3. **Tel** 20 94 60 30.

Yves Saint Laurent
Kurfürstendamm 52.
Map 11 A2.
Tel 883 39 18.

Men's Fashions

Anson's
Schlossstrasse 34.
Tel 79 09 60.

Mientus
Wilmersdorfer Strasse 73.
Map 4 F3, 5 A5, 11 A1.
Kurfürstendamm 52.
Map 11 A2.
Tel 323 90 77.

Patrick Hellmann
Kurfürstendamm 190–192.
Map 12 D2.
Tel 884 87 711.

Peek & Cloppenburg
Tauentzienstrasse 19.
Map 12 E1.
Tel 21 29 00.

Zegna
Kurfürstendamm 185.
Map 11 B2.
Tel 887 190 90.

Children's Clothing

H&M Kinder
Friedrichstrasse 78/80.
Map 8 F4.
Tel 200 739 88.

I Pinco Pallino
Kurfürstendamm 46.
Map 12 D1.
Tel 881 28 63.

Young Designers

Chapeaux
Bleibtreustrasse 51.
Map 11 B1.
Tel 312 09 13.

Esther Perbandt
Almastadtstrasse 3.
Map 9 C1. **Tel** 88 53 67 91.

Kaviar Gauche
Linienstrasse 44. **Map** 7 C1.
W kaviargauch.com

Lisa D
Hackesche Höfe, Rosenthaler Strasse 40–41.
Map 9 B2.
Tel 283 43 54.

Made in Berlin
Neue Schönhauserstrasse 19. **Map** 9 C2.
Tel 212 30 601.

MYKITA
Rosa-Luxemburg-Strasse 6.
Map 9 C1.
Tel 67 30 87 15.

NIX
Oranienburger Strasse 32.
Map 9 A2.
Tel 281 80 44.

Temporary Showroom
Kastanienallee 36a.
Tel 662 04 564.

Shoes and Accessories

Budapester Schuhe
Kurfürstendamm 43.
Map 12 D1.
Tel 88 62 42 06.
Kurfürstendamm 199.
Map 12 D1.
Tel 60 03 47 70.

Görtz
Kurfürstendamm 13-14.
Map 12 D1.
Tel 88 68 37 52.

Hut Up
Oranienburger Strasse 32.
Map 9 A2.
Tel 28 38 61 05.

Penthesileia
Tucholskystrasse 31.
Map 9 A2, 16 D1.
Tel 282 11 52.

Riccardo Cartillone
Oranienburger Strasse 85.
Map 11 C1.
Tel 281 28 21.

Schuhtick
Savignyplatz 11.
Map 11 C1.
Tel 315 93 80.
Potsdamer Platz Arkaden, Alte Potsdamer Strasse 7.
Map 8 D5.
Tel 25 29 33 58.

Perfumes

Body Shop
(in the main hall of Zoologischer Garten railway station).
Map 12 D1.
Tel 31 21 391.

Douglas
Kurfürstendamm 216.
Map 12 D1.
Tel 881 25 34.

Galeries Lafayette Parfümerie
Friedrichstrasse 76–78.
Map 8 F4.
Tel 20 94 80.

Harry Lehmann
Kantstrasse 106.
Map 11 A1.
Tel 324 35 82.

KaDeWe Parfümerie
Tauentzienstrasse 21–24.
Map 12 E1.
Tel 21 21 0.

Quartier 206
Friedrichstrasse 71.
Map 8 F3.
Tel 20 94 65 00.

Gifts and Souvenirs

Whether it is a piece of the Wall or a Prussian tin soldier, Berlin souvenirs are easy to come by. While most needs can be met on one of the main shopping thoroughfares, there are more exclusive options. If you are looking for something elegant, a piece of china made by Königliche Porzellan-Manufaktur Berlin *(see p137)* might be a good idea. Other good sources are the museum shops, notably the one in the Bauhaus Museum, with its designer household objects. For a child, a teddy bear is always an option – after all, the bear is the city's emblem. For handmade jewellery or contemporary art, head for Berliner Kunstmarkt Unter den Linden on a Sunday. In December, find the most beautifully crafted gifts on the numerous Christmas markets all over the city, the one on Gendarmenmarkt being particularly worthwhile.

Books and Music

The best places to buy books on art are the shops at major museums, where you will also find a good selection of cards, posters and general souvenirs. The best of these are in **Hamburger Bahnhof** *(see p114–15)*, **Gemäldegalerie** *(see pp126–9)*, **Museum Berggruen** *(see p168)*, **Schloss Charlottenburg** *(see p164–5)* and **Altes Museum** *(see p77)*.

The **Bücherbogen** chain offers a huge choice of books and has several outlets in the city. Other good stores include **Autorenbuchhandlung** or, if you want to combine shopping for books and art appreciation, **Artificium** has a gallery attached.

For English-language books or papers, **Saint George's** is the place to go, with its wide choice of both English and American literature. The **KaDeWe** also has a decent English-language section. **Prinz Eisenherz** has a good selection of gay literature. For second-hand books, try **Another Country** in Kreuzberg, which also operates a book exchange system. **Do You Read Me?!** in Mitte and **Motto Bookshop** in Kreuzberg both sell a wide range of fascinating magazines, including rare, small-distribution books published by independent publishers. In all of these shops the staff are usually very helpful.

Music lovers should head for **Cover Music** near the Ku'damm or, if it is classical music you are after, then **L & P Classics** has one of the finest selections. For a huge selection of old classical and jazz vinyl records, head to **Café Horenstein** in Wilmersdorf. If you happen to be short of funds, there is always the option of flicking through the second-hand CDs on offer at the Sunday antique market on Strasse des 17 Juni *(see p256)*. The market is always crammed with souvenirs and is a great huntingground for collectors of old vinyl records.

Toys

You won't have to travel far to buy a typical Berlin teddy bear – you can find them in stores all over the city, especially the gift shops in the Nikolaiviertel. If you're after a wider variety of toys, then **KaDeWe** *(see p159)* is the place to go. Like all the major department stores, KaDeWe offers a whole range of toys for children of all ages, but its teddy-bear section is second to none in Berlin. From the highly portable1-cm (0.5-inch) bear to the life-size 2-metre (80-inch) model, every kind of bear you can imagine is on sale here, so you shouldn't be disappointed. Also, the store can arrange a delivery to your home, so if your child has always dreamed of having an enormous teddy bear, this is a perfect opportunity to fulfil the dream.

Small manufacturers still make old-style wooden toys, from doll's house furniture to traditional jigsaw puzzles, and these make excellent gifts to take home. **Heidi's Spielzeugladen** on Kantstrasse and **Original Erzgebirgskunst** on Sophienstrasse are the best places to go for souvenirs of this kind. Train lovers hoping to extend their tracks and build more depots and stations should visit **Michas Bahnhof** on Nürnberger Strasse, the city's top provider of model train set accessories. An amazing range of goods is available here, including model trains from the past 100 years. They also ship internationally.

As an old Prussian capital, Berlin is also a good place to find Germanic lead soldiers; the best place to look is **Berliner Zinnfiguren Kabinett**. While most of the soldiers available are designed for children, collecting them is a popular hobby among adults, and the rarities often fetch very high prices on the market.

Flowers

It is very easy to find a nice bouquet in Berlin. Flower shops stand on nearly every street corner and the majority of them are open for business on Sundays. **Blumen-Koch** in Wilmersdorf offers an amazing selection of beautiful and colourful plants and is famous for its bouquets of exotic flowers, which are arranged and wrapped with real artistry.

China and Ceramics

The history of European china started in Germany in 1708. The alchemist Böttger, while searching for the secret of making gold, discovered instead how to make Chinese-style porcelain. Berlin soon became a major producer. **KPM (Königliche Porzellan-Manufaktur Berlin)** *(see p137)* is still in operation, and its products will satisfy even the most choosy of porcelain collectors. Plenty of newly made china is available, but if you are looking for something older, then an afternoon could be spent in some of the city's antique shops *(see pp256–7)*. Currently manufactured pieces can be bought in the KPM factory shop. Those who prefer Meissen porcelain will be able to find it in several shops along the Ku'damm.

While porcelain is expensive, an equally precious gift can be made of a ceramic dish or breakfast set, traditionally manufactured in Thuringia. With their characteristic blue and white patterns, a wide choice of exquisite Thuringian ceramics can be found in **Bürgel-Haus** on Friedrichstrasse.

Specialist Shops

If you are determined to find something unique, or even quirky, you might want to visit some of the interesting specialist shops – like **Knopf Paul**, which specializes in extraordinary buttons, or **Bären-Luftballons**, which offers a delightful variety of colourful and amusing balloons. There are also a number of shops which specialize in teas and tea-time accessories. **Tee Gschwendner** and **Berliner Teesalon** offer the best selection in this field.

Smart letter paper and good pens can be bought in **Papeterie**, but if you're still stuck for ideas, there's no harm in browsing through the specialist departments in **KaDeWe** *(see Toys)* where there's always something guaranteed to catch the eye. For gifts and clothing designed by local artists, visit **Aus Berlin** on Karl-Liebknecht-Strasse.

DIRECTORY

Books and Music

Another Country
Riemannstrasse 7.
Map 15 A4.
Tel 69 40 11 60.

Artificium
Rosenthaler Strasse 40/41.
Map 9 B1.
Tel 30 87 22 84.

Autorenbuch-handlung
Else-Urg-Bogen 599–600.
Map 5 C5.
Tel 313 01 51.

Bücherbogen
Savignyplatz. **Map** 11 C1.
Tel 31 86 95 11.

Café Horenstein
Fechnerstrasse 3.
Map 11 C5.
Tel 86 39 68 97.

Cover Music
Kurfürstendamm 11.
Map 12 D1.
Tel 395 87 62.

Do You Read Me?!
Auguststrasse 28.
Map 9 A1.
Tel 69 54 96 95.

Gemäldegalerie
Matthäikirchplatz 8.
Map 7 C5.
Tel 266 424 242.

Grober Unfug
Zossener Strasse 33.
Map 15 A3.
Tel 69 40 14 90.

Hamburger Bahnhof
Invalidenstrasse 50/51.
Map 8 D1.
Tel 266 42 42 42.

Hugendubel
Tauentzienstrasse 13.
Map 12 E1.
Tel (01801) 48 44 84.

KaDeWe
Tauentzienstrasse 21.
Map 12 E1. **Tel** 21 210.

Kulturkaufhaus Dussmann
Friedrichstrasse 90.
Map 8 F3.
Tel 202 51 111.

L & P Classics
Welserstrasse 28.
Map 11 C1.
Tel 88 04 30 43.

Lehmann's
Hardenbergstrasse 5.
Map 5 C4.
Tel 61 79 110.

Motto Bookshop
Skalitzer Strasse 68.
Tel 48 81 64 07.

Museum Berggruen
Schlossstrasse 1.
Map 4 E3.
Tel 266 42 42 42.

Prinz Eisenherz
Motzstrasse 23.
Map 11 B2.
Tel 313 17 95.

Saint George's
Wörther Strasse 27, Prenzlauer Berg.
Tel 81 79 83 33.

Toys

Berliner Zinnfiguren Kabinett
Knesebeckstrasse 88.
Map 5 C5.
Tel 315 70 00.

Heidi's Spielzeugladen
Kantstrasse 61.
Map 4 F5.
Tel 323 75 56.

Michas Bahnhof
Nürnberger Strasse 24.
Map 12 E2, 12 F2.
Tel 218 66 11.

Original Erzgebirgskunst
Sophienstrasse 9.
Map 9 B1.
Tel 282 67 54.

Flowers

Blumen Damerius
Potsdamer Platz Arkaden.
Tel 20 94 44 44.

Blumen-Koch
Westfälische Strasse 38.
Map 11 A4.
Tel 896 69 00.

China and Ceramics

Bürgel-Haus
Friedrichstrasse 154.
Map 8 F3.
Tel 20 45 26 95.

KPM
Wegelystrasse 1.
Tel 39 00 90.

Friedrichstrasse 158–164.
Map 8 F3.
Tel 204 55 835.

Specialist Shops

Aus Berlin
Karl-Liebknecht-Strasse 17.
Map 9 C3.
Tel 41 99 78 96.

Bären-Luftballons
Kurfürstenstrasse 31/32.
Map 11 C1.
Tel 26 97 50.

Berliner Teesalon
Stuttgarter Platz 15.
Tel 28 04 06 60.

Knopf Paul
Zossener Strasse 10.
Map 15 A4.
Tel 692 12 12.

Papeterie
Uhlandstrasse 28.
Map 11 C2.
Tel 881 63 63.

Tee Gschwendner
Kurfürstendamm 217.
Map 12 D1.
Tel 881 91 81.

Antiques and Objets d'Art

The antique and art markets in Berlin are booming. New galleries are opening all the time, particularly in the eastern areas of town. Spandauer Vorstadt is full of antique shops and contemporary art galleries, but the northern part of Mitte (the area around East of the Centre) is the focus of the Berlin art market. Constantly raising their standards, the galleries attract numerous art dealers and collectors, while non-commercial exhibitions organized by art societies like NGbK, NBK and KunstWerke add to the creative atmosphere. As for the antique trade, a walk through any of the city's main thoroughfares should show that it is active in just about every district.

Auction Houses

Berlin's oldest and most prestigious auction houses are **Gerda Bassenge** and **Villa Grisebach**, both of which organize sales at the start of the year and in the autumn. Bassenge specializes in graphic art, and a month before each sale an auction of books and autographs is held. A photographic auction takes place a few days after the main sale of graphic art. The prices are usually higher at Grisebach, which deals mainly in 19th-century paintings. Expressionists and modern classics often go under the hammer here. Another good auctioneer is **Kunst-Auktionen Leon Spik** on Ku'damm.

Galleries

If you are pressed for time, Spandauer Vorstadt in the northern part of Mitte might be the place to go. Since the fall of the Berlin Wall, some 30 galleries have been set up in the Linienstrasse, Auguststrasse, Sophienstrasse and Gipsstrasse areas. Among these are **Arndt** and **Eigen & Art**, both on Auguststrasse, **Contemporary Fine Arts**, **Carlier Gebauer**, **Max Hetzler**, **Mehdi Chouakri** and **Loock**. **Galerie & Buchladen Barbara Wien** and many other small galleries are on Linienstrasse. On so-called "open days" three or four times a year, all the galleries open at the same time to exhibit new collections. One is always in early October, during the Art Forum Berlin fair, providing a chance to spot the changing trends in contemporary art. It can also be enjoyable to walk this district on a Friday evening, when many galleries have opening parties (Vernissages).

Galleries near Kurfürstendamm, such as **Rodendahl, Thöne und Westphal**, offer high-quality art in a quieter atmosphere. Other galleries include **ATM Gallery, C/O Berlin** and **Michael Schultz,** as well as **Anselm Dreher**, **Barbara Weiss**, **Nature Morte** and **Galerie Stühler**. The latter offers a crossover of paintings, design and jewellery.

Antique Shops

Antique shops can be found in every district of Berlin. Near Kurfürstendamm and around Ludwigkirchplatz there are a number of high-class shops offering expensive *objets d'art*, including the exquisite Secession trinkets in **ART 1900**.

Furniture specialists can be found in Suarezstrasse in Charlottenburg, where original Thonets can be bought as well as modern designer steel items. Browse travel-related objects at **Antik Center**, or classic items from just a few decades ago at **Design 54**. Another place to go is Bergmannstrasse in Kreuzberg. In its mildly Oriental atmosphere you can often find valuable pieces among masses of junk. **Das Zweite Büro** in Zossener Strasse specializes in trading old desks, cupboards and filing cabinets, which don't come cheap, but the quality of the merchandise is excellent. Standing opposite Das Zweite Büro is **Radio Art** with its extensive collection of old radios and record players. Some other interesting shops to try are **Bleibtreu Antik** and **Lakeside Antiques**. There's a real market atmosphere in the arcades of the S-Bahn railway bridge near Friedrichstrasse where a host of street traders sell all kinds of knick-knacks, from clothes and books to cutlery and domestic accessories.

Flea Markets

Many Berliners spend their Saturday and Sunday mornings at flea markets, and after a coffee go for a stroll in the Tiergarten or to a museum. Trödel- und Kunstmarkt, on Strasse des 17 Juni near Tiergarten S-Bahn station, is the most popular market in town. It is divided into two parts, and the antique section deals with books and magazines as well as pricey rarities. If you have the time and patience to sift through the huge amount on offer, you are likely to find some great bargains. Arts and crafts trading takes place on the other side of Charlottenburger Brücke, and the goods on offer range from leather items and ceramics to colourful silk clothes and jewellery. Shops from all over Berlin are usually represented here.

From **Berliner Kunst- und Nostalgiemarkt an der Museumsinsel**, it is only a few steps to the museums. The stalls along Kupfergraben stand opposite the Pergamon- and Altes Museum, and art objects, books, records and other antiques are on display around the Zeughaus.

Young tourists and locals flock to the **Flohmarkt am Mauerpark**, occupying a stretch of land where the Berlin Wall once stood. This lively market offers antiques, curiosities, clothing, arts and crafts and home-made items every Sunday, and Saturdays in the summer. It's worth a visit just for the celebratory atmosphere with live music and street performers. Also worth a Sunday visit is the **Flohmarkt Boxhagener Platz** in Friedrichshain, one of the best small markets. For fabrics, as well as food, try the **Turkish Market** on Maybachufer in Neükolln each Tuesday and Friday.

The flea market operating in the car park near the Fehrbelliner Platz U-Bahn station opens at the weekends at 8am. You would do well to get there as early as possible, as it is full of experienced collectors who only need a few minutes to spot something valuable. If you are after memorabilia from the former GDR, you should try the stalls around Potsdamer Platz and Leipziger Platz. However, the quality and authenticity of what is on sale is often questionable.

The **Treptower Hallentrödel** market on Eichenstrasse offers everything under one roof, from old telephones and army boots to bathroom accessories and piles of very cheap books (5 for €2). The hall, a former bus depot, is worth visiting for its interesting architecture alone. Other flea markets to visit include **Antik & Trödelmarkt am Ostbahnhof**.

DIRECTORY

Auction Houses

Gerda Bassenge
Erdener Strasse 5a.
Tel 89 38 02 90.
Open 10am–6pm Mon–Thu, 10am–4pm Fri.

Kunst-Auktionen Leo Spik
Kurfürstendamm 66.
Map 12 D1.
Tel 883 61 70.

Villa Grisebach
Fasanenstrasse 25.
Map 12 D2.
Tel 885 91 50.

Galleries

Anselm Dreher
Pfalzburger Strasse 80.
Map 11 C2.
Tel 883 52 49.
Open 2–6pm Tue–Fri, 11am–2pm Sat.

Arndt
Potsdamerstrasse 96.
Map 13 C2.
Tel 20 61 38 70.
Open 11am–6pm Tue–Sat.

ATM Gallery
Eylauerstrasse 13.
Map 14 D5.
Tel 0176 34 64 222.
Open by appointment.

Barbara Weiss
Kohlfurterstrasse 41–43.
Map 16 D3.
Tel 262 42 84.
Open 11am–6pm Tue–Sat.

Carlier Gebauer
Markgrafenstrasse 67.
Map 9 A4.
Tel 24 00 86 30.
Open 11am–6pm Tue–Sat.

C/O Berlin
Hardenbergstrasse 22.
Map 9 A1.
Tel 28 44 41 60.

Contemporary Fine Arts
Am Kupfergraben 10.
Map 9 A2.
Tel 28 87 870.
Open 11am–6pm Tue–Fri, 11am–4pm Sat.

Eigen & Art
Auguststrasse 26.
Map 9 B1.
Tel 280 66 05.
Open 11am–6pm Tue–Sat.

Galerie & Buchladen Barbara Wien
Schöneberger Ufer 65, 3rd floor.
Map 13 C1.
Tel 28 38 53 52.
Open 1–6pm Tue–Fri, noon–6pm Sat.

Galerie Crystal Ball
Schönleinstrasse 7.
Map 16 E4.
Tel 600 52 828.
Open 3–8pm Tue, Fri & Sun.

Galerie Poll
Anna-Louisa-Karsch Strasse 9.
Tel 261 70 91.
Open 11am–6pm Tue–Fri, 11am–4pm Sat.

Galerie Stühler
Fasanenstrasse 69.
Map 12 D1.
Tel 881 76 33.

Loock
Potsdamer Strasse 63.
Map 8 D1.
Tel 394 096 850.
Open 11am–6pm Tue–Sat.

Max Hetzler
Goethestrasse 2/3.
Map 8 F5.
Tel 346 497 850.
Open 11am–6pm Tue–Sat.

Mehdi Chouakri
Schlegelstrasse 26.
Map 9 B1.
Tel 28 39 11 54.
Open 11am–6pm Tue–Sat.

Michael Schultz
Mommsenstrasse 34.
Tel 31 99 130.
Open 11am–7pm Tue–Fri, 10am–2pm Sat.

Nature Morte
Weydingerstrasse 6.
Map 8 F5.
Tel 030 206 548 77.
Open 11am–6pm Tue–Sat.

Rosendahl, Thöne und Westphal
Kurfürstendamm 213.
Map 11 C1.
Tel 882 76 82.
Open 10am–6pm Tue–Fri, 11am–3pm Sat.

Thomas Schulte
Charlottenstrasse 24.
Map 9 A3.
Tel 20 60 89 90.
Open noon–6pm Tue–Sat.

Antique Shops

Antik Center
Suarezstrasse 48.
Tel 208 26 81.

ART 1900
Kurfürstendamm 53.
Map 11 B2.
Tel 881 56 27.

Bleibtreu Antik
Detmolder Strasse 62A.
Map 11 B1. **Tel** 883 52 12.

Design 54
Suarezstrasse 54.
Tel 31 10 20 91.
Open 11am–6:30pm Tue–Fri, 10am–2:30pm Sat.

Lakeside Antiques
Neue Kantstrasse 14.
Map 4 E5.
Tel 25 45 99 30.

Radio Art
Zossener Strasse 2.
Map 15 A3.
Tel 693 94 35.
Open noon–6pm Thu & Fri, 10am–1pm Sat.

Das Zwieite Büro
Zopssener Strasse 6
Map 15 A3.
Tel 693 07 59.
Open 10am–6pm Mon–Fri.

Flea Markets

Antik & Trödelmarkt am Ostbahnhof
Erich-Steinfurth-Strasse.
Open 9am–5pm Sun.

Berliner Kunst- und Nostalgiemarkt an der Museumsinsel
Museumsinsel & Kupfergraben.
Map 9 A2.
Open 11am–5pm Sat & Sun.

Flohmarkt Boxhagener Platz
Boxhagener Platz.
Open 10am–6pm Sun.

Flohmarkt am Mauerpark
Bernauer Strasse 63–64.
Open 7am–7pm Sun.

Treptower Hallentrödel
Puschkinallee.
Open 10am–5pm Sat & Sun.

Turkish Market
Maybachufer Neukölln.
Open 11am–6:30pm Tue & Fri.

Food Products

Food specialities from all over the world can be found in Berlin, a fact which is due partly to the city's own lack of traditional cuisine. Gone are the days when local fare was restricted to pork knuckle with cabbage, cutlets, *Currywurst* and potatoes. Today the side streets and thoroughfares are teeming with the shops and restaurants of many nationalities – Italian, Greek, Turkish, Spanish and French, as well as Mexican, American, Japanese, Chinese and Thai. As befits any major European capital, the food is of the highest quality, and there are more and more shops providing organic products, from vegetables and wholemeal bread to various wines and beers.

Patisseries and Sweet Shops

Berliners certainly have a sweet tooth, for there are plenty of patisseries and sweet shops all over the city, and a wide range of cakes is available. A typical speciality is a doughnut known simply as a *Berliner*, but the majority of places offer a whole range of cakes along with French pastries and fruits. **Buchwald** is renowned for producing some of the best cakes in town, mainly to take away, but there are also a number of patisseries, or *Konditoreien*. Among the best of these are the two branches of the **Wiener Conditorei**, **Caffeehaus am Roseneck** and **Caffeehaus Neu-Westend**, where sweet tooths can find delicacies from Vienna.

Leysieffer shops, with their exquisite chocolates and pralines, are a serious temptation for chocoholics. Visitors should also try the large stores: **KaDeWe's Feinschmecker Etage** and **Galeries Lafayette's Gourmet** departments both have a wonderful range of confectioneries.

Cheeses

The largest selection of cheeses in Berlin can be found at the **Gourmet** in **Galeries Lafayette** which has a particularly broad choice from France. **KaDeWe**'s cheese department also offers a wide variety, while **Maître Philippe** sells only select cheeses from small producers. You won't find any fridges here, but the whole shop is air-conditioned and the aroma whets the appetite. A huge assortment of cheeses can also be found at **Vinaggio**. **Einhorn** specializes in international products, mainly sandwiches, pasta, meats and a wide variety of cheeses. **Salumeria da Pino** is also a must for cheese lovers.

Wines

Between them, **KaDeWe** and **Galeries Lafayette** have the biggest wine cellars, while smaller businesses usually specialize in wines from a particular region. **Der Rioja-Weinspezialist**, for example, sells only wines originating from northern Spain, while **La Vendemmia** specializes in Tuscan wines. A wide selection of German wines is available at **Viniculture**.

Meats, Cold Cuts and Fish

Berliners eat quite a lot of meat and meat products – the latter in particular are real German specialities. So if you are not vegetarian you should try something from the bewildering range of sausages and meat rolls. As well as the well-stocked departments in the big stores **KaDeWe** and **Galeries Lafayette**, small shops offer excellent-quality products. **Neuland Fleischerei Bachhuber** is good. It specializes in chemical- and hormone-free meats, while a broad selection of fish and game is offered in **KaDeWe's** delicatessen. **Rogacki** is another good fishmonger and **Kropp Delikatessen und Feinkost** is a well-stocked delicatessen where you can buy a variety of prepared meats.

Food Halls

The old 19th-century food halls are not as important today as they were before World War II, when they were the chief source of produce. The biggest of them all was on Alexanderplatz. The place used to teem with people 4 hours a day, but the hall wasn't rebuilt after sustaining damage during World War II. The GDR authorities had no use for such a large food hall, and with the advent of supermarkets there was no need for it.

Today there are five food halls: **Arminiusmarkthalle** in Moabit, the **Marheineke Markthalle** and **Markthalle Neun** in Kreuzberg, **Domäne Dahlem Hofladen** and **Markthalle Berlin-Tegel**. Most open all day Monday to Saturday (Markthalle Neun only on Thursday evening and all day Friday and Saturday). Typically, Berliners use the food halls to pick up the one or two speciality items they can't find in the supermarkets. Shopping in these halls is a good opportunity to try traditional German *Currywurst*: the outlets in these food halls are regarded as the best in town.

Markets

Markets offer an additional way of shopping for food. They take place twice a week, and one of the best is the **Winterfeldtmarkt**, which takes place on Wednesdays from 8am until 1pm and on Saturdays from 8am until 4pm. On Saturdays the opening hours are extended if the crowd is big, which it often is. You can buy everything from high-quality fruits, through vegetables and cheeses from all over the world to clothing and domestic accessories. Fast-food outlets offer falafel or grilled sausages, and the place is surrounded by bars and cafés full of clients and traders relaxing with a glass of beer. The atmosphere and range of goods on offer is truly international.

Türkisher Markt am Maybachufer is a big Turkish market which opens on Tuesdays and Fridays. It is popular with Turks living in Kreuzberg and Neukölln. The stalls offer all kinds of Turkish specialities. There are also markets in the city centre on Kollwitzplatz – the **Ökomarkt** and **Neuer Markt** on Thursdays and Saturdays and the **Markt am Wittenbergplatz** on Thursdays. In fact, Thursday is the day when Wittenbergplatz is invaded by farmers from all over the region offering a variety of products. You won't find any exotic fruits at these, but if you have had enough of tasteless supermarket tomatoes and apples, then they should provide a good alternative. Depending on the season, you can buy pickled gherkins *(Salzgurken)* from the Spreewald, asparagus from the Beelitz region and delicious, sweet aromatic strawberries. **Domäne Dahlem Ökomarkt** offers a good selection of organic foods on Wednesdays and Saturdays.

DIRECTORY

Department Stores with Food Halls

Galeries Lafayette Gourmet
Friedrichstrasse 76–78.
Map 8 F4.
Tel 20 94 80.

KaDeWe's Feinschmecker Etage
Tauentzienstrasse 21–24.
Map 12 E2.
Tel 21 21 0.

Patisseries and Sweet Shops

Buchwald
Bartningallee 29.
Map 6 F3.
Tel 391 59 31.

Caffeehaus Am Roseneck
Hohenzollerndamm 92.
Tel 895 96 90.

Caffeehaus Neu-Westend
Reichstrasse 81.
Tel 364 10 60.

Fassbender & Rausch
Charlottenstrasse 60.
Map 9 A4.
Tel 20 45 84 443.

Kolbe & Stecher Bonbonmacherei
Heckmann Höfe, Oranienburger Strasse 32.
Map 9 A1.
Tel 4405 52 43.

Leysieffer
Kurfürstendamm 218.
Map 12 D1.
Tel 885 74 80.

Leysieffer
Quartier 205, Friedrichstr. 68.
Map 8 F4.
Tel 20 64 97 15.

Wiener Conditorei Caffeehaus
Hagenplatz 3.
Tel 89 72 93 60.

Cheeses

Einhorn
Wittenbergplatz 5–6.
Map 12 F2.
Tel 218 63 47.

Maître Philippe
Emser Strasse 42.
Map 11 B3, 11 C3.
Tel 88 68 36 10.

Salumeria da Pino
Windscheidstrasse 20.
Map 4 E5.
Tel 324 33 18.

Vinaggio
Monbijouplatz 2.
Map 9 B2.
Tel 257 60 831.

Wines

Der Rioja-Weinspezialist
Akazienstrasse 13.
Tel 782 25 78.

La Vendemmia
Akazienstrasse 20.
Tel 787 125 35.

Viniculture
Grolmanstrasse 44–45.
Tel 883 81 74.

Meats, Cold Cuts and Fish

Kropp Delikatessen und Feinkost
Karl-Marx-Strasse 82.
Map 16 F5.
Tel 623 1090.

Neuland Fleischerei Bachhuber
Güntzelstrasse 47.
Map 11 C4.
Tel 873 21 15.

Rogacki
Wilmersdorfer Strasse 145–146. **Map** 4 F4.
Tel 343 82 50.

Food Halls

Arminiusmarkthalle
Arminiusstrasse 2–4.
Map 6 E1.
Open 7:30am–6pm Mon–Thu, 7:30am–7pm Fri, 7:30am–3pm Sat.

Domäne Dahlem Hofladen
Königin-Luise-Strasse 49, Dahlem.
Tel 66 63 00 23.

Marheineke Markthalle
Marheinekeplatz.
Map 15 A5.
Tel 6128 61 46.
Open 8am–8pm Mon–Fri, 8am–6pm Sat.

Markthalle Berlin-Tegel
Gorkistrasse 13–17.
Tel 43 43 849.
Open 8am–7pm Mon–Fri, 8am–4pm Sat.

Markthalle Neun
Eisenbahnstrasse/ Pücklerstrasse.
Open 5–10pm Thu, 10am–6pm Fri & Sat.

Markets

Domäne Dahlem Ökomarkt
Königin-Luise-Strasse 49, Dahlem.
Tel 666 30023.
Open 8am–1pm Sat.

Markt am Wittenbergplatz
Wittenbergplatz.
Map 12 F2.
Open 10am–6pm Thu.

Neuer Markt am Kollwitzplatz
Prenzlauer Berg.
Open 9am–4pm Sat.

Ökomarkt am Kollwitzplatz
Prenzlauer Berg.
Open noon–7pm Thu.

Türkischer Markt am Maybachufer
Maybachufer.
Map 16 E3, 16 F4.
Open 11am–6:30pm Tue & Fri.

Winterfeldtmarkt
Winterfeldplatz.
Map 13 A3.
Open 8am–1pm Wed, 8am–4pm Sat.

ENTERTAINMENT IN BERLIN

With so much on offer, from classical drama and cabaret to variety theatre and an eclectic nightclub scene, it is possible to indulge just about any taste in Berlin. During the summer months many bars and restaurants set up outdoor tables, and the area around Unter den Linden, the Kurfürstendamm, Kreuzberg and Prenzlauer Berg, in particular, seems to turn into one large social arena. The city really comes into its own at night, when its clubs, all-night cafés and cocktail bars give you the chance to dance till dawn. The city has many nightlife centres, each with a slightly different character. Prenzlauer Berg is best for mainstream bars, cafés and clubs, while Friedrichshain has a bustling nightlife, and Kreuzberg and Schöneberg have a vibrant gay scene. The Mitte district *(see East of the Centre, pp88–99)* offers a true mixture, its opera house and classical theatre surrounded by lively and inexpensive bars. On a Sunday, a quiet trip down the river or along the canals offers a pleasant way to unwind.

The Berlin Philharmonic Orchestra

Practical Information

There are so many things going on in Berlin that it can be difficult to find what you're looking for. The Information Centre offers basic information *(see p278)*, but for greater detail you can buy a copy of the listings magazines *Tip* or *Zitty*, which offer the widest range of suggestions. Information on festivals, sports events, cinema programmes, theatre schedules, cabarets and concerts can be found on websites www.berlinonline.de and www.visitberlin.de.

But if you've only just arrived in town and haven't made it yet to an Internet café or a kiosk, the chances are the bar you're sitting in, or your hotel foyer, has leaflets on the wall to point you in the right direction. And there is no end of posters around town telling you what's on offer.

Guides

You won't be short of cultural guides in Berlin. The fortnightly listings magazines *Tip* and *Zitty*, which cover the widest choice of events, are issued on Wednesdays, while the daily newspaper *Berliner Morgenpost* has daily culture pages, as do the other major newspapers *Taz*, *Berliner Zeitung* and *Tagesspiegel*. All of these can be bought at news kiosks.

For culture information in English, pick up a copy of the *Exberliner* magazine, which has feature stories and listings. It can be found at English-language bookshops, as well as a few cafés.

The monthly magazine *Kunst* (Art) is a dual-language guide to galleries and exhibitions. It also has an informative website (www.kunstmagazinberlin.de).

Tickets

Tickets can usually be bought two weeks before an event, and you can buy them directly at theatre box offices or make a telephone booking. Reserved tickets have to be picked up and paid for at least half an hour before a show. Students, pensioners and the disabled are entitled to a 50 per cent discount, but you will need to present appropriate

The Admiralspalast entertainment complex *(see p71)*

Berlin's Jazzfest features traditional jazz music *(see p268)*

documentation. You can also pre-book tickets at special outlets all over Berlin but they charge a 20 per cent commission. All the major theatres and concert halls have special wheelchair access, but the number of places for the disabled is limited; make it clear when buying a ticket that you need an appropriate place. Tickets to some theatres include a pass for public transport.

If a performance has sold out, you can always try to find tickets just before the show, for some of the pre-booked tickets may not have been collected. One agency which specializes in these last-minute purchases is called **Hekticket Theaterkassen**. You can buy tickets on the day, even an hour before a performance. If someone has already returned their ticket, you might be able to buy it at a 50 per cent discount.

Other agencies to contact for tickets are **Interklassik**, on Friedrichstrasse, and **Koka 36** on Oranienstrasse in Kreuzberg.

Information for the Disabled

In all the guides to theatres and concert halls the availability of wheelchair access is noted by a distinctive blue sign. The majority of the bigger theatres, halls and opera houses have special places for wheelchairs and seats reserved for people with walking difficulties. When buying a ticket you must specify your need, as the number of places is limited.

If you are disabled you should be able to commute without restriction on public transport, as the majority of U- and S-Bahn stations have lifts, and they are clearly marked on maps of the underground. Many buses now have special ramps and facilities for wheelchairs, but if you experience any difficulty members of the BVG staff will always help.

Public Transport at Night

The last U-Bahn trains run just before 1am, but buses and trams continue running every half an hour, making Berlin's night-time transport one of the most efficient in Germany. Bus and tram timetables are linked, and there are two major interchange points: one on Hardenbergplatz, near the Zoo railway station, and the other on Hackescher Markt. On Friday and Saturday nights you can also use all U-Bahn lines (except 4 and U55), which operate every 15 minutes throughout the night. Some S-Bahn lines also work at night over the weekend. Every ticket office and information point in town has brochures with details about night-time public transport.

Ornate Elephant Gate at the Zoo Berlin *(see p154)*

Afternoon with the children in the Museumsdorf Düppel *(see p189)*

DIRECTORY

Ticket Agents

Hekticket Theaterkassen
Hardenbergstrasse 29d.
Map 12 D1.
Tel 230 99 30.

Karl Liebknechtstrasse 13.
Map 9 D2.
Tel 230 99 30.

Interklassik
In Dussmann Kulturkaufhaus, Friedrichstrasse 90.
Map 8 F3.
Tel 20 16 60 93.

Koka 36
Oranienstrasse 29.
Map 16 E2.
Tel 61 10 13 13.
W koka36.de

Theatres

Thanks to Reinhardt and Brecht, Berlin became a landmark in the European theatre scene in the 1920s, and its success continues to this day. During the years of Nazi rule, many people working in the business were killed or forced to emigrate as the stage became a propaganda machine, but after World War II a revival spread through Berlin's theatres. At the heart of this revival were Bertolt Brecht and his Berliner Ensemble, and Peter Stein who ran the Schaubühne.

Modern History

Following the construction of the Berlin Wall, the number of venues doubled as each part of the divided city worked to build its own theatres. The Volksbühne in the East had its equivalent in the West called the Freie Volksbühne, and the eastern acting school, the Academy, was matched by a second Academy in the west.

The economic difficulties caused by the reunification of Germany forced a number of places to shut down, but the theatres of East Berlin managed to survive. In the west, the Freie Volksbühne and the Schiller-Theater (the largest stage in Germany) had to close, but the Volksbühne, under Frank Castorf, and the Deutsches Theater, led by Thomas Langhoff, continued to do well. Independent theatres have fared equally well in both parts of the city.

The theatre season runs from September to July, with its peak in May during Berliner Theatertreffen (Berlin Theatre Forum), when many other German theatre groups are invited to stage their plays. There are also a number of youth theatres which produce the work of young writers, and these follow the seasons of the major venues.

Repertoires are published in the listings magazines *Tip* and *Zitty*, and also displayed on yellow posters in U-Bahn stations and thoughout Berlin. Leaflets are available in many restaurants around the city.

Major Stages

The **Deutsches Theater** and its small hall **Kammerspiele** on Schumannstrasse is a top-class theatre and offers a varied repertoire of productions with very professional modern stagings. From the Greek classics to the modern classics and contemporary plays, the Deutches Theater has successfully staged them all. Tickets for these plays can be difficult to obtain, but it is worth persevering.

At **Volksbühne** you can see interesting performances of classical plays in modern settings, as well as adaptations of books or films or pieces written by young writers. Concerts, lectures and dance evenings are organized in the Red and Green Salon of the theatre, and with so much going on the Volksbühne now seems more of a cultural centre with a multimedia character than just a stage.

Although it was particularly important for German theatre in the 1970s and 1980s, **Schaubühne am Lehniner Platz** is no longer as popular as it was, which is a shame, for production values don't get any higher than this. The close attention to detail – on everything from the sets and scenery to the choice of music and the editing of the printed programme – is extraordinary, and distinguishes it from the other theatres in town.

The **Berliner Ensemble** (or BE for short) has been managed by such influential dramatists as Bertolt Brecht from 1949 and then Heiner Müller in 1970. The spectacles created by these two are still performed today. The whole theatre is magnificent, and it has some superb architecture including the stage; after each performance you can meet the actors in the canteen in the courtyard. Another venue well worth visiting is **Hebbel am Ufer, Hau Eins** – an ambitious place with a programme that includes contemporary plays and modern dance.

Other major venues include the **Maxim Gorki Theater**, which offers English subtitles, and the **Renaissance-Theater**. The **Schlosspark Theater** is a former state theatre that is now a private enterprise with an interesting repertoire.

Small Stages and Alternative Theatre

There are a number of alternative theatres in Berlin, each enthusiastically playing the works of what are generally lesser known authors. **Hebbel am Ufer, Hau Eins** is devoted to avant-garde theatre and dance and is considered to be the city's best alternative stage. The smaller boulevard theatres, like **Theater am Kurfürstendamm** or **Komödie am Kurfürstendamm**, offer different, lighter programmes.

Among other small theatres are **Bat-Studiotheater** and **Kleines Theater**. There are many other notable venues, including **Theater 89**, **Heimathafen Neukölln** and the **Vagantenbühne**.

To enjoy theatre in English, head to the **English Theatre Berlin**, which produces many of its own original productions, as well as classics and improvisational pieces.

Musicals, Reviews and Cabarets

There are four main musical theatres in Berlin, in addition to the many small venues which fit musicals into their more general repertoire. **Friedrichstadtpalast** and the historic **Admiralspalast**, both in the eastern part of the city, stage many of the new major shows as well as musicals and variety shows. A smaller stage at Friedrichstadtpalast hosts cabaret. The **Theater des Westens** in Charlottenburg is more traditional, while the

Theater am Potsdamer Platz is a modern theatre set up in 1999.

As for cabaret, there are probably as many acts in Berlin today as there were in the 1920s, usually performed by small itinerant groups which rely on the hospitality of theatres for a venue. **Distel**, in Friedrichstrasse, continues its success from GDR times, and **Stachelschweine** celebrates its popularity in western Berlin.

There are many more venues for musicals, reviews and cabarets. Among these are **Bar jeder Vernunft**, **Chamäleon Variété**, **Shake! Das Zelt am Ostbahnhof**, **Scheinbar**, **Wintergarten Varieté** and **Die Wühlmäuse**.

Tickets

It is usually possible to pre-book tickets two weeks before a performance. You can buy them directly from the box office of the theatre or by telephone booking. There are also ticket vendors all over town, but they usually charge a per cent commission. Even if the theatre or concert has been sold out, there is still a chance of buying something just before the performance, provided that not all pre-booked tickets have been collected.

Hekticket Theaterkassen specializes in this kind of last-minute ticket. If you are lucky enough to pick up a ticket on the day of performance, you may find it has been returned and reduced to half its former price.

DIRECTORY

Major Stages

Berliner Ensemble
Bertold-Brecht-Platz 1.
Map 8 F2.
Tel 28 40 80.

Deutsches Theater
Schumannstrasse 13a.
Map 8 E2, 15 A1.
Tel 28 44 10.

Hebbel am Ufer
Hau Eins
Stresemannstrasse 29.
Hau Zwei
Hallesches Ufer 32.
Hau Drei
Tempelhofer Ufer 10.
Map 14 F2.
Tel 25 90 00.
W **hebel-am-ufer.de**

Maxim Gorki Theater
Am Festungsgraben 2.
Map 9 A3.
Tel 20 22 11 15.

Renaissance-Theater
Knesebeckstrasse 100.
Map 5 C5.
Tel 312 42 02.

Schaubühne am Lehniner Platz
Kurfürstendamm 153.
Tel 89 00 23.

Schlosspark Theater
Schlossstrasse 48.
Map 4 E4.
Tel 789 56 67.

Volksbühne
Linienstrasse 227.
Map 10 D1.
Tel 30 24 06 55.

Small Stages and Alternative Theatre

Bat-Studiotheater
Belforter Strasse 15.
Tel 755 41 77 77.
W **bat-berlin.de**

English Theatre Berlin
Fidicinstrasse 40.
Map 14 F5.
Tel 691 12 11.
W **etberlin.de**

Heimathafen Neukölln
Karl-Marx-Strasse 141.
Tel 56 82 13 33.

Kleines Theater
Südwestkorso 64.
Tel 821 20 21.
W **kleines-theater.de**

Sophiensaele
Sophienstrasse 18.
Map 9 B1.
Tel 283 52 66.

Theater 89
Putlitzstrasse 13.
Map 8 F1.
Tel 31 16 11 90.

Theater und Komödie am Kurfürstendamm
Kurfürstendamm 206/209. **Map** 11 C2.
Tel 88 59 11 88.

Vagantenbühne
Kantstrasse 12a.
Map 12 D1.
Tel 312 45 29.

Musicals, Reviews and Cabarets

Admiralspalast
Friedrichstrasse 101.
Map 8 F2.
Tel 47 99 74 99.

Bar jeder Vernunft
Schaperstrasse 24.
Map 12 D2.
Tel 883 15 82.

BKA Theater
Mehringdamm 34.
Map 14 F4.
Tel 202 20 07.

Chamäleon Variété
Rosenthaler Strasse 40–41.
Map 9 B2.
Tel 40 00 59 30.

Distel
Friedrichstrasse 101.
Map 8 F2.
Tel 204 47 04.

Friedrichstadt-Palast
Friedrichstrasse 107.
Map 8 F2.
Tel 23 26 23 26.

Kalkscheune
Johannisstrasse 2 (behind Friedrichstadtpalast).
Map 8 F2.
Tel 59 00 43 40.

Scheinbar
Monumentenstrasse 9.
Map 13 C5.
Tel 784 55 39.

Shake! Das Zelt am Ostbahnhof
Am Postbahnhof 1.
Tel 29 04 78 40.

Stachelschweine
Europa-Center, Tauentzienstrasse 9–12.
Map 12 E1.
Tel 261 47 95.

Theater am Potsdamer Platz
Marlene-Dietrich-Platz 4.
Tel (0180) 54 444.

Theater des Westens
Kantstrasse 12.
Map 4 E5, 11 A1, 12 D1.
Tel (0180) 54 444.

Wintergarten Varieté
Potsdamer Strasse 96.
Map 13 C2.
Tel 58 84 33.

Die Wühlmäuse
Pommernallee 2–4.
Map 3 B5.
Tel 30 67 30 30.

Tickets

Hekticket Theaterkassen
Hardenbergstrasse 29d.
Map 12 D1.
Tel 23 09 930.
Karl Liebknechtstrasse 13.
Map 9 D2.
Tel 230 99 30.

Cinema

Berlin has always been the capital of German cinema, and it is likely to remain so. In November 1895, exactly two months after the Lumière Brothers presented their first moving pictures in France, brothers Emil and Max Skladanowsky showed a series of short films to a spellbound German public. Wintergarten Varieté-theater was the place where you could go to see those famous pioneering films of kangaroos fighting, acrobats tumbling and children performing folk dances. By 1918 there were already some 251 cinemas with 82,796 seats available in Berlin, and by 1925 the number of people involved in the film industry had reached 47,600. The history of UFA (Universal Film AG), established in 1917, is intimately linked to that of Berlin, for the company has its two studios here.

Big Screens and Big Films

Many cinemas can be found around Breitscheidplatz, near the Ku'damm, Tauentzienstrasse and Alexanderplatz. After the fall of the Berlin Wall, many new multiplex cinemas were built, the biggest being the **CinemaxX Potsdamer Platz** and the **Cinestar Sony Center**. At the Cinestar, mainstream Anglo-American movies are dubbed, rather than subtitled, but you can also see films in their original language here. Next to the Cinestar, the CinemaxX is the city's largest multiplex, with a total of 19 screens. Here cinema-goers can see all the latest Hollywood and German blockbusters. The **Zoo Palast**, historic seat of the Berlinale, now offers weekly screenings of films in their original language.

Next door to CinemaxX is the **IMAX** cinema – the biggest screen in Germany. It can only show films that are shot with an Imax camera, but the spectacle is always breathtaking. Its huge curved screen is 27 m (89 ft) across and covers approximately 1,000 sq m (10,750 sq ft). It shows a range of films including natural history, travel and underwater features, as well as a selection of 3D films that require special viewing glasses.

Each February, Potsdamer Platz is taken over by the **Berlin International Film Festival**, or Berlinale. Hundreds of films are screened, and Berliners often queue for hours to get hold of the popular tickets. You can also buy tickets online at the festival's website.

Three other areas of Berlin are known as cinema centres: East of the City, in Friedrichshain and in Prenzlauer Berg. For those curious about the days of the GDR, the **Kino International** on Karl-Marx-Allee, built in 1963, is typical of cinemas built in the Communist era. It's pretty austere and only has 551 seats.

Studio Cinemas

There are plenty of small studio cinemas scattered across town, and it is in these that new independent films and retrospectives of particular actors and directors are shown. Cinemas like **Hackesche Höfe Kino**, situated near Hackescher Markt, offer a pleasant break from the bustle of modern city life, and most have bars of their own. The café at Hackesche Höfe Kino offers light snacks as well as a wonderful fifth-floor view over the nearby neighbourhood.

The **Kino Arsenal**, on Potsdamer Platz, belongs to the Freunde der Deutschen Kinemathek (Friends of German Cinema) and is ideal for lovers of German film, for this is where you can see all the national classics. The venue has a detailed monthly programme which includes four screenings per day, many of which come with a small introductory lecture. Copies of the programme are distributed in bars all over town.

If you're interested in original language movies, **Cinéma Paris** in Charlottenburg is the place to go for French films, while the **Odeon** in Schöneberg specializes in English and American films.

There are also many tiny neighbourhood cinemas and *kino*-bars, which have their own charm. Among the best are the **Tilsiter Lichtspiele** in Friedrichshain, and the **Lichtblick Kino** in Prenzlauer Berg, which plays *Casablanca* at midnight every Saturday.

Open-Air Cinemas

Open-air cinemas start operating as soon as the weather allows. They can be found in parks and open spaces all across town. Some of the nicest are the **Freiluftkinos** Kreuzberg and Friedrichshain, as well as the **Openair** inside the Schloss Charlottenburg. All of these outdoor venues show a selection of current first-run films as well as the established classics. Screenings start when it starts to grow dark – around 9pm during summer.

Non-Commercial Films

Although most people tend to go to the cinema nowadays to see the latest blockbuster movie from Hollywood, it is still possible to track down some of the venues which show less popular films including documentaries and other non-commercial films.

The **Zeughauskino** specializes in non-commercial films. It co-ordinates its interesting and informative repertoire with exhibitions in the Deutsches Historisches Museum (the German Historical Museum), as well as showing its own series of documentaries.

Prices

Cinema tickets usually cost between €8 and €11 and students and senior citizens don't always receive a discount. Many cinemas declare Tuesday or Wednesday as Cinema Day, when tickets are €1–€2 cheaper. Some cinemas also organize so-called "Blue Mondays" when tickets are reduced to as little as €4.

In most cinemas there are usually three shows per evening, the first at 6pm and the last at around 10pm. Some cinemas accept telephone bookings, but you have to turn up to pay for your ticket at least half an hour before a show; otherwise, it may go to somebody else. Most ticket offices don't take credit cards, so have cash in hand. Twenty minutes of commercials precede most screenings, although some venues use this time to show short films by up-and-coming directors.

The Film Business

If you're interested in the business of film production, visit Studio UFA in Babelsberg, Potsdam. A must for all cinema fans, the **Studiotour Babelsberg** allows you to see a live film crew working on a current production *(see p207)*. You will also get a chance to see some classic film sets – some going back to the days of Marlene Dietrich – as well as samples of the latest technical wizardry.

A wide variety of books, in many different languages, about cinema and film can be found in **Bücherbogen** under the arcade of the S-Bahn railway bridge at Savignyplatz. Alternatively, you can try **Bücherstube Marga Schoeller** at 33 Knesebeckstrasse, near Kurfüstendamm.

DIRECTORY

Big Screens and Big Films

CinemaxX Potsdamer Platz
Potsdamer Strasse 5.
Map 8 D5.
Tel (040) 80 80 69 69.

Cinestar Sony Center
Potsdamer Strasse 4.
Map 8 D5.
Tel 26 06 64 00.

IMAX
Potsdamer Strasse 4.
Tel 26 06 64 00.

Kino International
Karl-Marx-Allee 33 (corner of Schillingstrasse).
Map 10 E3.
Tel 24 75 60 11.

Zoo Palast
Hardenbergplatz 8.
Map 6 D5.
Tel 25 40 10.

Studio Cinemas

Cinéma Paris
Kurfürstendamm 211.
Map 11 A2, 12 D1.
Tel 881 31 19.

Hackesche Höfe Kino
Rosenthaler Strasse 40–41.
Map 11 C2.
Tel 283 46 03.

Kino Arsenal
Potsdamer Strasse 2/ Sony Center.
Map 12 F2.
Tel 26 95 51 00.

Lichtblick Kino
Kanstanienallee 77.
Tel 44 05 81 79.

Odeon
Hauptstrasse 116.
Map 13 B5.
Tel 78 70 40 19.

Tilsiter Lichtspiele
Richard-Sorge-Strasse 25a. **Tel** 426 81 29.

Open-Air Cinemas

Freiluftkino Friedrichshain
Volkspark Friedrichshain.
Map 10 F1.
Tel 29 36 16 29.

Freiluftkino Kreuzberg
Adalbertstrasse 73. **Map** 16 E1. **Tel** 293 61 60.

Openair Schloss Charlottenburg
Spandauer Damm 10.
Map 4 E2.
Tel (01805) 44 70.

Film Festivals

Berlin International Film Festival
Every February, Potsdamer Platz.
Tel 259 200.
W berlinale.de

The Film Business

Bücherbogen am Savignyplatz
Stadtbahnbogen 593.
Tel 31 86 95 11.

Studiotour Babelsberg
August-Bebel-Str. 26–53, Potsdam (entrance Grossbeerenstrasse).
Tel (0331) 721 27 50.

Non-Commercial Films

Zeughauskino
Unter den Linden 2.
Tel 20 30 44 21.

Famous Films About Berlin

Berlin Alexanderplatz
Germany 1931, directed by Phillip Jutzi, based on Alexander Döblin's book.

Berlin Alexanderplatz
GDR 1980, directed by Rainer Werner Fassbinder.

Berlin Calling
Germany 2008, directed by Hannes Stöhr.

Berlin, Chamissoplatz
GDR 1980, directed by Rudolf Thome.

Berlin, die Symphonie einer Grossstadt (Berlin, Symphony of a Great City)
Germany 1927, directed by Walter Ruttmann.

Berlin – Ecke Schönhauser
GDR 1957, directed by Gerhard Klein.

Berliner Ballade (Berlin Ballad)
American Occupied Zone 1948, directed by Robert Stemmle.

Cabaret
USA 1972, directed by Bob Fosse.

Coming Out
GDR 1988/1989, directed by Heiner Carow.

Eins, zwei, drei (One, two, three)
USA 1961, directed by Billy Wilder.

Goodbye Lenin!
Germany 2003, directed by Wolfgang Becker.

Der Himmel über Berlin (Wings of Desire)
GDR/France 1987, directed by Wim Wenders.

Kuhle Wampe
Germany 1932, directed by Slatan Dudow, script by Bertolt Brecht.

Das Leben der Anderen (The Lives of Others)
Germany 2006, directed by Florian Henckel von Donnersmarck.

Die Legende von Paul und Paula (The Legend of Paul and Paula)
GDR 1973, directed by Heiner Carow.

Menschen am Sonntag (Men on Sunday)
Germany 1930, directed by Robert Siodmak and Edgar G Ulmer.

Lola rennt (Run, Lola, Run)
Germany 1998, directed by Tom Tykwer.

Sonnenallee
Germany 1999, directed by Leander Haußmann.

Classical Music and Dance

Berlin has one of the world's finest orchestras (the Berlin Philharmonic Orchestra) and two of the most beautiful concert halls (the Philharmonie and the Konzerthaus). The Berlin Philharmonic is pre-eminent among the city's three symphonic orchestras, all of which perform regularly in Berlin. There are three major opera houses to choose from and a smaller one for lovers of the avant-garde. The opera houses have interesting ballet programmes built into their repertoires, performed largely by resident dance companies. Throughout the year, the city also attracts international ballet groups. Apart from regular concerts, the city offers many festivals, two of the most popular being MaerzMusik and the Classic Open Air Festival on Gendarmenmarkt. Smaller concerts are organized in the city's many churches, halls and palaces.

Concert Halls

The **Philharmonie** is one of Europe's grandest concert halls, boasting excellent acoustics. It houses the Berlin Philharmonic Orchestra, which was founded in 1882 and achieved great popularity under the conductor Herbert von Karajan. In 1989, the orchestra was taken over by Claudio Abbado, a worthy successor, and since 2002 it has been directed by Sir Simon Rattle, an acclaimed British conductor. Tickets for popular programmes quickly sell out. Chamber orchestras perform in the smaller **Kammermusiksaal** attached to the bigger hall.

With its elegant surroundings, **Konzerthaus Berlin**, formally known as the Schauspielhaus *(see p67)*, is one of the best places to listen to classical music. The building was restored after World War II and now contains a large concert hall and a smaller room for chamber music. Classical concerts are also held at the **Universität der Künste** and the **Staatsbibliothek** (State Library).

Many churches in Berlin also open their doors for concerts throughout the year. Berliner Dom in Mitte is a spectacular venue with an excellent concert programme. For a guide to all these events, look up the listings magazines *Tip* or *Zitty (see p260).*

Opera and Classical Ballet

Among Berlin's three major opera houses, the **Staatsoper Unter den Linden** *(see p65)*, under the leadership of Daniel Barenboim, is a gem and is one of the leading opera venues in the world. This beautiful building underwent major restoration works from 2011 until 2015. The repertoire includes the traditional German classics, Italian opera, classical ballets and, to a lesser extent, contemporary pieces.

Komische Oper *(see p70)* is known for its broad range of lighter opera, for which you can nearly always find tickets. The ballet produced here is particularly innovative.

Opera productions at the **Deutsche Oper Berlin** are often modern and intriguing. The repertoire includes music ranging from major Italian operas and Mozart to Wagner and Saint-Saëns.

The **Neuköllner Oper** in the Neukölln district is an innovative and productive stage.

Modern Dance

Modern dance productions are held in **Hebbel am Ufer** at its three sites on Stresemannstrasse, Hallesches Ufer and Tempelhofer Ufer. In recent years, however, **Tanzfabrik** in Kreuzberg and **Sophiensaele** and **Radialsystem V** in Mitte have become equally dynamic centres of avant-garde dance, as has the International Choreographic Theater of Johann Kresnik in the Volksbühne *(see p262–3).*

Contemporary Music

The Berlin organization **Initiative Neue Music Berlin e.V.** publishes a website with information about current performances of contemporary music. It always includes **BKA** near Mehringdamm with its weekly programme of **Unerhörte Musik**.

Festivals

The Berliner Festwochen festival has been divided into **Musikfest Berlin**, held throughout September, and **spielzeiteuropa**, a theatre and dance festival stretching from October to December. Each festival promises a range of events and attracts famous orchestras and soloists from around the world.

Contemporary music festival **MaerzMusik**, held every March, sees numerous world premieres of newcomers and established composers alike.

The Young Euro Classic festival is a platform for the best young symphony orchestras from all over the world, who convene in Berlin's prestigious Konzerthaus every August.

Once a year, for Berlin Night of Theatres and Operas, around 60 of the capital's stages, connected by shuttle buses, open late and offer short productions to touring visitors.

Berlin Klassiktage is an annual summer festival of classical music with evening concerts held in historic settings all over the city.

A real treat for music lovers is the wonderful Classic Open Air Festival featuring opera and concerts that is held every summer on an open stage on Gendarmenmarkt, which is built especially for the occasion. Another musical feast is the Bach-Tage festival in Potsdam, which takes place every year in September.

Open-Air Concerts

Classical open-air summer concerts are staged at **Waldbühne**, in a beautiful leafy setting near the Olympiastadion. The venue seats 20,000 and once a year features the Berlin Philharmonic Orchestra. The atmosphere is relaxed and informal, with kids running around while parents eat and drink during the shows. After sunset, when the crowds light candles brought for the occasion, the atmosphere becomes magical.

Music in Palaces and Notable Buildings

During music festivals, recitals are often held in Berlin's beautiful historic buildings, and a concert in the Berliner Dom *(see p79)*, the Orangerie in Schloss Charlottenburg *(see pp164–5)* or Schloss Friedrichsfelde *(see pp182–3)* can be an unforgettable and delightful experience.

Various

The **Musikinstrumenten Museum** offers entertaining concerts on selected Sunday mornings, and as a part of the *Alte Musik Live* scheme you can listen to the music of old masters played on their original instruments. A special booklet covering the museum's various musical events is available from all theatres, concert halls and music shops. The Konzerthaus Berlin and Komische Oper have regular classical concerts, tours and demonstrations for children. Find a calendar of all classical music events in Berlin at the website www.klassik-in-berlin.de (English version is available).

The **Kulturkaufhaus Dussmann** shop offers the widest range of music in Berlin, with a stock of over 50,000 titles, and staff always ready to help you. Literary readings, lectures and other special cultural events are also staged at the store. **Gelbe Musik** is also more than a shop; it has a gallery specializing in contemporary music and co-ordinates many concerts and recitals.

DIRECTORY

Concert Halls

Konzerthaus Berlin
(Schauspielhaus)
Gendarmenmarkt 2.
Map 9 A4.
Tel 203 0921 330.
W konzerthaus.de

Philharmonie & Kammermusiksaal
Herbert-von-Karajan-Strasse 1.**Map** 8 D5.
Tel 25 48 80.

Staatsbibliothek
Potsdamer Strasse 33.
Tel 2660.

Universität der Künste
Hardenbergstrasse 33.
Map 6 E3.
Tel 31 85 23 74.

Opera and Classical Ballet

Deutsche Oper Berlin
Bismarckstrasse 35.
Map 5 A4.
Tel 34 38 43 43.

Komische Oper
Behrenstrasse 55–57.
Map 8 F4.
Tel 47 99 74 00.

Neuköllner Oper
Karl-Marx-Strasse 131–133, Neukölln.
Map 16 F5.
Tel 688 90 777.

Staatsoper Unter den Linden
Unter den Linden 7.
Map 9 A3.
Tel 20 35 45 55.
(Until 2015: Bismarckstrasse 110.
Map 5 A4.)

Modern Dance

Hebbel am Ufer

Hau Eins
Stresemannstrasse 29.
Map 8 E5.

Hau Zwei
Hallesches Ufer 32. **Map** 14 F2. **Tel** 259 00 427.

Hau Drei
Tempelhofer Ufer 10.
Map 14 F2.
Tel 25 90 00.
W hebel-am-ufer.de

Radialsystem V
Holzmarktstrasse 33.
Map 10 F5.
Tel 288 788 50.
W radialsystem.de

Sophiensaele
Sophienstrasse 18.
Map 9 B1.
Tel 283 52 66.
W sophiensaele.com

Tanzfabrik
Möckernstrasse 68.
Map 14 E4.
Tel 786 58 61.
W tanzfabric-berlin.de

Contemporary Music

Initiative Neue Musik Berlin e.V.
Klosterstrasse 68–70.
Map 10 D3. **Tel** 242 45 34.
W inm-berlin.de

Unerhörte Musik (BKA)
Mehringdamm 34.
Map 14 F3.
Tel 20 22 00 33.

Festivals

MaerzMusik
Berliner Festspiele GmbH
Schaperstrasse 24.
Map 12 D2.
Tel 254 892 18.

Musikfest Berlin/ spielzeiteuropa
Berliner Festspiele GmbH
Schaperstrasse 24.
Map 12 D2.
Tel 254 892 44.

Open-Air Concerts

Waldbühne
Glockenturmstrasse 1.
Tel (01806) 57 00 70.

Various

Gelbe Musik
Schaperstrasse 11.
Map 12 D2.
Tel 211 39 62.

Kulturkaufhaus Dussmann
Friedrichstrasse 90.
Tel 202 51 111.

Musikinstrumenten Museum
Tiergartenstrasse 1.
Map 8 D5.
Tel 25 48 10.

Tickets

Hekticket
Reduced and last-minute tickets only.
Tel 230 99 30.

Interklassik in Kulturkaufhaus Dussmann
Friedrichstrasse 90.
Tel 201 660 93.

KaDeWe Theaterkassen
KaDeWe department store (6th floor),
Tauentzienstrasse 21.
Map 12 F2.
Tel 212 122 77.

Rock, Jazz and World Music

To music lovers Berlin can mean anything from techno to the Berlin Philharmonic Orchestra, for the city has a thriving and multi-faceted music industry. Between its classical and ultra-modern extremes the full spectrum of musical taste is catered for, from bar-room blues to rock'n'roll and international pop. Whether it's a major event by a world-famous band or a small-scale evening of jazz improvization, you needn't look far to find what you want. The biggest events take place in sports halls and stadiums, but most of the action can be found in discos, bars and the city's various clubs *(see pp270–71)*. There are also a number of cultural centres where you can stop by to listen to modern music. The best way to find something for yourself is to get hold of a copy of the listings magazines *Zitty* or *Tip*, and look out for flyers and leaflets in bars.

Big Concerts

Berlin is always high up on the list when major pop, rock or jazz bands go on tour. While people flock from all over the country to attend these events, there are a number of smaller events which attract an equally devoted audience. Since the closure of the huge Deutschlandhalle, the big events take place in **Max-Schmeling-Hall** and the Velodrom *(see p273)*. For the really big crowds, events are usually held at the **Olympiastadion** *(see p178)* which has seating for 100,000. The **Waldbühne** next door has a capacity of 20,000 and hosts both classical orchestras and rock bands. **Kindl-Bühne Wuhlheide** is another equally flexible venue. Concerts and plays are also organized at the popular **Arena** in Treptow – a very large music hall, dating from the 1920s, which used to be a local bus depot. The massive **O2 World** arena is located in Friedrichshain. It hosts many of the large touring pop concerts, as well as sport events and other productions. For detailed information about what's on and where, consult the websites berlinonline.de and berlin.de, or the listings magazines *Zitty* and *Tip*.

Other Musical Events

There are plenty of smaller venues in Berlin where concerts are held. Among them are **Lido** and the famous **SO36** in Kreuzberg. The future of this legendary venue is uncertain, due to the gentrification of the area. See it before it disappears.

Schöneberg was notorious in the 1980s for its punk rock scene, but while those days are now over, there are still plenty of exciting things on offer here today. One of the most popular places in town is **Tempodrom** (check listings magazines for up-to-the-minute details).

Columbia Halle, which is located near Columbiadamm, is a well-known location for medium-size events, and so is the **Astra Kulturhaus** on Revalerstrasse, which hosts a range of indie, rock, punk and pop artists. If you are looking for particularly atmospheric concerts, try the **Passionskirche**, a church in Kreuzberg. Another good location to check out is the large **Kulturbrauerei** complex in Prenzlauer Berg. This former brewery now houses dozens of venues, playing a mix of world, rock and electronic music.

Jazz

Jazz lovers from all over the world descend on Berlin for the **Jazzfest Berlin**, and its accompanying **Total Music Meeting**, both of which are held each year. The former is more traditional, but the latter is devoted to modern experimental work. "Jazz across the Border" takes place in July; it is a festival at which all kinds of borders are crossed, not least those of musical inhibition.

As far as regular clubs are concerned, jazz is still very popular in Berlin, in spite of the pull of its perhaps better-known electronic and techno discotheques. The **A Trane** and **b-flat** are classical jazz bars where you can listen to small bands just about every night of the week.

Another great venue is **Quasimodo** on Kantstrasse, which has a relaxed and intimate atmosphere. Its concerts only start after 10pm, when performances at Theater des Westens have finished; the vibrations would otherwise disturb the neighbouring audience. The acoustics at Quasimodo are also excellent and many big names in jazz have performed on its stage. Another good venue for enjoying jazz is **Bilderbuch**, on Akazienstrasse.

Apart from the typical, classical jazz clubs, jazz can also be heard in many of the city's smaller bars, like **Kunstfabrik Schlot** on Kastanienallee. If it's a mixture of soul, rap and jazz you want to listen to, then head for the **Junction Bar** in Kreuzberg. The **Badenscher Hof Jazzclub** on Badensche Strasse is another great place for jazz. It has a varied programme of mainstream jazz, modern jazz and blues.

World Music

As a broadly cosmopolitan city with an increasingly multi-national population, Berlin is home to a wide variety of music. Lovers of world music should visit Berlin in May, when the large and lively Karneval der Kulturen takes place. The main event is an exciting street parade through Kreuzberg featuring marching bands and dance troupes playing an extremely diverse array of music. The presence of music from all parts of the world is never that far away.

The **Haus der Kulturen der Welt** on John-Foster-Dulles-Allee is an institution set up by the Berlin Upper Chamber to support this cosmopolitanism, and its main aim is to make non-European cultures more accessible to Germany. As music is one of the best ways of bridging cross-cultural differences, the Haus der Kulturen der Welt organizes all kinds of concerts at its own **Café Global** – one of the best Saturday-evening venues for listening to and dancing to music from all over the world. Details of the bands on offer can be found in a booklet which should be available in bookshops and restaurants around town.

A similar organization is the **Werkstatt der Kulturen** on Wissmannstrasse, which has been staging all kinds of cultural events for some years now. These include regular concerts and music festivals. Between them, the Haus der Kulturen der Welt and the Werkstatt are the most reliable providers of world music in town, but you can also find a number of bars and clubs that specialize in the music of one particular nation. Details of these can be found in the listings magazines *Zitty* and *Tip*, and on flyers all over town.

Latin American discos are becoming ever more popular throughout Berlin – **Havanna** in Schöneberg is one of the city's most popular and largest.

Irish music is also well represented in the city, and all you have to do is visit a few pubs. Live music is played in **Wild at Heart** on almost every night of the week.

Tickets

The price of tickets for major pop concerts can be astronomical, particularly if you want to secure a good seat. At the other extreme, you should be able to get into smaller clubs for €5–€12, but again, if a famous person or band is playing you will have to pay a good deal more. Often you will find the ticket price includes a drink at the bar.

Tickets for major events are likely to sell out quickly and should be booked well in advance; there are numerous ticket offices in the busier parts of town *(see p261)*.

If you just want to spend the night at a club, you should have no trouble buying a ticket at the door.

DIRECTORY

Big Concerts

Arena
Eichenstrasse 4.
Tel 533 20 30.

Kindl-Bühne Wuhlheide
Strasse zum FEZ 4 (An der Wuhlheide). **Tel** 530 79 53.

O2 World
Mühlenstrasse 14–30.
Tel 20 60 70 88 99.

Waldbühne
Glockenturmstrasse 1.
Tel (01806) 57 00 70.

Other Musical Events

Astra Kulturhaus
Revalerstrasse 99.
Tel 20 05 67 67.

Columbia Halle and Columbia Club
Columbiadamm 13–21.
Tel 69 81 28 14.

Kulturbrauerei
Schönhauser Allee 36.
Tel 44 35 26 14.

Lido
Cuvrystrasse 7.
Map 8 E5.
Tel 695 66 840.

Meistersaal
Köthener Strasse 38.
Map 8 E5.
Tel 325 999 715.

Passionskirche
Marheineckeplatz 1–2.
Map 15 A5.
Tel 69 40 12 41.

SO36
Oranienstrasse 190.
Map 16 E2.
Tel 61 40 13 06.

Tempodrom
Am Anhalter Bahnhof, Möckernstrasse 10.
Map 14 E1.
Tel 0185 55 41 11.

Tipi am Kanzleramt
Grosse Querallee, Tiergarten.
Map 7 C3.
Tel 39 06 65 50.

UFA Fabrik
Victoriastrasse 10–18.
Tel 75 50 30.

Jazz

A Trane
Pestalozzistrasse 105.
Map 5 C5.
Tel 313 25 50.

Aufsturz
Oranienburger Strasse 67.
Map 9 A1.
Tel 280 474 07.

b-flat
Rosenthaler Strasse 13.
Map 9 B1.
Tel 283 31 23.

Badenscher Hof Jazzclub
Badensche Strasse 29.
Map 12 D5.
Tel 861 00 80.

Bilderbuch
Akazienstrasse 28.
Map 13 A5.
Tel 78 70 60 57.

Jazzfest Berlin
Schaperstrasse 24.
Map 12 D2.
Tel 25 48 90.

Junction Bar
Gneisenaustrasse 18.
Tel 694 66 02.

Kunstfabrik Schlot
Edisonhöfe, Chausseestrasse 18.
Map 3 A4.
Tel 448 21 60.

Quasimodo
Kantstrasse 12a.
Tel 31 80 45 60.

Yorckschlösschen
Yorckstrasse 15.
Map 14 E4.
Tel 215 80 70.

World Music

Haus der Kulturen der Welt & Café Global
John-Foster-Dulles-Allee 10.
Map 7 C3.
Tel 39 78 70.

Havanna
Hauptstrasse 30.
Map 13 A5.
Tel 784 85 65.

Kulturbrauerei
Schönhauser Allee 36.
Tel 44 35 26 14.

Werkstatt der Kulturen
Wissmannstrasse 32.
Map 16 E5.
Tel 60 97 700.

Wild at Heart
Wiener Strasse 20 (Kreuzberg).
Tel 61 07 47 01.

Clubs

Berlin is considered the clubbing capital of Europe. Countless clubs with an atmosphere from trashy to classy attract visitors from all over the world. The years after the fall of the Wall provided a limitless supply of new locations, from old bank vaults to abandoned power stations, though some of these have closed to make way for more profit-oriented uses. Still, the city parties on and the endurance of Berlin's late-night scene is stunning. Parties rarely get going before midnight, and after-work and after-hours parties serve as a connection to the next night out. Few clubs specialize in a particular kind of music but rather reserve certain days of the week for different styles; find out what you are in for online, or through a number of free magazines and flyers distributed widely in bars.

Techno

Although the legendary Love Parade that used to lure over a million devotees into town has moved on, Berlin still considers itself to be the techno capital and looks on its clubs, with their striking locations, as cultural assets. **Berghain** is one of the world's biggest and most renowned techno clubs. Combined with its upstairs **Panorama Bar**, the former power station is a unique Saturday-night cathedral of techno and house but is not always easy to get in to due to its selective door policy. **Tresor**, Berlin's first techno club, moved from its old bank vaults to a post-industrial location in Mitte. The somewhat eerie place can absorb several thousand people and is open Wednesdays to Saturdays.

Watergate, in Kreuzberg, is located right beside the beautiful Oberbaumbrücke bridge on the banks of the Spree and is favoured by techno, D&B, minimal and house DJs from all over the world. Both sound system and visual effects are spectacular at this temple of hedonism that also sports a floating outside terrace.

Located inside a swimming pool complex that dates back to the early 1900s, the **Stattbad Wedding** is a club devoted to techno and house music. It attracts a hip, young crowd thanks to its renowned resident DJs.

On Thursdays, popular **Sage Club** in Mitte has mostly rock, less techno and house; it features live acts, DJs and theme nights. One of the dancefloors is adorned with a fire breathing dragon and instead of air conditioning, an outdoor pool provides welcome relief in the summer.

Discos

If it's a good old-fashioned disco you're looking for, with happy tunes and a little less of the techno, then **Sophienclub** is the place to go. It was famous even before the fall of the Wall and attracts a mixed crowd that is into classic and independent rock, soul, R&B, dance and pop. **FritzClub im Postbahnhof**, a multi-floor party and disco venue in two former mail cargo halls that accommodates up to 1,200 guests, is favoured by an under-25 student crowd that couldn't care less about dress codes. Also in Friedrichshain, **Matrix** is a booming club and disco, its vaulted brick catacombs bustling with a young crowd. **Narva Lounge** next door is a little more refined, with two dance floors, a cocktail bar and white leather booths to be seen in. Ritzy **Adagio** at Potsdamer Platz is styled like a medieval castle and attracts a good mix of both young and a little more mature party-goers. A stunning location and premises, with high ceilings, chandeliers and a dress code, is **Goya**, favoured by thirty-somethings who are eager to dance.

Trendy and Alternative Clubs

Twelfth-floor **WeekEnd** at Alexanderplatz is a beautifully designed bar-cum-rooftop-terrace club with a stunning view over downtown east Berlin. Resident and visiting DJs spin mostly hip-hop, electro, deep-house and funk. The most grown-up feature here is the prices.

For the quintessential Berlin experience, try retro-style **Kaffee Burger**, where the legendary "Russendisko" was born. Parties, often featuring Russian bands and DJs, are wild; the interior is a mix of 1950s Germany and Soviet realism. **ADS**, near Ostbanhof, has a programme spanning from techno raves to rock concerts to digital culture festivals, where experts in digital art, music and animation present their work to the public – culminating in a digital music party. **K17** is a rather dark "goth", punk and electro club playing different music on each of its four floors.

Bohannon is an unpretentious but nicely styled soul and oldies club with two bars in Mitte. It is frequented by a friendly and open-minded thirty-something crowd. Also located near Hackescher Markt, **Flamingo** is a trendy nightclub and cocktail bar on the riverfront. **Felix Club Restaurant** at the backside of Adlon Hotel may be as posh as the location suggests – but the symbiosis of Italian cuisine and relaxed clubbing works for Berlin's fashionable and wealthy.

For a more underground experience, try the **Cassiopeia** in trendy Friedrichshain (good for electro, house, funk, ska, old-school rap and reggae) that, apart from dance floors, features an outdoor rock-climbing tower. **SO36** in Kreuzberg is a classic and still worth a visit for a Karaoke or ballroom-dancing night, a punk or rock concert or one of the regular oriental gay parties.

The front part of **Oscar Wilde**, in the location of a popular 1920s dance hall on Friedrichstrasse, is an Irish pub, while the backroom has wild soul and hip-hop parties. There are also a couple of surviving old dance halls to go and waltz. Among the oldest is **Clärchens Ballhaus** in Mitte, shared by patrons of all ages dancing to an eclectic mix of German classics, chart hits and the Beatles.

Lounges

For those not sure whether they feel like dancing the night away, Berlin's lounges are good for a relaxed evening. In contrast to the clubs, they tend to be open every day. **PURO Sky Lounge** near the KaDeWe on Tauentzien is a very stylish rooftop club with great sunset views. Elegant **Solar** near Potsdamer Platz offers great views from the 17th floor. **40seconds** serves as a restaurant and bar before the DJs get going after 11pm. This exclusive penthouse venue also has incredible 360-degree views. **Spindler und Klatt** in Kreuzberg is a former grain warehouse now sporting lounge beds to sprawl on, one-stop dining and clubbing. In summer, the riverside terrace is a huge bonus.

Gay and Lesbian Clubs

Berlin has a very tolerant attitude to people with different sexual orientations. A big day for the whole city is the gigantic parade on Christopher Street Day, which takes place annually at the end of June. Berlin Pride Festival is celebrated for three weeks pre-ceding the CSD. Berlin's gay community meets at countless bars, clubs and discos, many of them found around Nollendorfplatz in Schöneberg, or in gay-friendly clubs like **Berghain/Panorama Bar**.

The city's most popular gay discos are **SchwuZ**, in Neukölln, and **Connection** on Fuggerstrasse. Many clubs usually frequented by straight people also have regular gay nights, such as Shade Inc at **Flamingo** on Wednesdays.

For lesbians, the best club is Café Fatal at **SO36**. It admits gay men to a Sunday dance.

Special Interest

You want to check the dress/undress code before heading out to legendary **Kit-Kat Club**. On most nights, guests are requested to shed most of their clothes on entering this adult playground. The techno and trance club has plenty of room to dance, but also to lie down and relax – which is practised by clubbers of all sexual persuasions.

DIRECTORY

Techno

Berghain/ Panorama Bar
Am Wriezener Bahnhof 20 (Friedrichshain).
Tel 293 602 10.

Sage Club
Köpenicker Strasse 76–78.
Map 10 D5.
Tel 278 98 30.

Stattbad Wedding
Gerichtstrasse 65.
Tel 467 973 50.

Tresor
Köpenicker Strasse 70.
Map 10 E5.
Tel 629 08 750.

Watergate
Falckensteinstrasse 49 (Kreuzberg).
Tel 612 803 95.

Discos

Adagio
Marlene-Dietrich-Platz 1.
Map 8 D5.
Tel 258 98 90.

FritzClub im Postbahnhof
Strasse der Pariser Kommune 8.
Tel 698 12 80.

Goya
Nollendorfpl. 5.
Map 13 A2.
Tel 419 939 000.

Matrix
Warschauer Platz 18 (U/S Warschauer Strasse).
Tel 293 69 990.

Narva Lounge
Warschauer Platz 18.
Tel 293 69 990.

Sophienclub
Sophienstrasse 6.
Map 9 B1.

Trendy and Alternative Clubs

ADS
An der Schillingbrücke 33–34. **Map** 10 F5.
Tel 212 38 190.

Bohannon
Dircksenstrasse 40.
Map 9 C2.
Tel 695 05 287.

Cassiopeia
Revaler Strasse 99.
Tel 473 85 949.

Clärchens Ballhaus
Auguststrasse 24.
Map 9 A1.
Tel 282 92 95.

Felix Club Restaurant
Behrenstrasse 72.
Map 4 F3, 8 E4.
Tel 301 117 152.

Flamingo
Kleine Presidentenstrasse 4a.
Tel 0179 326 7587.

K17
Pettenkoferstrasse 17.
Tel 42 08 93 00.

Kaffee Burger
Torstrasse 60.
Map 9 C1.
Tel 280 464 95.

Oscar Wilde
Friedrichstr. 112a.
Map 8 F1. **Tel** 282 81 66.

SO36
Oranienstrasse 190.
Map 16 E2.
Tel 614 013 06.

WeekEnd
Alexanderstrasse 7.
Map 10 D2.
Tel 246 31 676.

Lounges

40seconds
Potsdamer Strasse 58.
Map 13 C2.
Tel 890 642 20.

PURO Sky Lounge
Tauentzienstrasse 9–12.
Map 12 E1. **Tel** 263 678 75.

Solar
Stresemannstrasse 76.
Map 14 E1.
Tel 0163 765 27 00.

Spindler und Klatt
Köpenicker Strasse 16 (Kreuzberg).
Tel 319 881 860.

Gay and Lesbian Clubs

Berghain/Panorama Bar
(see Techno)

Connection
Fuggerstrasse 33.
Map 12 F2.

Flamingo
(see Trendy and Alternative)

SO36
(see Trendy and Alternative)

SchwuZ
Rollbergstrasse 26.
Tel 57 70 22 70.

Special Interest

Kit-Kat Club
Köpenicker Strasse 76.
Map 10 D5.

Sport and Recreation

Berlin is a sports-loving town, and every year the major sports events attract a growing number of fans and competitors. The Berlin Marathon, run in September, is now the third largest in the world, its 42-km (26-mile) distance tackled by runners and roller-skaters – able-bodied and disabled alike. The Bundesliga (German football league) cup final takes place in May in the Olympia Stadion. Crowds of each team's supporters converge on the city a few days before the game, and after the match they all join a huge party for the winners along the Ku'damm. The world tennis elite battle it out during the German Open championship every April.

Cycling

The flat terrain, numerous parks and countless special routes for cyclists – which reach a total of 850 km (530 miles) – make Berlin a cycle-friendly city. Bikes can be taken along on the S- or U-Bahn trains, which provide easy access to the three most popular routes – along the Havel river, around the Grunewald forest and around the Müggelsee, but make sure to buy a special bike ticket.

There are many places all over Berlin where you can rent a bike for €8–€15 per day *(see p293)*, provided you leave a deposit in cash. The best hotels and hostels in town also hire out their own bikes for guests. The route from the historic centre of Mitte to the Ku'damm via Tiergarten can be an unforgettable experience.

In January those lovers of two wheels meet during Berliner Sechs-Tage-Rennen in the **Velodrom** on Paul-Heyse-Strasse. You might have some problems buying a ticket as the event is very popular, so give them a call beforehand. For information concerning routes, events, tours or anything else you may need to know about cycling in Berlin, contact the **ADFC (Allgemeiner Deutscher Fahrrad-Club)**.

Golf

Just about every sporting discipline is catered for in Berlin, and golfing is no exception. The **Golfer's Friend Driving Range** golf club is located in the west of the city, on Cordesstrasse 3. It is open from 9am to 10pm on weekdays in summer, and from 10am on weekends. The hours are slightly shorter in spring, autumn and winter, and the range closes when it snows. A bucket of 30 balls costs €5. **Golf Berlin-Mitte** offers an indoor practice net.

There are two golf courses within Berlin: the **Golf und Landclub Berlin-Wannsee**, which has a large 18-hole course and a smaller one with 9 holes, and **Berliner Golfclub-Gatow**, which only has an 18-hole course, plus a 6-hole practice course. There are more than 20 golf clubs around Berlin, most of which have excellent restaurants and are situated close to hotels.

Swimming Pools

Public swimming facilities in Berlin are extremely clean and you can always swim there safely. Some of the best places to try are on the Havel river and the city's lakes. Swimming on natural beaches is free, but there are no changing rooms or toilet facilities.

Berlin also has a number of artificial beaches which are all manned by lifeguards. The best known is the **Strandbad Wannsee**, which was built in the 1920s and remains very popular today. Other excellent spots can be found around Müggelsee.

One of the most beautiful swimming pool complexes is **Olympiastadion** *(see p184)*, which was a venue for the 1936 Berlin Olympic Games. A special pool for diving has a 10-m (33-ft) tower with a lift. Alternatively, you can simply sunbathe on the steps and admire the view.

The three most beautiful swimming pools are situated in Mitte, Neukölln and Wilmersdorf. **Stadtbad Mitte**, on Gartenstrasse, is a painstakingly restored building which dates from the 1930s. It has a 50-m (164-ft) pool designed for sporting events as well as recreational swimming. **Stadtbad Charlottenburg**, on the other hand, offers a smaller pool which is more appropriate for relaxation than serious swimming; it is also beautifully decorated with Secessionist paintings. But if it's a swim in luxurious surroundings you want, then take a dive at the **Stadtbad Neukölln**; the extraordinary decorative mosaics, frescoes and marble-and-bronze ornamentation is enough to make you forget why you came here in the first place.

Two equally stunning experiences are guaranteed at the **Badeschiff Arena** on the river Spree in Treptow. In summer, the arena is a floating, open-air swimming pool on the riverbank. In winter, it is transformed into a space-like, enclosed swimming hall. The **Tropical Islands** water and fun park, southeast of Berlin, is a huge, artificial paradise set in a vast construction hall once built for zeppelins.

Badminton, Squash and Tennis

You won't have to travel far in Berlin to find facilities to play badminton, squash or tennis, as numerous courts are scattered all over town, from local parks to sophisticated sports centres. It is customary to bring your own sports shoes, but rackets are almost always available to rent.

The entrance fee in most cases includes the use of a sauna, and at **Sportoase** there are 15 badminton courts in addition to 8 squash courts. Other court facilities can be found in the telephone directory.

Other Sports

Every weekend in August, John-Foster-Dulles-Allee in Tiergarten is closed to traffic to become a genuine paradise for rollerblade and in-line skaters. Plenty of shops in the area offer skates and safety equipment at reasonable rates. For ice-skating fun, the **Horst-Dohm-Eisstadion** provides a 400-m- (1,312-ft-) rink. In snowy winters, Berliners like to go sledding down the Teufelsberg rubble hill in Grunewald.

If you fancy a boat trip, rowing boats are available for hire at many places along the banks of the lakes. In the Tiergarten you can rent them near Café am Neuen See and around Schlachtensee; the price is around €7–€10 per hour.

Fitness

There are always new gyms opening and others closing down in Berlin, so your best bet is to check the telephone directory for the most up-to-date listings. At many gyms you can buy a daily card, rather than becoming a member. But if your visit to Berlin is a long one, it may be worth joining. **Ars Vitalis** is the best independent fitness club and spa for men and women in Germany. **Fitness First** is one of the best options for women; it has five studios across the city and they are all large and well equipped. The main branch is directly beneath the TV tower in Alexanderplatz. A one-day ticket costs €19.

Spectator Sports

As a rule, Berlin's sports teams tend to be among the country's best, and rank highly in each of their respective leagues. Football matches of Hertha BSC take place in the Olympia Stadion and tickets are usually available at approximately €10–€36.

Alba Berlin is among the top basketball teams in Germany, and its matches in the **O2 World** can be attended by up to 8,500 fans. For international events it's best to pre-book tickets well in advance, and the price can vary between €10 and €64, depending on the match. Berlin also has a good hockey team, Eisbären Berlin, whose matches always sell out quickly.

Horse Racing

Lovers of horse racing have two tracks to choose from in Berlin. **Trabrennbahn** in Mariendorf is open all year and the races held here are strictly commercial. The **Galopprennbahn Hoppegarten** track, on the other hand, has a more approachable feel.

Marathon

Running a full marathon isn't everyone's cup of tea, but when you see the enormous crowds gathered to run the **Berlin-Marathon** in September, you may well wish you were one of the pack.

The route is one of the world's fastest, attracting top sponsors and athletes alike; the world record has been broken here several times. Thousands gather to cheer the runners, rollers and disabled athletes – the latter having their own group, which starts before the others.

DIRECTORY

Cycling

ADFC
Brunnenstrasse 28.
Tel 448 47 24.

Velodrom
Paul-Heyse-Strasse 26.
Tel 44 30 45.

Golf

Berliner Golfclub-Gatow
Sparnecker Weg 100.
Tel 365 00 06.

Golf Berlin-Mitte
Markgrafenstrasse 58.
Tel 280 470 70.

Golf und Landclub Berlin-Wannsee
Golfweg 22.
Tel 806 70 60.

Golfer's Friend Driving Range
Cordesstrasse 3.
Tel 326 03 250.

Swimming Pools

Badeschiff Arena
Eichenstrasse 4.
Tel 533 20 30.

Stadtbad Charlottenburg
Krumme Strasse 9.
Tel 34 38 38 60.

Stadtbad Mitte
Gartenstrasse 5.
Map 7 A1.
Tel 308 80 90.

Stadtbad Neukölln
Ganghoferstrasse 3.
Tel 68 24 98 12.

Strandbad Wannsee
Wannseebadweg 25.
Tel 803 5450.

Tropical Islands
Tropical Islands Allee 1, 15910 Krausnick.
Tel (035477) 605 050.

Badminton, Squash, Tennis

Sport Factory
Warener Strasse 5.
Tel 563 85 85.

Sportoase
Stromstrasse 11–17.
Map 4 F1, 4 F2.
Tel 390 66 20.

Fitness

Ars Vitalis
Hauptstrasse 19.
Map 13 A5.
Tel 311 65 94 70.

Fitness First
Panoramastrasse 1a.
Map 9 C2.
Tel 279 0770.

Other Sports

Horst-Dohm-Eisstadion
Fritz-Wildung-Strasse 9.
Tel 824 10 12.

Spectator Sports

O2 World
Mildred-Harnack-Strasse 14–30.
Tel 206 07 080.

Horse Racing

Galopprennbahn Hoppegarten
Goetheallee 1.
Tel (03342) 389 30.

Trabrennbahn Mariendorf
Mariendorfer Damm 222, Tempelhof.
Tel 740 12 12.
Open race times vary.

Marathon

Berlin-Marathon
Hanns-Braun-Strasse/Adlerplatz.
Tel 30 12 88 10.

CHILDREN'S BERLIN

When it comes to entertainment, people of all ages are catered for in Berlin, and children are no exception. There are numerous shops, theatres and cinemas to keep them occupied, not to mention circuses and zoological gardens. Additionally, there is the Deutsches Technikmuseum (German Museum of Technology), the Museumsdorf Düppel or the Kinder- und Jugendmuseum, all of which encourage children to take part in the displays. Tickets for children under 14 are almost always reduced, and very young children are often admitted for free. Restaurants often have special areas for toddlers.

The Potsdam train, always a favourite among children

Information

Berlin is very welcoming to its younger visitors. Families with children are entitled to public transport discounts, and children can travel free or at a reduced rate, depending on their age. For detailed information on the discounts and opportunities for children, contact **Berlin Tourismus Marketing GmbH**. This organization offers several discount cards which entitle the holder to public transport use and entry to various museums and attractions. Some versions of these cards are valid for one adult and up to three children. Ask about the Berlin WelcomeCard and the CityTourCard *(see p279)*.

Zoological Gardens

One of Berlin's zoological gardens can be visited the moment you arrive in town, as it is located opposite the Zoo railway station. The **Zoo Berlin** offers extensive parkland and many animal enclosures, as well as an excellent aquarium with the biggest collection of aquatic fauna in the world.

The second zoo, **Tierpark Berlin** in Friedrichsfelde, isn't quite so convenient but it is much bigger and can still be reached by U-Bahn. Covering a wide area around Schloss Friedrichsfelde, the Tierpark is the largest park in Europe.

Apart from these zoological gardens, a lot of the parks in Berlin contain mini-zoos where many different kinds of animals can be seen. In a garden behind the Märkisches Museum, for example, you can see a bear.

As well as the more exotic animals, however, it is also possible to see the familiar favourites. Small children will love the **Kinderbauernhof Auf dem Görlitzer**, which has a collection of domestic animals. Here geese, pigs and rabbits run happily around the Görlitzer Park.

Museums

Generally speaking, Berlin's museums are well set up for children. Perhaps the most entertaining is the **Deutsches Technikmuseum** *(see p148)*, where children can take part in all kinds of experiments. The **Ethnologisches Museum** *(see p185)* also prepares special exhibitions for children. On some days you can take part in a game with Mexican papier-mâché dolls, on others you can participate in a Japanese ceremonial bath. A visit to the **Museumsdorf Düppel** is an excellent way to show a child the workings of a medieval village. The Museum für Naturkunde *(see p113)* is another fun place for children, particularly the dinosaur sections and the dioramas of animals in their natural habitats. The **Kindermuseum Labyrinth** is another favourite.

Another great place to visit is the **Puppentheater-Museum**, which is always lively, and offers a chance for children to take part in minor performances.

Theatres

Established in 1969, **Grips Theater** is probably the most interesting theatre for children and teenagers. Its independent and ambitious programme attracts many spectators and one of its performances, *Linie 1*, was made into a film. Other venues worth trying are the **Theater an der Parkaue**, **Theater o.N.**, **Zaubertheater**

Children admiring Neptune's Fountain by the Town Hall

A visit to the medieval village at Museumsdorf Düppel

Igor Jedlin and the **Puppentheater Berlin**. Another option is to go to one of the city's many circuses, all of which prepare their programmes with children in mind.

Sports

Ice-skating in winter and roller-skating in summer are popular in Berlin, and football and swimming are popular year-round. You can swim in rivers, lakes and swimming pools (the **Berliner Bäderbetriebe** hotline offers useful information). Each district has its own ice-skating rink, but the **Horst-Dohm-Eisstadion** is outstanding with its 400-m (1,312-ft) run and large ice-hockey rink. **FEZ Berlin** offers a special daily programme for kids.

Other Entertainment

Berlin is full of wonderfully equipped children's playgrounds. Each neighbourhood has at least one, usually complete with climbing frames, ping-pong tables and mini soccer courts.

An ascent of the Fernsehturm (Television Tower) at Alexanderplatz *(see p95)* is a great way to treat a child, perhaps for afternoon tea. You can buy cake and juice in the tower's rotating café. A lift in the Funkturm (radio tower) in the Messegelände *(see p179)* offers an excellent view ofthe city, from a slightly lower height.

Cabuwazi is a children's circus-training group that offers workshops and performances. It operates five permanent big-top tents, the main one being at Görlitzer Park in Kreuzberg. **The Story of Berlin** is a fun way for both parents and children to experience the history of Berlin in a thrilling multimedia exhibit. And the **Berliner Gruselkabinett** (Berlin Room of Fear) is enough to frighten anybody.

For an out-of-the-ordinary experience, you can't go wrong at either the **Zeiss-Großplanetarium** or the **Planetarium am Insulaner**, where fascinating shows allow you to explore the known universe and to have a good look at the stars.

DIRECTORY

Information

Berlin mit Kindern
W berlin-with-children.com

Berlin Tourismus Marketing GmbH
Am Karlsbad 11.
Tel 25 00 25.
W visitberlin.de

Zoological Gardens

Kinderbauernhof Auf dem Görlitzer
Wiener Strasse 59b.
Tel 611 74 24.

Tierpark Berlin
Am Tierpark 125, Lichtenberg.
Tel 51 53 10.

Zoo Berlin
Hardenbergplatz 8, Charlottenburg.
Tel 25 40 10.

Museums

Kindermuseum Labyrinth
Osloer Strasse 12.
Tel 800 93 11 50.
Open 1–6pm Fri & Sat, 11am–6pm Sun & hols.

Museumsdorf Düppel
Clauertstrasse 11.
Tel 802 66 71.
Open Apr–Oct: 3–7pm Thu, 10am–5pm Sun & holidays.

Puppentheater-Museum Berlin
Karl-Marx-Strasse 135.
Tel 687 81 32.
Open 9am–3pm Mon–Fri, 11am–4pm Sun.

Theatres

Grips Theater
Altonaer Strasse 22.
Tel 397 47 40.

Puppentheater Berlin
Gierkeplatz 2.
Tel 342 19 50.

Theater an der Parkaue
Parkaue 29.
Tel 55 77 520.

Theater o.N.
Kollwitzstrasse 53.
Tel 440 92 14.

Zaubertheater Igor Jedlin
Roscherstrasse 7.
Tel 323 37 77.

Sports

Berliner Bäderbetriebe
Tel 22 19 00 11.

FEZ Berlin
Strasse zum FEZ 2.
Tel 53 07 10.

Horst-Dohm-Eisstadion
Fritz-Wildung-Strasse 9.
Tel 824 10 12.

Other Entertainment

Berliner Gruselkabinett
Schöneberger Strasse 23a.
Map 14 E1.
Tel 26 55 55 46.

Cabuwazi Circus
Wiener Strasse 59H.
Tel 54 46 90 94.
W cabuwazi.de

Planetarium am Insulaner
Munsterdamm 90.
Tel 790 09 30.

The Story of Berlin
Kurfürstendamm 207–208.
Map 11 A2.
Tel 88 72 01 00.

Zeiss-Großplanetarium
Prenzlauer Allee 80.
Tel 42 18 450.

DB
DB

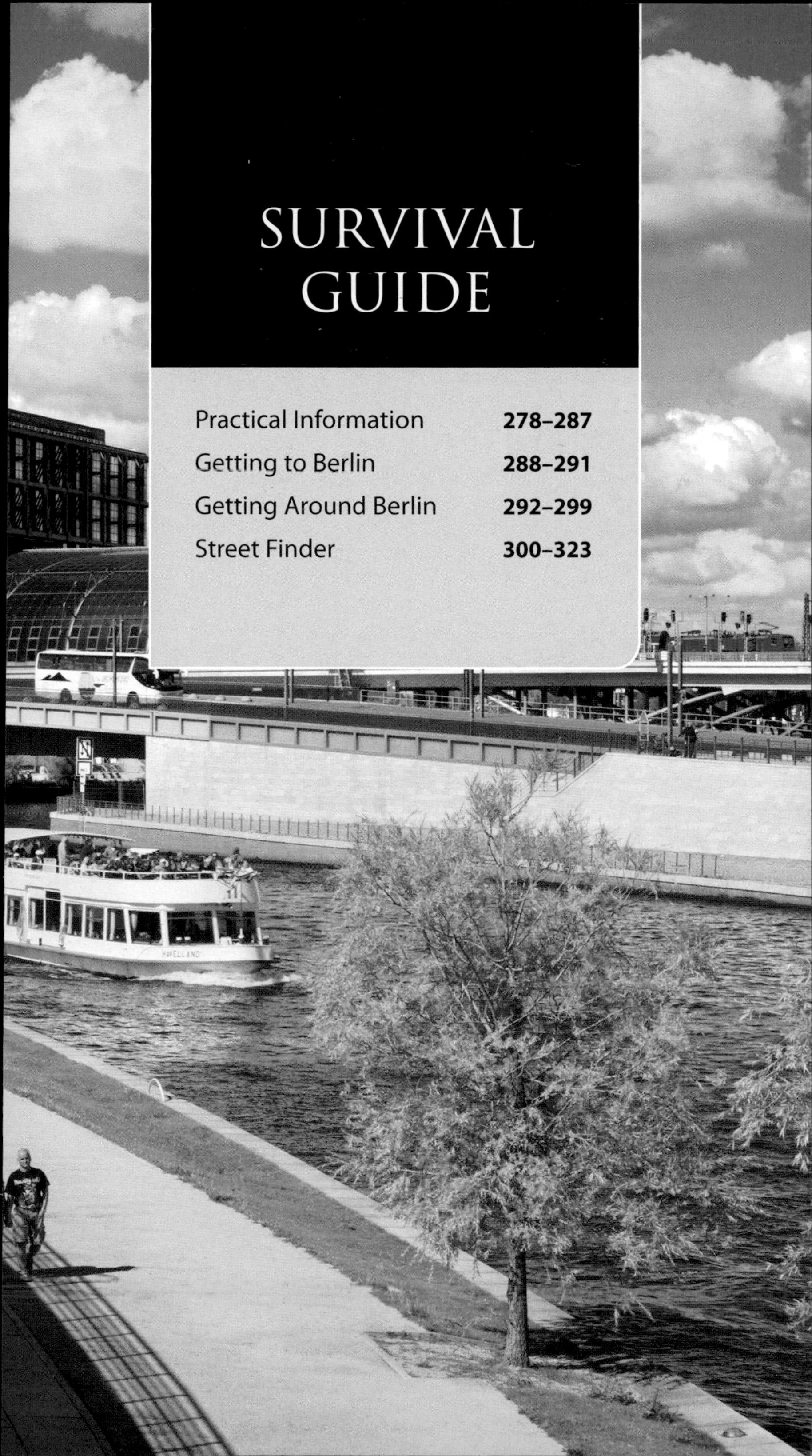

SURVIVAL GUIDE

PRACTICAL INFORMATION

Berlin is a tourist-friendly city, so you shouldn't have too much difficulty getting around. Many Germans speak English and Berliners are usually welcoming to newcomers. Cash machines, telephones and parking meters all have clear instructions, and public transport is of the highest standard *(see pp292–3)*. For reduced fares on public transport, buy yourself a daily or weekly travel card or a BerlinWelcomeCard, which also gives you discounted access to many museums. There are plenty of information centres in the busiest areas of town, and a number of different listings magazines and brochures are available. If you have Internet access, VisitBerlin.de is a good information source.

Visa and Customs

A valid passport is necessary for all visitors to Germany. Visas are not required for citizens of EU countries. A list, available from all German embassies, specifies other countries whose nationals do not need a visa for visits of less than 90 days. Non-EU citizens wishing to stay in Germany longer than three months will need a visa, obtained in advance, available from German consulates. All visitors should check requirements before travelling.

On arrival in Germany, you will not be charged duty on personal articles. As in other European countries, no drugs or weapons may be brought across the border. It is also forbidden to import any meat products from non-EU countries. The amount of cigarettes and alcohol allowed in or out of the country is restricted. Non-EU residents can bring up to 200 cigarettes (or 50 cigars, or 250g of tobacco), one litre of spirits (or four litres of wine), and up to €430 worth of personal goods (including perfumes and electronic items). You may be asked to pay extra tax on items deemed to be worth more than your personal allowance.

Embassies and Consulates

Most large countries have embassies in Berlin. They are spread across different parts of the city, a result of the period when Germany was divided. Some of the newer embassies are wonderful examples of modern architecture, such as the Nordic countries' joint mission in Tiergarten, while some older embassies retain the design ethos of the divided period, such as the Czech Republic Embassy on Wilhelmstrasse.

Tourist Information

There are many excellent tourist information centres in Berlin. The two biggest are at the **Neues Kranzler Eck** and the **Brandenburg Gate**, but others can be found at **Hauptbahnhof** and in the **Alexanderplatz TV Tower** near Alexanderplatz. The **Potsdam Tourismus Service** office is in central Potsdam, on Brandenburger Strasse.

For up-to-the-minute news, turn to the Internet; **VisitBerlin.de**, which is managed by **Berlin Tourismus Marketing**, is a very reliable source of information for tourists.

Tourist information centre in Berlin

Opening Hours

Offices in Berlin usually open from 9am to 6pm, with an hour's lunch break. Smaller shops open from 9:30 or 10am to 8pm, and on Saturdays most shops close at 4 or 5pm. Shops are closed on Sundays due to Germany's religious traditions. However, those in the main train stations remain open on Sundays; you can find supermarkets at Hauptbahnhof, Friedrichstrasse and Ostbahnhof.

Trading rules are relaxed in the month before Christmas, when most shops are open every day and for longer hours. For typical bank opening hours, *see p284*.

The Berlin CityTourCard, for discounted entry to many of the city's major sights

Museums and Historic Buildings

There are over 150 museums and galleries in Berlin, but exhibitions change and collections move continually. This guide covers the most important places, but plenty of information is also available on lesser-known museums and galleries. Tourist information offices can provide up-to-the-minute details.

A good information line is the **Info-Telefon der Staatlichen Museen zu Berlin** and its associated website, and there are also information centres devoted to the the Sanssouci

◀ Hotel Spreebogen on the Spree river

Sightseeing boat tour along the Spree

complex in Potsdam and the Pergamonmuseum. Contact the **Stiftung Preussiche Schlösser und Gärten Berlin-Brandenburg**, which is the authority in charge of most major gardens and castles in the region.

Museums and historic buildings are usually open 10am to 5pm (sometimes to 6pm), Tuesday to Sunday. Some museums, however, close on another day instead of Monday, and many museums are open late on Thursdays, and often allow free entry during these hours.

For reduced entrance prices, you may want to get hold of the Museen Pass Berlin, which allows three days' unlimited access to the major museums. This pass is sold at official tourist information centres. It can be used at all the national museums, including the whole Museum Island complex, the Kulturforum, Museen Dahlem and several additional institutions in Charlottenburg.

Other options for getting more value for your money are the **Berlin Welcome Card** (see www.VisitBerlin.de) and the **CityTourCard**, which both offer you public transport for three days, and discount entry to a long list of attractions. The conditions and attractions offered by both vary, so it's best to check which is most suitable for you.

Check event listings for the biannual Lange Nacht der Museen, which is held in May, when many museums stay open until midnight, with special shuttle buses put on to transport nocturnal visitors between them.

Guided Tours

There are many bus tours available in Berlin, all of which will, in 3 or 4 hours, introduce you to the city's chief historic buildings. A single ticket usually allows you to get off at any stage and rejoin the tour at different stops. However, if you want to save some money, the double-decker public transport bus No. 100 follows a similar route *(see p295)*.

If you would rather go on foot, walking tours are also possible – these provide a more leisurely tour of the city, stopping at all the major landmarks and museums.

A variety of cycling tours, or tours by **Segway** (two-wheeled electronic vehicles), provide fun ways to see the sights.

There are many different companies offering tours; some ask you to pay in advance, whereas others offer "free" tours, but may request a tip at the end (the tour guides often earn very little for their work).

If you are in Potsdam (*see pp192–207*) you can ride a train around town, which starts outside the Kutscherhaus Inn in Sanssouci.

Guided bus tour offering an overview of Berlin and its environs

Social Customs and Etiquette

Older Germans are quite formal upon first meeting, and may introduce themselves with their surname and a stiff handshake. Younger Germans tend to be more casual.

As in most of Europe, smoking is technically illegal inside public buildings, cafés, restaurants, bars and nightclubs. However, there are many establishments in Berlin which circumvent these laws by naming themselves a *Raucherkneipe* or smoking pub. It is quite common for people to smoke in public locations, and although this is increasingly discouraged it is rarely punished.

Language

German is the official language, but many places have signs in English. Most staff and locals speak some English, but Berlin is a good place to try German (*see pp350–52)*, as the locals are used to hearing their language spoken in many accents.

A refurbished antique public convenience in Kreuzberg

Public Conveniences

There are plenty of public toilets in Berlin, but you can also use the facilities in museums, stores and cafés. In some places the convenience comes with a charge, usually 50 cents.

Men's toilets are marked by the word *Herren* or a triangle with the vertex pointing downwards; ladies', by the word *Damen* or *Frauen*, or a triangle with its vertex pointing upwards.

Travellers with Special Needs

Not all of Berlin's streets and shops have been altered to cater for the disabled, but the majority of theatres, galleries and other sights do have the required facilities, such as wheelchair access. Detailed information about accessibility can be obtained from **Mobidat Infoservice**. Two other organizations to consult are the **Berliner Behindertenverband** and **Der Landesbeauftragte für Menschen mit Behinderung**. Both of these organizations can be contacted if you need to hire a wheelchair, a special bus, or even someone to help assist for the day.

Gay and Lesbian Travellers

Berlin is a relaxed and tolerant city, and is home to one of the largest and most diversified gay communities in Europe. There are many vibrant gay scenes across the city, with numerous bars, cafés and clubs. Areas which are recommended are the district near Nollendorfplatz U-Bahn station in Schöneberg, around Mehringdamm and Oranienstrasse in Kreuzberg, as well as much of Prenzlauer Berg and Mitte. The magazine *Siegessäule* is good for up-to-date information.

The Berlin Pride Festival is held at the end of June, and there are many other events and festivals held throughout the year. The **Schwules Museum** contains an exhibition about the development of gay rights and the gay community.

An ISIC card (International Student Identity card)

Travelling on a Budget

By European standards, Berlin is one of the cheapest cities and it is possible to get by with very little money. Travellers wishing to save can purchase a meal for a few euros at one of the many *Volksküchen*, or "people's kitchens", which can be found in a number of former squat buildings in the eastern districts. For a full directory check www.tressfaktor.squat.net.de.

If eligible, before arriving in Berlin it is worth getting hold of an **ISIC** card (or International Student Identity Card). This entitles you to a 50 per cent reduction on some museum entrance fees and to occasional discounts on theatre, plane and rail tickets. Another discount card, **EURO<26**, is available for people up to the age of 30. These cards are only valid in Europe, but can provide many discounts.

Germany's excellent *Mitfahrer*, or car-pooling systems, provide a free or cheap way to get between cities. The main ones are www.mitfahrgelegenheit.de and www.blablacar.de. Free accommodation-sharing schemes can be found at www.couchsurfing.com and www.hospitalityclub.org.

Revellers at the Berlin Pride Festival

Time

Germany is in the Central-European time zone, which means that Berlin is 1 hour ahead of Greenwich Mean Time; 6 hours ahead of US Eastern Standard Time, and 11 hours behind Australian Eastern Standard Time. From late March to late October, clocks are set forward 1 hour.

Electrical Equipment

Most electrical sockets carry 220V, although in bathrooms the voltage may be slightly lower for safety reasons. Plugs are the standard continental type, with two round pins. Buy a European travel adaptor before you leave home.

A stall at Öko-markt in Kollwitzplatz – an organic market

Responsible Tourism

Germany is among the most ecologically aware countries in Europe, with many well-established systems in place to help reduce negative environmental impact. About 15 per cent of the country's energy comes from renewable sources, a percentage expected to increase. The Green Party is one of Berlin's major parties, and one of the strongest in Europe. There are often many independent demonstrations on environmental and political grounds.

Most Berliners are passionate cyclists, recyclers, and "bio" food consumers. Given the extent of environmental awareness, it's quite easy to participate in impact-reducing schemes whilst visiting Berlin. Recycling bins can be found at many public locations, such as train stations. It's possible to eat ecologically by visiting one of the many outdoor organic markets across the city (the **Öko-markt** in Kollwitzplatz on Thursdays is regarded as one of the best). Here you can be sure of the food's origin and buy locally sourced produce. Many restaurants also choose to serve organic food. To see green building practices in action in the city, visit Potsdamer Platz, where many of the office buildings have grass roofs and water recycling schemes. The modern Reichstag building *(see p138–9)* is successfully powered by renewable energy.

There are a number of hotels in Berlin which claim to operate on ecological principles, using less harmful cleaning products, recycled and non-toxic furniture, or renewable electricity. Some accreditation schemes are available to help guide guests opting for the green choice, for example, **Green Key**. Check the green credentials of a hotel before booking – your query may encourage other hotels to adapt their practices.

Berlin is surrounded by nature reserves and there are many accommodation options located in forests with good connections to the city centre. Camping is possible, near Hauptbahnhof, for those wanting the greenest option.

DIRECTORY

Embassies

Australian Embassy
Wallstrasse 76–79.
Map 9 C4.
Tel 880 08 80.

British Embassy
Wilhelmstrasse 70.
Map 8 E4.
Tel 20 45 70.

Canadian Embassy
Leipziger Platz 17.
Map 8 E5.
Tel 20 31 20.

New Zealand Embassy
Friedrichstrasse 60.
Map 8 F2.
Tel 20 62 10.

South African Embassy
Tiergartenstrasse 18.
Tel 22 07 30.

US Embassy
Pariser Platz 2.
Map 8 E4. **Tel** 830 50.

Religious Services

American Church
Lutherkirche, Dannewitzstrasse.
Tel 813 20 21.

Anglican Church
St Georg, Preussenallee 17–19.
Tel 304 12 80.
W stgeorges.de

Huguenot
Französischer Dom, Friedrichstadtkirche, Gendarmenmarkt 5.
Map 9 A4.
Tel 229 17 60.

Jewish
Oranienburger Strasse 29.
Map 9 A1. **Tel** 88 02 80.

Muslim
Berliner Moschee, Brienner Strasse 7–8.
Map 11 A5. **Tel** 87 357 03

Protestant
Berliner Dom, Lustgarten.
Map 9 B3.
Tel 202 691 36.

Kaiser-Wilhelm-Gedächtniskirche, Breitscheidplatz.
Map 12 E1.
Tel 218 50 23.

Marienkirche, Karl-Liebknecht-Strasse 8.
Map 9 C3.
Tel 247 595 10.

Roman Catholic
St-Hedwigs-Kathedrale, Bebelplatz.
Map 9 A3.
Tel 20 348 10.

Tourist Information

Berlin Tourismus Marketing
Am Karlsbad 11.
Tel 25 00 25 (24-hour).
Fax 25 00 24 24.
W visitberlin.de

Brandenburg Gate
Pariser Platz, southern building. **Map** 8 E3, 15 A3.
Open 9.30am–6pm daily (to 7pm in summer).

Hauptbahnhof
Europaplatz 1, level 0, northern entrance.
Map 8 D1.
Open 8am–10pm daily.

Neues Kranzler Eck
Kurfürstendamm 22.
Map 12 D1.
Open 9:30am–8pm Mon–Sat.

Potsdam Tourismus Service
Brandenburger Strasse 3.
Tel (0331) 27 55 88 99.
W potsdamtourismus.de

Museums and Historic Buildings

Berlin Welcome Card
W berlin-welcomecard.de

CityTourCard
W citytourcard.com

Info-Telefon der Staatlichen Museen zu Berlin
Tel 266 42 42 42.
W smb.museum

Stiftung Preussische Schlösser und Gärten Berlin-Brandenburg
Tel (0331) 969 42 200.
W spsg.de

Guided Tours

Segway Tours
Tel 240 479 91.
W citysegwaytours.com/berlin

Travellers with Special Needs

Berliner Behindertenverband
Jägerstrasse 63d.
Tel 204 38 47.
W bbv-ev.de

Der Landesbeauftragte für Menschen mit Behinderung
Oranienstrasse 106.
Tel 90 28 29 17.

Mobidat Infoservice
Tel 322 94 03 00.
W mobidat.net
W wheelmap.org

Gay and Lesbian Travellers

Schwules Museum
Lutzowstrasse 73.
Tel 69 59 90 50.
W schwulesmuseum.de

Siegessäule
W siegessaeule.de

Travelling on a Budget

EURO<26
W euro26.org

ISIC
W isiccard.com

Responsible Tourism

Green Key
W green-key.org

Öko-markt
Kollwitzplatz, Prenzlauer Berg. **Open** mid-Mar–Dec: noon–7pm Thu; Jan–mid-Mar: noon–6pm Thu.

Personal Security and Health

Berlin is a relatively safe cosmopolitan city, with few serious security concerns. Crime isn't usually directed at tourists; the most serious incidents, such as car burnings (for which the city has a reputation), are usually targeted at rich residents living in formerly poor neighbourhoods. Nevertheless, as with all major European destinations, you should always be careful with your belongings, particularly during rush hours. If you do run into trouble, or need advice, you can always get help from the police.

Police officers in Berlin

Police (How to Report a Crime)

For serious crimes in progress, call the emergency police number, **110**. For all other crimes, you should call the non-emergency police number and ask to speak to an English-speaking officer. They will inform you of the address of the nearest police station and give you basic information about what to do next.

At the police station, you will be asked some questions and may have to sign a statement. The officer may ask for specific details, such as serial numbers or pictures of stolen items. If it is a more serious matter you may be asked to return to give evidence; smaller problems might be resolved in your absence.

If you are accused of a crime, you have the right to request that police contact your embassy (*see p281*), which should then provide basic assistance and may give you legal support or suggest a lawyer to represent you. You are not obliged to answer any questions and any interviews that are conducted must be carried out in the presence of a translator.

What to be Aware Of

Berlin, like most major cities, has a number of beggars who hassle tourists. It is common to be approached by women carrying cards written in English which request money. These people are often more of a nuisance than a threat. If you wish to help the homeless, it's more helpful to donate direct to a charity (www.berliner-stadtmission.de). Pickpockets can also be a problem.

Kottbusser Tor U-Bahn station is notorious for its drug pushers, so be careful there late at night. Like most big cities, few of the S- and U-Bahn stations are pleasant after dark, but they are often patrolled by guards – if you need help, you can approach them. Panic buttons on platforms can also be used in an emergency.

In an Emergency

The first number to call in an emergency is **112**, which connects you to the emergency call centre for medical, fire or police assistance. The police also operate a separate emergency number, 110.

If you spot a fire, phone the emergency number and ask for the **Fire Brigade**, or *Feuerwehr*, or use one of the emergency alarm buttons located in public areas.

Ambulances are operated by many different companies, but the emergency call centre will dispatch the nearest ambulance unit available. In less urgent circumstances you can request an ambulance or a doctor by calling the **Medical Services** number, which may take up to 2 hours to respond to a call.

On S- and U-Bahn platforms there are panic buttons that connect you to an operator, who will call the appropriate emergency service.

A special **Chemist Information** number is available offering information about chemists, which is helpful when searching for a pharmacist after hours. Another option is to contact your embassy, which should be able to inform you which doctors are able to speak your language. Other helplines include a **Poisons** emergencies service and a **Confidential Helpline for Women**.

Lost and Stolen Property

There is one central bureau for lost property in Berlin (the **Zentrales Fundbüro**) and this is where anything left in public is deposited. It is worth noting, however, that the BVG (Berliner Verkehrsbetriebe) has its own office (the **Fundbüro der BVG**) for items left on buses or trams or on the U-Bahn system. Some items left on S-Bahn trains may also be sent to the **Zentrales Fundbüro der Deutschen Bahn AG** in Wuppertal.

A public fire alarm

Unfortunately, tourists are more frequently targeted by thieves than any other group, which is why all valuables should ideally be kept in a hotel safe. Thankfully, serious robberies are rare in Berlin, but pickpockets are active, particularly in crowds and on the U-Bahn system. If you are unlucky enough to be the victim of street crime, you should report it to the police straight away. Remember to obtain a statement confirming what items were stolen – you

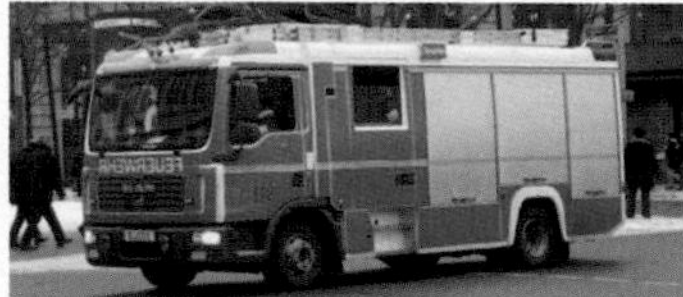

A German fire engine

German police patrol car, a common sight

will need this when it comes to making any insurance claims.

If you are travelling by car, don't leave photographic equipment or luggage in open view, and try to use a secure car park or hotel garage whenever possible.

Pharmacies and Hospitals

It's never hard to find a Berlin pharmacy, or *Apotheke*. There is one on almost every city block, and they are marked by large distinctive signs bearing the letter "A".

Symbol for *Apotheke* (pharmacy)

Pharmacies are generally open from 8am to 6pm Monday to Saturday. At least one pharmacy in each district is open after hours and on Sundays and public holidays. The addresses are usually posted near the door of any pharmacy, or can be easily obtained by calling the **Chemist Information** hotline. When visiting an after-hours pharmacy, you will be served through a window in the door and will have to wait outside while your prescription is provided. You may need a doctor's prescription to obtain certain pharmaceuticals, and the pharmacist can inform you of the closest doctor's practice. Visitors who require prescribed medication should ensure they take enough to cover their stay, in case it is not available.

There are many so-called *Drogerien*, such as the chain stores Rossmann and DM, which look like pharmacies but sell only toiletries and beauty products. Only *Apotheken* are authorized to sell pharmaceutical products.

There are several major hospitals in Berlin, all equipped with casualty units. The most central hospital is **Charité Mitte Campus** in Mitte. Call the emergency **Medical Services** number for information about your nearest hospital. When visiting a hospital or using an ambulance, you may be charged a €10 consultation fee even if you have health insurance.

An independent chemist in Berlin's city centre

Travel and Health Insurance

EU nationals holding a European Health Insurance Card (EHIC) are entitled to use the German health service, and usually receive free emergency treatment. Patients may need to pay for treatments and then reclaim the cost from the health authorities. All tourists should have travel insurance.

DIRECTORY

In an Emergency

Confidential Helpline for Women
Tel 615 42 43.

Fire Brigade and Ambulance
Tel 112.

Medical Services
Tel 31 00 31.

Poison Helpline
Tel 192 40.

Police
Tel 110 (Emergency).
Tel 4664 4664 (Non-Emergency).

Lost and Stolen Property

Fundbüro der BVG
Potsdamer Strasse 180–182.
Tel 194 49.
W bvg.de
Open 9am–6pm Mon–Thu, 9am–2pm Fri.

Zentrales Fundbüro
Platz der Luftbrücke 6.
Tel 90277 31 01.
Open 9am–2pm Mon, Tue, Fri & Sat, 1–6pm Thu.

Zentrales Fundbüro der Deutschen Bahn AG
Döppersberg 37, 42103 Wuppertal.
Tel 0900 190 599.

Pharmacies and Hospitals

Charité Mitte Campus
Chariteplatz 1.
Tel 450 50.

Chemist Information
Tel 11 880.

Banking and Local Currency

Unlike in many other countries, it is quite hard to travel around in Germany without cash. Credit card use is not prevalent, although it has been steadily on the increase. Many retailers – including major supermarkets – still refuse credit cards or foreign bank cards, as do smaller shops, cafés and bars. However, ATMs are easy to find in most areas if you need to withdraw cash using a credit or debit card.

Banks and Bureaux de Change

Most visitors use debit cards for safety. Cash can be exchanged at banks and bureaux de change *(Wechselstuben)*. The major banks, such as **Deutsche Bank** and **ReiseBank**, usually have similar rates of exchange, but some charge a commission; ask how much before commencing your transaction. Bank opening hours vary from branch to branch, but generally are as follows: 9am to 4pm (Monday, Wednesday, Friday) and 9am to 6pm (Tuesday and Thursday).

Bureaux de change are often located close to railway stations and airports. **Exchange AG** and Reisebank AG are among the most reliable places for exchanging cash or traveller's cheques. Others can be found downtown, around Joachimstaler Strasse in the west and Friedrichstrasse in the east. You can also exchange cash at hotel reception desks, but rates are often poor. Given the high commission rates sometimes charged by banks and bureaux de change, the most economical way to get cash can be to withdraw from an ATM.

ATM – a convenient method for accessing cash while in Berlin

ATMs

ATMs are easy to find and use. Most are operated by banks and are accessible 24 hours a day, in well-serviced lobbies.

Most ATMs have multiple-language menu options and accept all major credit and debit card systems, including Maestro, Cirrus, VISA and MasterCard. Less commonly accepted are American Express, Diners Club and other cards. Check the machine for the corresponding logos.

Note that some ATMs are operated by private companies which charge large fees, and some banks may charge you extra for using an international terminal.

One of the city's many banks where money can be exchanged

Always exercise caution while using ATMs; be aware of anyone standing close to you when using one and shield the numbered keypad when entering your PIN.

Debit and Credit Cards

You may find it difficult to get by using only a credit card. Cards are accepted in some hotels, shops and restaurants, but not all. A sign on the door should tell you if cards are accepted, and which brands they take – **VISA** and **MasterCard** are most frequently accepted, and sometimes **American Express** and **Diners Club** as well.

Some cafés and restaurants require a minimum purchase to use a credit card. If you are only ordering a snack, check that you have some cash in case your card is not accepted.

Many shops accept Electronic Cash cards, or EC cards, which are issued by German banks. Your regular bank debit card may be accepted in shops, but check before relying on this method of payment.

DIRECTORY

Banks and Bureaux de Change

Deutsche Bank
W deutsche-bank.de

Exchange AG
Friedrichstrasse 150–153.
Tel 20 64 92 96.

ReiseBank
W reisebank.de

Lost Cards and Cheques

American Express
Tel (069) 97 97 20 00.

Diners Club
Tel 07531 36 33 111.

MasterCard
Tel 0800 819 1040.

VISA
Tel 0800 811 8440.

The Euro

The euro (€) is the common currency of the European Union. It went into general circulation on 1 January 2002, initially for 12 participating countries. Germany was one of those countries, and the German mark was phased out in 2002. EU members using the euro as sole official currency are known as the Eurozone. Several EU members have opted out of joining this common currency.

Euro notes are identical throughout the Eurozone countries, each one including designs of fictional architectural structures. The coins, however, have one side identical (the value side), and one side with an image unique to each country. Both notes and coins are exchang- eable in all participating euro countries.

Banknotes

Euro banknotes have seven denominations. The €5 note (grey in colour) is the smallest, followed by the €10 note (pink), €20 note (blue), €50 note (orange), €100 note (green), €200 note (yellow) and €500 note (purple). All notes show the stars of the European Union.

5 euros

10 euros

20 euros

50 euros

100 euros

200 euros

500 euros

2 euros

1 euro

50 cents

20 cents

10 cents

Coins

The euro has eight coin denominations: €1 and €2; 50 cents, 20 cents, 10 cents, 5 cents, 2 cents and 1 cent. The €2 and €1 coins are both silver and gold in colour. The 50-, 20- and 10-cent coins are gold. The 5-, 2- and 1-cent coins are bronze.

5 cents

2 cents

1 cent

Communications and Media

The postal and telecommunications networks and services in Germany are very efficient. Letters addressed within the country are usually delivered within 24 hours. Public telephones are becoming rare, though they can be found at railway stations and in some busy public areas. Mobile telephone coverage is excellent, and you can buy a cheap pre-paid SIM card to use during your visit. Internet facilities are widely available, with Internet cafés in many locations. News and information services are excellent in Germany. There is a plethora of good-quality newspapers, magazines, and television and radio channels. For English-language news and information, the best place to turn is the Internet. The website VisitBerlin.de is a good information source and will keep you up-to-date with what is happening across the city.

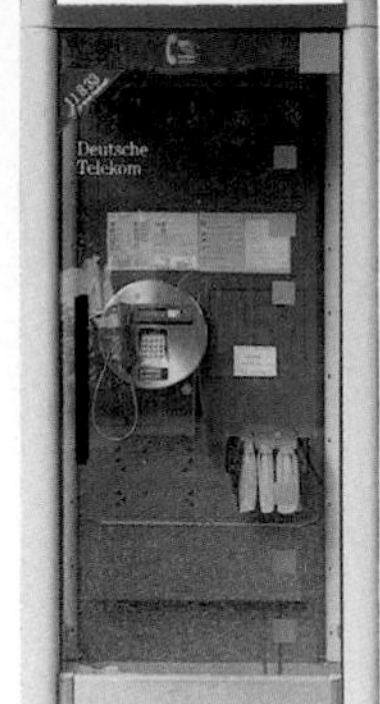

A typical Deutsche Telekom public telephone booth in Berlin

International and Local Telephone Calls

Although the number of public phone booths is constantly being reduced, Deutsche Telekom still operates a network across Berlin and Germany. Some accept coins, but more common are phones that take credit cards as payment. It is also possible to buy a pre-paid telephone card from newspaper kiosks, post offices and tourist offices. A small number of telephone boxes for long-distance calls are operated by other companies. These normally accept coins and credit cards.

If you are staying in a hotel, making telephone calls from your room is usually the least economical option. For long-distance calls, the cheapest option is often to visit an Internet and telephone café.

Internet and telephone centres often sell international calling cards, which can be used from any phone. The quality and value of such cards varies greatly. It is worth requesting a receipt upon purchase in case your card is faulty.

Mobile Phones

If you are travelling with a mobile phone it can be a good idea to buy a local SIM card with a German telephone number. This can help reduce the costs of using public or hotel telephones to call local numbers. Having a mobile is advisable in case of emergencies, for calling ahead to confirm bookings, or to find addresses. There are many companies offering cheap pre-paid SIM cards, for example, **BASE**, which you can insert into your mobile (check with your regular service provider about possible restrictions), or **Lebara**, whose packages include free minutes to over 40 countries. SIM card packages are sold at most supermarkets and convenience stores.

To add credit, buy a credit voucher from the cashier. Sometimes you will be asked to enter your phone number into a point-of-sale machine at the cashier, or you may be given a voucher with instructions on entering a code into your handset.

To call local numbers using your mobile phone, you will have to enter the local area code, 030 for Berlin and 0331 for Potsdam. If using an international mobile phone, you may need to add the national calling code (+49), remove the first zero, then complete the number as listed.

The Internet and Email

Internet centres are common throughout Berlin, particularly in areas of high ethnic diversity, such as Kreuzberg and Neukölln. They can be an economical way to check your email, and many locations offer printing services as well. Most Internet centres ask you to pay at the end of your computer session. Rates can vary greatly, so it's best to check before using a terminal.

If you are travelling with a laptop or mobile device, you can connect to the Internet at many cafés and libraries. Most wireless networks are password-controlled, and an access code is required, although it is usually provided free of charge to the customer.

An Internet café and shop

Important Numbers

- Germany country code 49.
- Berlin area code 030.
- Potsdam area code 0331.
- National directory inquiries 11 8 33.
- International directory inquiries 11 8 34.
- Emergency 112.
- To make an international call, dial 00 followed by the country code, area code and number, omitting the initial 0. Country codes: UK 44; Eire 353; Canada and US 1; Australia 61; South Africa 27; New Zealand 64.

German magazines on display at a street vendor stall

Postal Services

German post offices are easy to spot with their distinctive yellow **Deutsche Post** signs. Mailboxes, too, are an eye-catching yellow.

As in other European countries, you can send registered letters, parcels and money orders from post offices. They also offer stamps, telephone cards and the usual variety of postal stationery, as well as some banking services. If the office is closed, you can use automatic stamp and package machines, which have instructions in multiple languages.

When posting a letter, always check the labels on the mailbox. Some boxes are divided, with one side accepting mail for within Berlin only, and the other accepting everything else.

Opening times can vary widely, but most post offices in Berlin are usually open from 8am to 6pm on weekdays, and until 1pm on Saturdays. Those with extended hours, including Sundays, are at major railway stations and central areas, such as Bahnhof Friedrichstrasse in Georgenstrasse. Poste restante letters can be collected from a number of post offices, depending on the postcode they are addressed to. For the central Friedrichstrasse post office, the postcode is 10117, and for the Joachimstaler Strasse post office in West Berlin, use the postcode 10623.

As well as the nationalized Deutsche Post, Germany also has a private mail network, known as **PIN Mail**, which offers competitive prices for domestic mail and package delivery services. You can find their distinctive green-coloured offices in various locations across the city, and their mailboxes can be found in some newsagents.

Information about collection times

Slot for non-local letters

Slot for local letters

Typical Berlin-style mailbox found on street corners

Newspapers and Magazines

Newspapers can be bought in shops all over Berlin, but mostly they are sold by the city's numerous street vendors. In the evenings you may also find them on sale in bars and cafés. The most popular titles are the *Berliner Zeitung*, *Der Tagesspiegel*, the *Berliner Morgenpost* and *BZ*. Foreign-language papers can be found all over the city, especially at airport and railway kiosks. Some of the major department stores also have a good range of newspapers and magazines.

The two best magazines devoted to cultural events are *Zitty* and *Tip*, which cover the major (as well as minor) concerts, exhibitions and lectures held throughout Berlin. The very latest news can also be obtained from tourist information centres and the Internet. For visitors, VisitBerlin.de is essential for keeping up-to-date with events.

Television and Radio

You will be spoiled for choice when it comes to television channels. Apart from the national ARD and ZDF, there are many regional and private channels. Berlin has its very own channel, RBB, alongside national channels RTL, RTL2, SAT1 and PRO7. You can pick up special interest channels, like DSF for sport and VIVA or MTV for music.

In addition to these there is even an option for Turkish programmes in Berlin, and thanks to cable and satellite television you can easily tune into foreign programmes in English, American, French and many other languages. In hotels, television channels mainly cover the news, music and sport. For radio news in English, tune into the BBC World Service (94.8 MHz) and NPR Berlin (104.1 MHz)

DIRECTORY

Mobile Phones

BASE
W **base.de**

Lebara
W **lebara.de**

Internet

Internet Café
Schönhauser Allee 188, Mitte.
Open 8am–4am daily.

Postal Services

Deustche Post
Bahnhof Friedrichstrasse, Georgenstrasse 12.
Open 6am–10pm Mon–Fri, 8am–10pm Sat & Sun.
W **deutschepost.de**

PIN Mail
W **pin-ag.de**

GETTING TO BERLIN

Berlin lies at the heart of Europe and has excellent rail and air links with the rest of the continent. Its airport receives regular flights from major European cities as well as North America, the Middle East and southeast Asia. Likewise Lufthansa, the German national carrier, and airberlin offer flights to destinations around the world. The efficient railway network is as good as anywhere in Europe, and takes you to the centre of Berlin. One of the cheapest ways to travel to the city is by international coach, although this is usually the slowest form of transport. If you are travelling by car, the *Autobahn* (motorway) leads to the Berliner Ring (Berlin Circular Road), from where a number of exits are signposted to the city centre.

Quick boarding with an electronic boarding pass for Lufthansa Airlines

Arriving by Air

Schönefeld and Tegel airports are Berlin's main airports until Berlin Brandenburg Airport opens in 2016. This new airport will significantly increase the city's capacity to receive international flights, with airlines such as airberlin, Lufthansa, Condor, Air France and easyJet able to increase the frequency of existing flights and add numerous new destinations to their schedules.

Berlin receives many flights from destinations throughout Europe, North America and Asia. The most frequent flights are by **Lufthansa** and **British Airways**, offering flight connections from all over Europe and beyond. From North America, **Delta** and **United** fly to Berlin from New York. **easyJet** offers daily connections from London Luton and Gatwick airports, and **Ryanair** flies from London Stansted three times daily. **airberlin** has direct flights from New York and Los Angeles and indirect connections from London Stansted and Gatwick. Lufthansa's low-cost subsidiary **Germanwings** offers indirect connections to London and North America.

Tickets and Fares

When planning your trip to Berlin, it is worth shopping around, as prices can vary enormously. Some of the best deals are offered by inclusive tour operators such as **Tuifly** and **Thomas Cook**; see your local travel agent for details. Air fares are usually cheaper when booked well in advance, and discounts are available for children and students. Low-cost airlines, such as Ryanair and easyJet, can only be booked via the Internet. A useful source of up-to-date information on schedules and fares to Berlin is www.opodo.com, a site operated by a consortium of European airlines including Lufthansa. Another helpful site is www.skyscanner.net. If you are willing to travel at short notice, you may be able to find a last-minute bargain.

Berlin Brandenburg Airport

Following ongoing delays, Berlin's new airport is currently expected to open in 2016. It will ultimately replace the closed Tempelhof and Berlin's two remaining airports, Tegel and Schönefeld, which has been rebuilt and expanded. It is informally named after the late Willy Brandt, the former West Berlin mayor and chancellor of West Germany.

Berlin Brandenburg will have an initial capacity of 27 million passengers a year, an increase of about 5 million passengers from the previous airports. The design of the terminal will leave room for expansion, meaning that up to 45 million passengers could eventually pass through annually. The airport code will be BER, marked on all tickets

The 31-m (100-ft) observation tower at Berlin Brandenburg Airport

Lufthansa aeroplane

and baggage tags. The airport features a striking observation tower, designed by Berlin architects Karin and Ramsi Kusus. Visitors can climb the tower for a view over the airfield, which will have its own motorway exit on the A113 and excellent railway services.

Transport from the Airport

Schönefeld is located 20 km (12 miles) southeast of the city centre, and is easily accessible by rail and road. It is near to the new Berlin Brandenburg Airport and has good and affordable public transport connections.

The fastest way to the centre of the city is to take one of the frequent Airport Express trains operated by Deutsche Bahn. The RE7 travels via Ostbahnhof to Alexanderplatz, Hauptbahnhof and Zoologischer Garten; the RB14 takes the same route but continues on to Charlottenburg and Spandau; and the RE9 travels via Südkreuz and Potsdamer Platz to Hauptbahnhof. Trains run every 15 minutes. A ticket costs €3.20, and can be purchased from machines on the platform; the same ticket price applies for all forms of public transport – S-Bahn, U-Bahn and bus.

Another rail option is the local S-Bahn network, which is slower, with more stations. The S9 and the S45 trains both run from the airport every 10 minutes and connect with the city-wide S-Bahn system. It is also possible to connect to the U-Bahn network by taking a bus. The X7 and X11 shuttle buses go to Rudow U-Bahn station, from where the U7 line runs to the city centre.

From Sunday to Thursday, most public transport services run from 4am until midnight. After this time, a night bus service continues to operate. From the airport, you can take the N7 bus, which travels slowly to the central districts and connects to other bus lines. On Fridays and Saturdays, most public transport runs 24 hours across the city.

A convenient but more expensive option to get to the city centre is by taxi, which should cost between €30 and €40.

Tegel airport is located 5 miles (8 km) from the city centre and can be reached easily by bus or taxi, both of which stop in front of the main hall. A trip by bus to the city centre usually takes 25–30 minutes and costs €2.60. Alternatively, bus no. 128 links the airport with U-Bahn station Kurt-Schumacher-Platz on the U6 line, while bus no. 109 links to Jakob-Kaiser-Platz station on the U7 line. If travelling by taxi, a trip to the centre costs between €20 and €30.

Destinations listings on the departures board

Former Airports

Airport aficionados may like to explore Berlin's now-closed terminals, especially the historic Flughafen Tempelhof *(see p149)*. Built during the Third Reich, Tempelhof has since been transformed into a giant public park. At weekends the old airfield is full of kite-flyers, cyclists and urban gardeners. The old terminal is still in its original state, and is used for events and conferences. The future of the Tegel terminal is under debate; it may become a business centre or a university campus.

DIRECTORY

Airlines

airberlin
Saatwinkler Damm 42–43.
Tel (01805) 73 78 00.
W airberlin.com

British Airways
Budapesterstrasse 18b.
Tel (01805) 26 65 22.
W ba.com

Delta
W delta.com

easyJet
W easyjet.com

Germanwings
Tel (0900) 19 19 19.
W germanwings.com

Lufthansa
Friedrichstrasse 185–190.
Tel (01805) 805 805.
W lufthansa.com

Ryanair
W ryanair.com

United
W united.com

Tickets and Fares

Thomas Cook
W thomascook.com

Tuifly
W tuifly.com

Airports

Berlin Brandenburg Airport/Schönefeld Airport/Tegel Airport
Tel 60 91 11 50.
W berlin-airport.de

The engine of an ICE (Inter City Express) train

Arriving by Train

The standards of European public transport are generally very high, particularly in central Europe, so whichever rail link you take to Berlin your journey is bound to be comfortable. The city has excellent connections with most major German and European cities. There are direct services between Berlin and Zürich, Brussels, Prague, Amsterdam, Paris and Warsaw. Besides these lines, there are many convenient international routes to choose from, via other German cities.

Deutsche Bahn the national railway company, operates a famously efficient service that criss-crosses the country. The Regional Bahn (RB) and Regional Express (RE) trains operate routes around the greater Berlin and Potsdam area, while longer distances are served by Inter City (IC) and European City (EC) trains. For a luxurious experience, take an Inter City Express (ICE) service; these sleek trains are the most expensive mode of rail transport, but are also extremely fast and comfortable.

If you are thinking of staying in Germany for quite a while, and are keen to travel around a lot by train, one of the cheapest options is an **InterRail** card. This can be bought by persons of any age, from any European country (and a variety of neighbouring countries), and gives the traveller unlimited access to rail transport in a selection of European countries. Tickets can be bought online. North American visitors can enquire into **Eurail** cards, which are available through travel agents or online. The prices vary depending on your age and the number of countries you want to visit, and the duration of the pass; the younger the visitor, and the more limited number of countries you wish to visit, the cheaper the card.

Logo of Deutsche Bahn (German Railways)

At various times of the year, but especially in summer, there are often special deals offering discounted travel. Among these are weekend tickets and family tickets. It pays to visit the information desk and ask about the different fares currently on offer. There are also discounts available by booking online, for travelling in groups and for those under 26 years of age.

Berlin's central railway station, **Hauptbahnhof**, opened in 2006 and is one of Europe's biggest rail traffic hubs. With its two soaring glass and steel office towers and a vast main hall, the station is a spectacular sight. The Hauptbahnhof is the main station for all Deutsche Bahn trains with German and international destinations or origins. Several S-Bahn routes (S3, S5, S7 and S75) link the station with the city. A short U-Bahn line, the U55, travels from here to the Bundestag and Brandenburger Tor, and there are plans to extend this line to meet the U5 at Alexanderplatz. The station also has a Deutsche Bahn Customer Centre, a tourist office, a lost and found bureau, shops, restaurants, rental car agencies, a bank, late-night services and a supermarket that is open on Sundays.

The former West Berlin central railway station, the Bahnhof Zoo (now called Zoologischer Garten) has become a regional railway station, but with many U- and S-Bahn lines connecting here, it is still an important traffic hub in the western downtown area. The best place to obtain information about public transport is the BVG pavilion on Hardenbergplatz *(see p295)*.

Some trains coming from destinations in the south or east arrive in Ostbahnhof, a convenient station where you can easily exchange money and send mail. Ostbahnhof is linked to other districts in Berlin via S-Bahn.

Remember that the ticket for your journey to Berlin is also valid on all S-Bahn connections to other stations, providing you use it immediately on arrival. For details of train times and destinations, call the **Deutsche Bahn Information** line.

Covered platforms at the airy, modern Hauptbahnhof

Coach Travel

Wherever you can travel by train, it is likely you can also travel by coach (long-distance bus), and Germany is no exception. On international routes, the fast network of *Autobahnen* (motorways) enables coaches to nearly match the speed of trains. Some try to raise the level of comfort by showing videos and serving light refreshments, but coaches generally are less roomy and less comfortable than trains. It is often a matter of cost; coach travel is nearly always cheaper than rail travel.

After you have visited Berlin, you may decide to take a coach trip to another German city or further afield. If so, the place to go is the **Zentral-Omnibus-Bahnhof**, situated near the Internationales Congress Centrum in the west of the city, best reached via the Messe Nord/ICC S-Bahn station. This is the city's largest long-distance bus station, and you will find connections to towns all over Germany, as well as links to other major European cities.

The main coach companies that stop in Berlin are **Eurolines**, **Berlin Linien Bus**, **Student Agency Bus** and **Ecolines**. Some coach companies, on overnight journeys, offer more comfortable sleeper seats for a small extra charge.

Typical road signs indicating the *Autobahn* and a district in Berlin

Travelling by Car

Berlin is surrounded by a circular *Autobahn* or motorway (the Berliner Ring), which is linked to *Autobahnen* leading to Dresden, Nürnberg, Munich, Hannover, Hamburg and beyond. Numerous exits from the ring road are signposted into the city centre, but the road is so long that it is sometimes quicker to cut through town to get to

One of the many coach services available in Berlin

wherever you are going (although not during rush hour).

While driving around the city, keep an eye on your speed; the police are extremely vigilant at doing speed checks. Less-experienced drivers may feel a little uneasy on the *Autobahn*, as German drivers tend to zoom along at speeds reaching 200 km/h (125 mph). Keep to the right, unless you are over-taking. Always remember to check your side- and rear-view mirrors before switching to a left-hand lane. If you want to overtake, make sure there's nobody coming up behind. The speed at which fast cars come up behind you can be surprising. On some stretches of the *Autobahn*, lower speed limits are imposed depending on weather and road conditions. For assistance on the road, call ADAC Auto Assistance (*see p293*). If you are involved in an accident, call the police on 110.

Driving licences from all European countries are valid in Germany. Visitors from other countries need an international licence. You must also carry your passport and the standard documentation (including insurance certificate or "green card") if driving your own car. To rent a car you will need a credit card as well as a valid driver's licence. There are several places to rent vehicles around the city, including the major train stations and airports *(see p293)*.

As in most countries, German law is tough on drinking and driving. In the event of an accident, or being pulled over by the police, you may find yourself in serious trouble if alcohol is found in your blood-stream. It is better not to take the risk in the first place, and abstain from drinking.

DIRECTORY

Trains

Deutsche Bahn Information
Tel 0180 5 99 66 33.

Deutsche Bahn UK Booking Centre
Tel +44 (0) 8718 80 80 66.
W bahn.de

Eurail and InterRail
W raildude.com

Hauptbahnhof
Service point at northern entrance, ground floor.
Map 8 D1.
Tel 0180 599 6633.

Coaches

Berlin Linien Bus
Mannheimer Str. 33/34.
Tel 338 44 80.
W berlinlinienbus.de

Ecolines
Tel (069) 401 59 055.
W ecolines.net

Eurolines
Tel (069) 7903 501.
W eurolines.com

Student Agency Bus
W studentagencybus.com

Zentral-Omnibus-Bahnhof (Cental Bus Station)
Messedamm 4.
Map 3 C5.
Tel 30 10 01 75.

GETTING AROUND BERLIN

Getting around Berlin is easy and enjoyable, thanks to the wonderfully efficient public transport system. It's also a great city to experience by bicycle or foot. Most of its main sights are located in the city centre and can easily be reached by cycling or walking. More peripheral areas can be reached by public transport. U- and S-Bahn trains systems are by far the quickest way to travel, but the trams and buses are also reliable. If you happen to get a double-decker, they are excellent for sightseeing. Drivers, however, may find that Berlin isn't the easiest of cities to drive in, largely because of the endless road works. Building sites are scattered all over the city, and the number of parking spaces is inadequate in central areas, so congestion is bad and driving should be avoided if possible.

Lights at a pedestrian crossing indicating when it's safe to cross

Green Travel

There is almost no reason to use a car in Berlin, as public transport is extensive and efficient, even to the outer reaches of the city. You can buy day-, week- or month-long passes to make your visit cost effective (*see p294*). For long distance trips, there are many fast train connections, as well as safe and effective *Mitfahrer* car-pooling schemes that stretch across Europe (www.mitfahrgelegenheit.de).

The best way to see Berlin is by bicycle. There are more than 600 km (372 miles) of dedicated bicycle lanes, and drivers give cyclists respect when sharing the road. It's easy to hire a bike for a day, a week, or even an hour through **DB Call-A-Bike**, the public cycling scheme operated by Deutsche Bahn (*see p293*).

There are several hundred *Umwelt Taxis* (Environmental Taxis) operating in Berlin. They carry a sign to indicate that they use *Erdgas*, or natural gas, which is slightly less polluting than other fossil fuels.

Other green travel systems include Segway tours (*see p279*) and **Velo Taxi**.

Walking

German drivers are generally careful and watch out for pedestrians, but vigilance is still needed. Cyclists travelling at speed can be dangerous, as many cycle routes run along the pavements (sidewalks), only marked by a line or by a different colour (normally red). You can easily be hit, or at least scolded for being in the wrong lane.

When searching for a specific street address, keep in mind that street numbers sometimes increase along one side of the street and then turn around at the end and continue on the other side. Street signs on each corner include the numbers within that particular block.

Disabled visitors should contact **Mobidat Infoservice** or the **Berliner Behindertenverband** for advice on getting around, including wheelchair rental and other support services.

Driving

Driving around Berlin is not as straightforward as it is in some European capitals. Most of downtown Berlin (inside the S-Bahn ring) is a green zone, where only vehicles with an approved environmental badge are allowed. You can buy the badge online at www.umwelt-plakette.de. Most rental cars are covered.

Local drivers are mostly careful and don't break speed limits or enter junctions on yellow lights. You are allowed to turn right on a red light if a green arrow is also showing.

Petrol stations can be found right across the city. Some may require you to pay before your pump is activated.

You won't have a problem hiring a car in Berlin, as long as you show your passport and a valid driving licence; a credit card is the preferred method of payment. There are many hire

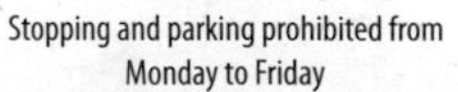

Stopping and parking prohibited from Monday to Friday

Parking permitted during working hours and at weekends only with a ticket

Parking Meter

Parking meters are used on most streets. You have to pay for parking depending on the parking zone; usually between 9am and 7pm on weekdays, and 9am and 2pm on Saturdays. Check signs for information.

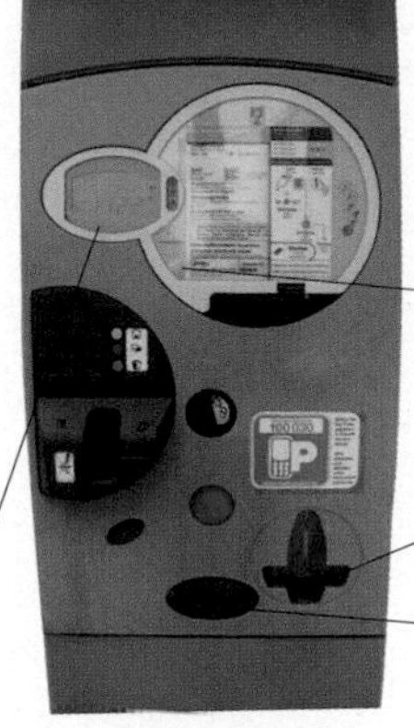

companies, including **Avis, Europcar**, **Hertz** and **Sixt**, with offices at the airports, railway stations and in the city centre.

If you experience any trouble on the road, you should call **ADAC Auto Assistance**.

Parking

Finding a parking place won't always be easy, especially during lunchtime, but with a bit of luck you should be able to leave your car in the middle lane of the Ku'damm or near Alexanderplatz. There are also parking meters on nearly every street, and many car parks.

Parking your car illegally is not worth the risk; Berlin traffic wardens are constantly on the prowl, and as well as giving you a ticket, they can have your vehicle towed. If your vehicle is towed away, you must call the **Berlin Police**. It can cost up to €250 to locate your vehicle. For a cheaper solution, search nearby streets – cars are sometimes simply moved rather than impounded.

Cycling

Most of the main roads have designated cycling lanes and traffic lights at intersections. When using bicycle racks, make sure your bike is locked and don't leave it for too long.

You can take your bike on U- and S-Bahn trains and trams but must enter the carriage by the correct door and leave your bike in the designated space. Bikes are prohibited on buses, except night buses, which can carry up to two at the driver's discretion. For all public transport an additional *Fahrrad* (bicycle) ticket is required.

Deutsche Bahn operates a fantastic public bicycle system. You can find ranks of their specially marked **DB Call-a-Bike** bicycles at train stations and major intersections. To rent one, register using the computer terminal found at each station by providing your credit card details. A one-off registration fee of €12 applies. The first 30 minutes are free, and then the cost is 8 cents a minute, up to a maximum of €15 a day or €60 a week.

You can also hire bikes at many cycling shops for similar or cheaper rates; one of the most reliable is **Fahrradstation**. Or take a ride in a **Velo Taxi**. You will be transported in an open-air coach on the back of a bike.

DB Call-a-Bike bicycles for rent

DIRECTORY

Walking

Berliner Behindertenverband
Jägerstrasse 63d.
Tel 204 38 48.

Mobidat Infoservice
Tel 322 94 03 00.

Driving

ADAC Auto Assistance
Tel (01802) 22 22 22.
W adac.de

Avis
Tel (01805) 21 77 02.
W avis.com

Europcar
Tel (040) 520 187 654.
W europcar.de

Hertz
Tel (01803) 33 535.
W hertz.com

Sixt
Tel (01805) 252 525.
W sixt.de

Parking

Berlin Police (towed vehicles)
Tel 4664 98 78 00.

Cycling

DB Call-a-Bike
W callabike.de

Fahrradstation
Dorotheenstrasse 30.
Tel (01805) 108 000. **Open** Mar–Oct: 10am–7:30pm Mon–Fri (to 6pm Sat, to 4pm Sun); Nov–Feb: 10am–7pm Mon–Fri (to 4pm Sat).

Velo Taxi
Tel 2803 1609. **Open** Apr–Oct.
W velotaxi.com

Buses, Trams and Taxis

Travelling by bus in Berlin is highly recommended. Buses are efficient, generally on time, and they travel useful routes – although some buses can get crowded during rush hour. Most of the major roads have special bus lanes so buses are punctual even when the main roads are congested. A double-decker bus is worth taking if you're new in town and want to have a good look round (see Useful Bus Routes map on the City Map). Trams are another particularly good option in the central and eastern parts of the city; like the buses and S-Bahn lines they are part of BVG and accept the same tickets.

BVG pavilion on Hardenbergplatz providing transport information

Tickets

The whole of Berlin is divided into three travel zones: A, B and C. Zone A covers the city centre, Zone B the outskirts of town and Zone C includes Potsdam and its environs. Travel between the zones is simple, with tickets available for each combination of zones.

The most expensive option is to travel by buying a single ticket, which is valid for 2 hours and valid on all forms of public transport, including S- and U-Bahn trains, with as many changes as you need. Travel is allowed in only one direction, so a second ticket is needed for the return journey. Short-trip (*Kurzstrecke*) tickets are cheaper, but can only be used for three stops on trains and six stops on buses or trams.

Tickets can be bought from ticket machines at U- or S-Bahn stations, on board trams or from the bus driver. You must validate your ticket before you start your journey by inserting it in a red or yellow time-stamping machine found near the ticket machines, at platform entrances and on board buses. Children under 14 years old are entitled to a discount (*Ermässigungstarif*) and those under 6 can travel for free. The One-Day Ticket (*Tageskarte*) is valid from the moment it is validated until 3am the next morning. Weekly cards (*7-Tage-Karte*) are valid for seven days, and have the added benefit of allowing you to travel with one extra adult and up to three children for free after 8pm on weekdays, or all hours across the weekend.

Berlin WelcomeCard ticket

Several tourist cards are available that combine public transport with discount entry to museums and attractions. The Berlin Welcome Card and the CityTourCard are both popular (*see p279*). For information about tickets and public transport in general, check the **BVG** website, visit a **BVG Pavilion** for all transport information, or check the **Ticket Information** line.

Travelling by Bus

Bus stops are marked by signs bearing the letter H, for *Haltestelle* or stop. All bus routes have a detailed time-table on display at each stop. Inner-city bus stops are equipped with digital screens indicating waiting times. Bus stops are often relocated due to road works. You can always find a replacement stop nearby.

Apart from its number, a bus will also have its destination on show; pay attention to this, as some buses shorten their routes outside rush hour. It is not always necessary to flag down buses at stops, but it can help. Enter via the front door and buy a ticket from the driver. If you are transferring and already have a validated ticket, show this.

Approaching stop names are announced automatically and are displayed digitally. Press the *Halt* ("Stop") button to get off; most stops are made "on request" only (especially in the suburbs). To exit, you must press a button to open the doors.

A typical single-decker bus

Types of Bus Service

There are several different bus services operating in Berlin, but all use the same ticket tariffs. Regular buses are marked by three-digit route codes and operate every 20 minutes between 5am and midnight. Important routes are serviced by Metro buses, marked by the letter M at the start of their route code. These operate 24 hours a day, and run every 10 to 20 minutes. Express buses, marked by the letter X, run every 5 to 20 minutes.

The night bus service begins operation after midnight and is a very reliable network. These buses are marked by the letter N and tickets can be bought direct from the driver. They operate every half-hour until about 4am, when the U-Bahn service resumes.

Routes 100 and 200

These special routes are served by double-deckers and include the most attractive parts of town. The buses operate between Bahnhof Zoo and Prenzlauer Berg, passing most of the city's interesting historic sights. For the price of a regular bus ticket, you can visit many of the locations as a more expensive tourist bus tour. The buses stop at Museum Island, Unter den Linden, Brandenburg Gate, the Reichstag, Potsdamer Platz, the Tiergarten and Kaiser-Wilhelm-Gedächtniskirche.

The BVG also operates a special historic bus tour called the Zille-Express, which makes a 50-minute circuit around the centre of Berlin, with commentary in German and English. The tour operates between April and October, departing from Brandenburg Gate every hour from 10:30am to 5pm. A trip costs €8 and is free for children under the age of 10.

Trams

Trams (*Strassenbahn*) operate in Mitte and the eastern parts of the city – a legacy from the city's division, when West Berlin tore up its once-extensive tram network. Despite servicing only

Modern tram operating in the former East Berlin quarter

Tram Stop

Every tram stop displays the appropriate tram numbers, timetables and maps. Buses sometimes also use the stops and are listed accordingly.

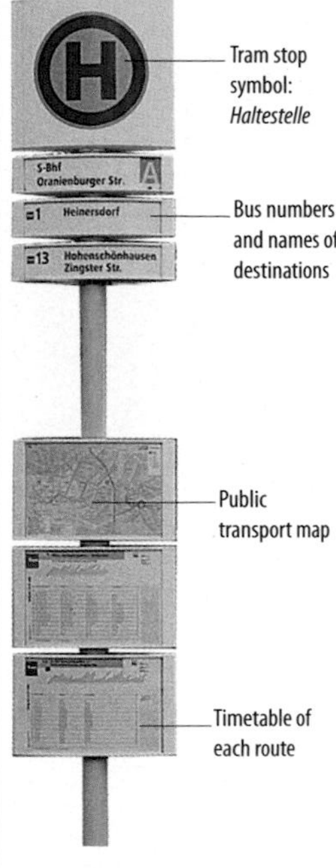

one-third of the city, trams remain a great way to get around, particularly if you are travelling from Mitte to any part of Prenzlauer Berg. The M10 is also a convenient route, connecting Prenzlauer Berg to Friedrichshain.

Important routes are serviced by Metro trams, marked by the letter M at the front of their route code. These trams run every 10 or 20 minutes, 24 hours a day. Other trams operate between 5 or 6 am and midnight, arriving every 20 minutes.

The network runs a mix of modern wheelchair-friendly low-floor trams and old carriages with stairs; look for wheelchair symbols on timetables for guidance on which service is most suitable.

Tram tickets can also be used on buses, S- and U-Bahn trains. You can purchase tickets using machines (coin only) on board.

Taxis

Taxis are a comfortable but expensive way of getting around Berlin. All taxis are of the same cream colour and have a big "TAXI" sign on the roof. You can easily hail one on the street or arrange a cab by phone, through **Taxi Funk** or **Würfelfunk**. You can also get a taxi from a designated rank in popular locations, such as train stations.

The fare is calculated by a meter on the driver's dashboard. If you are travelling 2 km (1 mile) or less, you can request the *Kurzstrecke* (short trip) for €4 – but only from taxis hailed in the street, and only if you inform the driver at the start of the trip.

A Berlin taxi with a yellow roof sign

DIRECTORY

Useful Numbers

BVG Information
(BVG-Kundendienst).
Tel 194 49.
W bvg.de

BVG Pavilion
Hardenbergplatz.
Open 6:30am–9:30pm Mon–Fri; 10am–5:30pm Sat & Sun.

Ticket Information
S-Bahn Berlin
Bahnhof Alexanderplatz.
Tel 29 74 33 33.
Open 6:30am–9pm Mon–Fri, 8am–9pm Sat & Sun.

Taxis

Taxi Funk Berlin
Tel 44 33 22.

Würfelfunk
Tel 210 101.

Travelling by U-Bahn, S-Bahn and Regional Trains

While in theory Berlin has two separate train networks – the U-Bahn and S-Bahn systems – in practical terms there is not much difference between them, and commuters use the same tickets for both. Strictly speaking, the U-Bahn operates as a metro system, with most of its trains running underground, while the S-Bahn is a longer-distance commuter service. In practice, however, there is a great deal of overlap between the two systems, and many stations have both S- and U-Bahn platforms. The U-Bahn is owned by BVG and the S-Bahn by Deutsche Bahn.

Train arriving at a station on a U-Bahn platform

U-Bahn

The U-Bahn network is very dense, with numerous stations very close together. Don't be confused by the name – "underground" trains also run on elevated tracks above the street in some sections. During rush hours trains are very frequent, usually arriving every few minutes. There are ten U-Bahn lines in total. The service closes down between around 12.30am and 4am, and is replaced by night buses. On weekends, all lines are open 24 hours, except the two short-line services, the U4 and the U55.

S-Bahn

The S-Bahn is faster than the U-Bahn, with stations spaced further apart. Trains run every 10 or 20 minutes, or more frequently in peak hours. There are a total of 15 S-Bahn lines, all running well beyond the confines of the city; four of them (S3, 5, 7 and 75) travel concurrently along the central line between Westkreuz and Ostkreuz. The Ring service (S41 and S42) is a convenient way to circle the city; it takes one hour to travel a complete circuit.

The S-Bahn has been plagued by problems due to cost-cutting over the years. If on your journey you face delays, it's worth noting you can use your ticket on the large red regional trains (RE and RB), which stop at most stations on the central line between Ostbahnhof and Zoologischer Garten.

Tickets

Tickets for S- and U-Bahn trains are the same as the tickets used on local buses and trams. The *Kurzstrecke* (short-trip) single ticket is also acceptable, although it is only valid for three S-/U-Bahn or five bus/tram stops. Vending machines stand at the entrance to each station, selling single tickets, and one- and seven-day travelcards and other tickets. The red or yellow validation machines can be found next to the ticket machines, or near the entrance to each platform.

You may notice that there are no gates to stop free-riders trying their luck on the trains, but attempting to travel free of charge can be risky. Trains are patrolled by ticket inspectors, who always work in plain clothes. They tend not to accept any excuses; fines for not having a ticket start at €40.

Signs and Trains

There's no mistaking a U-Bahn station, with its large rectangular sign and trademark white U on a blue background; similarly for S-Bahn stations, which have a round sign with a large white S on a green background. On metro maps each line is marked by a different colour and number.

The direction of the train is noted on the train and platform, which always give the final destination. When embarking, always check both the line number and the final destination of the train, as it is very easy to confuse your direction. All stations have maps of the local area as well as maps of the entire metro system. Maps of the network are also on view in the train carriages.

Train doors do not open automatically; you must push a

A distinctive yellow-and-red train, part of the rapid transit S-Bahn rail system

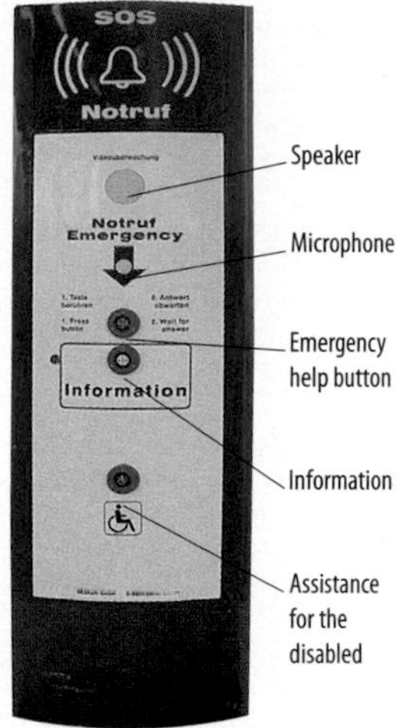

Information and emergency help point for the S-Bahn and U-Bahn

flashing button or pull a metal handle to open them. An alert sounds when doors are closing and the train conductor will announce, *"Zurück bleiben!"* ("Stay back"). During the journey the next station is announced inside the carriage and information is given on electronic screens.

Regional Trains

Operated by Deutsche Bahn *(see p290)*, the Regional Bahn and Regional Express (RB and RE) trains service the wider Berlin-Brandenburg region and beyond. They are a great way to get to Potsdam *(see pp192–207)* or other smaller towns near Berlin.

Tickets can be bought at automatic machines on station platforms, or from ticket offices. If travelling at the weekend there are special offers available, including a five-person ticket that lasts all day. A normal U- and S-Bahn ticket can be used to ride these trains within Berlin – which is particularly useful when there are delays on the S-Bahn line.

Regional trains depart from only a small number of stations, including Hauptbahnhof, Friedrichstrasse, Alexanderplatz, Ostbahnhof, Zoologischer Garten and Gesundbrunnen.

USING THE U- AND S-BAHN

1 Find the station you want on a map and see which line runs there. Do not forget to make a note of the final destination of the line so you can be sure of travelling in the right direction.

Map of U- and S-Bahn lines *(see inside back cover)*

2 Find the type of ticket you require on the touchscreen. After making your selection, the price is displayed and you can insert your coins, notes or credit cards.

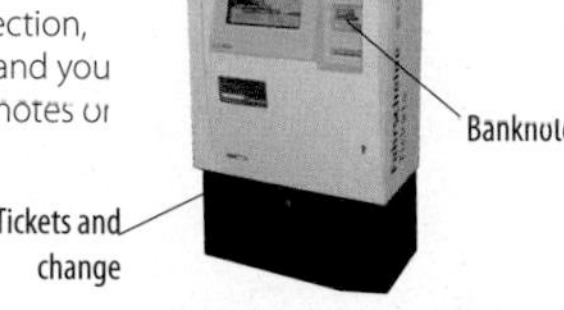

3 A ticket from the machine looks different from one bought on a bus or tram, but it will always contain information about its type and price.

Weekly travel card and one-day travel card

4 After entering the station you must validate your ticket in one of the red or yellow stamping machines located on the platform.

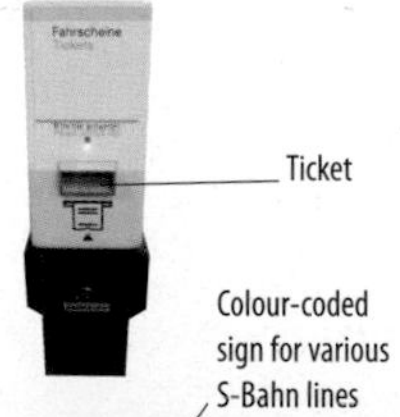

Colour-coded sign for various S-Bahn lines

5 Follow the signs to the appropriate platform and choose the correct side by checking the destinations of departing trains.

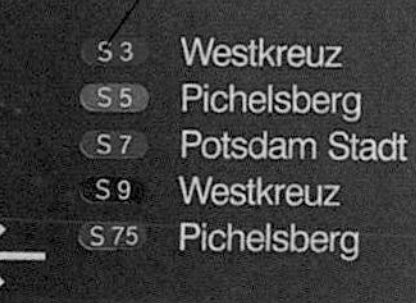

Information board indicating the destinations of departing trains

Sign indicating where to go for these U-Bahn lines

6 After leaving a train, proceed to the exit, signed *Ausgang*. If there are several exits, signs will tell you the names of the streets outside, while arrows will indicate the location of elevators and escalators.

A typical exit sign

Getting Around by Boat

The river routes of Berlin may not be as dense as those of Amsterdam or Venice, but the Spree and the Havel offer more than just a pleasure cruise in the sun. An extensive system of canals and lakes links the city centre with Potsdam, Spandau, Charlottenburg and the area of Müggelsee. All kinds of water transport are available, from rowing boats to catamarans and barges.

One of many tourist boats on the Spree river

Getting Around Berlin on the Water

One of the most relaxing ways to spend the afternoon in Berlin is to take a leisurely 3- to 4-hour journey by boat along the Spree river and the Landwehrkanal. There is no shortage of companies offering this kind of trip. Four of the most reliable are **Reederei Bruno Winkler**, **Stern und Kreisschiffahrt**, **Reederei Hartmut Triebler** and **Reederei Riedel**. Each has its own dock, but the routes they follow are similar. You can admire the historic buildings of Mitte as the boat passes by the Berliner Dom along Museum Island, before heading off to the government district and the Reichstag. You should have a good view of the Haus der Kulturen der Welt and the new city in Moabit shortly before entering the Landwehrkanal. This runs alongside the Zoological Garden and new city buildings on Potsdamer Platz, and passes through Kreuzberg on its way to the junction with the Spree at Oberbaumbrücke.

Most of the boats available along this route have enclosed lower decks and open upper decks, with a bar serving snacks and drinks. All the sights are explained by a guide along the way; the commentary is usually in German, but some companies can arrange for an English speaker.

Public Ferries

In addition to the many privately operated cruises, there are also six public ferry lines that are integrated into the public transport system. These are marked by a stylized F and use the same tickets as trains and buses. Most of them provide cross-river connections in locations to the east where there are no bridges. However, the F10 provides a particularly charming trip from Wannsee (near Potsdam) to the lakeside village of Alt-Kladow – a great budget option for those who don't want to pay a lot for a cruise.

Trips Along the Spree and Havel Rivers

If you want to try something a little more adventurous, there are longer trips to choose from, some of which cover the western lakes as well as the city centre. A pleasant route takes you along the Spree, past the Mitte district, to Treptow, Charlottenburg and Spandau. From here you can carry on along the Havel river to the Grunewald and the Wannsee, then take a trip past Pfaueninsel to Potsdam. To do this, enquire at Stern und Kreisschiffahrt. Companies Reederei Bruno Winkler and Reederei Hartmut Triebler offer similar trips starting at Spandau and Charlottenburg.

Other options include a trip from Tegel port to Spandau and Wannsee, or a journey from Treptow to Köpenick. If you really want to, you can cover the whole of Berlin by boat, starting from Tegel in the north and finishing at Köpenick in the southeast, all within 5 or 6 hours.

Longer Journeys Around Berlin

For even longer tours, you may decide to take a whole day exploring the rivers, canals and lakes of Berlin. From Treptow you can take a boat to Woltersdorf which takes you

Boat moored along the river in the summer

One of the larger boats available on the Spree

through the charming lakeland area of Müggelsee. This region really is one of Berlin's greatest treasures and is ideal for anyone searching for a quiet place to relax. There are many man-made beaches to choose from, as well as summer gardens and cafés – and a large white fleet of ships to show you around Berlin. Müggelsee is best visited on a warm summer's day, when you can easily spend a few hours on one of its beaches.

Another adventurous idea is to take a voyage along the Teltowkanal from Treptow to Potsdam. From here, **Weisse Flotte Potsdam** can take you not only to Wannsee and the other familiar routes around town, but also to Caputh, Werder and to many other sights to the south and west of Potsdam.

Boat Hire

It is possible to charter a small boat to use for several hours or longer. **Bootsverleih Spreepoint**, on the shores of Müggelsee in the east, hires motor-boats to those with the appropriate licences, or you can find a chartered boat at the **Solar Boat Pavilion** in Köpenick. For a trip through the centre of the city, the **Spree Shuttle** offers private boat tours of the main sights.

Reederei Riedel company logo

Potsdam and its lakes and rivers teem with boat rental companies; check with the Potsdam Tourismus Information Centre *(see p281)* for contact details.

DIRECTORY

Boat Tours

Reederei Bruno Winkler
Mierendorffstrasse 16.
Tel 349 95 95.
W reedereiwinkler.de

Reederei Hartmut Triebler
Bratringweg 29.
Tel 37 15 10 52.

Reederei Riedel
Planufer 78.
Tel 67 96 14 70.
W reederei-riedel.de

Stern und Kreisschiffahrt
Puschkinallee 15.
Tel 536 36 00.
W sternundkreis.de

Weisse Flotte Potsdam
Lange Brücke 6.
Tel (0331) 275 92 10.

Boat Hire Companies

Bootsverleih Spreepoint
Müggelseedamm 70.
Tel 64 11 291.
W spreepoint.de

Solar Boat Pavilion
Müggelheimer Strasse 10
Tel 01606 309 997.

Spree Shuttle
Lausitzer Strasse 36.
Tel 611 80 01.
W spree-shuttle.de

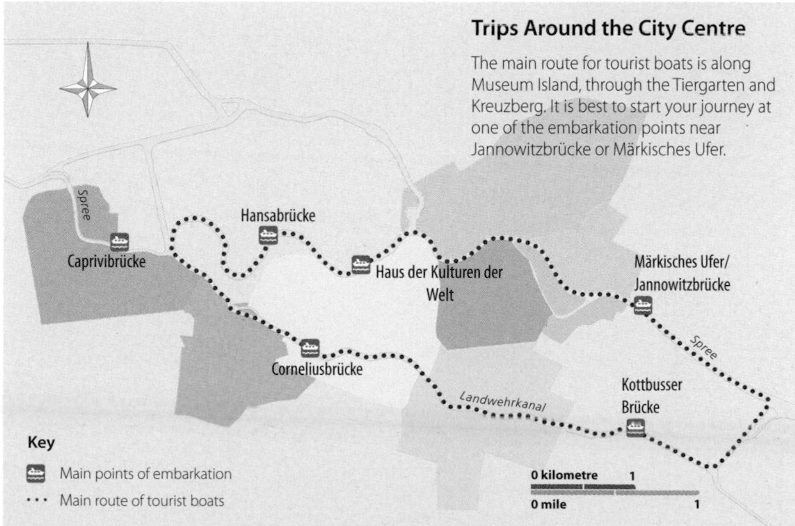

STREET FINDER

Map references given for historic buildings, hotels, restaurants, bars, shops and entertainment venues refer to the maps in this section of the guidebook only.
A complete index of street names and all places of interest can be found on the following pages. The key map below shows the area of Berlin covered by the *Street Finder*. The maps include all the major sightseeing areas, historic attractions, railway stations, bus stations and the suburban stations of the U-Bahn and S-Bahn, as well as the ferry embarkation points. The names of the streets and squares in the index and maps are given in German. The word Strasse (Str.) indicates a street, Platz a square, Brücke a bridge and Bahnhof a railway station.

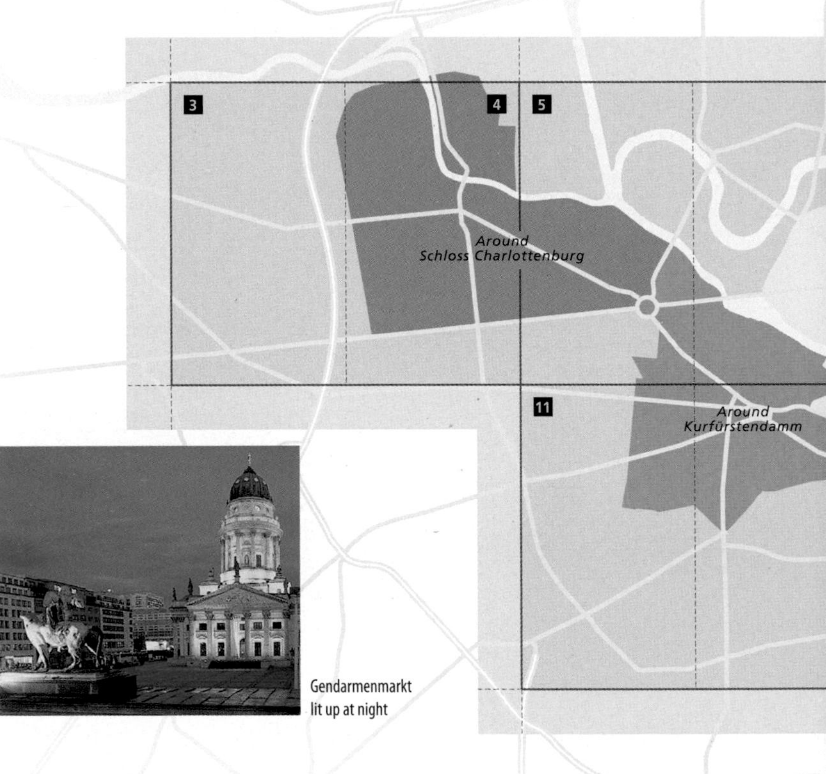

Gendarmenmarkt lit up at night

Key

- Major sight
- Place of interest
- Other building
- S-Bahn station
- U-Bahn station
- Railway station
- Bus station
- Tram stop
- Hospital with casualty unit
- Police station
- Tourist information
- Church
- Synagogue
- Railway line
- Pedestrianized street
- Autobahn (motorway)

Scale of Maps 1–16

0 metres 200

0 yards 200

1:12,200

Palm house in the Botanischer Garten

Rococo Chinesisches Haus in Park Sanssouci, Potsdam

Modern business centre of Potsdamer Platz

Street Finder Index

E

F

G

H

I

J

K

L

1
A
B
C
Gesundbrunnen
SWINEMÜNDER BRÜCKE
SCHWEDTERSTRASSE
RAMIERSTRASSE
BRUNNENSTRASSE
VOLKSPARK HUMBOLDTHAIN
GLEIMSTRASSE
RÜGENER STRASSE
SWINEMÜNDER STRASSE
GUSTAV-MEYER-ALLEE
LORTZINGSTRASSE
Voltastrasse
MAUERPARK
HUSSITENSTRASSE
DEMMINER STRASSE
VOLTASTRASSE
WOLLINER STRASSE
VINETA-PLATZ
RUPPINER
USEDOMER STRASSE
WATT-STRASSE
STRALSUNDERSTRASSE
BERNAUER STRASSE
ACKERSTRASSE
HUSSITENSTRASSE
Bernauer Strasse
RHEINSBERGER STRASSE
ARKONA-PLATZ
GARTENSTRASSE
STRELITZER STRASSE
ZIONKIRCHSTRASSE
FEHRBELLINER STRASSE
Gedenkstätte Berliner Mauer
ANKLAMER STRASSE
PARK AM NORDBAHNHOF
SOPHIEN-FRIEDHOF
BERGSTRASSE
VETERANEN STRASSE
WEINBERGS PARK
Nordbahnhof
INVALIDENSTRASSE
ACKERSTRASSE
BERGSTRASSE
Naturkundemuseum
EICHENDORFFSTRASSE
CHAUSSEESTRASSE
WEINBERGSWEG
Rosenthaler Platz
TIECK-STRASSE
BORSIGSTRASSE
NOVALISSTRASSE
TORSTRASSE
LINIENSTRASSE
ROSENTHALER STR.
KLEINE HAMBURGER STR.
KOPPEN-PLATZ
KL. AUGUSTSTR.
JOACHIMSTR.
Brecht-Weigel-Gedenkstätte
8
9

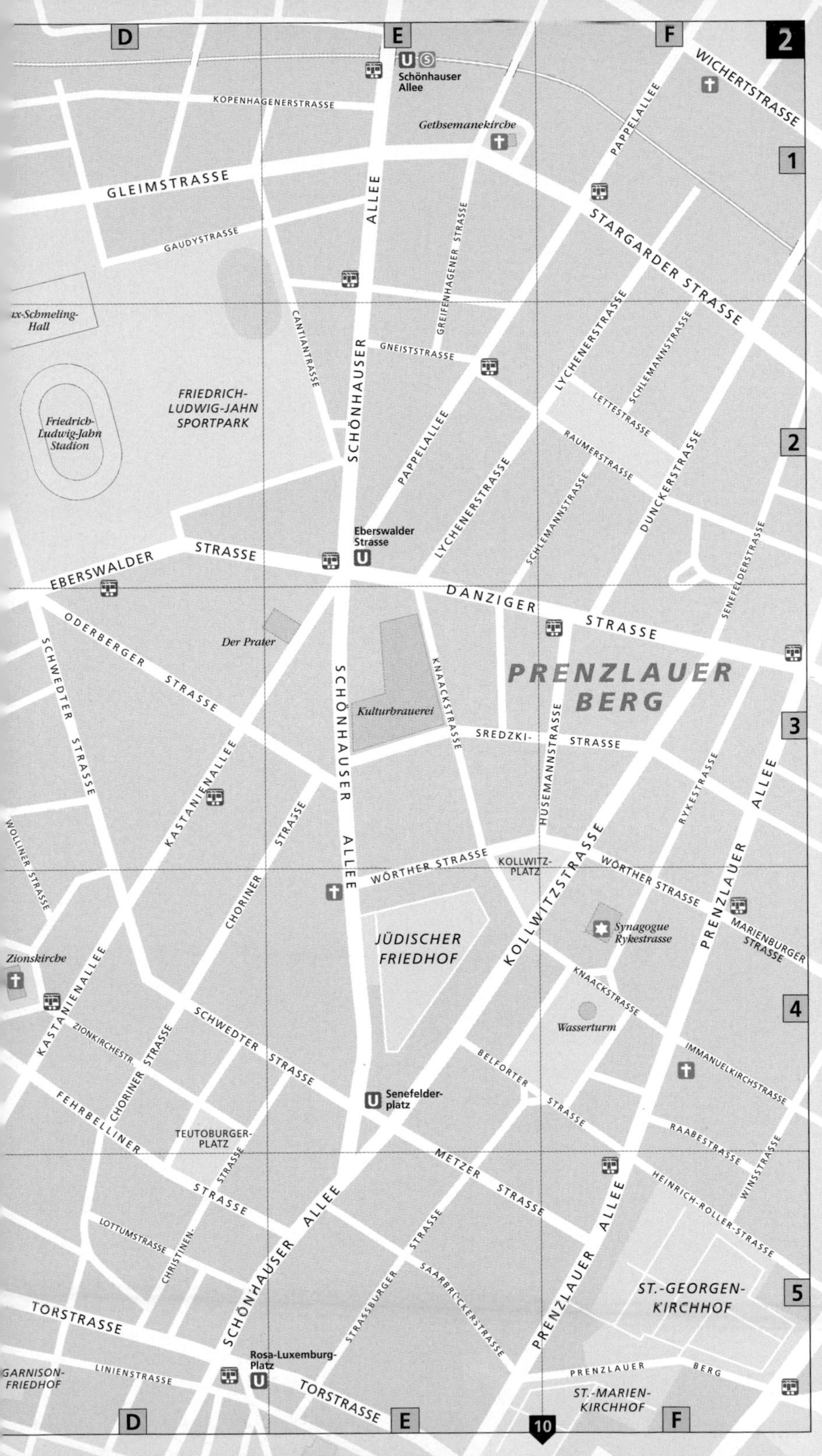

D
E
F
2
Schönhauser Allee
KOPENHAGENERSTRASSE
Gethsemanekirche
WICHERTSTRASSE
PAPPELALLEE
1
GLEIMSTRASSE
ALLEE
GAUDYSTRASSE
GREIFENHAGENER STRASSE
STARGARDER STRASSE
Max-Schmeling-Hall
CANTIANSTRASSE
SCHÖNHAUSER
GNEISTSTRASSE
LYCHENERSTRASSE
SCHLEMANNSTRASSE
FRIEDRICH-LUDWIG-JAHN SPORTPARK
Friedrich-Ludwig-Jahn Stadion
LETTESTRASSE
RAUMERSTRASSE
PAPPELALLEE
2
LYCHENERSTRASSE
SCHLEMANNSTRASSE
DUNCKERSTRASSE
Eberswalder Strasse
EBERSWALDER
STRASSE
SENEFELDERSTRASSE
DANZIGER
STRASSE
ODERBERGER
STRASSE
Der Prater
SCHWEDTER
STRASSE
KNAACKSTRASSE
PRENZLAUER BERG
Kulturbrauerei
SREDZKI-
STRASSE
3
KASTANIENALLEE
HUSEMANNSTRASSE
RYKESTRASSE
ALLEE
WOLLINER STRASSE
STRASSE
ALLEE
WÖRTHER STRASSE
KOLLWITZ-PLATZ
WÖRTHER STRASSE
PRENZLAUER
CHORINER
KOLLWITZSTRASSE
Synagogue Rykestrasse
MARIENBURGER STRASSE
JÜDISCHER FRIEDHOF
Zionskirche
KASTANIENALLEE
KNAACKSTRASSE
4
Wasserturm
SCHWEDTER
STRASSE
ZIONKIRCHESTR.
STRASSE
IMMANUELKIRCHSTRASSE
BELFORTER
STRASSE
FEHRBELLINER
CHORINER
Senefelder-platz
RAABESTRASSE
TEUTOBURGER-PLATZ
STRASSE
METZER
STRASSE
WINSSTRASSE
STRASSE
ALLEE
HEINRICH-ROLLER-STRASSE
LOTTUMSTRASSE
CHRISTINEN-
SCHÖNHAUSER
STRASSE
SAARBRÜCKERSTRASSE
PRENZLAUER
ST.-GEORGEN-KIRCHHOF
5
TORSTRASSE
STRASSBURGER
Rosa-Luxemburg-Platz
GARNISON-FRIEDHOF
LINIENSTRASSE
PRENZLAUER
BERG
ST.-MARIEN-KIRCHHOF
TORSTRASSE
D
E
10
F

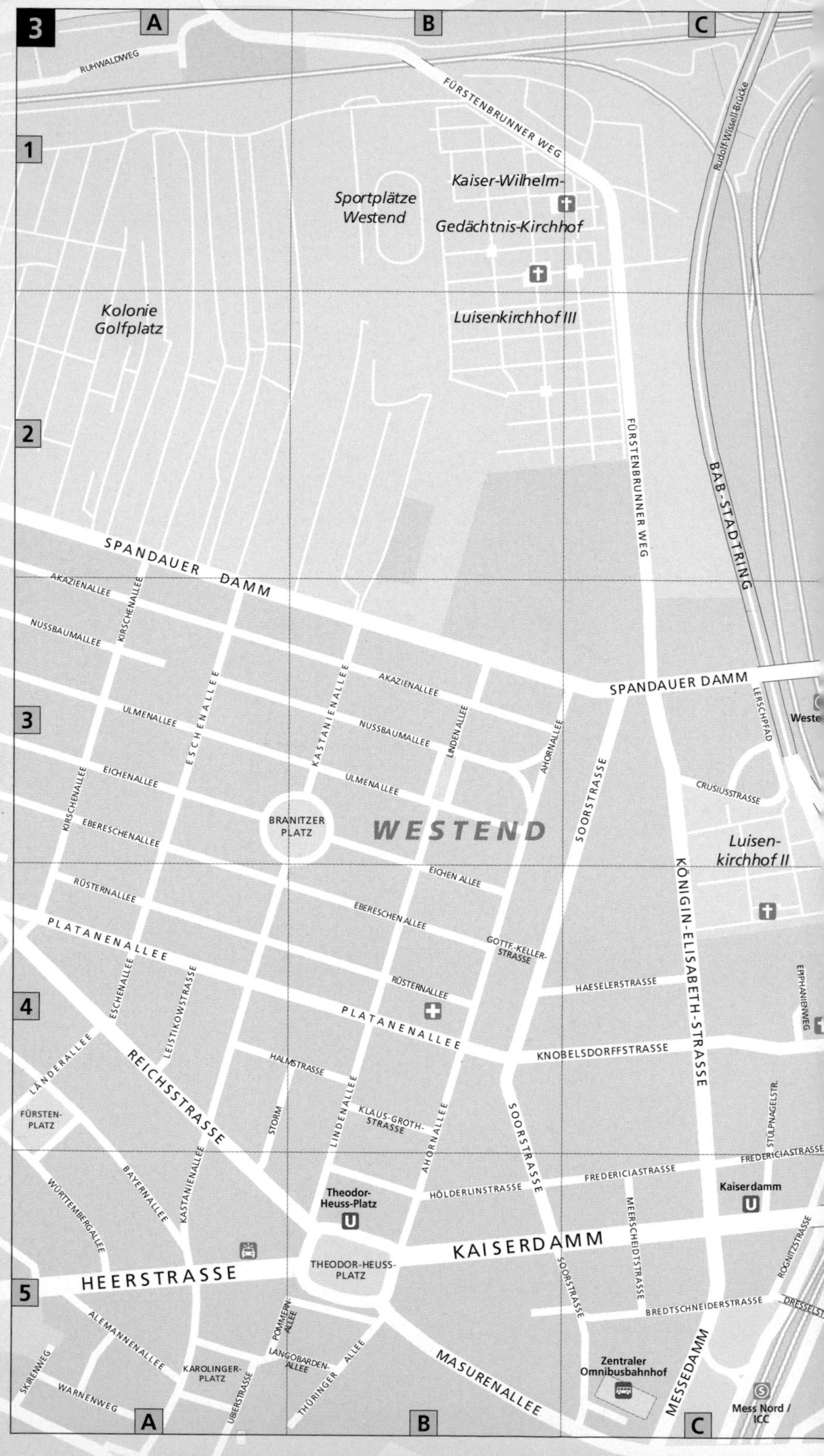
3
A
B
C
1
2
3
4
5
RUHWALDWEG
FÜRSTENBRUNNER WEG
Sportplätze Westend
Kaiser-Wilhelm-Gedächtnis-Kirchhof
Luisenkirchhof III
Kolonie Golfplatz
Rudolf-Wissell-Brücke
BAB-STADTRING
SPANDAUER DAMM
AKAZIENALLEE
NUSSBAUMALLEE
KIRSCHENALLEE
ESCHENALLEE
KASTANIENALLEE
LINDENALLEE
AHORNALLEE
ULMENALLEE
EICHENALLEE
EBERESCHENALLEE
BRANITZER PLATZ
WESTEND
SOORSTRASSE
LERSCHPFAD
CRUSIUSSTRASSE
Luisenkirchhof II
KÖNIGIN-ELISABETH-STRASSE
RÜSTERNALLEE
PLATANENALLEE
GOTTF.-KELLER-STRASSE
HAESELERSTRASSE
EPIPHANIENWEG
LEISTIKOWSTRASSE
REICHSSTRASSE
HALMSTRASSE
KNOBELSDORFFSTRASSE
LÄNDERALLEE
FÜRSTEN-PLATZ
STORM
KLAUS-GROTH-STRASSE
STÜLPNAGELSTR.
FREDERICIASTRASSE
WÜRTTEMBERGALLEE
BAYERNALLEE
Theodor-Heuss-Platz
HÖLDERLINSTRASSE
Kaiserdamm
MEERSCHEIDTSTRASSE
ROGNITZSTRASSE
KAISERDAMM
HEERSTRASSE
THEODOR-HEUSS-PLATZ
BREDTSCHNEIDERSTRASSE
DRESSELSTR.
ALEMANNENALLEE
POMMERN-ALLEE
LANGOBARDEN-ALLEE
MASURENALLEE
Zentraler Omnibusbahnhof
MESSEDAMM
SKIRENWEG
KAROLINGER-PLATZ
WARNENWEG
ÜBIERSTRASSE
THÜRINGER ALLEE
Mess Nord / ICC

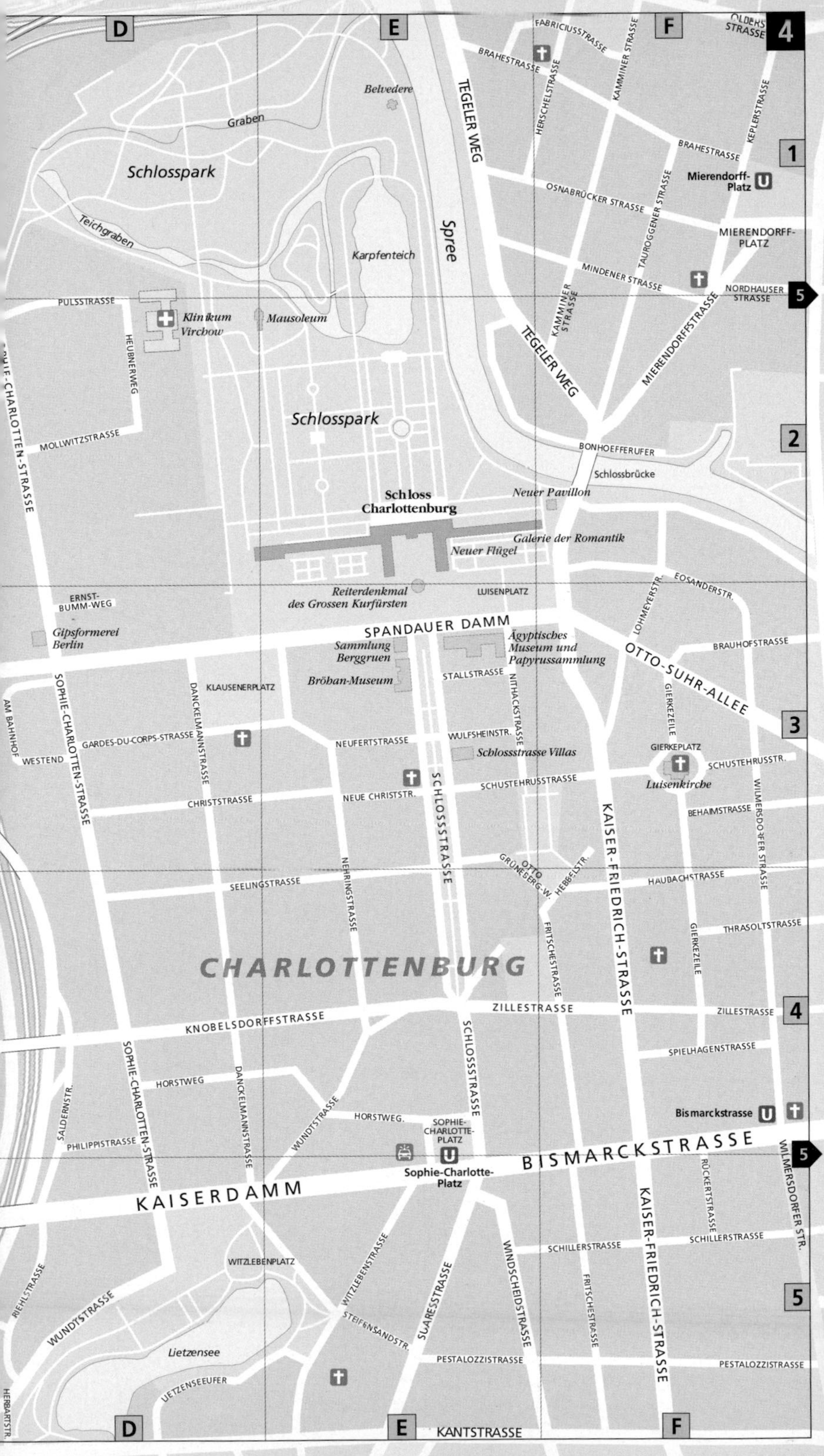

D
E
F
4
1
2
3
4
5
5
5
Schlosspark
Graben
Teichgraben
Belvedere
Karpfenteich
Spree
TEGELER WEG
Klinikum Virchow
Mausoleum
Schlosspark
Schloss Charlottenburg
Neuer Pavillon
Galerie der Romantik
Neuer Flügel
Reiterdenkmal des Grossen Kurfürsten
LUISENPLATZ
SPANDAUER DAMM
Gipsformerei Berlin
Sammlung Berggruen
Bröhan-Museum
Ägyptisches Museum und Papyrussammlung
OTTO-SUHR-ALLEE
Schlossstrasse Villas
Luisenkirche
Mierendorff-Platz
MIERENDORFF-PLATZ
BONHOEFFERUFER
Schlossbrücke
CHARLOTTENBURG
KNOBELSDORFFSTRASSE
ZILLESTRASSE
BISMARCKSTRASSE
KAISERDAMM
Sophie-Charlotte-Platz
Bismarckstrasse
KAISER-FRIEDRICH-STRASSE
SOPHIE-CHARLOTTEN-STRASSE
SCHLOSSSTRASSE
Lietzensee
LIETZENSEEUFER
WITZLEBENPLATZ
KANTSTRASSE
PESTALOZZISTRASSE
SCHILLERSTRASSE

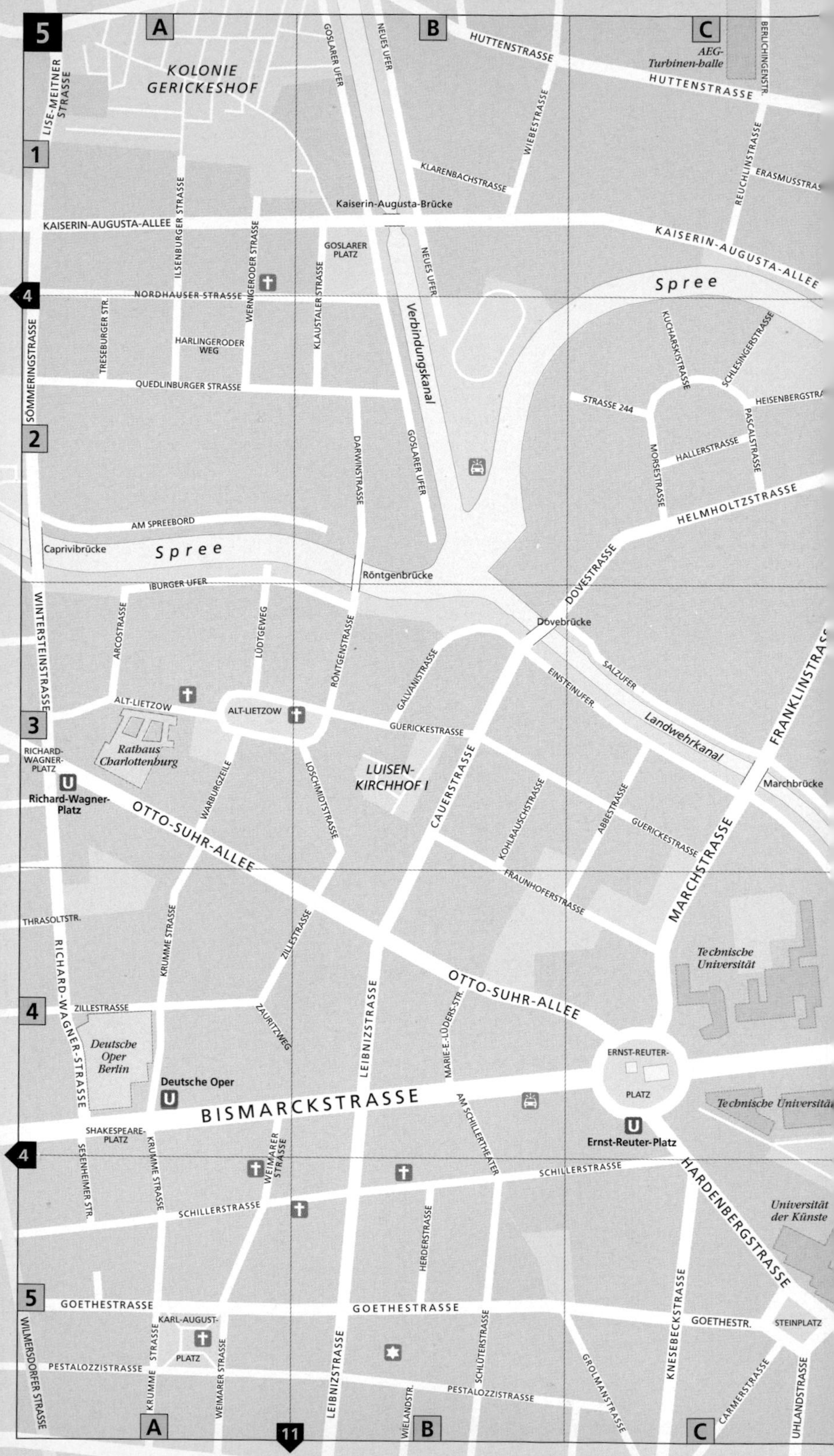
5
A
B
C
KOLONIE GERICKESHOF
LISE-MEITNER STRASSE
HUTTENSTRASSE
AEG-Turbinen-halle
BERLICHINGENSTR.
GOSLARER UFER
NEUES UFER
WIEBESTRASSE
KLARENBACHSTRASSE
REUCHLINSTRASSE
ERASMUSSTRASSE
ILSENBURGER STRASSE
Kaiserin-Augusta-Brücke
KAISERIN-AUGUSTA-ALLEE
GOSLARER PLATZ
WERNIGERODER STRASSE
NORDHAUSER STRASSE
KLAUSTALER STRASSE
Spree
Verbindungskanal
TRESEBURGER STR.
HARLINGERODER WEG
QUEDLINBURGER STRASSE
SÖMMERINGSTRASSE
KUCHARSKISTRASSE
SCHLESINGERSTRASSE
STRASSE 244
HEISENBERGSTRASSE
PASCALSTRASSE
MORSESTRASSE
HALLERSTRASSE
DARWINSTRASSE
HELMHOLTZSTRASSE
AM SPREEBORD
Caprivibrücke
Röntgenbrücke
IBURGER UFER
WINTERSTEINSTRASSE
DOVESTRASSE
Dovebrücke
ARCOSTRASSE
LÜDTGEWEG
RÖNTGENSTRASSE
GALVANISTRASSE
SALZUFER
EINSTEINUFER
FRANKLINSTRASSE
ALT-LIETZOW
GUERICKESTRASSE
Landwehrkanal
RICHARD-WAGNER-PLATZ
Rathaus Charlottenburg
LUISEN-KIRCHHOF I
LOSCHMIDTSTRASSE
CAUERSTRASSE
Marchbrücke
Richard-Wagner-Platz
WARBURGZEILE
KOHLRAUSCHSTRASSE
ABBESTRASSE
OTTO-SUHR-ALLEE
FRAUNHOFERSTRASSE
MARCHSTRASSE
THRASOLTSTR.
KRUMME STRASSE
ZILLESTRASSE
LEIBNIZSTRASSE
Technische Universität
RICHARD-WAGNER-STRASSE
MARIE-E.-LÜDERS-STR.
ZAURITZWEG
Deutsche Oper Berlin
Deutsche Oper
ERNST-REUTER-PLATZ
BISMARCKSTRASSE
AM SCHILLERTHEATER
SHAKESPEARE-PLATZ
Ernst-Reuter-Platz
SESENHEIMER STR.
WEIMARER STRASSE
SCHILLERSTRASSE
HARDENBERGSTRASSE
Universität der Künste
HERDERSTRASSE
GOETHESTRASSE
KNESEBECKSTRASSE
GOETHESTR.
STEINPLATZ
KARL-AUGUST-PLATZ
SCHLÜTERSTRASSE
GROLMANSTRASSE
PESTALOZZISTRASSE
WILMERSDORFER STRASSE
CARMERSTRASSE
UHLANDSTRASSE
WIELANDSTR.
1
2
3
4
5
11

D
E
F
6
MOABIT
WALDENSER STRASSE
WALDSTRASSE
EMDENER STRASSE
OLDENBURGER STRASSE
BREMER STRASSE
JONASSTR.
BREDOWSTRASSE
BUGENHAGENSTRASSE
WILHELMSHAVENER STRASSE
STROMSTRASSE
LÜBECKER STRASSE
ARMINIUSSTR.
Rathaus Tiergarten
TURMSTRASSE
1
BEUSSELSTRASSE
GOTZKOWSKYSTRASSE
OTTOSTRASSE
OTTOPLATZ
Turmstrasse
TURMSTRASSE
KLEINER TIERGARTEN
ZWINGLISTRASSE
ALT-MOABIT
ALT-MOABIT
7
ALT-MOABIT
ZINZENDORFSTRASSE
JAGOWSTRASSE
ESSENER STRASSE
BOCHUMER STRASSE
KREFELDER STRASSE
STROMSTRASSE
Gotzkowskybrücke
ELBERFELDER STRASSE
Lessingbrücke
Spree
HOLSTEINER UFER
2
LEVETZOWSTRASSE
DORTMUNDER STRASSE
BUNDESRATUFER
LESSINGSTRASSE
CLAUDIUSSTRASSE
WIKINGERUFER
FLENSBURGER STRASSE
Bellevue
AGRICOLASTRASSE
JAGOWSTRASSE
SOLINGER STRASSE
Hansabrücke
HANSAVIERTEL
TILE-WARDENBERG-STRASSE
ALTONAER STRASSE
BARTNINGALLEE
HANSA-UFER
HANSEATENWEG
WULLENWEBERSTRASSE
HANSAPLATZ
3
Akademie der Kunste
Hansaplatz
SCHLESWIGER UFER
FLOTOWSTRASSE
KLOPSTOCKSTRASSE
ALTONAER STRASSE
HÄNDELALLEE
GUTENBERGSTR.
SIEGMUNDS HOF
BACHSTRASSE
SALZUFER
HÄNDELALLEE
EINSTEINUFER
ENGLISCHE STRASSE
Fauler See
SALZUFER
Tiergarten
STRASSE DES 17. JUNI
4
STRASSE DES 17. JUNI
Charlottenburger Brücke
TIERGARTEN
GROSSER WEG
MÜLLER-BRESLAU-STRASSE
Neuer See
7
Landwehrkanal
THOMAS-DEHLER-STR.
HERTZALLEE
FASANENSTRASSE
Lichtenstein-brücke
DRAKESTRASSE
5
RAUCHSTRASSE
Newton Sammlung
ZOOLOGISCHER GARTEN
CORNELIUSSTR.
JEBENSSTRASSE
HARDENBERG-PLATZ
KATHARINA-HEINROTH-UFER
Ludwig-Erhard-Haus
Bahnhof Zoologischer Garten
D
E
12
F

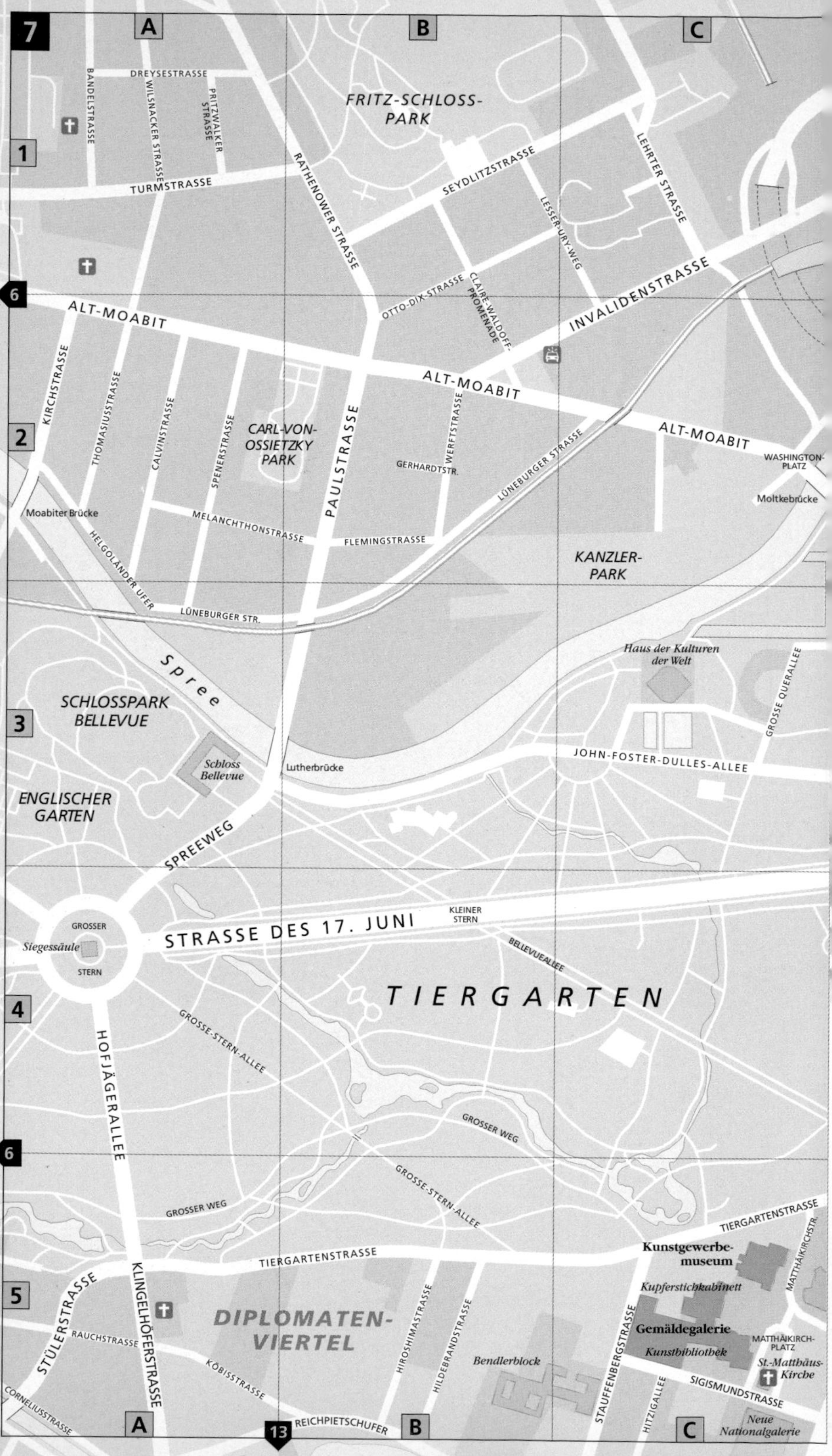
7
A
B
C
1
2
3
4
5
6
13
DREYSESTRASSE
BANDELSTRASSE
WILSNACKER STRASSE
PRITZWALKER STRASSE
TURMSTRASSE
FRITZ-SCHLOSS-PARK
RATHENOWER STRASSE
SEYDLITZSTRASSE
LEHRTER STRASSE
LESSER-URY-WEG
OTTO-DIX-STRASSE
CLAIRE-WALDOFF-PROMENADE
INVALIDENSTRASSE
ALT-MOABIT
KIRCHSTRASSE
THOMASIUSSTRASSE
CALVINSTRASSE
SPENERSTRASSE
CARL-VON-OSSIETZKY PARK
PAULSTRASSE
WERFTSTRASSE
GERHARDTSTR.
LÜNEBURGER STRASSE
WASHINGTON-PLATZ
Moltkebrücke
Moabiter Brücke
HELGOLÄNDER UFER
MELANCHTHONSTRASSE
FLEMINGSTRASSE
KANZLER-PARK
LÜNEBURGER STR.
Spree
Haus der Kulturen der Welt
SCHLOSSPARK BELLEVUE
Schloss Bellevue
Lutherbrücke
GROSSE QUERALLEE
JOHN-FOSTER-DULLES-ALLEE
ENGLISCHER GARTEN
SPREEWEG
GROSSER STERN
Siegessäule
STRASSE DES 17. JUNI
KLEINER STERN
BELLEVUEALLEE
TIERGARTEN
HOFJÄGERALLEE
GROSSE-STERN-ALLEE
GROSSER WEG
TIERGARTENSTRASSE
Kunstgewerbe-museum
MATTHÄIKIRCHSTR.
Kupferstichkabinett
Gemäldegalerie
Kunstbibliothek
MATTHÄIKIRCH-PLATZ
St.-Matthäus-Kirche
STÜLERSTRASSE
KLINGELHÖFERSTRASSE
DIPLOMATEN-VIERTEL
RAUCHSTRASSE
KÖBISSTRASSE
HIROSHIMASTRASSE
HILDEBRANDSTRASSE
Bendlerblock
STAUFFENBERGSTRASSE
HITZIGALLEE
SIGISMUNDSTRASSE
Neue Nationalgalerie
CORNELIUSSTRASSE
REICHPIETSCHUFER

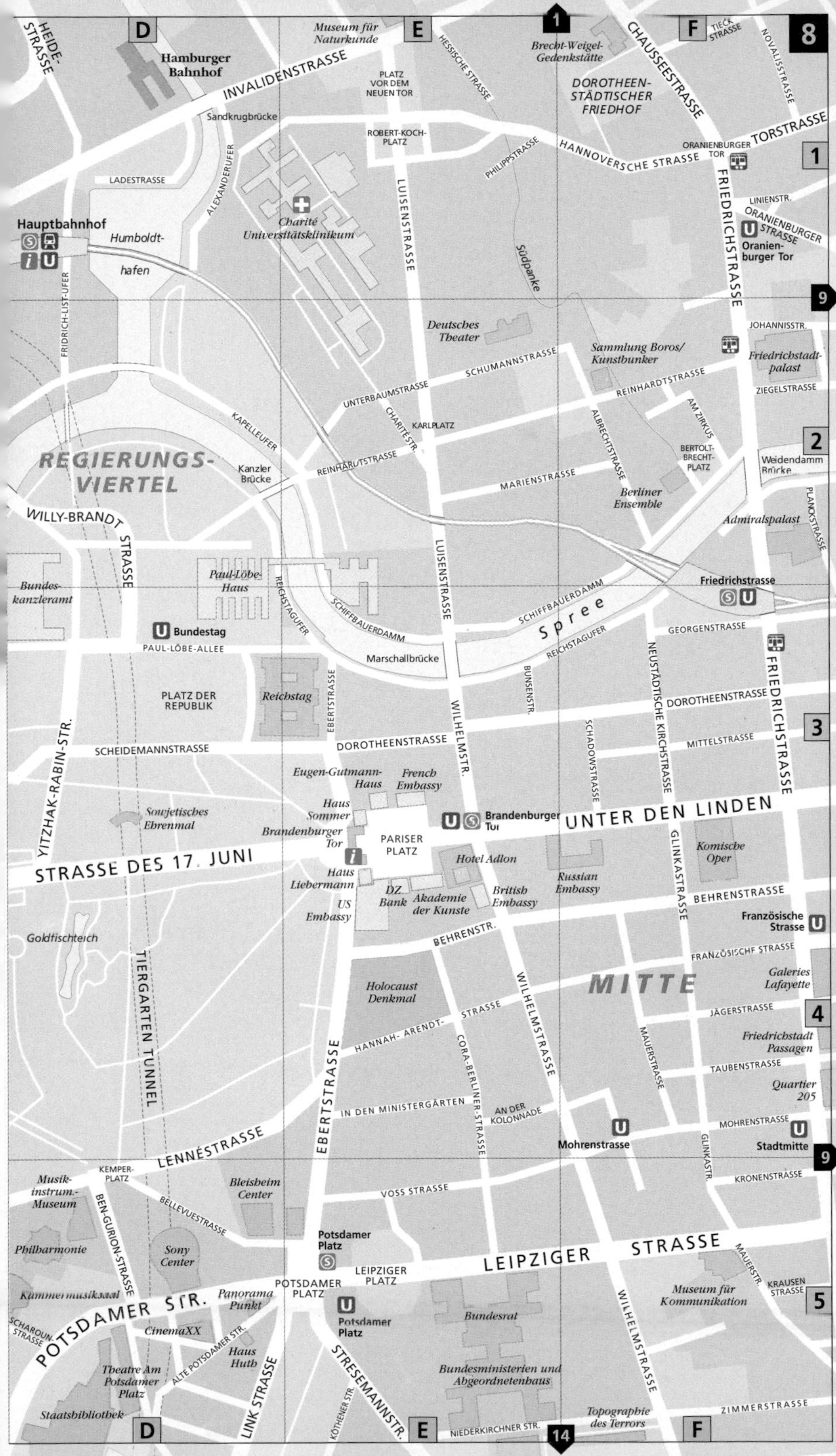
8
D
E
F
1
Hamburger Bahnhof
Museum für Naturkunde
Brecht-Weigel-Gedenkstätte
DOROTHEEN-STÄDTISCHER FRIEDHOF
INVALIDENSTRASSE
CHAUSSEESTRASSE
TORSTRASSE
HANNOVERSCHE STRASSE
FRIEDRICHSTRASSE
LUISENSTRASSE
Charité Universitätsklinikum
Hauptbahnhof
Humboldt-hafen
Oranienburger Tor
Deutsches Theater
Sammlung Boros/ Kunstbunker
Friedrichstadt-palast
REGIERUNGS-VIERTEL
Berliner Ensemble
Admiralspalast
Friedrichstrasse
Spree
Bundeskanzleramt
Paul-Löbe-Haus
Bundestag
Reichstag
PLATZ DER REPUBLIK
UNTER DEN LINDEN
Brandenburger Tor
PARISER PLATZ
Hotel Adlon
Komische Oper
Russian Embassy
British Embassy
US Embassy
STRASSE DES 17. JUNI
Sowjetisches Ehrenmal
Goldfischteich
TIERGARTEN TUNNEL
MITTE
Holocaust Denkmal
Galeries Lafayette
Friedrichstadt Passagen
Quartier 205
Mohrenstrasse
Stadtmitte
Französische Strasse
LEIPZIGER STRASSE
Potsdamer Platz
Sony Center
Philharmonie
Musikinstrum.-Museum
Bleisheim Center
POTSDAMER STR.
Bundesrat
Museum für Kommunikation
Topographie des Terrors
Staatsbibliothek
Theatre Am Potsdamer Platz
14
9

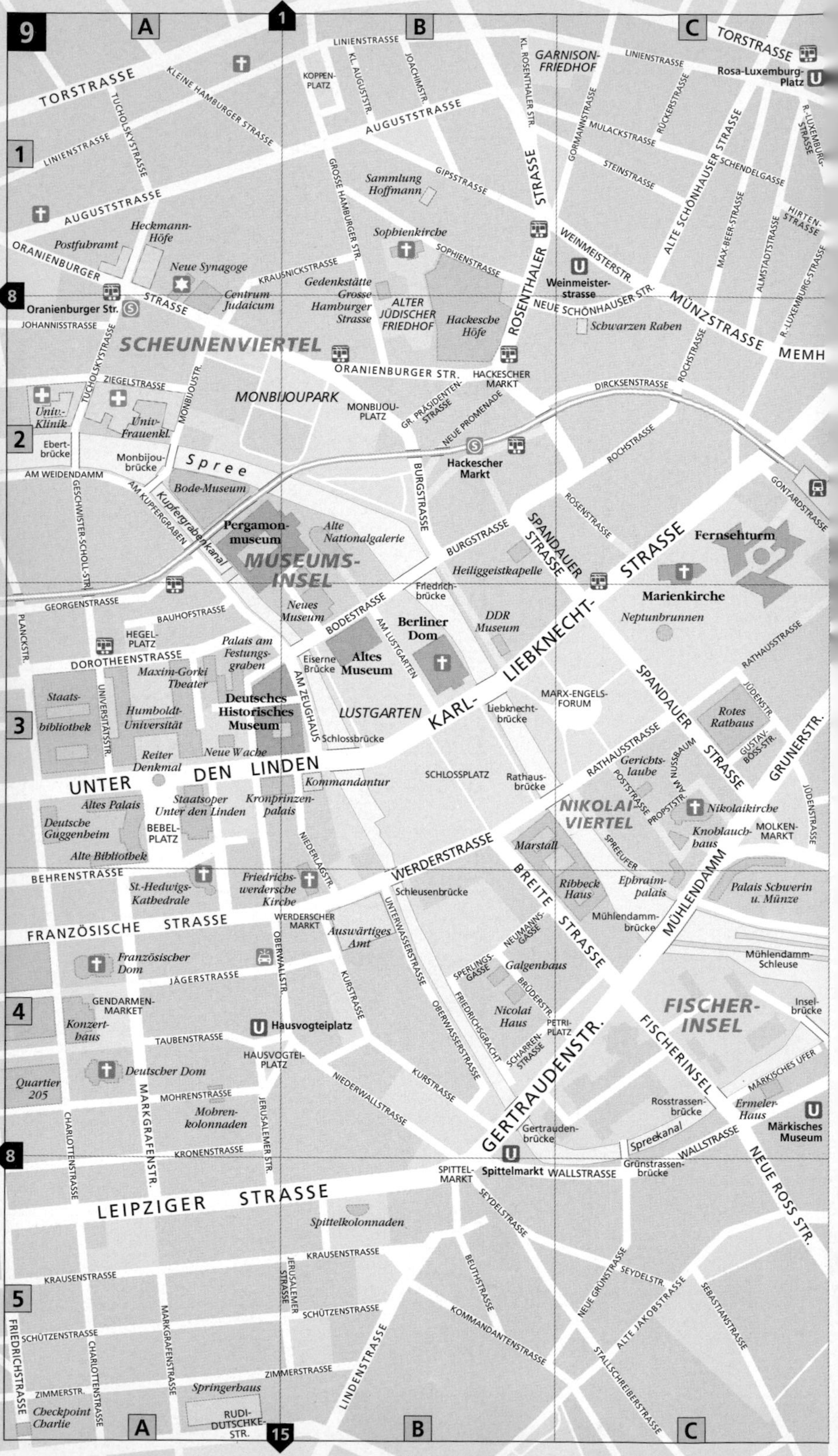

9
A
B
C
1
2
3
4
5
8
15
TORSTRASSE
LINIENSTRASSE
KLEINE HAMBURGER STRASSE
TUCHOLSKYSTRASSE
KOPPEN-PLATZ
KL. AUGUSTSTR.
JOACHIMSTR.
KL. ROSENTHALER STR.
GARNISON-FRIEDHOF
Rosa-Luxemburg-Platz
R.-LUXEMBURG-STRASSE
AUGUSTSTRASSE
GORMANNSTRASSE
MULACKSTRASSE
RÜCKERSTRASSE
STEINSTRASSE
ALTE SCHÖNHAUSER STRASSE
SCHENDELGASSE
GROSSE HAMBURGER STR.
Sammlung Hoffmann
GIPSSTRASSE
ROSENTHALER STRASSE
Heckmann-Höfe
Postfuhramt
ORANIENBURGER STRASSE
Neue Synagoge
Sophienkirche
SOPHIENSTRASSE
WEINMEISTERSTR.
MAX-BEER-STRASSE
ALMSTADTSTRASSE
HIRTEN-STRASSE
Weinmeister-strasse
KRAUSNICKSTRASSE
Gedenkstätte Grosse Hamburger Strasse
Centrum Judaicum
ALTER JÜDISCHER FRIEDHOF
Hackesche Höfe
NEUE SCHÖNHAUSER STR.
MÜNZSTRASSE
R.-LUXEMBURG-STRASSE
Oranienburger Str.
JOHANNISSTRASSE
Schwarzen Raben
SCHEUNENVIERTEL
ROCHSTRASSE
MEMH
ORANIENBURGER STR.
HACKESCHER MARKT
ZIEGELSTRASSE
MONBIJOUSTR.
MONBIJOUPARK
DIRCKSENSTRASSE
Univ.-Klinik
Univ.-Frauenkl.
MONBIJOU-PLATZ
GR. PRÄSIDENTEN-STRASSE
NEUE PROMENADE
Ebert-brücke
Monbijou-brücke
Spree
Hackescher Markt
ROCHSTRASSE
AM WEIDENDAMM
Bode-Museum
BURGSTRASSE
GONTARDSTRASSE
GESCHWISTER-SCHOLL-STR.
AM KUPFERGRABEN
Kupfergrabenkanal
Pergamon-museum
Alte Nationalgalerie
ROSENSTRASSE
SPANDAUER STRASSE
Fernsehturm
MUSEUMS-INSEL
BURGSTRASSE
Heiliggeistkapelle
KARL-LIEBKNECHT-STRASSE
Friedrich-brücke
Marienkirche
GEORGENSTRASSE
BAUHOFSTRASSE
Neues Museum
BODESTRASSE
DDR Museum
Neptunbrunnen
PLANCKSTR.
HEGEL-PLATZ
Palais am Festungs-graben
Berliner Dom
AM LUSTGARTEN
RATHAUSSTRASSE
DOROTHEENSTRASSE
Eiserne Brücke
Altes Museum
Maxim-Gorki Theater
AM ZEUGHAUS
MARX-ENGELS-FORUM
JÜDENSTR.
Staats-bibliothek
UNIVERSITÄTSSTR.
Humboldt-Universität
Deutsches Historisches Museum
LUSTGARTEN
Liebknecht-brücke
SPANDAUER STRASSE
Rotes Rathaus
GRUNERSTR.
Schlossbrücke
GUSTAV-BÖSS-STR.
Reiter Denkmal
Neue Wache
RATHAUSSTRASSE
Gerichts-laube
AM NUSSBAUM
UNTER DEN LINDEN
Kommandantur
SCHLOSSPLATZ
Rathaus-brücke
POSTSTRASSE
PROPSTSTR.
Altes Palais
Staatsoper Unter den Linden
Kronprinzen-palais
NIKOLAI-VIERTEL
Nikolaikirche
JÜDENSTRASSE
Deutsche Guggenheim
BEBEL-PLATZ
NIEDERLAGSTR.
Marstall
SPREEUFER
Knoblauch-haus
MOLKEN-MARKT
Alte Bibliothek
WERDERSTRASSE
MÜHLENDAMM
BEHRENSTRASSE
St.-Hedwigs-Kathedrale
Friedrichs-werdersche Kirche
BREITE STRASSE
Ribbeck Haus
Ephraim-palais
Palais Schwerin u. Münze
Schleusenbrücke
FRANZÖSISCHE STRASSE
WERDERSCHER MARKT
Auswärtiges Amt
UNTERWASSERSTRASSE
Mühlendamm-brücke
NEUMANNS-GASSE
Mühlendamm-Schleuse
Französischer Dom
OBERWALLSTR.
SPERLINGS-GASSE
Galgenhaus
JÄGERSTRASSE
KURSTRASSE
OBERWASSERSTRASSE
FRIEDRICHSGRACHT
BRÜDERSTR.
GENDARMEN-MARKT
Nicolai Haus
FISCHER-INSEL
Insel-brücke
Konzert-haus
Hausvogteiplatz
PETRI-PLATZ
TAUBENSTRASSE
HAUSVOGTEI-PLATZ
SCHARREN-STRASSE
GERTRAUDENSTR.
FISCHERINSEL
Deutscher Dom
MÄRKISCHES UFER
Quartier 205
MOHRENSTRASSE
Mohren-kolonnaden
NIEDERWALLSTRASSE
KURSTRASSE
Rosstrassen-brücke
Ermeler-Haus
Märkisches Museum
CHARLOTTENSTRASSE
MARKGRAFENSTR.
JERUSALEMER STR.
Gertrauden-brücke
Spreekanal
WALLSTRASSE
KRONENSTRASSE
Spittelmarkt
SPITTEL-MARKT
WALLSTRASSE
Grünstrassen-brücke
NEUE ROSS STR.
LEIPZIGER STRASSE
SEYDELSTRASSE
Spittelkolonnaden
KRAUSENSTRASSE
KRAUSENSTRASSE
JERUSALEMER STRASSE
BEUTHSTRASSE
NEUE GRÜNSTRASSE
SEYDELSTR.
SEBASTIANSTRASSE
SCHÜTZENSTRASSE
KOMMANDANTENSTRASSE
ALTE JAKOBSTRASSE
FRIEDRICHSTRASSE
SCHÜTZENSTRASSE
CHARLOTTENSTRASSE
MARKGRAFENSTRASSE
LINDENSTRASSE
ZIMMERSTRASSE
STALLSCHREIBERSTRASSE
ZIMMERSTR.
Springerhaus
Checkpoint Charlie
RUDI-DUTSCHKE-STR.

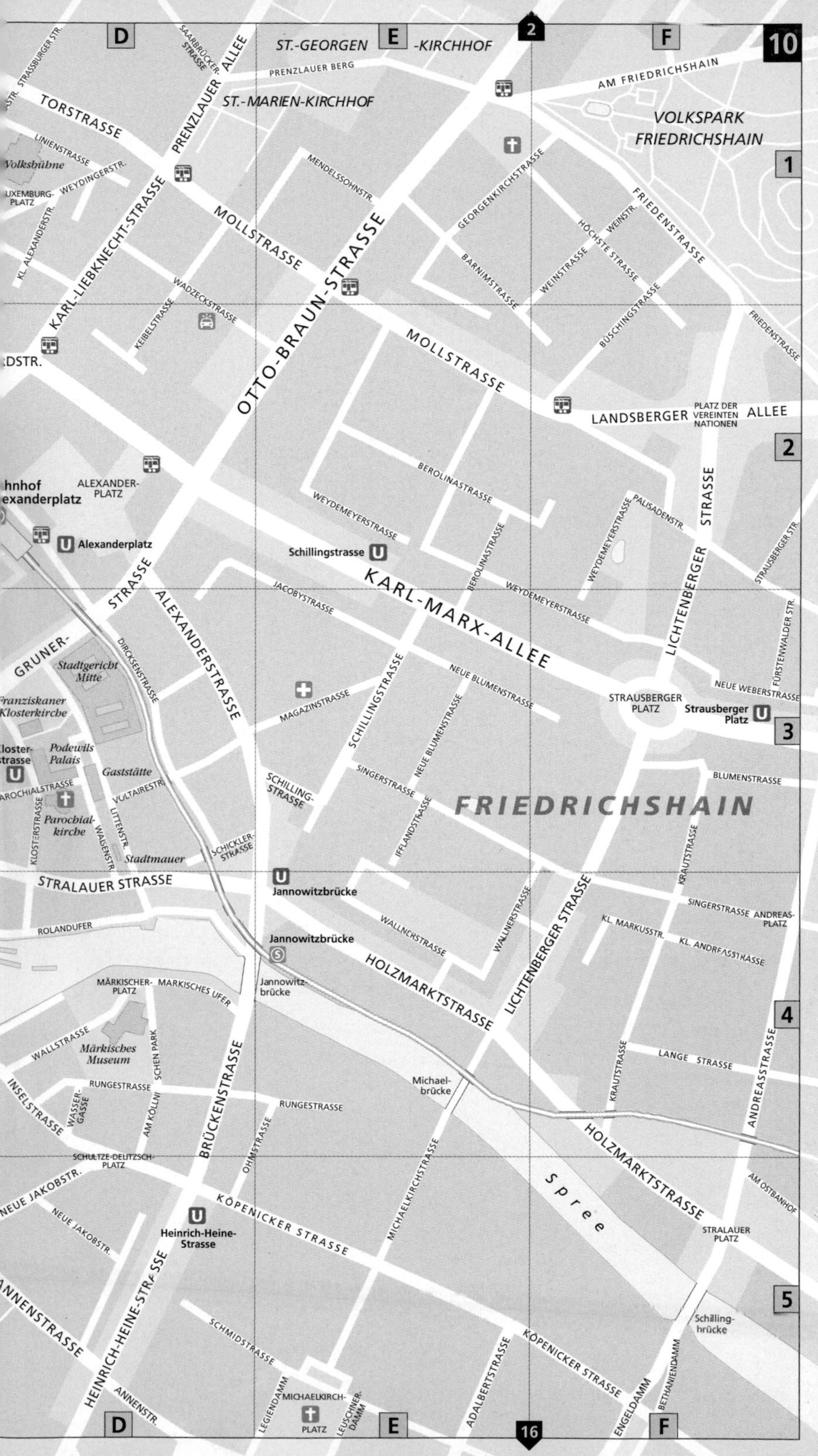
D
E
F
2
10
1
2
3
4
5
16
ST.-GEORGEN -KIRCHHOF
ST.-MARIEN-KIRCHHOF
VOLKSPARK FRIEDRICHSHAIN
PRENZLAUER BERG
AM FRIEDRICHSHAIN
PRENZLAUER ALLEE
SAARBRÜCKER STRASSE
STRASSBURGER STR.
TORSTRASSE
LINIENSTRASSE
Volksbühne
WEYDINGERSTR.
LUXEMBURG-PLATZ
KL. ALEXANDERSTR.
KARL-LIEBKNECHT-STRASSE
MOLLSTRASSE
MENDELSSOHNSTR.
OTTO-BRAUN-STRASSE
GEORGENKIRCHSTRASSE
BARNIMSTRASSE
WEINSTRASSE
HÖCHSTE STRASSE
WEINSTR.
FRIEDENSTRASSE
BÜSCHINGSTRASSE
WADZECKSTRASSE
KEIBELSTRASSE
MOLLSTRASSE
LANDSBERGER ALLEE
PLATZ DER VEREINTEN NATIONEN
BEROLINASTRASSE
WEYDEMEYERSTRASSE
PALISADENSTR.
LICHTENBERGER STRASSE
STRAUSBERGER STR.
FÜRSTENWALDER STR.
ALEXANDER-PLATZ
Alexanderplatz
Schillingstrasse
KARL-MARX-ALLEE
JACOBYSTRASSE
BEROLINASTRASSE
WEYDEMEYERSTRASSE
GRUNER-STRASSE
ALEXANDERSTRASSE
DIRCKSENSTRASSE
Stadtgericht Mitte
Franziskaner Klosterkirche
Klosterstrasse
Podewils Palais
Gaststätte
PAROCHIALSTRASSE
Parochialkirche
KLOSTERSTRASSE
LITTENSTR.
WAISENSTR.
VOLTAIRESTR.
Stadtmauer
SCHICKLERSTRASSE
MAGAZINSTRASSE
SCHILLINGSTRASSE
NEUE BLUMENSTRASSE
SCHILLINGSTRASSE
SINGERSTRASSE
IFFLANDSTRASSE
STRAUSBERGER PLATZ
Strausberger Platz
NEUE WEBERSTRASSE
BLUMENSTRASSE
FRIEDRICHSHAIN
KRAUTSTRASSE
STRALAUER STRASSE
Jannowitzbrücke
ROLANDUFER
WALLNERSTRASSE
WALLNERSTRASSE
LICHTENBERGER STRASSE
SINGERSTRASSE
ANDREASPLATZ
KL. MARKUSSTR.
KL. ANDREASSTRASSE
HOLZMARKTSTRASSE
MÄRKISCHER PLATZ
MÄRKISCHES UFER
Jannowitzbrücke
WALLSTRASSE
Märkisches Museum
KÖLLNISCHEN PARK
RUNGESTRASSE
INSELSTRASSE
WASSERGASSE
AM KÖLLN
BRÜCKENSTRASSE
RUNGESTRASSE
OHMSTRASSE
Michaelbrücke
LANGE STRASSE
KRAUTSTRASSE
ANDREASSTRASSE
HOLZMARKTSTRASSE
Spree
AM OSTBAHNHOF
STRALAUER PLATZ
SCHULTZE-DELITZSCH-PLATZ
NEUE JAKOBSTR.
NEUE JAKOBSTR.
Heinrich-Heine-Strasse
KÖPENICKER STRASSE
MICHAELKIRCHSTRASSE
ANNENSTRASSE
HEINRICH-HEINE-STRASSE
SCHMIDSTRASSE
ANNENSTR.
LEGIENDAMM
MICHAELKIRCHPLATZ
LEUSCHNERDAMM
ADALBERTSTRASSE
KÖPENICKER STRASSE
ENGELDAMM
BETHANIENDAMM
Schillingbrücke

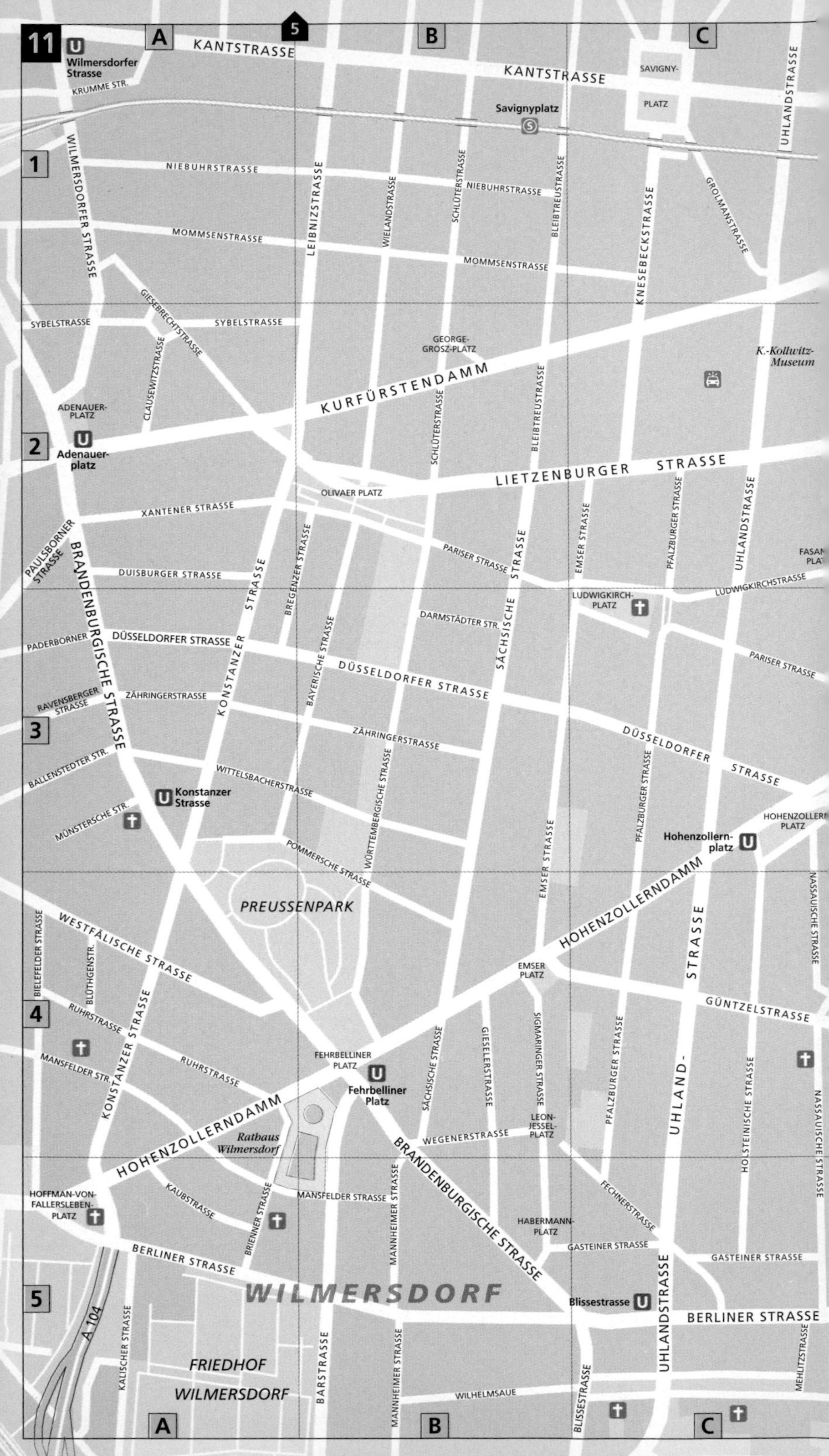
11
A
B
C
5
1
2
3
4
Wilmersdorfer Strasse
Kantstrasse
Krumme Str.
Savigny-Platz
Savignyplatz
Uhlandstrasse
Niebuhrstrasse
Mommsenstrasse
Wilmersdorfer Strasse
Leibnizstrasse
Wielandstrasse
Schlüterstrasse
Bleibtreustrasse
Knesebeckstrasse
Grolmanstrasse
Sybelstrasse
Giesebrechtstrasse
Clausewitzstrasse
George-Grosz-Platz
Kurfürstendamm
K.-Kollwitz-Museum
Adenauer-Platz
Adenauerplatz
Lietzenburger Strasse
Olivaer Platz
Xantener Strasse
Paulsborner Strasse
Brandenburgische Strasse
Duisburger Strasse
Konstanzer Strasse
Bregenzer Strasse
Pariser Strasse
Sächsische Strasse
Emser Strasse
Pfalzburger Strasse
Ludwigkirchplatz
Ludwigkirchstrasse
Darmstädter Str.
Paderborner
Düsseldorfer Strasse
Bayerische Strasse
Ravensberger Strasse
Zähringerstrasse
Ballenstedter Str.
Wittelsbacherstrasse
Konstanzer Strasse
Münstersche Str.
Württembergische Strasse
Pommersche Strasse
Preussenpark
Hohenzollernplatz
Hohenzollerndamm
Nassauische Strasse
Bielefelder Strasse
Westfälische Strasse
Blüthgenstr.
Emser Platz
Güntzelstrasse
Ruhrstrasse
Mansfelder Str.
Fehrbelliner Platz
Giesebrechtstrasse
Sigmaringer Strasse
Holsteinische Strasse
Rathaus Wilmersdorf
Wegenerstrasse
Leon-Jessel-Platz
Uhlandstrasse
Hoffman-von-Fallersleben-Platz
Kaubstrasse
Brienner Strasse
Mansfelder Strasse
Mannheimer Strasse
Fechnerstrasse
Habermann-Platz
Gasteiner Strasse
Berliner Strasse
Wilmersdorf
Blissestrasse
A 104
Kalischer Strasse
Barstrasse
Friedhof Wilmersdorf
Wilhelmsaue
Mehlitzstrasse
Fasan Plat

12
D
E
F
6
13
1
2
3
4
5
ZOOLOGISCHER GARTEN
C/O Berlin
Theater des Westens
KANTSTRASSE
HARDENBERGSTR.
BUDAPESTERSTRASSE
BUDAPESTER STRASSE
OLAF-PALME-PLATZ
Kaiser-Wilhelm-Gedächtniskirche
BREITSCHEID-PLATZ
Europa-Center
Neues Kranzler-eck
Jüdisches Gemeindebaus
FASANENSTRASSE
KURFÜRSTENDAMM
Kurfürstendamm
JOACHIMS-TALER PLATZ
Uhlandstrasse
TAUENTZIENSTRASSE
NÜRNBERGER STRASSE
BURGGRAFENSTRASSE
WICHMANNSTR.
KEITHSTR.
KURFÜRSTENSTRASSE
ANSBACHER STRASSE
BAYREUTHER STRASSE
KEITHSTRASSE
RANKESTRASSE
MARBURGER STRASSE
LOS-ANGELES-PLATZ
AUGSBURGER STRASSE
MEINEKESTRASSE
JOACHIMSTALER STRASSE
WITTENBERG-PLATZ
Wittenbergplatz
KaDeWe
PASSAUER STRASSE
KLEISTSTRASSE
AN DER URANIA
EISLEBENER STRASSE
Augsburger Strasse
WÜRZBURGER STR.
BAYREUTHER STR.
LIETZENBURGER STRASSE
RANKEPLATZ
SCHAPERSTRASSE
BUNDESALLEE
FÜRTHER STR.
KELHEIMER STR.
ETTALER STRASSE
FUGGERSTRASSE
WELSERSTRASSE
MARTIN-LUTHER-STRASSE
NÜRNBERGER PLATZ
GEISBERGSTRASSE
MEIEROTTOSTRASSE
SPICHERNSTRASSE
GRAINAUER STRASSE
KULMBACHER STRASSE
BAMBERGER STRASSE
MOTZSTRASSE
GOSSOWSTRASSE
Spichernstrasse
Viktoria-Luise-Platz
REGENSBURGER STRASSE
VIKTORIA-LUISE-PLATZ
WINTERFELDTSTRASSE
NACHODSTRASSE
LUITPOLDSTRASSE
LUITPOLDSTR.
HOHENSTAUFENSTRASSE
NIKOLSBURGER STR.
PRAGER STRASSE
HEILBRONNER STRASSE
MÜNCHENER STRASSE
SCHWÄBISCHE STRASSE
NIKOLSBURGER PLATZ
TRAUTENAUSTRASSE
PRAGER PLATZ
SPEYERER STRASSE
TRAUNSTEINER STRASSE
TRAUTENAUSTR.
LANDHAUSSTRASSE
Güntzelstrasse
PRINZREGENTENSTRASSE
BARBAROSSASTRASSE
LANDSHUTER STRASSE
BERCHTESGADENER STRASSE
ASCHAFFENBURGER STRASSE
PENZBERGER STRASSE
FREISINGER STRASSE
GÜNTZELSTRASSE
NÖRDLINGERSTR.
ROSENHEIMER STRASSE
THARANDTER STR.
HELMSTEDTER STRASSE
JENAER STRASSE
STÜBBENSTR.
WESTARP-STRASSE
BAYERISCHER PLATZ
GRUNEWALD-STRASSE
GRUNEWALDSTRASSE
BERLINER STRASSE
Bayerischer Platz
BOZENER STRASSE
MERANER STRASSE
INNSBRUCKER STRASSE
SALZBURGER STRASSE
APOSTEL-PAULUS-STR.
WARTBURGPLATZ
GOTHAER STRASSE
Berliner Strasse
BOZENER STR.
WARTBURGSTRASSE
GERDAUER STRASSE
BADENSCHE STRASSE
NORDSTERNSTR.
MEININGER STRASSE
JOHN-F.-KENNEDY-PLATZ
WILHELMSAUE
BABELSBERGER STRASSE
KUFSTEINER STRASSE
AM RATHAUS
Rathaus Schöneberg
BELZIGER STRASSE

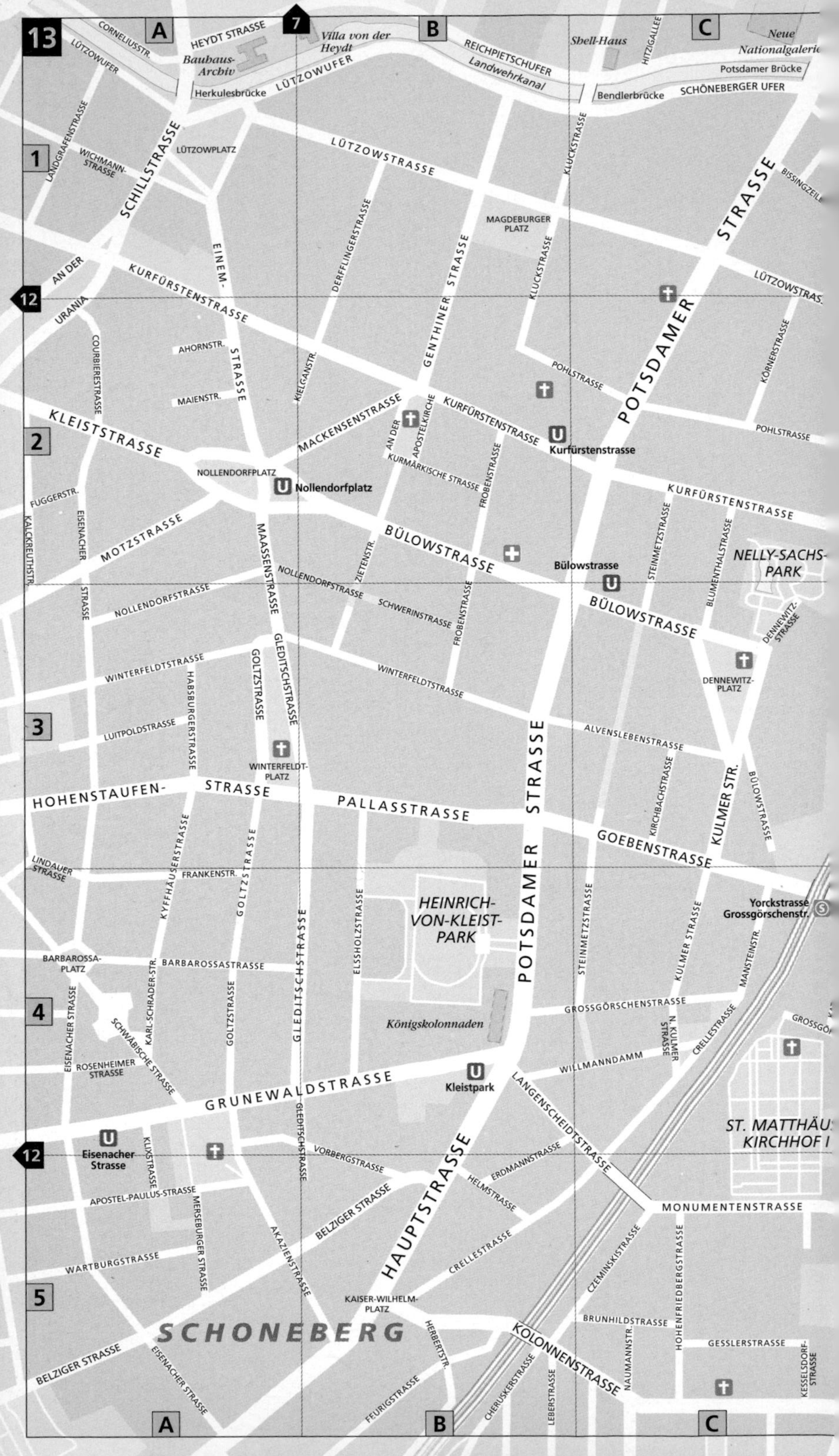

13
A
B
C
7
12
1
2
3
4
5
Villa von der Heydt
Bauhaus-Archiv
Shell-Haus
Neue Nationalgalerie
HEYDT STRASSE
CORNELIUSSTR.
LÜTZOWUFER
Herkulesbrücke
REICHPIETSCHUFER
Landwehrkanal
Bendlerbrücke
SCHÖNEBERGER UFER
Potsdamer Brücke
HITZIGALLEE
LÜTZOWPLATZ
LÜTZOWSTRASSE
SCHILLSTRASSE
LANDGRAFENSTRASSE
WICHMANN-STRASSE
KLUCKSTRASSE
MAGDEBURGER PLATZ
BISSINGZEILE
AN DER URANIA
KURFÜRSTENSTRASSE
EINEM-STRASSE
DERFFLINGERSTRASSE
GENTHINER STRASSE
POTSDAMER STRASSE
COURBIERESTRASSE
AHORNSTR.
MAIENSTR.
KIELGANSTR.
POHLSTRASSE
KÖRNERSTRASSE
KLEISTSTRASSE
MACKENSENSTRASSE
AN DER APOSTELKIRCHE
KURMÄRKISCHE STRASSE
FROBENSTRASSE
Kurfürstenstrasse
NOLLENDORFPLATZ
Nollendorfplatz
FUGGERSTR.
KALCKREUTHSTR.
EISENACHER STRASSE
MOTZSTRASSE
MASSENSTRASSE
ZIETENSTR.
BÜLOWSTRASSE
Bülowstrasse
STEINMETZSTRASSE
BLUMENTHALSTRASSE
NELLY-SACHS-PARK
NOLLENDORFSTRASSE
SCHWERINSTRASSE
DENNEWITZ-STRASSE
WINTERFELDTSTRASSE
GLEDITSCHSTRASSE
GOLTZSTRASSE
HABSBURGERSTRASSE
DENNEWITZ-PLATZ
LUITPOLDSTRASSE
WINTERFELDT-PLATZ
ALVENSLEBENSTRASSE
KIRCHBACHSTRASSE
KULMER STR.
HOHENSTAUFEN-STRASSE
PALLASSTRASSE
GOEBENSTRASSE
LINDAUER STRASSE
FRANKENSTR.
KYFFHÄUSERSTRASSE
ELSSHOLZSTRASSE
HEINRICH-VON-KLEIST-PARK
Yorckstrasse Grossgörschenstr.
KULMER STRASSE
MANSTEINSTR.
BARBAROSSA-PLATZ
BARBAROSSASTRASSE
KARL-SCHRADER-STR.
GROSSGÖRSCHENSTRASSE
Königskolonnaden
N. KULMER STRASSE
CRELLESTRASSE
SCHWÄBISCHE STRASSE
ROSENHEIMER STRASSE
WILLMANNDAMM
GRUNEWALDSTRASSE
Kleistpark
LANGENSCHEIDTSTRASSE
Eisenacher Strasse
KULMSTRASSE
VORBERGSTRASSE
ERDMANNSTRASSE
ST. MATTHÄUS KIRCHHOF I
HELMSTRASSE
HAUPTSTRASSE
APOSTEL-PAULUS-STRASSE
MONUMENTENSTRASSE
MERSEBURGER STRASSE
BELZIGER STRASSE
AKAZIENSTRASSE
CZEMINSKISTRASSE
HOHENFRIEDBERGSTRASSE
WARTBURGSTRASSE
KAISER-WILHELM-PLATZ
BRUNHILDSTRASSE
SCHONEBERG
HERBERTSTR.
KOLONNENSTRASSE
GESSLERSTRASSE
NAUMANNSTR.
KESSELSDORF-STRASSE
CHERUSKERSTRASSE
LEBERSTRASSE
FEURIGSTRASSE

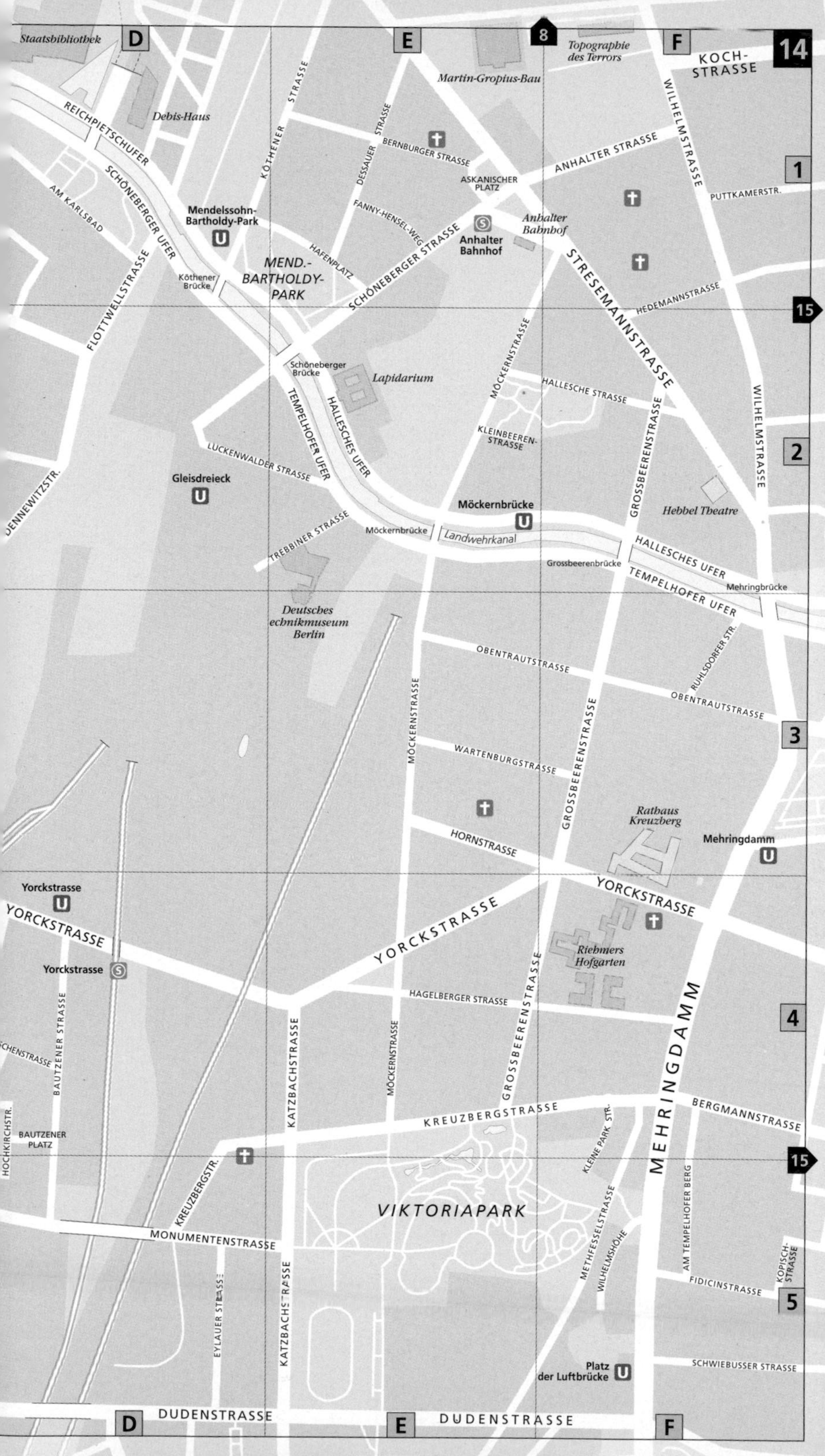
Staatsbibliothek
Debis-Haus
Martin-Gropius-Bau
Topographie des Terrors
KOCHSTRASSE
14
REICHPIETSCHUFER
SCHÖNEBERGER UFER
AM KARLSBAD
KÖTHENER STRASSE
DESSAUER STRASSE
BERNBURGER STRASSE
ASKANISCHER PLATZ
ANHALTER STRASSE
WILHELMSTRASSE
PUTTKAMERSTR.
FANNY-HENSEL-WEG
Mendelssohn-Bartholdy-Park
Anhalter Bahnhof
HAFENPLATZ
SCHÖNEBERGER STRASSE
MEND.-BARTHOLDY-PARK
Köthener Brücke
FLOTTWELLSTRASSE
STRESEMANNSTRASSE
HEDEMANNSTRASSE
MÖCKERNSTRASSE
Schöneberger Brücke
Lapidarium
HALLESCHE STRASSE
TEMPELHOFER UFER
HALLESCHES UFER
KLEINBEEREN-STRASSE
GROSSBEERENSTRASSE
LUCKENWALDER STRASSE
Gleisdreieck
DENNEWITZSTR.
Möckernbrücke
Hebbel Theatre
TREBBINER STRASSE
Landwehrkanal
Grossbeerenbrücke
Mehringbrücke
Deutsches Technikmuseum Berlin
OBENTRAUTSTRASSE
RUHLSDORFER STR.
WARTENBURGSTRASSE
Rathaus Kreuzberg
Mehringdamm
HORNSTRASSE
Yorckstrasse
YORCKSTRASSE
Riehmers Hofgarten
HAGELBERGER STRASSE
MEHRINGDAMM
BAUTZENER STRASSE
KATZBACHSTRASSE
KREUZBERGSTRASSE
BERGMANNSTRASSE
HOCHKIRCHSTR.
BAUTZENER PLATZ
KREUZBERGSTR.
KLEINE PARK STR.
VIKTORIAPARK
AM TEMPELHOFER BERG
MONUMENTENSTRASSE
METHFESSELSTRASSE
WILHELMSHÖHE
KOPISCHSTRASSE
FIDICINSTRASSE
EYLAUER STRASSE
Platz der Luftbrücke
SCHWIEBUSSER STRASSE
DUDENSTRASSE
D
E
F
1
2
3
4
5
8
15

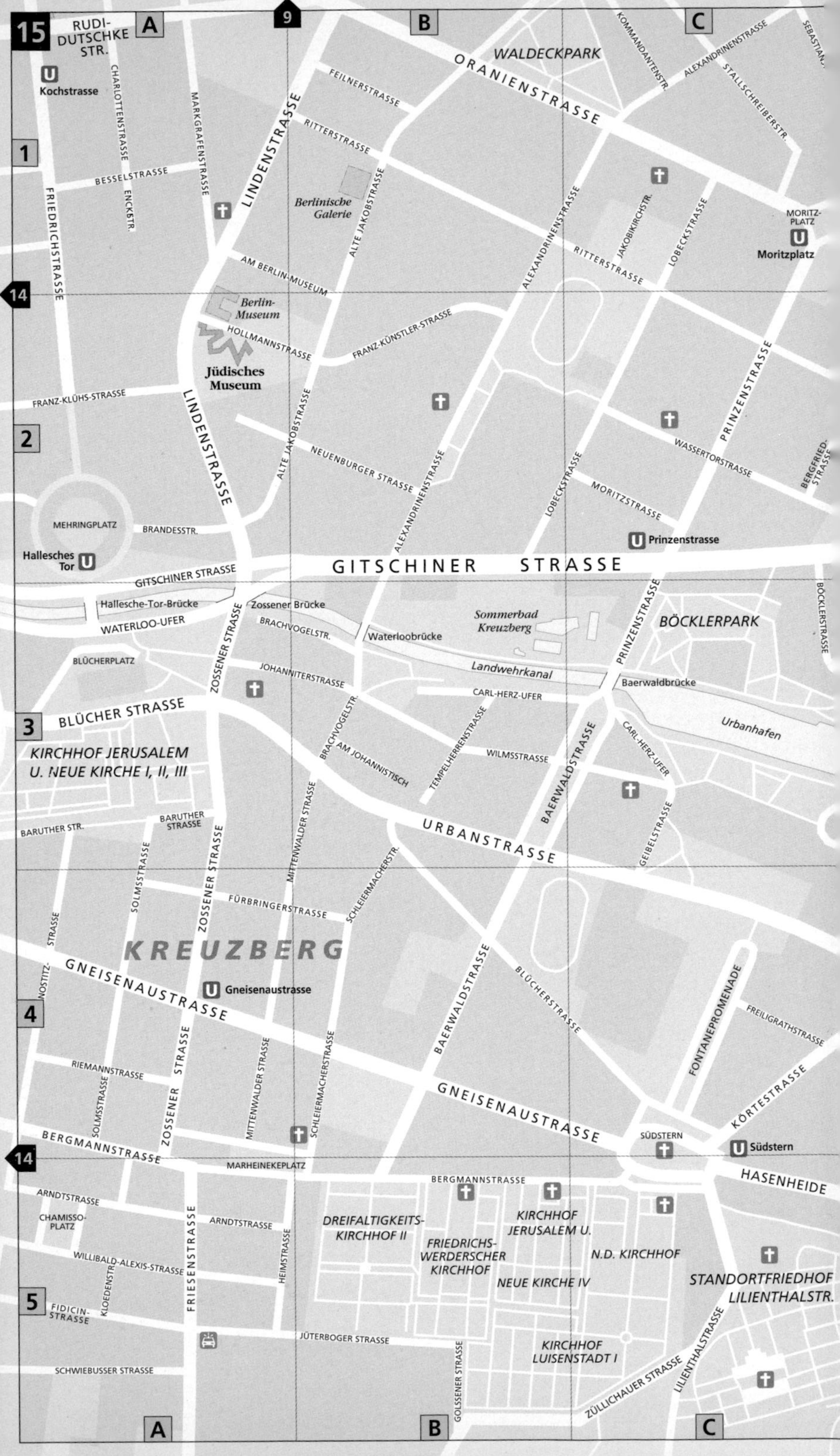
15
A
B
C
1
2
3
4
5
9
14
RUDI-DUTSCHKE STR.
Kochstrasse
CHARLOTTENSTRASSE
MARKGRAFENSTRASSE
LINDENSTRASSE
FEILNERSTRASSE
RITTERSTRASSE
WALDECKPARK
ORANIENSTRASSE
KOMMANDANTENSTR.
ALEXANDRINENSTRASSE
STALLSCHREIBERSTR.
SEBASTIAN-
BESSELSTRASSE
ENCKESTR.
FRIEDRICHSTRASSE
Berlinische Galerie
ALTE JAKOBSTRASSE
JAKOBIKIRCHSTR.
LOBECKSTRASSE
MORITZ-PLATZ
Moritzplatz
AM BERLIN-MUSEUM
Berlin-Museum
HOLLMANNSTRASSE
FRANZ-KÜNSTLER-STRASSE
Jüdisches Museum
FRANZ-KLÜHS-STRASSE
NEUENBURGER STRASSE
WASSERTORSTRASSE
PRINZENSTRASSE
BERGFRIED-STRASSE
MORITZSTRASSE
MEHRINGPLATZ
BRANDESSTR.
Hallesches Tor
Prinzenstrasse
GITSCHINER STRASSE
Hallesche-Tor-Brücke
Zossener Brücke
WATERLOO-UFER
BRACHVOGELSTR.
Waterloobrücke
Sommerbad Kreuzberg
BÖCKLERPARK
BÖCKLERSTRASSE
BLÜCHERPLATZ
JOHANNITERSTRASSE
Landwehrkanal
Baerwaldbrücke
CARL-HERZ-UFER
ZOSSENER STRASSE
BLÜCHER STRASSE
TEMPELHERRENSTRASSE
Urbanhafen
AM JOHANNISTISCH
WILMSSTRASSE
KIRCHHOF JERUSALEM U. NEUE KIRCHE I, II, III
BAERWALDSTRASSE
GEIBELSTRASSE
BARUTHER STR.
BARUTHER STRASSE
MITTENWALDER STRASSE
URBANSTRASSE
SOLMSSTRASSE
SCHLEIERMACHERSTR.
FÜRBRINGERSTRASSE
NOSTITZ-STRASSE
KREUZBERG
GNEISENAUSTRASSE
Gneisenaustrasse
BLÜCHERSTRASSE
FONTANEPROMENADE
FREILIGRATHSTRASSE
RIEMANNSTRASSE
KÖRTESTRASSE
SCHLEIERMACHERSTRASSE
SÜDSTERN
Südstern
BERGMANNSTRASSE
MARHEINEKEPLATZ
HASENHEIDE
ARNDTSTRASSE
CHAMISSO-PLATZ
FRIESENSTRASSE
HEIMSTRASSE
DREIFALTIGKEITS-KIRCHHOF II
FRIEDRICHS-WERDERSCHER KIRCHHOF
KIRCHHOF JERUSALEM U.
N.D. KIRCHHOF
NEUE KIRCHE IV
STANDORTFRIEDHOF LILIENTHALSTR.
WILLIBALD-ALEXIS-STRASSE
KLOEDENSTR.
FIDICIN-STRASSE
JÜTERBOGER STRASSE
SCHWIEBUSSER STRASSE
GOLSSENER STRASSE
KIRCHHOF LUISENSTADT I
ZÜLLICHAUER STRASSE
LILIENTHALSTRASSE

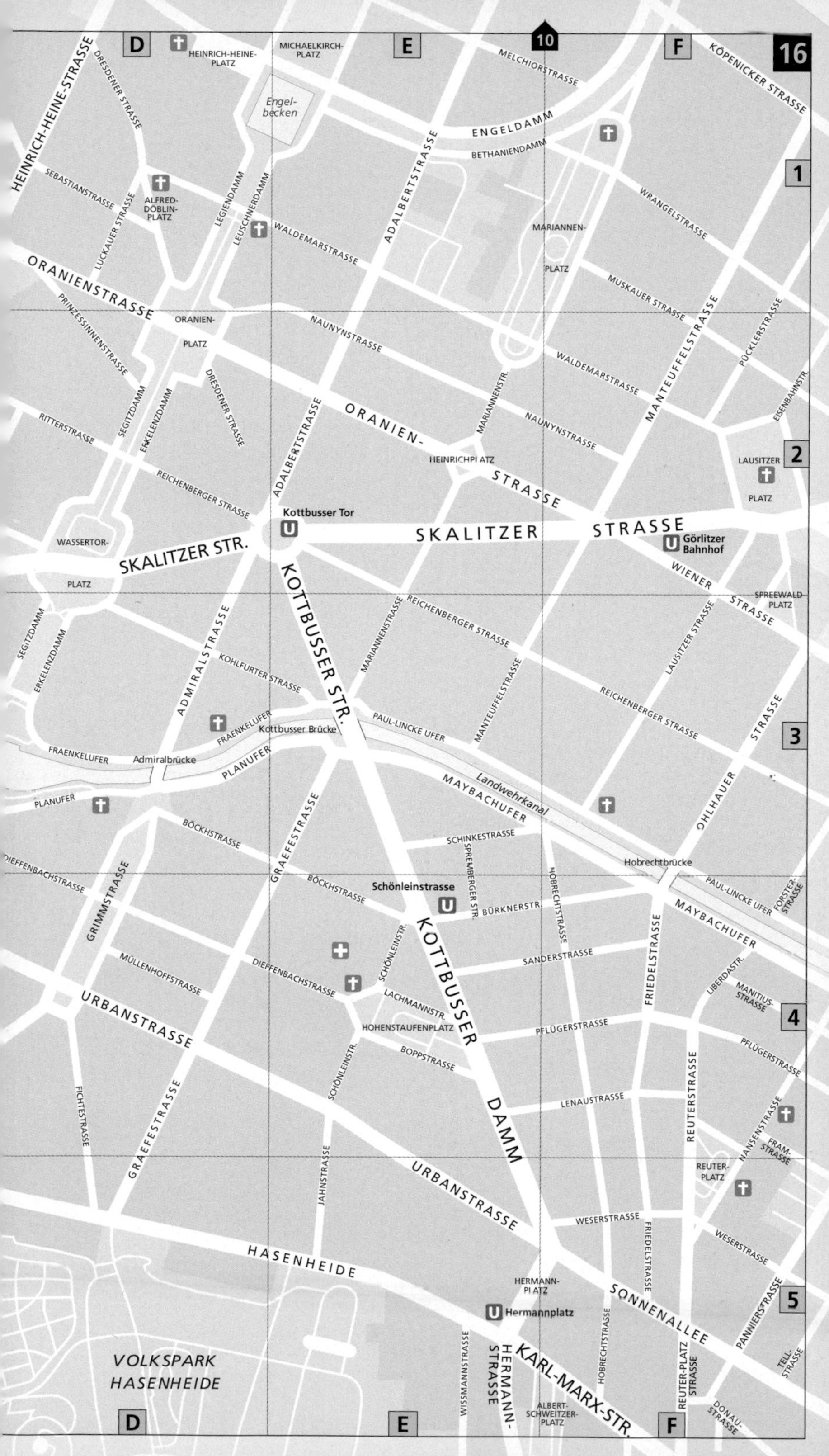
16
D
E
F
10
1
2
3
4
5
HEINRICH-HEINE-STRASSE
HEINRICH-HEINE-PLATZ
MICHAELKIRCH-PLATZ
Engel-becken
MELCHIORSTRASSE
KÖPENICKER STRASSE
ENGELDAMM
BETHANIENDAMM
DRESDENER STRASSE
SEBASTIANSTRASSE
ALFRED-DÖBLIN-PLATZ
LUCKAUER STRASSE
LEGIENDAMM
LEUSCHNERDAMM
WALDEMARSTRASSE
ADALBERTSTRASSE
WRANGELSTRASSE
MARIANNEN-
PLATZ
MUSKAUER STRASSE
MANTEUFFELSTRASSE
PÜCKLERSTRASSE
ORANIENSTRASSE
ORANIEN-
PLATZ
NAUNYNSTRASSE
PRINZESSINNENSTRASSE
WALDEMARSTRASSE
EISENBAHNSTR.
SEGITZDAMM
ERKELENZDAMM
DRESDENER STRASSE
ADALBERTSTRASSE
ORANIEN-
STRASSE
MARIANNENSTR.
NAUNYNSTRASSE
HEINRICHPLATZ
LAUSITZER
PLATZ
RITTERSTRASSE
REICHENBERGER STRASSE
Kottbusser Tor
WASSERTOR-
PLATZ
SKALITZER STR.
SKALITZER
STRASSE
Görlitzer Bahnhof
WIENER
STRASSE
SPREEWALD-PLATZ
KOTTBUSSER STR.
MARIANNENSTRASSE
REICHENBERGER STRASSE
SEGITZDAMM
ERKELENZDAMM
ADMIRALSTRASSE
KOHLFURTER STRASSE
LAUSITZER STRASSE
MANTEUFFELSTRASSE
REICHENBERGER STRASSE
FRAENKELUFER
Kottbusser Brücke
PAUL-LINCKE UFER
FRAENKELUFER
Admiralbrücke
PLANUFER
OHLHAUER
STRASSE
Landwehrkanal
MAYBACHUFER
PLANUFER
BÖCKHSTRASSE
SCHINKESTRASSE
SPREEMBERGER STR.
HOBRECHTSTRASSE
Hobrechtbrücke
DIEFFENBACHSTRASSE
GRAEFESTRASSE
BÖCKHSTRASSE
Schönleinstrasse
BÜRKNERSTR.
PAUL-LINCKE UFER
FORSTER-STRASSE
GRIMMSTRASSE
MAYBACHUFER
KOTTBUSSER
SCHÖNLEINSTR.
SANDERSTRASSE
FRIEDELSTRASSE
MÜLLENHOFFSTRASSE
DIEFFENBACHSTRASSE
LIBERDASTR.
MANITIUS-STRASSE
LACHMANNSTR.
URBANSTRASSE
HOHENSTAUFENPLATZ
PFLÜGERSTRASSE
PFLÜGERSTRASSE
BOPPSTRASSE
SCHÖNLEINSTR.
DAMM
REUTERSTRASSE
LENAUSTRASSE
FICHTESTRASSE
GRAEFESTRASSE
NANSENSTRASSE
FRAM-STRASSE
REUTER-PLATZ
JAHNSTRASSE
URBANSTRASSE
WESERSTRASSE
WESERSTRASSE
FRIEDELSTRASSE
HASENHEIDE
HERMANN-PLATZ
SONNENALLEE
Hermannplatz
PANNIERSTRASSE
VOLKSPARK HASENHEIDE
WISSMANNSTRASSE
HERMANN-STRASSE
KARL-MARX-STR.
HOBRECHTSTRASSE
REUTER-PLATZ STRASSE
TELL-STRASSE
ALBERT-SCHWEITZER-PLATZ
DONAU-STRASSE

General Index

Page numbers in **bold** refer to main entries

A

B

G

H

T

Acknowledgments

Dorling Kindersley would like to thank the following people whose contributions and assistance have made the preparation of this book possible.

Design and Editorial
Managing Art Editor Kate Poole
Editorial Director Vivien Crump
Art Director Gillian Allan
Consultant Gordon McLachlan
Factcheckers Jürgen Scheunemann, Petra Falkenberg
Translators Magda Hannay, Anna Johnson, Ian Wisniewski
Proofreader Stewart Wild
Indexer Hilary Bird
Revisions Team Louise Abbott, Namrata Adhwaryu, Ashwin Raju Adimari, Asad Ali, Gillian Andrews, Brigitte Arora, Claire Baranowski, Marta Bescos Sanchez, Tessa Bindloss, Arwen Burnett, Divya Chowfin, Lucinda Cooke, Vidushi Duggal, Joel Dullroy, Nicola Erdpresser, Emer FitzGerald, Camilla Gersh, Mohammad Hassan, Kaberi Hazarika, Claudia Himmelreich, Jessica Hughes, Claire Jones, Bharti Karakoti, Priya Kukadia, Rakesh Kumar Pal, Maite Lantaron, Delphine Lawrance, Jude Ledger, Carly Madden, Franziska Marking, Kate Molan, Catherine Palmi, Susie Peachey, Rada Radojicic, Erin Richards, Ellen Root, Simon Ryder, Sands Publishing Solutions, Azeem Siddiqui, Sadie Smith, Annie Stein, Andrew Szudek, Maria Taari, Leah Tether, Helen Townsend, Conrad van Dyk, Ajay Verma, Deepika Verma, Hugo Wilkinson

DTP Samantha Borland, Lee Redmond

Additional Illustrations Paweł Pasternak

Additional Photography Amir Akhtar, Francesca Bondy, Britta Jaschinski, Claire Jones, Catherine Marshall, Ian O'Leary, Jürgen Scheunemann

Additional Text Joel Dullroy, Claudia Himmelreich, Jürgen Scheunemann

Special Assistance
Dorling Kindersley would like to thank the staff at the featured museums, shops, hotels, restaurants and other organizations in Berlin for their invaluable help. Special thanks go to the following for providing photographs and pictures: Heidrun Klein of the Bildarchiv Preussischer Kulturbesitz; Frau Betzker and Ingrid Jager of the Bröhan Museum; Margit Billeb of the Centrum Judaicum; Brucke-Museum; Deutsche Press Agency (DPA); Renate Forster of the Deutsches Technikmuseum Berlin; Andrei Holland-Moritz of Forschung- und Gedenkstätte Normannenstrasse (Stasi-Museum); Matthias Richter of Konzerthaus Berlin and the Berlin Symphony Orchestra; Georg Kolbe Museum; Carl Kamarz of Stiftung Preussische Schlösser und Gärten Berlin and the Berlin and Potsdam Palaces; Thomas Wellmann of the Museum of the City of Berlin; Hamburger Bahnhof; Annette Jäckel of DeragHotels for providing photographs of the interiors of DeragHotel Grosser Kurfürst; Reinhard Friedrich; Hans-Jürgen Dyck of Haus am Checkpoint Charlie; Gaby Hofmann of Komische Oper Berlin; Gesine Steiner of Museum für Naturkunde; Ute Grallert of Deutsches Historisches Museum; Elke Pfeil of the Brecht-Weigel-Museum; Ingrid Flindell of the Käthe-Kollwitz-Museum; Sylvia U Moller of Villa Kastania; Manuel Volsk of the Savoy Hotel; Sabine Rogge of the Grand Hotel Esplanade Berlin; Claude Borrmann of the Hotel Palace Berlin; Gerald Uhligow of the Einstein Café; Hotel Adlon; Hotel Brandenburger Hof and Restaurant Die Quadriga; Hotel Kempinski; Rockendorf's Restaurant; The Westin Grand Hotel.

Photography Permissions
Dorling Kindersley would like to thank the following for their kind permission to photograph at their establishments: Margaret Hilmer of the Berliner Dom; Kaiser-Wilhelm-Gedächtniskirche; Galeries Lafayette; KaDeWe; Frau Schneider of BVG (Berlin Underground System); Deutsche Bundesbahn for allowing photography of the Zoo railway station; Dorotheenstädtischer Friedhof for allowing photographs of the tombs; Flughafen Schönefeld for allowing photography of the airfield; Annie Silbert of the Zoologischer Garten Berlin for allowing photography of the animals and attractions; Hilton Hotel; Carlos Beck of the Sorat Art'otel, Berlin; Manuel Volsk of the Savoy Hotel, Berlin; Sabine Rogge of the Grand Hotel Esplanade; Claude Borrmann of the Hotel Palace Berlin; Gerald Uhligow of the Einstein Café; the Olive restaurant; the Bamberger Reiter restaurant; Sklepo for allowing photography of its interiors and porcelain. Count Lehmann of Senatsverwaltung für Bauen, Wohnen und Verkehr for providing cartographic information as well as copyright for the use of maps; Ms Grazyna Kukowska of ZAIKS for her help in securing permission to reproduce works of art.

Picture Credits
a = above; b = below/bottom; c = centre; f = far; l = left; r = right; t = top.

Works of art have been reproduced with the permission of the following copyright holders: Richtkräfte (1974-77) Joseph Beuys ©DACS, London 2011 114br; *Pariser Platz in Berlin* (1925–26) Oskar Kokoschka ©DACS, London 2011 69bl; *Mother and Child* Käthe Kollwitz ©DACS, London 2011 158c; *Girl on a Beach* Evadr Munch ©ADAGP, Paris and DACS, London 2011 121tc; *Head of the Faun* (1937) Pablo Picasso ©Succession Picasso/DACS, London 2011 36tr, *Woman in a Hat* (1939) Pablo Picasso ©Succession Picasso/DACS, London 2011 169tl; *First Time Painting* (1961) Robert Rauschenberg ©DACS, London/VAGA, NY 2011 114bl; *Farm in Daugart* (1910) Karl Schmidt-Rottluff ©DACS, London 2011 130tl; *Mao* (1973) Andy Warhol © Licensed by the Andy Warhol Foundation for the Visual Arts, Inc./ARS, NY and DACS, London 2011 114cr.

The publisher is grateful to the following individuals, companies and picture libraries for their permission to reproduce their photographs. The works of art have been reproduced with the consent of the copyright owners.

Admiralspalast: S. Greuner 260br; **Alamy Images:** Agencja Fotograficzna Caro 296br; Pat Behnke 54-5; Bildarchiv Monheim GmbH 187cl; David Crausby 283bl; Colstravel 2-3; dpa picture alliance 283cla; Adam Eastland 18br; Gavin Hellier 56; Imagebroker 160, 208, 216-7; JLImages 150; Leslie Garland Picture Library 138br; LOOK Die Bildagentur der Fotografen GmbH 10cra, 154tl; Eric Nathan 95cra; Novarc Images 154bl; Joern Sackerman 11bl; Peter Widmann 88; Woodystock 72; **Aletto Kudamm:** 220br; **Allstar:** cinetext 145tc; **AMJ Holding GmbH & Co. Kg:** Steffen Janicke 67br; **Austria restaurant:** 241bc; **Berger + Parkkinen Architekten Ziviltechnik GmbH:** 44br; **Berlin Brandenburg Airport:** Marion Schmieding/Alexander Obst 288br; **Berlin Tourismus Marketing GmbH:** 114cl, 280cr; visitBerlin.de/adenis 279tl; visitBerlin.de/Koch 167br, 290bl; visitberlin.de/Philip Koschel 107tr; visitberlin.de: 113tl; visitBerlin/Mathesius 278crb; visitBerlin.de/Meise 278bl; **Berliner Dom:** 78br; **Berliner Festspiele:** Bianka Göbel 261tl; **Berliner Sparkasse:** 284bl; **Berliner Verkehrsbetriebe (BVG):** 294cb, 294cla, 297tr, 297c, 297cr, 297cra; **Berlinische Galerie:** *Stadtwandelverlag* (2004) © Florian Bulk and *Dreiheit* (1993) © Brigitte and Martin Matschinsky-Denninghoff 145br; **Bildarchiv Preussischer Kulturbesitz:** 24 all pics, 26cb, 26bl, 33cla, 33cl, 33cra, 34 all pics, 35tr, 36tr, 36br, 37ca, 37br, 69bl, 74cla, 82-3 all pics, 83-4 all pics, 87br, 118 all pics, 119cra, 122-3 all pics, 126-7 all pics, 128-9 all pics, 130tl, 185tr, 185crb, 200tc; Jorg P Anders 20cl, 30cl, 75ca, 121tc, 124c, 124br, 125crb, 125cb, 181bc; Margarete Busing 36c; Ingrid Geske-Heiden 34tl, 77cra; Klaus Goken 62t, 34crb, 80t; Dietmar Katz 45crb; Johannes Laurentius 77bl; Jürgen Liepe 34cra, 77cla, 168b; Jürgen Zimmermann 30tl; **Brandenburger Hof:** 224bc, Die Quadriga 238tl; **Bröhan-Museum:** 169bl; **Centrum Judaicum:** 104tr; © **Charité - Universitätsmedizin Berlin:** 112ca; **Circus Hotel, Berlin:** 222br; **Corbis:** Atlandtide Phototravel 116; Christian Charisius 280bl; Dpa/Britta Pedersen 286br; Blaine Harrington III 100, 192; Hemis/Rene Mattes 32, Jon Hicks 276-7; Andreas Schluter 166tl; Sygma/Aneebicque Bernard 229tl; Adam Woolfitt 228cla; Michael S. Yamashita 229c; **Michael Day:** 179cr; **Derag Livinghotel Henriette:** 223tc; **Deutsche Bahn AG:** 293br; **Deutsche Press Agency (Dpa):** 10bl, 50cla, 52cra, 52bl, 69tr, 149br, 155br, 201br; **Deutsches Historisches Museum:** (Zeughaus) 8–9, 27clb, 27tr, 28-9, 29tr, 30tl, 30cb, 30br, 31tl, 35bl, 39tl, 60-1 all pics; **Deutsches Technik-museum Berlin:** 34bl; **Dreamstime.com:** Rumifaz 59crb; **ECB:** 285tc; **European Commission:** 285; **E.T.A. Hoffman:** 237bl; **Fernsehturm Sphere Restaurant:** 233tr; **Filmpark Babelsberg:** 207 cla/crb/bl; **Fischers Fritz:** 232br; **Gedenkstätte Berlin Hohenschönhausen:** 174br; **Gedenkstatte und Museum Sachsenhausen:** 181cr; **Georg Kolbe Museum:** 178tc; **Getty Images:** David Bank 13br; Halfdark 287tr; Image Source 12tc; Siegfried Layda 179bc; John Macdougall 282cla; Florian Seefried 115bl; **Guglehof, Berlin:** 234br; **Gullivers Bus GmbH:** 291tr; **Hamburger Bahnhof:** 114bl, 114br, 115cr; **Haus am Checkpoint Charlie:** 43br; **Haus der Wannsee-Konferenz:** 189tl; **Hotel Adlon Kempinski:** 70tl, Restaurant Quarré 226cl; **Hotel Pension Funk:** 221tr; **Imageworkshop Berlin:** Vincent Mosch 135br; **Jewish Museum Berlin:** 146tr, 147br; Deutsches Technik-museum Berlin 147clb; Jens Ziehe, Berlin 146cl; Leo Baeck Institute, New York 146tr; **Kafers Dachgarten:** 236tr; **Käthe-Kollwitz-Museum:** 158b; **KaDeWe:** 53b; **Komische Oper Monika Rittershaus:** 51br, 70br; **Konzerthaus Berlin:** 67tl; **Kurhaus Korsakow:** 239b; **Courtesy of Lufthansa AG:** 288cla, 289tl; **Max und Moritz:** 240tl; **Nhow Berlin:** 225tl; **Meyer Nils:** 30crb, 42tr; **Motel One Berlin Alexanderplatz:** 220t; **Museum für Naturkunde:** 113br; **Pasternak, Berlin:** 235tr; **Philharmonie:** 119tl; **Popkomm:** 261bc; **Potsdam Museum:** Mathias Marx 206cl; **Presse- und Informationsamt des Landes Berlin:** BTM/Drewes 47bl; BTM/Koch 47cla, 133tl; G. Schneider 53cra; Landesarchive Berlin 133br; Meldepress/Ebner 130bc; **Partner fuer Berlin:** FTB-Werbefotografie 132cl, 147cr; **Radeberger Gruppe:** KG: 230cla, 230cr, 230bl, 230fcla; **Robert Harding Picture Library:** 31CRB; **Rocco Forte Hotel de Rome:** 218br; **Rosa's Dance Co.:** 261cr; **Courtesy the Company Sarah Wiener:** 114tr; **Photo Scala, Florence:** Volk Ding Zero (2009) © Georg Baselitz 115tc; **Schneider, Guenter:** 43tr; **Schirmer, Karsten:** 260cl; **Jürgen Scheunemann:** 51cra, 142tr, 143tl; **Spindler & Klatt:** 243b; **STA Travel Group:** 280tc; **Staatliche Museen zu Berlin-preussische Kulturbesitz/kunstgewerbemuseum:** Irmgard Mues-Funke 125tl; **Stadtmuseum Berlin:** 20, 23TL, 23BR, 25tr, 26t, 28cla,137tr; Hans-Joachim Bartsch, 21br, 22tl, 22bc, 29br, 87tr; Peter Straube 90bc, 92tr; **Stasimuseum/ ASTAK e.V:** JOHN STEER 175TR **Stiftung Preussische Schlösser und Gärten Berlin:** 18tr, 23c, 164cl, 164cb, 165 all, 194br, 196cla, 196br, 197tc, 197crb, 197br, 197bl, 202cl, 202br, 203cra, 203ca, 203bc, 203bl, 202br; Daniel Lindner 165crb; **Superstock:** age fotostock 13tr, Blaine Harrington 190-1; imagebroker.net 12bl, Julie Woodhouse 170; **Tim Raue, Berlin:** 237tr; **Topography of Terror Foundation:** Uwe Bellm 142cla, 144tr; **View Pictures:** William Fife 45bl; **Villa Kastania:** 219bc; **Restaurant Volt:** 242tl

Front endpapers - **Alamy Images:** Gavin Hellier Rtl, imagebroker Lclb, JLImages Lbc, Peter Widmann Rtr, WoodyStock Rbr; **Corbis:** Atlandtide Phototravel Ltr, Blaine Harrington III Rtc.

Jacket Front and Spine – **4Corners:** SIME / Luca Da Ros

Map Cover – **4Corners:** SIME / Luca da Ros.

All other images © Dorling Kindersley. For further information see: www.dkimages.com

Special Editions of DK Travel Guides

DK Travel Guides can be purchased in bulk quantities at discounted prices for use in promotions or as premiums. We are also able to offer special editions and personalized jackets, corporate imprints, and excerpts from all of our books, tailored specifically to meet your own needs.

To find out more, please contact:

in the United States **SpecialSales@dk.com**

in the UK **travelspecialsales@uk.dk.com**

in Canada DK Special Sales at **general@ tourmaline.ca**

in Australia **business.development@pearson. com.au**

Phrase Book

In an Emergency

Where is the telephone?	**Wo ist das tele-fon?**	*voh ist duss telefon?*
Help!	**Hilfe!**	**hilf**-*uh*
Please call a doctor	**Bitte rufen Sie einen Arzt**	**bitt**-*uh* **roof***'n zee ine-en artst*
Please call the police	**Bitte rufen Sie die Polizei**	**bitt**-*uh* **roof***'n zee dee poli*-**tsy**
Please call the fire brigade	**Bitte rufen Sie die Feuerwehr**	**bitt**-*uh roof'n zee dee* **foyer**-*vayr*
Stop!	**Halt!**	**hult**

Communication Essentials

Yes	**Ja**	**yah**
No	**Nein**	**nine**
Please	**Bitte**	**bitt**-*uh*
Thank you	**Danke**	*dunk-uh*
Excuse me	**Verzeihung**	*fair*-**tsy**-*hoong*
Hello (good day)	**Guten Tag**	**goot**-*en tahk*
Goodbye	**Auf Wiedersehen**	*owf*-**veed**-*er-zay-ern*
Good evening	**Guten Abend**	*goot'n* **ah***b'nt*
Good night	**Gute Nacht**	*goot-uh* **nukht**
Until tomorrow	**Bis morgen**	*biss* **morg***'n*
See you	**Tschüss**	*chooss*
What is that?	**Was ist das?**	*voss ist duss*
Why?	**Warum?**	*var*-**room**
Where?	**Wo?**	**voh**
When?	**Wann?**	**vunn**
today	**heute**	**hoyt**-*uh*
tomorrow	**morgen**	**morg***'n*
month	**Monat**	**mohn**-*aht*
night	**Nacht**	**nukht**
afternoon	**Nachmittag**	**nahkh**-*mit-tahk*
morning	**Morgen**	**morg***'n*
year	**Jahr**	*yar*
there	**dort**	**dort**
here	**hier**	**hear**
week	**Woche**	**vokh**-*uh*
yesterday	**gestern**	**gest***'n*
evening	**Abend**	**ah***b'nt*

Useful Phrases

How are you? (informal)	**Wie geht's?**	*vee gayts*
Fine, thanks	**Danke, es geht mir gut**	*dunk-uh, es gayt meer goot*
Until later	**Bis später**	*biss* **shpay**-*ter*
Where is/are?	**Wo ist/sind...?**	*voh ist/sind*
How far is it to...?	**Wie weit ist es...?**	*vee* **vite** *ist ess*
Do you speak English?	**Sprechen Sie Englisch?**	*shpresh'n zee* **eng**-*glish*
I don't understand	**Ich verstehe nicht**	*ish fair*-**shtay**-*uh nisht*
Could you speak more slowly?	**Könnten Sie langsamer sprechen?**	**kurnt**-*en zee* **lung**-*zam-er* **shpresh***'n*

Useful Words

large	**gross**	**grohss**
small	**klein**	**kline**
hot	**heiss**	**hyce**
cold	**kalt**	**kult**
good	**gut**	**goot**
bad	**böse/schlecht**	**burss**-*uh*/**shlesht**
open	**geöffnet**	*g'***urff**-*nett*
closed	**geschlossen**	*g'***shloss***'n*
left	**links**	**links**
right	**rechts**	**reshts**
straight ahead	**geradeaus**	*g'***rah**-*der*-**owss**

Making a Telephone Call

I would like to make a phone call	**Ich möchte telefonieren**	*ish mer-shtuh tel-e-fon*-**eer***'n*
I'll try again later	**Ich versuche es später noch einmal**	*ish fair-zookh-uh es* **shpay**-*ter nokh ine-mull*
Can I leave a message?	**Kann ich eine Nachricht hinterlassen?**	*kan ish* **ine**-*uh nakh-risht hint-er*-**lahss**-*en*
answer phone	**Anrufbeantworter**	*an-roof-be*-**ahnt**-*vort-er*
telephone card	**Telefonkarte**	*tel-e*-**fohn**-*kart-uh*
receiver	**Hörer**	**hur**-*er*
mobile	**Handy**	*han-dee*
engaged (busy)	**besetzt**	*b'zetst*
wrong number	**Falsche Verbindung**	*falsh-uh fair*-**bin**-*doong*

Sightseeing

library	**Bibliothek**	*bib-leo*-**tek**
entrance ticket	**Eintrittskarte**	*ine-tritz*-**kart**-*uh*
cemetery	**Friedhof**	**freed**-*hofe*
train station	**Bahnhof**	**barn**-*hofe*
gallery	**Galerie**	**gall**-*er-ree*
information	**Auskunft**	**owss**-*koonft*
church	**Kirche**	**keersh**-*uh*
garden	**Garten**	**gart***'n*
palace/castle	**Palast/Schloss**	*pallast/shloss*
place (square)	**Platz**	**plats**
bus stop	**Haltestelle**	**hal**-*te-shtel-uh*
national holiday	**Nationalfeiertag**	*nats-yon*-**ahl**-*fire-tahk*
theatre	**Theater**	*tay*-**aht**-*er*
free admission	**Eintritt frei**	*ine-tritt fry*

Shopping

Do you have/ Is there...?	**Gibt es...?**	*geept ess*
How much does it cost?	**Was kostet das?**	*voss* **kost***'t duss?*
When do you open/ close?	**Wann öffnen Sie? schliessen Sie?**	*vunn* **off***'n zee* **shlees***'n zee*
this	**das**	*duss*
expensive	**teuer**	**toy**-*er*
cheap	**preiswert**	**price**-*vurt*
size	**Grösse**	**gruhs**-*uh*
number	**Nummer**	**noom**-*er*
colour	**Farbe**	**farb**-*uh*
brown	**braun**	*brown*
black	**schwarz**	**shvarts**
red	**rot**	**roht**
blue	**blau**	**blau**
green	**grün**	**groon**
yellow	**gelb**	**gelp**

Types of Shop

antique shop	**Antiquariat**	*antik*-**var**-*yat*
chemist (pharmacy)	**Apotheke**	*appo*-**tay**-*kuh*
bank	**Bank**	**bunk**
market	**Markt**	**markt**
travel agency	**Reisebüro**	**rye-z***er-boo-roe*
department store	**Warenhaus**	**vahr***'n-hows*
chemist's, drugstore	**Drogerie**	*droog-er*-**ree**
hairdresser	**Friseur**	*freezz*-**er**
newspaper kiosk	**Zeitungskiosk**	*tsytoongs-kee-osk*
bookshop	**Buchhandlung**	**bookh**-*hant-loong*

bakery	**Bäckerei**	beck-er-**eye**
post office	**Post**	posst
shop/store	**Geschäft/Laden**	gush-**eft**/**lard**'n
film processing shop	**Fotogeschäft**	**fo**-to-gush-**eft**
self-service shop	**Selbstbedienungsladen**	selpst-bed-**ee**-nungs-lard'n
shoe shop	**Schuhladen**	shoo-lard'n
clothes shop	**Kleiderladen, Boutique**	klyder-lard'n, boo-**teek**-uh
food shop	**Lebensmittelgeschäft**	**lay**-bens-mittel-gush-eft
glass, porcelain	**Glas, Porzellan**	**glars, port-sell-ahn**

Staying in a Hotel

Do you have any vacancies?	**Haben Sie noch Zimmer frei?**	harb'n zee nokh **tsimm**-er-fry
with twin beds?	**mit zwei Betten?**	mitt tsvy bett'n
with a double bed?	**mit einem Doppelbett?**	mitt ine'm **dopp**'l-bet
with a bath?	**mit Bad?**	mitt **bart**
with a shower?	**mit Dusche?**	mitt **doosh**-uh
I have a reservation	**Ich habe eine Reservierung**	ish **harb**-uh ine-uh rez-er-**veer**-oong
key	**Schlüssel**	shlooss'l
porter	**Pförtner**	**pfert**-ner

Eating Out

Do you have a table for…?	**Haben Sie einen Tisch für…?**	harb'n zee tish foor
I would like to reserve a table	**Ich möchte eine Reservierung machen**	ish **mer**-shtuh ine-uh rezer-**veer**-oong makh'n
I'm a vegetarian	**Ich bin Vegetarier**	ish bin vegg-er-**tah**-ree-er
Waiter!	**Herr Ober!**	hair **oh**-bare!
The bill (check), please	**Die Rechnung, bitte**	dee **resh**-noong bitt-uh
breakfast	**Frühstück**	**froo**-shtock
lunch	**Mittagessen**	**mit**-targ-ess'n
dinner	**Abendessen**	**arb**'nt-ess'n
bottle	**Flasche**	**flush**-uh
dish of the day	**Tagesgericht**	**tahg**-es-gur-isht
main dish	**Hauptgericht**	**howpt**-gur-isht
dessert	**Nachtisch**	**nahkh**-tish
cup	**Tasse**	**tass**-uh
wine list	**Weinkarte**	vine-kart-uh
tankard	**Krug**	khroog
glass	**Glas**	**glars**
spoon	**Löffel**	**lerff'l**
teaspoon	**Teelöffel**	tay-lerff'l
tip	**Trinkgeld**	**trink**-gelt
knife	**Messer**	**mess**-er
starter (appetizer)	**Vorspeise**	**for**-shpize-uh
the bill	**Rechnung**	**resh**-noong
plate	**Teller**	**tell**-er
fork	**Gabel**	**gahb**'l

Menu Decoder

Aal	**arl**	eel
Apfel	**upf'l**	apple
Apfelschorle	**upf'l-shoorl-uh**	apple juice with sparkling mineral water
Apfelsine	**upf'l-seen-uh**	orange
Aprikose	**upri-kawz-uh**	apricot
Artischocke	**arti-shokh-uh-**	artichoke
Aubergine (eggplant)	**or-ber-jeen-uh**	aubergine
Banane	**bar-narn-uh**	banana
Beefsteak	**beef-stayk**	steak
Bier	**beer**	beer
Bockwurst	**bokh**-voorst	a type of sausage
Bohnensuppe	burn-en-zoop-uh	bean soup
Branntwein	brant-vine	spirits
Bratkartoffeln	brat-kar-toff'ln	fried potatoes
Bratwurst	brat-voorst	fried sausage
Brot	brot	bread
Brötchen	bret-tchen	bread roll
Brühe	bruh-uh	broth
Butter	**boot**-ter	butter
Champignon	**shum**-pin-yong	mushroom
Currywurst	**kha**-ree-voorst	sausage with curry sauce
Dill	**dill**	dill
Ei	**eye**	egg
Eis	**ice**	ice/ ice cream
Ente	**ent**-uh	duck
Erdbeeren	ayrt-**beer**'n	strawberries
Fisch	**fish**	fish
Forelle	for-**ell**-uh	trout
Frikadelle	Frika-dayl-uh	rissole/hamburger
Gans	ganns	goose
Garnele	**gar**-nayl-uh	prawn/shrimp
gebraten	g'**braat**'n	fried
gegrillt	g'**grilt**	grilled
gekocht	g'**kokh**t	boiled
geräuchert	g'**rowk**-ert	smoked
Geflügel	g'**floog**'l	poultry
Gemüse	g'**mooz**-uh	vegetables
Grütze	**grurt**-ser	groats, gruel
Gulasch	**goo**-lush	goulash
Gurke	**goork**-uh	gherkin
Hammelbraten	hamm'l-**braat**'n	roast mutton
Hähnchen	haynsh'n	chicken
Hering	**hair**-ing	herring
Himbeeren	him-beer'n	raspberries
Honig	**hoe**-nikh	honey
Kaffee	kaf-**fay**	coffee
Kalbfleisch	kalp-flysh	veal
Kaninchen	ka-**neensh**'n	rabbit
Karpfen	**karpf**'n	carp
Kartoffelpüree	kar-toff'l-poor-ay	mashed potatoes
Käse	**kayz**-uh	cheese
Kaviar	**kar**-vee-ar	caviar
Knoblauch	**k'nob**-lowkh	garlic
Knödel	**k'nerd**'l	noodle
Kohl	**koal**	cabbage
Kopfsalat	**kopf**-zal-aat	lettuce
Krebs	**krayps**	crab
Kuchen	**kookh**'n	cake
Lachs	**lahkhs**	salmon
Leber	**lay**-ber	liver
mariniert	mari-neert	marinated
Marmelade	marmer-**lard**-uh	marmalade, jam
Meerrettich	may-re-tish	horseradish
Milch	**milsh**	milk
Mineralwasser	minn-er-**arl**-vuss-er	mineral water
Möhre	**mer**-uh	carrot
Nuss	**nooss**	nut
Öl	**erl**	oil
Olive	o-**leev**-uh	olive
Petersilie	payt-er-**zee**-li-uh	parsley
Pfeffer	**pfeff**-er	pepper
Pfirsich	**pfir**-zish	peach
Pflaumen	**pflow**-men	plum
Pommes frites	pomm-**fritt**	chips/ French fries
Quark	kvark	soft cheese
Radieschen	ra-**deesh**'n	radish
Rinderbraten	**rind**-er-brat'n	joint of beef
Rinderroulade	**rind**-er-roo-lard-uh	beef olive
Rindfleisch	**rint**-flysh	beef
Rippchen	**rip**-sh'n	cured pork rib
Rotkohl	roht-koal	red cabbage
Rüben	rhoob'n	turnip
Rührei	**rhoo**-er-eye	scrambled eggs
Saft	**zuft**	juice
Salat	zal-aat	salad

Salz	**zults**	*salt*
Salzkartoffeln	*zults-kar-toff'l*	*boiled potatoes*
Sauerkirschen	*zow-er-***keersh***'n*	*cherries*
Sauerkraut	*zow-er-krowt*	*sauerkraut*
Sekt	**zekt**	*sparkling wine*
Senf	**zenf**	*mustard*
scharf	*sharf*	*spicy*
Schaschlik	*shash-lik*	*kebab*
Schlagsahne	*shlahgg-zarn-uh*	*whipped cream*
Schnittlauch	*shnit-lowhkh*	*chives*
Schnitzel	**shnitz***'l*	*veal or pork cutlet*
Schweinefleisch	**shvine***-flysh*	*pork*
Spargel	**shparg***'l*	*asparagus*
Spiegelei	*shpeeg'l-eye*	*fried egg*
Spinat	*shpin-art*	*spinach*
Tee	**tay**	*tea*
Tomate	*tom-art-uh*	*tomato*
Wassermelone	*vuss-er-me-lohn-uh*	*watermelon*
Wein	**vine**	*wine*
Weintrauben	*vine-trowb'n*	*grapes*
Wiener Würstchen	*veen-er voorst-sh'n*	*frankfurter*
Zander	**tsan***-der*	*pike-perch*
Zitrone	*tsi-trohn-uh*	*lemon*
Zucker	**tsook***-er*	*sugar*
Zwieback	*tsvee-bak*	*rusk*
Zwiebel	**tsvee***b'l*	*onion*

Numbers

0	**null**	**nool**
1	**eins**	**eye***'n***s**
2	**zwei**	**tsvy**
3	**drei**	**dry**
4	**vier**	**feer**
5	**fünf**	**foonf**
6	**sechs**	**zex**
7	**sieben**	**zeeb***'n*
8	**acht**	**uhkht**
9	**neun**	**noyn**
10	**zehn**	**tsayn**
11	**elf**	**elf**
12	**zwölf**	**tserlf**
13	**dreizehn**	**dry***-tsayn*
14	**vierzehn**	**feer***-tsayn*
15	**fünfzehn**	**foonf***-tsayn*
16	**sechzehn**	**zex***-tsayn*
17	**siebzehn**	**zeep***-tsayn*
18	**achtzehn**	**uhkht***-tsayn*
19	**neunzehn**	**noyn***-tsayn*
20	**zwanzig**	**tsvunn***-tsig*
21	**einundzwanzig**	**ine***-oont-tsvunn-tsig*
30	**dreissig**	**dry***-sig*
40	**vierzig**	**feer***-sig*
50	**fünfzig**	**foonf***-tsig*
60	**sechzig**	**zex***-tsig*
70	**siebzig**	**zeep***-tsig*
80	**achtzig**	**uhkht***-tsig*
90	**neunzig**	**noyn***-tsig*
100	**hundert**	**hoond***'t*
1,000	**tausend**	**towz***'nt*
1,000, 000	**eine Million**	**ine***-uh* **mill***-yon*

Time

one minute	**eine Minute**	**ine***-uh min-***oot***-uh*
one hour	**eine Stunde**	**ine***-uh* **shtoond***-uh*
half an hour	**eine halbe Stunde**	**ine***-uh hullb-uh* **shtoond***-uh*
Monday	**Montag**	**mohn***-targ*
Tuesday	**Dienstag**	**deen***s-targ*
Wednesday	**Mittwoch**	**mitt***-vokh*
Thursday	**Donnerstag**	**donn***-ers-targ*
Friday	**Freitag**	**fry***-targ*
Saturday	**Samstag/ Sonnabend**	**zum***s-targ* *zonn-ah-bent*
Sunday	**Sonntag**	**zon***-targ*
January	**Januar**	**yan***-ooar*
February	**Februar**	**fay***-brooar*
March	**März**	**mairts**
April	**April**	*april*
May	**Mai**	*my*
June	**Juni**	**yoo***-ni*
July	**Juli**	**yoo***-lee*
August	**August**	*ow-***goost**
September	**September**	*zep-***tem***-ber*
October	**Oktober**	*ok-toh-ber*
November	**November**	*no-***vem***-ber*
December	**Dezember**	*day-***tsem***-ber*
spring	**Frühling**	**froo***-ling*
summer	**Sommer**	**zomm***-er*
autumn (fall)	**Herbst**	**hairpst**
winter	**Winter**	**vint***-er*

MARTINA COLE

REVENGE

headline

Copyright © 2013 Martina Cole

The right of Martina Cole to be identified as the Author of the Work has been asserted by her in accordance with the Copyright, Designs and Patents Act 1988.

First published in Great Britain in 2013
by HEADLINE PUBLISHING GROUP

First published in Great Britain in paperback in 2014
by HEADLINE PUBLISHING GROUP

1

Apart from any use permitted under UK copyright law, this publication may only be reproduced, stored, or transmitted, in any form, or by any means, with prior permission in writing of the publishers or, in the case of reprographic production, in accordance with the terms of licences issued by the Copyright Licensing Agency.

All characters in this publication are fictitious and any resemblance to real persons, living or dead, is purely coincidental.

Cataloguing in Publication Data is available from the British Library

ISBN 978 0 7553 7563 9 (B-format)
ISBN 978 1 4722 1457 7 (A-format)

Typeset in ITC Galliard by Avon DataSet Ltd,
Bidford-on-Avon, Warwickshire

Printed and bound in Great Britain by Clays Ltd, St Ives plc

Headline's policy is to use papers that are natural, renewable and recyclable products and made from wood grown in sustainable forests. The logging and manufacturing processes are expected to conform to the environmental regulations of the country of origin.

HEADLINE PUBLISHING GROUP
An Hachette UK Company
338 Euston Road
London NW1 3BH

www.headline.co.uk
www.hachette.co.uk

For Darley and Adele,
with all my love

Prologue

The Lord shall smite thee with madness

Deuteronomy 28:28

2012

'Hello! Are you not listening to me? My little girl has been missing for three *fucking* days. I think that might be worth your attention, don't you?'

Michael Flynn was so angry he was almost spitting his words down the phone. Over six feet tall and with a heavy build he was a big man and, as everyone in the room knew, he was more than capable of great violence. He was paying them for their expertise, which they currently seemed to be lacking in. In fact, they were irritating the arse off him with their stupidity.

'Her mother is giving me serious grief, and that alone is a fucking bugbear. I need to know where she is, people! So I think you lot had better get me the information I need before I start to think you're all mugging me off. I know she isn't exactly what you might call a wilting fucking violet and, believe me, when I locate her I will personally launch her into outer space for this. But I want her found. You are the *Filth* – this is what you fucking do! You locate errant fuckers. So you had better start doing it quickly. I am not a man who is known for his patience, and I have a very low threshold for idiocy.' He slammed down the telephone.

Jamie Gore listened to his boss rant at the policemen in his employ. Everyone knew that Jessie Flynn, Michael Flynn's daughter, was about as dependable as a Nigerian marriage broker; therefore, she held no importance whatsoever to anyone, especially to the police. She could get away with anything – from possession of any substance, including a bomb, should she ever purchase one, and that was all thanks to her father's influence. He'd paid the Old Bill handsomely to *ignore* her over the years; now suddenly he wanted them to make her a priority? Bit of a turnaround there. He spoke up. 'Look, Michael, with all due respect, you know your daughter as well as we do, she could be fucking anywhere. She goes on the missing list regularly . . .'

Michael Flynn was dark-haired and dark-skinned, he had the Irish gypsy in him there was no doubt about that. He was a handsome fuck, and his good looks were part and parcel of his persona. Both men and women were attracted to him, and he had always used that to his advantage. His startling blue eyes were now trained on Jamie Gore, and the man felt the first prickle of uneasiness at the intensity of his gaze.

'You having a fucking laugh, Jamie? You think I brought you lot here for nothing? My old woman is like a fucking lunatic! My little Jessie is on the missing list! No one, and I mean *no one*, has seen her for *three fucking days*! I know she is a lazy mare, I know she lives on her own fucking time-zone, and I know she is the biggest pain in the rectum since records began. But she is still my baby girl. So my advice would be to fucking well find her! Track her down, let me know where she is so I can deliver her back to her mother and then we can go home.'

Michael looked around the room, and he knew that every bloke in there was thinking the same thing: Jessie Flynn was probably tucked up in bed with another lowlife, another fucking no-mark she had picked up on her travels. She was a trollop of the first water, having been sleeping with the enemy since she was fourteen years old. He wondered how many of his workforce had serviced her at one time or another. She was a beautiful-looking girl, with the morals of a fucking alley cat. It didn't matter – he still wanted to know where she was. More to the point, her mother *needed* to know. Josephine was deeply concerned for her daughter's whereabouts.

Jessie was not a girl you could lose sleep worrying about all the time – she stumbled from one disaster to the next (usually the disaster was a man), but she always seemed to come out on top. He made sure of that. She came home at some point and then her mum would be so pleased to see her there would be no retribution of any kind. That was the trouble. Michael personally believed that his daughter needed a fucking good slap, but his wife would never agree. If Jessie murdered the neighbours with an axe and it was caught on CCTV, his wife would say, 'Well, they must have upset her.' Jessie could do no wrong in her eyes.

He too had indulged her once, when she had been small and still lovable, but that had changed the moment she discovered the power of her sexuality and the harm it could bring to the father she had once adored. He had given up trying to force any kind of fatherly rules or regulations on her. Jessie wouldn't listen to him anyway – she was a girl after his own heart in many respects. She did exactly what she wanted, and she did that with the maximum amount of energy she could muster. But she was a whore, and that fact broke his heart. Not that he could ever let that be known – in his game that would be seen as a weakness.

He sighed heavily. The men in this room were some of the hardest men in the South East; they *all* worked for him and were pleased to do so. He was a hard man, everyone knew that, but he prided himself on being a fair man, a decent man in some respects. These were men who were at the top of their particular games, and he used their nous and their instincts for his own ends – and made sure that they earned a good fucking wedge at the end of the day. Michael Flynn was a one-off; in his world he was a man who was not only feared, but who had also earned the respect of his peers, and who had managed to rise to the top without treading on too many people's toes. He had embraced his partners in crime, and made sure that they earned enough to prevent them coveting what he had. Now he had the partnership and the major earn from every Face in the country – well, in Europe, if truth be told. And the men he dealt with owed him, respected him for his achievements, and did not begrudge him his percentage because, without him, most of them would never have got as far as they had. He had worked his way up the ladder, realising early on that to keep on top you had to have a loyal and willing workforce, and that if you wanted to earn a place of importance in the criminal world, you also needed a very lucrative and honestly run legitimate business, as well as the wherewithal to not only invest heavily in other people's businesses, but to also be able to offer them a modicum of protection should Lily Law decide to investigate them at any time.

Well, Michael basically owned Lily Law, and it was not fucking cheap. He paid out a serious fucking wedge to the Old Bill, and they, for their part, did fuck-all the majority of the time to earn their crusts. It was one of the things that really irritated him, but they were what his old partner Patrick Costello used to call a 'necessary evil'. He had worked hard to get them in his pocket, and many of them had *him* to thank for their additional wages, nice cars, and kids' educations. Because of that, he held all the major cards: he could negotiate a prison sentence, he could make certain charges disappear, he could fit up anyone who he felt was getting a bit too big for their boots. It was a win-win situation. No one had ever had that much power over the law before. He had orchestrated that by himself, and now he was a man who was settled at the top. No one in his game would ever feel the urge, or indeed the need, to try and take his place and run his businesses. He was too shrewd for all that old fanny. His legit businesses were huge earners as well – he could explain away everything he owned. In short, Michael Flynn was virtually untouchable.

But now he was looking out at the men he knew as friends, not just as business associates, and he felt the prickle of shame wash over him. His daughter going AWOL was not something they saw as in their remit to sort but, as they were on his payroll, they had no option but to listen to him and offer their help in any way they could.

His Jessie's reputation had preceded her as always. They all assumed she was drugged and/or drunk out of her head somewhere, because that was what she was famous for. Twenty-two years old, and she was already a legend in her own lunchtime. She had been excluded from every school he sent her to, and instead she had embraced the underworld from an early age – from the drug dealers, to the scumbags who hung around the council estates, the burglars, gas-meter bandits with homemade tattoos – she spent her time in filthy squats until he brought her back home to her mother time and again. After cracking open a few heads, of course.

Michael had given up on her completely by the time she was sixteen. Once he had found her naked on a filthy mattress in a condemned house in Hackney with a junkie three times her age, who had given her not only a black eye but a dose of gonorrhoea as well. He had known then that he had no choice but to step away from her emotionally. He loved her, but he could not get through to her. Nevertheless, he had gone back and almost kicked the man to death for doing that to his baby. He had vented his anger, looking around at how she had been living. She was available to any man who tipped her the wink and who she thought would anger her father, and bring him shame.

He didn't understand it. She had had a home that was not only full of love for her, but was beautiful. She had everything she could have desired: the chance to go to a good school, and a good life ahead of her. But, from fourteen years of age, she had made it her business to find the lowest of the low, and make a home there for herself with them, and she had broken her mother's heart in the process. Unlike her father,

her mother still felt her daughter could turn her life around, redeem herself. But Michael refused to get involved any more; she was his Achilles heel, his only real weakness. Her antics were common knowledge in his world, and it was only his status that stopped people from gossiping openly about her.

He had tried everything, and she had fought him every step of the way. She was his daughter, and he would protect her as much as he could but, in his darkest moments, when he heard about her latest escapades, or the police informed him she had been arrested once more, he had wished her dead, and he hated himself for that.

Seeing the suffering she caused his wife made him resent Jessie all the more. Jessie had broken her mother early on. She still cared what happened to her daughter; she hoped that she would come home one day, and it would be forgotten, and they would live a normal life together, like everyone else. Michael knew better. He just provided Jessie with the means to live her life, but at least her need of money allowed him to police her in some ways.

Jessie had given birth to a child at sixteen, but the child was no more to her than a doll she dressed up on special occasions. She left him to be brought up by her own mother. Michael loved the bones of his handsome little grandson, who had more of the Flynn family in him than whoever had been the fucking piece-of-dirt culprit. Not that Jessie had any fucking idea of her son's parentage of course; the poor child had been no more than a whodunnit and, with Jessie, that meant it could have been literally *anyone.* Oh, he'd accepted the reality of his Jessie a long time ago. He loved her, but he didn't *like* her one bit.

Now her mother was worried about her and, if he was really honest with himself, so was he. He understood her much more than she had ever realised; she was a ponce of Olympian standards, but she had never missed an opportunity to pick up her allowance. She should have been at his offices the day before to pick up the money, but she had been a no-show. That was not like his daughter at all – she craved money like a junkie craved a fix. She spent like a woman with no fucking arms – on clothes, shoes and, unfortunately, men. His Jessie never missed her cash payment; she had her credit cards as well, but he could monitor them, so she knew the value of a pound. Jessie was a druggie, a drunk and a waste of space, but she was never late for her allowance. He made sure that it was far too lucrative for her to turn down.

So where the fuck was she?

Jessie Flynn opened her eyes, and fear enveloped her.

It was pitch dark, and she was aware that she was bound, both her hands and her feet tied. For all her exploits, she had never found herself in a predicament like this. She was racking her brains to work out not only who the fuck she had upset recently, but who would have the guts to do this to her knowing who her father was. She knew, on one level, she was in serious trouble, but she was still having a problem accepting that.

She was Jessie *Flynn*, for fuck's sake! Her dad was the biggest Face in town. That had always meant she was immune to aggravation of any kind – even when she caused outrageous problems for herself, those problems were automatically negated by her father's timely intervention.

She strained her eyes to see where she was being held captive, but the darkness was total. There was nothing to see at all – just a pure blackness. She was actually truly frightened, and that shocked her. She had never felt real fear before – it was an alien concept – and she swallowed down the scream that she could feel building inside her throat. She would never let anyone know that she was scared or worried about anything. All her life she had lived behind a mask of defiance, and she was not going to let this situation freak her out.

She took a few deep breaths to calm herself; her heart was hammering in her ears, and she could hear it so loudly it was like a drum beating in the room. It bothered her more than she liked to admit. It was too quiet, that was the problem; there was no sound other than her own breathing, her own heartbeat.

Instinctively, she knew that was not a good sign. This was not a situation that she could interpret or make any sense of. She was not unused to waking up somewhere strange, without any memory whatsoever of how she had arrived there. She would often see a man asleep beside her and have no idea who he was or where she had come across him. But she would find out eventually; she would talk to them and gradually she would get the gist of how she had arrived in their bed and, somewhere in the back of her mind, she would dredge up something to explain the events of the night in question.

This was different. She was tied up and she was in pain. Her arms felt like they were being wrenched from their sockets, and her ankles were tied so tightly she couldn't feel her feet.

She felt the fear rising inside her once again, and she fought it down; whoever had done this to her would never get the satisfaction of hearing her cry out into the darkness, or calling for help. She was shrewd enough to know that, wherever she was, crying out for help would be futile. If there was any chance of being heard her mouth would have been taped shut. The silence around her was complete, like the darkness; she was not somewhere random passers-by would stumble across, let alone somewhere that noise would cause people to panic or phone the Filth. She was being held captive for some reason – she just hoped that the reason would be explained to her sooner rather than later.

She was cold, and she could smell the mustiness of the mattress she was lying on – the place was damp, so she could even be underground. The silence and the stench made her think that might be the case. She knew, deep in her guts, that she was not here for any reason that might benefit her.

She closed her eyes tightly because, once more, she was feeling the urge to shout her lungs out, however futile. She needed to use the toilet, she felt a sudden urge to open her bowels; she was coming down fast, and she could feel it. She had not eaten properly for a few days and, now that she was sobering up, she was becoming even more afraid of the dangerous predicament she found herself in. She tried to bring her hands out from behind her back, but she couldn't. They were tied together so tightly, every movement caused a burning pain. It occurred to her suddenly that she was still fully clothed, so whoever had done this to her did not seem to have touched her in a sexual way. She was not sure that was a good thing either – that would have been something she could understand, could even control. Everything in her life until now had been about using her feminine wiles to get what she wanted.

She took a few more deep breaths, but the panic lingered close to the surface. She closed her eyes tightly and tried to relax her body, but it was hard. Her arms were screaming now; she had probably been tied up for a good few hours, and her trying to move around was causing the pain. She tried to wiggle her fingers – a voice in her head was telling her to keep the circulation going. Tears formed in her eyes, and she blinked them away furiously. She was not going to show her fear to anyone, that was simply not in her make up.

This had to be a kidnapping. The thought gave her a thrill of anticipation – if that was the case then her dad would pay them and that would be it. Though she also knew her dad would never rest till he had tracked them down – not for taking her hostage, of course, but for trying to have him over. She suspected he wouldn't actually bother to pay them if it was left up to him – it was her mum who would insist. Her mum was all he cared about really, and his grandson, of course. Her son was the only saving grace Jessie had; her dad couldn't control her life, so he was determined to control his grandson's. He loved him though. She saw that, and it hurt her.

She managed to turn over on to her belly, and that eased the pain in her shoulders. She had never in her life felt so vulnerable or so alone, and she was craving a drink. Not water – though even that would be welcome. No, she was craving a real drink. She needed a large vodka or a Scotch, just something to take the edge off. Valium at least would help her relax and work out what she was going to do. It occurred to her that for the first time in years she was stone-cold sober, without the crutch of either chemicals or alcohol.

She heard the scraping sound of a heavy door opening somewhere in the distance outside the room where she was tied up like a kipper, and she felt the unmistakable prickle of genuine terror.

Detective Inspector Timothy Branch of the Serious Crime Squad was annoyed even though he had always known that this day would come. He was not a fool – no matter what Michael Flynn might think. He had been aware from the first moment he had taken the man's money that he was, to all intents and purposes, now owned by him. He would be called on at some point to repay the favour; he had just not expected it to come so fucking soon. In fairness, this actually was a police matter – a missing daughter was not something to take lightly. He shouldn't feel so angry about being summoned into his offices by Flynn, or about the man demanding, in a loud and threatening manner, that he wanted results.

'Take the opportunity to earn your fucking keep, you useless fucking ponce!'

That hurt. Timothy knew when he was being taken for a cunt, and the man he was dealing with was not someone who could be palmed off with legal jargon, more's the pity. He knew he had to deliver, and deliver sooner rather than later.

Michael Flynn was like a man demented. 'She disappeared three days ago, Branch, and I have it on good authority that she was last seen in a pub in Upney. She scored some coke and grass, and she left around midnight, and no one has seen her since.'

Timothy Branch nodded, as if he was in full accord with everything he was hearing. His carefully modulated pseudo-posh voice was like a red rag to a bull, though he wasn't aware of that just yet. He was a snob, and a social-climbing arsewipe who had no qualms about taking money on the side to bankroll his wife's pretentious upper-middle-class lifestyle, and who had believed that his expertise would never be compromised by his association with a known villain. His stupidity and his arrogance were exactly the reasons why he was on Michael's payroll in the first place; without someone like Flynn on his side, he had no chance of hitting the big time.

'I will put out a missing persons report, Michael, but, in all honesty, she will probably turn up as per usual, we both know that.'

Michael looked at the man he had been paying handsomely for so long, and it occurred to him that he had been paying out a decent wedge to a complete fucking moron. Timothy *had* to have known that at some point he would be called on to deliver, that the day would come when he would be asked to do a favour of some description. Now he was being asked to do something that he should be doing *anyway* – look for a missing girl – but he was not really demonstrating the level of motivation that Michael's regular payments should have guaranteed. In fact, he was not showing the least bit of willing, and that alone was irritating. He was showing no consideration of how much he had pocketed over the last few years, or how his rise through the ranks of the police force had been orchestrated by the same man he was now attempting to mug off.

Michael Flynn was not in the mood for this kind of aggravation; the last few hours had been a revelation to him as to how deeply his daughter and her fucking lifestyle had impacted on him personally. He was now being treated like a fucking tourist by a no-mark who relied on him for a second wage, and that was not something he could allow. 'You useless fucking cunt! All the money I have slipped your way, and you treat me like a fucking greebo! Like a fucking no one!' He dragged the terrified man from his chair, savouring his fear, and his dawning comprehension of exactly who he was dealing with. 'I expect the best, because that is what I have paid for over the years, and you are two seconds away from making me regret my decision to put you on my payroll. A decision that I can easily rectify – and that, my friend, would of course mean that you would have to return every penny I fucking shoved your way over the years. You avaricious useless fucking ponce! I hate dishonest Old Bill more than anything. If I ever get a capture it had better be from one I couldn't buy off. That's an honest nicking, you see, and I could swallow that. But Filth like you are only there to do what I fucking request of them.'

Timothy Branch lay on the floor of his own office, with his arms over his head to protect himself from another onslaught from Michael Flynn. He was well aware that everyone in the station could hear the conversation and would know exactly what was going on. He was waiting for the beating that he was convinced was going to come. He had made a mistake of Olympian standards, and he could not rectify the situation because he had brought it on himself. He had honestly believed that being a policeman, a *senior* policeman, would have guaranteed him immunity from this sort of behaviour. He had assumed that Flynn, for all his money and reputation, would have thought long and hard before he raised his hand to a member of the police force. But he had been very wrong. Flynn's power went far deeper than he had ever anticipated. The fact that no one had come to his aid was a real lesson for Timothy Branch. The outer offices were now deathly quiet; everyone out there was listening to this exchange and he knew his humiliation was now complete.

Then the office door opened with a bang, and Chief Superintendent Dennis Farthing came into the room like an avenging angel, all cigarette smoke and false teeth. Timothy Branch felt relief washing over him, until he heard the man say with mock sincerity, 'A sorry business this, Michael, but don't you worry, my friend – I will have my best men on it, of that you can be assured. Jessie is a priority, I guarantee.'

Michael Flynn felt the anger seeping out of him. This was what he wanted – a promise that everything that could be done to find his daughter was being done. His wife needed that, she needed to know that Jessie was being treated as a priority, that he was using his considerable power to locate her child. But, deep down in his gut, he knew that something was not right, that this was far more serious than anyone really thought. Jessie never missed a pay day, and she never went twenty-four hours without ringing her mother. Even drugged out of her brains, she still rang her mum for a chat, because she knew that if she didn't get in touch Josephine would worry herself sick. Jessie knew that her mum needed to hear from her, that she wasn't a well woman in her own way. It was Jessie's only real saving grace that she rarely let a day go by without a call to her mum.

Now it was almost four days since anyone had seen or heard from her. If Michael was honest, he was feeling more uneasy by the hour.

Josephine Flynn was having trouble breathing. It was a warning before she got one of her panic attacks, so she sat down in her chair and tried to regulate her breaths. She hated herself for her weakness, but she had always suffered with her nerves. She could feel her heartbeat slowing down, and she closed her eyes in relief.

She savoured the calmness that washed over her, the feeling of normality and the knowledge that she had conquered her demons, if only for a little while. She opened her eyes slowly, and looked around sadly; she knew she should motivate herself, tidy up, *do* something constructive. But she wouldn't because she never did. No matter how many times she convinced herself that she was ready to finally do it, to finally take control of her life and her surroundings, when it came to the crunch, she *never* did anything that made a real difference.

She noticed that the curtains were open; Michael must have snuck in and opened them while she was sleeping. She knew that if he had not opened them she wouldn't have bothered. She liked them closed, she liked to shut out the world, the *real* world. Michael always argued that they had such wonderful views – all farmland and no other houses in sight. He thought that would make her feel better, make her feel easier in herself. But he didn't understand that the view outside the windows was irrelevant, she had no interest in it whatsoever. She had no real interest in anything other than her immediate surroundings.

She got up slowly, and went to her dressing table. Michael had left her a pitcher of fresh water, and she smiled at his kindness. She poured a glass out for herself, and then she meticulously counted out her medication. She swallowed the pills quickly, comforted by the feel of them in her mouth as she forced them inside her with huge gulps of the fresh water her husband knew she needed. She felt better immediately; she had taken her first step into the day, a day that was as fraught for her as every other day in her life.

She went back to her chair, and settled herself down again. Everywhere she looked was cluttered – piles of photographs, newspapers, or used jars. Shoes were piled in the corners, and her clothes were strewn all over the floor. Rubbish was kept in bin bags, and she had placed them lovingly against the walls. The clutter was her armour against the world – it made her feel safe. She could look at something that she had kept for reasons known only to herself, and she could smile in remembrance of a memory long gone – a memory no one cared about but her.

Now her Jessie was gone. No word at all, and Josephine knew in her gut that something bad had happened to her daughter.

She opened up her make-up bags which were never far from her side and, pulling a large mirror towards her, she began the long and painstaking artistry she used to create the image that allowed her to face the world as best she could.

Michael Flynn was tired. He had not slept properly for two days and, even though he had not believed it possible, he was deeply concerned for his daughter's safety. She was selfish, greedy, manipulative and devoid of any real morals, and that was exactly why she never failed to turn up for her allowance. She had very expensive tastes, and she liked to be able to indulge herself; she wasn't as low rent as she made out.

She was never off his radar no matter what anyone else might think or what he might let them think. She was always going to be his baby. She was a girl who made it very difficult to love her, who knew exactly how to rattle his cage. It was something she had made her mission in life; hurting him was something she enjoyed so much she had even left her own son behind in her pursuit of his unhappiness. He had taken on responsibility for the child along with his wife although, to his daughter's chagrin, it had not been a chore for them. In fact, it had been almost like a rebirth for them both, inasmuch as they had adored their grandson from the moment he had entered the world. Jessie, on the other hand, had not been miraculously changed by giving birth to her own flesh and blood, as her mother had been convinced would be the case. Instead she had abandoned her little son at the first available opportunity, and she had drifted in and out of his life ever since. Michael hated her for that, even more than he hated her for how much she had hurt her poor mother.

Jessie thought she herself was the only person worth a

day's interest. But that was his daughter – an arrogant fucker, who had no moral compass whatsoever. She saw everyone around her as someone to be used for her own ends, and that included her own child, her own flesh and blood. Michael had been forced to accept that about her over the last few years and it had not been as easy as everyone had believed. It had been very hard for him. Because he had loved her with a vengeance. She was his baby girl, his only child. She was also a selfish, vicious, bitter, manipulative, avaricious, devious, two-faced ponce, whose only interest in life seemed to be getting drunk, drugged, laid, or a combination of all three. She had been the apple of his eye once, and now she was someone he had to live down on a daily basis. It was only his standing that stopped him from hearing the real gossip concerning her, and he knew that was a good thing because if she pushed him too far, he knew he might finally do something to get himself nicked.

He was staring at the phones in his office, hoping that whoever had her would just ring him up and let him know she was OK. Then, once he had paid them off, and his Jessie was accounted for, he would hunt the bastards down like the fucking rabid dogs they were, and personally make sure that they never again put any other parents through such agony. He would take great pleasure in ensuring they disappeared from the world around them in as much pain and terror as physically possible.

He was taking his daughter's disappearance personally; whoever was behind it was trying to prove a point. This was about him. It had to be. Inside his head, he could not help wondering if his daughter was a part of it all. She was capable of anything, as he knew better than anyone. But he hoped that he was wrong. For all that had happened, he hated to think she was capable of trying to rip him off and, if she *was* trying to do that, he would personally make sure that everyone involved would be made aware of how irritated their actions had made him, his Jessie especially. If she *was* involved, that would be the last straw, and he would have to take drastic action against her.

There were some things that could never be forgiven. Some things that could finally cause a body to turn on their own.

Jessie woke up once more, and she was immediately aware that there was somebody else in the room with her.

It was still pitch dark. Still cold and damp. She knew that she couldn't be the first to speak – her dad had always told her: when in doubt, shut your trap. If you kept your own counsel, eventually the others would feel the need to explain themselves, and he had been right. She had learnt that the hard way. So she didn't say a word.

She could hear the shallow breathing of whoever was now in the room with her and, more to the point, she knew that they could also hear her breathing. They would know that she wasn't asleep any more. She was very much awake. It was a terrifying experience. She had never once, in her whole life, needed to worry about someone else's reactions to her or her antics. No matter what had happened to her, no matter what she had said or done, she had always known that her father would be in the background, and the reason why she would ultimately be safe no matter what she did.

No one was willing to confront her because that would mean they would have to deal with *him*. That was something no one in their right mind would even consider. It was her get-out-of-jail-free card, the reason she pushed everything as far as she could. It was why she had been able to fuck her father over again and again. He had always made sure that she was untouchable. She had thought she was invincible because of her father – it was something she relied on. No matter what she did, no matter how much trouble she had landed herself in, her father had always made sure that it had all gone away. It was something she had seen as another of his weaknesses, as another reason to do whatever she wanted. After all, no matter what she did, he bailed her out. He made sure that her actions did not infringe on his lifestyle in any way and that was what it was all about. She knew his reputation was everything to him. Well, she was his daughter, his only child, and she had made damn sure that his reputation as a parent was worth nothing. She had enjoyed that, enjoyed the knowledge that her actions had undermined him, and made him see that he was not worth anything really.

But now she didn't know what to think. She would have to play this one by ear. She was in serious trouble. Whoever was behind this was not someone who cared about her or her family name.

She was so scared. She wasn't alone in this darkness, and she knew that she wasn't going anywhere anytime soon.

Josephine Flynn looked at her little grandson and smiled. He was beautiful – dark-haired and blue-eyed – his grandfather's double. He even had Michael's mannerisms. It was uncanny considering Jessie had no idea who had fathered him. Josephine believed that Michael's genes were so strong they had cancelled out any that the culprit contributed. She hoped so, for the child's sake; his father could be anybody – that was the honest truth. Jessie had only had the child because an abortion was out of the question as far as her father was concerned. It was also the only thing that would make her mother turn against her daughter. Still, Josephine liked to think, in her lighter moments, that her daughter wouldn't have been capable of doing something so heinous.

Jessie knew how she had struggled to have *her*. She had lost all her other children – some even after Jessie's birth. A child, Josephine believed, was God's gift, and to refuse such a wonderful offering was beyond forgiveness. So Jessie had calmed down, stopped her drinking and drug-taking for a while, and she had brought this handsome gorgeous boy into the world. Jessie had then walked out of her own child's world when he was two days old; she had given him over to her parents without a backward glance. That had hurt Josephine more than anything else her daughter had done, even if she was happy to take him on. Jessie had only been sixteen, and Josephine had hoped that giving birth might have made her daughter grow up, start to understand that all actions had their own set of consequences. But she had been wrong, very wrong – if anything, it had just made her daughter worse.

Jessie had not even bothered to name her own child, and that, for Josephine, summed up the whole situation. So she had named him herself – Jake – and Jessie had not voiced an opinion either way.

Jake was six years old now, but he wore clothes for an

eight year old. He was bright as a button, already reading and writing well beyond his years, and showing every sign of being academic. Well, he had not inherited that from his mother! Jessie had always been a poor student – not because she wasn't clever, but because she was lazy. Jessie had always taken the path of least resistance. Josephine blamed herself; they had waited so long for Jessie to come along, and she had ruined her from day one. She regretted that now. Her mother had been right all those years ago. She had warned her that Jessie was a girl who needed to be chastised, who had a strong will that needed to be curbed.

Michael, in fairness, had allowed her free rein with Jessie's upbringing. He had never forced his own opinions on her where the child was concerned, even when she had known he had every right to call the shots. Michael loved her too much – he always conceded to her and her wants. He adored her, and she loved him all the more for that, because she knew that her problems would have made a lesser man run away as fast as his legs would carry him. But her Michael had never once made her feel anything other than cared for and cherished.

She watched as her grandson looked around her cluttered bedroom, and she waited for what she knew was coming.

'It's very dark in here, Nana. Why don't you come into the garden with me? You could push me on my swing if you liked.' The hope was in his voice, as always.

Josephine smiled sadly. 'That's what we have Dana for, Jake. She's much younger than Nana and she can run after you. How about after your swing, we have dinner with Granddad, and then we can all play a game together?'

Jake Flynn shrugged; it was no more than he had expected. 'OK. Will my mummy be coming to see me soon?'

It was a loaded question, and one he asked occasionally when he remembered he had a mummy. Josephine swallowed down the sadness inside her as she answered him brightly, 'You'll see her soon. You know that she is *very* busy. But as soon as she gets some time off from work, she will come straight here to see you.'

Dana O'Carroll was a good nanny – she knew when to intervene and, grabbing the child's hand, she said loudly in her thick Irish brogue, 'Come on now, Jake, let's go and play, shall we? Your nana needs to sort out a few things.'

Josephine watched them as they left the room, and she closed her eyes in distress. Pulling herself from her chair, she looked at herself in the full-length mirror that Michael had bought for her all the way from France. It was very old, and had cost a small fortune. She loved it. She saw a very beautiful woman, well dressed with perfect make-up, and sad green eyes. She didn't look her age, and her figure was still to be envied. Her thick blond hair had to be coloured now; a girl came every month and saw to that, her nails, and her waxing. She had always been a woman who had looked after herself in that respect. She suspected she could still turn a few heads – that's if she ever left the house, of course – and she knew that Michael was proud of her. He had always made her feel like the only woman in the world, and he still treated her like a queen.

If only Jessie had tried to understand him, meet him halfway even, she knew they would not be in this situation. But Jessie always had to have the last word, and had understood that, because of her mother's problems, she had the upper hand. Jessie hated that her mother's world was so small, and she blamed her father for everything that had happened. No matter how hard Josephine had tried to explain the truth, Jessie had not believed her. Now she was terrified that her daughter had taken up with someone who had harmed her, hurt her little girl in some way.

Jessie had a knack for finding that type of person – men who used her, who treated her like she was nothing and discarded her without a backward glance. Men who she sought out, and who she paid for, bankrolled with her father's money, and who she knew would make him angry because she was throwing her life away just to hurt him. Now, it seemed she had finally picked the wrong one – a man who she couldn't control.

It had been too long. Her Jessie never went a day without talking to her – whatever she thought about her father, she loved her mother. They were very close, and it was only the knowledge that she would find it hard if she didn't see or hear from her little girl that had stopped Michael from sidelining his Jessie for good. He felt it would do her good to have to earn her own keep, and see what the world was like without his name to protect her; Josephine had argued that if he did that she would be in danger of losing her altogether. Her real fear was that Jessie would end up on the streets, selling herself to whoever for enough money to get stoned. Now she wondered if he had been right all along, and a short, sharp shock, as he put it, might have done Jessie some good.

She picked up her favourite rosary. It had been a present

from Michael on their wedding day – it was not expensive, it was very plain, made from olive wood, but it meant the world to her.

She kissed the Cross of Christ, and blessed herself quickly. Then she walked from her bedroom into her large sitting room. There she knelt down before the crucifix that dominated the room, and she began the first decade of the rosary. She normally enjoyed the Joyful Mysteries but, since Jessie's disappearance, she was now concentrating on the Sorrowful Mysteries. She could feel the despair that Mary, the Mother of Jesus, must have felt when her son had been taken from her. All she wanted, all she was praying for, was a phone call. Just something to let her know her daughter was safe.

'Is he fucking sure? How are we supposed to plot his daughter's last movements? I mean, in all honesty, where would we start? She could have been literally anywhere.' Marcus Dewer was genuinely perplexed. He was also feeling worried – like many of Michael's workforce, he was guilty of having known Jessie Flynn in a biblical sense. If he was honest, on more than one occasion. Now she was on the missing list, and he was terrified that Michael would find that out. Like most people, he believed she was on the nest somewhere, drugged out of her brains and oblivious to all the aggro she was causing.

Jamie Gore shrugged. 'It is what it is, Marcus. She likes this part of Brixton because she can score here. So let's get parked, and start asking round.'

Marcus sighed, and parked the BMW neatly. He looked

at the photo of Jessie; she was a pretty girl, there was no doubt about that.

'This is fucking stupid! Everyone knows there's a price for information on her. The whole of the Metropolitan Police are scouring the Smoke. So what we are supposed to find out I don't know.'

Jamie Gore secretly agreed with his friend, but he was too shrewd to say that. 'Marcus, do me a favour, will you? Shut the fuck up, and do what the man is paying us for. Who knows – we might stumble on to something accidentally. In fact, I think we should poke our heads into a few skag houses. You know what junkies are like – the fucking Third World War could erupt and they wouldn't even notice until they ran out of heroin. So there's a chance, albeit a very slim one, that they might not know about her being missing. And don't forget, Marcus, if we find out something important, we will be greatly rewarded.'

Marcus nodded, but he wasn't convinced. He was more worried that they would be the ones to find her, overdosed and dead as a doornail. *That* wasn't the kind of news he would relish giving Michael. It was what the majority of people believed had happened to Jessie Flynn – they were waiting for her body to turn up, and no one wanted to be the one who found it.

Jessie was weak. The man who was holding her only gave her the minimum of water; she was always thirsty, although the hunger wasn't so acute any more. She couldn't work out how long she had been down here in the darkness. She seemed to sleep a lot, so she guessed that he was putting something in the water to keep her sedated. At least he had untied her hands although she was still manacled around her ankles, and the chain was attached to an iron hoop on the wall behind the mattress. She was still in darkness – the only time there was any light was when he brought her water. He had a torch, but it blinded her, so she covered her eyes. She had a feeling he wasn't interested in her seeing him anyway. She played the game – that was all she could do.

He had still not spoken to her, and that frightened her more than anything else. She had threatened him, abused him, told him that her father would be searching for her, and he had not reacted in any way. He had shone the torch and shown her an old chamber pot where he expected her to do her business. She had railed at him, cursed him, but there had been no reaction.

She had woken up earlier because she could hear him moving around outside the door. She swallowed down the rising panic that was getting harder and harder to control. She didn't know what she was supposed to do, what he wanted from her. She could smell her own faeces, could feel the dirtiness of her body and clothes. She had waited for him to rape her, or assault her, but he had done nothing. He brought her some water at regular intervals, and he emptied the chamber pot at some point, and he had also left her a blanket. She could only assume he had kidnapped her, and he was waiting for her father to pay the money. He would pay it – her mother would make sure of that. But why was it taking so long?

She kept thinking of every serial-killer film she had ever watched, every book she had ever read about men who abducted young women, and tortured and raped them. Only in the books and the films, there was always a detective on their trail who you knew would eventually save the girl and kill the maniac; you knew that because the detective *always* solved his case no matter how obscure the clues. The maniac would also often be in direct contact with the police, would be taunting them and, as the reader or viewer, you would be cheering on the detectivc, knowing all along that he or she would eventually work it out. But that was not real life. She worried that he was going to come in at some point and really hurt her, and she was so terrified about that.

Her initial arrogance was gone; she was not only stone-cold sober for the first time in years, she was also acutely aware that she wasn't ready to die. She loved her son in her own way, and she wanted to see him again, see her mum, be hugged by her once more. She had to wonder if this was something to do with her dad – he had stepped on a lot of people's toes. Surely she should have been out by now if it was about money? What if this man was holding her as a grudge against her father? Or what if he was a serial killer and her father's name and reputation meant nothing to him?

She pushed her fist into her mouth to stop herself from screaming; she still had enough strength left to make sure she didn't show him her fear. She wouldn't show him how scared she was until she absolutely had to. She would beg him on her knees if that was what he wanted, she would do whatever she needed to try and get herself out of this situation.

She pulled the blanket around her, and she forced herself to try and think rationally. But it was hard to concentrate – the darkness was so intimidating, so final. And the man who held her was still an enigma. Until he spoke to her or acknowledged her presence in some way, she knew she couldn't even begin to understand exactly what she was dealing with. She felt the tears running down her face, and she didn't even try to stop them.

'Come on, Jake, eat your dinner up.'

Michael winked at his grandson, as always amazed at the love the child could engender in him. Considering the circumstances of his birth, Michael had always been in awe of the feelings he had for this child.

'I'm eating my dinner, Granddad, so I can grow up big and strong like you.'

Michael sighed. He remembered when his Jessie had been like this little lad, innocent, trusting and eager for her parents' company. All that had changed when she was fourteen. Overnight she had become a different person – difficult, awkward, full of hate. Everyone said it was teenage angst, that she would grow out of it. But she hadn't, she had gradually got worse, and she had become out of control. Now she was missing, and he didn't know what more he could do.

Book One

We will either find a way, or make one

Hannibal

Do not trust in extortion or take pride in stolen goods,
though your riches increase, do not set store by them

Psalm 62:10

Chapter One

1979

Michael Flynn looked around the dingy offices with interest. This was where Patrick Costello, the legendary East-End Face, orchestrated the serious earns for the Costello family. Up to now, Michael had been working for one of Patrick's collectors – a ponce named Jimmy Moore – but what he really wanted was to be in the thick of the Costello business. He knew he could learn a lot from Patrick Costello.

Patrick Costello was now nearly fifty, although he looked younger than his contemporaries. He had done a nine-year stretch in his twenties, and he had used his time inside wisely. He had been in for murder and, as a lifer, he had been afforded the opportunity to better himself, and he had taken advantage of everything that was open to him. He had taken up body-building, and he had also gained himself a degree in English Literature, understanding, for the first time in his life, the power that education could bring.

Since his early release, Patrick had a different approach to the Life. He had done his time, and he was not about to make that mistake again. Now he made sure that everything he was involved in could never be traced back to him. He paid his people to ensure that they would take the fall if everything was to go pear-shaped, and he paid well.

His brother Declan was just five years younger than Patrick, but he was like a big, overgrown schoolboy, all jokes and friendly camaraderie. He had a wide, open face that screamed honesty and shielded from most of the world the fact that he was capable of great violence. Coupled with the fact that he never forgot or forgave anything he might see as an insult, he was a very dangerous individual.

Declan was the one that most of the Costello workforce dealt with on a daily basis, and that was how both brothers liked it. Declan enjoyed issuing orders more than planning operations, and Patrick was more than happy for him to do that, while Declan, in turn, was happy to let his older brother make the big decisions and decide where and how they would invest their money. *He* couldn't organise a Papal Mass in the Vatican on his own.

Patrick was the head of the family. He made sure that everything ran smoothly, orchestrating every move that the Costellos made. He had a few men on his own personal payroll too. They had started out in the family business but, seeing their capabilities, Patrick had offered them a new path. When they came into his *personal* employ, they then saw the side of the Costello family business that was as lucrative as it was dangerous. Patrick trained them up personally, and they answered to him and no one else. The main criteria for working alongside him was the ability to keep everything on the down-low and if the person *did* get a capture, for whatever reason, they were expected to take the consequences involved without question. They knew they would be well compensated for their trouble.

Now Michael Flynn was getting the chance of a face-to-face with Patrick Costello and he didn't intend to waste it.

He could hear Patrick coming up the stairs, back to his office, and he waited patiently for him.

Patrick came through the doorway beaming. 'Sorry about that, son, but you know the old adage – no rest for the wicked, eh?'

Michael grinned in response.

Patrick stood by his desk for a few moments looking at Michael intently.

Michael held the man's gaze easily, but it unnerved him nonetheless. Patrick Costello looked more dangerous than ever in his own domain. Michael could see that Patrick's reputation as a man who was not to be crossed was more than warranted. Michael had never in all his life felt so vulnerable or so nervous. But he kept his emotions in check.

Patrick smiled suddenly. 'Don't be nervous of me, Michael. I have been hearing good things about you, son, and I want you to come and work for me – personally.'

Michael was so amazed at what Patrick Costello had said he couldn't even answer him.

Patrick smiled at Michael. He could see not just the amazement but also the sheer *want* in the boy's eyes. He had chosen well. Michael Flynn was much younger than any of the other men he had taken on, but the lad had already established himself as a good earner. Even more importantly, he already had a reputation as a young man who never discussed anything with anyone.

Patrick had been impressed by Michael's dealings with Jimmy Moore. *He* was a useless cunt, who was hated by everyone he came into contact with – even his relatives. He bullied everyone around him, thinking he could get away with it because his uncle, Terry Gold, was a well-known Face. Yet Michael Flynn – who Patrick Costello knew was more than capable of taking care of himself, especially when it came to a runt like Jimmy Moore – had been sensible enough to keep his cool, do his job. He'd also kept his mouth shut about Jimmy Moore's skimming – something Patrick intended to have a word with Declan about putting a stop to quick-sharp – until he knew exactly what the score was. That was the type of person that Patrick Costello liked to have on his side. This lad would happily work for him and, if push came to the proverbial shove, he would do his time inside with the minimum of fuss.

'I don't know what to say, Mr Costello . . .'

'Before you answer me, Michael, you need to understand something. My half of the business is very clandestine. I make sure that the serious earns are not only fucking lucrative, but also so secret that no more than two or three people have any real knowledge of the actual scam they are involved in at any given time.'

He was watching Michael intently, so Michael nodded slightly as if in total agreement. He was being sounded out – how he reacted now would be the making or the breaking of him, and would either guarantee him a place with Patrick, or see him back with Jimmy once more.

Patrick sighed, as if he was debating within himself whether Michael was worthy of his attention. 'I believe that fewer people in the know ensures the absolute integrity that serious earns demand, and I only deal with serious earns. I *know* – within hours – if anyone on my personal payroll has spoken out of turn or been foolish enough to let their mouths run away with them. I'm explaining this so you know where I am coming from, and so you know exactly what is expected of you.'

Michael still didn't say a word. If truth be told, he didn't know what to say. Instead he waited patiently for Patrick to continue.

'Declan is a fucking star. He fronts the family businesses, as you well know. But what I say now is for your ears only.'

Michael nodded firmly this time; he was giving this man his word.

'Declan, God love him, couldn't work out how to find his own cock with a detailed map and a police sniffer dog. So I have a couple of men who do the actual money side of it all and Declan does what he's good at – making sure that everything runs smoothly. Now, I am telling you all this because I trust you. I run the family and Declan takes his lead from me. I work on the more dangerous enterprises, behind the scenes, so to speak.'

Michael watched Patrick warily as he walked to the large old-fashioned filing cabinet by the back wall. Opening up the top drawer, he took out a bottle of Johnnie Walker whisky. He came back to the desk and, settling himself into his large leather chair, he poured out two generous measures of the whisky into two chipped tea cups, before passing one to Michael. Then, taking a deep drink, he carried on talking as if there had been no interruption at all. 'I like you, Michael.

I can see a great future for you. You're very young but, in your case, I see that as a good thing. I want to take you under my wing, and teach you the business that eventually you will be responsible for. I will guarantee you a fucking serious wedge, but that wedge is because if it should all fall out of bed, for whatever reason, *you* will be the one looking at a big lump. Do you understand that, Michael? If it all goes pear-shaped then you will be expected to take the fall. That is why you get the big bucks, son.'

Michael sipped at his whisky before answering. The chemical burn as it crept slowly through his body was almost welcome. He was finally understanding exactly what was being asked of him. Patrick was not even attempting to sugar-coat it. He was being brutally honest, and that meant a lot to Michael. He spoke, and sealed his fate.

'I understand what you're saying and, if you still want me, I'm in.'

Patrick grinned; it was what he had expected. He had chosen well as usual. If the boy had backed out, he would not have held it against him, but the people he recruited had to know the score from the off. He liked to be clear *exactly* what they were getting into, and *exactly* what he expected from them. Once they came onboard, he owned them.

'You're a good lad, Michael. I don't normally bring in youngsters like you, but I need someone who can understand this new world that's emerging. I hear great things about you, and I know personally that you can keep your trap shut. If you listen to me and use your loaf, the chance of getting any kind of capture is very remote. But the chance *is* there, as it is with any criminal enterprise. You need to understand that.'

Michael shrugged. 'I know the score. I appreciate that you have been so honest with me, but I knew from an early age that getting my collar felt was an occupational hazard. It goes with the territory. I am not a fool, Patrick. I know the downside to this business and, if for whatever reason I *do* get banged up, I know I will get my head round it, and do my time. As you know yourself, that's all you can do.'

If Patrick Costello had liked Michael before, now he found that he had a sneaking admiration for him as well. He had it all, this youngster – good looks and a seriously sensible attitude. Now he needed to make sure that Michael was tied to him for ever. He had to make him a party to something that would not only guarantee the boy's allegiance, but would also bind them together, give them a bond of sorts.

'Well then, Michael Flynn. Welcome aboard.'

Chapter Two

Josephine Callahan was dressed to impress; from her long, thick blond hair, styled in the latest fashion, to her high-heeled stiletto shoes, she looked every inch the part of the girlfriend of a man like Michael Flynn. He expected her to look good when he took her out, and she understood why. He was making a name for himself, and he needed a girlfriend who was his equal. She had been seeing him since she was fourteen years old. He had been nineteen then, but the age difference had never bothered anyone. Now, at seventeen, she was his in every way that mattered. They were a couple, and engaged to be married. She could not have asked for anything more. They were a match made in heaven.

Josephine's dad, Des Callahan, was a Face – not a well-known Face, not someone people were really scared of, but he wasn't a mug either. He had done seven years for a bank robbery, and he had done it without complaint which had earned him respect. It hadn't been easy for his wife and daughter when he'd been put away, though – without a regular income coming in they'd struggled, relying on the goodwill of his bosses. By the time he got out, Des had learnt his lesson. This time he planned for the future, putting his ill-gotten gains into legitimate businesses in case he was ever unlucky enough to get another serious capture. Her mum, Lana, now ran a café on the A13 and a betting office in Dagenham. They were both booming businesses these days, and her dad, although not exactly retired, was in a position where he could pick and choose his work.

Josephine was an only child, adored by both her parents, and now by Michacl, who was everything they could have wanted for her.

Tonight he was taking her to a housewarming party at Patrick Costello's. Patrick was Michael's new boss and Josephine knew how important it was for her to be accepted by the Costellos too. She loved Michael so much – she was determined to make him proud of her.

Chapter Three

Declan Costello was already feeling drunk, and he was aware that his brother Patrick would not like it. He had been drinking since the early afternoon, even though he had known that he should have arrived at the party sober as a judge. But with the information he had learnt today weighing heavily on him, it was no wonder he felt the need to seek oblivion.

He could see Patrick's wife Carmel frowning at him with her usual disgust, so he studiously ignored her. She was a royal pain in the arse, forever acting like she was something special. If she wasn't married to his brother she would be in a council flat two minutes' walk from her mother's, like most of her mates. He had never understood what his brother saw in her. She was such a fucking snob and she had no real personality. Declan wasn't exactly Mr Charisma, but at least he worked for a living. Carmel had nothing going for her except a pretty face and a large pair of knockers, end of.

Feeling her eyes on him, he decided to escape the party and made his way to Patrick's office in search of his brother and another drink.

Opening the door, he was surprised to find Michael Flynn alone inside.

'All right, Declan? Have you seen Patrick yet? He said he wanted a quick word. What a lovely drum, eh? I don't think I've ever been in a place like this before in my life. It's like something from a film.'

Declan grinned amiably. He liked young Michael Flynn. He was a good kid and talented at his job. Anyone who could put up with that ponce Jimmy Moore without trying to bail out had to have something going for them. Michael was the only person so far who had worked for Jimmy and not requested a move. Declan wouldn't fancy Jimmy's chances if it ever came to a straightener between the two, but he admired the lad for not rising to the bait. He knew his place, and that Jimmy wasn't worth any aggravation.

His brother had great plans for this young man, and he was pleased about that. Patrick had a knack of finding people who were not only astute and willing to work, but were also willing to take the flak if the need should ever arise. His older brother had no intention of ever being banged up again.

'That's exactly what I was just thinking to myself!' he lied conversationally. 'It's fucking handsome all right, Michael. Too much space for me, mate. There's about twenty acres comes with this lot. I like to be in the Smoke personally. All this country air can't be good for you!'

Michael laughed. Declan was clearly very drunk. He was a dangerous fucker if you weren't careful but, if you used your loaf and kept on his good side, he was good company. Michael had learnt the importance of giving certain people their due. That was why he rarely drank more than a few drinks in certain company, and why he made it his business to always say something nice to the people who could influence his career.

He answered craftily, 'I don't know about that, Declan, but they do say the country air makes you randy. It's all those fucking farmers' daughters – all that space and not enough geezers.'

Declan roared with very loud laughter; he did like a dirty joke.

Unlike his brother, Declan had never married. He enjoyed plenty of female company, but never felt the desire for one woman above all others. He preferred variety. He used the women who came into his life, but he was good to them and, for the few weeks that they caught his attention, he lavished his money and time on them.

'I never thought of that, young Michael! I better get around the local pubs, have a look at the strange on offer. Now, where is that lovely little girl of yours?'

Michael was pleased at the compliment; she was a real looker was his Josephine. She was a cut above the usual girls and he knew that.

Before he could answer, the door to the office opened wide and Patrick Costello made a grand entrance.

'Hello, boys, how d'you like my new house then?' Patrick looked expectantly from Michael Flynn to his brother.

Michael was about to speak when Declan broke in furiously with, 'You had to do it, didn't you, Pat, eh? I asked you not to and you still did it.' Declan suddenly looked fit to be tied.

Patrick Costello didn't reply.

Michael just stood there, unable to say a word. He didn't know what it was about anyway. It was the first time he had ever seen Declan so angry, and it seemed that Patrick sensed that as well. This outburst had come out of nowhere.

'The whole Golding family are dead, burnt to death in their beds. Except for the son – it seems he was staying overnight at his mate's. Two little girls died though. Twelve and fourteen. How must you feel, Patrick? All that mayhem for five hundred quid.'

Michael Flynn felt physically ill.

'It wasn't anything to do with me, Declan. I can only assume the man owed other people money. Let's face it, he was a fucking ponce.'

Declan laughed at his brother's arrogance. 'Who the fuck do you think you are, Patrick, eh? Well, remember, things like this have a nasty habit of coming back on you. It's called karma. And no matter what you say, how much you might deny it, I know this was your handiwork.'

He stormed out of the room.

Michael Flynn looked at Patrick Costello. Michael was white-faced, ashen, knowing that *he* had been the one who had caused such carnage.

Patrick shrugged. 'Hard lines, son. Typical fucking Golding, though, lying about his whereabouts as usual.'

Patrick could see the terror on the lad's face and, pouring him a large brandy, he gave it to him, saying, 'Get that down you, son. You're in shock. But no one knows the truth except us. These things happen occasionally. Shit happens.'

Michael gulped down his brandy.

'The man lied to me, Michael. He said they were all going away for a few days.' He sighed heavily. 'What's done is done, son. Just make sure we keep it close to our chests, OK?'

Michael nodded. He didn't know what else to do.

'I have explained the downside of the business to you, and now you are finding it out for yourself. Take my advice, son: if you want to get on in this game, you need to learn how to tune out the shit you don't need. It's a fucking tragedy, but if Golding hadn't been such a lying cunt, none of this would have happened.'

Michael was nodding, desperate to believe what the man was saying.

Patrick looked into Michael's eyes, and he said warily, 'If this is all too much for you, tell me now. We can part company, and no hard feelings. But I need to know I can count on you, Michael.'

Michael Flynn wasn't going to lose this opportunity; it was what he had dreamt of all his life. 'You can count on me, Patrick.'

The man grinned. 'I had a feeling you were going to say that!'

Michael Flynn knew then and there that he had burnt his boats. He had come into this business with his eyes open, and he had always known that people were sometimes murdered. It could happen to any of them, for a host of reasons. Just like the big prison sentence was always going to be there, hanging over his head. It was the chance you took if you chose the Life. He couldn't let an accident, a fucking misunderstanding, cloud the rest of his life. He would put it out of his mind, force it from his psyche. After all, he had only done what Patrick Costello had asked of him – that was what he was being paid to do, and that was what he wanted to do with his life. He had made his choice.

Chapter Four

'Oh, for fuck's sake, Mum, it's just a telephone. Anyone would think we were living in the Middle Ages the way you carry on. I had to get a phone put in for work, OK? But you are more than welcome to use it if you want.'

Hannah Flynn could hear the underlying annoyance in her son's voice. In the three months since he had started working for Patrick Costello he had changed drastically.

'And who would I be calling on the telephone, I ask you?'

Her voice held a questioning note that irritated her son all the more. Anyone would think she had never seen or heard of a telephone in her life. It had never occurred to him until now how few friends his mother actually had. She was only forty-one; anyone would think she was in her dotage the way she carried on.

Michael sighed heavily, forcing himself to be pleasant. 'I really don't know, Mum. But if you need the doctor, for example, or the fire brigade, you can call them. Now, if anyone rings for me, just take a message. I've left a pad and pencil by the phone, OK?'

She nodded, rolling her eyes angrily. She could hear her

son's growing impatience with her and it hurt her deeply. 'Are you coming home at all tonight?'

Michael shrugged before saying testily, 'I don't know, Mum. I keep telling you, it depends on what I have to do. But look on the bright side for once, I can always ring you now, can't I? Tell you not to wait up for me. I'm not a kid any more, Mum, for fuck's sake.'

Hannah knew when to back off. She had always prided herself on understanding her son better than he did himself. Since he had been working for Patrick Costello, Michael had become a different being. He had grown up and away from her almost overnight, and her hold over him was all but gone. He loved her, she knew that, but he didn't talk to her now, not like he used to. She knew hardly anything about his life outside the home, and that wasn't going to change. Working for Patrick Costello was like working for MI5 by all accounts. She was not happy, but she knew when to retreat.

Forcing a smile, she said generously, 'No, Michael, don't be ringing me at all hours. You get yourself off, son, and I'll see you tomorrow.'

That was what he wanted to hear. Hugging her quickly, he left the house. As she heard his car pulling away, she closed her eyes tightly in frustration. He gave her so much, and she knew that she should be grateful for that, but he was all she had. With no husband or lover, he was her everything. She had devoted her life to him, and she felt that he owed her.

Nowadays, she was nothing more than the woman who washed and ironed his clothes, and provided him with a meal whenever he wanted one. He kept his own hours, and she never knew when she would see him. This was not what she had expected from him, but she had to tread warily. He was determined to marry that young Josephine and, now he was starting to earn, she realised it wouldn't be long before he did just that.

She was losing her hold over him, and she couldn't let that happen. Not without a fight anyway.

Chapter Five

Patrick and Declan were holding court in a public house near enough to the docks to make a good meeting place, yet far enough away so the meetings didn't look dodgy. It was a great pub, and the Costellos were regular punters. Their main workforce were happy to hang out there and, as it wasn't that big, it was also easy to keep an eye on the clientele, watch the comings and goings.

Michael walked into the bar just after nine. He was well dressed for the occasion, in a slim-cut, dark blue suit, an outrageous lilac paisley shirt, open at the neck, and chunky gold cufflinks that had his initials etched on them. They had been a present from Patrick Costello and he wore them at every available opportunity.

His thick dark hair was still long, but it was now cut and styled professionally. Michael had always been aware that his good looks made women love him, and men admire him. As well as the looks and the build, he also had the added bonus of a nice disposition.

He made his way to the bar, and he was gratified to see that Patrick Costello already had a drink waiting for him. He caught sight of Terry Gold watching him intently, but he didn't react in any way. Terry had not been pleased by the turn of events and Michael's inclusion in the Costello inner circle; his nephew Jimmy had been *his* boss after all. Terry Gold was well aware of Jimmy's business practices, robbing everyone he dealt with hand over fist. Michael knew that Terry Gold was probably wondering if *he* might have mentioned that to anyone of importance. He was insulted by the man even thinking that about him. As if he would do that! He wasn't a fucking grass.

'You're looking sharp lately, Michael, I didn't recognise you when you walked in.'

Michael laughed, but he was a bit embarrassed at Patrick's words. He had changed in a lot of ways, but now he had money he could afford to look good. He felt he needed to dress as befitted his new station in life.

'Do you like it? I got it in Ilford from some Jewish geezer. It's the most I've ever spent on clothes in my life.'

Patrick laughed loudly. 'You look the dog's knob! All that old bollocks in the Bible about clothes don't make the man – they fucking do! A nice bit of clobber makes you feel good about yourself. You can wear a suit well and all, boy, you've got the build for it.'

Michael didn't know how to accept the compliment, so he took a large gulp of his whisky and soda. He had started drinking Scotch because the Costellos were whisky drinkers. But, if he was honest, he didn't really like the taste.

'You did well this week, Michael – I'm pleased.' Patrick swallowed down his drink, and motioned to the barman for another.

The juke box came on suddenly, and drowned out the

noise of the men talking. It was 'Unchained Melody' by The Righteous Brothers. Michael sighed with contentment; he loved this song. He guessed that one of the older men had put it on and, as he glanced around the packed bar, he felt a thrill that he was part of this world.

Patrick motioned with his head, and Michael followed him through the throng to the men's toilets. Inside, Patrick waited patiently for the men using the urinal to leavc. Michael noticed that they each did just that. He was impressed with Patrick's ability to get whatever he wanted.

Once they were alone, Patrick looked into the large mirror that took up half the wall and, as he smoothed his hair down, he said quietly, 'I need you to sort something out for me.'

Michael nodded. 'Whatever you need, Patrick. You know that.'

Patrick turned from the mirror. 'You're a good kid, Michael. You are going to go far.'

He faced the mirror once again, admiring himself from all angles. He had this young lad's total loyalty, he already knew that. The boy had a natural decency about him, he was a straight arrow there was no doubt.

'I need you to take out Terry Gold, Michael. He has to disappear off the face of the earth, and it has to be done as quietly and as unobtrusively as possible. No one can know that we were involved. This is just between you and me, no one else can ever know about it.'

Michael was shocked, but he knew better than to show that. Instead he looked into Patrick Costello's eyes. He could see the man searching his face for some kind of reaction. The air around them was suddenly heavy, full of menace. In this game, Michael was well aware he would be asked to prove his worth, his loyalty, time and again. He couldn't lose his nerve if he wanted to be a serious player in the Life. He had to show that he was capable of *anything* that might be asked of him. So he shrugged nonchalantly, aware that he had just made a life-changing decision.

'Consider it done.'

Chapter Six

'It's got to be something you ate, Michael.'

Josephine was genuinely concerned, and Michael hated that he had to lie to her. But ever since he had agreed to take out Terry Gold, he had been throwing up.

'Yeah, you're probably right, love.'

Josephine placed a cold flannel on his forehead. It felt good, there was no doubt about that.

'I'll get you a cup of weak tea. You lie back and rest.'

He nodded, but as he looked around her bedroom, he fought down the urge to vomit all over again. It was such a girly room with its pink paintwork and flowery wallpaper. Her kidney-shaped dressing table was painted white, and she had made pink satin curtains for it which hung in regimented pleats around the outside.

She had actually done a really good job, but he hated it and the frills and the frippery that she lived with. She loved clutter – that was just one of her little foibles. He wasn't used to it. His mother was not a feminine woman in that respect – his home had always been clean, unadorned and, in some ways, quite masculine. It had never occurred to him before but, whereas Josephine and her mum could spend hours deciding on a colour scheme or choosing a particular material, his mother had never really bothered herself with anything like that. He thought it might be something to do with the lean years they'd endured when Des was put away. They'd had so little for so long now they seemed never happier than when they were buying new bits and pieces. But it was all a bit much for him.

As much as he hated Josephine's bedroom in its girly glory, another part of him loved that she cared so deeply about such things. Her femininity was something that she gloried in and was one of the things that had attracted him to her. Josephine was a man's woman. A natural carer, she wanted nothing more from her life than to be his wife, rear his children, and look after the home he would provide for them.

He closed his eyes tightly, determined not to think about Patrick Costello's request. It was one thing to kill without realising it – another entirely when you *knew* what you were doing.

He heard Josephine come back into the bedroom. Opening his eyes he looked into her beautiful face, and he knew then and there that if he wanted to provide any kind of a decent life for her and his children, he had to man up and follow the path he had been offered. The path he had chosen.

'Go and see the priest, Josephine, set a date for the wedding.'

Josephine's eyes were stretched to their utmost; he could see the joy that was such a huge part of her personality radiating from them. Josephine could find the joy in anything, she could find the good in any situation. She was a girl who always expected the best out of everything and everyone, and he wanted to make sure that was exactly what she would always get.

'Oh, Michael, are you sure? What about your mum? You know she thinks we should wait.'

Michael laughed. 'Oh, sod my mum. We know what we want, darling. Sort it for next year. Big as you like, where you like and no expense spared.'

Josephine sat on the bed beside him and, smiling happily, she sipped at the mug of tea that had been meant for him. This wedding was what she had been longing for, and now it was finally happening.

Michael adored her and, as he listened to her chattering on about the dress of her dreams and the cake she had always wanted, he was content. He had burnt his bridges, the decision was made, and he felt much lighter in himself.

Chapter Seven

Ever since Michael Flynn had been given royal status by Patrick and Declan Costello, Terry Gold had been feeling nervous. It was just a matter of time until his nephew's skulduggery would finally come to light.

The Costellos were men of the world – they knew that an element of skimming was inevitable, that any cash business was open to a bit of creative accounting. It was what made their world go round. But Jimmy had been stronging it. Terry had told him time and again that while a few quid was deemed acceptable, a serious rob would only be frowned upon by the powers-that-be. Jimmy, though, was not a person who took kindly to any kind of criticism; he saw himself as *entitled* to everything. It was his buzz word.

Terry had his own creds where the firm was concerned: he had always been a good earner, always played it straight, more or less. He was a hard man in his own right, and his uncle's reputation was something Jimmy had played on. And Terry had let him get away with murder, because he was family. He had never envisioned that Jimmy's gofer would suddenly become the man of the moment. No one could have seen that one coming – not even Doris Stokes – and, according to his old woman, *she* knew everything.

He had been a fool, he could see that now. He had let Jimmy go too far and had even defended him. Until Jimmy had come onboard, though, Terry had never once had his credibility questioned. Not that anyone had actually accused him of anything yet, but he knew that Jimmy's reputation was a reflection on him. He had brought Jimmy into the fold, and he had failed to keep the boy under control. No one had really given a toss, until that ponce Flynn had been brought in as a worker. Jimmy had loathed everything about him on sight, from the lad's good looks to his quiet demeanour, and Michael's rep as a fighter – a fighter to be feared – had not endeared him to Jimmy either.

In fairness, Michael Flynn had never retaliated even though Jimmy had treated him like dirt, but Michael's quiet acceptance of Jimmy's bad behaviour had only made matters worse. It was an insult in itself, as if Jimmy was beneath his notice. Then, as Jimmy upset more and more people, he wouldn't take onboard the fact that, in their world, you had to know your own limits.

Eventually the Costellos would be forced to do something about Jimmy. They would have heard whispers already, especially Patrick – he had eyes and ears everywhere. Patrick Costello was the brains of the outfit. Declan had his own creds and was respected and feared by the people who worked for him, but Patrick was in a different league. There was plenty of talk about him and his private band of workers, but no one had any real information. It was all supposition and rumour, but the fact that he had now taken Flynn under his wing meant he had watched him for a good while.

Still, it wasn't Flynn who he should be nervous of – it was

Jimmy. Since Michael Flynn had been catapulted into the big leagues, it was eating at Jimmy like a cancer.

Terry Gold sighed heavily. He could hear his wife chatting away to his sister in the kitchen. He loved his sister dearly, although he wondered how the fuck she had given birth to a no-mark like Jimmy.

As he made his way to the kitchen, he caught the aroma of roast chicken, and he felt a little bit better. He loved his food and, if he had to confront Jimmy, he would be much happier doing it on a full stomach.

Linda Gold smiled at her husband as she busied herself with making the dinner. She was concerned about Terry though. He looked very worried lately, and that wasn't like him at all. She opened the oven and, as she lifted the chicken out, ready to baste it once more, she said quickly, 'Oh, I nearly forgot, Terry. Declan phoned. I said you'd call him back.'

Chapter Eight

Jimmy Moore was angry, and he wasn't a man who could hide his emotions. All this questioning of his business practices was getting on his nerves. As far as Jimmy was concerned, he did what the job required, and that was that. He might skim a little on the side, but that was just a perk of the job. At the end of the day, he still managed to deliver a decent wedge every week.

He poured himself a large glass of vodka. It had no real taste or smell, but it did the job required, and that was enough for him. He glanced around his office. It was a real shithole, but why would he care about that? It was no more than a base for him to work out of. His uncle Terry was always on at him to clear it up, make sure that there wasn't anything that could be seen as incriminating evidence hanging around. As if the Filth were ever going to come near here!

His uncle Terry was turning into a right tart lately. He couldn't see that it was the 1970s, not the fifties any more. He couldn't see that the world was changing on a daily basis. He had been Jimmy's role model all his life, but now Jimmy hated that the man he had tried so hard to emulate was, in reality, no more than a fucking dinosaur. *He* was young, he could see where the world was heading. From the punks to the skinheads, the message was as clear as a fucking bell: you had to look out for number one. There was no other choice.

He lit a cigarette, and pulled on it slowly, savouring the taste of the tobacco. He had a bit of coke in his wallet, and he was sorely tempted to have a quick toot. But his uncle would suss him out and they would end up arguing again.

Jimmy glanced at his watch; his uncle was late. It was after ten, and he had been the one to insist that Jimmy be there by nine-thirty at the latest. He sighed.

Hearing the outer door open, he downed his vodka quickly. It was strange, though – he had not heard a car pull up or seen any headlights. Normally his uncle parked right outside, it was impossible to miss him. The silly old fucker had probably parked up the road. He was paranoid lately, seeing skulduggery around every corner.

The office door opened, and Jimmy was startled to see Declan Costello's minder, Danny Briggs. Danny was a large man of West Indian origin, with dreadlocked hair, and a body-builder's physique. He was carrying a large machete and, as Jimmy registered the significance of that, he was too stunned to even try and defend himself.

Chapter Nine

'It's awful, isn't it, Mum?' Josephine was as shocked as everyone else about Jimmy Moore's death.

Lana Callahan sighed. 'Well, he was a fucker, Josephine. I hate to say it because his mum's lovely. But, be honest, he was a lairy little fucker.'

Josephine didn't answer; she was still shocked by the brutality of the murder. The local news had reported that he had received over twenty blows from a machete, and that the police were encouraging anyone who had been in the vicinity between nine and eleven p.m. the previous evening to contact them with any information.

Josephine's father had remarked at the end of the news bulletin, 'Well, that says it all, girls. The plod have more chance of arresting Bill and Ben for smoking Little Weed than catching the fucker responsible.'

'His poor mum, though.'

Lana lit a cigarette and, pulling on it gently, she inhaled the smoke. As she blew it out, she said honestly, 'It's a tragedy, all right. But he upset a lot of people with his bad attitude. Look at how he treated your Michael. He's a saint, that boy. Let's face it, Michael can have a row if needs be – and how he kept his hands off that little fucker God only knows. But that's the point, really, isn't it? Unlike Michael, Jimmy didn't have a sense of place, didn't have the savvy to know when to back off, he didn't have the brain capacity to realise that the only thing he had in his favour was his uncle. Michael swallowed his knob because he had enough sense to know that, until he earned his own creds, he had to take whatever Jimmy dished out.'

Josephine was staring at her mum now; the turn that the conversation had taken was scaring her. She didn't like Michael's name being used like that. She was frightened that Michael might be a suspect.

'Michael was with us, Mum, you know that as well as I do.'

Lana shook her head slowly in disbelief; sometimes her Josephine really was as thick as shit.

'No one's saying that, love. If you listened to me, you'd know that all I was trying to say is that your Michael has self-control. That is very important in his line of work. I think that his ability to keep his emotions in check is why Patrick Costello took him on. The Jimmy Moores of this world never really prosper, Josephine, whereas the people like your Michael are a rarity. They are reliable, dependable, see?'

Josephine smiled then, her relief almost tangible. 'I see what you mean now. For a minute there I actually thought you were going to say that Michael might have been in the frame.'

'Oh, for Christ's sake, Josephine, have a day off, will you!' Lana looked at her lovely daughter – she was a real beauty. But the girl's propensity for worrying about nothing bothered her mother. Josephine had never really come to terms with her father's sudden – albeit temporary – disappearance from their life. Though they had visited Des regularly, Josephine had never been comfortable in the prison environment. She had hated visiting him in Parkhurst and, even when Des had been sent to the open prison on the Isle of Sheppey prior to his release, she had still found it difficult to cope with her father's predicament. Even worse was remembering how rough life had been without him. Oh, they'd managed to keep a roof over their heads, but times had been tight and Lana had had to budget down to the last penny. Now, luckily, their businesses provided the Callahans with guaranteed financial security, but Lana knew Josephine had never forgotten that time. She'd never take the relative luxury they lived in these days for granted.

Now she had fallen head over heels for Michael Flynn. And, if Lana knew anything, young Michael was going to rise up to the highest echelons of the Costello firm. Her daughter needed to understand that, when you tied yourself to men like Des and Michael, you had to accept the possibility that they might be put away, and Josephine could find herself exactly where Lana had been all those years ago.

It was an occupational hazard for them, but it was hard on the woman left behind, alone with kids and an empty bed. You had to learn to deal with it, and that was basically that. Perhaps it was time she opened her daughter's eyes to the world she had chosen.

Chapter Ten

Michael was tired, and he had to stifle another yawn. It was late; the weather had turned over the last few days, and the night air was heavy with icy fog. It was bitterly cold for early October, and the Indian summer they'd been enjoying had disappeared overnight. The weather report had even said there was snow in Scotland – the best fucking place for it as far as he was concerned. He hated the cold, always had. The long nights depressed him – even as a kid he had dreaded the clocks going back an hour. You got up while it was dark, and it seemed wrong somehow. Days shouldn't begin like that, days should begin with light and sunshine. Even a weak winter sun was preferable to no sun at all.

But tonight the fog would serve a purpose. He looked around him – all he could see were the dark shapes of the trees, and the muddy track he had driven over an hour earlier.

He had thought he would be nervous, frightened, but now he'd set things in motion he had no real feelings either way. This was something that had to be done, and he had no option other than to get it over with, and get on with his life. He had already killed – a whole fucking family – even though he had not known what he was doing at the time. But he had learnt how to deal with it. Once you accepted something it was so much easier to live with – no matter how bad it might be. He had planned every step meticulously this time and, so far, it had all fallen into place. He hoped that everything else would be as easy.

He was not a fool, and he had made sure that he had every contingency in place. He had pondered this for hours on end, planned every detail, trying to work out as many different scenarios as possible. He was convinced that he was covered, no matter what might happen.

He glanced at himself in the rearview mirror, pleased at how calm he appeared. If the police should happen upon him, and ask why he was sitting alone in a car in the middle of nowhere, he had a perfect alibi ready. He had blankets, a flask of soup, and a pair of binoculars. He was a twitcher he'd claim; tell them he often slept in his car so he could get up at the crack of dawn and pursue his hobby. He even had a notebook prepared to show them, if necessary, filled with times, dates, places and what species of bird he had seen. It was probably a step too far, but he had been determined to make sure he had covered every angle. Now he just wanted to get it over with. He was bored, cold, and dying for a decent drink.

As he arched his back to loosen his muscles, and allowed himself a large, noisy yawn, he saw the glare of headlights as a car crawled slowly up the dirt road ahead of him. He relaxed back into his seat, took a long breath, and held it deep inside, until the car pulled up beside his, then he exhaled slowly.

This was it.

He got out of his car quickly, and the cold night air was enough to chase away the last vestiges of tiredness. He smiled amiably as he slipped into the passenger seat of Terry Gold's Mk IV Cortina. Michael was pleased to see that Terry had used his usual car. That would make things much easier for him.

'Brass monkeys out there, mate, I'm freezing.'

Terry smiled apologetically. 'I had a bit of trouble finding this place, Michael. Not exactly the A13, is it?'

Michael smiled, and Terry Gold was impressed at how straight and white Michael's teeth actually were.

'You got the gear then, Terry?'

Terry Gold sighed in mock exasperation. ''*Course* I have. Be a bit pointless coming all the way out here if I didn't, for fuck's sake!'

Michael laughed. Terry Gold had to be as thick as proverbial shit. There was no way in hell he would have fallen for any of this. But greed was a great incentive to so many people. When Michael had told Terry casually that, if he could lay his hands on a couple of keys of coke, he had a buyer who was new to the game, caked up with money, and who wanted the transaction to be as private as possible, Terry Gold had nearly bitten his hand off. Terry had always had one eye on the main chance, it was second nature to him.

It didn't matter that Terry suspected Michael had had a hand in his nephew's murder. Jimmy's death had been overlooked, but everyone in the know was aware that the Costellos had wanted it. Terry Gold had no choice but to swallow – what else could he do? And this was an opportunity he couldn't turn down.

'It's in the boot, Michael.'

They got out of the car together, and Terry lit himself a cigarette. Michael watched as he busied himself opening the boot, pulling up the carpet where he had hidden the three keys of coke in the space where the spare wheel should have been.

Michael shook his head. How fucking predictable could you get? The first place the Filth would look if they were to search your motor was the boot.

As Terry leant into the boot to pull the heavy bundles free, Michael slipped a small lead cosh from his coat pocket. The first blow was enough to subdue Terry and knock him out. The next fifteen blows were just insurance; there was no way this ponce was ever going to recover no matter what might happen in the next couple of hours. Michael pushed the body into the boot and slammed the lid shut. Then, whistling under his breath, he got into the driving seat and started the car. He drove it deeper into the woodland until it was impossible to drive any further.

Getting out of the car, he leant in from the driver's side and took the handbrake off. Then he used all his considerable strength to push the car, and its grisly contents, into a large, deep and extremely filthy lake. He had to wade into the freezing water and keep pushing until the car finally slipped down and disappeared out of sight into the murky depths.

Satisfied that it was gone, and that no one would know it was in there, Michael finally made his way back carefully in the darkness to his own car. His trousers and shoes were already hampering him and, opening the boot of his BMW, he quickly stripped himself. Once he had dressed in clean clothes and new boots, he got into his car, put the heater on full blast, and drove slowly back through the lanes. When he finally pulled out on to the A2, he put on his radio, and drove home at top speed, feeling good. He had achieved something.

Terry Gold's disappearance was a nine-day wonder. His nephew's bloody demise had been a violent lesson to anyone in the firm who harboured similar dreams of getting ahead by skimming. But the disappearance of Terry Gold, a happily married man who adored his family and always put them first, really frightened everyone who knew him.

No one was ever arrested or even suspected of having any involvement in Terry's disappearance. On the other hand the Costellos didn't ask around about him either. They didn't discuss it, let alone speculate as to what might have occurred and that, in itself, spoke volumes. Not that anyone said that out loud, of course, but it didn't stop people wondering.

Chapter Eleven

Michael glanced at his reflection in the mirror behind the bar, pleased with how he looked. He was a man to respect; having the Costello brothers' favour gave him the creds he needed to carry out his new businesses with the minimum of real effort. No one in their right mind was going to give him any kind of aggravation.

Since taking out Terry Gold six months ago, he now had his own personal earns. Patrick had given him the lion's share of three very lucrative pubs, and a new nightclub they had recently opened in East London. All he had to do was show his face on a regular basis and collect the takings from his managers – it was so easy it felt almost wrong. He was coining it in, and he had to do fuck-all. But he was shrewd; this was just the opener. Once Patrick had seen for himself how Michael coped and what he could earn from the venues, he would then be asked to do some real work. Patrick was thrilled with him, and he had rewarded him well for proving that he was a man who could be trusted. It was just a matter of time until the serious graft was offered him. Michael couldn't wait.

Josephine was standing at the far end of the bar, and he watched her for a few minutes. She was chatting away to her friends and, as he observed her, he couldn't help smiling. Everyone liked her – she had no side to her and that was her greatest asset.

As usual she was the best-dressed bird in the whole place. She had a knack for finding the clothes that really suited her figure. She always looked well groomed, from her hair to her make-up to her nails. Even if she was only popping to the shops for a pint of milk she made sure she had her make-up on and her hair done. It was all part of her charm. He loved her femininity. She was fragile, vulnerable and she needed him so much. He *wanted* her to need him, to depend on him. That was how it should be.

The music was blaring out, and he was pleased to see that the place was already filling with people. It was still early, and Friday night was ladies' night. The girls got in the club for free before ten thirty and, by the time the pubs turned out, the place was thronging with women and girls of every shape and size.

Catching her eye, he motioned to Josephine to join him and, as she walked towards him, he saw the bouncers giving her the once-over. It was gratifying, but she was his – and everyone knew that.

'It's really taking off, Michael, don't you think? You must be well pleased.'

He grinned. 'It's all right, Josephine, we're getting there. Listen, darling. I have to go and sort a few bits out. You be all right with your mates for a while?'

''Course! You go and do whatever you need to.'

He kissed her gently on the lips. 'I won't be long, darling, promise.'

Josephine looked into his eyes; he was so good to her, always had her best interests at heart. 'You know where I am!'

He watched her as she went back to her little clique of mates, before making his way to his offices. He walked through the foyer of the club, pleased to see that there was already a big queue of people waiting to get in. He saw the doormen searching the ladies' handbags, not just for weapons – a girlfriend was the obvious choice to smuggle in a knife or firearm – but for alcohol as well.

As he slipped through the heavy brocade curtains that led into the offices, he was whistling under his breath. Life was definitely good.

Closing the heavy door behind him, he savoured the relative quiet. The music was now no more than a muted drone. He loved this office, it was his sanctuary. It had pale cream walls and expensive oak furniture. There weren't any windows, but that was a plus really – it added to the security that was necessary when large amounts of money were involved. The big, heavy safe was bolted to the floor behind his desk, dominating the room. It was not just used for the storage of the money that the club accumulated, but also for certain other items of value.

He sat down behind his desk, and busied himself going over the invoices for the alcohol and food. He had a good manager in – the guy was young, granted, but so was Michael – and he had known him for a long time. He trusted him implicitly, and knew that Paulie O'Keefe had the gift of numbers. He could not only keep two sets of books going – a must for anyone in a cash business like this – but he also had the added bonus of being big enough and ugly enough to ensure that people would think twice before they crossed him. Michael and Paulie were a good team. The only way he could survive was by surrounding himself with people he could trust. He had learnt that from Patrick Costello.

There was a gentle tapping on the door and, sitting back in his chair, Michael called out, 'Come in.'

As expected, Paulie O'Keefe entered the room. With the heavy build of an Irish navvy, he seemed to fill the room with his presence. Michael was a tall man, but Paulie was big everywhere, from his huge legs, like tree trunks, to his giant head. He had short, thick red hair and small piercing blue eyes. His mouth was thick-lipped, and he had a nose that seemed to have been flattened across his cheeks. He had the look of the fool about him, but Michael knew that he was actually a genius, especially when it came to numbers. He was perfect for the job in hand and, once people got over his appearance, they soon learnt that nothing got past him.

'Fucking hell, Paulie, you seem to grow bigger every time I see you!'

Paulie laughed. 'What can I say, Michael, I like me grub.'

Paulie sat down gently in the large leather club-chair opposite Michael and, taking out a pack of Benson & Hedges, he lit one leisurely.

'Well, we are well in profit, Michael. It's like printing dough, honestly.'

Michael nodded in agreement. 'I know. I went over everything last night. This place is already paying for itself. Everyone's happy, I can tell you that.'

Paulie smiled, acknowledging the compliment. Then, leaning forward in his chair, he said quietly, 'There is one bugbear though, Michael, and I can't do anything about it without your say-so.'

Michael frowned. There weren't many things on God's green earth that Paulie O'Keefe couldn't sort out by himself. Michael felt a distinct tightening in his guts, and prepared himself for bad news.

'Come on then, Paulie. Out with it.'

Paulie O'Keefe stared at his friend for long moments before saying angrily, 'It's that flash little cunt Rob Barber. He's been coming in here mob-handed, and he runs up huge tabs – never paid one of them to my knowledge – and he causes a fucking fight every time. Now, the bouncers are wary – after all, he is a Barber. No one wants to be the one to cause a fucking turf war. But he has to be tugged, Michael. I kept this quiet because I knew you would go mad if you found out. But last week he went too far. He was coked out of his fucking brains and, to cut a long story short, he ended up smacking some little bird in the mouth. I told him to fuck off out of here myself, and he went without too much trouble. I think even he knew he had gone too far. But we have to make a stand, Michael.'

Michael sighed heavily. This was trouble with a capital T all right. The Barbers and the Costellos had always had an uneasy alliance. The Barbers were Notting Hill boys, and they had no interest in East London, or South London come to that.

Jonny and Dicky Barber were not men whose company was sought after. The Barbers were no more than violent thugs. Unlike the Costellos, they had not adapted to the changing times, they still ruled their little empire with only violence and intimidation. Consequently, although they made a living, they were hated. Their empire was also shrinking. The Jamaicans were not easy to subdue – anyone who had ever dealt with them knew that. Now they were a force to be reckoned with in their own right. They had the monopoly in Brixton, Tulse Hill and Norwood, as well as a strong presence in Notting Hill, Shepherd's Bush and the surrounding areas. They were the new Irish, for fuck's sake – everyone with half a brain knew that. They were happy to work beside you for the earn, had plenty to bring to the table and, most importantly, had the contacts needed to supply the product for the growing trade in cannabis.

Now Rob Barber, the youngest brother, an idiot with the IQ of a fucking amoeba, had the gall to come to *his* club, and try to fucking mug him off?

Paulie could see the anger building inside Michael. He had to be the voice of reason, but he had not had any other choice here. Rob Barber had shit on their doormat, and that could not be tolerated. Still, it had to be sorted with finesse. 'Listen to me, Michael. My first instinct was to take the fucker out the first night he rolled up here, but I knew that would only cause more trouble. So I swallowed because, as big a cunt as he is, there are still his brothers and their firm to deal with. Patrick and Declan have to be in on this, mate. You have to see the logic of that. They must have the final say.'

Michael knew that Paulie was right, but it was the principle as far as he was concerned. That little shit Rob Barber would have known that it was *his* name on the door here, that the Costellos had given the club to *him*. Rob Barber had really been challenging Michael, and that was hard to overlook.

He had earned his place in the Costello family, he was respected by everyone in his orbit. When Patrick Costello singled a person out, it was assumed – rightly – that the person concerned had done something very noteworthy indeed. Something that warranted their meteoric rise through the ranks. To be treated so disrespectfully by someone like Rob Barber – a man who was a laughing stock – was fucking outrageous.

He had to calm down; he knew that giving in to his emotions was a futile exercise. He needed to keep a clear head, think this through properly. 'You're right, Paulie, we need to sort this with care. But you should have told me the score from the off. It should never have gone as far as it has. And I can tell you now, mate, Patrick will already know everything there is to know. He has ears everywhere – I learnt that very early on. I left you to it, and I know you were only trying to sort it out yourself to save me any aggro but, in future, you tell me anything of relevance sooner rather than later, OK?'

Paulie nodded. 'I didn't want to bother you with it. I honestly never thought it would go so far. But you're right, Michael, in future I'll know better.'

Michael smiled then, a big, bright smile. 'Oh, and tell all the doormen he's barred on my express order and if Rob Barber wants to discuss it, he can come and see me – personally.'

Chapter Twelve

'Are you looking forward to us getting married, Michael?'

Michael opened his eyes slowly at Josephine's question. He was just about to fall asleep, he was so tired, even though it was the middle of the afternoon. It had been a long, stressful week.

''Course I am, you silly mare.' He tightened his hold on Josephine, pulling her naked body even closer to him. 'You don't half ask some daft questions, you know.'

Josephine laughed. 'I just love hearing you say it!'

She was lying against him; they were a perfect fit together and she lived for these stolen moments in her bed. Her mum and dad were at the betting shop today going over the books, so she and Michael were safe for a few hours. She suspected her mother knew they were sleeping together but she knew they wouldn't talk about it out loud. She loved to be alone with Michael like this. She knew that he loved her, and she understood that he had a lot of things to take care of when they were out. She was happy to stand with her friends, chat, have a laugh, and wait for him to come and claim her. But, sometimes, she wished that he would forget about his work just for one night, and take her out like he used to, just the two of them. Now they were either in his club or one of his pubs. He would be here, there and everywhere, and she tried not to mind too much, but it was hard sometimes.

He'd fallen asleep, was snoring now, and she sighed. She didn't really have that many friends, the majority of the girls were just hangers-on. They were nice enough, she supposed, but she was aware that the main attraction was that she was Michael Flynn's girlfriend. They wanted to be a part of *his* world; they all flirted with him when he was beside her, throwing blatantly provocative looks his way. She could see that he wasn't interested in any of them, though – he loved her, she was certain of that.

She was better looking than any of them anyway. She'd always been aware of her beauty – accepted it as a fact of life. One of her earliest memories was somebody saying to her mum what a beautiful child she was. She wasn't a bighead – she didn't use her looks for attention; after all, she only had eyes for Michael. One of the nuns at her school had said to her that she was a lucky girl because she was beautiful inside and out. The nun had also told her that beauty could be a scourge, and to remember that looks faded eventually, but the beauty inside her was for ever. She had liked hearing that. It had the ring of truth to it.

She remembered the first time she had seen Michael. She had been fourteen years old, and she had been walking home from school. She had looked across the busy high road, and seen the most handsome boy ever, standing stock still, and he had been staring at *her*. She had smiled at him suddenly, as shy as she was then, and that had been it. He had walked over the road, dodging in and out of the traffic, and she had waited for him as if it had been the most natural thing in the world.

Once they were married she would feel much better. It would be different then, she wouldn't have to go out with him, night after night. She would have a home to look after, babies to take care of. She couldn't wait. She wanted a girl first, a little girl who would help her take care of her siblings. As they were both only children, she and Michael agreed that they would have a houseful of babies. All gorgeous, and all wanted.

She fell asleep beside him thinking of names for her babies that were waiting to be born.

Chapter Thirteen

Patrick and Declan Costello were both listening intently as Michael explained the situation that Rob Barber had caused in the nightclub.

His voice expressed no emotion as he gave them both the facts. This was something that had to be decided by the Costellos; his personal anger would play no part. Still it was hard for him to keep his personal opinions to himself.

He made Paulie O'Keefe sound like the hero of the hour, careful to emphasise that he had only wanted to keep Michael out of anything that might cause unnecessary trouble with the Barbers and that was why he'd kept silent at first. He could see Patrick nodding his head as if he could understand that kind of logic. It wouldn't have been through any cowardice – everyone knew that Paulie O'Keefe was more than capable of standing up for himself should the need arise. Paulie had the reputation of a real marler, a fighter's fighter. Once he was set off, he would bite, kick, punch, head-butt, use any available weaponry, no holds barred. He was also known to easily take on more than one opponent if necessary. No, that Paulie O'Keefe had not demolished young Rob Barber was the feat in itself here.

Declan was annoyed, Michael could tell that much. He hated the Barbers with a vengeance. They had a history. Many years before, Declan had beaten Dicky Barber to the proverbial pulp. Dicky Barber had been the one to insist on the fisticuffs; he had confronted Declan outside a pub in Woolwich of all places. He had challenged Declan to a fight and, once provoked, Declan had been more than happy to oblige.

Jonny Barber had taken no action at the time. He had enough sense to know that Dicky Boy had brought all the grief on himself. *He* had sought out the fight, and he had lost. There was nothing to be done. The fight had been in public, and Dicky had been the instigator. Jonny chose his battles shrewdly and he'd had a feeling that, if it ever came down to it, the Costellos would not be easy to topple. They were a bigger firm in every way, and they were well liked. It was better to retreat on this occasion, and Jonny had made sure that Dicky Boy had done exactly that. This was something Patrick Costello had known within days.

'Rob Barber has to be thirty-five if he's a day! "Young Rob Barber", my arse. He's a cunt. Even Jonny don't trust him, and he's his own brother! What does that tell you?' Declan's voice was laced with anger and disgust.

Patrick poured them a large whisky each. He stood by the windows, looking down at the empty warehouse, picturing it in his mind as it might have been many years before, packed to the brim with casks of brandy, or bolts of different coloured silks. It would have been a hive of activity then, the whole place ringing with noise.

'It's a piss-take all right, Declan. But I think that this is a job for Superman.' He turned back towards his brother and Michael. 'You want him badly, Michael, I can tell.'

Michael smiled grimly.

'He was after you, my son. *You're* the one he wanted, and you know that. He was stronging it in *your* club. Now, thanks to Paulie O'Keefe and his good intentions, that ponce probably thinks that you haven't got the bottle to face him. He thinks you've tried to swerve him.'

Michael stood up abruptly, and Patrick and Declan Costello were both suddenly reminded of how dangerous the lad could be if provoked. Michael's biggest asset was his ability to control his temper. Not many people could do it so well. Patrick himself could, but Michael was the only other person he had ever encountered who was able to do it so absolutely. It was a rare gift, and it showed a strength of will that was as powerful as it was unique. In the world they inhabited, the capability for violence was the norm, but very few could channel that violence and use it like a deadly weapon.

Michael was genuinely furious now. Patrick wanted him to show his real feelings, knowing that he needed to vent his anger. This was personal. Rob Barber had come looking for *him*. He had invaded his personal space. Michael was the new kid on the block, and people like Rob saw that as an invitation, a chance to enhance their own reputation at the expense of someone else. Rob Barber would never have fought him one-to-one; Michael knew that his reputation as a fighter would have put paid to that. No, Rob Barber would need a knife or a gun, a posse of people around him. He was a coward.

'I want him all right, Patrick, of course I fucking do! But I know enough to keep my private opinions to myself, and I have enough self-control to make sure that I don't cause trouble for anyone else. If I *had* gone after him, you both know that I would have nigh on fucking killed him.'

Patrick Costello started laughing, and Declan, swallowing his drink in one gulp, joined in.

Michael Flynn stood there as the Costello brothers roared with laughter and, despite himself, he started to laugh as well.

Patrick wiped his eyes on his coat sleeve. 'You are so like me, Michael. Always thinking of the big picture. You try and work out what might happen if you were to let your natural instincts run riot. I know exactly what it's like.' He was tapping a finger into his temple now, his face screwed up with seriousness. 'I knew as a kid that I had too much anger inside me, that I had to learn how to contain it. As young as I was, I had the ability to kill someone when the anger took over. You are the only person I have ever met who has the same affliction, Michael. And, like me, you have learnt to control it.'

Michael recognised the truth of the man's words. He could see Declan watching them both, fascinated as he listened to his brother explain himself as if it was the first time he had ever really understood him. The discomfort that Patrick's words had created was evident.

Patrick sighed heavily, as though he was tired out from all the talking. 'You can have Rob, Michael. Declan, you can finally finish off that ponce Dicky. And, as for Jonny Barber, I have wanted to take that ponce out for years. Now we have no other option. Rob has seen to that, the useless fucker.'

Michael smiled. His smile was so endearing. No one looking at it could ever have believed that it could hide so much hate and so much anger.

Patrick poured them each another drink and raised his glass in a toast. 'We need to plan this well. Do it quickly and quietly.'

Michael nodded. 'I agree. We need to let things calm down. Take them unawares.'

Patrick Costello was hearing exactly what he wanted. This was something to be done with finesse. Done properly, it was a message for everyone out there with dreams of the big time. He said quietly, 'On the plus side, boys, once the Barbers are out of the frame, we will be without any natural predators!'

Declan nodded his agreement as they clinked glasses. 'Couldn't have put it better meself, bruv.'

Chapter Fourteen

Hannah Flynn watched her son as he ate his dinner. He had always attacked his food, and she enjoyed watching him eat. He savoured every mouthful and, like any mother, she loved to watch her child devouring what she had provided. Not that she had ever cooked elaborate meals on a daily basis; she didn't enjoy cooking so she had never bothered with anything fancy. Until now it had never really mattered. Now that her son was so embroiled with the Callahan family, she was making an effort to keep him around.

Lana Callahan, on the other hand, cooked meals as if her life depended on it, and she was teaching young Josephine the finer points of Irish cuisine, as she called it. A contradiction in terms if ever Hannah had heard one. Lana Callahan cooked all the old Irish recipes Hannah's granny had cooked. It annoyed the life out of her. *She* was actually far more Irish than any of them. She had been born in Ireland for a start – and she still had the accent to prove it. Second-hand Irish, that's all *they* were. They had no knowledge really of where their family had come from originally, and had no contact with people there. They'd never even been to Ireland.

According to Michael, Lana was a really good cook, and

Josephine was following in her mother's footsteps. She was a veritable fecking saint, if her son was to be believed – the Holy Mother of God should watch herself. There was a serious contender for the crown of Queen of Heaven in Josephine Callahan.

They were taking him over, and that he was *letting* them was apparent. Michael acted like he was already a member of the Callahan family, he spent so much time round there. Hannah didn't know how she could compete but even after nearly four years, and a wedding all planned and paid for, she still couldn't accept the girl as a permanent fixture in her life.

Instead, she was determined to spoil him while she could. She was on the offensive now, cooking for her son and giving him the benefit of his Irish heritage herself. 'You're enjoying that, son. I can see that.'

Michael smiled, his mouth full of stew. It was rare for his mum to cook something so delicious. Other than Christmas dinner, his old mum wasn't known for her culinary skills. Breakfast had always been cereal and cold milk – winter or summer. She'd never once made him a packed lunch – just given him money to go to the local chippy. He never complained; what he didn't have he couldn't miss. But the Callahan family had opened his eyes and he liked the way they lived. Meals were something to be enjoyed in their house, something to be shared together as a family. It was an alien concept to him at first, but now he found that he looked forward to it. The way they talked about their day, and sat there when they were finished eating, just enjoying being in each other's company, was something he wanted for his children.

'It's lovely, Mum. I was absolutely starving as well, so it's much appreciated!'

Hannah was suddenly struck with pangs of guilt. Michael wasn't averse to cooking for himself if the need arose. Eggs and bacon were his forte. He had cooked that for them both most Sundays after they had been to Mass. She had let him do it – eventually, she had even expected it. Now she was sorry. She had always prided herself on her feminist beliefs, even though, if she was truthful, she was just lazy. She had not even bothered to get up and see him off to school once he was old enough to look after himself. He had been quite happy so she had always felt that it was pointless both of them getting up when she was so tired. After all, she had always worked so they could live. She had expected him to do his bit from an early age, and he had never questioned her methods. Until now. Hannah realised her son was very old-fashioned in some respects. He liked having a decent meal waiting for him when he came home; he expected his laundry to be hung up in his wardrobe, crisply ironed. That was how things were done in the Callahan household. He didn't even bother to give her a thank you for her trouble any more; he seemed to think it was expected of her. It was as if he had taken a step away from her; she was frightened that, if she wasn't careful, he would step away from her for good.

She gazed at him, still amazed that she'd produced such a handsome man. He was really a looker, he could actually have been a male model if he had been that way inclined. There were plenty of them now, on TV adverts and in all the magazines. They were real men too – not like the nancy boys of old. Her Michael could have been in films, he was *that* fecking handsome. He had the rugged good looks that most men would kill for. He could have *any* girl he wanted, yet he had eyes for no one except Josephine Callahan. He was throwing himself away, but he could not see that. He was obsessed with her.

She decided to change the subject. 'How's it going with the Costellos, son?'

Michael shrugged as usual. She knew he was not going to give her bell, book and candle. He never discussed anything with her any more.

'Great. There's a party at Patrick's house tomorrow, why don't you come? It's his wedding anniversary. It will be a great night, Mum. Plenty of drink, great food, and a live band as well. You should really think of coming along with me and Josephine.'

Hannah grimaced. She had known about the party for weeks, but he'd said not a word to her about going with him. 'Oh, you and young Josephine wouldn't want me with you.'

Michael shook his head. His mother was such a bitter pill these days. He knew that Josephine had asked her to come with them ages ago but, as usual, she had totally blanked her.

It was starting to irritate him. She still treated Josephine as if she was no more than a casual acquaintance of his, even though they were on the verge of getting married. He had tried to keep the peace, tried to pretend that there wasn't any problem, but it was getting harder and harder to keep up the pretence. His mother went through stages of acknowledging Josephine existed. Then she would revert to ignoring her, and Josephine would allow her to treat her like shit. It wasn't on. He had really had enough.

'Josephine would love you to come with us, Mum, as you know.'

Hannah sighed and, looking at her son quizzically, she said haughtily, 'Oh, I don't think that's really the case now, Michael, do you?'

Michael hated her when she was like this. She had always acted as if everyone that he liked or he wanted to be involved with had something chronically wrong with them, and as if he was too young or too stupid to see that for himself. He had always backed down, feeling guilty for wanting other people in his life. His mother had been enough for him when he was a kid, but he saw that he had never made friends unless his mother had given them her seal of approval. Now he was a grown, successful man, but she still expected him to choose her over everyone else in his life.

'Why do you do this, Mum? Why do you always have to try and make everything such a fucking drama? You were invited, you know that.'

Hannah could sense the anger that her son was trying so hard to contain. She had pushed him too far. If only she could stop herself, enjoy his company while she had it, without trying to force him to prove that she was the only person he would ever love. But she couldn't do that. He was *hers*, her only child, her only boy, and she was not able to let him go. He *owed* her. The few years with Josephine were nothing compared with the lifetime with her. He would see that at some point.

'Josephine is forever inviting you out somewhere, Mum,

and you are always saying that you can't make it. Well, listen to me. One of these days she'll finally take the hint and blank you, and who could blame her, eh?'

Hannah wanted to explain that she could not help herself. Josephine was like a thorn in her side. The day he had met that little bitch had been the beginning of the end for her and her son. Now with the wedding nearly upon them, she knew that she would have to accept her, at least on the surface. She had no choice. But it was so hard. Josephine Callahan was like a big balloon; bright and beautiful on the outside, but if you popped the fucker with a well-aimed dart, just hot air inside. Why could her son not see that? Josephine was not woman enough for a man like her Michael. He would tire of her eventually, that was a given.

'Listen, Michael, I don't accept her invitations for the simple reason I don't want to spend a whole day looking in clothes shops! Jaysus, Michael, you tell me one time you ever knew me to go shopping for a whole fecking day! I'd rather boil me own shites.'

Michael had to laugh; in fairness, she was telling the truth. But it wasn't about that – it was about showing willing, about accepting Josephine as her future daughter-in-law, as a part of the Flynn family. She knew that as well as he did.

'But you have money to spend now, Mum! You're not that old, you still look pretty good. Shopping is what women do these days, Mum, they like to keep themselves looking nice. Lana looks fantastic for her age, she dresses so well that sometimes people think that her and Josephine are sisters!'

Hannah laughed in derision. This was too much for her now. 'So who thinks that then, eh? Did this person happen to have a white stick and a fucking dog by any chance? *Sisters!* Now I've heard fecking everything.'

Michael pushed his plate away angrily, knocking over his glass of Guinness in the process and revealing the bitterness he tried so desperately to keep in check.

'Do you know what, Mum? Josephine's right about you. You are so fucking *negative*. No matter what she tries to do, no matter what she says, you never give her a chance. She got tickets for that West End show you said you wanted to see, and you turned her down flat. You actually sneered at her as if anyone wanting to go was a fucking moron.'

Hannah shook her head in self-righteous denial. 'You are wrong there, son, I'm telling you.'

'I was there, Mum, remember? I *saw* the way you reacted and I swallowed my knob because Josephine asked me to. I was all for having a fucking straightener once and for all. I tell you now, Mum, if it had been left to me, this would have been over a long time ago.'

Hannah was watching her son wide-eyed. She was aware that she had to try and rein herself in, but it was too late. Michael was so angry and disappointed in her, she had no option but to let him vent his spleen.

'Then she got tickets to go and see The Dubliners, and you still fucking blanked her. I grew up listening to you telling me how The Dubliners were the greatest Irish band of all time. You have every album they have ever made, yet you passed up the chance to see them live. I thought you would have snatched her hand off, but, oh no, you were too busy making sure she knew her place in your fucking world. The Dubliners were the soundtrack of my childhood,

Mum. I know every word to "Danny Boy", "Boolavogue", "Four Green *fucking* Fields", "Kevin Barry" and "The *fucking* Galway Shawl". The one chance you had to go and see them in the flesh, and you said no because poor Josephine asked you to go with her. She is a nice girl, Mum, because anyone else would have told you to get fucked years ago. You sit round her mum and dad's, and everyone knows you don't really want to be there. You act like you are doing us all a favour or something. Well, don't bother in future. If you can't get along with my *wife*, then I have no option, do I? If I have to choose between you, I'll choose my Josephine.'

Michael could see the genuine hurt on his mother's face. He was all she had, but that had been her choice – she had never wanted anyone else. And, even though he loved her with his entire being, he knew he had to put a stop to this. She'd had it her own way for far too long. Josephine had done everything physically possible to try and find some kind of common ground, find something that might bring them closer. It was clearly never going to happen. He could see that now. His mother was just too Irish, too focused on him and too proud. If she had her way, he would still be living at home with her when he was forty-five.

Michael was a man in his own right, a man to be reckoned with. He was not a kid, and he was not going to humour her. It stopped now.

Hannah just stared at her son, unable to believe that he had said such awful things to her. She knew he had meant every word. She had asked for the majority of it – even she could see that. But he was her only child. She had reared him single-handedly, and devoted her whole life to him. What else did she have?

The doorbell rang loudly, shattering the silence that lay between them. She felt the urge to scream in anguish, to give her pain an outlet, make her son understand how much he was hurting her, see his disloyalty before it was too late.

Michael was out of his chair like a bullet out of a gun, evidently relieved to get away from her. It was as though he wanted nothing more at this moment in time than to be as far away from her as physically possible.

Hannah was fuming. She knew who it was. Trust Josephine Callahan to turn up now. If she didn't know any better, she would think she had planned it.

Chapter Fifteen

Jonny Barber was nearly sixty years old. He had pretty much looked that age since his early forties. At only five feet eight inches, he wasn't tall; but with his barrel-chest and bow legs he made quite an impression. His thick black hair had started to go grey in his late twenties, and he'd worn it as a steel-grey crew cut ever since. It was the only haircut that suited him. He was not a handsome man but his eyes were unforgettable. Like both his brothers, he had inherited his mother's big blue eyes framed with long, dark eyelashes. These were so striking that people always gave him a second look. He couldn't blame them – he knew they were wasted on him. His eyelashes were the envy of many a woman, and they also explained why he had been married three times. His eyes had the power to make a certain kind of woman forget about the rest of his face, though his reputation and large bankroll were also a great help.

These days, Jonny was a worried man. He had heard that his youngest brother Rob had been making a nuisance of himself as usual. Only this time it seemed he had been foolish enough to take his anti-social personality outside his home turf and all the way across London to the East End. He had decided to go and pick a fight with young Michael Flynn, a lad who had a good reputation and never looked for trouble, but was more than capable of looking after himself if it should find him. He was also one of Patrick Costello's workers. Patrick, as everyone knew, let his brother Declan run the main business, while he dabbled in everything and anything that was illegal and lucrative. He wasn't only talking drugs. From acquiring prestige cars for the booming Arab markets, to firearms of any kind, including sawn-off shotguns for the bank-robbing fraternity, and army-issue heavy artillery, you named it, Patrick Costello could get it. Jonny Barber had even heard a whisper that the man could procure Semtex if the price was right.

Over the years, the Costellos had made a good name for themselves; they outclassed the Barbers in every way, and that they had never once encroached on the Barbers' turf was something Jonny really appreciated. The Costellos had integrity. They still lived by the old code, and that meant that you never trespassed on anyone else's pavements. Jonny knew that if they had wanted to procure his family's turf, they were more than capable of doing it. The Costellos had the manpower and the money. He should have followed their example, but he had never bothered to look outside of his own front yard. Now it was too late.

Dicky had tried to take them on years before, and failed dismally. Declan Costello had hammered the fuck out of his brother, and there was no way he could have retaliated. Dicky had been in a pub in Woolwich, drunk as a skunk. He had eyeballed Declan in the same drinking establishment and, in a moment of utter fucking alcohol-induced lunacy, had challenged him.

Jonny was well aware his brother Dicky could have a row – there was no doubt about that – but Declan Costello was another matter. Once riled he had no off button. However many times he was knocked down, he got back up, and kept coming. Not that he had ever been knocked down by a single man – it took a good few to achieve that. Declan could take on the entire British Lions rugby team, and still be the only one standing at the end of the fight. *No one* who knew Declan would ever be stupid enough to take him on. Even Roy 'Pretty Boy' Shaw, the bare-knuckle boxer and a seriously hard man, had joked that he would fight any man alive except Declan Costello.

Jonny had heard at the time that Declan had tried everything in his power to get out of having the fight, but Dicky, being Dicky, had been like a dog with a bone. Eventually, Declan had lost his cool. The rest was history.

Now Rob had seen fit to pick a fight with Michael Flynn, a man who everyone knew was destined for greatness, who always treated the people around him with the utmost respect, but who had proved himself on more than one occasion as a vicious fucker if roused.

Jonny sighed in exasperation. This was not something he had expected. He had assumed that even a fucking moron like young Rob would have had enough sense to keep away from someone like Flynn. With relatives like his, who needed fucking enemies?

He had to take action so he'd called a family meeting. As usual his two brothers were late. It was a fucking farce. He might as well be pissing in the wind. Dicky would take Rob's side, he was prepared for that. But he was going to make sure that his brothers were left in *no* doubt that, if they didn't comply with his demands, he would personally take them out himself. *He* was the head of this family and he was fighting for the whole firm – for everything that they had worked for. They were not strong enough to take on the Costellos. So they were just going to have to use their powers of persuasion to try and defuse the situation before they found themselves in the middle of an all-out war.

Chapter Sixteen

Father Riordan had always liked young Michael Flynn. He thought of him as a kind-hearted lad. Considering the fact that he had been brought up by that Hannah, a woman who had the face of an angel and the personality of a Doberman pinscher, he thought the lad had turned out very well. He was delighted to be performing the wedding ceremony for young Flynn and his lovely fiancée Josephine Callahan. He thought they made a wonderful pair.

Oh, he had heard the gossip, of course. Michael Flynn worked for the Costellos, both of whom were regular churchgoers and men who were generous to a fault. Father Riordan had only to mention the missions and they were putting their hands into their pockets. He wouldn't mind a few more like the Costellos in his parish, if he was to be brutally honest, as long as he didn't know too much about what they got up to. They were like so many of the second-generation Irishmen – they did what they needed to feed their families, and who could blame them? It was a hard world, all right; he knew that himself.

'So, Michael, are you excited about the big day?'

Michael grinned happily. 'I can't wait, Father. It can't come round quick enough for me.'

Father Riordan was thrilled at the lad's devotion; so few wanted the church ceremony these days. When he looked around the church on a Sunday he nearly fainted at the sight of the young girls, dressed like whores, with no bras, thick black eyeliner and faces like a smacked arse because they had been dragged to the service by their parents. Parents who were as bewildered as he was by this new generation. It wasn't Ireland, that was for sure.

'Well, not long now, Michael, and Josephine will not only share your name, but she will share the rest of your life with you. The sacrament of marriage is a serious event in anyone's life. It's pledging your love and your allegiance to each other in the eyes of the Lord God Himself.'

Michael bowed his head. 'That's the plan, Father. She is everything to me.'

As they sat side by side in the church, Michael felt a peace settle over him. He loved the church and the solitude that it afforded him. He had often come here as a child to sit and think. For him there was nowhere else in the world where a body could be so utterly alone as in a Catholic church.

He was a believer, of course, in his own way. He had a deep respect for his religion, and he knew that it was something that would always be a part of his life, even if there were a lot of the teachings he couldn't help question. That was just part of growing up; all in all, he still needed the stability it afforded him.

Josephine shared his beliefs and it was something they would pass on to their children. It was important that they learn that they were a part of something so big and powerful, that would be with them for their entire lives.

'You ready to make your confession, Michael?'

'Yes, Father, of course.'

Michael knew he had to make a good Act of Contrition before his marriage. He wanted to be able to take Communion on his wedding day without any blemish on his soul whatsoever. A Catholic marriage was a blessed sacrament. There would be no divorce; his marriage was for life and for the life thereafter. Michael knew how serious it was.

Father Riordan wished with all his heart that he had more young men like Michael Flynn in his parish. Decent young Catholics were getting rarer by the year.

'Come on, then.'

Michael followed the priest into the confessional box. He knelt down immediately, appreciating the softness of the leather beneath his knees. It was quite dark inside. He knew that the priest was now his conduit to the Lord Himself, and it was something he had never taken lightly. This was so powerful a thing that even the laws of the land had no authority in the confessional box. Whatever he told the priest could never be repeated and, as long as he was truly repentant, his sins would be forgiven and his soul would be once more without blemish.

He blessed himself quickly, wanting to get this over as soon as possible. 'Forgive me, Father, for I have sinned. It has been over two years since my last confession.'

Father Riordan blessed him, taking his time over it. He always enjoyed hearing confession. It was such a personal, private thing, the opportunity to talk to God Himself in person. You could unburden yourself of your sins and worries, and ask His forgiveness, knowing He would not refuse you. He would not stand in judgement of you or turn away from you. Father Riordan believed that this was the mainstay of the Catholic religion – the concept of the power of forgiveness and the knowledge that if you made a good confession you would be cleansed of your sins. You would be without stain, have a pure soul – for a short while anyway. You could take Holy Communion with a light heart, knowing you were in a state of grace. It was a very powerful thing to the true believer.

Michael bowed his head, and he started to speak quietly and respectfully. 'I have sinned, Father. I have used profanities, taken the Lord's name in vain. I have also had bad thoughts, terrible thoughts. I have not always honoured my mother.'

Father Riordan had expected as much. He smiled to himself. He had heard much worse than that over the years. 'Go on, my son.'

'I have also taken Josephine into my bed on more than one occasion. I know that I should not have done that. I should have waited, treated her with more respect. And I will do that now. I will wait until we are married in the eyes of the Church. I will make sure that our children are born in holy wedlock.'

Father Riordan already knew all about this. Josephine had been confessing that sin regularly for a long time, and she had not felt the urge to stop doing it. He understood that the weakness of the flesh was the scourge of youth, but he kept his own counsel. He was more astounded at Michael's honesty. The lad was being far more truthful than he had expected. He was also being so humble and painfully honest, that it was making the priest feel almost as if he was eavesdropping. It was years since he had heard such old-fashioned terminology; it was as unexpected as it was welcome. He could hear the total commitment in Michael's voice as he promised to wait until his wedding night so he could take his bride without sin.

There was a silence then. A long silence. But he could hear Michael's breathing – it was shallow and fast.

'I also have to confess to something else, Father. A mortal sin. A sin that I know will be difficult for you to understand.'

There was an edge to Michael's voice now. Father Riordan could feel a distinct change in the air around them. He knew, immediately, that whatever Michael was going to say to him, he did not want to hear. But he had no choice. He had to hear the confession, it was out of his hands. He was filled with a sense of trepidation, of the fear that always accompanied the unknown. He felt hot suddenly, sweaty. He knew he had to do his duty, to listen to Michael, and not judge him – no matter what he might say. He took a deep breath to steady himself before saying, 'You can say anything in here, Michael. Remember, you are not talking to me, you are talking to the Holy Father Himself. You can tell Him anything. I can never repeat anything I hear in the confessional. You know that. It's not for me to judge. I can only offer you an Act of Contrition.'

Michael sighed gently. Then, lifting his head up, he said softly, 'I have killed, Father.'

Chapter Seventeen

Patrick Costello was tired. He had been up since early morning, and now he was knackered. His anniversary party was about to start and he was fed up with it already. He loved his wife dearly, but she was what was known as 'high maintenance'. If anyone else gave him the grief that she did, he would have shot them in cold blood without a second's thought. Luckily, Carmel was a good girl, a great mother and, he had to admit, he loved her. But she had been on his back for the last few days about their wedding anniversary. It was like talking to the Antichrist; *everything* he said was wrong. She had decided that *he* had insisted on having an anniversary party, and he had been intelligent enough to go along with everything she said without a word. She could make him feel that he was in the wrong even when he knew, without a shadow of a doubt, that he was totally in the right. If truth be told, he actually admired her for that. She was one of the few people in his world who was not scared of him, and that was why he loved her so much. If she had feared him, he would have walked all over her. They both knew it. Declan had hated her since day one, but he had accepted that she was what his brother wanted. As Carmel also hated Declan with a vengeance, it had made no odds.

Tonight, Patrick had to entertain everyone in his world, and make sure that they enjoyed themselves. It was part and parcel of being the main man; every person he had invited into his home was not only grateful to be a part of his celebration, but the invitation conveyed the message that they were doing a good job. Patrick had always understood the need to make everyone on his payroll feel that they were appreciated. Declan might be who they dealt with on a daily basis, but Patrick made sure that everyone in the firm knew that he was aware of them and what they did. It was important to remind people that they were valued.

He poured himself a large brandy from the bar in the room he'd commandeered as his hideaway. It was the only room in the house that his wife had not been allowed to decorate. It was a man's room. The walls still had the original wood panelling and the flooring was a dark oak. He liked wood – it was honest, uncomplicated. He had two chairs – one on either side of the original Adam fireplace – both battered looking. They were as old as the hills, but the antique leather had cost a small fortune. The only other piece of furniture was a large bookcase he had picked up at an auction, which doubled as a bar, and there was a set of French doors that led out to the garden. He had no photographs or knick-knacks, nothing of a personal nature, but he liked it like that.

He settled himself into a chair, waiting for Michael and Declan to arrive; they needed to talk before the party got into full swing.

Declan arrived first; he was dressed to impress, and Patrick could not help laughing at him. He was wearing a bespoke suit, dark blue with a pale silver pinstripe, a deep blue shirt, and hand-made shoes. For the first time ever, Declan actually looked smart.

'Look at you!'

Declan grinned, but he was clearly embarrassed. 'I know! I went to see the bloke that Michael uses. He is a fucking magician I'm telling you, bruv.' His big head was bright red, even his ears were flushed. Patrick felt a rush of affection for his brother. He was pleased to see him looking so good.

'I can see that. I have never seen you look so smart! Fuck me, I never thought I would see the day!'

Declan went to the bookcase and busied himself by pouring a drink. 'I see Michael has already started on a new earn. He has a real knack for sniffing out the money shots. I only heard about it through one of my blokes. He mentioned that he had seen Michael over in Ladbroke Grove. He was drinking with that Winston Oates – he's the main man where drugs are concerned, as you know yourself. I assume he is making a point to the Barber brothers as that's their turf, so to speak.'

Patrick was startled; he had heard nothing about Michael having a new earn. He had always prided himself on knowing everything about everyone around him – even his brother Declan was not immune. He had always believed in the adage that knowledge is power. Now he was wondering if he was getting lax in his old age, if his affection for Michael was clouding his judgement. He had not even asked about the boy's movements recently; he had trusted him implicitly. Patrick had always been in possession of a healthy but suspicious nature – it was something he had always prided himself on. He trusted no one, and that was why the Costello brothers were so successful. But it seemed that Michael Flynn had achieved the impossible. For the first time ever, Patrick had not thought to have one of his main earners watched. He couldn't believe that he had been so remiss. He trusted Michael – of course he did – but large amounts of money could be a terrible temptation to even the most loyal of men. History was filled with examples of how money – second only to a seriously good shag – could turn the most level of heads.

Declan observed his brother's reaction and couldn't help feeling a small twinge of satisfaction; it was very rare that he knew something of interest before his older brother. He had only found out about Michael's meeting by accident but, unlike Patrick, who had a pathological fear of taking anyone on face value, he really did believe that Michael Flynn was as straight as a die. He hoped that he had not caused the boy any unnecessary aggro – he knew from bitter experience that Patrick could turn on a coin if he felt that he was being mugged off in any way. He was dangerous was Patrick, especially if he felt he had been overlooked in some way. He always had to be the fucking main man. He decided to backtrack.

'Listen, Pat, I might have that all wrong, mate. I heard it from Cecil Thompson and, let's be fair, he was never the sharpest knife in the fucking drawer, was he? His wife had more cocks than a geriatric chicken, and he never had a fucking clue – it was only when his youngest came out blacker than Nookie's knockers that he suspected there might be skulduggery afoot!'

Patrick laughed and the tension eased. He knew that Declan was trying to smooth it over, sorry that he mentioned Michael. He sussed out that Declan enjoyed telling him something that he was not aware of – it was a rare enough occurrence and, for Declan, it was like winning the pools. Still, he was on his guard now.

'Michael will be here soon. Let's just see what he has to say, shall we?'

Chapter Eighteen

Josephine was wearing a cream-coloured silk dress that fitted where it touched and, even though she had no skin on show other than her arms, it showed off every curve she was in possession of to its full advantage. She looked stunning and she knew it.

She had added cream leather high heels, and a thick black belt that emphasised her tiny waist to complete the outfit. Michael liked her to look good, because he loved showing her off. He was proud of her and appreciated how she looked after herself, and he especially loved it when she dressed herself up like this. There was no cleavage on show – just as he wanted it – nothing that could be seen as provocative, yet she looked sexier than if she was wearing a micro-mini skirt with thigh-high boots.

Her hair fell down her back; it was lightly curled and lacquered. It looked natural, even though it had taken her hours to perfect it. Her eye make-up was not too heavy, but she was wearing a deep wine-coloured lipstick as her only splash of dramatic colour, which finished off her whole look perfectly.

She was pleased to see the reactions from everyone at the

party as she'd walked into the room with Michael. He wanted her to be noticed and she was more than happy to oblige. She loved getting dressed up, it was something she knew she was good at.

Michael handed her a glass of champagne, and she took it from him carefully. Michael was considered an important man, and she had to make sure that she was seen as worthy of his attention. After all, they were going to be married soon, and that fact alone guaranteed her respect from the people around them. Still, a man like Michael was seen as fair game by most of the women in their world, but she had sworn to herself that she would make sure that he never had any reason to look anywhere else for attention. She herself had seen the women who had married their men, had a few kids and then let themselves go, got fat and frumpy. They stopped wearing make-up and taking care of themselves. It was easy to let your guard down with a wedding ring on your finger and believe that having a man's kids was enough to keep the man of your dreams beside you, loyal to you because you had produced their flesh and blood.

As if! It was the seventies, and the power of marriage was slowly being eroded. Divorce was no longer just for the rich and famous, it was now becoming a part of everyday life. Josephine was determined that her Michael would always see her as the girl he had met and married, not as the woman he had tied himself to. She would not become a whining, overweight baby-maker who lost the knack of enjoying the life that was on offer. Those were the women she secretly despised. She believed she was too shrewd to fall for all that old fanny.

For now she intended to warn off any women who saw themselves as contenders for her position as Michael's girl. If she had to fight them off physically, if that is what it took to keep him beside her, she would, though she hoped it never came to that. Instead, she was making a name for herself as a beauty, as a fashion plate, and she wanted everyone to remember how good she looked each time they saw her. She was going to make sure that nothing interfered with them or their lives together. Still, she'd be a fool not to be a bit intimidated by just how important he was becoming, and how his status would make him even *more* attractive to certain women. Her mum had made sure she understood the ways of their world. There were pug-ugly men who, without their status as hard nuts, would be hard pushed to pull a muscle – let alone anything else. She knew that a lot of those men had walked out on their families for the lure of youth. It was pathetic, but it was a fact of the life they lived with. But it was not going to happen to her. Michael loved her and, if she used her loaf, that would never change.

She gulped her champagne down quickly, suddenly gripped by a feeling of anxiety. She swallowed hard and took a deep breath. Calm again, she lapped up the attention, which served to remind Michael of just how good she was for him, and how wonderful their life together would be.

She saw Patrick's wife Carmel beckoning her over; as usual she was surrounded by the other women at the party. Patrick's wife was never alone. Carmel's so-called 'friends' agreed with everything she said and waited for her to take the lead on all matters. It was almost embarrassing to watch at times. Carmel Costello loved being the queen bee, and she played the part to perfection. If she decided to dance, then they all danced. If she drank shots, they each followed suit. And if she decided that one of the girls had offended her in some way, they immediately became persona non grata to everyone, pushed out of her circle brutally and very publicly. Carmel Costello made her wishes very clear.

It was childish really, but Josephine knew that she had to follow suit and do what was expected as Michael's wife-to-be. She already had a level of security because of Michael's position in the firm as Patrick Costello's boy wonder. Michael was not going to fuck *that* up; he'd worked hard to get where he was and he would do whatever was needed to keep himself on the up and up.

This was the game they were both having to play. Josephine had joined a group of women whose husbands' livelihoods were dependent on the Costello brothers, and that was something none of them, Josephine included, could ever forget.

Chapter Nineteen

Colin Dawes was a man who went out of his way to avoid trouble of any kind. He wasn't a coward – he could look after himself – but he had never seen the logic of going out and actively looking for trouble. In his experience, it eventually found its way to your door anyway. Now, he was in a quandary as he stood outside Jonny Barber's office. He had known Jonny since they were little kids and, as big a bastard as Jonny could be, Colin couldn't stand aside and see him taken out without giving him a heads-up of some description. It was only fair.

The problem was, Jonny wasn't a man who encouraged friendly conversation; he had no time for anyone other than his brothers so approaching him wouldn't be easy. But Jonny had seen him all right in the not-too-distant past, and that counted for a lot where Colin was concerned. He was a decent man, or at least he tried to be anyway. He knew he had to do the right thing and he owed Jonny Barber.

Colin took a deep breath and pulling himself up to his full height – just over six feet one inch – he rapped loudly on Jonny's office door, before walking in to face him. He consoled himself with the fact that he was doing what he would want someone to do for *him* if the need ever arose.

Jonny Barber had never really liked Colin Dawes. He suspected it was because Colin had the knack of being popular by his very nature. Even at school, Colin had managed to make friends with everyone around him. Admittedly, Jonny couldn't really fault him for that, but he found Colin's obvious camaraderie with all and sundry very unsettling. He just wasn't comfortable with people like Colin Dawes; he always felt wrong-footed around him.

Nevertheless, Colin Dawes had worked for the Barbers for a very long time, and Jonny recognised that he owed him a private audience for that reason alone. His loyalty had never once been questioned, he'd never given them cause for any doubt, unlike the majority of the men on the Barbers' payroll, who Jonny personally wouldn't trust to look after his mother's mangy old cat without a written statement of support from the RSPCA. His brother Dicky had played a hand in that. He had picked fights with everyone at some time or another – it wasn't even personal, it was just his nature. In all honesty, Jonny wasn't entirely without blame. Just like Dicky, he had never been blessed with a sunny nature, and he had caused his fair share of bad feeling with the people he employed. Thanks to his brother's natural antagonism towards most of the human race, he had never been in a position to relax his guard and put his trust in the people around him. Dicky could have more fights than Joe Frazier in a twenty-minute timeframe. Dicky had made a career out of alienating everyone on their payroll at one time or another. Now Jonny was worried it might come back to bite them on their arses. His younger brother was basically a fucking moron.

'All right, Colin? What can I do you for, mate?' He was trying to be friendly, jovial even. It was hard though. He was still waiting for his brothers to make an appearance.

Colin smiled, trying to look relaxed. He was still a good-looking man, even at his age. Colin had always put his looks down to his aversion to alcoholic beverages of any kind. He had never liked the taste of drink, even as a lad and, seeing the trouble that it could cause, he was very glad about that. Give him a cup of tea any day. Alcohol not only reduced people's inhibitions – it was also a fuel for bad tempers. It fanned flames that caused serious damage to everyone involved.

He was nervous, and he took a breath to steady himself. 'Look, Jonny. I don't want to cause trouble, mate. You know me – I keep out of everything, but I can't stand by and see you made a mug of.'

Jonny Barber was looking at Colin Dawes as if he had never seen him before in his life. He had not expected anything like this – certainly not such raw honesty. 'What the fuck are you prattling on about?'

Colin had no choice, he had to tell it like it was. Jonny was not going to make it easy for him, but it was too late to back out now.

'Rob and Dicky have taken a few blokes, and they are on their way over to Patrick Costello's house where, incidentally, he is having a big fucking party to celebrate his wedding anniversary. Rob and Dicky seem to think that they can easily gain entry into Patrick's home, and then they plan to take out the Costello family en masse. I assume they didn't discuss any of this with you, because you would have told them that they were on a death wish. It's fucking lunacy, Jonny. But you know young Rob – he's got a serious fucking hard-on for Michael Flynn, and Dicky has always wanted to pay back Declan Costello for past misdemeanours.'

Jonny Barber was unsure if he was actually awake. This could only be some kind of nightmare brought on by narcotics or some kind of serious illness. No one in their right mind would think – even for a moment – that they could take out the Costello brothers. And certainly not in their own fucking *home*, for fuck's sake! It was so blatantly outrageous a claim, yet so like something Dicky was capable of, he knew that it could only be the truth.

He understood that Colin Dawes was only trying to help, was doing him what he felt was a favour – being loyal and decent even. But he wished Colin Dawes had kept his big fucking trap shut.

Jonny wasn't sure if he was willing to get involved. He would rather have been able to say, in complete honesty, that he had known nothing about any of this, and that it was as big a surprise to him as it was to everyone else. Thanks to this cunt, he couldn't do that now.

There was no way in hell that his brothers would be able to walk away from this. It was never going to happen. The fucking Flying Squad would be hard pushed to infiltrate Patrick Costello's house, even with a warrant and a tag team from the SAS. Patrick Costello had always made sure he was well protected from any outside aggravation. He was a man who was always two steps ahead and who, therefore, had put in place security that might be needed should any threat arise.

Jonny felt faint suddenly. His head seemed to be filling up with hot air, he couldn't breathe properly. He felt himself choking; his mouth was so dry, he had no spit left. He had only the sticky dryness that came from extreme fear. His chest felt tight, as if a steel band was squeezing all his breath out of him. His heart was beating so loudly in his ears it was drowning out everything else. He knew that he was on the verge of collapsing. For the first time in his whole life he was experiencing acute terror on a grand scale, and it was coupled with the knowledge that there was nothing he could do about any of it.

He was clutching his chest, but he was dismayed because he wasn't having the heart attack he so dearly craved. He was aware that he was already thinking clearly again, and that his natural instinct for self-preservation was kicking in. Even as he realised that, he felt guilty because he knew that he should be at least *trying* to do something to help his brothers out. But they had already made their beds. They had not seen fit to tell him what they had planned, so he could do nothing for them now. They had undertaken this madness alone – and they would have to take the consequences alone.

He had been left out of the loop because they had both known he would have forbidden it. So fuck them for the treacherous bastards they were! He could only look out for himself now, guard his own interests, and try to salvage what he could from what was, in reality, a situation that was fucking unprecedented in the world they inhabited. He would have to make damn sure that the Costellos and that ponce Flynn were given every assurance that he personally had no knowledge whatsoever of his brothers' suicidal mission. It was about self-preservation. His brothers were as good as dead already; he had no option but to try and save his own arse if it was in any way possible. But he didn't really hold out much hope.

'How about a drink, Colin? And then you can tell me everything you know, eh?'

Colin Dawes was thrilled by the invitation, unaware that he was actually being kept there as Jonny Barber's alibi for the evening and that he was putting his own life in danger if it all went pear-shaped.

Chapter Twenty

Patrick Costello's wife Carmel was a woman on a constant mission in life.

She was confident she had her husband's affection – his love even – but it was something she had to work for all the same. And she did just that. He treated her like a goddess, and always made sure she was given her due as the mother of his children. No matter what might happen in the future, even if he ever did get a capture by the Filth for some reason, he had provided for his family. Not that anything like that was really on the cards. Her Patrick was far too big nowadays. But, if it *did* come to pass, she knew she would still be able to live the lifestyle she had become accustomed to. She had access to his offshore accounts – he had given that information to her to ensure that she felt safe – and she never worried about the future.

Patrick was older than her; he had married later in life and taken those vows seriously. Even so, Carmel was a realist. Patrick saw himself as a good husband, as well as a good Catholic, but he was also a man. And not just any man, but a Face in a world of permanent strange, where good-looking and very willing young women were plentiful. There were far too many girls in the Life just like she had been, with the same goal in mind, and the same determination to get what and who they wanted, whatever the cost. She knew men with second, third and even fourth wives. That would never happen to *her* – *she* would keep her status come hell or high water.

These young girls – who seemed to multiply every year – had the edge, because they were younger than her, fresher, without the scars of childbirth and without the curse of familiarity. She made herself known to each and every one of them so they would be in *no* doubt of what they would be up against should they decide to try and challenge her position. However much Patrick adored her, she would not let her guard down for one second. She was determined to be the *only* Mrs Costello, and she was not going to give that status up without a fight. His only way out of this marriage was death – and not hers either. She made sure that she was surrounded by her own clique of girls and women that she felt were not a threat to her or her lifestyle. She knew every female in her husband's orbit, and she made sure that she was a permanent fixture in every part of his social life. Patrick might think she was being paranoid – he was a great guy, a good father, and a loyal husband. But he didn't comprehend the lengths that certain women were prepared to go to in order to get what they wanted.

Carmel was not going to give any fucker the chance to try and muscle in on what was rightfully hers. She had always worked – and she continued to do so every day – to keep her home and, more importantly, her place in the Life. It was a good life in so many ways, but it was also very difficult because she could never let herself relax, could never take her eye off the ball. She was constantly on alert, and it was exhausting. But she had to protect herself and her children from being ousted by a younger model.

Now they were having an anniversary party and, even though Patrick had made sure it was a great night and was treating her like royalty, she still couldn't bring herself to truly relax and enjoy it. She had made him organise it. She might tell everyone that it was all his idea, but it was all hers really. Occasions like tonight made a point to everyone. The Costellos were together, they were happy and nothing could come between them. It was a moment of triumph.

If only she could enjoy it and her husband's company. But she couldn't relax any more.

She caught sight of Michael Flynn's fiancée, Josephine Callahan. The girl was absolutely stunning, there was no doubting that. She was also a really nice person, and Carmel hated that she was so jealous of her, but she couldn't help it. Josephine was not only gorgeous, she was *young* – as young and as innocent as the day was long. It was an irresistible combination to most men.

Michael Flynn, though, was all over her like the proverbial rash, and Josephine had eyes for no one but her Michael. They were a lovely young couple, and she had no reason for the jealousy she was feeling towards them. Nevertheless, Josephine Callahan was another one to be watched like a hawk, and watch her she would. Keep your friends close, and your enemies closer – what a true statement that was. Patrick had asked her privately to take the younger girl under her wing, to look after her and ease her into the fold so to speak;

after all, Carmel knew the score from personal experience. Even though her husband had shown no interest in the girl other than the fact she was Michael's intended, Carmel still felt the ugly pain of jealousy, coupled with a feeling of fear. That fear was *always* going to be there. She might act like she had everything under control, that she was in charge of everything around her – from her family, to her home and the people she brought into her personal orbit – but it was all a sham. Deep inside, she had never really known a truly happy day since she had married Patrick Costello. Once she had landed him, she had spent every minute since trying to keep him. And it was not easy.

Carmel had too much pride to let anyone, especially Patrick Costello, kick her to the kerb. She had invested too much of her time and effort to end up a has-been. From the moment he put a ring on her finger, she had made it her mission in life to keep him by her side.

Chapter Twenty-One

Michael was in a good mood. His Josephine looked the dog's gonads at the party tonight, and he was excited about his forthcoming nuptials. He really was a man in love.

He'd been feeling very wholesome since his confession. He didn't like being with Josephine knowing he had committed murder. It felt a bit off, even though he had chosen to do it and had known it was expected of him. There was a part of him that was secretly unnerved that his initial qualms about taking someone's life now seemed completely out of proportion. He wasn't exactly *pleased* by what he had done, but there was no getting away from the fact that it had been much easier than he had thought it would be to actually do it. He could argue that he'd been put into an impossible position. When Patrick made the request, he'd had no choice but to agree.

Father Riordan had taken his sins and wiped them away. It had been so easy, and he felt much better in himself now he had atoned for it. He felt lighter, as if the weight of the world had been taken off his shoulders. He would never again underestimate the power of his religion.

As he went into Patrick's office he was smiling; he felt

fantastic. 'Hello, boys, you will not believe what I have got to tell you.'

Patrick grinned before saying sarcastically, 'Well, let me guess. Is it to do with you, a dealer in Notting Hill, and the possibility of a cannabis-based business?'

Michael just laughed loudly. 'Fucking hell, Pat! There was me thinking that I had manoeuvred us a right good earn, but I should have known better! You cannot be surprised, you're always a fucking step ahead. You're like Secret Squirrel. Un-fucking-believable!'

Declan was interested in how his brother would react to Michael's news. He almost wished he'd kept his trap shut earlier. He trusted the boy implicitly – he should have known nothing was certain with his brother. But Michael was his blue-eyed boy, for fuck's sake! Declan wasn't bothered by the favouritism. He was more than happy with his earns. Patrick's interest had never been in the bread and butter side of the business, he had always craved the more exotic earns. Declan was quite happy that Patrick left him to get on with it. His brother was a difficult man to work alongside, with a terrible need to control everyone, everything, and every deal that he saw as being within his personal remit. He was basically a massive pain in the arse. Declan loved him dearly, but he was aware that he had never been quick enough mentally for Patrick. He had always known his brother was the brains of the family, but he didn't feel inferior to his brother in any way. He was proud of him, and he was more than happy with his place in the Costello businesses.

Declan saw in Michael Flynn the same quick brain, and the same resolve that was so much a part of Patrick's make up. It was why his brother had taken to the lad, and why he himself understood the boy's importance to the firm.

Declan watched his brother as he flexed his muscles and made his point.

'You know me, Michael. I always like to know the score. I make sure that I am never in a position of weakness. It's nothing personal, Michael, I just feel that it's in my interest to know everything about everyone.'

Michael was not fazed. He would have done the same himself. 'I'm impressed, Pat. But I think you'll see the logic of it.'

Patrick sipped at his drink noisily before saying, 'He's Jonny Barber's boy, Michael.'

Michael shrugged nonchalantly. Declan was impressed with the boy's complete disregard of his brother. He had such confidence in himself, it was a pleasure to listen to him. He would not be another of his brother's yes men. But Michael Flynn was not arrogant – he genuinely wanted to bring in an earn.

'We want the Barbers out of the way, so what's the fucking difference? They're all cunts. Why do you think I cultivated Oates when I got the chance? He's an all right geezer, and the Barbers have treated him in a diabolical fashion. None of the people they have around them are even remotely happy with the circumstances of their employment. They shit on their own doorstep, rip off their own – they don't seem to understand that times have changed. I have done no more than open up a dialogue with Oates and he was thrilled, believe me. It's the next step, Pat.'

Patrick was listening to the boy intently. Michael had no

side, he was as honest as he was loyal. He had proved that already.

'You're right, mate. But I wouldn't be the boss if I didn't flex my muscles now and then. It never hurts to show that you're aware of what's going on. It's the reason we are so fucking successful, son. Remember that.'

Michael knew he had been both praised and subtly warned. He wasn't too bothered about either. He had no reason to worry – he had done nothing more than set up a good deal. He knew how to play the game. People like Patrick Costello needed to be reassured, needed to know that the people he put his trust in appreciated him. Michael was more than willing to give him what he saw as his due. It was a small price to pay for what he was getting in return, and he did respect him.

'I won't ever forget that, Patrick, don't you worry. I want you to know that I am grateful for every opportunity and every penny that I have earned from being a part of the Costello family. I just wanted to bring something to the table. It's a big earn, Oates likes me and, to be honest, I really like him. He's a decent bloke. But I'm not a fool – I guessed you would already be two jumps ahead.'

It was exactly what Patrick wanted to hear. He relied on the network of people he had accrued over the years, people who were willing to give him the full monty about anyone and everyone around him. Even Declan wasn't immune to his interest – that was something Patrick was not proud of, but he couldn't help himself.

'You're a good kid, Michael. I know that.'

The office door crashed open, and they were all surprised

to see Douglas Marshall burst into the room. Dougie was no more than a soldier, one of Declan's crew of heavies, and his interruption was not appreciated at all.

'What the fuck are you doing, Dougie?'

The words were spoken by Declan and the inference was that he had obviously lost his mind.

'I'm sorry about this, Declan, but the fucking Barbers have turned up looking for a fucking row.'

Chapter Twenty-Two

Dicky Barber was drunk enough to be reckless, but not so drunk he couldn't hear the warning bell that was clanging loudly in the back of his mind.

As he looked at the men policing the gates of Patrick Costello's home, he could see that they would happily die before giving the Barbers and their entourage entrance. They were just standing there, completely unconcerned at the turn of events, armed, of course, and adamant that the Barbers were not on the guest list.

Dicky knew they had made a colossal fuck-up. Neither of them had thought it through. Dicky wished he wasn't so drunk. The reality of the situation was dawning on him, and he knew he and his brother looked every inch the complete cunts they were.

Rob, however, was experiencing no such qualms. He was still determined to make his mark, make a public statement to the world. But, as a man who had never once had the nous to plan ahead, to try and cover any eventualities that might occur if things were to go wrong, he was not taking onboard that the men who had accompanied them were now backing away, realising they were outnumbered and outclassed. He was being treated as a minor irritation, and not as a serious problem.

Rob was quite affronted that they had not been granted immediate access to the Costello home. He had believed they would be ushered in like visiting royalty. But they were still outside the gates, and that was not going to change.

Rob was shouting now. 'Just tell him we are here, will you? It's a fucking party, ain't it? We are fucking guests.'

A heavyset man in his late fifties stood in front of the gates. He sighed. It was like dealing with football hooligans – all drink and bravado and not a brain cell between the lot of them.

'As I said before, you are *not* on the guest list. I would strongly advise you to put the weapons away and get yourselves home.'

The security was much heavier than they had anticipated. Dicky had counted at least seven men on the gates alone, and that was without the security for the cars that lined the country lane leading up to the property. These men were not about to be intimidated by anyone, and they were more than willing to do what they were paid to do.

Still, it was a shock to see just how Patrick Costello actually lived. Even from outside the electric gates, the house looked like something from a film set. It was lit up like Battersea Power Station for a start, and the drive – if they ever got past the gates, of course – appeared to be a good seven hundred yards long. The night air was filled with the sound of music, conversations and laughter. Everyone in that house was completely unaware that anything was amiss.

Dicky had already clocked the brick wall that surrounded the property, knew that it was as secure as Parkhurst. No one was getting in there without a fucking Sherman tank.

The only thing they had achieved tonight was signing their own death warrants, after showing the world just how amateur the Barbers actually were. It was a joke – a bad one at that.

Costello's drum was full of just about every Face in the Smoke and the surrounding areas. But not the Barber brothers. That said it all really. If they had any kind of status they would have been in there now, enjoying the hospitality like everyone else.

Dicky felt the cold fingers of fear envelop him as he looked around and saw the men they had brought with them reassessing their chances of getting away from here alive. It had already gone too far. *They* had gone too far the minute they had arrived on Patrick Costello's doorstep. It was the man's anniversary, a party to celebrate his family life. His kids were somewhere in there, for fuck's sake.

Dicky knew that even if they backed away now, they were still dead men. This was a real piss-take, an insult of Olympian standards. It was a drunken fucking faux pas that was so outrageous it could never be overlooked.

Jonny had been right: the Costellos *had* given them respect, and allowed them to work their own turf, even though they could have taken it from them easily. He could see that now. Fucking stone-cold sobriety and hindsight could often be a truly terrible thing. Drink was a fucking curse – it caused more trouble than it was worth. It gave people false courage and, even worse, it had the added bonus of fuelling the smallest of fires until it was suddenly a raging inferno of hatred and anger.

Rob already had his shotgun out; it was a small-gauge sawn-off, not really a weapon for something like this. Dicky Barber cringed with embarrassment. This really was fucking amateur night, and Dicky hated that he had, once more, let his hate rule his head.

But Rob needed to prove himself, needed to show that he was not about to cry off and walk away. He was going to make his mark.

'You don't fucking scare me, you cunts.'

Dicky saw his brother raise his firearm and knew he was going to use it. He watched helplessly as his brother was taken out within seconds by a crossbow.

It was as quiet as it was lethal. It was all over.

Chapter Twenty-Three

The party was in full swing and Josephine was watching Carmel Costello closely. She could see the woman was getting more and more irritated by the second, and she couldn't blame her. Patrick Costello had hardly shown his face all night and, as it was his party, that was not only rude, it was also worrying her personally, because Michael had not been near or beside *her* either.

The music was good, the food was fantastic, and the drink was flowing like water. All around her people were having a great time but, like Carmel, she couldn't help wondering where the fuck the men were.

She saw Carmel slip out of the large living room, and she followed her up the staircase and across the landing into the master bedroom. She could see how upset Carmel really was, and she couldn't blame her. It had to be a work situation of some description, but surely, on a night such as this, work could take a back seat?

She tapped gently on the bedroom door and then, without waiting for an answer, she slipped inside, closing the door quietly behind her. Carmel was sitting on a king-size bed and, for the first time ever, Josephine saw her with her guard down. She was wiping her eyes with a tissue, and she looked very fragile, very vulnerable. Josephine had never realised how thin Carmel actually was. Looking at her now, she seemed to have disappeared into her clothes. It was awful. She seemed older, defeated somehow. Her lovely face, always so perfectly made-up, and always with her trademark smile, looked haunted. It was a real eye-opener for Josephine.

Josephine went to her without even thinking about it and, putting her arm around the woman's shoulders, she hugged her gently, aware that Carmel needed comforting, needed someone to share her burden.

'Are you OK, Carmel?'

Carmel Costello looked around her sadly. The room was beautiful, it was something most women could only dream of. She had walked into this room once and felt that she had finally got it all, had finally made it. Yet it meant nothing to her now, at this moment in her life. It was as if the house, the cars, the lifestyle she craved were nothing more than an illusion because, until tonight, she had never felt such acute loneliness. Patrick had disappeared and left her alone at his own party, and that had hurt her more than she had thought possible.

Oh, everyone was enjoying themselves and they would assume that Patrick, being Patrick, had important business to attend to; it wasn't in any way a slur on her. But it had hurt. Being left alone for so long and putting on a brave face was difficult when all she really wanted to do was stab him through the heart. She had not realised how much she had wanted him to be beside her, how much that would have meant to her.

It was nice being comforted by young Josephine. She believed the girl meant well and wouldn't broadcast every word spoken by her to the nation. She could trust her, she felt that and, for the first time in years, she let herself say what she really meant – she needed to get it off her chest.

'I'll be all right in a minute, Josephine. It's just sometimes I could kill Patrick. He's left me out there on my own for hours. It's our night – he could at least remember that. I feel such a fucking fool.'

Josephine sighed. 'Tell me about it, Carmel. Michael's on the missing list as well, and Declan too. It has to be work. Something that needs sorting sooner rather than later. You're right to be upset, but I bet you it's something *very* important. Patrick worships you, anyone can see that.'

Carmel could see the girl was trying to make her feel better, and she appreciated that. It was kind of her to try and lift her spirits. But Carmel was feeling truly grieved. Josephine was too young and too innocent to understand the life she was getting into. She would soon learn the reality. It was easy to be so cavalier when it wasn't *her* husband who had left his own party.

'Listen to me, Josephine. Michael is just like my old man – he will always put his work first. Unlike most men, the work they are involved in can't be left till the morning. The world they live in means they are on their guard every second of every day. Literally anything can happen and, when it does, they have no choice but to make sure any problems are sorted, pronto. It means you had better get used to being alone most of the time, get used to worrying that the Filth will somehow take him from you, get used to looking over your shoulder constantly because you never know what the future might hold. You have to learn to look out for number one so that, if the worst does happen, you have made sure you have covered your own arse. It's a world of illusion, a world of pretending and putting on a front. It's a world that I really wish I had never entered. It's a world I craved, and one that I now feel trapped in.'

Josephine was shocked at Carmel's words – at the vehemence and also the truth of them.

Seeing Josephine's face, Carmel felt awful, sorry now that she had ever spoken. 'I'm sorry, Josephine love, take no notice of me. I'm just angry, that's all. I have a houseful of people, and Patrick has bloody well left me to it, and on our anniversary, if you please.'

Josephine just hugged the woman tightly once more, aware that Carmel regretted letting her guard down, showing her weakness, admitting her unhappiness.

'Listen, Carmel, I know I come across as a bit wet at times, and I know you have just told me the truth. But I love Michael and, no matter what happens, like you with Patrick, I will always stand by him. So don't worry about me. I'm stronger than I look!'

Up close, Josephine could see the fine lines around Carmel's eyes, and she could sense the woman's sadness. For the first time ever, she had seen the real Carmel Costello, and it had been a real eye-opener. She felt desperately sorry for her, more so because she knew how much Carmel Costello valued her reputation as a woman always in control.

'Come on, Carmel, let's get back to the party, shall we? If

I was you I would go in that office and give him a piece of my mind!'

It was the right thing to say and Carmel laughed. 'You're right, Josephine. Come on, let's get back downstairs.'

But her words stayed with Josephine; she knew that she would never forget them.

Chapter Twenty-Four

'What a fucking abortion that was! The Barbers have to be on something to actually think they could come here.'

Michael was as shocked as the Costello brothers at the turn of events. It was unbelievable. He turned to Patrick, saying angrily, 'Dicky's still breathing by all accounts, but Rob's on his last legs. Still, he is one strong fucker, I'll give him that. I've said to go and pick up Jonny. Then, when the party's over, we can finish this once and for all.'

Patrick nodded. He was absolutely outraged at the whole turn of events.

Declan was watching him carefully, and he could see the signs that denoted Patrick's true nature. His brother rarely allowed himself the luxury of giving his natural inclinations free rein, but he would now no doubt. Patrick would make sure that the Barbers paid for their sins a hundredfold, and who could blame him? It was a monumental piss-take but, worse than that, it was utterly fucking disrespectful. If the Barbers had planned it properly, and given them a run for their money, at least they would have had *some* respect. But to show up like that, without a fucking thought, was no more than a diabolical liberty. It had kept Patrick from attending his own party. It had caused him untold aggravation. A wedding, an anniversary, a birthday, a christening, or a fucking funeral – these were sacrosanct. They were private family functions and they were, because of their very nature, taboo. Anywhere wives, children or close family were all together was off-limits. This kind of action was something that only a fucking lunatic would even consider, especially when it involved a family like the Costellos.

Michael changed tack, trying to play it down when he could see that Patrick was becoming unhinged. *That* wasn't something that would benefit any of them.

'I've kept it quiet so far, Pat. No one here knows anything has occurred, but it will probably get out at some point. The Barbers' entourage are long gone – the fucking tossers were willing to serve up Jonny to get a pass. I've got people disposing of them as we speak. So, as fucking outraged as we are, everything is under control. It's sorted.'

Declan laughed suddenly, he had always had a strange sense of humour. 'Look on the bright side, Pat – saved us petrol money, eh? We've got them now. Jonny won't give us any trouble. From what I can gather he had nothing to do with the night's entertainment, but he'll know it's over for them.'

Patrick looked around him. He was still reeling from the shock of how close the Barbers had got to them. To his home. His family.

Michael had done well. He had organised the security with Declan, and he had not underestimated the need for men who were not only fearless, but who were also sensible enough to know that any trouble needed to be dealt with as quietly as possible. The use of a crossbow was genius.

'Imagine turning up somewhere like this with a fucking sawn-off! It just tells you how fucking ignorant and cheap they really are. Imbeciles. Fucking morons.'

The door opened then, and Carmel Costello stood there like the avenging angel. 'Patrick Costello, it's our wedding anniversary, remember? And you have spent most of the night in here! Are you thinking of joining your wife and guests at any point?' Carmel was fuming, that was evident.

Patrick immediately looked contrite. He knew she had a point, and she would be bringing this up till her dying day. His voice was soft as honey as he placated her. 'Look, Carmel darling, there's been a bit of aggro with your present, and I've been in here on the blower trying to sort it out. I'm so sorry, love.'

It was exactly what she wanted to hear, and she forced a smile on to her face. Patrick had apologised, and he was finally joining the party, so at least she might salvage something from the evening.

Chapter Twenty-Five

Jonny Barber was resigned to his fate. It was all over bar the shouting – the only thing he could do now was try and take whatever came his way with aplomb.

He was sitting in a damp, dark cellar somewhere, waiting for the Costellos to arrive and finish what his idiot brothers had started. Knowing Patrick Costello, he would want to finish this job off personally – and who could blame him? Jonny would have done the same thing himself.

He was cold – not that that mattered much in the grand scheme of things. He could hear his brother, Dicky, muttering away under his breath, and he guessed that he had come to the same conclusion as he had. They were living on borrowed time. Dicky had taken a beating; he had put up a good fight, but come off worst.

Jonny sighed heavily. He was still reeling from the turn of events. Rob, his baby brother and the bane of his life, should already be dead, but not him! The moron was fighting for every breath, lying on the filthy floor. The crossbow had hit him square in the chest, but it had obviously missed his heart. Jonny was surprised at the lack of blood, though he knew that a weapon such as a knife, or a crossbow dart in this case, stopped the bleeding if it was left in situ. If a knife was pulled out of a stab wound it brought tissue, muscle, guts, all sorts with it, and caused serious bleeding. If the knife was left in the wound, then it was unable to do any real damage – it stopped the bleeding for a start. Ironically, the dart was the reason his brother was still alive.

He could hear the conversation that was going on behind the door. The noise was comforting in some ways – there was a radio on somewhere; he could hear the music in the background. It almost sounded normal.

He sighed. He had tried to talk to Dicky, but he was already away with the fairies. Terror at the realisation of what he had brought on them all had robbed him of his reason. Lucky Dicky.

At least he was assured that his family would be all right. Patrick Costello was a lot of things but he was first and foremost a gentleman. Jonny thought back on the road that had brought him to this. He had been a man who had embraced violence; he had lived by it and, like his brothers, he had enjoyed it. The Barbers had been big fish in a very small pond – now that pond would be owned by the Costello brothers. Jonny had no doubt that all the people who had been forced to pay homage to *him* would be overjoyed at his sudden demise; there were very few who would have been willing to stand by his side. Oh, hindsight was a wonderful thing.

His old dad's favourite saying had been 'those who live by the sword, die by the sword'. He should know – the wife-beating ponce. He had finally beaten his wife once too often, and had then been taken out by his own sons. What goes around comes around, that was another of his old man's sayings.

Jonny Barber was astounded by how calm he was about his own situation, and how easily he seemed to have accepted his fate.

But when Patrick Costello was making him watch as Michael Flynn tortured his brothers to death, and he could hear their screams of agony ringing in his ears, he finally snapped out of his stupor. There would be no mercy; they were sending out a message that would be heard and remembered by everyone in their orbit for many years to come.

Chapter Twenty-Six

'For fuck's sake, Mum, give me a break, will you? All you ever seem to do lately is moan. I can't be doing with it. Fuck the priest! Why would I give a flying fuck about what he thinks of me?'

Hannah Flynn watched her son warily. She had heard the gossip about him, and about his growing reputation as Patrick Costello's right-hand man. Part of him had been gone from her a long time ago – Josephine had seen to that. But now the Costellos had him too and, between the lot of them, there was nothing left for her.

She rolled her eyes towards the ceiling, trying her hardest to keep her temper under control.

'I'm just saying Father Riordan is a good man who's always liked you, Michael. So I know that somehow you must have offended him for him to be avoiding you. He hasn't said anything outright, but there's clearly something radically wrong between you two. You must have said or done something to upset him and I'm telling you now, Michael, I don't care how hard you think you are, you will always be my baby, my *only* son – that will never change – but I want to know what you've done.'

Michael was just as annoyed. Father Riordan had no right to react in any way about something said to him in the confessional – that was supposed to be between him and God. The priest was irrelevant, he had nothing to do with any of it.

His mother, on the other hand, needed to be placated, and sooner rather than later. She set great store by the Catholic Church, and she saw the clergy as above everyone else because of their great faith. He actually agreed with her about that; it *was* something to be in awe of. To devote your life to Christ, and the good of others, was something he would never, ever understand, but that didn't stop him from having complete and utter admiration for the people who were willing to do it.

'Father Riordan caught me on a bad day, Mum. I might have fucked him off. I'll sort it out, OK?'

'Well, you'd better. I thought I had brought you up better than that. He's going to conduct your marriage ceremony, a holy sacrament which will bind you to that girl for the rest of your life. There's no such thing as divorce for us, remember.'

Michael nodded his agreement. 'I have no intention of *ever* getting divorced from my Josephine, Mum, so you can rest easy about that much anyway. And I will see the priest and apologise to him, so wind your neck back in, will you? He shouldn't be so fucking touchy anyway. I put more than enough poke into his bin, as you know yourself.'

That was true. Her son gave a lot of money towards the Church's charitable causes. He was more than generous and, until now, Father Riordan had been very vocal in his praise of her son's contributions to the parish.

Hannah was almost placated, but she couldn't shake the feeling of worry. The marriage was going ahead, and she had no option but to accept it. It was out of her hands, and her son had made his opinion very clear about that. He was besotted with the girl, and Josephine Callahan – soon to be Flynn – was as besotted as he was. Hannah should be pleased that her boy was settling down. If only her future daughter-in-law didn't irritate the life out of her.

The doorbell rang and she watched as her son nearly broke his neck to answer it. She could hear Josephine's voice in the hallway – it was like nails on a blackboard to her – but she plastered a smile on her face, and prepared to greet her son's intended with as much warmth as she could muster.

Chapter Twenty-Seven

Lana Callahan had heard the talk about the Barbers' untimely end; she knew enough about the Life to understand that, for the Costellos, the talk about the men's violent deaths could only enhance their reputation.

It was common knowledge that the Barbers had brought it on themselves; everyone knew that their bodies were never going to be found – not in this lifetime anyway, if ever. They were long gone, but the story of their demise continued to be whispered about. The police might have their suspicions, but there was nothing concrete for them to pursue – not that they would feel comfortable accusing the Costellos of anything anyway. Considering the Costellos paid the London Filth very generously to be left in peace, it wasn't in anyone's interest to rock the boat. Even the Serious Crime Squad had expressed little or no interest in the Barbers' sudden disappearance. Ultimately, *they* had wanted them off the streets and they weren't in the least bit bothered how that had come about.

But Lana was now finding herself becoming increasingly worried about her daughter's beau – and wondering exactly what he was capable of. She liked Michael Flynn a lot and she knew that he loved her daughter, but she couldn't help wondering how much her daughter really knew about the man she was marrying.

She herself hadn't fully comprehended, until this had happened, that he had another side to him. He hid it well, but it was there nonetheless. He had a kink in his nature, she knew that now for a fact. He had the capacity to completely disengage with anything that he felt was necessary to his own wellbeing, his peace of mind.

Her husband had told her, on the QT, the true story about the Barber brothers' final hours but, unlike Des, who seemed to think that Michael's part in the brutal murders was something to be applauded, she couldn't help worrying about what kind of a man her daughter was tying herself to.

Since Des had regaled her with their soon-to-be son-in-law's violent exploits, she had found herself watching him carefully. She'd observed him smiling and laughing as if nothing had happened – as though he had not a care in the world. He was still carrying on as normal and, in her heart of hearts, she felt that was wrong – very wrong. She understood that violence was a part of his life – it was a part of life for anyone in the criminal world. For people like the Costellos, violence gave them the edge, made their names and guaranteed them their place in society. She'd found it easy to accept until it had suddenly appeared on her doorstep.

She had been so pleased that Josephine had found a man like Michael, who could look after her, provide for her and give her a good life. Now she wasn't so sure. If only she didn't know so much about him; but Des had been proud to tell her how her daughter's husband-to-be had proved himself to Patrick Costello as a man capable of anything. He had seen it as an achievement to celebrate, something to be admired. He thought Michael Flynn was a high flyer, and he was over the moon that he was going to take their only child to the top with him.

It felt wrong to her now; violence should not be treated so matter-of-factly. Michael actually frightened Lana. He was marrying her daughter, and Josephine might think she understood what she was getting herself into, but she didn't. Josephine was a kind, trusting, loving young woman; Lana was convinced that if she ever knew the real truth about Michael it would destroy her. She was madly in love with him, and Lana knew that, even if she told her what she knew about Michael, Josephine wouldn't believe any of it.

She wished Des had kept his big mouth shut; he might think Michael was the dog's bollocks but now, thanks to him, *she* thought Michael was a dangerous fuck.

Chapter Twenty-Eight

Father Riordan could feel the sweat dripping from every pore in his body as Michael Flynn watched him closely. He knew that he had no right at all to stand in judgement over another human being, but the knowledge of the young man's crimes was something he couldn't forget about. It was on his mind every waking hour. He had listened to adulterers and wife beaters, he had made himself listen to people's deepest, darkest secrets, and he had always been able to tell himself that they had not told *him* – they had been confiding in the Lord God Himself. But not this time. This was something he couldn't find it in his heart to overlook. This was murder. It could never be rectified.

Now here was Michael, with young Josephine Callahan, listening to him eagerly as he talked about the importance of the marriage vows, about it being a blessed sacrament, and how they were expected to always remember that they had been joined together in Holy Matrimony by God Himself, when all the time *he* knew that Michael Flynn was a killer. Even worse, thanks to him, Michael had no guilty conscience about his act. It was over with, he had been forgiven. And Father Riordan had been the one to hear his confession. It was torturing him.

'Are you all right, Father? You look a bit peaky.'

Josephine seemed genuinely concerned about him and, as the priest looked into her lovely face, he saw the kindness there. This was a girl who was going to marry a man he knew was a murderer. He forced himself to smile at her and act normally.

'I'm not feeling too good to be honest, Josephine. I think I'm coming down with the flu.'

Josephine was instantly contrite, sorry that they had bothered him when he was obviously feeling unwell. 'Oh, listen, Father, we can do this another time. You get yourself off to bed. You know that we are both more than ready to be married. It's not long now, is it? I can't wait.'

Father Riordan was still smiling. 'You're right, Josephine, I shouldn't be here at all tonight. The last thing you two need is the flu! I'll see you both soon, OK?'

Michael stood up slowly and, grinning happily at Josephine, he said jovially, 'You go on, darling. I want to talk to Father Riordan in private for a minute.'

Josephine nodded, then she kissed the priest gently on his cheek. As she left the pew, she blessed herself before the altar, and the two men watched as she walked sedately out of the church.

Michael Flynn looked at the priest for long moments; he could almost feel the man's fear emanating from him. He was annoyed that Father Riordan, his confessor, his parish priest, was acting so oddly.

'What exactly is your problem, Father?'

The man didn't answer him – he couldn't even meet his eyes. This was an outrage as far as Michael was concerned. He had confessed his sins, as required by his Church, especially before his wedding day. Who the hell did Father Riordan think he fucking was? The cheek of him.

'You can't stand in judgement of me, Father, and we both know that. You're acting strangely, and I really don't like it. I confessed to you so I could get married free and clear. That's the *Church's* teaching, not mine. I've repented for all my wrongdoings and as far as I'm concerned we are square, mate. But if you don't sort yourself out, we are going to have a serious problem.'

It was a threat, and Father Riordan knew it. He had never thought for one second that his chosen life in the priesthood would eventually make him question not only his faith, but everything that he had ever believed in. This handsome young man, who came to Mass every Sunday, gave generously to the parish, who looked like any decent God-fearing individual, was about to marry a lovely young girl and live happily ever after, was a devil in disguise. He had made a choice. He had known that he had committed a mortal sin, and he had only confessed so he could put it behind him and get married with a clear conscience. Father Riordan was well aware that Michael Flynn felt no real sorrow for what he had done – he was playing at being repentant. But true repentance was the whole point of the confessional – without being truly sorry for your sins, it was meaningless.

'Are you listening to me, Father?'

The priest looked into Michael's eyes; whatever he did now would lay the foundations for the future. He prayed silently for the strength that he needed.

'I'm listening to you, Michael. But I don't feel that I can see you again. I know that I am failing you as a priest, but I have to follow my own heart, my own conscience.'

Michael was very quiet. He could see that Father Riordan was serious. Michael knew that he wasn't being awkward or deliberately obtuse. This was a real dilemma – for both of them.

'I trusted you, Father. Now I feel that was a big mistake on my part.'

The priest shook his head vigorously. 'No, Michael, you didn't make a mistake. Anything you might have told me in the confessional is sacrosanct. I can *never* repeat it to a living soul, and I wouldn't, I can assure you of that. But I can't act like it never happened, Michael. I have to go away from here.'

Michael sighed; he liked Father Riordan, he was a decent enough man. 'Look, Father, I'm sorry if my actions have caused you problems but, as far as I knew, I wasn't talking to you, was I? Anything that I *might* have said, was between me and my God. I think that you are overreacting. I mean, for fuck's sake, this is exactly what you lot sign on for, isn't it?'

The priest stood up. He could never hope to make this man understand how confused he was feeling, or why he felt the need to leave not only his parish, but his home and his whole life. Michael would never understand that just because *he* could live with his own actions, it didn't mean that everyone else could. It was a waste of time.

'Michael, look after young Josephine – she loves the bones

of you. I'll talk to Father Barry. He'll be more than happy to officiate at your wedding. You've both known him since you were little children anyway.'

Michael nodded sadly. He held out his hand and Father Riordan shook it heartily. He didn't know what else to do.

Book Two

Pride only breeds quarrels, but wisdom is found in all those who take advice

Proverbs 13:10

Chapter Twenty-Nine

1989

'For fuck's sake, Josephine, anyone would think we were fucking hard up, darling!'

Michael was laughing, but Josephine knew that he was actually annoyed. He spent money like it was going out of fashion on all manner of frivolities, and she didn't mind that; after all, he was the one earning it. But she couldn't understand why he got so annoyed with her because she liked to budget, liked a bargain. She could see him eyeing the mound of toilet rolls that she had piled up in the utility room, shaking his head in mock despair. All of the spare rooms were filled with her bargains and bulk-buys.

He just couldn't see that it made her feel good about herself, made her feel secure. She held her temper. She knew from experience that anything she might say would fall on deaf ears, and today she was not going to get involved in any arguments. She poured them both mugs of tea. It was her way of ending any dispute they might have, and it had always worked.

Michael smiled to himself, understanding that the conversation was now over. He was happy to oblige. 'Thanks, darling. I need this.'

Josephine smiled gently, and Michael was, as always, taken aback at how deeply he loved his wife. It never failed to amaze him how even a smile from her could tear at his heart. He adored her, and he wished that he knew how to make her feel better.

'You out all day, Michael?'

He nodded. 'I'll be home for dinner though – I'm only meeting Patrick to sort out a few bits and pieces. Nothing really important. Let's watch a film tonight, eh? Open a bottle of wine.'

Josephine laughed at his deliberate nonchalance. He was trying to make everything better and she loved him for that. 'That sounds good to me, Michael.'

'It's a date, then.'

Josephine leant against the granite worktop, and sipped her tea. She was never happier than when they were like this, easy in each other's company, and without the spectre that she felt was between them. No matter what Michael did or said to reassure her, she knew that, as much as he loved her, they were both aware of the void in their lives.

She swallowed down the sadness inside her. Michael couldn't cope when she felt like this, and he wouldn't leave her on her own if he thought she was obsessing about their life together and how she had let him down. He was so good to her, and she knew how lucky she was to have a man like him.

'Go on, get yourself off, Michael. I'm cooking a lamb casserole for us tonight, so ring me and let me know what time to expect you.' She kissed him softly, and walked with him to the front door.

He hugged her tightly to him, and she could feel the love he had for her. But instead of making her feel secure, all she felt was her failure as a wife. As he pulled out of the driveway, she closed the door and, leaning against it, she exhaled wearily. It was getting harder and harder to keep up her act.

The house was huge – much too big for just the two of them – but when they had bought it, they had assumed that they would be filling it with their children. Sons and daughters that they could love, cherish. They had meticulously planned for the big family they had both wanted. They had picked out names for the children-to-be, even chosen schools. They had never once allowed for the fact that she might miscarry each of those children, one after the other, with shocking frequency.

But she had done just that, lost every one in a blaze of blood and pain. It was so unfair. She had seen every doctor available, they had spent thousands of pounds, and they were still childless. Josephine was unable to keep a child alive in her womb for any length of time.

Now she was pregnant once more and this time she wasn't telling *anyone* – especially not her husband. *This* time, when the child they had created was expelled from her womb, she would carry the burden alone. She couldn't bear to look at his face again, first seeing the hope for her pregnancy then, eventually, witnessing his disappointment when it ended prematurely, seeing his pity for her, because she couldn't do the one thing that came naturally to every other woman in the world. It was the pity in his eyes that she found the hardest to endure.

No, she would carry this baby alone, with no doctors, no

family involvement whatsoever. She would just wait and see, and accept the outcome alone. The days of crying for hours on end were gone and she was not going to let Michael be hurt any more. She would shoulder this all herself. It was the least she could do. She couldn't get his hopes up again. It was cruel enough for her – she would protect him from it this time.

Chapter Thirty

Patrick Costello had been up half the night fighting with Carmel, and he was tired out. These days he was really feeling his age. His Carmel could keep a row going for fucking hours – she relished every second of it. Years ago he had too – the passionate fighting, followed by the even more passionate making up. Then it had been about making love for hours on end, picnics together in bed, champagne cocktails he would make for them, followed by more sexual gymnastics, and protestations of their undying love for one another. It was another lifetime.

Nowadays, as he tried to explain to his wife, he could only manage one or the other – the fucking or the fighting. Unfortunately for him, his Carmel was a born arguer, and she loved nothing more than a knock-down, drag-out fight on a regular basis. It had been nearly three in the morning before she had finally let him sleep and, the worst thing was, he *still* didn't know what the fuck they had been arguing about. He had to smile though, she was a game old bird, there was no doubting that. She never ceased to surprise him. She could pick a row with a deaf mute if the fancy took her. That had been what had attracted him to her deep down. Sure, she was a smashing-looking bird and good in the kip, but the fact she had never been in awe of him had stood her in good stead once upon a time. He had respected her for that. Now, he hated that she needed to have a tear-up on a regular basis; to prove that he still loved her he had to fight with her. He loved her as much as he was capable of loving anyone, but that didn't stop her getting on his nerves. Her constant need for attention was wearing thin – the dramatics that had once been so exciting were draining him.

As the mother of his children, Carmel would always have a hold on his affection. His daughters were not exactly kids to be proud of, though. They were such a disappointment to him, even though he loved them dearly. They were both lazy, lacking in intelligence, and unable to understand the concept of hard work, let alone the importance of actually getting a job. He had trusted her with the girls, and couldn't help feeling she had failed them.

He sighed, deciding not to think about any of that now – it already took up too much time, and it was a pointless exercise.

He glanced around his new offices; they were a bit over the top for his tastes, if he was being honest, but it was all about top show these days. He resented weighing out for it; he had eventually bowed to Michael's wishes, as he had known he would. The boy was more often right than wrong. But it still galled him – he paid more for these offices a year than he had paid for his first house. It was fucking mental but he accepted that to be seen as legitimate, they needed to *look* legitimate. That meant they actually had to run everything from the offices from which they ran the more legitimate businesses. It was sensible, but it was also against his natural inclinations. The fact that the businesses they ran from here were all very lucrative made no difference to him; Patrick was a born thief which was never going to change as long as he had a hole in his arse. He would always crave the illicit pound. He could have had a legal earn if he had chosen that route in life, but where was the real fucking profit for anyone with that old shite? Paying fucking tax for a start, employing accountants, and all the other old fanny that would have entailed.

This wasn't a country that had ever encouraged free enterprise. As soon as a profit was made, the government slaughtered you with taxes, and then they taxed your work-force to boot! The whole fucking concept of tax went against his beliefs. Nevertheless, Patrick was a realist, and Michael was right about making sure the legit businesses were seen to pay the taxes required of them and, more to the point, visibly profitable enough to explain away the cars they drove and the homes they lived in. It was a different world now; it was hard to launder the dead money – it needed to be absorbed into real businesses and, he had to admit, the lad had a knack for doing that. Times had changed all right, but he still bitterly resented every penny that he paid out to the government.

Michael breezed into the offices and, seeing Patrick Costello's dark countenance, he laughed loudly. 'For fuck's sake, Pat, you look fucking knackered, mate. Sorry I'm late. Traffic.'

Patrick smiled despite himself; only Michael would have

the front to say that to him. 'Don't start me off. Carmel had the urge for a fucking all-nighter. If any man had a fucking reason to find a new bird, it's me.'

Michael had heard it all before. Patrick had always been very vocal about his wife's ability to fight him on a whim, and at any hour of the day or night, by all accounts. It sounded so tiring to Michael – he could never have lived a life like Patrick and Carmel Costello. She was a raving nutbag, and that was being nice about her. But she was not a woman who endeared herself to the people around her. She was arrogant for starters. She looked down her nose at basically everyone around her, and she treated the people who worked for Patrick and Declan with such obvious disdain that it was impossible for them not to see it. He would *never* have tied himself to a woman like Carmel, he knew that much. She had delivered Patrick's children with the minimum of fuss, but that was as far as her usefulness had gone. That Patrick was not as enamoured of his wife – or her tantrums – as he had once been, was more than evident lately. But Michael knew better than to give an opinion either way. That was the easiest way to destroy a good friendship, and the easiest way to get himself killed. Women like Carmel were inclined to cause as much trouble as possible if they felt they were being ousted from their position.

'Well, that's your business, mate.'

Patrick laughed. He was well aware that Michael loathed his Carmel, and always had. She had that effect on most people. The only person his Carmel had ever liked was Josephine Flynn, and that was only because poor Josephine actually liked his wife.

'You're a diplomat, Michael. So, tell me, how is everything going?'

Michael was all business suddenly, glad to be away from the personal – and the dangerous. 'Well, it's good news about the mortgage businesses. I told you they would be a lucrative earn, and they are. Serious money is coming in now, Patrick, and best of all, it's being encouraged by the government. Buying your own house is available to everyone these days, and our brokers are doing well. It's such an easy fucking earn. It's also a good way of laundering money, Pat. Buying a house for cash and then remortgaging it, means the money from the mortgage company can then be put into legitimate bank accounts. It can be moved about, buying and selling other properties, for example, investing it into businesses, clubs, whatever. I've been moving a lot of the money into Spain, investing in the property market in Marbella and Benidorm. The good thing about Spain is there's no extradition so, for a lot of our investors, that's a fucking added bonus. They can get out there easily – it's a lot closer than South America, put it that way.'

Patrick Costello already knew everything that Michael was telling him. It rankled with Michael that, after all this time, Patrick Costello should still feel the need to keep an eye on him. But he would never change; Michael had no choice but to accept it. All of that aside, Patrick Costello still trusted him more than he had ever trusted anyone. It was just the nature of the beast.

Patrick was happy with the news. They were coining it in, making real money, getting a fantastic return for their initial investments, and that was only because of Michael

Flynn. *He* had the foresight to see the opportunities that Spain and Portugal had to offer long before anyone else. He had been adamant about investing not just money, but their time and effort, into the new ventures. He had insisted, from the start, that they needed to not just make their mark but, more importantly, they needed to ensure that they put their own people in the key positions ready for the future.

It was already paying off big time – plus they had guaranteed for themselves the foothold that ensured that anyone else who might feel the need to invest out there had no other option but to talk to them first. Patrick Costello knew that this lad had sewn up Spain and the surrounding areas. He had also done it legally.

'The Spanish don't give a fuck about anything, Michael, they just want people to bring their money out there. Tourism has already fucked the economy. They are far too reliant on it already, just as you predicted. Whole communities are now dependent on the hotel industry. You were right about that, mate. I bow down to you, you're a fucking genius, son. But I always knew that, didn't I?'

Michael accepted the man's praise as his due. He loved Patrick Costello; he had been very good to him, and Michael had made sure that he had earned not only his trust, but also his respect. That was why knowing that Patrick still felt the need to spy on him rankled. It offended him and his sense of loyalty. But he couldn't say a word – that would be tantamount to mutiny.

Michael could never admit to Patrick that he was aware of it. His position in the Costello family gave him not just a serious earn, but also guaranteed him a place in the London underworld that he could never have occupied without Patrick Costello taking him under his wing and giving him his personal attention. He could never, ever forget that; he would always be grateful for the man's interest in him, and the opportunities he had been afforded because of it.

'Listen, Patrick, I think we should go and have a couple of drinks, a bit of lunch, and discuss a few business opportunities that I think might be in our interests.'

Patrick Costello was more than game. He always enjoyed listening to the lad's ideas – Michael Flynn had the knack of sniffing out an earn before anyone else. But, more than that, Patrick Costello genuinely enjoyed his company. 'Lead the way, my son. I'm up for all that.'

Chapter Thirty-One

Declan Costello woke up with a blinding hangover. He opened his eyes warily – the sunlight was already giving him gyp. He squinted his eyes and attempted to look at his watch, but it was a pointless exercise. He brought his right arm as close to his face as possible – all he could see was a blur. His watch was a solid gold Rolex, with a gold face and gold numerals. He could see fuck-all, let alone the time.

He looked around him groggily; he recognised the bedroom at least. It was the boudoir of one Samantha Harker. He had found himself here on more than one occasion and, in his defence, he had never remembered actually arriving. He pulled himself up in bed and, putting the pillows behind his back, he leant into them, using the headboard as a backrest. He could smell himself – a mixture of sweat, alcohol and Samantha Harker. He scrabbled around on the bedside table and, as he knew he would, he found his cigarettes and lighter. He lit a Benson & Hedges, and pulled the smoke into his lungs lazily.

The room was actually very clean. Samantha was a good housekeeper – he remembered that from past experience. Her flat was spotless, and quite well decorated, considering.

She was a nice enough girl and a game bird. *Great* pair of tits, and not bad-looking. She was very young though.

He felt a sudden flush of shame wash over him – he was old enough to be her father. She was the only girl that made him feel like this. Yet here he was, once more in her bed. He closed his eyes in annoyance.

He could hear her moving about in the kitchen. Her flat was so small, it was like being in a fucking envelope. The bedroom door opened a few minutes later, and Samantha came into the room, smiling that big smile of hers, and bringing him a mug of tea. Her little girl was, as always, hot on her heels. The child was like a miniature of her mum. She had the same blue eyes, the same thick blond hair, and the same wide smile. She stood at the end of the bed, and he could sense her watching him.

'Here you are, Declan, a nice cup of tea.'

He took the steaming mug of tea carefully. Samantha always acted as if he didn't owe her anything, and why wouldn't she? He owed her fuck-all.

Samantha sat on the bed beside him. She was devoid of make-up, and her dressing gown hid the killer body that he knew so well. 'What a great night again! Honestly, Declan, I really did enjoy myself.'

He smiled, unsure what to say to her.

Samantha looked closely at the man she had spent the night with on more than one occasion and seeing the way he was acting – as if his being in her bed was something to be ashamed of – she felt the burning anger that only humiliation could bring. He was the only man she had ever allowed into her home, into her bed, since she had given birth to her daughter. She had felt such an affinity with him from their first meeting, she had truly believed they had made a genuine connection. He was much older than her, but that didn't bother her at all. She had been attracted to his personality, his strength, and his kindness. She had felt all of that straightaway. She had also felt a deep physical attraction to him that she had never felt for anyone else before. He had sought *her* out after their first meeting; she had never once looked for him – she had too much pride in herself for that. He had pursued her, as she had known he would. Now he was suddenly acting like she was beneath him, and that hurt.

She opened her arms, and pulled her little daughter on to her lap, hugging the child to her. Declan watched her warily. He could feel the atmosphere changing, knew that he was naked, and had no option but to wait for his opportunity to get his kecks on, and run like the fucking wind as far away as humanly possible.

Samantha looked into his eyes for long moments. She was still hugging her little daughter tightly, and he could see how the child enjoyed her mother's embrace, and how much affection there was between them.

'Listen, Declan, I don't like you treating me like this. You act like this has never happened before, but it has – many times. I've fallen in love with you, Declan, I think you already know that. But I will not let anyone treat me like a whore. If you don't want to see me again, then you can fuck off, OK?'

Declan wanted to hold her, tell her it was going to be all right. But he couldn't. 'You could be my daughter, Sam. I'm far too old for you. I'm trying to be the good guy here.'

Samantha smiled sadly. 'Well, it's a pity you didn't think about that before we got so involved. It's OK to sleep with me in secret, then? Thanks a bunch, Declan. You know where the door is.' She stood up and, with as much dignity as she could muster, she carried her daughter out of the room.

Declan lay there in Samantha Harker's bed, wishing with all his might that he was anywhere else in the world. He could hear Samantha in the kitchen, chatting away to her little girl, pretending that everything was fine, but beneath the love he could hear in her voice for her child, there was a deep abiding sadness.

Declan Costello had never felt so guilty about anything in his whole entire life.

Chapter Thirty-Two

Carmel Costello watched her two daughters with growing irritation. They argued constantly with each other and with her. They treated her like she was no more than a servant. Assumpta, the eldest, had become her nemesis; she would argue that black was white if it meant going against her own mother. Gabriella, too, would gladly pick a fight with her own fingernails – she was as spoilt as her older sister, and even more inclined to argue just for the sheer hell of it.

Patrick always tried to insinuate that they took after her! As far as she was concerned, they were their father's daughters. They were completely spoilt – they had never once had to do anything for themselves, and they never *were* going to do anything for themselves. She had given them everything they had wanted, and they repaid her by demanding that she give them even more. To be fair, she had used them to make Patrick do whatever she had wanted him to do. The girls had been her bargaining chips, her way of making him toe the line, and he had done everything she had asked of him.

Now the girls were completely out of her control. They were both without a conscience, without any moral compasses whatever. They were as spoilt as she was but, unlike her, they didn't have the brain capacity to understand that it took more than a temper tantrum to get what they wanted from a man like their father.

Patrick was disappointed in the girls and she was as disappointed in them as he was. The girls' education had cost a small fortune, and they didn't have a single qualification between them. She had been so sure that they would both be achievers, would both make their parents proud of them. It had never occurred to her that they would end up no better than if they had been brought up on a council estate. She had assumed the fact they went to a very expensive private school would have at least guaranteed them a place in society, would have given them something that could have helped them to get on in life. But it had been a waste of time and a waste of money.

She was also becoming aware that her husband saw these daughters of his as the product of *her* machinations, *her* insistence that he let her sort it all out, because he was incapable of understanding the economics of a female's education. But she was not to blame – it was her daughters who had failed them both, who had not understood that they were in a position to make something of themselves, who had both left a very expensive education with no more than a backward glance, and nothing whatsoever to show for any of it. Even she had read more books than they had, and that was saying something. She had simply assumed the school would see to everything they needed for a decent education – they were getting paid enough money after all. It had never occurred to her that the school would take the money and run.

Patrick saw his daughters as no more than the spoilt brats they were. He was absolutely right about that, of course. Now she had to break the news to him that Assumpta was pregnant. She was losing him, she knew that much; he already saw her as the architect of everything that had gone wrong with the family. This could be the final straw.

The girls were still at it. It was amazing really to see them in action. When they were fighting they really didn't have any care for anyone else around them.

'Assumpta, shut up for five fucking minutes and talk to me, will you?'

The girls both looked at their mother with abject shock at her words.

'Your father is going to go fucking ballistic when he finds out you are in the club. So, if I were you, darling, I would think long and hard about his reaction to your news. I would also make sure that the father is on hand, or at least give him a name. By Christ, I never thought that I would look at you two and feel such shame!'

Assumpta and Gabriella exchanged glances. It suddenly occurred to them both just how serious the consequences of their lifestyles might be.

When Assumpta looked at her mother, Carmel saw the fear on her eldest daughter's face. She had finally broken through to both of her girls.

'Your father is going to want to kill whoever is responsible, take my word on that. So, please, Assumpta, use your brain for once, and try and make this as painless as possible for everyone concerned.'

Carmel Costello had finally won her daughters' full

attention and, even though she knew it was only because they needed her to stand between them and the man who had fathered them, it was still something of a coup for her.

Chapter Thirty-Three

Michael had just come through the back door of his house and, as he was taking his sheepskin coat off, he called out loudly, 'Oh, Josephine, you're not going to fucking believe this, darling. It's so fucking mental.'

Sitting in her daughter's kitchen, Lana Callahan was all ears; she knew a serious bit of gossip when she heard it. She shook a warning finger at her daughter, and Josephine smiled. She always told her mother everything eventually anyway.

Michael bounced into the kitchen, all dark good looks and natural confidence. That was his way. He always seemed to be happy with his surroundings; no matter what the situation might be, nothing ever seemed to faze him. He sounded shocked, though, about whatever he had heard. Lana suspected that this was one of the few times he had let his usual guard down.

The sight of his mother-in-law, however, sitting to attention at his kitchen table, stopped him in his tracks. She wasn't his biggest fan, he knew that, but she was a woman who liked to know what was going on first-hand. And she was like the grave.

So, grinning nonchalantly, he said in a pseudo-dramatic voice, 'This is something you might regret hearing, Lana, I'm warning you now.'

Lana laughed. She loved to hear the latest gossip, but she was more than capable of keeping it to herself; she knew the danger involved in repeating things she heard in this house, especially when it concerned people like the Costellos and their ilk.

Josephine opened the fridge and took out a can of lager and, as she opened it, she looked at her husband craftily, and said, 'Come on then, Flynn, don't keep us in suspense.'

Michael took the beer from her and, after taking a deep drink, he wiped his mouth carefully. Then he waited for his wife to sit back down at the kitchen table before he said seriously, 'Assumpta Costello is pregnant. Patrick is going off his fucking nut.'

He waited for the reaction he expected, but it didn't arrive. Instead, his wife and her mother didn't act even remotely surprised. He had expected them to have been agog, as shocked as he was at the news.

'Has she named anyone yet, Michael?' Josephine kept her voice as neutral as possible.

He shook his head, unsure now if this revelation was actually as secret as he had first believed. Patrick had not said a word to him personally about any of it, he had heard it from Declan. Now he had a good idea why Patrick was keeping it so close to his chest. If his own wife and her mother were not shocked at the news of Assumpta being pregnant, that could only mean they knew something that he obviously didn't.

Michael shrugged carelessly, but he was a bit miffed. 'I don't know about that. Declan only told me because of Patrick's extremely erratic behaviour of late. He has been so unpredictable, so fucking angry with everything and anyone. Patrick is obviously keeping all of this well under wraps, and who can blame him? But he is like a bear with a fucking sore arse and, when he finally does fucking let rip, God help the poor fucker responsible. He is like a man possessed. He's ashamed into the bargain – I bet that's the real fucking problem actually. After all, she's still a kid, really.'

Josephine and her mother still didn't say a word to him about Assumpta or her predicament. That was irritating him. He felt pushed out, as if he was a mug or a fucking outsider, who wasn't deemed fit to know anything of importance. His good mood was slowly evaporating, and he was regretting his eagerness to discuss any of this with his wife or her mother. His amiable demeanour was gone in seconds and the women were immediately alerted to his changed mood. His voice was flat now, his irritation more than evident as he said sarcastically, 'I am now assuming that you two ladies know more about this drama than I do. So come on – spill. I'm all ears.'

Josephine really didn't want to be the one who told her husband about his closest friend's daughter – well, *daughters* if all the talk was true. They had certainly kept it in the family anyway. If they had not been Patrick Costello's daughters, their antics would have been the talk of the town for a lot longer and with much more graphic detail. As it was, only a few of the women who were married to men with access to the inner circles had felt safe enough to discuss it amongst themselves, and they had never talked about it to anyone outside. It was far too dangerous. No one would want to be the person who informed Patrick Costello about his daughters' private lives.

But both of his daughters had been putting themselves out there for a long time, with anyone and everyone who would have them, if the gossip was to be believed. Now Assumpta was pregnant, and it was going to be a whodunnit, there was no doubt about that. If there had been a regular bloke involved, then Patrick might have swallowed it, but that wasn't the case. Assumpta had been taking on all-comers for a long time, and she was as brazen as she was available. It had been common knowledge amongst the women in the Costello world but, as always in these situations, the men had no inkling whatsoever.

Josephine could not help resenting the fact that girls like Assumpta managed to get a baby without even trying, and grow it inside them without any problems whatsoever. If they didn't choose to abort the poor child, they just pushed it out with the minimum of fuss. They treated childbirth and pregnancy without any kind of respect, they had no concept of the importance of what their bodies had achieved. Pregnancy was no more than a problem for them. It was just something they could choose to either continue with or, the more likely scenario, remove from their bodies, and then carry on their lives as if none of it had ever happened, as if they had never been lucky enough to have a baby inside them. A little baby that was healthy and snug inside a womb that would not let them down, would not suddenly expel the poor child from their bodies, leaving them not only devastated but, with each painful, bloody failure, feeling less and less of a woman, unable to do the one thing that was expected of them. It was so fucking wrong. *She* wanted, *needed* a child more than anything else in the world, yet she had miscarried one after the other. The only baby she had managed to carry longer than a few months had died inside her, and she had gone through the whole pain of early childbirth knowing she would get nothing at the end of it.

She realised that her mother was talking to Michael. She forced herself to listen to their conversation, but she was so hurt, so angry at life.

Michael was shaking his head in amazement now, his earlier annoyance with his wife and mother-in-law gone. He listened closely to Lana as she told him the score about Patrick's daughters; she was very knowledgeable about them, and their lifestyles – that much was obvious to Michael. It seemed that the women knew far more than the men around them about what was actually going on.

He found himself believing everything that Lana was telling him about the Costello girls and their carryings on. There was a ring of truth in what she was telling him which he couldn't ignore. He felt the same burning heat of humiliation and anger that his friend would be feeling at his daughters' shame, and he was sorry to the very heart of him.

'If Patrick knew that his daughters were laying down with all and sundry on a regular basis he would go off his fucking tree. The men who they have been with can't have known whose daughters they were cavorting with, surely? No one would dare to touch them knowing they were Patrick Costello's girls.'

Lana shrugged, irritated now. She had not trusted her daughter's husband since the night the Barber brothers had gone on the missing list. He was a dangerous man, who acted like he was normal, but it was all a sham. If she had had her way, her daughter's wedding would never have gone ahead. Her husband loved him, though; he saw him as the son he had never had, thought the sun shone out of his arse, as did her daughter. But she had sussed the real Michael, and his complete ignorance about men and the lure of girls like the Costellos incensed her. It just proved to her how foolish these men could really be.

'You listen to me, Michael Flynn. You'd be surprised at just how low some men are willing to sink. From what we've heard, those girls have been at it for years. Carmel Costello might not be my favourite person, but she didn't deserve what those girls have done. She tried to give them a decent start in life. Patrick Costello, the big-headed bully that he is, has to come to terms with his daughters' actions. It won't be easy for him, but he has no other option. So remember this for the future, Michael – it takes two to tango. If she can name the father of Patrick Costello's first grandchild – and that is what her child is, remember, *his* grandchild, his flesh and blood – I will eat my fucking knitting.

'And another thing, Michael, while we are all being so honest. I would lay good money on the child being black, or at least dark-skinned. But I expect you and the Costellos will sort it out. "Who would sleep with Patrick's daughter?" This from a man who knows first-hand what men are capable of, who prides himself on his knowledge of the world around him. Patrick Costello is going to get the shock of his life, and do you know something? I'm glad. It's about time you realised that you are not the be all and end all. There is always someone who will sneak under your radar, and take what's yours, destroying everything you hold dear without you even noticing it.'

Michael was utterly taken aback at his mother-in-law's vehemence. He had only sought to give his wife a bit of gossip, as he usually did when he came home. He told her everything about his life, his work – he always had done.

Josephine, however, had been very quiet throughout this conversation. She had left her mother to tell him what they knew about Assumpta and her unfortunate situation. In truth, he had heard *far* more about the Costello girls and their sexual gymnastics than he felt comfortable with. He could *never* let Patrick know that he was aware of any of this.

Lana, he realised, had enjoyed giving him the truth about the situation. Lana had never really been right with him since before his marriage to her only daughter. She had seemed to change overnight. He had put it down to his own mother's interference, and Lana's natural concerns for her only daughter. Now, though, he couldn't help wondering if she just didn't like him. She had once been his biggest fan – now she had no real care for him at all. Every time Josephine had lost a child, Lana had been there, holding her daughter's hand, and he had seen her watching him closely, as he grieved the loss of his child with his wife. He had felt her blaming him for each one, even as he guessed that she didn't want her daughter to carry his spawn.

While they were childless, Lana felt that she had the upper hand. As though the marriage wasn't really consummated and, therefore, it could be dissolved. She didn't understand that, as much as he wanted a child, he would always want Josephine more. She was everything to him, and she always would be. It was Josephine who craved a child. He didn't care any more one way or the other. He just wanted his wife, his Josephine.

He smiled amiably, unwilling to let this woman know that she had affected him in any way. 'Well, Lana, that's told me, all right. In future, I will keep my fucking trap shut.'

Josephine could sense the animosity coming not only from her mother, but also from her husband. He had every right to feel aggrieved. Her mother had no right to treat him as she did, to show her contempt for him, and the life he lived. He provided her with everything she could want and more. Josephine knew that she had to say something to her mother. She had to show Michael that she understood how he was feeling, that she was on his side, as she always had been and always would be.

'That's enough, now. I think it's time you went home, Mum.'

Lana looked at her daughter in disbelief. She was being asked to leave, *told* to leave. It wasn't a request, her daughter was aiming her out the door all right. It was a dismissal.

Michael smiled genuinely then. He was pleased that Josephine could see his point of view, understood how he hated it when her mother treated him with such contempt in his own home.

Lana felt her face flush with humiliation. Josephine treating her so shabbily hurt her deeply, but she couldn't retaliate.

'Come on, Mum, Dad will be wondering where you are.'

Lana walked out of the room with as much dignity as she could muster. In the entrance hall of her daughter's home, she picked up her coat from the arm of the large leather sofa that was all but lost in the huge space that Lana had always admired. Her daughter's home was not just big, it was also very beautiful, Josephine had the money needed for such a property. Michael had always given her daughter whatever she wanted but, even knowing that, Lana still couldn't bring herself to forget what he really was or what he was capable of.

Josephine held the front door open, and Lana walked out of the house quickly. But she couldn't resist one last jibe; she was so offended at the treatment she'd received, which she felt was so unfair. She wanted nothing more than her daughter's happiness. Josephine was a lot of things, but she wasn't happy. How could she be with a violent thug like Michael?

'I can't believe you are really doing this to me, Josephine. I would give you the world on a plate if I could and you know that.'

'Oh, I do know that, Mum, I always have. But Michael is my husband, and he has already given me the world on a plate, in case you haven't noticed. He has also given you and Dad a good earn. You've never been so well off. And if I have to choose between you both, you know it will always be him, Mum.'

Lana walked away. As she got into her car, she heard the front door close loudly behind her.

Michael hated seeing his wife so torn. He wanted to protect her from anything that might harm her. It was his job as her husband. He opened his arms and pulled her into them. He could feel her body relaxing into his, knew that she was where she wanted to be.

'I'm so sorry, Josephine. I don't know what that was about.'

She hugged him tightly, enjoying the feel of him, the smell of him. He felt so safe, so strong. 'Oh, forget about it, Michael.' She wanted to change the subject. Make it all go away. 'How much does Patrick know about his daughters, do you think?'

He sighed in consternation. 'I really don't know. Declan told me about it in confidence. Patrick hasn't said a dicky-bird – now I know why. If what your mum said is true, and I think it probably is, Patrick will have a hard time taking all that onboard. Who wouldn't? He thought the sun rose and set with his girls. They were his reason for living. His kids, his flesh and blood.'

Josephine didn't answer that. She hoped that *her* flesh and blood, this pregnancy, would finally come to fruition and give them the one thing they couldn't buy. Just one child would be enough – that's all she wanted.

'I tell you this much though, Josephine. Whoever Assumpta names as the culprit will wish they had never been fucking born.'

Chapter Thirty-Four

Patrick Costello was practically hyperventilating, such was the vehemence of his anger. He knew he had to be alone for a while, so he had come into his office and poured himself a very large whisky. He sipped it slowly, savouring the strong taste, and the burn as he swallowed it down. He needed the alcohol to give him at least a modicum of inebriation, to take the edge off feeling too much.

This had never happened to him in his life before. He was never unable to control his emotions. His daughter's pregnancy was bad enough but, coupled with her bare-faced refusal to name the culprit, his usual aplomb was rapidly deteriorating. He took another large sip of the whisky, praying for it to calm him down and give him some kind of peace. He needed to deaden his emotions for a short while, until he could once more control himself – and his actions.

He was going to kill someone soon – that was a given – and, if his daughter didn't answer his questions, there was a good chance that the dead person might actually be *her*. It was her reluctance to name anyone as the father which had finally convinced him there must be more than one person in the frame. If it had been a love job, she would have come clean. He could have accepted that, could have understood the power of youth, of being in love for the first time. He wasn't a complete fucking moron, he could have overlooked such behaviour if it was down to love. He would still have been angry, but he would have allowed for his daughter, his baby, to have been caught up in her hormones.

But it wasn't like that at all. This was devoid of any romance and, therefore, of any reason he could have found to forgive her. She had no idea who was the father of her child and she didn't seem to care either. It was as if the child she was carrying inside her was nothing more than an inconvenience. She just wanted it gone from her, aborted, taken away as soon as. It was actually her complete disregard for the child inside her that really concerned him. His Assumpta, his lovely girl he had adored, was treating her pregnancy as simply a problem to be solved. She did not seem to comprehend the enormity of what was happening to her, that she was now the guardian of another human being, a child that *she* had created. She didn't understand that, as Catholics, they had no option but to bring the child into the world, and love it unconditionally, no matter the circumstances of its conception. That was the whole ethos behind being a fucking Catholic in the first place – especially an Irish Catholic. You sinned, and you then lived with that sin. You *loved* that sin, and you cared for that sin until it wasn't a sin any more – it was the best thing to have happened to you, a gift from God Himself. It was given to you for a reason – to make you a better person, and show you the miracle of life, and how it can bring you peace, and more love than you could ever imagine.

Assumpta just wanted it gone from her, as if she was drowning an unwanted kitten.

The door of his office opened quietly, and he stood still as a statue. His daughter was there. He could smell her, the perfume she wore, the heavy scent of her make-up. She had always worn far too much make-up. She was a beautiful girl, and he had never understood her fascination with painting her face. But he had allowed it. He had given his wife the final say on the girls and their lifestyles. Now he was sorry, even though he knew that his Carmel had done her best by the girls. She was as baffled as he was about Assumpta and her predicament. He stood stiffly, looking out of the window, seeing the beauty of the view, all the while forcing down his anger, his disappointment and his shame that his daughter had really thought that he would not have a problem arranging for her to have her child scraped out of her. One wrong word from his daughter now, and he would likely seriously harm her.

Assumpta looked at her dad. For her whole life he had only been there as a provider – her mum had been the main carer. She had done her best, but she had always been more interested in how she herself looked, or in how they were dressed.

Assumpta had been sexually active since her early teens. Her reputation meant nothing to her. She was a Costello and *that* had given her the power over everyone in her orbit since she could remember. Everyone was nice to them because they were Costellos – no other reason. She had started sleeping around to prove to herself that she could transcend the Costello name. If only she knew then what she knew now.

She was already four months gone, and all she wanted was for her dad to make it go away and let her start her life again, properly this time, sensibly, with the gift of hindsight. Now she knew the pitfalls, she was more than willing to learn her lesson. Whatever it took, she would do it.

'I'm sorry, Dad.'

Patrick closed his eyes in distress. She sounded so young, so innocent. This was his baby, his first-born. This was the girl who adamantly refused to give him the name of her child's father.

He gulped at his whisky. Then he said as calmly as humanly possible, 'Just tell me who the father is. That is all I want to know.'

Assumpta swallowed down her annoyance. If he only knew the circumstances, he might understand her reluctance to broadcast it to the nation. But if he did, he would realise that she couldn't say exactly who the father was. She had a vague idea, going by the dates, but that wasn't going to be enough for her father. 'I wish I could turn back time, Dad. But I can't, no one can. I just want the opportunity to put this behind me and start again.'

Patrick turned around then, and looked at his daughter. She was so pretty, all tits and teeth – a real brahma. Her hair was thick and shiny, her eyes were deep blue, and she had his mum's high cheekbones. She was a Costello all right – physically, anyway.

'You're having this fucking baby, Assumpta – get that through your thick head. As a Catholic, I can't believe that you ever thought otherwise. If you *don't* have your baby, Assumpta, I will cut you off from this family without a second fucking thought. I swear that to you in the name of the Christ Child Himself. I will never forgive you as long as you live. You will be as dead to me as the child you murdered.'

It was over. Patrick Costello looked at his daughter and knew that he had finally beaten her. His threat to cut her off had frightened her more than anything else. That troubled him, but he firmly believed that the child would be the making of her. It was the only thing left that could redeem her in his eyes.

Assumpta knew that she had no option but to do as her father insisted. He had shown her how serious he was, and he was not going to change his mind. This child she was carrying meant more to him than it could ever mean to her. She hadn't thought for a second that anyone in her family would welcome her pregnancy; she had banked on her parents wanting the child removed as quickly and quietly as possible. That *her* father, Patrick Costello, really believed in the sanctity of life had been something she had never thought possible. But she could not have been more wrong. The stories she had heard about him all of her life suggested the opposite. His capacity for great violence, the myths about his involvement in the death and the disappearance of people who had thwarted or challenged him, implied that her father was a murderer.

To now find out that this same man was adamant that abortion was unacceptable, was a sin against God, scared her. She had always assumed that his churchgoing was just another scam, nothing more than a public show, a pretence to make him look like a good, decent man. That her father *actually* believed in the Catholic Church, and its most basic of beliefs, forced her to reappraise her position.

But she had one last argument up her sleeve. One she hoped would cancel out everything else her father had said.

'Dad, I have to tell you something.'

Patrick shrugged. He could be magnanimous now – he had won the war. 'Go on, then.'

'This baby I'm carrying might be black.'

Patrick could hear the hope in her voice. She genuinely thought that a black child might be enough to make him turn against everything he had ever believed in. This daughter of his would never cease to amaze him.

'And?' He made sure his voice was as nonchalant as possible.

Assumpta was rattled by his reply. 'I just thought you should know, that's all.'

Patrick laughed. 'The fact you said "might" tells me all I need to know about you. But I couldn't give a flying fuck if it was sky blue with pink spots. It's going to be born and it will bear the Costello name. It will be my first grandchild and, as such, it will be given every opportunity I can provide for it and, hopefully, unlike its mother, it will have the brains to make something of itself.'

Assumpta turned to leave, and Patrick fought the urge to kick her arse out of the door. She had disappointed him in more ways than one. It wasn't the pregnancy itself – he would have come to terms with that eventually – but his daughter's disregard for her own child's welfare, and her complete indifference to it had really shown him how selfish she was. He had to admit that he was ashamed of his daughters – both of them. They were cut from the same cloth, and so self-absorbed they couldn't see further than their own needs and wants. He had grown up with nothing; they had been given all they could desire from an early age. His girls knew the price of everything, but the value of nothing.

There was poor Josephine Flynn, who had more right to motherhood than this whore of his, and yet she had lost child after child, denied the one thing that she craved. Well, his Assumpta was finally going to learn the harsh realities of life. She was going to have her child and, if she had any nous whatsoever, she would finally understand about consequences.

He had heard all the tales about his daughters. Declan had given him the gossip, so he wouldn't hear it from strangers. He had been shocked but, more than anything, he had been so hurt. That he had unknowingly harboured such poisonous vipers, such vacuous females, had really shown him the truth of his life. Carmel, God love her, had trusted them implicitly. She was even more outraged than he was about their exploits.

Everyone around him had known about his daughters, and the lifestyle they had chosen to pursue, while he was left in the dark. It was the worst kind of betrayal for a man like him who prided himself on never being taken unawares. He had no option but to face it, hold his head up, and front it out.

But if anyone *ever* had the nerve to say anything to his face, he would kill them without a second's fucking thought.

He was going to find out who the father of his grandchild was, and the names of every single man who had taken his daughters to bed behind his back. Patrick's reputation was everything to him; it was something he had to fight for, and he would do exactly that.

Chapter Thirty-Five

'Listen, Pat, this has all got to stop, mate. You are making a fucking fool of yourself.'

Michael Flynn was asking for trouble, but he had no choice. Patrick was out of control, he seemed to have completely disconnected from reality. He had never seen anything like it in his life.

Declan stood watching him. Michael knew that he had not really believed that he would actually say anything to Patrick, even though they had planned this together. Patrick wasn't a man who encouraged any kind of criticism about himself, in fact he had a serious problem dealing with it. But something had to be done, and Michael was the only person with the balls to do it.

Patrick looked at Michael. The contempt in his voice was evident. It was not something he had ever thought he would hear directed at him, let alone from young Michael.

'I don't give a flying fuck what you might think, Michael. You need to remember that you work for me, mate, not the other way around.'

Michael steadied his voice, aware that he had to try and defuse the situation. But, by the same token, this had to be sorted, things had to be said. 'And you need to remember who *you* are, Patrick. If you have any brains you will stop this fucking witch-hunt. Think about it. If your daughter actually *knew* who had knocked her up, don't you think she might have fucking mentioned it by now? I really do understand how you're feeling, but you are making a laughing stock of yourself. It's a joke, Pat. You're not the only man whose daughter is having a baby on her own. It's the eighties, it isn't even a fucking big deal these days.'

Patrick recognised that, on one level, Michael was speaking the truth. He was chasing after nothing. But he just couldn't stop himself. He hated that his daughter had let herself down so much and that, at the same time, she had let him down, shamed him in the worst way possible. He blamed Carmel. She was a fucking disgrace, she had failed him miserably. She was another trollop, another user. It was a family trait, by all accounts, and his daughters had not inherited it from him. That's if they *were* his daughters, of course. He was wondering about that now. He couldn't eat or sleep. His whole life was consumed with thinking about his daughters, the lives they had led, and his complete ignorance of it all. He couldn't believe that he had been so naïve. He had always told his girls how lovely they were, how beautiful they were; he had treated them like princesses, totally convinced of their goodness. He had assumed they understood the importance of decency, had cherished their virginity, known the value of self-respect. But that had been a complete fucking myth on his part. They had apparently lain down for anyone who gave them the time of day. He had never once even suspected them of anything untoward. Now he could only wonder what else he had missed, what else had been going on beneath his nose. Every day he was finding it harder to believe they were his flesh and blood.

Even Declan and Michael were suspect to him now. He had given them the same trust, and now he could only wonder at his own foolishness. His Carmel was the most suspect, as far as he was concerned. She had been in charge of the girls after all. Now he was constantly reminded of Carmel's past. She had hardly been a wilting fucking virgin when he had met her, but she had been much younger than him, and she had pursued him with a fucking vengeance until she got him. He had happily signed on for life, for a family and a home. She had supplied the family, he had supplied everything else. He had given her and his girls everything that money could buy, contentedly settled down with Carmel, and he had never once given her cause to doubt him or his loyalty. But could he really say the same about her? He wasn't so sure any more.

Michael sighed; he could see that Patrick wasn't listening to him, was unaware that he was even in the same room. 'Are you even listening to me, Pat? I'm talking away to you and you're off with the fucking fairies again. Get a grip, will you? We are already haemorrhaging fucking money. You keep missing meetings, and when you *do* bother to turn up you pick fights with men you have known all your life – men who rely on you because they trust you, because you have always been so reliable in the past. If you don't fucking sort your head out, Patrick, we will be seconded. We are already losing custom but, worst of all, we are losing face. Our credibility is shot thanks to you.'

Declan could see that his brother was too far gone to listen to reason. Patrick was already tuning Michael's voice out. When he had these episodes, he had the knack of only hearing what he wanted to hear. In truth, his brother rarely listened to anything he didn't want to hear anyway. It was part of Patrick's psyche, his inability to ever be wrong. It was this unpredictability that gave him the edge over everyone else. He was not going to listen to anything unless it suited him, unless it was directly concerned with this latest fixation. Michael had never really experienced Patrick like this before; Declan knew how dangerous it could make him.

He had always accepted that his brother lived outside normal human parameters. It had once been his strength, the reason he instilled fear into everyone without even trying. Anyone with half a brain could see that Patrick Costello was marching to a different beat to the rest of the world. Now his brother had descended into utter chaos. This latest episode went far deeper than ever before. Declan had seen him paranoid, but never against his own. Who would ever have thought Patrick could have been brought so low by his own children?

Assumpta had destroyed her father. She had unknowingly unearthed the man's only known weakness, and Declan, like Michael, could see that, if they weren't careful, someone else was going to step up and take over the businesses. This kind of weakness was treated with the scorn it deserved in the world they inhabited. Patrick was far too influential to let something so personal take precedence over anything else. This kind of trouble was sorted quietly, and that suited everyone concerned. It was the law of the pavement, and was how it would always be. It was how the Costellos had made their mark, how they had taken over someone else's business. The trick was to make sure that the same thing never happened to you.

Declan shook his head, and said quietly, 'Leave him, Michael. You're wasting your fucking time.'

Michael knew that Declan was right. Patrick was oblivious to them. It was frightening, but Michael couldn't help his morbid fascination at the man's obvious lunacy. Patrick looked wrong; he was not just manic, he was without any kind of boundaries or guidelines. Everything that kept them at the top of their game was now going to destroy everything they had worked for. It was unbelievable, and Michael was well aware that he had to be the one to take control, because Declan wouldn't.

Chapter Thirty-Six

Josephine was happier than she had been for a very long time. She was still pregnant, and she was still the only person who knew about it. She was not going to tell anyone until she had to. She had let everyone down so many times in the past, she wasn't going to chance it again. The pain of each loss became more acute – it never lessened. Everyone she saw would give her clichés and pity. It was the pity she hated the most. She could feel this baby inside of her every minute of every day. She felt different this time, she was convinced of that. It felt right somehow. It was her secret to keep, this was her own private happiness. Her silence meant no one was watching her every move, questioning every expression on her face, asking if she was feeling ill, or if she was off-colour, telling her to sit down or lie down as if she was dying or something, searching her face constantly for the first signs of pain, followed by the miscarriage they had been expecting all along. No one forcing her to rest, or sitting with her so she never had any time on her own. It was wearing having so many people caring for you, tiring trying to be upbeat and constantly pretending that you weren't terrified of losing yet another baby down the toilet. This was so much better for her. This was far more relaxing.

She rubbed her belly gently, caressing her child and hoping that this time she might actually get the chance to hold this one in her arms.

Michael's mother was the real bugbear; she felt the woman almost wished the losses on her daughter-in-law. She was a vicious old bitch who saw Michael as hers and no one else's. A child, a *living* child, would cement their marriage and she believed that was something Hannah didn't want. She felt awful even thinking it, but it was the truth.

She heard Michael's car as it crunched on to the driveway. He was early; she had not even thought about any dinner for them – not that he would care, of course.

She could hear him as he walked around the side of the house – he always came through the back door. It was a running joke between them. He said it was his council-house upbringing: out through the front door and in through the back.

Josephine automatically put the kettle on. He always expected a cup of tea. They had become so predictable. She wondered if that was because they had not been blessed with a child yet. A child didn't allow for such routine. It was the reason why people could never make plans, or guarantee their days. A child was also the reason why people like them got married in the first place.

'Good girl, I'm dying for a cuppa.'

Josephine plastered a smile on her face. Then, turning to her husband, she said as gaily as she could, 'Name me one time you have ever come in this house and not had a welcoming cup of tea. It's me job, isn't it? It's what I live for, Michael, catering to your every whim!'

He laughed with her and felt himself relax. It was hard sometimes; Josephine could be sensitive. He adored her with a passion, but he knew that she felt the absence of a child acutely. She would never believe he didn't care either way. She was a very beautiful woman, and she was the only woman he had ever wanted – ever would want. If only she could believe it.

'I want my whims catered to, Josephine. I think you can cater to them tonight, actually,' he said teasingly.

She poured them both out mugs of tea and looked at him assessingly. 'I think I can just about manage that, Michael, if you're good.'

Michael grinned, happy his wife was so cheerful. He wished he felt the same, but all the worry about Patrick was getting to him. He sat down at the kitchen table wearily, and waited for Josephine to bring him his tea. She sat down beside him, and he smiled gently at her. The kitchen table seated eight people comfortably, it could accommodate ten at a push. It was scrubbed pine and, like everything else in the house, tasteful, expensive, and underused.

They had bought this house with such high hopes and, gradually, those hopes had been shattered. Now the house felt too big for the two of them. It seemed to scream loneliness, and it never felt cosy any more. But it was the only home they knew, and leaving it would be like admitting they had failed, and accepting they would never have a child. If, and when, they moved out it would have to be Josephine's choice – never his. It could only be her decision.

She was so pretty, he never tired of looking at her. Suddenly, he noticed that she looked different somehow. 'You look like you're putting on a bit of weight, girl.'

Josephine was pleased at his words. It meant she was doing everything a pregnant woman should do. She really wanted to share the news with him, but she knew she couldn't. They had been there so many times before. If she lost this baby at least he wouldn't have to grieve with her again.

'I think I have actually, Michael. But I'm pleased about it. I lost so much weight after the last baby. I think this means I am finally getting back to normal, eh?'

Michael felt so sad. He understood how hard it was for her to mention anything about the babies she had lost.

'You always look good to me, Josephine, you know that. But I think you're right, mate.'

Josephine sipped her tea, then she changed the subject quickly. 'Did you manage to talk to Patrick?'

Michael scowled angrily. 'Don't go there, Josephine. He's lost the fucking plot. He's always been a bit touched, as you know. That is why he's so successful. He has an air of controlled violence, and no one in their right fucking mind would ever want to cross him. But that's gone now. He is fucking strange. Even Declan is fed up with him.'

Josephine had expected as much. She had seen Patrick for herself, and she had sussed out that he was not firing on all cylinders. He was acting stranger by the day. Carmel was at her wit's end. She wasn't able to cope with the man he had become.

'Carmel told me that he doesn't ever sleep now. He paces

the house all night long. The girls are terrified of him. Poor Assumpta feels responsible. Carmel told me that two nights ago he was nearly arrested. He walked into their local off-licence and threatened the bloke behind the counter – accused him of following him. It was only the fact that the local Filth were aware of who he was that saved him from being nicked. They rang Carmel and she had to go and get him. She said he was like a maniac. She's scared of him, what he's capable of.'

Michael had already heard that story from Declan. Patrick had never been the full shilling, but he was now ninety pence short of a fucking pound. It was amazing how much he had deteriorated in the last few weeks. 'Declan told me the story. But he also said that Patrick has lost it before. He's had what the doctors called a "psychotic break" on more than one occasion, just never as pronounced as this. In fact, according to Declan, Patrick has been under a fucking shrink since he was a little kid! He has been as mad as a fucking brush since junior school. As you can imagine, I was thrilled to bits to hear about that at this late stage.'

Michael was baffled by Patrick, and he didn't know what to do about him. This was something that no one could ever have planned for. Now, though, it was here, and it needed sorting out. Declan, as per usual, was leaving the real work to Michael. He didn't want his brother's latest escapade to become common knowledge. He also didn't want to have to sort his brother out personally. He didn't want any responsibility at all – especially the kind that involved him having to make decisions about his older brother. But that was understandable in a way.

'Patrick needs to be put away somewhere – for his own good, let alone everyone else's. He is so fucking far gone, Josephine, I've never seen anything like it in my life. People are already talking about him. He has picked fights with men who we have dealt with for years, accused them of all sorts. These are hard men, but they're not fucking stupid. They can see first-hand that Patrick Costello is a dangerous fuck. He always was – granted – but now he looks and sounds like a fucking card-carrying looney. It can't go on, can it? I have to do whatever is needed to sort this situation out.'

Josephine understood that Michael was unloading his worries on to her. He had always used her as his sounding board – she knew she was the only person he trusted enough to speak so openly to. It helped that she often told him what she knew he wanted to hear.

Josephine shook her head sadly. 'No, you're right, it can't go on, Michael. Patrick needs someone to take the reins for a while, give him time to sort his head out, look after everything so no one can take advantage of him. Only you can do that for him, Michael. You run everything anyway – everyone knows that. Patrick obviously needs specialist help, and I know Carmel would welcome any support she could get. Reading between the lines, I think she would leave him if it was possible. But you and I both know that is never going to happen. He would see her dead first.'

Michael nodded his agreement. Josephine spoke the truth: Carmel was living on borrowed time. He pulled her from her chair, and on to his lap. He squeezed her to him, enjoying the familiar feel of her body against his. He loved the smell of her hair – she was always so fresh and clean. Even now, without any make-up on, she was still a really good-looking woman. He could feel the extra weight she had gained, and he was happy about that. She had been so thin after losing the last baby. He had been worried about her, but he had known from past experience that she didn't need to be constantly reminded of what had happened. Or question if it could have been avoided somehow. She just carried on as usual – it was her way of coping. But he knew that she grieved inside, that she hurt much more than she would ever have admitted to him or anyone else. He just respected her wishes, and he let her cope in the only way she knew how. If she cried in the night, he held her, comforted her. But, other than that, he played along with her, and pretended nothing had happened.

'I can feel love handles, Josephine! I think you might be getting fat!'

She laughed delightedly at his words. 'I eat lots of chocolate when I'm on my own. I put on a nice sad film, and then I break out the Cadbury's Fruit and Nut!'

He liked hearing her sounding so happy again. It felt as if she was almost back to normal again. He hoped so. He missed her when she was grieving. It was mad really – all the money he earned, and all the love she had inside her, and they couldn't have the one thing that they really wanted. The one thing *she* really wanted. Then there was Assumpta, who was carrying a child she really didn't want. Any other father would have seen it aborted, for no other reason than the girl was a fucking idiot and no one in their right mind would trust her with a baby. She had enough trouble stringing a coherent sentence together. It was so unfair.

He sighed, and hugged his lovely wife tightly to him. As his mum always said, if it was meant to be, then it would happen for them. He wanted it to happen not just because his Josephine deserved it, but because he would finally feel she had everything he had promised her all those years ago, when they were just starting out and life still held endless possibilities. She had never asked for anything, she had always been there for him, and he knew how lucky he was in that way. Nothing he could ever do would change her feelings for him, she loved him without any strings, or any kind of expectations.

She was his world, and that would never change.

Chapter Thirty-Seven

Carmel Costello looked awful, but for once she didn't care. This wasn't about her – this was about her husband.

'Assumpta, will you please shut up! If he hears you carrying on again he will be up here on top of us. Just ignore him.'

Assumpta knew that her mother was talking sense, but her father's shouting was getting too much now. It had been going on for hours. 'Just make him shut up, Mum, please make him stop! He's giving me a headache.'

Carmel grabbed her daughter's wrists tightly. The girl was getting hysterical, and she didn't blame her. Nevertheless, this was something her daughter had brought on herself – had brought on them all with her behaviour. Carmel's job was to emphasise to her daughter the seriousness of what was actually going on.

'Listen to me, girl, and you better listen good. That man down there is not in his right mind. He is capable of *really* hurting us. You know that he cannot be talked to when he is like this. If I thought I could calm him down don't you think I would have been down there hours ago? I'm the one person who has ever been allowed to disagree with him, and that's only when he lets me. Right now, he is beyond reason and if you don't shut the fuck up, he will be up here like an avenging angel and then we will really be in trouble.'

Assumpta was truly terrified now. Her father had been ranting without pause for hours on end, and it wasn't going to let up any time soon.

'Just keep quiet, let him get it out of his system, and hope to God that it's sooner rather than later.'

Chapter Thirty-Eight

Declan was tired out. It was the third time in twenty-four hours that Carmel had rung him to come and help with Patrick. If only Patrick would agree to go into hospital. But he was adamant that he was not going to do *that* again.

He was so fucking paranoid. He was convinced that everyone was plotting against him. It was like dealing with a six-foot toddler, who had no intention of doing anything other than exactly what they wanted.

'Please, Patrick, will you just let me speak for a few minutes?'

Patrick was still manic. Declan could see the toll the lack of sleep was having on his brother. He had seen him like this before, but never this bad. He was all over the place, unable to relax for even a few minutes. It was pitiful to watch him.

'I don't need to do fucking *anything*, Declan. I know that you will just talk shite to me again. I'm telling you what I've told you over and over: I am *not* going into a hospital. I don't *need* to go into a hospital. What I need is to sort things out. What I *need* is to fucking finally remove the people who are standing in my way. Don't you get it? I am surrounded by cunts, absolute cunts.'

Declan sighed. This was going to go on for a while. Carmel wanted to have him sectioned but she was too frightened to be the person to orchestrate that. She wanted Declan to do it and who could blame her?

He knew he *should* do it. It was in all their interests – especially Patrick's – but he couldn't. He couldn't bring himself to put his brother away. It was never going to happen. But seeing him like this was almost as bad. All his life Patrick had been on the borderline, but he had always managed to eventually control himself. His strength of mind was awesome. Patrick had always been very unpredictable but, in the past, he had accepted that about himself. He had understood his own weaknesses and fought to bring them under some kind of control.

It was finding out about his daughters that had tipped him over the edge this time. Declan had heard the rumours about them – especially Assumpta. More than a few people had seen fit to put him wise about his nieces and their lifestyles. The men who had approached him had been sensible enough to know that if Patrick ever got wind of his daughters' antics there would be hell to pay, and they had wanted Patrick to curb his girls before something like this happened. Declan had listened to the gossip, but he had no intention of telling his brother anything.

Carmel hadn't connected with her girls once they had grown up. In Declan's opinion, she was incapable of any real connection with anybody – she was too selfish, too self-absorbed. As long as the girls were well dressed, and their make-up was perfect, she didn't care about anything else. It wasn't that she didn't love them in her own way, it was more down to Carmel's inability to show interest in anyone other than herself. He had never liked her, but he had to admit she did do her best for Patrick. He believed that, in her own way, she loved him – at least as much as she was capable of loving anyone other than herself.

His brother was talking to himself and some of his mutterings were sending chills through Declan's body.

'I know that we have got to take Ozzy Harper out, Declan. We'll go over to his house tonight, and just shoot him, end of. Quick, clean and neat. It will send a message to everyone then. All the people who have been running me down, slagging me off, taking me for a cunt, will know that they are living on borrowed fucking time. They'll realise that, eventually, I will get round to them as well – and I will do just that, Declan. I swear on our mother's fucking grave. I will take them out, each and every one.'

Patrick was deadly serious, and Declan was appalled. He smiled at his brother, aware that he had to talk him out of this lunacy. It was getting far too fucking dangerous. He was actually contemplating killing a man they had known all their lives, who was a real friend, a decent bloke – and a hard man in his own right.

'I think Ozzy is away, Patrick. I heard he was in Spain. He has a gaff out there, remember? In Marbella. We've stayed there many times.'

Patrick's eyes were darting everywhere. Declan knew his brother was now wondering if *he* could be trusted. Patrick's paranoia was getting worse by the minute. He had to sort this out before Patrick really went postal. Imagine if Patrick had decided to kill someone, and no one was with him to talk him out of it! It could literally cause fucking murders. Or what if his brother took against Carmel or his girls again? He was more than capable of killing them – he had killed before, after all. Only then, he had planned it out beforehand, and it had been nothing more than a means to an end. Now it was just an idea that popped into his head, and he felt honour bound to see it through to the bitter end.

Patrick was confused. 'Are you sure that Ozzy is away, Declan?'

Declan nodded. He glanced around his brother's office, saw that the door was closed and the French windows locked tight. He knew Carmel and the girls were upstairs, prisoners in their own home.

'Why don't we go and meet Michael? He will know for definite where Ozzy is. That way we can be sure, can't we? Michael always keeps tabs on everyone, it's in his nature.'

Declan picked up the phone on the desk casually, and rang Michael's house. He explained quickly and loudly that Patrick wanted to kill Ozzy, but no one was sure if he was in Spain at the moment, so could Michael please meet them at their old offices at the scrapyard. That way they could talk it over together, and plan what they were going to do about it. The scrapyard was the best place because, as Patrick said, all their other offices were bugged.

At the other end of the line, Michael listened to Declan quietly. He could hear the desperation in his voice, and understood that Patrick was obviously completely out of control now.

He kissed Josephine gently on the lips and left her curled

up on the sofa watching TV. 'I won't be long, darling. I have to pop out for a while.'

Josephine was used to her husband's odd hours. She smiled her goodbyes. 'See you later, Michael. Try not to be gone all night.'

He didn't answer her.

Chapter Thirty-Nine

Patrick and Declan arrived at the scrapyard and, as expected, Michael was already there. The lights were on in the Portakabin that passed for office space, and Declan noticed that the night watchman and his Doberman were gone. He understood the significance of that. He could not change anything that was going to happen. It had gone too far now.

Patrick didn't seem to notice anything out of the ordinary, however, and he walked quickly towards the offices.

Declan followed his brother slowly into the Portakabin, sorry that it had to come to this, but knowing that there was nothing else to do now. Patrick was a liability, and that could not be tolerated.

Chapter Forty

Michael had planned for this and was leaving nothing to chance. He had given the nightwatchman a decent few quid, and he had willingly gone home with his Doberman who was his closest friend. She was in whelp so, as far as he was concerned, she had earned a few days off. It wasn't the first time he had been asked to leave his post for unexplained reasons. As he was a man who had no interest in anything or anyone – which was exactly why he had been given the job in the first place – he left without question.

As Patrick walked into the offices, Michael was already in place. He was clear that Declan shared his opinion about Patrick and his latest escapades. The fact that Declan had arranged for the meet to be here said it all. This was the only place secure enough to do what was needed. It was quiet, it was dark, and it had the added bonus of being somewhere that Patrick Costello would feel safe.

'You all right, Michael?'

Michael nodded. Even now, Patrick Costello was impressive. He seemed to fill the space with his personality, with his natural charisma. So few people displayed that kind of edge – it was what separated the men from the boys, the real criminals from the wannabes. Even now, completely off his fucking tree, the man still had more nous than most of the people around him. It was such a shame that the man's mental capabilities had finally let him down. The same capabilities that had given him the lead role in the criminal underworld for so long, were now the reason he couldn't ever be trusted again.

Michael walked towards his friend with a smile of greeting on his face, holding out his right hand. As Patrick gripped it, ready for the handshake he expected, Michael pulled him towards him quickly and with his left hand he plunged an eight-inch blade into Patrick's heart.

It was over in seconds.

Michael held Patrick as he crumpled in his arms, and carefully lowered him to the floor, giving him as much dignity as possible. He stood over him with his brother Declan as he bled out. He hoped that the man had not suffered too much.

'Oh my God.' Declan was nearly in tears. He knelt beside his brother's lifeless body.

Michael shrugged. 'My old mum used to say, Declan, I'm glad you think of Him as yours as you will need Him one day. She is a good Catholic, I'll give her that.' He poured two large brandies and, passing one to Declan, he said gently, 'You know this had to happen, mate. It's better this came from us than from someone else, someone who could use it to their advantage. It was quick, and almost painless. We did what was needed and we did it for the right reasons. Remember that.'

Declan knew that Michael was right, but it still felt wrong.

For all Patrick had become, he was still his brother. 'I know you're right. But I wish it hadn't come to this.'

Michael didn't answer him. There was nothing he could say to make Declan feel any better. This was one of those things that happened in their world. It wasn't malicious, it was just necessary.

'I want it to look like a robbery, Declan. No one will believe that, of course, but it will satisfy the Old Bill and Carmel will get the insurance.'

Declan nodded. It occurred to him that with his brother's demise, he now, to all intents and purposes, worked for Michael Flynn. Michael was now the new king on the block. Not that he cared – he wouldn't want that kind of responsibility for all the tea in China – or should that be all the heroin the Chinese could supply? He knew Michael was thigh-high in that kind of shit.

Michael was already the go-to man, and Patrick's untimely departure would only give him more power. He wondered if Michael knew just what he was taking on. Without Patrick behind him, Michael Flynn would have to prove his own worth in more ways than one.

It didn't occur to Declan that Michael had always prepared for any and every scenario. He was a man who never once left anything to chance, who thought everything out from every angle possible – that was the reason Patrick had taken him on in the first place. And he had taught him well. Patrick had seen a kindred spirit in Michael Flynn. He had passed on the knowledge needed to be a part of the world Patrick had so carefully created. It was a world of extreme violence, where *everyone* was suspect, where money was made in huge quantities by people who needed not only Patrick's permission but also his know-how. Patrick Costello had never offered an earn until he had worked out every scenario humanly possible. It had been why people saw him as a safe partner. He never took risks, he would lose money before he would ever put himself or anyone he was involved with in any danger. It was what he was good at and why he was so well respected. Now he was gone and, like everyone in the world they inhabited, people would mourn his passing but, other than that, once the shock wore off, he would become just another story people told. It was brutal, but true. Patrick had one flaw: his natural capacity for lunacy. It had been his downfall. It had happened to many men before him. It was also the reason they eventually died violent deaths.

Michael Flynn was always going to get the top spot, it had just been a matter of time. In fairness, Declan knew that Michael would never have sought it unless there had been a good reason. He had thought the world of Patrick, and he had appreciated the man's interest in him and his trust. Declan knew that Michael had only done what was needed, but it still left a bitter taste.

Michael was more than ready to take control of the Costello business – in all honesty, he couldn't wait to get started. After a decent period of mourning, of course.

Chapter Forty-One

Michael felt fantastic. Everyone was giving him their condolences, while letting him know, at the same time, that they were willing to carry on as usual. *That* was the important thing – he needed to be seen as capable of taking over Patrick's role.

He was aware that his hand in Patrick's death – albeit without any hard proof – was already being accepted as a fact of life. Patrick's behaviour before his demise had been seen, noted, and, therefore, his untimely death had been judged a necessary evil.

Now at the man's funeral, Michael Flynn was being fêted as Patrick Costello's natural successor by everyone who mattered. It was more than he could have hoped for. He had been quite happy to fight his corner if needs be – he had worked hard enough for it, after all. But, in reality, he knew that Declan's acceptance of his leadership had been what had really sealed the deal. For all Declan might act the fool, he was far more on the ball than he let on. That he had stood back, today of all days, and let Michael take centre stage spoke volumes. He would always remember that, and appreciate it. He knew that Declan really missed his brother, and so did he. He had loved Patrick Costello – he had been the father he had never known. But Patrick had been the one to teach him the number-one rule – sometimes things had to be done and, as hard as it might be, you could never let emotions cloud your judgement. He had understood that from day one and, like Patrick, he had been determined never to allow his emotions to let him down.

Carmel Costello sat through the service, pleased at the turnout for her husband, but even more pleased that he was gone. She could breathe again, and her daughters could relax. Thanks to Michael, they were safe in every way. Assumpta had got rid of her child already, and now they were all going to move to the house they owned in Spain. For the first time in ages she could actually breathe easily, and relax like a normal person. She finally had Patrick off her back. Not that she hadn't loved him – she had in her own way, and she had lived with his strangeness when necessary – it had been a small price to pay for everything else she had got from the relationship. But, as the time had gone on, he had become a difficult man to deal with, and this last lot had really made her realise just what she was actually dealing with. He had terrified her and the girls, and she had known there was no talking to him, that he was beyond her control.

Carmel had wanted Patrick because of his money and what he could offer her. His reputation had given her security, and that had been his big attraction for her. She had believed that her tantrums and his allowing her to have her say, demand what she wanted, had been because *she* had some kind of control over the life they led. But that had been a sham. Providing she ultimately did what he wanted, he tolerated her antics and that was all. The last few months had opened her eyes, shown her exactly what she had tied herself to, and how precarious her life with him actually was. Patrick was dangerous.

Michael had given her not just her freedom, and her daughters' freedom, but he had also given her the one thing she had never really known existed until now. He had given her peace of mind.

She had watched the way that everyone had gone to Michael, offering their condolences – and their fealty. She hadn't cared that she was relegated to second place. None of that mattered – that was poor Josephine's problem now. She would soon see how difficult it was to be with a man who had to fight every day of his life to keep what he had and who saw skulduggery at every turn. It was hard work.

Chapter Forty-Two

Father Riordan was watching the congregation with a heavy heart. He had tried to leave this parish, but he had been made to stay, against his will. He looked at Michael Flynn, and he wondered at a God who could let a man like that loose on the world, a man who paid his dues to the Church, and who actually believed that he was a good Catholic. It was against everything he had always believed. Oh, he knew of priests back home who had happily heard confessions from the men in the IRA, who saw them as no more than products of their environments, but that could never be him. He believed that the fact that poor Josephine had not been given a child was his God's way of making sure people like Michael Flynn didn't bring any more of his ilk into the world. But that didn't explain why so many other violent men in the parish seemed to have child after child, year after year.

He waited patiently as the coffin was carried from the church on the shoulders of men who were all as violent as they were fêted. He would give Patrick Costello the full funeral Mass, as was his right – he was a Catholic and he was entitled to it. But Father Riordan was also aware that the man was another violent criminal, and he had died by the sword, or by the knife, which was the same thing really. It stuck in his craw. He had no option but to do as he was asked – he had to do as his religion commanded him. Jesus had been a prisoner, unfairly captured, tortured and humiliated. Finally he had died on the cross for the sins of the world – for men like these. His job was to never have an opinion or judge anyone, but it was hard, knowing what he knew about them.

He saw that Michael Flynn and Declan Costello were the lead pallbearers, and they did what was expected of them both with the maximum of respect for the man they were burying. It was the least they could do for the man they both loved in their own ways and, if the gossip was true, who they robbed of his life. It was an open secret, and it would never be questioned. Michael Flynn was too powerful for that now. He was untouchable.

In their world, Patrick Costello had been given a good send-off. He had been given his due, for what that was worth.

But Father Riordan hated that he was again a part of it, and he could not do anything about that. He hated that this was what his life had become.

Chapter Forty-Three

'That went well, Michael. Patrick would have been happy with the day.'

Michael smiled sadly. 'I hope so, Declan. None of us wanted this.'

Declan was aware Michael was only speaking the truth even if it hurt. 'Well, Carmel's happy, anyway!'

Michael laughed – Declan had got that much right. Carmel was over the moon at her husband's death, and who could blame her?

'In fairness to her, Declan, she did what she could for him. Somewhere nestled between those expensive tits of hers is a heart. I feel sorry for her, but even she knew it was all over for him.'

Declan sipped his beer. The wake was being held at Michael's house. No one seemed to think that was strange – it was common knowledge that Declan wasn't in a position to host such an event, and the word on the street was that Carmel and her daughters didn't want the responsibility of such a huge undertaking.

It was a big funeral. People had come from all corners of the globe, as was expected. They were not just paying their respects to the man they knew and loved – they were also making sure their earns were safe.

Josephine had done a fantastic job. The whole thing was perfect. The food had been catered – it was expensive and plentiful and she had arranged for waitresses and bar staff to serve the drinks. Now everyone was happily drunk and reminiscing, as was expected at a funeral such as this. Michael's house was plenty big enough to hold such a huge party, and he knew that the fact it was at his *home* would just reinforce his credibility, as well as giving him the opportunity to prove how successful he was. He knew how important it was for him to be seen as a man of means with money behind him. The lifestyle was everything; it was what would define him to the people he'd be dealing with. This was a win-win situation for him, but he was glad that it was nearly over and he could finally get back to normal.

Still, it was nice to see his house full, and watch his wife play the hostess; she did it so well. He was going to make sure that the men he dealt with got the personal touch. He would invite them here with their wives for dinner. He would bring this house to life, and give his Josephine the opportunity to shine. He was so proud of her today. She had taken the onus off Carmel and, at the same time, she had made sure that people saw that he was the real deal. He couldn't help feeling as he looked around him that he was where he deserved to be. He had worked for this. He had learnt from the master, and now he could feel pride in what he had achieved.

He was still a young man, yet he had just inherited the biggest prize of all. He had taken on Patrick Costello's mantle, and no one had questioned that. Michael knew he had his creds, but he had still expected at least one person to challenge him. He planned his defence down to the last detail – he was not going to give anything away without a fucking fight. He was prepared to wipe out anyone who even looked like they might want to try it on. Yet he had been wrong. It seemed that everyone accepted his new role. Personally, he would have been straight in there, sooner rather than later; if he was in their shoes, he would have done everything in his power to take him out. This was the only chance anyone was going to get to push themselves ahead in the game for a long time, Michael was determined about that.

Declan brought him over a large whisky, and he took it gratefully.

'Old Joey Murphy is on top form. He loves a fucking Irish funeral. He wants to sing.'

Michael laughed. It was the icing on the cake. He dragged Declan over to the old boy; he was eighty if he was a day, and an old IRA man. He could cause a fight in an empty house with a drink in him. He had buried his children – three handsome sons. Two had been murdered, the youngest had died in prison of cancer. He was a real character, and he was always given the respect he was due. He was a great singer of Irish songs.

'Come on, Joey, how about "The Wild Colonial Boy"? Patrick always loved that one.'

Joey was thrilled to be singled out, and he sang the song with real feeling, knowing that everyone would join in the chorus.

Michael saw Josephine watching him, and he winked at her, before opening his arms wide. She walked into his embrace unhesitatingly; this was where she always wanted to be.

As the singing swelled around her, Josephine laughed delightedly. The baby was hanging in there, and she felt wonderful. Michael was so caught up in the aftermath of Patrick's death, he still hadn't noticed anything. That was what she wanted. She didn't want anyone to know about her pregnancy – all she wanted was to be left alone long enough to know if this baby was going to be there for the duration. Patrick Costello had inadvertently given her the time she needed to carry this baby inside her without a fuss, and she would always be grateful to him for that. Michael hugged her tightly suddenly, and whispered in her ear, 'I love you, Josephine Flynn.'

And, looking up at him and smiling brightly, she mouthed back, 'I know.'

Chapter Forty-Four

'It's a lot of fucking money, Declan, and I think you deserve to know about it. Now Patrick's gone, it's my call. I never understood why he kept you out of the loop anyway, to be honest. It didn't sit right with me but, while he was alive, I had no option but to let it slide.'

Declan didn't answer Michael. He recognised that Michael was trying to be fair and give him an in. He looked at Michael in his expensive suit, with his perfect haircut; he knew how best to present himself to the world. Men like his brother and Michael Flynn would always want more – it was what made them get up in the morning. They couldn't settle for anything other than being the best, being the main man. They were incapable of ever being content with what they already had. But that wasn't Declan.

'Look, Declan, I just want us to be clear about everything. You are a Costello after all, and I want to bring you into everything so we are both aware of what is going on.'

Declan saw his reflection in the window; he had never liked these offices any more than Patrick had. This was all Michael's idea. Michael had brought them into a new world, and given the Costello name a polish that had been sorely needed.

'Look, Michael, I appreciate what you're trying to do but, honestly, I never wanted anything to do with Patrick's side of the business. I chose to take a step back a long time ago. I only ever partnered him in the day-to-day. I know you mean well, but I have no interest in any of his other businesses – I never did. That was why he wanted you onboard. So do me a favour, mate – leave me out of it.'

Michael was silent for a long while as he digested what he had been told. He had half expected something like this, but he had also wondered if, now that Patrick was out of the frame, Declan might want to be more involved in the real money side of everything. Michael knew that Patrick loved his brother, but didn't exactly consider him as an equal, as someone to respect. Now he saw that Declan was genuinely happy to leave him to it, he was quite happy to do just that. In fact, this suited him down to the ground.

'If that's what you want, Declan. I just wanted you to know that the offer was there.'

Declan grinned. 'I know that, mate, but I am fine as I am. You know something? You're much more like Patrick than you admit. You have the same drive that he had. I never had that myself. I'm easily contented, happy with what I've got.'

Michael knew Declan was speaking the truth. He admired his honesty, but another part of him abhorred the man for his weakness. He had just offered him an in to a world of real money, of real power, and he had refused it point-blank. Well, Michael had done what he felt was the right thing, and now he had no option but to carry on by himself.

'I just felt that I should give you the opportunity, that's all, Declan. If you're happy for me to carry on as before, then that's what I'll do.'

Declan shrugged nonchalantly. 'That suits me, Michael.'

Chapter Forty-Five

Josephine was listening to her mother with half an ear. She was already regretting inviting her round. Her mum resented her life with Michael, and that bothered her more than she liked to admit.

'. . . That is what everyone thinks, anyway.' Lana was watching her daughter warily. She had expected a reaction to her words, but it seemed that her Josephine was either unwilling to say anything, or she hadn't been listening. 'Have you bothered to listen to a word I've said?'

Josephine snapped back to reality as she heard the anger in her mother's voice. 'I'm sorry, Mum, I was miles away. What are you on about this time?'

Lana sighed in annoyance. 'I was just saying that people are talking about Patrick Costello's death. No one thinks it was really a mugging.'

Josephine looked at her mother, and felt the urge to slap her face. She knew what she was insinuating, and this wasn't the first time she had tried to bring this conversation up. Josephine stood suddenly. They were, as always, in her kitchen. She had made them both a lovely lunch, and she had tried to pretend that she was enjoying it. But she wasn't.

Her mother had been a pain in her arse for a long time now. Well, she was fed up. She couldn't allow her mother to get away with this, not again. 'Just what are you trying to say, Mum?'

Lana could see the bristling anger that her words had caused. It just added fuel to her belief that Michael Flynn had been behind Patrick Costello's death. Everyone thought that, except this daughter of hers.

'I'm not trying to say anything, love. I am just telling you what people are whispering.'

Josephine gave a deep low chuckle as if she was really tickled about something. 'Do you know something, Mum? I couldn't give a flying fuck about what "people" are saying. What I *do* know is my Michael had better not hear it. He wouldn't like to think that "people" are accusing him of murder, because that is what you're trying to say, isn't it? At least that's what you seem to be insinuating anyway.'

It finally dawned on Lana that her daughter would stand by her husband no matter what, even knowing what her husband was capable of. It didn't bother her at all. 'I never said anything of the kind.'

Josephine flapped her hands in front of her mother's face. 'Oh, Mum, will you stop it! It's all you go on about. Now, I am telling you for the last time, any more of this and I will aim you out the door. I mean it.'

Lana knew that her daughter was more than capable of doing just that. 'I wouldn't hurt you for the world, Josephine.'

Josephine looked at Lana, so upset at her mother's words that she was nearly in tears. 'But you *do* hurt me, Mum, you know you do. Every time that you try to say something bad about Michael, you hurt me. I can't do this any more, Mum. It has to stop. What you don't seem to understand is that I don't *care* what he might have done. I don't *care* what you or anyone else thinks. I love him, and he loves me. Nothing else matters.'

Lana was heart-sorry to see her only child so distressed. If only she would see Michael as he truly was. But that wasn't ever going to happen, she knew that now. Even if Josephine did know the whole truth about her husband, she wouldn't care – she had just admitted that.

'I'm sorry, love. I won't ever say another word, I swear. I just worry about you.'

Josephine sat back down, the fight was gone from her. 'Well, don't. Me and Michael are fine. He takes good care of me, Mum. If you bothered to take any notice you would see that for yourself.'

Lana sighed. 'I *can* see that, Josephine. I know he loves you. I know he provides for you. But I'm your mum, it's my job to worry about you. If you had a child of your own you'd understand what I'm saying.'

It was the final insult, and Josephine hated her mother for bringing that up, using motherhood to gain an advantage over her. Well, she had a baby inside her now. But not for anything would she share that with her mother. Instead she walked out of the kitchen leaving her mother sitting there, and up the stairs to her bedroom where she felt no one could hurt her.

Chapter Forty-Six

'This is completely unbelievable. Do you know how much money this is potentially worth, Michael?'

Michael Flynn was smiling. ''Course I do, Jeffrey. More money than you could shake a fucking stick at. But it's dangerous. It'll mean a serious fucking lump if it ever comes to it.'

Jeffrey Palmer laughed. 'I'd already worked that one out. But it's got all the hallmarks of a classic earn. Right up my street.'

Jeffrey Palmer was in good shape for his forty-five years. He had classic good looks too. Men liked him – he was a man's man – and women loved him, which he used to his advantage at every opportunity. He had a good reputation, and he had worked hard for it. He had been a grafter all his life, but he had gone as far as he could. He had accepted that – he'd basically had no choice. Patrick Costello had taken against him, and he had never been able to find out why, but the man had never offered him as much as a crumb from his table. On the rare occasions they had been in the same place, Patrick had barely acknowledged him. Jeffrey didn't know why – what he *did* know was that it certainly wasn't because of anything he had done. He had racked his brain for a reason why the man treated him like a leper, but he could not come up with a thing. He had always given Patrick Costello the respect he commanded, never once said a word about him that could be misconstrued in any way. If Costello had wanted a straightener with him, it had to come from Costello himself. He had more sense than to go looking for trouble. It had rankled though; he had felt slighted, humiliated. But he had eventually accepted it was just one of those things. Patrick Costello was well known for his ability to take against a body overnight. He was a dangerous fuck, and Jeffrey Palmer watched his back; Patrick Costello had not been averse to making people he didn't like disappear if the fancy took him. He was known to get others to do his dirty work – not just as proof of loyalty to him but, more importantly, to make sure the person in question was capable of doing whatever he might ask of them. His death had been tragic for many people, but there were many more who could suddenly breathe a lot easier.

This offer from Michael Flynn was not only going to ratchet him up a notch, it was also going to bring him into the world of serious villainy, and all that entailed.

Michael Flynn was watching Jeffrey closely. He was pleased to be bringing him onboard. Patrick had always taken against the man and Michael knew why. He had taken a real dislike to him for no reason other than he had a thick head of hair, and three strong sons. He was also one of the few men that Patrick Costello couldn't intimidate. Michael knew that the man was wondering why he was being given such an in suddenly. Why he, Michael Flynn, had not respected Patrick

Costello's wishes, and kept him outside in honour of the man everyone knew treated him like a son.

'You're very quiet, Jeff.'

Jeffrey Palmer shrugged, but he didn't answer him. He was waiting to hear what the score was, and that was something Michael could understand. Patrick had always told him to let other people talk to find out what you really wanted to know.

Michael spoke. 'I know you're wondering why I've offered you this opportunity, especially as Patrick wasn't exactly your biggest fan. But, for all that, he did admire you. He admired that you never challenged him, or bad-mouthed him. He was a funny fucker. He didn't like you, but he's gone now, and I think you are perfect for what I want.'

Jeffrey Palmer looked around him. He was in Michael Flynn's home, in his private office, and he was impressed at the way the man lived. It wasn't just about having money. Michael lived like a real businessman and his home reflected that. It wasn't the usual mix of expensive shite and ostentatious furniture. Michael's home was like his own – on a larger scale, of course. Like Michael Flynn, Jeffrey had married a decent girl, with a bit of savvy, and the intelligence to grow into the money that was coming in, who read the right magazines, and educated herself about how the other half lived. It was only a shame that Michael and his wife had not been blessed with a child to complete their family.

Jeffrey looked at Michael, and said seriously, 'I never knew why Patrick treated me like he did. I resented him for it, but I also knew there was nothing I could do to change it. The fault, whatever that might have been, wasn't on my side.

But I can tell you now, Michael, you won't regret bringing me onboard. This is perfect for me, mate. I have already dipped me toe in, so to speak, and I am aware of the main players we will have to deal with. But I assume that's why you want me.'

It was what Michael wanted to hear. 'I know you're up to speed on the people concerned, but you must remember that this time you will be dealing with them on my behalf. That means you will be the main man – none of them can shit without your say-so now, and they will accept that. They need me to smooth their paths for them, and I will do that as always, but remember, like you, they are still working for me. You will be required to remind them of that, yet oversee everything personally. This will also give you not just added status, but more money than you can imagine. It's already up and running, Jeffrey, all I want from you is to take it over, and then report to me. I'd advise you to put someone in place to oversee your usual earns. This lot is going to take up all your time, believe me.'

Jeffrey Palmer was impressed, but not really shocked; he had expected nothing less. He knew that Michael Flynn would insist on his total dedication to the cause he had offered him, and he was more than willing to do that. This was the opportunity of a lifetime. 'That is a given, Michael. When do you want me to start?'

Michael laughed loudly, with genuine humour; he had known from day one that Jeffrey Palmer would bite his hand off for this opportunity. Getting up, he poured them both large whiskies and, when they were once more settled, he said seriously, 'I will walk you through it, from start to finish, do the introductions to the hierarchy – that's who you will be dealing with from now on. I know you have already tapped into them for your own gain, and that is a big plus as far as I am concerned. Just keep in mind that you are there for me in the future.'

It was a warning.

Jeffrey Palmer smiled. He had good teeth – teeth that he had inherited from his mother, and his sons had been lucky enough to inherit them too. His mother was Irish, strong as an ox, and he could see himself in her. His father, on the other hand, had never been more than a distant memory. He had been murdered when Jeffrey was two years old, shot to death over a game of poker. It wasn't a death worth commemorating; the man had been a piece of shit. Jeffrey had always sworn that his life would amount to something, that he would not be the kind of man his father was – an East-End bullyboy, whose only aim in life was to drink, gamble and engage in small-time villainy to achieve those ends. Jeffrey had made something of himself, lived down his father's name, and his father's memory. Now, thanks to Michael Flynn, he would be able to reach his full potential.

'Listen, Michael, I will do whatever is needed. You know that. I have to ask, though, how much product are we dealing with?'

'A lot more than anyone realises, Jeff. We are shifting about ninety keys a week, and that's just the cocaine. It's big business. We supply everyone who's anyone. Nothing moves without my express say-so.'

Jeffrey Palmer was suitably impressed. He was also working out his cut of the take. 'I understand. It's a big responsibility.'

Michael nodded his agreement, before saying sarcastically, 'I know.'

Michael finished his drink, enjoying the burn as the whisky went down. He was pleased with Jeffrey Palmer. He would do a good job but, more than that, everyone would know that if Patrick Costello was still in the mix, Jeffrey Palmer wouldn't have got a look-in. It was Michael's way of letting everyone know that he was his own man. He would make any changes he thought necessary, and on his own terms. He had to make sure the people around him were all *his* men. Patrick Costello had taught him the importance of loyalty, and how giving certain people not just your trust, but also the chance to earn from that trust, was worth more than anything. He knew the truth of that first hand, and now he was going to use that knowledge to his advantage. In his own way, he had loved Patrick Costello; he had been like a father to him. But, like Patrick, he knew that, where business was concerned, emotions had no place. He had the capacity to overlook such trifles; he had understood that when Patrick had insisted he carry out murder for him. He knew now that if he had failed, he would still be no more than a drone, a nobody, and that was something he would always thank Patrick Costello for. He had educated him on the finer points of being a player in the Life. Without him, Michael would be nothing.

Chapter Forty-Seven

Josephine was busy; she had cleaned the house from top to bottom, and now she felt she could face the task of clearing out her overfull wardrobes. She was piling clothes up on the floor, trying to decide which to take to the charity shop, but she was finding it hard, she needed all of them. She was happy, still pregnant, feeling good, and that was what she was focusing on. Michael was so wrapped up in his new role, he didn't have time to think about her. That suited her, she was quite happy enjoying this by herself. This time it was going to be different, she felt that in every way. She felt stronger, more in control of everything this time. It was scary and exhilarating keeping such an enormous secret to herself.

She caught a glimpse of herself in the mirrored wardrobes. She could see the swelling under her clothes and she wanted to cry with happiness. She had to do it this time if it killed her. Unlike with the other pregnancies, she felt full of energy, without the familiar dragging feeling inside her belly, or the constant tiredness. She woke up feeling rejuvenated, ready for each new day. She had gradually lost contact with all her old school friends – they had all had babies, and she had not been able to stand it in the end. She still saw them socially, but that was about it. She had hated herself for the jealousy she had felt every time she had seen them hold the babies they had produced, hated herself for not being happy for them, for the bitterness she felt. It was nature, a natural thing that was expected of any woman, and yet she had been denied it over and over again. But not this time.

She heard Michael bounding up the stairs; as always he had come in search of her. It was so touching. She felt a rush of love wash over her. He stood in the bedroom doorway, and she marvelled at the sight of him. He was such a good-looking man, and he still had the power to excite her, make her want him.

'You having a clear-out, then?'

She smiled at him, happy to see him. 'Not before time, Michael. I'm starting on your wardrobes next.'

He grinned. 'Go for it. I'm enjoying seeing you so lively.' He was quiet for a few moments before saying softly, 'It suits you.'

Josephine laughed. 'What suits me?'

He was beside her now, and pulling her into his arms. She loved the feel of him, he made her feel so safe and secure.

He kissed her forehead gently, before saying, 'Being pregnant, Josephine. It suits you, darling. But when were you going to tell me?'

She pulled away slightly to look into his eyes, and she could see the sorrow there, mixed with bewilderment and happiness. 'How long have you known, Michael?'

He hugged her to him closely. 'A while, Josephine. I've been waiting for you to tell me yourself.'

She wanted to cry, but she couldn't. He knew, and now

she felt a fool – of course he would have known. He wasn't stupid. But she had really believed she had kept it secret, and that she had done so for his benefit, not hers.

'Oh, Michael, I didn't tell anyone, not a soul – no one knows. I thought if it all went wrong, I wouldn't have to live with the feelings of inadequacy. I wouldn't have to listen to the well-meaning clichés. If no one knew I could deal with it all myself.'

Michael felt the tears come into his eyes at her generosity of spirit. She wanted to save him hurt, and that was such a selfless act on her part. 'You silly bitch! I sussed a while ago. I wish you would listen to me, Josephine. If we have a baby I will be made up, but for you more than for me. As long as I have you I don't need anyone else. I swear that on my immortal soul.' He hugged her even tighter, raining kisses all over her face.

Josephine knew he was speaking the truth, but it still didn't make her feel any better. 'I'm so sorry, Michael, I just wanted to do this by myself. I would have told you eventually. I'm amazed that you noticed, to be honest.'

Michael was offended. 'Of course I did, Josephine! You're my world, for fuck's sake.'

Josephine looked into the handsome face she knew so well. She could see his anger, mingled with his despair, and she hated herself for causing it. He had only ever loved her, given her his love and his protection no matter what. 'Can you do me one favour, Michael? Keep this between us, please. I don't want anyone to know about it. If I lose it, I don't want it to be common knowledge. I couldn't go through that again.'

Michael sighed heavily. ''Course, darling. Whatever you want to do is fine by me.'

'Thanks, Michael. It's just I can't pretend any more. Your mum is always making remarks about how we should have a family by now, and my mum acts like miscarriages happen to everyone. It's too raw for me. Every time it goes wrong I feel such a fucking failure. I feel so bereft. If I do lose this baby, Michael, I want it to be a private grief this time. I want it to be our sorrow, no one else's.'

Michael could hear the longing in his wife's voice, the need for a child, and the fear that once more she would be denied that, because her body would let her down as it always had. He would gladly hand over every penny he had if it would give her a child of her own, and the peace it would bring to her.

'I promise you, Josephine, I won't say a word.'

She nestled into his arms, and he felt the overwhelming love for her that had never changed. He loved her unconditionally. 'How are you feeling, though? Do you feel all right in yourself?'

She nodded and, pulling away from him again, she looked up into his face. 'That's just it, Michael, I feel great. I feel better than I ever have before. This time it feels so right. I can't explain it. If it's going to happen for us, I think it will be this time.'

'Oh, my darling, I hope you're right.'

As he pulled her into his body once more, he was praying that she was right this time. But whatever happened, he knew he had no choice; he had to look after her as best he could.

Chapter Forty-Eight

Declan was tired out. He had a new little bird and she was more than willing in every way possible. She was only twenty-two, and she was built for pleasure. She had a lovely little face, blue eyes, thick blond hair and creamy skin, coupled with a pair of thirty-six D cups. She was also gifted with a mouth like a docker, and that, unfortunately for her, coupled with her desire to be married, was her main drawback. Declan was already on the look-out for a new conquest. Deirdre, though, was not about to be sidelined.

He had been here before – many times – and he had always managed to extricate himself from the lady in question. He wished they would listen to him from the off; he *told* them he wanted nothing from them other than a good time. He would always give them a nice parting gift – generally a few quid – or, if they were a bit posh, an expensive piece of jewellery. Deirdre, though, seemed determined to be around for the duration.

As he stood by the bar in the nightclub he had just opened with Michael, he felt irritation wash over him. Girls like Deirdre were born to be used – it was their lot in life. He could see her out of the corner of his eye – she was wearing fewer clothes than a professional athlete, and she was giving him the evil eye as if he might actually give a fuck. He was glad to see Michael walking over to him and, as they shook hands, he turned his back on his offending girlfriend with relief.

'What a fucking success, Declan! It's fabulous. Well done.'

Declan was pleased. He had worked hard on this place. He had acquired it as payment for a long-term debt. The man involved had a real passion for the gee-gees; unfortunately, the gee-gees didn't have a passion for him. Declan had given him a good deal on the loans, and a generous time span for paying him back. Neither had been appreciated, of course, but that was a compulsive gambler for you. The man in question had eventually been given no other option than to sign the place over and walk away, debt-free.

Declan had revamped it, renamed it, and now all he had to do was sit back and coin it in. It was a gold mine. It was located in East London with plenty of pubs and restaurants nearby and, best of all, it was now licensed for everything from live bands to boxing matches. The Costello firm, run by Michael Flynn, still owned enough Filth to guarantee anything they might feel they wanted. This was going to be a real earner; it had five bars over two floors, a huge dancing area, a glitterball that could pass for a spaceship and, like all their premises, the only people who could deal drugs were in their employ.

'I think it will pay us well, Michael.'

Michael grinned. 'I don't think you need worry about that, mate. I would worry about that bird behind you, though – I think she's out for a fight.'

Deirdre was tapping him on his shoulder, as if she had every right to be there. He rolled his eyes at Michael, who he could see thought this was absolutely hilarious. He turned slightly towards her and, opening his arms in a gesture of supplication, he said, 'What now?'

Deirdre looked at him with barely concealed malice.

Michael could see that Declan was not in the mood for a drama; this was *his* night, and he was clearly embarrassed because it was happening in front of him. Since Patrick had gone, Declan treated Michael with the same respect he had always given his older brother. It was instinctive. Although he had refused Michael's offer of a partnership, he still treasured his own place as a Costello, and the respect that demanded.

'What do you mean by that?'

Michael looked at the girl properly; she was a looker, but then all Declan's amours were lookers. He wouldn't bother otherwise – womanising was his hobby. This one had a mouth on her, though, and she wasn't going without a fight. Declan was willing her to take the hint and go away. But Deirdre was far too drunk, and full to the brim with righteous anger. She was going to have her say publicly and as loudly as possible.

Michael stepped forward and, grabbing her arm roughly, he said quietly, 'If you don't fuck off, you filthy little skank, I am going to get my blokes to drag you out of here and then I will personally see to it that you can never show your face within a ten-mile radius. I can do that. Declan can do that too but, unlike me, he's a nice guy. Now do yourself a favour, and fuck off.'

Deirdre was frightened now. This was Michael Flynn, and he was a Face, a real Face. That he had threatened her was something to be taken seriously, and she knew it. His words had sobered her up and, when he pushed her away from him, she nearly lost her balance.

Michael put his arm around Declan's shoulders, and she saw him pull Declan around till they were both facing the bar which meant they had their backs to her. It was the ultimate insult. Michael Flynn would not be in any company that reflected badly on him, or his world, he had made that more than clear. She walked away quickly; all she wanted now was to go home and lick her wounds.

Declan watched her walk away in the mirrors behind the bar area and, shaking his head slowly, he said gratefully, 'Michael, that was fucking priceless.'

Michael laughed. He knew they were being observed, and he played the game, but was annoyed that the situation had ever arisen, especially on a night such as this. They were being watched by everyone, which was all part and parcel of the world they inhabited. People knew who they were, and they wanted to be a part of it, no matter how small that part might be. They were interesting because of *who* they were. They were the people who between them ran more or less everything around them, including this new nightclub. He certainly wasn't about to let a slag like that make a scene, and show him up. He would cut her fucking head off first and ram it down her neck.

He was smiling jovially though as he said, 'You, my old friend, need to fucking grow a pair, and grow them fucking soon. Never, and I mean never, let a cunt like that think she has the right to cause a scene. It's a sign of weakness but, worse than that, it's a reflection on us. We are men who rely on our reputations – without them we are nothing. The fact she thought she could cunt you in front of me is fucking outrageous. Like I am going to swallow that, for fuck's sake! I wouldn't take that shit off my Josephine and I'm fucking married to her.'

Declan didn't answer for a while, he didn't know what to say. But he knew that Michael was right. Deirdre would have caused the Third World War if Michael hadn't stopped her, and she would have loved every second of it. He should have nipped it in the bud. 'I'm sorry, Michael. You know me – I like the lairy ones. But you're right. It will never happen again, I will make sure of that.'

Michael gestured for two more drinks, and the barmaid was there in nanoseconds. 'Good. I'm glad to hear it. Now, let's enjoy the night. We have to mingle with the punters, give them their money's worth, but I need a few more drinks first!'

Declan laughed. 'Welcome to my world!'

Michael was pleased to see Jeffrey Palmer and his crew making their way across the dance floor. He felt himself relaxing. He knew that, by the end of the night, everyone who was anyone would make their way over to him, and he would give them free drinks, and listen patiently to their life stories. It would guarantee the club's success, and he would have done his bit for public relations.

The music was loud, the place was packed out, and his expert eye was making sure the bouncers were all where they should be, and the bar staff were fast and efficient. It was second nature to him now, making sure everything was running smoothly, looking out for flaws, and working out a solution to any problems he might encounter. Patrick Costello had taught him well, and as he listened to yet another tale of derring-do from a wannabe Face intent on impressing him, he realised just how much he actually missed him.

Chapter Forty-Nine

Jermaine O'Shay was a very large Jamaican – he was into body-building, and he spent at least two hours a day in the gym. He was not a handsome man, but he was imposing, standing at over six feet tall and naturally big-boned. He was a man who looked dangerous. His size guaranteed that, as did his bald head, along with his permanent scowl. Women, however, loved him. He was a man who knew the power he wielded, and who used it to his advantage. In reality, although he was capable of great violence should the situation merit it, he was actually a nice guy. Like Michael Flynn, he understood the need to exude a persona. And, like Michael Flynn, he ruled his little empire with a mixture of fear tempered with kindness. He surrounded himself with people he trusted, who he could relax and be himself with. Patrick Costello had offered him a partnership, and that had been a defining moment in his life. He had known how to import drugs, and he had made a good living from that. Patrick Costello had then entered his life, and shown him how, not only to utilise his contacts, but how to maximise his return. With Patrick Costello's backing, he had become a big player almost overnight.

Now, though, he was in a quandary. Michael Flynn was a perfect replacement for Patrick Costello, he could never refute that. Nothing had changed – it was as if Patrick Costello was still alive. Jermaine had dealt with Michael Flynn, as per usual, and everything had been fine. But now, Michael suddenly wanted him to deal with Jeffrey Palmer, and he wasn't sure about that. He liked the way things were – he wasn't a man who relished change.

He was sitting in the bar of his private club, nursing a rum and Coke. His club was just off the Railton Road, and only accessible to certain people. It was small, but his clientele liked that. It was a place where people could relax without worrying about what they might say or who they said it to. He catered for people like himself, who needed to keep a degree of privacy, and who were also willing to pay for that.

He heard Michael before he saw him. He was greeting the doorman as usual and, as he walked down the stairway into the bar, he was laughing. Jermaine stood up, and Michael shook his hand firmly. He then stood aside and Jermaine found himself shaking Jeffrey Palmer's outstretched hand.

There wasn't anyone tending the bar so early in the day, so Jermaine walked behind the counter himself. 'What can I get you?'

Michael Flynn sat down on the banquette in the corner. It was newly re-covered in gold and green brocade. Jeffrey Palmer sat beside him, looking around him with interest. Jermaine was glad he had upgraded the place. He had a sneaky feeling that this wasn't Jeffrey Palmer's usual kind of drinking establishment.

'A couple of whiskies, mate, and not any of that fucking

knock-off either! I nearly lost the enamel off my teeth last time.'

Jermaine laughed. 'I told you, man, if you're putting Coca-Cola in it, you don't deserve the good stuff. My old dad would turn in his grave if I allowed a decent Scotch to be diluted with that shit.'

Michael nodded. 'He has a point, in all fairness, Jeffrey. But, when I come down here, I have to put something in the drinks – otherwise I would be flat out in no time.'

Jermaine grinned. 'Call yourself a fucking Irishman?'

Jeffrey laughed with them. 'Was your dad Irish then, Jermaine? I mean, with your name being O'Shay? It don't get more Irish than that, does it?'

Jermaine brought the drinks to the table and, sitting down beside them, he answered, 'My great-granddad was Irish, but it's been all black since then.'

Jeffrey wasn't sure how to react, and Jermaine could see that. He liked that he didn't want to offend in any way. That showed him the man wasn't racist – not outwardly anyway. Only time would tell.

'If you go to Jamaica, everyone has some Irish in them somewhere. Some even have blue eyes. It's fucking surreal. There are Patricks and Seans everywhere. We also like the Guinness – my mum used to call us the sunburnt Irishmen.'

Michael laughed loudly; he had heard this before, many times. He knew that Jermaine was proud of his Irish heritage, and even more proud of his Jamaican roots.

Jeffrey sipped his drink, and was pleased when he realised it was a good Irish malt. Like Jermaine, he had not been looking forward to this meeting; he had only dealt with the men who worked for Jermaine until now. A few keys here and there, mainly cocaine, and a lot of grass. When possible, he scored some Blond. Lebanese Gold was a really sought-after product. Unlike the Black, which came from Afghanistan, the Gold always guaranteed a mellow buzz. There was a lot of Blond coming in from the States – Acapulco Gold – but it was the Lebanese that people were willing to pay for.

Michael was quiet, watching the two men as they circled each other. He knew that neither man wanted it, but both these men would do their best to accommodate him. He supplied their wages because, without his permission, they basically couldn't operate. He was in the wonderful position of allowing people to earn without hindrance. If he was involved, he could guarantee the minimum police interference, and the opportunity to work with like-minded individuals, giving them the chance to not only expand their businesses, but also their earnings.

'Jeffrey, if you do take over from Michael, we will have to meet regularly, at least twice a week. I need to know everything at least a month in advance. I'm sure Michael has explained all that.'

Jeffrey was surprised to find he was almost enjoying himself. Jermaine O'Shay was a man much like himself, aware of his own capabilities, and who disliked change. Like himself, Jermaine had no option but to work with whoever Michael Flynn told him to work with. That was a difficult thing for men like them, who were the head of their own firms, and respected by the people they employed. He was now on Jermaine O'Shay's turf, in the man's own drinking club, so he had to be the one who bent over. Like Michael Flynn,

Jeffrey knew the value of humility, how it could be used to gain an advantage. It was a deadly weapon if employed properly. It could mask the violence that lurked underneath.

'Oh, yeah, I understand how this needs to work, mate. I just hope you are OK about us working together. I've been in touch with some of your boys for a while now, as I'm sure you already know. Now that Michael has given me this opportunity, I just want to make a success of it.'

Michael was impressed. He had hoped that Jeffrey Palmer would understand the situation with Jermaine, and work with him, but he had not expected Palmer, who could turn on a coin if the fancy took him, to humble himself for the greater good. It pleased him; he felt he had chosen wisely.

Jermaine O'Shay walked back behind the bar and, bringing back the bottle of malt, he poured them each another large drink, before saying sincerely, 'To us. The new order.'

Michael grinned. 'I'll drink to that.'

He was tired out. He had never completely understood just how much Patrick Costello had actually done until now. He had assumed that Patrick had given *him* the lion's share of the work. Now, though, he realised that the real money was what Patrick had concentrated on, and that was a full-time job in itself. Michael was having to work day and night to keep on top of everything and, even though he was given the same respect as Patrick Costello, he didn't have a Michael of his own, so he was having to gradually farm the lesser work out. He had not been too bothered at first, knowing that he just had to find the right people for the right jobs, and that might take time.

Josephine being pregnant again had changed everything.

He needed to get things in place as soon as possible so he could concentrate on her. She was a diamond, never complaining about his late nights, always ready to listen to him. He knew she would stand by him through anything life might throw at them. Now it was his turn, and he wanted to be there for her. He would do anything to see that this child came into the world. She deserved a baby so much, and her craving for a child of her own was painful to watch. He owed her this, and no matter what happened, he was going to be there beside her.

Chapter Fifty

'Michael, will you go out, please? I am *OK*.'

Her husband was starting to get on Josephine's nerves now. He was always asking how she was, staying in with her, offering everything from back rubs to cups of tea. It was wearing her out. All this attention was really irritating, and he watched her like a hawk.

'I just want to help you, darling.'

Josephine sighed. 'You want to help me, do you?'

Michael nodded. He looked like a lost Boy Scout. 'Of course I do.'

'Then go out, will you? I know you have loads of stuff to sort out. I also know you want to help me. But all I want is a bit of space. I am OK! I feel good. But you're making me feel nervous, like you're waiting for this to go wrong.'

Michael was devastated. He was trying to be the good guy. He was worried about her, and he *was* worried that she might lose the baby. It would obliterate her, as it always had. 'Oh, darling, I just want you to know you are my priority. I spend so much time out and about. I love you. I want to be there for you.'

Josephine smiled sadly. 'I love you, Michael, you know

that. But you are like a fucking bad smell lately, hanging around here. You're normally out all hours of the day and night. I've never once questioned that, have I? I accept that it's part and parcel of your job. Now, though, if I even fart, you're standing behind me. It is driving me mad. I can call you if I need you.'

Michael was looking at his wife, saw the way she was trying to keep as calm as possible, and knew he was getting on her nerves. He was getting on his own fucking nerves! But his real fear was that, if she lost this child too, she would not cope with it as well as she seemed to think. She was convinced this time was different somehow, but he wasn't so sure. He felt it might be wishful thinking on her part, and who could blame her? She saw the doctor regularly, and everything seemed fine, but that was how it had been in the past. He would gladly give ten years off his life, if it meant she could have a child of her own.

'Look, Josephine, I know what you're saying, darling. But I care about you, and I worry about you.'

Josephine closed her eyes in distress. Sometimes men were so thick! It was all about Michael really, but he couldn't see that. He was waiting for her to fail again. Oh, he never said that, of course! But she knew him better than anyone else in the world. He was scared for her if this all went pear-shaped again.

'Well, do you know what, Michael? Don't worry about me, OK? Just let me be. You're stressing me out, can't you see that? I have sat here night after night, all on my Jack Jones, for years, and I have learnt to live with that, live with your work, and the odd hours. I even have a routine. Bet you never knew that. I watch certain programmes, I have a nice bath, I go to bed and I read. I've learnt to cope *without* you and I like a bit of peace in my own home. So I am begging you, Michael, *please*, will you stop treating me like a fucking invalid? I know that this child might not come to term, I know that better than anyone, believe me. Been there, done that, remember? Many times. Go out, do your job, and let me do mine.'

Michael could see that Josephine was serious, and she had a point. He was letting the business slide, and that was not good for either of them. He should be out there, sorting out the mess that Patrick Costello had left behind. But he also felt he should be there for his wife.

'All night that phone has been going in your office, Michael, but you won't answer it. You just sit here like a nun at a stag do. You make me nervous. Answer the fucking thing, and do what's needed.' She grabbed his hand tightly. 'I know how difficult it's been for you. Patrick left a big hole. You have a lot to contend with, so will you just get on with it? I feel like I'm keeping you from your business. I don't want that, Michael, and, if you're really honest, neither do you.'

The office phone was ringing again, and she could see that Michael was torn once more. 'Answer the fucking thing, will you, Michael? Put us all out of our misery.'

He laughed despite himself. He knew how lucky he was to have her. She never asked anything of him, she just accepted him for who he was. She wasn't a fool either, she knew the score – knew what he was all about. He stood up, and walked from the room to answer the phone.

Josephine lay back against the sofa cushions, and sighed in relief. She cupped her belly with her hands, content with the new life she had inside her, and the promise of some well-needed peace and quiet. Michael had to let her deal with this in her own way. She didn't need a babysitter, she just needed to feel in control of her own life. She closed her eyes, tired out. She just wanted her bed and some sleep.

Michael came back into the room a few minutes later, and she could see he was worried about something.

'I have to nip out, darling.'

She smiled gently. 'All I can say is, thank fuck for that!'

Chapter Fifty-One

Declan was seriously worried. *He* had never had to deal with a situation like this before – his brother had made sure of that. Patrick knew the value of speed in these kinds of situations. Michael was finally on his way, but it just wasn't good enough. He should have been here ages ago, and he would tell him that as well. Michael was like a fucking ghost these days, drifting in and out at his leisure. It was a travesty. He was supposed to be the big boss now, and it seemed to Declan that Michael Flynn had dropped the fucking ball. He needed to up his game, because the people he dealt with looked for weakness and, if they found it, they went in for the kill.

He sat down. The Portakabin was too hot, stuffy, and it fucking stank. He lit a cigar, and puffed on it deeply. The smell of his big Churchill would mask anything and, as this place stank like a Turkish wrestler's jockstrap, he welcomed the tobacco's distinct aroma.

He could hear the swearing and threats coming from the other room, and he closed his eyes in annoyance. This wasn't his gig – this was Michael Flynn's territory. He didn't like being dragged into it all, but he had no choice in the matter.

Someone had to do something before it got out of hand. This was the kind of situation that could easily cause a war.

He saw the headlights of a car as it pulled up outside, and he waited patiently for Michael to join him. He was really aggravated, but he knew he had to keep a lid on it until this was all sorted out. One thing at a time, had always been Patrick's mantra, and Declan chose to live by it.

Michael opened the door and, as he walked in, Declan saw that the man was already angry. 'Tell me this is a fucking joke, Declan.'

Declan shook his head, nervous suddenly. Michael Flynn looked fit to be tied, and that wasn't a good thing. 'Like I'd bring you out at this time of night for a fucking laugh. I've been trying to get you all evening. This is your fucking business, Michael, not mine.'

Michael knew he was right. He should have answered the phone – no one rang the house unless it was important. Josephine was his only weak spot, his Achilles heel. He had fucked up big time.

'So, come on then, what fucking happened?'

Declan realised that the man in the next room had suddenly gone quiet. He assumed that he had heard Michael's voice, and was now rapidly sobering up and wondering how he could get out of the situation he had caused.

Declan puffed on his cigar for a few moments. 'Jeffrey Palmer was in the new club having a few drinks, and who should turn up there mob-handed, full of drink, drugs and God knows what else? Only Kelvin McCarthy. He homed straight in on Jeffrey. It was fucking outrageous, Michael. Jeffrey was good in all fairness, he swallowed a lot. More than I fucking would have if it was me. But it got out of hand. Jeffrey was going to give him a well-deserved slap, and Kelvin pulled a gun on him – in full view of everyone. Thank fuck we were in the top bar. Most of the people there know the score. But it was fucking hairy, I tell you. He would have shot him and all, but young Danny Kirby wrestled the gun off him. He is worth watching, that lad. He saved us all a fucking serious nightmare tonight. Anyway, to cut a long story short, I have got Kelvin in there.' He gestured towards the door that led to the other room in the Portakabin. 'We bundled Kelvin out of there as fast as we could. But Jeffrey Palmer is not going to let this drop, and who could blame him? It was a public humiliation. It's just that Kelvin's father is a different kettle of fish as you know. Christie McCarthy is a fucking known Face, and he has a big crew behind him. He also has a son who is about as much use as a nun's cunt. The bugbear is he is *still* his son.'

Michael looked around him quickly, his mind working overtime. This was a real problem in more ways than one. He admired and respected Christie McCarthy. He was one of the few people they didn't do business with although they had requested his services on occasion. Christie McCarthy was actually the only person capable of taking him on. He was also one of the few people that Patrick Costello had genuinely liked. They had grown up together, and they had always had a good relationship. Christie McCarthy pretty much kept himself to himself. He had long-term businesses that were not just very lucrative, but were also specialised. He was the go-to man if you needed someone to disappear permanently but, for whatever reason, you couldn't be seen to be involved. He was also a very experienced mediator who could not only solve certain problems between the warring factions, but who was also guaranteed to be without any bias whatsoever. That was his expertise. He had made his living from his ability to facilitate any kind of meeting, even between sworn enemies. He would then act as the mediator for their talks, and no one had ever dared to take advantage of him, use the meeting for their own ends or for payback. Christie McCarthy wasn't a man who would allow anything like that to happen; after all, this was his bread and butter. He could also provide any service that might be needed, from a getaway driver to a bent barrister. His forte was his wide range of contacts and his reputation as a man who delivered.

But now his son had been the catalyst for a situation so serious it could easily deteriorate into a fucking war.

Michael walked into the other office. Kelvin McCarthy was sitting on an old typing chair tied up like a kipper. Michael could see the fear in the boy's deep-blue eyes. He was his father's son, there was no doubting that. He had the same arched eyebrows and thick black hair and, like his father, his face had the dark shadow of a man who needed to shave twice a day. He was Christie's living image – a handsome fucker – but that's where the similarity ended. Personality-wise, he was the antithesis of his old man. He was a weak-willed, vicious bully, who traded on his father's name, and his father's reputation. Well, he had picked a fight with the wrong people this time.

Declan walked into the room behind him, and Michael knew he was wondering, along with Kelvin McCarthy, what was going to happen. His incarceration had clearly thrown Kelvin off kilter. He had not expected to be treated so roughly, nor so carelessly. Never before had anyone ever dared to bring him to book. He had always been given a pass, and his father had smoothed things over.

'How old are you, Kelvin?' Michael's voice was casual, even interested.

Kelvin could detect no real anger, and he felt himself relax a little. The fact he had been brought here worried him. He knew enough about the Life to realise that Michael Flynn wasn't a man to be crossed lightly and that even his father would balk at a face-to-face with him.

As he was sobering up, and coming down from the pills he had popped like sweets, he understood for the first time in his life that he was in real trouble.

'I'm twenty-six.'

Michael didn't answer him immediately. He just stood there looking at him. Under the man's gaze, Kelvin felt the first flush of shame wash over him.

'Did you hear that, Declan? He's twenty-six years old, for fuck's sake.'

Declan Costello knew how to play the game, so he said nonchalantly, 'I heard him all right.'

'Fucking amazing though, isn't it, Declan? Twenty-six, and a completely fucking useless cunt. That has got to hurt your old man – he has to be ashamed of you, Kelvin. Can I call you Kelvin, by the way?'

Kelvin McCarthy nodded his agreement. He didn't know what else to do; he had never been in a situation like this in his life. ''Course you can. It's my name, after all.' He tried to lighten the heavy atmosphere that permeated the room, acting like he wasn't bothered about being trussed up like a chicken and unable to move.

Michael Flynn stared at him for long moments. Kelvin McCarthy watched him warily. His eyes were ice cold; he looked capable of anything. Kelvin knew instinctively that he *was*. He possessed no fear of anyone or anything.

'You can call me Mr Flynn.'

Kelvin McCarthy was suddenly feeling very frightened, and that was an alien concept to him. All his life, he had been cushioned by his name. Now he was feeling the terror that being at the mercy of a man like Michael Flynn could elicit. Kelvin McCarthy was a coward really. He had always traded on his father's name, and that had been enough to get him what he wanted, and guarantee him a level of protection. He wasn't so sure about that any more. But he still believed that, whatever happened, no one would harm him because his father was Christie McCarthy, and that alone gave him the criminal equivalent of diplomatic status. His father's name and his reputation was like money in the bank. He had worked with everyone who mattered, from Jack Spot to the Krays and the Richardsons, and had carved for himself a unique place in the world of villainy. He provided a service that no one else could even attempt to emulate. His word was his bond. His whole business relied on his reputation as a man of the utmost integrity, who could be trusted without question. That was his father's main strength, and why his father was so respected in his world. It was also why he felt that even someone like Michael Flynn would think twice before he did anything that might cause a rift between them.

Kelvin watched Michael warily. The man was completely relaxed, and that alone was unnerving. He was acting as if this was an everyday occurrence.

'So, Kelvin, what do you think I should do with you?'

Declan Costello walked from the room, and busied himself pouring them both large whiskies. He had a feeling they were going to need them. Michael was baiting the boy, and he hoped that Kelvin had the brain capacity to give him the answers he expected. He didn't hold out much hope though – he could see the boy was rattled.

Michael accepted the glass of whisky from Declan, and took a large gulp. He was enjoying Kelvin's fear. He needed to be made aware of his actions. 'I mean, think about it from my point of view. You came into my club, and you then caused a big fucking scene. You even had the fucking audacity to pull a gun on a very good friend of mine. I mean, think about it logically, Kelvin. I can't let this go, can I?'

Kelvin McCarthy was hurting everywhere. He was bound tightly, and he couldn't move his arms at all. He was also tired out. He had the hangover from hell, and Michael Flynn was treating him like a fucking no one. He was threatening him, and Kelvin McCarthy felt that he should remind the man of who he was actually dealing with. He was scared, but he was also aware that his father would not allow anything to happen to him. His natural arrogance was coming to the fore. He was safe as the proverbial houses. Michael Flynn wasn't going to really harm him – he wouldn't dare. His dad had always stepped in and smoothed everything over. He had stepped over the line, and he would have to pay dearly when his dad learnt the whole story. But that was the point

– his dad would ultimately be the one to punish him for his sins, no one else. That was how it had always been.

He sighed theatrically. He could feign abject contrition in his sleep; he had been doing it since he was fifteen and his dad had found out he was a thief. 'Look, Mr Flynn, I admit it. I fucked up big time. It won't happen again, believe me. I have learnt my lesson the hard way. But this is dragging on too long now, OK? My joints are screaming with pain, and I can't feel my hands. I've been tied up like this for fucking hours. My dad will be wondering where I am. The people I was with last night will eventually have to tell him what happened – that's if he hasn't heard already, of course – but I will explain to him that it was all my fault. I swear to you both, on my mother's life, that I will walk away from this without any malice towards you whatsoever.'

Michael Flynn listened to him intently, but he showed no reaction to his speech.

Declan walked from the room slowly and, once more, seated himself behind the big old desk that his brother had bought at an auction years before. He picked up the bottle of Glenfiddich and poured himself out another generous measure. He knocked it back quickly, and immediately poured himself out another large glass. The dawn was breaking. He could hear cars in the distance, the sound of people going to work, to jobs that paid the same wage week after week, year after fucking year. It was completely alien to him, that kind of life. But, as Patrick had always said, without people like them, Britain would be fucked. They were the people who kept the country going, who worked in the industries that made Britain great. They were the backbone of the country; without them and the work ethic they possessed, Patrick had always said Britain would die on its feet. There was a beautiful logic in there somewhere, a brutal truth that couldn't be denied. He sighed heavily, and looked at Michael warily through the doorway. He was still standing there, not even a movement or a word to indicate he had heard anything that Kelvin McCarthy had said.

Michael could see the confusion on Kelvin's smug face. He had expected a reaction to his little speech. But Michael knew, deep in his heart, that he was never going to give this ponce a swerve. He looked at the man once more. He had everything a man could want. He was big, handsome, he had a fuck-off head of hair, and a father who would have gladly given him the earth on a plate. But he viewed his own father as nothing more than a fucking weapon, used him as a guarantee so he would never have to pay for his mistakes personally. That a man like Christie McCarthy could produce such a fucking weak-willed, avaricious, lazy, vicious, useless ponce like this was beyond Michael's ken. He would rather be childless than have to own up to fathering someone as heinous as Kelvin McCarthy. Even now, the man thought his name could excuse everything he had done. Michael was so disgusted, and so ashamed for Christie McCarthy, a truly great man. To know that he had produced such a fucking ingrate must be the worst thing a man could experience.

Michael went into the office where Declan was sitting quietly and, pulling out an old chair from the back of the room, he sat opposite him, and held out his empty glass. Declan filled it for him, and they both smiled suddenly.

'Patrick would never have sat there like you. He just couldn't have done that, Michael, you know? He had to be in the position of power always. This is the first time I have ever sat behind this desk! What does that say about me?'

Michael laughed. 'I know that better than anyone, believe me. It wasn't deliberate, Declan. It was just his nature. He had worked hard for his position in life, and it meant a lot to him.'

Declan could see the truth of that, and he was amazed that Michael had understood his brother so well, and what made him tick. 'You're right. Patrick always wanted more. Nothing would ever be enough for him. Like you!'

'I suppose so.'

Michael got up and, walking to the main door, he picked up a crowbar that was always there in case of emergencies.

Declan shrugged. 'This will cause a lot of trouble, Michael, but you know that, don't you?'

Michael was busy feeling the weight of his chosen weapon, moving it from hand to hand. He grinned. 'I know that, Declan. But even Christie McCarthy will have to accept that this time his boy has trodden on the wrong fucking toes. I can't swallow this, and neither can you. It was a blatant fucking public outrage. I will sort Christie McCarthy out, if necessary. But, whatever happens, that cunt in there is on his way out.'

Declan shrugged. He had expected this from the off. It was why he had brought the man here, and sent everyone involved home. This was not going to end happily for anyone concerned.

Michael went through to the back office a few minutes later. He had finished his drink first.

The first blow split Kelvin's head open, the second exposed his brain. He was dead almost immediately, so then Michael concentrated on the man's body. He was going to make an example of him. No one was going to be in any doubt about what was in store for them if they dared to cross him.

Chapter Fifty-Two

Josephine woke up slowly, and smiled lazily. Michael was asleep beside her, his arm around her waist. She felt her baby move inside her, and she felt a rush of happiness. Every time she felt it moving, she knew that it was still alive. She closed her eyes and said a quick prayer of thanks. She had been saying the rosary every day, the Joyful Mysteries, mostly. She wasn't comfortable with the others, least of all the Sorrowful Mysteries. She had also been saying the Thirty Days' Prayer, and the Creed. She had always loved the Creed. It was so beautiful. She prayed to Mary, Our Lady, a mother herself, to please protect her child, and guide it safely into the world. She was sure that her prayers would be answered. If it didn't happen this time, she was never going to try again; she would accept her barren state, and get on with her life.

She crawled out of the bed, making sure she didn't wake Michael up. He worked so hard, and she had forced him out of the house the night before. Now she felt bad about that. He was only trying to protect her.

She walked down to the kitchen, and put the kettle on. As usual, she opened the back door to let the air in. She loved that she had such a huge garden, and that it was so beautiful. The gardener came three days a week, and he kept it pristine. She had her own little herb garden, and a small patio that allowed her to sit outside and enjoy her garden at her leisure. She knew how lucky she was to have so much, she really did appreciate what her Michael had given her. She knew just how hard he worked for his family, and how lucky she was to have a man like that.

She made a cup of tea, and sat down at the kitchen table. She caressed her belly; it was really starting to show now. Her mum had to have guessed, but she had not said a word. Josephine loved her for that. Her mum had been her best friend, until she had taken against Michael practically overnight. They were suddenly at loggerheads, but her mother had the sense to know when to retreat, and she had done just that. No one was going to say a word against her Michael without a fight. If she had to make a choice, there would be no competition – Michael would win hands down. Every time her mother tried to slip a criticism in, she turned on her without hesitating. It had worked too. Her mother's complaints were now few and far between, thank fuck. Her dad loved him at least! As Michael always said, two out of three wasn't bad.

She sipped her tea. She would kill for a cup of coffee, but apparently it wasn't good for the baby, so she had stopped drinking it. She heard a car crunch to a stop on the drive. It was only eight a.m. She yawned noisily. Who could this be? It must be one of Michael's workers. They all seemed to have the code for the gates.

She went through the reception hall, and opened the front door. Two men pushed past her, knocking her backwards.

'Where is he?'

Josephine looked at the men in her entrance hall, absolutely terrified. They were huge and very aggressive. She recognised one of them, but she couldn't place him.

'He's not here. He hasn't been home all night.' She was not going to let them get any advantage over her husband, she knew that much.

'Look, love, don't fuck me about. I ain't in the mood for games. Where the fuck is he?'

Michael was at the top of the stairs, and she looked up at him fearfully. She couldn't believe it. He didn't seem to be the least bothered about them coming to his house, her home. He walked slowly down the stairs, saying, 'Have a bit of respect, lads. My wife's pregnant.'

Both men looked at her, and she pushed out her belly to emphasise her condition.

'I expected you at some point, but I thought you would have the decency to come to my offices. After all, I didn't bring my grievances to your front door, did I?'

No one said a word, and Josephine waited with bated breath, wondering what the next step would be. Michael was beside her now and, smiling pleasantly, he said gently, 'Put the kettle on, darling. Make us all a cup of tea.' Then he walked into his office, and the two men followed him, like lambs to the slaughter.

Chapter Fifty-Three

Michael closed the door to his office quietly. He gestured amiably to the two men to take a seat and when they were both settled comfortably – though looking thoroughly chastened at learning of his wife's condition – he bellowed at them loudly, 'How dare you! How dare you bring your fucking grievances into my home! My home, where my wife resides, and where I expect her to be safe and left in fucking peace. You dare to fucking come here like the avenging angels, and then expect me to swallow such outrageous fucking behaviour without retaliating?'

When Michael was really angry, he was formidable. He concealed his temper beneath the usual friendly countenance he showed to the world most of the time, whilst maintaining his reputation as a man whose temper, when roused, was without equal. He had nurtured this unpredictability over the years, ensuring that his reaction to any situation could never be guaranteed. That had stood him in great stead – it was the reason why these two men were unsure now of what he was actually capable of. Oh, he remembered the guilt he had felt over the Goldings' death and the angst he had felt over his first kill. It had all been easier than he had ever believed. He had been given a baptism of fire all right – Patrick Costello had ensured that. But it had shown him how simple the kill actually was. Now his reputation was set – his reaction to any given situation, on the other hand, was something no one could ever foresee. It was why these men were suddenly so fucking subdued. He had not been even remotely bothered by their presence on his doorstep; they had assumed it would give them the edge – instead, it had given him the advantage. They had come to his home in anger without taking the time to think it all through. That alone was a fucking insult in itself.

Michael Flynn genuinely felt for Christie McCarthy. The man's anguish was evident and he had every right to feel as he did. He had lost his son and that was a terrible thing for anyone to endure. But all that really mattered in their world was righting a wrong – that was the bottom line. Kelvin had pushed his fucking luck big time, he had taken a dirty great liberty, and he had been punished for it. That was it, as far as Michael was concerned, but he was willing to try to build a few bridges.

'Look, Christie, I know how you're feeling, mate, I respect that. But you know, as well as I do, that Kelvin was long overdue for a fucking hammering of some sort.'

Michael waited for a reply. He wanted to give this man a pass; he had no argument with him personally. But Christie's silence was making it difficult. Well, fuck him! He needed a fucking lesson in etiquette.

'Do you know what I really think? I think that *you* should have reined your boy in a long time ago. I mean, I couldn't believe my fucking ears! He actually pulled a gun on Jeffrey

Palmer, in *my* fucking club! In full view of the paying public, I might fucking add, disrespecting me and my premises.' Michael was getting even more annoyed now at having to explain himself. 'Do you honestly think that I should have swallowed my fucking knob? Done nothing? Your son baited that man for ages, he insulted him into the ground, and the only reason Jeffrey Palmer didn't retaliate and kill the cunt there and then, was because he was on *my* premises. He knew if he entered into the fray – bearing in mind that he had every right to sort that lairy little cunt out – he would now be in the same condition as your boy: dead as a fucking doornail. I cannot, and will not, allow such behaviour on my premises. I don't care who it is.'

Christie McCarthy knew that Michael had only done what he would have done himself in the same position. But this was still about *his* son. As useless as the boy had been, he was his own flesh and blood.

Michael was leaning on his desk, with his arms folded across his chest. He looked every inch the main man; he had something about him that told people he was not to be underestimated. Like Patrick Costello, he had an edge to him. McCarthy had dealt with dangerous men before – it was par for the course in the world they lived in – but, occasionally, the world threw up someone like Michael Flynn or Patrick Costello. They were few and far between, and the fact that they lived by such a completely different code was the reason they were so successful.

Christie McCarthy was a man who had his creds, and he had come here for a fight – not just to avenge his son's death, but to show people that some things needed to be redressed.

He glanced at his close friend, Sam Dunne, his sister's husband, and a man who he knew would always be there if needed. Like him, Sam was subdued.

'He was still my son, Michael, my boy, and you fucking murdered him.'

Michael shrugged nonchalantly. This was starting to irritate him now. It was all going on too long. 'Well, you know what? He didn't give me much fucking choice, did he? I'm not going to enter into a big discussion about this. I had to do what I did, and you both know that. I'm sorry to the heart of me for offending you, Christie. I have the greatest respect for you, but this was just business. It wasn't personal. If I had let his actions slide, you know I would never have lived it down!'

Christie was shaking his head in denial, so Michael bellowed, 'He asked for it, and he fucking got it! Not before time, either. You should have seen this coming, mate. He used your name, and he lived off your reputation like a fucking leech. I'm only saying to you what everyone else has been saying about him for donkey's years. I didn't want to do anything to him. As you know yourself, this kind of thing is a last resort, for fuck's sake! But it happened. Whatever you might think, I did what I had to do.'

Sam Dunne couldn't look Christie in the face. He was with Michael Flynn every step of the way. He loved Christie McCarthy like a brother, but that son of his had always been trouble. It was awful to know Kelvin was dead, for a father to know that his son had been murdered, but it had to be a relief for him in some ways. Christie had been plagued by the lad's antics for years. He spent money like water; he couldn't hold a job down, he had stolen from his own family. He had been devoid of any kind of decency whatsoever, he had lived his whole life believing he was entitled to everything. Now he had been taken out by Michael Flynn, and Sam Dunne was seriously regretting his impulsive actions in coming here. But family was family.

Michael could see how hurt Christie McCarthy was about his son. He didn't like to see the man so upset, but he wasn't going to sugar-coat everything; the man knew he had spawned a fucking moron of Olympian standards. He attempted to swallow his anger once more, and said gently, 'Look, Christie, I can't really apologise for what I did, all I can say is, I hope you can let this go. I don't want to fall out with you about it. I have no fight with you – I had no fight with him till he brought one into my club. But if you can't get over this, then tell me now.'

It was a threat, and Christie recognised it. Michael Flynn was getting bored, he wanted this over. He had apologised in his own immutable way, had tried to explain his action, and given Christie the respect he was due.

Christie had far more sense than his son – he knew when to let things go. Michael Flynn was also the main employer for many of the men he had to deal with on a daily basis – he was his bread and butter, really. It rankled – the death of a child wasn't something to be forgotten overnight, even if that child had been on a death wish for many a long year – but his earlier anger had diminished.

'I don't want to carry this on. You're right, Michael – my son should have known better. I knew he was a fucking waster. He broke my heart. I gave him every opportunity to work for a living, to have a life in the real world, but he fucked it up every time. I don't want to fall out with you over this. It is hard to say it, but he ain't worth all this. He never was.'

Michael smiled widely. He could be generous now, magnanimous. He had got what he wanted. 'I'm glad to hear that, Christie. I would have hated to have us at each other's throats. When I saw you two in my hallway, and my poor wife looking so fucking frightened, I was all for killing you both, just for the piss-take. I really didn't think we would get this far. It shows you how wrong first impressions can be, eh?' He held out his hand and Christie McCarthy shook it heartily. Then Michael turned to Sam Dunne, and did the same. It was all friendly now, the atmosphere lighter, and both Christie and Sam knew they had dodged a bullet. Michael was relaxed, acting like he was relieved that they had understood his terrible predicament and forgiven him.

'Let me pour us a drink. I'm so pleased we managed to get past this shit.' He poured them large brandies, personally serving them, making sure they were comfortable, offering them seats and cigars, treating them with the utmost respect, making them feel valued, acknowledging their status in his world.

'A toast. To the future.'

They all raised their Waterford crystal glasses, knowing that Michael Flynn had won the day. Everyone would find out that they had folded, that Christie had been forced to overlook his son's demise, and accept Michael Flynn's actions without any recourse whatsoever.

'I never wanted to fight with you, Christie.'

Christie McCarthy took a big gulp of his drink to steady his nerves. 'I know that, Michael. I know you had no choice. I can see that now.'

Michael was still smiling his big friendly smile, as he said nonchalantly, 'By the way, Christie, just one last question. I will never mention this again, but it's important that I know. Which treacherous ponce gave you the code to my fucking gates?'

Chapter Fifty-Four

Lana was on her third glass of wine. She was what she called 'merry' and, as Josephine topped her glass up, she laughed loudly. 'Oh, thank you, darling! This is just what the doctor ordered!'

Josephine laughed with her. This was the mum she loved, the mum she had grown up with – full of fun and mischief, always up for a good laugh. She had missed this. She hated them being at loggerheads, especially when it was over her Michael.

Lana looked at her daughter with her usual critical eye. For all her traumas, her Josephine was still a lovely-looking girl – well, woman now. She had kept her natural beauty, even after all the miscarriages and the stillbirth. The only real change had been her daughter's quietness; with every loss she had gradually lost her natural ebullience and her lust for life. Over the last few years she had become like a recluse – she rarely left the house now.

She still shopped twice a week, and that was it. But how she shopped! Talk about bulk buying! Everywhere you looked there were boxes, all piled up on top of one another. She used to keep them out of sight – now the whole place looked like a warehouse. Who the fuck bought twenty-four cans of soup at a time? There was only the two of them. As Des joked, if the bomb dropped, they could live round Josephine's for a year, and never eat the same meal twice. She had laughed with him, pretending everything was all right, but it worried her, as a mother. She knew that things were not OK with her daughter; her girl wasn't right in her mind.

This house had once been spectacular. Tastefully decorated, each item of furniture had been agonised over, carefully selected, and put into place with love and pride. Now, though, every room had boxes piled up everywhere. Josephine shopped like she was feeding the five thousand. A case of this, two cases of that. What really bothered Lana was that Josephine acted like it was perfectly normal. This was a very big house, yet her daughter was having to use *every* room to store her purchases. But Lana knew better than to say anything – she was not going to rock the boat in any way now that they were finally back on track. She kept her own counsel where Michael was concerned too. Josephine was not going to listen to anything detrimental about him, but Lana knew she must have heard the rumours going round. Look at all this about Kelvin McCarthy for a start – it was the talk of the town.

There was something she needed to pluck up the courage to ask her daughter though – something she couldn't let go. It was far too important. She gulped down her wine for more Dutch courage. It was really lovely; one good thing about Michael Flynn for all his faults – and they were legion – was he only bought the best.

'I'm a bit pissed, Josephine!'

Josephine laughed happily. 'I could have told you that, Mum!'

Lana laughed with her daughter, pleased to see the girl so happy for once. 'Josephine, my love, I have to ask you this, darling, as your mum – please don't be cross with me. Are you pregnant again?'

Josephine looked at her mother, sorry to her soul that her mum had not asked her the question straight out but had needed a few drinks to pluck up the courage. She knew that this was *her* fault. She had deliberately built a barrier between her and her mum. A barrier that had alienated her from her own mother so much she was too scared to ask her a perfectly natural question. She was nearly eight months gone now. She knew she should have told her mother already. She was an only child, she was all her parents had. She felt so guilty, and so disloyal. Her mum loved her more than anything, and she knew that without a doubt.

She was nearly in tears as she said brokenly, 'I didn't tell *anyone*, Mum. Neither did Michael – I wouldn't let him. I didn't want to get everyone's hopes up again. That way, if I lost this baby, I wouldn't have to face everyone, see their disappointment along with my own. I would have just coped with it myself this time. I didn't tell you in case it went wrong again. I couldn't bear to put you through it.'

Lana felt as if her own heart was going to split in two. Her daughter's words were so sad. But she could understand the girl's logic. It had been so traumatic for her, losing her babies time and time again. She had hated witnessing her girl's pain, watching her beautiful daughter die inside a little bit more with every failure. She had held her while she cried her heart out, wishing she could take her girl's overwhelming sense of loss and pain on herself, so her daughter wouldn't have to experience it. But that wasn't possible; all she could do was be there for her, and pray for the best.

'Oh, darling, I understand. But I want to help you in any way I can. I would have kept it to myself. I'm your mum, Josephine. I know we have had our differences, but never forget that you are everything to me. All I want is your happiness, darling.'

Josephine hugged her mum tightly, relieved now that she knew what was going on. 'I didn't even tell Michael at first, Mum. He noticed eventually, of course, but I couldn't bring myself to tell anyone else about it. As mad as this might sound, I feel different this time. I feel like this time I can do it. This baby moves about a lot. I can feel it's alive. I wish I had told you, Mum. I know I can always trust you, no matter what. I am so sorry.'

For the first time in ages, Lana actually felt close to her only child. She held her daughter tightly, marvelling at her firm, round belly, and the familiar feel of her daughter's embrace. It had been so long since she had held her in her arms. Her knowledge of Michael Flynn had caused the rift between them, and she knew now that she could not allow her personal feelings for Michael to cloud her relationship with her only child. She had no option – her daughter needed her, and that was enough.

'I can't even imagine what you've been through, darling. But I promise you, I will always be there for you, Josephine, no matter what.'

Josephine could feel her mother's tears mingling with her own. The guilt was completely overwhelming her now. She knew how much her mum loved her; never once in her life had she ever felt unwanted or neglected. Her mum and dad had lived for her, and she had always known that. She had chosen her husband over her mum, and that had been hard, but she knew she would do the same again, if needed. He was everything to her, and he always would be.

'Please, Mum, promise me you won't say anything bad about Michael again. I just can't stand it. He has stood by me and loved me through everything. He was happy to forget all about having babies, just so I wouldn't have to go through any more heartache. That is why I didn't tell him about this baby till I had to. I love him more than anything, and he loves me, Mum, I know that.'

Lana sighed gently. 'I won't say a word about anything or anyone. I promise.' She had learnt her lesson as far as all that was concerned. That her Josephine had chosen Michael over her had given her a reality check. She wasn't going to lose her daughter again, that was for sure. Michael Flynn was not someone she wanted in her daughter's life, she knew him for the man he really was. But her daughter didn't see him as anything other than her knight in shining armour, and she knew she would never disabuse her of that notion. It was pointless to even try. But she would watch him like a hawk, and pray every day that her Josephine would eventually see him for what he was.

Chapter Fifty-Five

Michael was watching Declan eat; the man was a veritable force of nature. He could consume his own bodyweight in steak, and still have room for a dessert. He was like a machine; he ate with a dedication that was almost inspiring, he enjoyed his food so much.

Michael was at the head of the table, of course, Declan was sitting to his right, and the other eight seats were taken up by people they worked with who were important enough to join them for dinner once a month. Declan couldn't see the value of it at all. He just saw a big bill at the end for Michael to pay. These people worked for them – surely *they* should be paying the bill? They gave them their earn, for fuck's sake! Yet Michael insisted that they wine and dine them. In Declan's mind, this was completely fucking ludicrous. But he couldn't see the money that they were bringing into the firm on a regular basis – Declan only saw the money they earned personally. He couldn't see the big picture – that these men brought in far more than they earned. But then, Declan didn't really understand the economics of the big earns. Michael made him come to these dinners, because he was his business partner. He had tried to educate him on the finer points of the businesses he ran, but Declan genuinely had no real interest whatsoever. Michael knew that these dinners were worth every penny. The men around him were all good earners, and they appreciated that he singled them out and showed them how much he valued them. He knew that, to keep people onside, you had to make them feel a part of everything, give them your time and, better still, your interest. It was a good night out for everyone concerned as well – good food, good wine and good company.

He sat back in his chair, feeling very relaxed. He had imbibed a few glasses of red wine, and he was enjoying the company. Jeffrey Palmer was on his left, in pride of place. He was always a good bloke to have around; Michael liked him a lot and, since the removal of young McCarthy, Jeffrey Palmer had done everything possible to show his appreciation. He was grateful to Michael Flynn for taking care of a very awkward situation for him, and he would never forget that.

Michael couldn't tell him that the main reason the boy had been dispatched was because he had dared to pull a gun on *his* premises. He could not let that go – no matter who might be involved. He would have taken out anyone, no matter who they were or who they worked for. It was the principle.

'What a great night.'

Michael smiled easily as always. He was good at that. 'I like it here, Jeffrey. It's a great place – a delicate mixture of bankers and wankers!'

Jeffrey laughed with him. 'That is a great analogy, and very true! But listen, Michael, I want to run something by you. I had a visit from an old mate this week. He did a big lump in the nick, but he has been out a good while. He now lives in Spain. He has a couple of nightclubs in the 'Dorm, and he has the contacts to procure any drugs required – in any quantity.'

Michael Flynn sipped his wine; he was not going to join in this conversation until he had to.

Jeffrey Palmer knew the game, but he had downed a few drinks, and he felt secure. Michael Flynn had done him the favour of a lifetime and he wanted to return the favour. He grabbed Michael's arm roughly, pulling him closer. 'Look, Michael, from what he tells me, he can undercut anyone.'

Michael pulled his arm away roughly. Leaning forward, he looked into Jeffrey's eyes, as he said sarcastically, 'Well, fuck me, Jeff. Let's ring him now, shall we?'

Jeffrey Palmer was taken aback at Michael's reaction and, as far as Michael was concerned, so he fucking should be.

'Listen, Jeffrey. We deal with people who are well under the plods' radar, who can supply very good gear, and who have always proved themselves to be very reliable. Never once have we ever had even the threat of a tug. Yet you want me to wipe out a friendship *and* a business partnership that goes back fucking donkey's years – a partnership that I have recently given to you, remember – and for what exactly? An ex-fucking-con who lives in fucking Benidorm of all places – the arsehole of the world. What the fuck are you on?'

Jeffrey Palmer knew that he had just made a major fuck-up. He had listened to his friend's spiel and, as he had been promised a much bigger margin on what he was shifting on a weekly basis, it had seemed a far more lucrative venture for all concerned. He had foolishly assumed that Michael Flynn would bite his fucking hand off. But now he understood that he had not only discussed his dealings with an outsider but, to compound his offence, he had been willing to step over the man that Michael Flynn had introduced him to, who he had offered him a partnership with. A partnership he had accepted, and he had been so grateful for the opportunity. He was earning a fucking fortune, more money than he had ever earned in his life, and he was throwing it back in Michael Flynn's face. That was not a good move. He could see the disgust on Michael's face, and felt physically ill.

'I am a bit miffed, Jeffrey. To be brutally honest, I can only assume that you have discussed our arrangements with your fucking "friend" from Benidorm, and told him all our business – times, dates and, more importantly, weights. That's all private business, as far as I am concerned. I thought you understood the importance of loyalty and secrecy. I can't see any reason to discuss our business with anyone outside of our little circle. But from what you just said, you have obviously told your mate, Mr *fucking* Benidorm, everything about us, from delivery to distribution. Otherwise, how would he have known he could undercut us?'

Michael was absolutely fuming. Of all the people on his payroll, Jeffrey Palmer was the last person he would have believed capable of something like this. He sat back in his chair, concealing his fury, and smiled amiably at the men around him. The waitresses here were stunning-looking girls, and they were waiting for the dessert orders. The girls who waited on them knew they were guaranteed a big tip. The bigger the tits, the bigger the tips – it was another reason why they got such wonderful service.

'I think some cheeses for me, and a nice glass of vintage port. I'm not a dessert man, as you all know.' Michael was laughing and joking as if nothing untoward had occurred.

Jeffrey Palmer was devastated. He had ruined, in less than a few minutes, a reputation that had taken him years to build. He waited a moment, watching the men at the table laughing and drinking, before leaning towards Michael, seizing his opportunity for another private word.

'Look, Michael, I am so sorry. I just saw the money, I didn't think it through properly. My mate is a straight arrow, though – safe as houses. He did a sixteen. You probably know him – Charlie Carter? Out of Notting Hill?'

Michael shrugged his annoyance. 'Like I'd fucking care about all that. I couldn't care if he was Saint John the fucking Baptist. He still had no right to be told my business.' Bending forward once more, he looked into Jeffrey Palmer's face, searching it as if he was looking for another weakness.

'Look, Jeffrey, I am so fucking outraged, I can't believe what you said to me. It's not just the fucking disregard for everyone you are working with – me included – it's the knowledge that you felt comfortable telling a stranger how we all work. That is almost like grassing. Telling someone else about our business practices. You are a fucking liability. Can't you see that? I brought you in, trusted you, and paired you up with a man I have worked beside for fucking years. You were *my* replacement, for fuck's sake. You seem to have overlooked not just me, and what I gave you, but also the reaction of the people you have been dealing with on my behalf.'

All around, the men were telling jokes, and Michael sat

back in his chair ready to join in. He had given Palmer enough of his time. He wasn't going to let him have another say now. As far as he was concerned he could go fuck himself.

Garry England, a young up-and-coming money launderer, was holding court. He was a really funny man – he could tell a joke like a professional comedian. Michael ignored his cheese board. He had lost his appetite. He busied himself lighting a cigar instead. He gestured to the maître d', and the man brought a bottle of Remy XO to the table, returning to place a brandy snifter in front of each of the men. The maître d' knew that the brandy that this lot would drink would cost more than the food. With the good wines and the aperitifs, this would be a serious bill. Michael Flynn was a valued customer in more ways than one. It gave them status to have Michael Flynn dine there on a regular basis. He was a good tipper, always made sure that everyone who waited on him got a decent wedge at the end of the night. He also made sure that none of his guests ever caused any disturbances, no matter how much they might have drunk.

Michael opened the bottle of brandy, and poured himself a large measure. Then he passed the bottle on to Declan. Michael sipped the liquid, savouring the taste. He did like a nice brandy. Patrick Costello had educated him, explaining the finer points of a good brandy and a good wine. Patrick Costello had told him, in confidence of course, how he had paid a mad French bloke – a sommelier from one of London's leading hotels – to teach him about wines, and how to appreciate them. Patrick had admitted to him that he had been amazed at the man's knowledge, and at how much he had learnt from him. And Patrick, in turn, had enjoyed passing his knowledge on. Michael would always thank him for that.

Garry England was telling everyone at the table a funny story about when he was a kid and he had gone with his mum on a visit to Parkhurst to see his dad. Declan was already giggling like a teenager; he had heard the story before. Michael couldn't concentrate though, he was still reeling from the shock that Palmer had actually attempted to replace the man he had introduced him to, a man he had worked with for years, who he trusted implicitly.

Jeffrey Palmer had been his choice. He had recruited him personally to be his replacement. He had trusted him to take over. That was the real bugbear – he had trusted a man who had not understood the enormity of what had been offered him, who had not had the intelligence to understand exactly what he was dealing with. It was a real melon scratcher, as his mum would say.

Chapter Fifty-Six

A very pretty girl carried their coffees into the spacious office that Michael used when he was in Canary Wharf. This was where the legitimate businesses were located, and where some of the more exotic business was also conducted. They were luxurious, and they were private. There was a whole workforce here who actually worked for their living.

Declan Costello was tired out and he sipped his coffee carefully.

Michael Flynn watched the big, overweight man opposite him with affection. Declan looked like a social worker, his suit was a tad too small, and his shirt was cheap. His whole look was unkempt and slightly soiled. But Michael trusted him. Declan Costello was a man who looked like an affable fool, but was actually a dangerous fuck when crossed.

'I need your advice, Declan. I know I can trust you, so please tell me what you think.'

Declan sighed. He knew that Michael was in a quandary; he had surreptitiously listened in to his conversation with Jeffrey Palmer and, like Michael, he had been mortified. More so because it had been Jeffrey Palmer talking such bollocks, a man who should have known better. But it was always the chosen ones who overstepped the mark.

'I did try and warn you, Michael. Patrick always said, the more you give people, the more they want. He was on the money. Why do you think he recruited you? As young as you were, he trusted you from the off, but you also had the added advantage that Patrick actually liked you. He saw your potential, and he was right. I know he made you prove yourself to him, prove that you were capable of what he asked of you – that was his way of sounding people out. But, on reflection, he brought you in out of nowhere, didn't he? He didn't bring up someone from the ranks, someone he knew, he had already worked with. He brought you straight in over all their heads.'

Michael digested the man's words; there was a logic there that couldn't be denied.

'You need to think long and hard about the people you put in place, Michael, and eventually you need to find yourself a number two. I've said this to you before. It's a big fucking responsibility for one person.'

Michael listened carefully. He respected Declan's opinion. He had a lot more going for him than anyone realised. Patrick used to joke that Declan was like a tree who didn't quite manage to reach the top branches, but he was a lot shrewder than people gave him credit for.

'I am aware of all that, Declan, but I'm asking what do you think about Jeffrey Palmer? I can't believe he opened up to Charlie Carter! The man's a fucking card-carrying, paid-up moron, who now knows *who* we deal with, *how* and *when* we deal with them, and *what* we earn from them. That is a dangerous fucking combination. What was that cunt thinking? I would have laid money on him having the nous to keep his fucking business to himself.'

Declan laughed. 'He was thinking about *money*, Michael. What else? You might guarantee him a good fucking wedge, but I bet Carter can offer him a better one. They are mates as well, and that is the danger, see? Jeffrey can't see that he is dealing with people you chose, who you know are safe, who have proved their worth over and over again. Jeffrey Palmer doesn't know anything about them, he's never even heard of them. He can only see his mate, and the benefits of working with someone he knows well. He has been told he can earn a lot more money if he can persuade you to change suppliers. It's the old story, Michael. Though I have to say, Charlie Carter will swallow a tug. He is a man who knows when to shut his trap.'

Michael sighed heavily. 'I know all that, Declan. You are hardly giving me a fucking lesson in life are you? What do you think I should do about it? That is the fucking question.'

Declan smiled lazily. 'You want me to suggest you take out Palmer, Carter and anyone else who you think needs to be silenced? Well, I won't, Michael. I think you need to give Palmer a good fright, and Carter as well. After all, they aren't going to confront you, or try and usurp your position, are they? I bet they are at panic stations already. But, remember this, if you stay your hand now, Jeffrey Palmer will never forget how close he came to dying. It's a learning curve for him.'

Michael laughed. 'If Patrick were here they would all be in blindfolds and smoking their last cigarettes.'

Declan shook his head. 'You're wrong. Patrick would have used this against them, and guaranteed their loyalty for life. Unless, of course, he was on one of his fucking mental half hours, then he would have killed everyone anyway, whether they had fucked him off or not.'

They laughed together then, knowing how true that was.

'Fucking hell. He could turn on a coin, could old Patrick.'

Declan nodded his agreement. 'You're preaching to the converted here, Michael. I lived with it all my life, remember? That is why I am telling you to think about this carefully. Patrick was a hard man, and he had a lot of respect, but he made a lot of unnecessary enemies over the years. He took against people on a whim, for no real reason, and that caused us untold aggravation at times, believe me. Ultimately, *you* had to take him out for the greater good.'

Michael closed his eyes; he hated to be reminded of his part in Patrick's death. Declan was right in what he was saying but, even though Michael knew all that, and agreed with everything the man had said, he still felt, deep down, that Jeffrey Palmer had crossed a line, gone too far. But he kept his own counsel; he had asked for Declan Costello's opinion, and the man had given it to him.

Chapter Fifty-Seven

Josephine was looking at herself critically in the mirrored wardrobes; she had a bump, but not a huge one. She caressed it instinctively, but the baby had not moved for two days, and now she was starting to feel panic rising inside her. Although she was eight months pregnant – the longest that she had ever carried a child – she was feeling nothing but dread. If this child had died, she knew she would never have another.

She was naked except for her dressing gown, a long flowing silk affair that had cost a small fortune, and it looked good on her. It was a pale pink colour, and with her thick blond hair and deep blue eyes she knew that it suited her complexion perfectly. Even pregnant, she still wanted to look good for Michael. She took a step closer to the mirror and pulled the dressing gown around her, tying it loosely. Her face was pale, gaunt; she could see fear reflected in her eyes.

Turning away, she walked to her bed and, picking up the clothes she had laid out earlier, she slowly started to dress herself. Her doctor had told her that if she felt she needed to see him at any time all she had to do was call. Michael had made sure of that. He had probably offered the doctor what he would call a 'sweetener', but which was, in reality, a very large amount of money – hard cash and tax free. She wasn't complaining though. She sat on the side of the bed and, bending over carefully, she slipped her maternity knickers over her feet. Michael called them her 'passion killers'. She stood up and pulled them into place.

She was putting her bra on when she felt a stabbing pain shoot through her abdomen. It was so sharp that it immediately took her breath away. She waited for it to pass, then she slipped her dressing gown on again. Sitting back on the bed, she waited nervously to see what, if anything, was going to happen to her next. She was not going to ring Michael or her mum or anybody until she knew what was going on. She would finish getting dressed, ring the doctor, and then she would drive herself to the hospital. She was determined not to panic; she was going to keep herself as calm as possible. Her doctor had told her that this was a normal pregnancy, and she was to treat it as such. There had been no bleeding or cramps, no feelings of illness or nausea. She had not felt her usual fragility, as if the child inside her womb was already too weak to go full term. There had been nothing untoward this time, and she needed to remember that. But until she held a baby of her own in her arms, she would not take anything for granted. She had suffered that kind of disappointment too many times before.

Chapter Fifty-Eight

'I hope she manages it this time, though why it was such a big secret I don't know. Let's face it, Michael, you could have told me! Anyone would think I was a stranger on the street instead of your own mother the way you treat me these days. I suppose the house is piled up with baby powder and nappies again. If she had a squad of ten, she couldn't use half the stuff she buys. It's ridiculous.'

Michael had heard enough. With Hannah, it was a constant barrage of complaints – then she wondered why they didn't want her around. Her snide remarks about grandchildren broke Josephine's heart. She made him feel guilty because he didn't seek her out every day, even though it was her own fault. She was so fucking bitter and twisted. As if he didn't have enough to deal with in his life without listening to her going on.

'Oh, for fuck's sake, Mum! Will you give it a rest!'

Hannah shut up. Her son's voice was full of anger and irritation. She pursed her lips together tightly, so she wouldn't react. Her son was worried about his wife, and that was natural. But he should still remember who had reared him, fed him, clothed him all his life.

Michael felt the urge to throttle his mother. She could make a saint swear. She was sitting there now, acting like butter wouldn't melt, while his poor Josephine was being examined by the doctor.

He made his way back to his wife, wondering why on earth he had bothered to go and update his mother on Josephine's progress. It was a complete waste of time.

He walked into Josephine's hospital room, a bright smile nailed to his face. He couldn't let her see how worried he was. If it went wrong this time, she would never get over it – he knew that much.

Lana was holding her daughter's hand, and he was pleased to see that Josephine was laughing at something her mother had said to her.

'Hello, Michael. The doctor said that everything is going fine! We heard the heartbeat, didn't we, Mum?'

Lana grinned. 'We did. Strong as an ox by the sounds of it.'

Michael sat on the bed. 'How long do they think?'

Josephine shook her head, and shrugged nonchalantly. 'Don't know. Still waiting for my waters to break. Could be here for ages!'

She would happily stay there for days if necessary and he knew that. All she wanted was for everything to be all right.

'Is your mum OK?'

Michael rolled his eyes. 'Same as always, Lana – about as much fun as a broken back.'

Lana laughed at him. 'No change there then!'

Josephine was watching her husband sadly. She knew how much he loved his mum, but she was not the easiest person to be around. Josephine was well aware that Hannah had never liked her much, but it had not mattered at first. If she had given her a few grandchildren, it would have made a big difference to their relationship. 'She doesn't mean it, Michael.'

Michael waved his hand impatiently. 'Sod her, Josephine.'

The midwife came in, and Michael automatically stepped away from his wife. He watched as she smiled and nodded, as always eager to please, to do the right thing. He prayed once more that this time God would bless them with a living child. He wanted a baby, of course, but if it wasn't meant to be, then, for him, that was that. He couldn't watch her go through this again. This time it seemed to be going normally but, with their track record, he wasn't going to let himself get excited about it.

The midwife was a heavyset West Indian woman, with a loud voice, and an infectious laugh. Josephine loved her, and he watched as the woman examined his wife, while chatting and joking with her, putting her at her ease. He was glad that he had paid to go private, it was worth every penny. Only the best for his Josephine. He loved her more than life itself.

'Did you hear that, Michael? My waters have broken! It's all go now.'

Carmen Presley was pleased with her charge's progress; the girl had been so unlucky in the past, and no one was taking any chances. But everything seemed to be going as planned.

Michael smiled happily, but he was relieved when Lana said pointedly, 'Get us a cup of tea, Michael, will you, darling?'

As much as Lana disliked her son-in-law, she felt sorry for him. She could see that he was terrified, and she knew that it was fear for her daughter. Whatever he was, she believed he loved Josephine.

As he left the room, she clasped her daughter's hand, and said another Hail Mary. Like Michael, she wanted this baby for her daughter more than she had ever wanted anything in her life.

Chapter Fifty-Nine

Declan Costello was in the top bar of their newest nightclub, The Gatsby. He was holding court, and enjoying every second of it. His latest amour, Sinead, a petite blonde with huge breasts and delusions of grandeur, was by his side. She was pretty enough, green-eyed with high cheekbones and full lips but, unfortunately for her, she had about as much personality as a tadpole. It had only been a week and already Declan was getting bored with her. The only women who lasted for a while with him had one thing in common other than being good-looking – a sense of humour.

Declan looked around him. Everyone, from Jeffrey Palmer to Jermaine O'Shay, had turned out to wet the baby's head. Even the Notting Hill lads had come over to the East End – an almost unheard-of situation. But Michael Flynn was popular and everyone wanted to congratulate him on the birth of his first child. Christ Himself knew they had waited long enough for it.

Jermaine was drinking whisky and, as usual, he had women lining up to talk to him. Tonight, though, he wasn't interested in the strange around him; he just wanted to share Michael's night with him.

The club was packed out, and the music was loud and pumping, the beat resonating through the floor.

Michael Flynn finally arrived just after midnight and, as he walked up the stairs to the top bar, Whitney Houston's 'I Wanna Dance With Somebody' came on. Laughing excitedly, Michael made his entrance by dancing erratically, and singing the lyrics at the top of his voice.

'Fucking hell, Michael! You pissed already?'

Michael was so happy, it was almost painful to watch him. After all these years, poor Josephine had finally managed to produce a child for them.

'Drunk? Am I fuck, you cheeky bastard! I'm happy. Get me a large Irish, mate.'

Everyone was clamouring to congratulate him; he was shaking hands and hugging people all around, his happiness infectious.

'So, come on then, what did she have?'

Michael looked at Declan in disbelief. 'Didn't you tell them?'

'No, I kept schtum. That's for you to know, and for that lot to find out! It's your news, mate. Not mine.'

Michael felt almost tearful at Declan's generosity of spirit. He understood how big this moment was for him and, even though he would not have minded Declan telling the people around them his news, he appreciated that Declan had left it to him.

'Come on then, Michael, what you got? It can only be one or the other!'

Michael was laughing once more. Then, standing up straight and clearing his throat theatrically, he announced,

'Jessica Mary Flynn was born today on the tenth of September nineteen eighty-nine weighing in at six pounds, five ounces. She is her mother's double, and she's fucking gorgeous.'

The cheer that went up from everyone was so loud it drowned out the music. Declan pushed a glass of whisky into Michael's hand, and he downed it in one go. Then, giving Declan his empty glass, he shouted, 'More!'

Michael had already noticed that Jeffrey Palmer was there with some of his crew, looking very sheepish. He had clocked Jermaine O'Shay too. Michael smiled at the people there; it was a great crowd, and he knew that they were there for him, to celebrate his good news with him. Almost every Face in London was in this bar tonight and, as he looked around him – at young Garry, as always telling jokes and making people laugh, and at Orville Cardoza, a Rastafarian of advanced years who was capable of extreme violence at the least provocation – he suddenly felt at peace with himself, and with his life. His little daughter was a miracle. She had arrived with the minimum of fuss, and he had never seen Josephine more beautiful – the look of triumph on her face had said it all. She had finally achieved the one thing she craved more than anything else in her life. As she had cradled her daughter in her arms, he had closed his eyes tightly and thanked God for finally answering their prayers.

He had another large whisky put into his hand and, once again, he swallowed it down quickly. 'Keep them coming, boys. Tonight I am going to get fucking plastered.'

The men around him were cheering him loudly. Arnold Jameson, a young Jamaican guy with a bald head and a taste for outlandish shirts, hugged him tightly. 'I remember getting my first baby. Your own flesh and blood. It's a real trip, ain't it, maw?'

Michael hugged him back. Until now he had not thought of it like that. His little girl, his brand spanking new little baby, was his flesh and blood.

Chapter Sixty

Josephine lay in the hospital bed, tired and sore, but also elated. She watched her little daughter as she slept in the Perspex crib beside her bed, fascinated by each breath and each snuffle. She was still worried that this was all a dream, and she would wake up in her own bed, covered in sweat and silently crying into her pillow.

She looked down at her body; already her belly had gone down – she didn't look like she had just given birth. She had laughed about it with the midwife, and another new mum who had popped her head around the door asking if it was OK to come in and say hello. She had really loved that. Talking babies with another mum was something she had never thought she would ever do. It was so natural, and they had chatted together for ages. Then she had fed her little Jessica – already she was Jessie, Michael had seen to that. Her mother had never allowed her name to be shortened – she was Josephine, never Jo. Yet she had already accepted Jessie for her daughter; it suited her somehow, she looked like a Jessie.

Even Hannah had not been able to ruin this day for her. Unlike her mother and father who had held the baby, cooed to her, and shared in her first few hours in the world, Hannah had refused the offer to hold her grandchild, and she had left without even saying goodbye. Michael had not even noticed his mother's absence; he was as besotted with Jessie as she was. He just gazed at his new daughter with complete and absolute awe. She was a lovely child already; she had been born pink and creamy, not even any blood or vernix on her. She could see herself in her daughter's features. Her mum had said Josephine had been *her* double, the image of her as a baby, and she was going to bring in the pictures to prove it. Michael was so dark, Josephine had thought the child would resemble him, dark-haired and apple-cheeked. But she wasn't – she was fair-skinned, and honey-blonde, just like her mum.

Josephine knew she should try to sleep – she was whacked out – but it was impossible. She wanted this day to last for ever. It was the best day of her whole life. She felt truly alive for the first time in years. Michael had been so good, pretending he didn't care if they had children or not, but she believed, deep inside, that he *did* care. She hugged herself with glee. She was finally a mother, she was someone's mum, and that felt so good. She looked at her little daughter, lying there so defenceless, so vulnerable, and she whispered softly, 'I promise you, my little Jessie Flynn, that I will never let you down. If you need me I will always be there for you.' She meant every word. It never occurred to her that sometimes you couldn't protect your children, no matter how much you might want to. Life just didn't work like that.

Chapter Sixty-One

Michael took a deep breath, and counted to five slowly in his head. Josephine was feeding little Jessie, and he had walked into his kitchen, barefoot, in only his boxer shorts, gasping for a cup of coffee, and stubbed his toe on a new pile of boxes that seemed to have appeared overnight. He had hopped around in agony, while cursing under his breath.

Instead of laughing as expected, Josephine had deliberately ignored his pain. He had hoped that now she had a baby to care for the bulk buying would stop. He had always thought her need to buy so much was because of her failure to have a child of her own. He had ignored it, telling himself that if it made her happy then that was enough. But now it was starting to annoy him. In the last six months, she had got worse not better. He glanced quickly at the boxes as he sipped his coffee. More fucking food – like they didn't have enough already! Twenty-four tins to the case, and there were five cases. Two were full of baked beans, one was spaghetti, and the other two were chilli con carne of all things. She cooked wonderful food for them – they rarely opened a tin of anything. It was getting beyond a joke.

He sat down, and smiled at his wife and daughter. Little

Jessie pushed her bottle away, and gave him a huge gummy smile. She was absolutely gorgeous, there was no doubting that. Her eyes were a deep blue and framed by long, dark eyelashes. Everyone commented on her eyes – even complete strangers, they were that remarkable. She seemed to look into your soul, she peered so intently. Even his mother had eventually succumbed to her charms.

'Morning, my darling.'

She started to crow at him, grinning and grabbing her own feet, and he laughed as Josephine tried to get her to finish her bottle. He kissed his wife on the forehead gently. 'Morning, my other darling.'

Josephine smiled at him, but she could sense his frustration, and she hated it. She knew that, on one level, he had a point about her buying, but it wasn't as if they couldn't afford it. Possessing the things that she purchased made her feel secure somehow. It had started so long ago, it was normal for her now. And if things were on special offer, she just saw it as a way of saving money.

'She is looking happy enough.'

Josephine grinned. 'She's already had her breakfast. She loves her food, Michael.'

He felt his heart constrict with his love for her. If only she would admit that her compulsive buying was getting out of hand. The house they lived in was huge by anyone's standards, but she was gradually filling it up with more and more boxes of food, talcum powder, even bloody dried milk. She bought stuff they would never even use, like the tins of chilli con carne, and the boxes of dried fruits. It was completely without logic. If they lived to be a hundred, they could never use it all. In the spare bedroom, she had piled up box after box of cereals, every kind. Big packs that were all out of date, along with tins of tuna and tins of pilchards.

'She'll need a big appetite won't she, Josephine? There is more cereal in this house than in fucking Tesco.'

He saw the hurt on his wife's face and immediately felt bad, as though he was in the wrong. Her eyes were filling up with tears, and he sighed. 'I don't want to hurt you, Josephine, but surely you can see that this is getting out of hand? Look around you, darling. This place is like a fucking warehouse. We don't even eat any of it. I tried to use a tin of beans the other week and you nearly bit my head off.'

Josephine rolled her eyes in exasperation. 'There were tins in the cupboard. You didn't need to open the case up. I explained that to you.'

He picked up his daughter, pulling her from his wife's lap. 'Listen to what you're saying, Josephine. Who gives a flying fuck where a tin of beans comes from, I ask you? And, as we have more beans in this house than a fucking army canteen, I would have thought you'd have welcomed someone actually *eating* the fuckers. They aren't ornaments, are they?'

Josephine was nearly in tears now. He forced himself to lower his voice, calm down. 'I've got a couple of lads coming round today. They are going to move all the boxes into the garages, OK? I want this place clear when I get home tonight. It's not a fucking depot, all right? It's our home.'

She didn't answer him, just looked at him with those huge pained eyes.

'I'm sorry, darling, but it's arranged now.' He stood up, playing with his little daughter, determined not to look at his wife and cave in as per usual. This time the house was being cleared, he was going to make sure of that. One of the rooms off the kitchen was a spacious old-fashioned larder. There were over sixty jars of jam on the shelves, forty jars of honey and, more worryingly, he had counted thirty-two tin openers in one of the drawers. Everywhere he looked, there was evidence of her hoarding, and it scared him more than he liked to admit. It wasn't normal. He had seen her wiping the tins over with a damp cloth, and placing them back into the boxes they had arrived in. Who the fuck did things like that? He had to put his foot down. They had a child to look out for now. She needed to start getting with the program. He had hoped that her finally having a baby would have sorted out her eccentricities, but instead it seemed to have exacerbated them. He loved her more than life itself, but he knew that things were not right.

'She's getting to be a right lump, isn't she?'

Josephine nodded. 'She is. Like I said, she loves her grub.'

'Well, she won't fucking starve in this house, will she?' He laughed as he spoke, trying to lighten the mood, but Josephine didn't react in any way at all.

Chapter Sixty-Two

Declan was extremely irritated – almost fuming, in fact – and that was a very unusual occurrence for him. He was a man who rarely let anything throw him off kilter. He saw that as a weakness, a character flaw – not that he had ever said that out loud. His brother and Michael were his polar opposite in that respect. Chasing the dollar was why people like them got up in the morning.

Well, he liked the world he had created for himself. He ran a good business, and he ran it very well. Declan believed wholeheartedly that he had more than enough for his needs. He earned a good wedge, he had shagged more women than he could shake a tenner at, and he genuinely liked his life. He didn't want marriage or children really. He was happy enough playing the eternal bachelor. What he didn't like was discord, especially among the ranks. He was very easy-going, but the people who worked for him knew that, if they pushed their luck, he was capable of great vengeance if the need should arise.

But now Michael Flynn needed a serious fucking talking-to and he was going to give it to him, please or offend. This should never have been allowed to go so far, and Michael knew that better than anyone. It took a lot to make Declan angry but, when he finally succumbed to anger, he could be a very dangerous individual. Michael would do well to remember that.

He glanced at his watch. Michael was already over an hour late, and that added to his irritation. Tardiness was the greatest insult of them all; arrangements were made to suit those concerned – it was the height of rudeness to overlook other people's needs.

He heard Michael arrive; he hailed people as always with his usual bonhomie and smiling face, but Declan knew Michael Flynn was not the amiable, hail-fellow-well-met cunt that he pretended to be. He was a vicious fucker, who could pass in company as a well-heeled, well-dressed businessman. And that was fine, so long as he remembered that, while he had been playing happy families for the last six months, he had inadvertently dropped the proverbial ball. He had a fucking seriously damaging break in his ranks, and it needed to be addressed sooner rather than later.

Josephine's problems were common knowledge and as much as everyone felt for him – after all, no one wanted a fucking nutbag on the team – Michael needed to remember the golden rule: family life came second to everything else.

As Michael made his entrance into the office, it took all of Declan Costello's willpower to stop himself from smacking him one. If ever a man needed to be brought down a peg, Michael Flynn was that man.

Chapter Sixty-Three

Hannah was holding her granddaughter on her lap, amazed at the love she felt for the child. The only other person to ever make her feel such overpowering love had been her son, and where had that got her? But little Jessie had crept into her heart, and now the thought of being parted from her was a real torment. She had even tempered her usual sarcastic remarks, frightened that if she pushed too far the child would be taken beyond her reach.

She could see herself in her, although no one else would admit that. She had her eyes, and her own mother's cupid bow lips. It was unbelievable really, the child's hold on her. Hannah adored her, and that was something she had never envisaged.

Hannah watched surreptitiously as Josephine oversaw the removal of her boxes of crap from the house. Not before time either, as far as she was concerned; it was like an obstacle course to get in, and Michael should have put his foot down years ago. She could see the panic in her daughter-in-law's eyes as the house was gradually emptied of her purchases. Despite herself, she actually felt sorry for the girl. Anyone would think she was being asked to give her family away. For the first time, Hannah realised that her daughter-in-law had a real problem.

'Come and sit down, Josephine. I've hardly spoken to you since I got here!'

Josephine looked at her in distress. 'I'll be with you in a minute, Hannah. I just need to make sure that everything is put away properly, where I can find it . . .'

Hannah stood up with the child in her arms, and walked to where her daughter-in-law was standing. She was at the back door and, as she went to follow the young men out to the garage, Hannah grabbed her by the arm.

'Leave it be. I don't want to upset you, but you're acting strange, love. These young men Michael sent here to move everything out of the house can see how strange you're acting. People talk, love, you know that as well as I do. Don't give them the opportunity for a story. If not for yourself, then for Michael. He can't be seen as having any kind of weakness. Now, come and sit down, and I'll make a fresh pot of tea.'

Josephine knew that the woman was right; she wasn't acting rationally. She shouldn't care about what was happening. But it wasn't that easy. She couldn't help the way she felt. Watching everything leave the house was like witnessing the death of a loved one. She felt bereft and vulnerable.

Hannah pulled her gently away from the door. 'Sit down and nurse your baby. I can see how hard this is for you, Josephine, but you have to let it go.' She passed the child to her daughter-in-law, and watched as her natural maternal instincts took over.

Josephine sat down at the kitchen table and Hannah

breathed a sigh of relief. Little Jessie was so good-natured, and she thanked God for that much at least. She wasn't a cross child and rarely cried.

'She is so contented, Josephine. I've never seen such a contented child in all my born days. That is all down to you, and your wonderful mothering.'

It was the right thing to say. Josephine smiled with pleasure at her words, and Hannah Flynn finally understood the reason her son loved this girl so much. She literally didn't have a bad bone in her body. She felt a moment's shame at the way she had treated her over the years. She had never given the girl a chance. She had always resented the way she had replaced her in her son's affections. It was only Jessie's birth that had softened her up. Now she saw the girl as she really was – a frightened young woman, who needed her kindness and understanding. She was a troubled soul, all right, and she needed help. Her Michael knew that and if Hannah had not been so selfish, so bitter, he would have turned to her for help. Instead he had protected the girl from her, knowing she didn't have a great opinion of her anyway. For the first time ever, Hannah felt truly guilty.

Chapter Sixty-Four

Michael held his hands out in a gesture of supplication. He knew that his late arrival would not be overlooked by Declan – tardiness was his pet hate.

'I'm sorry, Declan, but I had to sort some stuff out at home.'

Michael looked immaculate as always; the man had clearly spent a long time on his appearance. It was Michael Flynn's only vanity, he never looked anything other than perfect. Declan knew that his haphazard approach to life was the antithesis of Michael's. Declan was getting larger by the month and he had never been what anyone would call a looker. Unlike Michael Flynn, however, he didn't care about that. Michael, though, looked every inch the part of the well-heeled Face, from the expensive gold watch to his perfect haircut.

'You know why I called this meeting, so let's not fuck about, eh?'

Michael laughed at his friend's attitude; only Declan would dare to talk to him like that – only Declan could get away with it. He shook his head slowly in mock disbelief. 'OK, hold your fucking horses! It's sorted, all right?' He was being deliberately contrite, apologising without saying a word.

'I'm gonna need a bit more than that, Michael, and you fucking know it.'

The smile was gone now, and Declan was reminded of just how hazardous confronting someone like Michael Flynn could be. Like Patrick, his late brother, the man was capable of literally anything if crossed. He would do well to remember that, even if he had the man's respect and his affection.

'I know what you're saying, Declan. Believe me, I've tried to build bridges. I've given them every opportunity to sort the situation out between them. Jeffrey Palmer was willing to swallow his knob. He knew he had dropped a humungous fucking bollock from the off. But Jermaine O'Shay has been a real pain. He just won't let it go – not even for me.'

Declan sat down suddenly, and looked out of the large picture window that had a really magnificent view over the river. It was a cold day, overcast, a typical March morning. The threat of spring was in the air, and London looked like shit. He sighed. He could already see exactly where this was going. If Michael Flynn requested a personal favour, he expected the person to agree immediately.

'So what are you saying, Michael?'

Michael dragged a chair over to where Declan was sitting, and settled in beside him. Then, after a few moments, he said quietly, 'I've thought about this long and hard. I even asked Jermaine, as a friend, to overlook Jeffrey's faux pas, put it behind him. They are both good men. But he won't.'

Declan looked at Michael, saw the suppressed anger in his face, and the way that Michael was trying to hide it. But

Declan knew him too well. 'So what are you going to do about it?'

Michael grinned amiably, all white teeth and stunning good looks. 'What else can I do, Declan? I have been left with no fucking choice. They have to go.'

It was as Declan had expected. He couldn't change anything even if he wanted to. 'I see. Both men are well connected. It will be noticed.'

Michael smiled easily once again. 'I should hope so too! This is a fucking warning, mate. It's my way, or no way.'

Declan watched quietly as Michael picked imaginary dirt from his trousers using his manicured nails, pretending everything was normal.

'When are you going to do it?'

Michael looked over the river; he loved this view, he loved these offices. They spelt success to him. His legitimate businesses were booming, and that was important. He knew that if you earned enough legit money, it made it so much harder for anyone to find a reason to investigate your finances. He paid a lot of money out to keep his life on track – not just to accountants and secretarial staff, but also to the police, and the people the police dealt with. But it was worth every penny spent. He had more Filth and CPS on his bankroll than the Metropolitan Police. He paid off people all over the country. It made good business sense.

He looked at Declan, knew that the man was not sure about the latest developments. That wasn't unexpected, but he knew Declan would go along with him as always. '*We* are going to do it tonight, mate. I've arranged a sit-down at the scrapyard.'

Declan nodded his agreement, as Michael knew he would.

'I think I've been good, actually. Normally, I would have taken them out much earlier. But now I've had enough.'

Chapter Sixty-Five

Jermaine O'Shay was wary. He didn't trust Michael Flynn as far as he could throw him. As far as Jermaine was concerned, Palmer should have been removed from the equation the minute he fucked up. But Michael Flynn had been determined to find a way to sort everything out. He had understood Jermaine's problem – had agreed with him, sympathised – but he had still wanted him to let it go. He had even asked him to swallow as a personal favour to him.

As if that was ever going to happen. Jeffrey Palmer wasn't a cunt, but by the same token, he had tried to treat Jermaine like one. Palmer had a good rep, was well liked, but then so was he. This was about respect, and Michael Flynn needed to understand that. His assurance that he had sorted everything out just wasn't good enough. It had gone pear-shaped from day one. Palmer had tried to tuck him up and there was no way Jermaine O'Shay was going to back down. He was going mob-handed to this meet and, if it all went off, he would be prepared.

Chapter Sixty-Six

Jeffrey Palmer sipped his whisky, and felt himself relax. This had not been anything like he had expected. Declan and Michael were both friendly and chatty, making sure he was comfortable, asking if he needed anything else.

The scrapyard was legendary, and this was the first time he had been there. Everyone knew that this was where Michael and Patrick had conducted their real business. It was also a big earner in its own right; he had been told that over a million pounds' worth of scrap went through the place every year.

'I hope we can sort everything tonight, Jeff. I don't like discord within my workforce. It causes unnecessary aggro for everyone.'

Jeffrey sipped his drink, savouring the taste of the whisky. 'You know I don't want it either, mate. I dropped a fucking big bollock, and if I could fucking take it back I would. I just got a bit overenthusiastic, that's all. I was blinded by the earn.'

Michael laughed at the man's honesty. 'Well, you will know for the future.'

The headlights from a car played over the ceiling, and

Michael got up from his chair behind the dilapidated desk, and walked to the door. Opening it wide, he said gaily, 'Get yourself in, mate. It's fucking freezing.'

Jermaine got out of his car, and Michael saw he had two men with him. They were both close to Jermaine O'Shay, had worked for him for years. Michael Flynn ushered them into the Portakabin, before closing the door. Then, rubbing his hands together noisily, he said jovially, 'It's fucking taters out there tonight, all right. Colder than a witch's tit.'

The Portakabin was warm and inviting. Motioning to Jermaine with his hands, Michael watched as he sat down in the only other available chair. His two minders stood awkwardly by the doorway. The Portakabin was already filled to capacity; none of the men there were exactly small.

'I thought I said to come alone, Jermaine?' Michael's voice was cold now. His face without his usual smile, without any emotion whatsoever, looked very different, like a mask.

Jermaine O'Shay was not going to be intimidated. He had two of his best men with him and he was here to fight his corner, and remind Michael of who he worked with, and why he was so well thought of. He was partner to some of the hardest men who walked the earth. This was not a fucking friendly sit-down, as far as he was concerned. This was him, making a point, once and for all. This had gone on too long now, and he was bored with it.

'Well, as you can see, Michael, I didn't. I haven't come here to negotiate.'

Alarm bells rang for Jeffrey Palmer – there was going to

be trouble. He swallowed the last of his whisky quickly. He could see that Declan Costello was as nervous as he was. This was not going to end well, he knew that much.

Michael laughed gently. 'Do you know what, Jermaine? I fucking knew you would come mob-handed. I said that to you, didn't I, Declan?'

Declan nodded his agreement. 'You did at that, Michael. That's why we made provision for just such a situation.'

Jermaine O'Shay frowned. This was not what he was expecting at all.

Declan got up and opened the door that led to the other office.

Michael Flynn called out happily, 'Come in, guys, your moment in the spotlight has arrived at last.'

When Jermaine O'Shay saw the Barker brothers enter, he felt his heart sink like a stone in his chest. There were four Barker brothers, they were each born within a five-year period, and looked like clones. They were all over six foot, heavily built, with a natural penchant for extreme violence. Born from a Jamaican father, and a second-generation Dutch mother, they were handsome fucks, with coffee-coloured skin and dark blue eyes. They were Michael Flynn's private army, and he paid them well. He had their loyalty but, more importantly, he had their friendship. They only worked for the people they *wanted* to; they were known throughout England as men of courage, men of good character who couldn't be owned. They had always stood alone, and that was why they were so sought after. Now they were standing there with machetes in their hands, and smiles on their faces, eager to get down to business.

'I think this is what is called in France, a *fait accompli.* Basically, mate, you're fucked.'

Jermaine looked at his men then, still expecting them to back him up. But they were both standing by the doorway, staring straight ahead.

Michael shrugged nonchalantly. 'I asked you to swallow, Jermaine, but you refused. Months of aggro you've given me.'

Jermaine O'Shay was still not going to be intimidated. 'You know I deserve better than this, Michael. Remember who I work for.'

Michael laughed again. 'Oh, don't worry about me, Jermaine. I don't shit without planning it out first.' He put his hand on Jeffrey Palmer's shoulder and squeezed it. 'I never wanted this, remember that.'

He went to his desk and opened up one of the drawers, taking out a small axe. 'But I always do my own dirty work.'

He split open Jeffrey Palmer's skull with one massive blow. 'I think that is what the Jamaican Yardies call a permanent parting.'

No one moved, or batted an eyelid.

Jermaine O'Shay felt the spray of blood hit his face. It was outrageous. He watched in disbelief as Michael chopped the man's head off. Declan was looking at Jermaine with resignation and sorrow. He had tried to warn him, but he wouldn't listen.

Michael Flynn was drenched in blood now, it was like a scene from a cheap horror film. Jermaine tried to stand up, tried to defend himself, but his own men forced him back on to the chair, and held him in place.

Michael laughed once more. 'I hope you realise, Jermaine,

that this is nothing personal. I liked you. I liked Jeffrey. But I will not be crossed. I will not be treated like a cunt by anyone. I gave you every chance I could. But you insisted on throwing it all back into my face. So fuck you.'

He took his time with Jermaine O'Shay, knowing that this night would be whispered about and remembered by all present. It was about credibility, about teaching people a lesson. It was about making sure the people you employed never forgot who they were dealing with. It was about making a point for the future. Even the Barker boys were impressed, Declan could see that. Like them, Michael Flynn actually enjoyed this.

Chapter Sixty-Seven

Josephine heard Michael come in and glanced at the alarm clock on her bedside table. It was four a.m. She had just fed the baby, and was settling herself into bed again. She waited a few minutes, expecting him to sneak into the bedroom as he usually did. But he didn't come.

Then she heard the shower turn on in the main bathroom. He always used the shower in their en suite, and she wondered why he would suddenly need a shower in the middle of the night.

She got out of the bed, and walked silently out of the bedroom, and across to the bathroom. She slipped through the bathroom door, shutting it quietly behind her. It was a large room, with black marble tiles from floor to ceiling, and an antique bath that had cost a fortune. The walk-in shower was big enough for five people. She saw his clothes on the floor. They were soaked in blood. She instinctively reached for them and saw Michael watching her from the shower as she bundled them up quickly.

'Bring the towels down when you're finished, Michael.'

His eyes followed her as she left the room, before he turned back to finish his shower.

When he came downstairs she was burning everything in the large fireplace in his office. He passed her the towels he had used, and she threw them on to the blaze without a word. She didn't want this mess in her home.

'Is that everything?'

He nodded.

'You're safe, then?'

He pulled her into his arms, and held her tightly. ''Course I am, you silly mare.' He kissed her hair. She was trembling.

'We've got a baby now, remember.'

Michael smiled as he pulled away from her gently, and looked deep into her eyes. 'How could I ever forget? It's all for you and her now.'

She smiled back brokenly. 'I know that, Michael. I know.'

Book Three

He who brings trouble to his family will inherit only wind, and the fool will be servant to the wise

Proverbs 11:29

Chapter Sixty-Eight

2004

'That is one lairy little mare, Josephine. Don't you let her get away with it.'

Lana was furious, and Jessie Flynn knew her nana had a right to feel like that. She was heart-sorry for what she had said to her, but she had been goaded.

Josephine didn't answer. Instead she kissed her daughter on the cheek, and walked her to the front door. 'Declan is dropping you off at the disco, and your dad or I will pick you up, OK?'

Jessie sighed theatrically, still ashamed about swearing at her nana, but at least her mum understood why she had done it. 'I know, Mum. Why change the habits of a lifetime?'

'Well, we worry about you, darling, that's all.'

It was said easily, but the underlying warning was there. Jessie was well aware that her father would never let her out of the house if it wasn't for her mother.

'I'm sorry for shouting at Nana.'

Josephine smiled sadly. 'I know that, lovely. She means well, try and remember that. She was the same with me.'

'I know. But I hate having to fight for my freedom, Mum.'

Josephine laughed delightedly at her daughter's dejected

countenance. She was a real drama queen, a natural actress.

'Look, darling, if it was left to your father you'd never leave the fucking house. I've told you before, the best way to manage him is to let him think he is in control.'

Jessie rolled her big blue eyes with annoyance. 'I'm nearly fifteen, Mum, I'm not a child any more.'

Josephine pushed her away gently. 'Well, the jury's still out on that one, mate. Have a good night.'

She watched her daughter as she climbed into her uncle Declan's Mercedes. As she waved her off she felt a stab of fear. Jessie looked eighteen even without any make-up on – she was her daughter all right. Done up she looked like a grown woman. But she wasn't, that was the trouble. She was twenty-five in her body, but still a child in her mind. Older men looked at her with interest, and why wouldn't they? She didn't look like a schoolgirl; she had ripened far too early, bless her heart. It was a godsend that she was Michael Flynn's daughter, that alone gave her the protection most girls of her age didn't have. She was a beautiful girl, and that wasn't a mother talking. Her Jessie was a true stunner, in every way that counted for this generation.

She went back into the kitchen, prepared for the fact that her mother was going to give her an earful about why Jessie should never be allowed out without a chaperone. Her mum worried about Jessie looking so much older than her years, and she did too. But, by the same token, her Jessie had her head screwed on. It was strange because Jessie was much closer to Michael's mum than hers. Who would ever have thought that? Hannah seemed to understand her granddaughter in a way that Lana couldn't comprehend. If she didn't know better, she might actually think her own mother didn't like her only grandchild. Lana always seemed to be finding fault with her. It hurt Josephine because her Jessie was a good kid, but all Lana saw was the girl's appearance, and she seemed to insinuate that Jessie being well developed was a black mark against her somehow. It wasn't something that anyone could have prevented. Nature had endowed her daughter with good looks, a great figure and a bone structure to die for. She was a sensible girl, who had never given them a day's worry, and that was the most important thing as far as Josephine was concerned.

Lana was still fuming at being called an old bitch. 'Did you hear the way she spoke to me, Josephine? Who does she think she is? You need to put a stop to that fucker's gallop, I'm telling you.'

Josephine looked at her mother, saw the way she was bristling with indignation, determined to make her point about her only grandchild, and suddenly she heard herself bellowing loudly, 'Oh, Mum, will you give it a rest, for fuck's sake? She's fourteen years old! Get off her back, and give her a chance.'

'You let her get away with murder. You are making a rod for your own back, madam.'

Josephine was trying hard to keep a lid on her anger. 'Do you know what, Mum? Jessie is a fucking good kid, she does well at school, she goes to Mass without a fight, she helps out around the house. She never pushes her luck. She is my baby and, unlike you, I don't look for flaws, or weaknesses. She's still a kid, Mum, so let her be one while she has the chance.'

Lana sighed. She couldn't help it but she didn't like the child – didn't trust her. She was still waters, deeper than the ocean, that fucker. She would be proved right eventually. She *loved* her granddaughter – of course she did – but there was no liking there. Jessie Flynn was so selfish, so arrogant, so self-assured it was sickening to witness. She wouldn't be a kid for long. Already she knew too much. She had never understood the word no but, then again, she had never heard it. Everything she had ever wanted, she had been given. Michael would pluck the moon out of the sky if she asked him to. She was the only child, late arriving, and she was treated like fucking royalty. But she was also sneaky. Even as a little kid she had known she possessed the upper hand in the relationship with her parents. She was an accident waiting to happen, she would not toe the line for much longer, Lana would put money on that.

She looked at her daughter, who she loved with a vengeance and, modulating her voice, she said carefully, 'All I'm saying, Josephine, is she plays you like a fucking banjo.'

Josephine laughed. ''Course she does, Mum! It's called being a teenager. It's what they *do*. But she knows that me and Michael wouldn't put up with too much nonsense from her. She is still young enough to listen to what we say to her. Now, do you want another glass of wine or not?'

Lana nodded. Josephine poured the wine, and Lana turned her thoughts to her daughter. Josephine rarely left her house now – more often than not it was Lana who did the shopping for the family these days. Josephine was becoming more insular by the week, and young Jessie wasn't a fool – she would be bound to use that to her advantage. It was human nature. She had a lot of her father in her; she was stubborn just like him, and she was prone to serious anger when thwarted. She was her mother's double in her looks, but she had inherited none of her mother's kindly nature. Like her father, she rarely showed anybody her real self. She had inherited Michael's temper too. It had occasionally surfaced over the years and, just like Michael's, when it did finally erupt, it was a powerful force in its own right.

Chapter Sixty-Nine

Michael was exhausted, but he had no choice but to carry on. He was negotiating a deal that would bring him millions over the next few years if it came off. He had planned it down to the last detail; it had taken nearly a year to bring to fruition. Now he was almost there. He was working with a huge Colombian cartel personally, and he was only too aware how dangerous that could be. *These* people were not impressed with anyone, anywhere, and it had taken him a lot of time and effort to convince them he was a viable partner. He had his own rep as a bad man in Europe, but compared to them and the world they moved in the Europeans were fucking amateurs. These men were a law unto themselves; they would shoot their own mothers if they deemed it necessary to the cause, and were more than capable of torturing and murdering a rival's child to prove a point. They inhabited a world where a human life was valued cheaper than a can of Coke. It was a different ballgame altogether.

Now he, Michael Flynn, was fronting one of the biggest deals ever negotiated on British turf. And, once it was in place, he would be the undisputed king of Europe. No one could have a shit, shave or a shampoo without asking his permission first.

He looked out of his office window over the Thames. He loved this view; it made him feel invincible. He surveyed his domain. London was all his. He had bought, fought and forced his will on everyone who mattered, and it had paid off.

The offices had been recently revamped, and he wasn't sure he liked the results. With the white walls and bleached oak flooring, there was nothing remotely attractive about it – it looked far too impersonal for his tastes. He missed his old desk – an antique captain's desk. It had been bulky and scuffed, but it had character. Now he sat at a very expensive modern desk that was basically two planks of highly polished wood, held together by willpower and two pieces of eight by four. It had six spindly legs, which didn't exactly fill him with faith it would stay up, and it was without even one single fucking drawer to give it an iota of usefulness. Even the chair he sat on was uncomfortable – yet it had cost more than his first car. But it was all about front – he knew that better than anyone – and it impressed people he dealt with.

He was getting old, he supposed. He was turning into the very people he had loathed as a young man. Yearning for the past; now, of course, he understood why they had felt that way. He still wouldn't let anything be done over the Internet. He was classed as a dinosaur because of that, but he didn't care – he didn't trust it. They could shove cyberspace up their arses. For the right price, like most things in this life, it could be abused. He didn't trust anything that had the power to reach millions of people at a stroke. It seemed to him that computers bred laziness and apathy. People were too quick to trust in something that they couldn't build themselves, that they had to rely on other people to maintain for them, and at great cost as well. It was a recipe for disaster. He particularly worried about leaving a trail that could be discovered without the person involved even leaving their office. No, he wasn't prepared to join the cyber rats.

He worked in a world where the fewer people in the know the better. He still relied on private meetings and word of mouth. Fortunately for him, so did the Colombians. Now they had finally agreed to meet him on his own turf. It was the last step. That they had felt confident enough to come to him was a coup in itself. They needed to show him that they trusted him, and he had to prove to them that he could guarantee them the protection needed. He had done just that. They had landed safely in England, and no one had questioned them.

It was dark now, the lights were on across London. It was funny, but he always thought that London looked more impressive by night. It looked more alive to him, full of possibilities and secrets. He glanced at his watch, a diamond Rolex with a platinum face. It was just after nine p.m. They would be here in the next ten minutes or so. He glanced around him. He had everything ready. The drinks cabinet – that he personally thought looked like a fucking cheap filing cabinet – had every alcoholic beverage known to man, and the leather sofas were placed strategically so everyone could interact together without having to move about too much. There was also food in the kitchen, should anyone request it.

Salvatore Ferreira was an extremely cautious man. Michael

appreciated that trait. He rarely left his native Colombia. Michael had taken over a whole floor of one of the top London hotels to guarantee Salvatore his privacy, and also to give him the chance to enjoy the luxury such an establishment could provide.

He heard the soft thrumming noise that heralded the arrival of the private lift and, settling himself into his chair, he waited patiently to begin the meeting he had been waiting for for a year, and which would cement his legendary status in the criminal underworld once and for all.

Chapter Seventy

'Listen, Declan, I didn't want to be the one to tell you this, believe me, but what else could I do, for fuck's sake?'

Peter Barker, the eldest of the Barker brothers, looked into Declan's face with its usual blank countenance. But his colour was high, he was flushed red. Declan could tell the man was angry, and so he fucking should be. This was a piss-take, especially now when everyone knew there was something serious in the wind.

'Look, don't shoot the fucking messenger, mate – I'm trying to do the right thing here.'

Declan shook his head. This was the last fucking thing he needed tonight. The music from the nightclub was loud, even through the heavy fire doors of the offices. He hated the music they had to play in the clubs these days; it was fucking abysmal – it sounded like electrical interference to him. Declan sighed and, as calmly as he could, asked, 'Who did you say told you this, Peter?'

Peter took a large joint out of his jacket pocket and, after lighting it, he puffed on it fiercely before he answered his friend's question. 'I told you already, Declan – it was Jack Cornel. He was full of it. The stupid-looking northern ponce!

I was all for hammering him, but my brother Billy stepped in. He reckons that this is about nausing up Michael's meeting with the Colombians – though how they know about it is fucking suspect in itself. You and I know the Cornels have never been happy answering to him. Michael never gave them their due, and they fucking knew it. They are so fucking full of themselves. They still seem to think that the North is a fucking no-go area for us lot down here. The M1 passed right over their fucking heads, I tell ya.'

Declan laughed at the man's words despite himself. He could be funny, could old Peter Barker. He had a dry humour which wasn't everybody's cup of tea, but always hit the proverbial nail on the head.

'So they have come down south, determined to cause fucking havoc, have they?'

Peter nodded sagely. 'Basically, yeah. They think that if they cause problems for Michael, the Colombians will see the error of their ways. That's the real worry. Michael won't want any kind of issues, will he? That stands to reason.'

Declan let this information sink in. The Cornel brothers had been a thorn in everyone's side for a long time. They were without scruples, devoid of even the most basic of social graces, and they had taken over the North East almost by accident from the Dooleys. Jack Cornel had shot one of them over a debt and, as the older Dooley brothers were on remand, he had not yet been challenged about his foolishness. The Cornels were relatively new to the real game – up to now, they had been no more than cannon fodder. It had been assumed that they would be removed tout suite. But it had not happened. No one had ever seen the Cornels as a serious threat; now, it seemed, they were under the misapprehension that they were hard enough to take on Michael Flynn and the whole South East. What planet they were inhabiting was up for debate all right. It was ludicrous, and it could not have come at a worse time. Jack Cornel was a natural-born fighter, but his younger brother, Cecil, was a fucking looney. He was definitely two bob short of a pound note. He didn't fight as such – he just attacked with whatever weapon came to hand. Jack Cornel was a fucking exhibitionist; he would love nothing more than to cause a row with Michael in public. He was too thick to see the folly of his actions – all he would see was the glory of people knowing he had dared to do such a thing. As for Cecil, an original thought in his head would die of fucking loneliness; he would follow his brother's lead. It was a fucking abortion. Of all the times the Cornel brothers could have chosen to get themselves killed stone dead, they had to go and pick now, when Michael Flynn was negotiating the biggest deal in criminal history.

'Oh, Jesus Christ. Michael will go fucking apeshit when he finds out.'

Peter Barker grinned. 'I had worked that one out for myself, Declan.'

Declan Costello held his head in his hands; he was absolutely mortified. 'Round them up, Peter. But try and keep it on the down low.'

Peter took a deep toke on his joint before saying huskily, 'It will be a fucking pleasure, Declan, believe me. It's already in hand actually – I took it upon myself to presume!' He shook his head in wonderment. 'It never ceases to amaze me,

Declan, just how fucking thick some people actually are. But as my old nan used to say, you can't educate a fucking haddock.'

Chapter Seventy-One

Jessie was pleased to see her mum waiting outside her school, and she jumped into the car happily. She knew how hard it was for her mum to drive at night; she had guessed far more about her mum and her problems than she let on.

'I thought Dad might be picking me up. You know what he's like about me getting home at a reasonable time!' She was genuinely amazed that her mum had come to get her. She rarely left the house these days if she didn't have to. It was something she knew was wrong, but no one would ever say it out loud. It worried her that her mother didn't go anywhere any more, and it scared her that everyone acted as if it was normal.

Josephine smiled nervously as she pulled away from the kerb tentatively. 'He was unavoidably detained, as usual! Work stuff. How was your night anyway, darling?'

Jessie laughed with delight. 'It was a good night, Mum, a right laugh.'

Josephine could hear the pleasure in her daughter's voice. 'That's how it should be at your age.'

Jessie didn't answer; she was still basking in the night's events.

'I thought Natalie needed a lift home?'

Jessie shrugged easily. 'No, she's walking home with some of the other girls.' She wished it was her – she would love to walk home with everyone, exchanging gossip, and talking about the next party on Friday night that they were all looking forward to. Jason Ford had asked her to go with him. But that was never going to happen – she was always dropped off, and then picked up and taken home safely. It was her life, and she had to accept that.

'By the way, Mum, I'm staying at Natalie's house on Friday night. We're going shopping Saturday early. I told her mum it was OK.'

Josephine yawned. ''Course it is! We'll get you picked up when you're ready to come home.'

Jessie grinned happily. 'Thanks, Mum.' She knew her mum would never question her staying over at Natalie's. They had been friends since infant school, and they lived in each other's pockets. Natalie was going to tell her mum she was staying at *hers*, and they would then be able to go to the party in peace. She couldn't wait. Jason Ford was going to get the shock of his life on Friday. She was determined to show him she was a lot more grown up than he realised. She had been mad about him for over a year, and now he had actually asked her out. If her mum or dad knew about him, she would be grounded until she was old and grey. Her dad was like her minder! Yet she knew that he was not lily-white himself. She had heard all about him and her uncle Declan, but when she tried to ask her mother about the stories she'd been told, her mum had been less than forthcoming. She loved that they cared so much about her, but she also resented that they never gave her any freedom. She lived so far away from her friends, and that alone made her feel like an outsider.

The name Flynn gave her a certain cachet. She was the daughter of a man who was feared and respected in equal measure and that was her cross to bear. She had been treated like royalty all her life, and she had known from a young age that was because of her father. Even her teachers were wary of her father; that had been a real eye-opener for her. She wasn't a complete fool. People called him the Crime King of England – and a violent thug. It was awful, especially as her friends knew all the gossip too. But he was still her dad, no matter what people might say about him. She had a good life, and she appreciated it. Whatever he might be, he was the man she looked up to, and who she adored.

Nevertheless, she was going to lie and cheat her way to the party on Friday night. She was going to have a good night out, by hook or by crook.

Chapter Seventy-Two

Salvatore Ferreira was not as big as Michael had expected him to be. In fact, he was quite short – only about five nine – but he was built like a brick shithouse. Anyone looking at him would know immediately that he was more than capable of great violence. It was there in his eyes. He had the look of the gutter; his eyes were without any kind of emotion whatsoever and that was the real giveaway. Michael knew he had the same look. It was why they had both advanced so far in their careers. It was what made most people take a step back from them.

Salvatore Ferreira was dark-haired, dark-eyed and dark-skinned and he possessed a very proud countenance. Michael understood that as well – without that innate arrogance neither of them would have achieved anything of note. Michael was pleased to see that the man was very well dressed in a bespoke suit, handsewn shoes, and without the usual South American need for loud, garish jewellery. He looked just what he was: a well-heeled businessman.

They shook hands affably; each had a very strong grip. Sizing each other up, they were both pleased with what they saw in their prospective business partner. Michael knew his size gave him the edge, he was a powerful-looking man. Patrick Costello had told him many years before, 'Always walk into a place like you already own it, and the chances are that eventually you fucking will.' It was good advice, and something that he had never forgotten.

'It's an honour to have you here, Salvatore.'

His tone conveyed the respect the man required from him. After all, he was the main supplier, the benefactor – without him, Michael would never have been able to guarantee such huge amounts of drugs to the people he dealt with. This was something that had never been done before on such a large scale. Thanks to Ferreira, he had an endless supply of cocaine that was purer than anything else on the market. It could be cut over and over again, and still be purer than anything in Europe. Everyone was a winner.

'I am pleased to be here, Michael. My first time in London. Already I am in love with this country.'

Michael grinned. 'It's a funny old town, Salvatore. But it is also one of the biggest tourist destinations in the world. The Queen sees to that, mate. We may be a small country, but we are a rich one. Europe has always looked to us for guidance. We are the main players, as we always have been.'

Salvatore sat down on the black leather sofa gracefully. Michael knew he had come out of one of the worst slums on earth, that he had no real education – except what the Catholic priests had beaten into him on the odd occasion he had gone to school. Yet he was feared and respected by everyone he dealt with. There was more to this man than met the eye. He was not what Michael had been expecting. He had been told, on good authority, that the Colombians were basically fucking animals, without any social graces, but he had cast his net wider for information, and found out a lot more about the man by himself. You didn't live as long as Salvatore unless you had something going for you up top. Salvatore was already coming across as a man after his own heart, who had embraced the financial aspects that his career had provided for him, and who had then learnt how to carry himself in any company.

The two men had bonded immediately. They saw themselves in one another, and that was something they understood the value of. It was important to have trust – without it they were doomed. It didn't escape Michael's notice that Salvatore had left his men outside the door, and he was glad that his decision to meet the man alone had paid off.

Michael sat down beside Salvatore. 'I am so pleased that you came to England in person. I know how much that proves your belief in me. I wanted to show you that I have the money *and* the strength needed for such a venture – to not only finance this business arrangement, but also to police it and, more importantly, to guarantee you that there is *nothing* I am not prepared for.'

Salvatore nodded easily. 'I know this. I have done my homework, as you say. I would never have ventured this far from my homeland, unless I was sure of that beforehand.' He took a long drink of the brandy Michael had poured him, then he said honestly, 'But I have to ask you this, Michael, face to face – how are you going to deal with the Russians? They have always had the monopoly in Europe. The Russians, and their counterparts the Eastern Europeans, are like us

South Americans in many ways. They come from countries that are more corrupt than you could even imagine. They are ruthless, and they are here in London already. They don't play by the rules. They also have their own suppliers. True, it's always shit stuff – as you know, they are better with heroin and it's a completely different market. That aside, I need to know that you can control them, and that you have already implemented plans to ensure that they can never interfere with our business should they decide to. This is not something I would enter into lightly, you know that. You have guaranteed that you have the monopoly in Europe, and I believe you. If I didn't, I wouldn't have journeyed all this way. I just want you to reassure me that nothing and no one can interfere with our plans.'

Michael was irritated. He had already proved to Ferreira that he had everything under his control – that was why the man had come over to England in the first place! The Russians were already onside, as he had informed him; they were quite happy to let him supply whatever was needed. Once he was onboard with the Colombians, they didn't really have a choice. It was a done deal. There was too much aggravation in Afghanistan and Pakistan these days for the crops to be safe. It wasn't so easy for the Russians any more – they were not as welcome as they had been in the eighties and nineties. The Americans were all over them like a rash, and they were concentrating more on finance deals and investing heavily in property, especially Dubai, Croatia and Greece. Michael knew that Salvatore had been told this, and more than once. He also knew that Salvatore Ferreira would not have taken his word for it, he would have found out what he needed to know himself.

Michael swallowed down his frustration. This was nothing personal, it was just Ferreira flexing his muscles, and making sure that Michael understood exactly what was expected of him. He was warning him that any problems that might arise would be his alone, and he would be expected to sort them out quickly and with the minimum of fuss. The man was a businessman, and at least he had the grace to say this to him on the quiet, man to man, without an audience. Still it rankled. But Michael had listened to his mentor Patrick Costello well. He could hear his voice now saying quietly in his ear, 'Never let anyone know what you're thinking, Michael, never show them anything of importance. The earn is the prize, never forget that.'

Walking casually to the bar, he picked up the bottle of Remy XO. Then, pouring them both another drink, he sat back down beside Salvatore Ferreira on the leather sofa, smiling as if he had just been blessed by the Pope himself.

'I can assure you, Salvatore, that no one will interfere with our business. I own fucking everyone of importance, from the police, to the Customs, to the fucking High Court judges. I can access anyone needed.'

Salvatore Ferreira nodded; he had expected no less. He had made his point, he could be magnanimous now. 'I believe you, Michael. But I had to ask, you understand that?'

Michael took a large sip of his brandy and, shrugging nonchalantly, he said carefully, swallowing down the raw anger that was threatening to overwhelm him, 'Of course I do, Salvatore. I would do the same in your position. Now,

I thought I would take you to one of my clubs in the West End.'

Salvatore was watching him closely, and Michael knew this was some kind of test.

'I like the English girls. Proper blondes!'

Michael sighed heavily, rolling his eyes in mock annoyance. 'I had a feeling you would say that!'

Chapter Seventy-Three

Jack Cornel believed himself to be an intelligent man – if he had been allowed to have a decent education, he knew he could have made something of himself. His biggest problem was his arrogance, which he had worn like a shield since childhood. All his life he had sought arguments with anyone that he felt might be looking down on him. He had a huge chip on his shoulder. He hated to be treated like a nobody. His father had been a well-known drunk and his mother an even bigger one. The Cornel boys had grown up in a filthy council flat, the result of haphazard parenting, and had to live with the stigma of having the Cornel name.

They had not just witnessed violence – they had been the recipients of it since they could remember. It had been a hard upbringing. Jack had tried to protect his younger brother from his parents' viciousness and their complete disregard for the two children they had somehow created.

His father had finally beaten his wife to death when the two boys were thirteen and ten respectively. They had then had to try and survive in the care system. Too old for adoption, and much too disturbed for fostering at a residential care home, they had eventually been placed in a lock-down facility that catered for children either sent there by the courts for serious offences or, like the Cornel brothers, because no one knew what to do with them. It was a severe and harsh environment, and they stayed until eventually the social workers released them one after the other on to an unsuspecting public. By then they were past redemption, inured to pain and, without the skills to adapt to society, they had lapsed into the world of petty villainy. Burglars, thieves and liars, they had simply existed, until Jack shot a Dooley. That one act had made him believe he was now capable of moving them up in the world, thereby making a real name for themselves. Jack Cornel saw this as his chance to shine, and he was determined to make the most of the opportunity. He had assured his brother Cecil that, with Dooley's murder behind them, they were finally on the road to public recognition and wealth.

Chapter Seventy-Four

Declan was watching the Cornel brothers as they drank themselves stupid in a private club Michael had acquired a few years previously, in lieu of a heavy debt. They were with a couple of young lads, both up-and-coming Faces, who knew exactly what was wanted from them. The Cornels had walked into the club with the lads, without a second's thought, and that alone proved just how gullible they were. They were not even on their own home turf.

It was pitiful. The Cornel brothers actually believed that Michael Flynn was going to arrive here at some point, with the Colombians in tow. As if that would ever happen! As if anyone truly in the know would think that a man like Michael Flynn would actually come to a shithole like this, and bring his overseas guests with him.

He had told the bar staff to give them what they wanted, and to make sure the drinks were large and plentiful – the drunker these prats were the better. The Dooleys had made a major fuck-up by not paying the Cornels out for their brother's murder. The fact that they were on remand didn't really mean anything – they were running everything from the prison, business as usual. Rumour had it that they had a problem with the brother who had died, but so what? No one in the world they lived in would swallow something so outrageous. It was their brother, for fuck's sake! And that needed sorting out. It was a piss-take, an insult to them as a family, and especially when it was perpetrated by people like the Cornels – a pair of prize cabbages, whose combined IQ was equivalent to a fucking mongoose.

Whatever the rights and wrongs of the situation, Declan blamed the Dooleys' tardiness for the Cornels thinking they were on course for the big time. Now the Cornels were *his* problem, and that wasn't something he would forget in a hurry. The Dooleys owed him. He was doing their dirty work for them after all, and he was going to make sure they compensated him for his aggravation. It was going to be a very expensive oversight on their part.

He stepped back into the office quickly. They were drunk as cunts, but Jack would know there was something amiss if he saw him there.

He had told the doorman to clear the club by two a.m. The Cornels would think they were getting a lock-in. His lads had already told them they had arranged it so they could be there when Michael arrived. They were drunk and vulnerable and, as far as Declan Costello was concerned, that was exactly as it should be. The treacherous pair of filthy, dirty bastards! Wanting to fucking shoot Michael Flynn dead, and then to assume that would be enough to give them credibility, turn them into real Faces, real villains. They thought he would allow them to step into his shoes without a fight? It was so demented, it was almost comical.

Declan Costello could feel the beating of his heart as his

anger smouldered. If the Barkers had not given him the heads-up tonight could have been a bloodbath; it could have brought the Filth down on everyone concerned, including the visiting Colombians, and that was something, he had a feeling, that would not have been taken lightly.

He lit a cigarette, and pulled on it deeply. It was just coming up to one o'clock. Michael would be there within the hour, and that was when the Cornel brothers would finally realise the error of their ways.

Chapter Seventy-Five

Michael Flynn watched Salvatore Ferreira as he cheerfully succumbed to the charms of the beautiful Bella. She was one of his top-earning lap dancers. She wasn't as young as she looked, but that didn't really matter. She had the thick blond hair, blue eyes and creamy skin of a real English rose. She also had a very posh accent, and that went a long way with the clientele. She was really from Dagenham, but she had taken elocution lessons, ballet lessons, and had shrugged off the mantle of an Essex girl, creating a whole new persona for herself. He admired her. She had the sense to realise that this wasn't a job with a pension, she knew that her shelf life would be short, but could be very lucrative if she played her cards right. He had guaranteed her three grand, cash, to keep Salvatore amused: go home with him, and make him feel like a king. In fairness, she deserved a fucking BAFTA. What a performance! He caught her eye, motioned towards the door, and Bella was off her pole, and in Salvatore's lap within nanoseconds.

Michael Flynn walked them out to a private car five minutes later and, winking lewdly at a very drunken Salvatore Ferreira, he waved them off gratefully. He had done his bit, and now he could finally concentrate on the other business of the night. He was being driven by a young lad called Davey Dawkins, a good kid, who drove the car without ever trying to start a conversation. Michael appreciated that tonight more than usual. He was so angry he was quite literally capable of murder.

Chapter Seventy-Six

Josephine couldn't sleep – it was a long time since she had slept through the night. Even sleeping tablets didn't work any more. She had her own bedroom now. When Michael was out all hours, she didn't have to go to bed without him and pretend everything was OK. She could come in here and watch her TV programmes, sit in peace surrounded by her private things – her 'knick-knacks', as Jessie called them. Though they weren't really knick-knacks as such. The boxes she kept in here were full of important papers and magazines. She also had all of her daughter's school work from the first day she had attended – all her pictures, drawings, report cards. She even had the wrappers from sweets her daughter had eaten over the years. She couldn't part with them. Michael didn't think keeping everything Jessie had ever touched was normal. She didn't care. He didn't understand the bond between a mother and her child. She had every item of clothing that her daughter had worn. It was boxed up now, of course, washed and ironed. She knew exactly where everything was – every Babygro, every bib, everything she had kept she could find should she wish to.

Her bed was a double, with an antique mother-of-pearl headboard, and crisp white linen. There was no other furniture in here now, except for her chair and her TV. She didn't need anything else; she was quite happy to give the extra room over to her boxes of memories.

Sitting in here she was surrounded by her whole life. Michael hated it. He felt she dwelt too much on the past, when she should be enjoying the present or looking forward to the future. It was hard for him to understand how attached she was to her treasures. He was different to her; his life was mainly lived outside the house – he was always off somewhere – and he wanted her to be the same. Her journeys out into the world were getting rarer and rarer; she preferred the comfort and safety of her own home. She didn't drive much any more either, she only got into the car if she had to for her daughter's benefit. She knew, deep inside, that she was gradually becoming even more of a recluse, but she didn't care. She had all she needed here in her own home.

She looked down at her legs; they were still shapely. She was a good-looking woman, and she took good care of herself – she always put on her make-up and dressed well. Michael still wanted her; he enjoyed her body as he had years before. She still wanted him, and loved the feel of his arms around her. But she had no desire to go out with him any more. She cooked him meals that a professional chef would be proud of, she always made sure the table was dressed with everything from the finest glassware to the best linen. She kept a home for him that was the envy of many a man. All she asked in return was that he allowed her to live her life her own way.

She walked over to the French doors and, opening them, she went out to the small balcony. Sitting at the table, she looked at the sky. It was a clear night, the moon was full, and the stars were glittering above her. She shivered in the cold night air and, picking up the glass of white wine she had left out there earlier, she took a deep drink. Jessie was asleep, and she envied her daughter for a few moments. It had been so long since *she* had really slept, she had forgotten what it was like. She wished she didn't suffer from insomnia, that she could get into bed and relax like everyone else. Just to lie down and drift off peacefully was a luxury she couldn't enjoy any more. Instead, she was wide awake, straining her ears for the sound of her husband's car crunching on the drive. Once he was home safe, she always felt better.

It was when she was alone in the night like this that she couldn't stop herself thinking about things she knew were better left alone. Michael's lifestyle frightened her; she remembered late at night that the world he inhabited was a violent, bloody world. It was a world that she knew he loved, and one that she had never truly understood until the night she had seen him as he really was, covered in blood, and calmly washing it away without any emotion whatsoever. She had helped him – it had been instinctive; she had done what a wife in her position was expected to do for the man she had married. But it was a moment that changed everything. After that night, she had suffered from violent nightmares for weeks, and that was when her insomnia had begun. She was afraid of sleeping, afraid of the nightmares that would take hold, and she had never recovered. His lifestyle, what she knew he was capable of, terrified her. She'd thought she'd understood; seeing it first-hand was completely different.

She knew he would never harm her or his daughter; he loved them more than anything in the world, but that, in itself, was part of the problem. She didn't feel she could live up to his expectations of her, she hadn't even been able to give him a child for years. Now she worried that he saw her need for staying at home as a flaw. It was, she supposed, but it was how she coped. Even though he never said anything to her outright, she knew that her refusals to accompany him anywhere hurt his feelings. She didn't want to do that to him – she loved him with all her heart. But it was getting harder and harder for her to venture outside her home. Just picking up Jessie tonight had been so nerve-racking that when she had finally got back to the house, she had been sweating profusely.

Every day, her world shrank a bit more. She could only ever really feel safe inside her own home, with all her things around her. This need she had to feel safe was powerful. She had to step away from the world that Michael inhabited. It was a world that had gradually crippled her.

She just didn't want to fight it any more. Tonight she had made her mind up, admitted the truth to herself at last, and made a firm decision not to leave her sanctuary again. She felt almost tearful with joy. Michael would eventually accept her decision. Michael would never risk her actually telling him the truth, the real reason why she was like this.

Picking up her empty wine glass she went back into the warmth of the house. She would have another glass of wine, and watch a nice DVD. That was how she passed the hours away, because sleep was a luxury that all the money in the world couldn't buy.

Chapter Seventy-Seven

Jack Cornel was drunk, and he was not a friendly drunk at the best of times. He was, in actual fact, a paranoid drunk, looking for problems where none existed, and willing to follow his hatred wherever it might take him. He was already looking for a row, a reason to kick off. He had been waiting all night for that ponce Flynn to arrive and now he was bored. He had come to London to take out Michael Flynn. Every time he thought about it he felt the excitement stir in his belly. This was going to give him and his brother the kudos that they craved. He wanted to step into the limelight, show people what he was capable of, convince the world that he was not a man to be ignored.

Cecil was also drunk. Unlike his older brother, though, drink mellowed him out. He loved the world, and everyone in it. Jack watched as Cecil staggered to the men's room, all smiles and camaraderie. He was disgusted by his brother's antics – he was like a fucking big girl's blouse, so gormless it was embarrassing to watch him. Jack Cornel had one thing in his favour: even as drunk as a skunk, he was shrewd, and he never missed a chance that came his way. He had an inbuilt cunning that copious amounts of alcohol seemed to bring to the fore; he was one of the few people who actually functioned far better while under the influence of alcohol.

Glancing around, he noticed that the club was already almost empty. When he saw the doorman watching him, he knew immediately, without any doubt whatsoever, that there was something radically wrong. Years of living round two hopeless alcoholics had prepared him for the worst, and it had also taught him the need to have an escape plan at all times. He had not trusted the two young fellows who promised him Michael Flynn on a plate. He had felt from the off that they were just stooges. But he *had* counted on them producing the man in question at some point. He would then have happily taken his chance and, as he was in possession of two firearms, he felt his chances were much better than average; all he needed was a decent shot. He wasn't about to play games – he just wanted to get in there, take the fucker out, and then bask in the glory.

Now, though, he felt the cold fingers of fear on his neck. There was something more going on here. He swallowed down his drink quickly, before turning to his young hosts and saying craftily, 'I need a piss, lads, and I need to make sure that my little brother is still capable of cognitive thoughts and behaviour! Fill us up again – the night is young.'

He walked towards the men's room slowly and carefully, knowing he was being observed from all angles. Inside the toilet, he looked at his younger brother, who was trying unsuccessfully to drain his bladder without soiling himself and his trousers too badly.

Cecil looked in the mirror at his brother and he grinned idiotically. 'What a fucking great night, bruv!'

Jack Cornel rolled his eyes. His brother was never a man who could hold a drink inside him – he either pissed it out, or spewed it all over the floor. It was a cross he always had to bear, but tonight it annoyed him more than usual. Ignoring his brother, he walked into the stall. There was a window in there. It took him two minutes to open it – someone had painted it shut, so he had to use his penknife to open it. Once it was open he stood on the toilet bowl and climbed outside, calling to his brother to follow him. They found themselves in a small alleyway. Scaling a three-foot wall that took them on to another level, Jack grabbed his brother none too gently by the arm and pulled them both up a flight of rickety stairs until, finally, they were out on the street.

'What's going on, Jack?'

Jack Cornel didn't even bother to answer.

By the time they were missed, the two brothers were long gone.

Chapter Seventy-Eight

'What do you mean, Declan? How could you have fucking lost them?'

Michael Flynn was genuinely perplexed. This wasn't happening, surely? The Cornels were fucking idiots. How the fuck had they escaped?

Declan Costello was mortified; this was like amateur night. 'Look, Michael, that Jack is a lot more fucking with-it than we gave him credit for. He followed his brother into the john, and they went out the fucking window. No one could have foreseen that.'

Michael Flynn was looking at Declan Costello as if he had never seen him before in his life. He was so outraged at the man's complete fucking dereliction of his duty, he wasn't sure he could be trusted not to hammer him into the ground.

'This is fucking unbelievable! I have been entertaining the Colombians all night. All you had to do was keep an eye on two northern fucking wankers, and you are telling me that they outwitted you? They scrambled out of the crapper window, and no one fucking noticed anything? Are you telling me no one was outside?'

Declan shook his head in abject denial; he was reeling

with amazement. He had kept a low profile, waiting for Michael to arrive, and now it was completely fucking naused up in the worst way possible.

'Was he armed?'

Declan nodded once again. 'He had two firearms, a Glock, and a smaller handgun.'

Michael laughed sarcastically. 'Oh, that is just fucking great. Just what I need – a drunken fucking northerner after my blood, running the streets of London without a care in the fucking world. You useless crowd of cunts. If anything happens to cause problems with Salvatore, I will personally hunt every fucker involved down, and I will kill them myself.'

Declan looked around. Everyone in the club was looking at the floor; no one wanted to catch Michael's eye, or bring his wrath down on their heads.

Michael was in total shock. He was in the process of making a deal with one of the most dangerous men on the planet, and nothing – *nothing* – could go wrong. If Salvatore Ferreira thought that there was even a minuscule chance of aggro he would back off faster than a transvestite at a tractor pull. Salvatore had travelled to England because he had been assured that nothing could happen to him while he was here. If he was dragged into a police investigation because the Cornel brothers decided they wanted to chance their arm, it would cause murders – literally.

'Get out there, Declan. I want everyone we have on our payroll looking for them. There's a twenty-grand bonus on each of the Cornels' heads. Find them, and find them soon.

I'm going home. I assume you already have people watching my drum? The last thing we need is my wife and daughter put in the frame.'

Declan nodded. ''Course. Give me some credit, for Christ's sake.'

Michael stormed out of the club and, as soon as he was gone, Declan turned to the doorman. They were terrified for their lives, knowing they had made a major fuck-up.

'Patsy, get on the blower and get four of your guys over to Michael's drum sooner rather than later. I will organise getting everyone out on the pavements. We need to find the Cornels and, when we do, I will fucking skin the bastards alive myself.'

Chapter Seventy-Nine

Jessie Flynn woke up suddenly and, turning on her bedside lamp, she listened intently. Whatever had woken her from her sleep was still going on. She could hear her mother's voice shouting at someone. Her mother *never* shouted at anyone. She was one of the most inoffensive people on the planet. This was not something she had ever experienced before in her life. But she could hear panic and fright in her mum's voice.

Jumping out of bed, she ran from her bedroom, and across the large landing to her mother's room. 'What's happening, Mum? What's going on?'

Josephine was at her balcony doors and, at the sound of her daughter's voice, she turned quickly towards her, saying quietly, 'Go back to your room, darling, and lock your door. Don't argue with me, just do what I say.'

Josephine didn't want the men on her drive to know her daughter was in the house with her. They were after trouble. They wanted Michael, and she knew they were not leaving without a fight.

'Have you phoned the police, Mum?'

Josephine shook her head angrily. ''Course not, and don't

you either! Just do what I said, will you!' She was almost shouting at her daughter now, and Jessie was getting more frightened by the second.

She could hear a man's voice shouting angrily, 'I'm warning you, lady, open the fucking door or I'm blasting my way in.'

Jessie watched in shocked amazement as her mother shouted back loudly, 'Go on then, I dare you. But it won't be easy. A fucking cannon couldn't get through there. My husband will fucking be here any minute, and he will kill you. He will fucking take you out, mate, and laugh while he does it.'

She shut the balcony doors and pulled the wooden shutters across, locking them quickly. Then, as she ran from the room, Jessie followed her mother down the stairs, and into her father's office.

'Mum, we need to phone the police!'

'No, we don't! They are the last people we want on the fucking doorstep!'

Jessie Flynn couldn't believe her ears. 'Mum! We need to get the police here now!'

Josephine was opening the large safe Michael used for his cash, and Jessie watched as her mother removed a large shotgun. Priming it expertly, she pushed her daughter out of the door roughly and, standing in the hallway with the gun aimed at the front door, she bellowed, 'For the last time, Jessie, will you do what you're told for once. We don't need the police, OK? I've already rung for help. Now will you just *move it*!'

Jessie heard the urgency in her mother's voice, and she

ran up the staircase quickly, but she turned at the top of the landing, and watched her mother – her quiet, kind-hearted mother – calmly lock all the downstairs doors, before she once more positioned herself in the centre of the hallway, the gun cocked, her lovely face set into a grimace of hate.

This was unbelievable – it was like something from a TV programme! There were men outside trying to get in, trying to burgle them and, instead of phoning the police, her mum was preparing to take them on single-handed. It was wrong. It was terrifying. This was something that the police should be dealing with, surely? Her dad knew the police, they were always round the house having meetings with him.

She was shaking with fear now. She sat on the top stair and, pulling her nightdress over her knees, she watched her mother as if she had never seen her before. And she hadn't – not this mother, anyway. This was a woman Jessie had never met before. This was a woman Jessie was actually frightened of.

She heard glass shattering – the men had smashed through the back door. She saw her mother turn towards the locked and bolted kitchen door, the gun poised, and ready to discharge. This was a nightmare. None of this was happening.

'I'm armed, and I will blow you away, you bastards. I'm warning you now. Go while you still have a chance.'

The sound of cars screeching to a halt on the gravel drive was loud, and she saw the relief on her mother's face. Then she heard her dad's voice.

Her mother opened the front door quickly, and her father was inside the house. She could hear the sounds of his men's feet as they scrambled around. He was holding her mother to him tightly, kissing her hair and talking to her in a low voice, calming her down, making her feel safe.

Jessie watched silently, aware that none of them had even noticed her. She moved quickly and quietly, so she was out of view, tucked behind the banisters at the top of the stairs, and hidden by the darkness. She heard her father ask where she was, and her mother tell him she was locked in her bedroom. She saw him sigh with relief.

'Who are these people, Michael? What are they after?'

She saw her dad take the shotgun from her mother's arms carefully.

'I'm so sorry, Josephine. This was an accident. It should never have happened, darling. You didn't call the police, did you?'

Jessie saw her mother shake her head quickly. ''Course not. But I tell you now, another ten minutes and I would have. They were nearly inside our home! Our *home*, Michael! Jessie was terrified. *I* was fucking terrified.'

Michael was holding his wife tightly once more. Jessie could see the love they had between them, and she felt the tears come. It was so powerful to see them like that, holding each other so tightly, so attuned to each other's needs, and looking so perfect together. Then she heard her father chuckle, and she knew that the danger was over, that everything was going to be OK.

'You're a fucking diamond, Josephine, and no mistake. Fucking shotgun primed and ready to use just like I taught you. I am so proud of you, darling. Defending your home, your baby. I always knew I had picked a good one, and this proves it!'

Jessie was astounded to hear her mum laugh shakily at her father's words. 'I was scared to death, Michael, I can tell you that much.'

'I know that, darling. Now you go up and sort out our little Jessie. Tell her it was a robbery gone wrong, and it is all fine now. Bless her, she must have been terrified. I need to shoot out for a while, but I will leave some blokes here, so don't worry. This is a one-off, darling. A fucking complete outrage, caused by two fucking imbeciles known as the Cornel brothers who, for some reason, got the breaks they needed by complete accident. It should never have got this far! After I have dealt with them – and, believe me, they will rue the day they travelled down south to front me up – I will then deal with the men in my employ who let this fucking abomination happen.'

Jessie ran back to her room quickly and, locking the door behind her, she went to her bedroom window, watching as the men her father employed forced the two culprits into the back of a Range Rover. She could hear the two men protesting, and see the way they were being punched and kicked violently. She was still shaking with fear as she watched her dad walk over to the Range Rover, and take a piece of lead piping from one of his men, before dragging one of the robbers out of the Range Rover, and on to the driveway. She watched the man's head burst open as her father struck him over and over again with such force she could see the man's skull and his blood spraying everywhere.

She could hear her father screaming in anger, 'You dared, you *dared* to come to my home! My fucking home! I will kill you. I will fucking kill you stone dead!'

The other men just stood there, watching her father as if it was the most natural thing in the world. The violence was so matter of fact, and she didn't know how she was supposed to deal with it. The whole driveway was lit up like Battersea Power Station, so she watched it all in glorious technicolour.

She was still vomiting into the expensive porcelain sink in her beautiful en suite bathroom when her mother banged on her door, demanding entry.

Everything she had heard about her dad was true. She had finally seen it for herself. But it was her mother's actions that had really shocked her. That had made her realise just how little she knew about the people she lived with. Suddenly, she felt she didn't know anything any more.

Chapter Eighty

'Listen to me, Jessie. I know exactly how this looks, but you're too young to understand the reality of what happened here tonight.'

Josephine was heartbroken. She had never wanted her daughter to have to experience something so frightening. She had made coffee for everyone, left them clearing up downstairs, and then brought her daughter into her bedroom. Locking the door behind them, she had tried to explain as best she could that sometimes things happened, and there was nothing anyone could do to prevent them.

Jessie was staring at her mum, her lovely, quiet, kind-hearted mum, who everyone thought was as soft as shit and treated with kid gloves. Her entire life, she had believed that her mum was weak. Jessie had always felt that she needed to be protected, and Jessie had been willing to do just that. But it had been a lie. Her lovely mum, who had her 'problems', was actually capable of literally anything. Her mother obviously knew all about her dad and his business. Jessie knew her mother would have shot those men without a thought if the need had arisen. She had handled that shotgun like a pro. She was a liar; like her dad, her mother was a great big whopping liar. Here she was, acting like butter wouldn't melt, when it was all an elaborate act. Everything in her life had been a big pretence.

'Please answer me, Jessie. Talk to me, darling.'

Her mum sounded so genuine. It was amazing – she actually sounded as if she cared. She was once more all nervous tension; she even looked anxious, her voice quivering with emotion.

'I don't know what you want me to say, Mum.'

Josephine was relieved to hear her daughter actually speaking. She had not said a word for so long. 'I just want you to understand that what happened tonight was a one-off. It wasn't supposed to happen. None of it. Please, Jessie, you have to understand that, darling. Your dad would die before he would ever have let you see that.'

Jessie nodded slowly, unsure what else she was supposed to do.

Josephine Flynn could understand the way her daughter was feeling. She had been party to something that she had no experience of, and Josephine remembered only too clearly how disturbing it was to witness it first-hand. But there was nothing anyone could do about that now. Most importantly, Jessie needed to understand that she could *never* discuss it with anyone outside their family. There were some things that were best kept private.

Grabbing her daughter's hands in hers, Josephine squeezed them tightly, as she said huskily, her voice choked with emotion, 'Come on, Jessie love. You must have guessed that your dad wasn't the usual. I mean, I know you must have heard things about him.'

Jessie was sitting beside her mum on the bed, and she could feel the warmth of her mother's hands as she gripped hers tightly. It felt wrong. She wanted to pull her hands away, push her mother as far away from her as possible. But she still loved her mum more than anything. This made no sense to her. She was just a kid, only fourteen years old. She didn't know how to react to the night's events. She had been a witness to extreme violence and murder – something that would have frightened her had she seen it on a movie screen, let alone in real life. Now here was her mum, acting like it was nothing, as if it could be explained away and forgotten about.

Josephine brought her daughter's hands up to her mouth, and kissed her fingers gently, so desperately sorry for the girl's predicament. She'd do anything to take the pain away instead of having to make her daughter understand the importance of family loyalty, and how easily a careless word could destroy the life they had together.

'Look, Jessie, I know you can't understand any of this now, but you will one day. When you're older and wiser, you will understand why I am asking you to forget about tonight. I need you to promise me that you will never ever tell *anyone*, not even your nanas, about this. You've already guessed how serious this situation is. You're not a foolish girl. Remember, your father needs your loyalty now, and so do I.'

Jessie watched her mother carefully. She understood then that her mother would always put her father first, no matter what. She had sacrificed her own peace of mind for her husband many years before, and that was why she was so strange. Jessie did understand about the loyalty that her mother was asking of her. Family loyalty, along with being Irish Catholic, had always been seen as very important. Now her mother was asking it of her, and she couldn't refuse. No matter what she might be feeling deep down inside, she suddenly realised that she could never, *ever*, turn against her own family. It was a real moment of revelation for her. The knowledge that, even after all she had witnessed, all she now knew about her parents, if push ever did come to shove, she would never breathe a word to anyone. The fear that had overwhelmed her was suddenly replaced with another fear – the fear of losing the only life she had ever known. She had no other choice, and she would do what was expected of her.

Chapter Eighty-One

Declan Costello had been drinking heavily all day long, but he was still as sober as a judge. There wasn't enough alcohol in the world to get him drunk at this particular moment in time. He had really dropped the fucking ball. He should have had Michael Flynn's back from the off. He had happily taken a good wedge from Michael, he had been expected to sort out the minor businesses as he had always done, as well as any aggravation that might cross his path – especially any that might impinge on the serious businesses. He had become lazy; he had waited on Michael's word for everything, and that wasn't the deal – he knew that.

The Cornel brothers should have been taken out by him quickly and quietly, and Michael should never have had to be involved personally. Michael should have been told the details *afterwards*, secure in the knowledge that a threat like them had been dealt with. Instead, the Cornels had made it all the way to Michael Flynn's front door, and he had not even given the man's family any protection. The man's wife and daughter had been left hanging, vulnerable and defenceless, and that was *his* fault. The fact that Josephine had apparently turned into Bonnie Parker aside, Declan was aware that he had a lot to answer for.

He had fucked up. Michael was going to come for him, and he had no defence to offer. His brother Patrick, who had loved him dearly, would *never* have swallowed that – Declan would already be dead by now. Declan couldn't forgive himself for the trouble he had caused.

He looked across the bar; there were only two barmaids in – the club was very quiet today. The barmaids were both good girls. Estelle was in her fifties, but she looked good for her age – she could serve three people at once, and she was also adept at removing drunks if the need arose. She was all bleached-blond hair and long red nails. The other girl was a lot younger, perma-tanned, with thick, dark hair, heavily made-up brown eyes and impossibly pert breasts; she was on the look-out for a Face with a good few quid and preferably his own home. She had given him the nod more than once, but he could never remember her name for the life of him.

'Come on, girls, off you go. I'm locking up early today.'

Estelle had her coat on in seconds, and Declan watched gratefully as she steered the other barmaid up the stairs. He heard the door slam shut behind them.

He had sent all his workers out and about, and he was waiting patiently for Michael Flynn to arrive. He was not going to try and justify his actions, he was prepared to take his punishment. He loved Michael's daughter Jessie as if she was his own child, and that he had not even thought to see to her safety – or her mother's for that fact – was the biggest shame of his life. He had made two fatal mistakes – not only had he underestimated the Cornel brothers, he had let down Michael Flynn.

Chapter Eighty-Two

Hannah Flynn was worried about her granddaughter – not an emotion she had ever experienced before. Jessie, however, had managed to find her way into her heart. She loved the girl as much as she could love anyone. She saw herself in her at times. Hannah Flynn had always had a way of carrying herself – she walked tall, straight-backed, and with a natural grace. Jessie had inherited that along with her intelligence.

Josephine didn't have a brain in her head – she had the conversational skills of a twelve year old. All she had ever been interested in was fashion, clothes and shoes. She was a wonderful cook, though, and she kept a good table. Jessie, on the other hand, was very sharp, quick-witted. She was a girl who read voraciously, and to whom learning came naturally. She was capable of so much, and Hannah knew that whatever the girl decided she wanted to do with her life, she could do it.

But today young Jessie had looked seriously ill when she called at the house. Josephine had practically thrown her out, and Hannah wasn't going to forgive that in a hurry. She had not made it further than the entrance hall, before she was back in her cab and on her way home.

There was something going on in that house, and she would get to the bottom of it if it was the last thing she ever did in her life.

Chapter Eighty-Three

Every time Jessie closed her eyes, she relived the night's events. She felt physically ill, sickness roiling inside her belly, and breathless, unable to calm her fears.

Her bedroom was huge – bigger than most people's front rooms. It was very beautiful and she had always loved it. The walls were covered with a pale pink silk which had cost a fortune but from the moment her mum had shown it to her she had wanted it. Her double bed had been brought over from France – hand-carved, it would not look out of place in a palace. The curtains on her windows were a deeper pink than the walls, the floor was white oak, and every piece of furniture, from her bedside cabinets to the dressing table, was hand-picked and very expensive. Until today, she had never thought about the cost – suddenly it seemed to be important to her. She looked around her, saw the bookcase with her favourite books, the pictures of her life exquisitely framed, showing her smiling so happily – and completely unaware of the real world that she was living in. Unaware that, one day, that safe, happy world would explode in her face.

She closed her eyes, wanting desperately to blot it out.

Her lovely bedroom that was the envy of her friends, which she once had loved so very much, where she had felt safe and secure, was where she now felt trapped.

The door opened and her mother came into the room quietly. She had a tray in her hands with a glass of milk and a plate of cookies. Jessie waited for her mother to come to her and, as she sat on the bed, Jessie saw the sorrow in her eyes, and felt the deep sadness that enveloped her mother.

'Try and eat something, Jessie. For me.'

Jessie sat up abruptly, knowing that her mother would have to move away from her.

Josephine stood up awkwardly and, when her daughter had finally settled, she placed the tray across her lap. 'Drink the milk at least, Jessie.'

Jessie picked up the glass, and obediently took a few mouthfuls of the milk.

'There's a good girl. You'll feel better now.'

Josephine was so worried about her daughter. It had only been a day, but she hated that her child had been traumatised by the events of the night before.

Jessie pushed the glass roughly into her mother's hand. 'I'll feel better now, will I?'

Josephine placed the glass on the floor carefully. Then, sitting down on the bed, she looked at her lovely daughter for long moments before saying angrily, 'No, Jessie. You *won't* really feel better, darling. *I* know that, and *you* know that. Last night was a fucking nightmare, darling, and I would give anything to change it. But I can't. We can't phone the police like normal people. We can't talk about it to anyone *ever*. We have to make sure that no one knows what happened. It's not ideal, but it's how things are for people like us. I'm telling you, from personal experience, Jessie, you just have to find a way to deal with it.'

Jessie knew that her mum didn't realise she had seen as much as she had. Her mother really did believe that she had locked herself in her bedroom, and that was something Jessie needed her to believe. Her mother could never know what she had actually witnessed, and neither could her father. She actually didn't want them to know. The less they thought she knew about it, the better for all concerned.

Chapter Eighty-Four

Michael Flynn was bone weary. He looked tired and gaunt, he needed a shave and a shower – his usual good looks had deserted him.

Declan Costello stood quietly before him, a broken and shamed man. He was also in need of a bath and a shave; his clothes, like Michael's, were soiled and wrinkled.

Declan opened his arms wide in a gesture of supplication, as he said sorrowfully, 'What the fuck can I say, Michael? I naused it up from the start. I don't know what I was thinking. The Barkers were trying to do me a favour. If I'd had any fucking sense, I should have told them to deal with it. Instead, I honestly thought you would want to sort it yourself.'

Michael was so angry at Declan's explanation that he was frightened to say anything to him until he had harnessed his anger.

Declan could see that Michael was fighting to control himself. 'I'll get us both a drink, Michael.' Once behind the bar, he poured them both large whiskies.

Michael was trying to control his breathing. He had every right to be angry, and every right to exact any revenge he felt was warranted. But he knew that Declan didn't feel any malice towards him, and that he had not expected the Cornel brothers to be such a slippery pair of bastards. Declan Costello had been guilty of nothing more than sheer stupidity and laziness.

Michael gulped his drink, savouring the burn as it hit his belly. He could feel the energy coming back into his body and, swallowing down the rest of the whisky, he placed the glass on the bar gently, before leaning his body over the counter and picking up the whisky bottle. He poured himself out another large measure of Scotch. His back was turned away from Declan, and his voice was rough, as he said disgustedly, 'Do you know what fucking annoys me more than anything about you, Declan? That you can stand there like the orphan of the fucking storm, all sad-eyed, and ready to take your punishment, yet you know exactly what you did wrong. You know why my fucking wife and daughter were terrorised in their own fucking home. So what I want to know is, why didn't you think this through before it got out of hand?' He turned to face Declan, to look him in the eyes.

Declan just shrugged his huge shoulders; he was as bewildered as Michael. 'I was already well pissed by the time Peter Barker came to see me. I can't condone my actions. I need a day or two so I can think things through properly. Why do you think I didn't want the partnership when you offered it to me? I can't think on my feet. I run the same fucking businesses I did when my brother was in the big seat. I thought I was doing the right thing. I didn't think of the consequences. I certainly never dreamt the fuckers would go on the trot. Fuck me, Michael, they could barely stand up!'

Michael finished his whisky in one gulp. Then, sighing heavily, he brought the whisky tumbler down on to Declan's head with all his strength, and began beating the bloodied man viciously and deliberately.

When he was finished, Michael went into the men's rest room and washed his hands carefully, before tidying himself up as best he could. He left the club quickly; his car and driver had been waiting for him patiently. There were also two of his doormen waiting outside. As arranged, as soon as he drove away, they slipped into the club and began the job of cleaning up the mess that Michael Flynn had left behind him.

Chapter Eighty-Five

Michael had showered, and changed into a pair of black jogging bottoms and a crisp white T-shirt. As he walked across the landing from his bedroom to his daughter's, he could hear his wife pottering about in the kitchen below. It was a good sound, the sound of a home, of normality.

He tapped gently on his daughter's door, before walking into the dimness of her bedroom. Her TV was on, providing the only light, but the sound was down. She was lying in her bed and, as she turned to look at him, he forced a smile on to his face.

He knelt down beside her bed. She could smell the shampoo and soap that he always used – it was a familiar scent, something that had always comforted her until now. She looked up into his face, as she had so many times before, only this time it was different. He wasn't the dad she had loved and adored any more. He was a stranger to her. This was a man she didn't trust.

'You all right, Jessie?'

She nodded. He put his arms around her and hugged her tightly. He could feel the stiffness in her slim body, knew that she was still traumatised by the events of the last twenty-four hours. He relaxed his hold on his daughter and, settling her back on to her pillows, he sat beside her on the bed. He could see that the fright lingered, and he knew she was never going to forget what had happened. But he continued to smile down at her, as she watched him warily.

'Listen to me, Jessie. That was never supposed to happen. It was a complete one off. I swear that to you, darling. Burglars! Fucking creepers! They are the scum of the earth. Anyone who wants to nick someone else's hard-earned cash is filth. Never forget that, my little darling. But they weren't banking on your mum were they, eh?' He was trying to make light of everything, make a big joke of it. 'Did you see her, Jessie? With my shotgun! She looked like Calamity Jane!'

Jessie didn't answer, and that bothered him. She had always been able to say what she wanted to him – that was part of their closeness.

'She was only trying to protect you, darling. There are some bad people in the world, and sometimes bad things happen. But it's over now. It's all sorted out. Daddy's here.'

Michael could see his daughter's sad face, still full of fear. It was ridiculous. He was with her now – she had no reason to be scared of anything.

'I want to go to sleep.'

Michael watched his daughter closely. Her voice sounded different, there was no inflection in it, no emotion whatsoever. She had been truly affected by the Cornels. If he could, he would happily murder the fuckers all over again for that.

'OK, baby. But promise me you will try and put this behind you. You're a Flynn, and that means nothing or no one can ever hurt you.'

Jessie could hear the cold arrogance in her father's voice as he said his name and, without thinking, she said sarcastically, 'The name Flynn didn't seem to do us much good last night, did it?'

Michael was almost as shocked as she was by her words. He stood up quickly. She could see the anger she had caused, but she didn't care any more.

'There wasn't any burglary, Dad. No police were called either – I know that much.'

Michael didn't answer her for a while. Then, smiling sadly, he knelt down beside her bed once more. 'You're nearly fifteen. When I was your age I knew a lot more than people gave me credit for. So I'll say this, Jessie – me and your mum love you more than anything in this world, and everything we do is for you. Never forget that.'

She looked him straight in the eye as she said quietly, 'I won't.'

He stood up slowly. Something had changed between them, and he knew that it wasn't for the good. 'If I could change the last few days I would, Jessie. You know that, darling.'

She did. He would do anything for her – last night's events proved it.

'But you can't, Dad. No one can.'

She saw the mask slip from her father's face; he was still very angry, she could see that as plain as day. He looked like he was going to explode, but within seconds he was smiling at her once again. The smile that she had always coveted, that had been such a big part of her daily life.

'What I *can* promise you, though, is that I will *never* allow anything like that to happen to you or your mum again.'

She was watching him carefully, and he sensed that she was still not convinced by his promise to keep her safe. She was so beautiful – she was Josephine all over again, from the thick hair to the arched eyebrows. It was uncanny, the striking resemblance between them. But one thing he realised now, was that she didn't have her mother's nature. Jessie was not as warm or forgiving as the woman who had birthed her. There was an underlying steeliness in his Jessie that was reminiscent of *his* mother. He could be wrong; after all, the poor girl had just been through a terrible ordeal, and he mustn't lose sight of that. But there was something else going on here, he could feel it. He bent down and kissed his daughter lightly on her cheek, aware that she didn't respond.

'You try and get some sleep.'

Jessie watched her dad as he left the room. A part of her wanted to call him back, wanted to tell him that she knew what he had done to that man, and she still loved him. But another part of her was reeling from what she had seen him do. At least her mum had tried to be honest with her. Her lovely mum, who looked like she wouldn't hurt a fly, who everyone thought was as soft as soap, but who was far stronger than anyone would have believed. Her whole world had been stripped bare, and she had been left with nothing. Her life had been a sham, built on nothing more substantial than lies and deceit.

Chapter Eighty-Six

Josephine was sitting at the kitchen table, a large glass of white wine in her hand and a cigarette between her lips, when Michael finally joined her.

She could see from his expression that his visit with his daughter had not gone well. She should have warned him, but she had not wanted to cloud his thinking. She could see Jessie had been seriously affected by the events of the previous night.

Michael sat down wearily, and she poured him a glass of wine. 'I made you a few sandwiches, Michael. I can cook you something if you want? A bit of egg and bacon?'

He shook his head slowly. 'These are fine, mate.'

He grabbed a cheese and pickle sandwich and bit into it eagerly. He was hungrier than he had realised. He took a large sip of his wine, and savoured the crispness of it.

'It's still early days, Michael. She'll come round.'

He nodded his agreement. 'I hate that she had to go through that. I hate that you did! For fuck's sake, Josephine, those fuckers got right the way to our door. I will never forget it.'

Josephine smiled weakly at her husband. She hated to see him like this. She always made sure that she never let him see her own fears. She was still shaking inside but she could never let him know that. It had taken everything she had to face those men and defend her home.

'I just want to forget it, Michael.'

'I should be in the West End now. Salvatore wants to be wined and dined every night. I've had to send young Alex Martin in my place. He's going to take him clubbing. He's a good lad. He'll keep him out till the morning, and give me a bit of breathing space.'

'Did Cecil tell you how they knew about the Colombians?'

'Did he fuck! He was clueless. Jack was the brains of that outfit, and that's a contradiction in terms, I can tell you. That Cecil was as thick as shit. I have never in my life met someone as dense as him. He made Trigger look like a fucking applicant for Mensa.'

Josephine laughed despite herself. 'Your mum turned up today. You know her – she's like a bloodhound. I had her out the door in record time though. She sussed that there was something going on.'

He finished his sandwich, not bothering to answer. The fact that someone like Jack Cornel had managed to get so close to him had really thrown him. It had shown him just how vulnerable he was, even now when he was such a major player. He had been foolish to think that his name was enough to guarantee his safety, but he had not allowed for nutters like the Cornels. The last few days had shown him the cracks in his armour, had forced him to re-evaluate everything he had believed in. Patrick Costello had once said to him that there was nothing lonelier than being a success. How true that was.

Chapter Eighty-Seven

Natalie Childs was looking at her oldest and best friend in abject amazement. 'You can't be serious, Jessie!' Her voice had risen until it was almost a screech, she was so shocked at her friend's words.

'Oh, yes! I'm very serious, Nat.'

Natalie was still reeling from the shock of Jessie's latest revelations. Jessie Flynn had become a completely different person recently. The girl she had known and loved was long gone. This girl – the new Jessie – was not just without shame, she was brazen. This new Jessie was already getting a name as a whore, and she seemed to relish it.

'If you don't watch it, Jessie, you are going to end up in so much trouble.'

Jessie just shrugged nonchalantly. 'I don't care, Natalie.'

Natalie was scared for her friend; she couldn't understand what had happened to Jessie or why she was suddenly acting so strangely. 'Your mum and dad will go apeshit if they find out.'

Jessie could hear the bewilderment in Natalie's voice, and she felt a moment's sorrow for her friend. But Natalie could never understand her life, no one could. Unless they lived in her family's chosen world, it was impossible for anyone to understand. She looked at her friend's lovely face, so full of concern for her, and she wanted so much to set her mind at rest, but she couldn't do that.

'How the fuck will they find out? If you do what I ask, and say I am with you, nothing can go wrong, can it?'

Natalie wasn't sure. She didn't like all this lying and scheming. It wasn't a part of her life and, up until a few months previously, it hadn't been a part of Jessie's life either. Now Jessie lied about everything.

'What if your mum rings the house to talk to you? She's friends with my mum, remember? Have you thought of that?'

Jessie just laughed; she didn't care either way, that was obvious. 'So what if she does? If it was left to my mum and dad I would never leave the house without an armed guard. If I get busted, that's my problem, Nat, not yours. Anyway, if my mum did decide to ring, she would ring me on my mobile.' Jessie busied herself lighting a cigarette; after pulling the smoke deeply into her lungs, she said dismissively, 'I really don't give a flying fuck, Natalie. If I did get a capture, you know I'd take the flak – you wouldn't be dragged into anything. If that's what's bothering you, then forget it. I don't need anything from anyone, mate.'

Natalie knew when she was beaten and, as usual, she would do exactly what Jessie wanted her to. It had been like that since they were little kids. Jessie had always been the boss of the relationship and Natalie had never minded until recently. Now all Jessie wanted from her these days was an alibi. Unlike Jessie, Natalie had no interest in pubs or clubs, in meeting men who were far too old, and who expected far too much in return for the drinks they provided.

Jessie Flynn was getting a real reputation, but that didn't seem to bother her in the least. She was fifteen years old, but with her make-up and her clothes she looked at least twenty-five. She also had a way with her that belied her youth; she seemed so much older than her years. Everything about her friend, though, was an elaborate act. No matter how much Jessie tried to pretend that she was a grown-up, Natalie knew different. But she was still her friend, and that counted for a lot more than Jessie realised.

'OK. So who are you meeting this time?'

Jessie grinned mischievously. She had got what she wanted. Stretching her whole body slowly and luxuriously, she laid herself across Natalie's bed like a cat. Every movement was sensuous, dripping with her youthful sex appeal.

Natalie had always been envious of Jessie; she had developed very early, and now she had a body that any woman would kill for. She was high-breasted, with a slim waist and long legs. With her good looks and her amazing hair, it was a dangerous combination.

Natalie was pretty enough, but she knew she wasn't in Jessie Flynn's league. Men had been watching Jessie since she was thirteen, and who could blame them? She was stunning.

'Come on, Jessie, spill!'

Jessie stretched herself once more, a deliberate, sexual movement that made Natalie feel uneasy. It was too calculated, too deliberate.

'His name is Bill, and he is a builder. He is really good-looking, Nat.'

Natalie was intrigued despite herself. 'How old is he?'

Jessie pouted sexily. 'Late thirties. I'm not really sure, to be honest.'

Natalie looked suitably scandalised, and that pleased Jessie. It was exactly the reaction she had wanted to create.

'You will be careful, Jessie, won't you? Promise me.'

Jessie laughed in delight. 'Don't worry about me. I'm always careful, Nat.'

Natalie Childs shook her head slowly in disbelief; she couldn't believe her friend was so willing to take such chances, knowing the trouble it could cause. Everyone knew her dad wasn't a man to cross – not that she would ever say that to Jessie outright, of course. Her family's name and reputation had never been spoken of outright, but it had always been there between them. Jessie's father was a dangerous man, and if he found out what his Jessie was getting up to, Christ Himself only knew what the consequences would be. Jessie just didn't seem to give a damn.

'You're mad, Jessie. You can't keep all this up for ever.'

Jessie laughed, a deep husky chuckle that sounded far too old and knowledgeable for her years. 'You're probably right, Nat, but I really couldn't give a fuck either way.'

Chapter Eighty-Eight

Terence Brown was not a tall man, but what he lacked in height he made up for in width. He spent a lot of time in the gym, and his body showed that devotion. He wore clothes to accentuate his build. He wasn't a handsome man, but had an interesting face, and he looked very amiable and friendly. People assumed he was approachable – his countenance led people to think he was willing to open up a dialogue with them. Unfortunately, that was not the case.

Terence Brown was a man who could pick a fight with a novice nun if the mood was on him. He saw the majority of the people in the world as no more than an irritation, none more so than the people who insisted on attempting to engage him in pointless conversations. He made his living by collecting outstanding debts; they were always for huge amounts of money, and employing Terence Brown was the last resort. He could track any debtor, no matter where in the world they might have travelled to. He was like a bloodhound. He could sniff the fuckers out, and track them down with an ease that was as fast as it was unexpected.

His reputation was his greatest asset, and he used it to his advantage. He took thirty-five per cent of the monies that he collected, plus the ten grand up front he insisted on, to be paid whether he collected the debt requested or not. It was for his expenses and his time, and he saw that as his due. He was known and respected as a man who did the job required of him, not only quickly but, more importantly, *quietly.* If Terence Brown arrived on a doorstep, the person concerned made sure that they found the money needed as quickly as humanly possible. He was known to dispose of anyone who was unable to pay him. He saw failure to pay as a grave personal insult to him, and his retaliation as a reminder to anyone he might call on in the future. Terence Brown had carved a good life for himself, against the odds, and it was something he was proud of.

He glanced around the pub. It was Friday night, and it was packed out as usual. He paid for his drink, and sipped it carefully as he scanned the bar. It was just after ten and the place was buzzing – the music was loud and the conversations were louder. A bird he hooked up with occasionally was already walking towards him, and he smiled widely at her. She was a great-looking girl, all blond hair, minimal clothes and fake tan. She was also a good laugh. That was the main attraction for him – so few people caught his attention, but her sense of humour impressed him. She was looking for a Face, he knew. He wasn't going to get caught up in that shite, though. If, and it was a big if, he ever did decide to marry, it wouldn't be to someone who had lain down with anybody who bought her a few drinks and paid for the odd meal.

'I thought that was you, Terence!' He grinned at her, happy that she never made the mistake of pretending they had a real relationship. So many girls in her position tried to manufacture a closeness that wasn't there.

'I was passing, so I thought I'd pop in, Jan, and see if you fancied a quick drink?'

Janice Evans smiled widely. She liked Terence Brown a lot, he was always so nice to her, and she had a feeling that he liked her much more than he let on. 'That sounds lovely, Terence. I'll have a JD and Diet Coke.'

He ordered her drink, and Janice was chatting away, laughing and joking, when she realised that Terence wasn't listening to a word she was saying. She followed his gaze, and saw that he was watching a couple at the bar with an interest that wasn't exactly healthy. She grabbed his arm tightly and, as he looked down at her, she said huffily, 'Are you all right, Terence?'

Pulling a twenty out of his pocket he gave it to her, saying, 'Get another couple of drinks, Jan. Large ones, eh?'

She took the money, and turned back towards the bar, but she was annoyed. The girl he was staring at was very young, and that didn't sit well with what she knew of Terence Brown. He wasn't interested in many women, she had worked that out herself. But she shrugged her thoughts away; Terence wasn't the kind of man she could ever question, he wouldn't allow a woman to feel she had any hold over him. But he had never looked at anyone else while he had been in her company and she had liked that about him. Seeing him staring so intently at such a young girl bothered her. Even worse, she was annoyed with herself for caring so much.

Terence Brown suddenly found himself in a very serious

quandary, and he was not sure what he should do. This was a situation that he could never have envisaged happening to him in a million years, but it was something that he couldn't ignore and walk away from in good conscience. It was a fucking dangerous situation. A very *delicate* situation, that needed to be handled with tact and diplomacy. Luckily he was more than capable of doing that; the people he worked for used him because of his ability to keep his mouth shut. He saw himself as a man of principle, with old-style morals, which were very important to him. He had no choice – he had to do what was right.

Terence had worked for Michael Flynn on many occasions. Michael had always given him his due and he liked and greatly admired Michael. He had been invited into Michael's home and had broken bread there on more than one occasion. He'd spent many happy hours talking with the man who had always treated him with the utmost respect and never been anything other than charming to him.

Now, as he stood at the bar of this complete shithole of a pub – a place only the lowest of the low would frequent – he couldn't ignore the fact that Michael Flynn's young daughter was there, dressed like a pole dancer, and in the company of a man old enough to be her father.

He took the drink that Janice Evans gave him, and gulped it down. Then he pulled Janice towards him roughly, shouting to be heard above the music. 'Here, Jan, who's the bloke over there with the leather jacket and the Churchill shoes? Do you know him?'

Janice nodded quickly. If Terence Brown was asking questions there was a good reason for it.

'He comes in here all the time. Billy something-or-other. He's a builder out of Silvertown. A complete fucking waster, always on the pull – married with a couple of kids, by all accounts. The young girl he's with started coming in a few weeks ago. She's jailbait, if you ask me. She's already been with half the blokes in here from what I've seen of her. Anyone who buys her a few drinks is in with a chance!'

Terence Brown frowned at her words. 'Listen, I need to make a quick phone call. Do me a favour, Janice – will you keep an eye on them for me? I think he owes someone I know a good few quid, the treacherous cunt.'

Janice grinned happily, pleased that Terence Brown was asking her for a favour, happy to be a part of his life however small.

Chapter Eighty-Nine

Billy Thomas was drunk. It was late, and he knew his wife was going to give him grief for weeks, but he didn't give a toss. It was worth it. This little beauty was a real find; she was game for anything, as long as he supplied her with a good drink and a few lines. She was very young – younger than she let on – and he didn't reveal he knew the truth about her. She was fifteen years old at most – a real fucking draw for him; he liked them young and stupid. Treat them like grown-ups and they were so thrilled they would do anything he asked of them. She was his dream date.

He parked his work van neatly outside the flat conversion he was working on in Rainham. Jessie was nearly asleep, lying against his shoulder, and he kissed her gently, before slipping his tongue between her lips, licking the inside of her mouth roughly. She responded eagerly as he knew she would.

'Come on, mate. I've been waiting for this.'

As they got out of the van, Billy Thomas was already hard as a rock; he had been thinking about this all day, and he had planned ahead. He opened the front door quickly and, pushing Jessie inside, he didn't turn on any lights, just shut the door quietly behind them.

'Come on.'

He dragged her into the front room which was empty except for an old sofa. Pushing her down on to it, he kissed her roughly before getting up and walking into the kitchen. Jessie could hear him as he poured them both drinks.

She smiled happily. He had really come up trumps. She liked that he had planned – gone out and bought the alcohol, and then brought it here in readiness for the night's entertainment. The knowledge that he had done all that for her was a real power trip.

It was dim in the room with the only light coming from the lamp post outside, but she noticed that the walls had recently been plastered. The whole place smelt of damp and neglect. Even the sofa looked dilapidated. As her eyes adjusted to the dimness she could see it was filthy. It stank of cigarettes and fried food. But who cared? It was comfortable, and more than adequate for what she wanted.

Billy brought the drinks in and handed her a plastic glass full of vodka and Coke. 'Get that down your neck. Plenty more where that came from.'

Jessie took a deep draught; it was nearly all cheap vodka, as she had expected. She lay back against the arm of the sofa, and she could see his excitement as she gave him her glass, and casually started to undress herself. She was not wearing that much anyway and, as she pulled her top over her head, and dropped it on to the floor, she heard his intake of breath. She was without underwear – she knew the power of that from previous experience. Billy was already putting the drinks on to the floor, his whole world focused on her and her body. Her breasts were heavy and well shaped, enough to make any man fold, and Jessie enjoyed the power she had as she exposed them to the air. She lifted her skirt up around her hips, opening her legs wide, and she could hear the change in the man's breathing, feel his mounting excitement, as she pulled him into her arms, and kissed him deeply, pulling at his shirt, trying to rip it open.

'Come on, Billy boy, you know what to do.'

Billy Thomas was in a state of pure ecstasy. He jumped up quickly, tearing his clothes off with abandon. This was the best he'd ever had. This young girl was a fucking dream come true for him, and she was his – all his. It was as if all his Christmases and birthdays had arrived at once. He had never felt so aroused by anyone in his life. She was like a porn star, willing to do anything he wanted her to do. In this light, she looked her age – so fucking young and vulnerable. She was a schoolgirl in a woman's body, and it was a huge turn-on.

But as he finally thrust himself inside her, all hell suddenly broke loose.

Chapter Ninety

Terence Brown was more disgusted than he had ever felt in his life. Seeing a man like Michael Flynn shamed like this was unprecedented. The girl was screaming in terror, and he automatically grabbed her and placed his hand over her mouth. The noise she was making had to be stopped as quickly as possible – the last thing any of them needed was the fucking Filth arriving on the scene, all notebooks, bright eyes, and awkward questions.

Billy Thomas was being severely reprimanded by Michael Flynn, as he should be, the filthy piece of shit. He had more than earned this fucking hammering. He was a nonce, a fucking beast. The girl was only a kid for all her tits and make-up. It was a disgrace – what man in his right mind wanted a young girl? A child? Michael Flynn was really giving him the large. It occurred to Terence Brown that Billy Thomas was not going to leave this room alive. But that was his look-out – he had asked for it, and he was getting it.

Jessie could see everything that was happening around her and, as the reality of her situation sank in, she stopped trying to fight her way out, stopped trying to scream. Instead she closed her eyes tightly, and waited for it to be over.

Terence grabbed the nearest thing to him with his free hand, trying to cover the girl's nakedness with Billy Thomas's new shirt.

Michael Flynn was still beating the man with his fists and his feet, using all his considerable strength, but Terence knew the man was already dead. No one on earth could have survived that kind of a beating – it was impossible. The girl was quiet now, and Terence guessed that it had finally occurred to her that this was her fault – she was the instigator of everything that had happened. It was outrageous.

Michael Flynn continued kicking Billy Thomas long after the man had died. When his anger finally subsided, the man was no more than a bloody piece of meat, unrecognisable as a human being.

Michael Flynn looked at his only daughter for long moments before bowing his head in shame. '*You* did all this, remember that, Jessie. You caused this.'

Jessie Flynn stood up then and, dressing herself quickly, she said harshly, 'Oh no, *you* did this. It's what you do, Dad. Remember?'

Chapter Ninety-One

Josephine Flynn was absolutely devastated. Everything that she had been told about her daughter had hurt her like a physical blow.

'Oh, Jessie, what possessed you? For fuck's sake, have you no shame? Have you no fucking decency?'

Jessie laughed nastily. 'Oh, have a day off, will you, Mum? Acting all fucking shocked. I might have fucked a few blokes but, in the grand scheme of things, that's nothing really, is it? I never *killed* anyone, did I? I've never murdered anyone.'

Josephine stared at her lovely daughter; she saw the beauty she had inherited from herself, and she saw the coldness she had inherited from her father. Her Jessie was every bit as vicious as the man she seemed to hate so much.

Grabbing her daughter roughly by the hair, she forced her head back until she could look straight into her face. 'Don't you fucking *dare* try to bullshit me, lady. I'm warning you now, Jessie, don't push me too far. I might seem like a fucking pushover, but I'm not. Far from it. We *trusted* you, lady. Whatever you might think of us, we *trusted* you. So the real world has finally arrived on your doorstep – get over it. But don't you *ever* try and justify your own fuck-ups by blaming me and your dad. All we did was love you. We gave you the world, and don't you ever forget that.'

She threw her daughter away from her angrily, watching as she fell to the floor, unable to find it in her heart to comfort her child and make it better. At this moment she hated her – hated her for what she had done to her father, to them all. Her daughter had chosen her own road, and it was a road that she would find very lonely, and very hard.

'You broke your father's heart, I hope you know that, and I'll never forgive you for it. He loved you more than life itself. You stupid, stupid girl. You knew that we weren't like other families – don't pretend you didn't. You knew all about us, I know you did, so stop trying to pretend different. Your nana Flynn made sure of that. I know she's filled your head with her spite and her anger the last few months.'

Jessie pulled herself up slowly from the kitchen floor, grabbing at the black marble worktop to steady herself. She was in so much pain, hurting all over. She could see clumps of her hair on the flooring. That her mum could have attacked her like that was something she would never have believed possible. Even after everything that had happened, it was her mother's anger that had really been the eye-opener for her. Her mother had always been the one person she had felt she could rely on no matter what. She knew now, though, that her mum would always put her father first – he was her only real interest. It was a learning curve all right. She could see the truth of everything her mother really stood for now, and it was just another let-down for her, just another lie they lived with.

She had been brought up to believe that her family were blessed, and lived so well because her father worked so hard.

She had never questioned that – why would she? The man she had loved was a thug who used violence to earn a living. His lifestyle had nearly caused the death of her mother and herself, but no one seemed to think that was of any importance. Now her mother was actually trying to tell her that she was disappointed in *her*? That *she* was the one in the wrong? It was outrageous. How could her mother not see her point of view?

'I saw everything that night, Mum. You with the shotgun, acting like fucking Calamity Jane. I saw everything that went on – I was watching. You hypocrites, telling me what to do all the time, watching me like a hawk, the *good* girl, the *good* daughter, pretending we were a *normal* family, when it was a lie. We could have died that night.'

'But we didn't, did we?'

Jessie sighed heavily, unable to believe her mother's attitude.

Josephine poured herself a large glass of wine and, taking a long drink, she sat down at the kitchen table. Lighting a cigarette, she puffed on it for a while before saying sadly, 'So you saw everything that night. I'm sorry, I really am. But you also saw a man murdered earlier tonight, a man you were sleeping with. Fifteen years old, and already a seasoned mistress! Yet that doesn't seem to be bothering you too much – in fact, if it wasn't for you, he would be alive and kicking, darling. So let me ask you this – how can you justify that? It seems to me you are more like your old man than you realise, lady.'

Jessie Flynn didn't answer her mother, she didn't know what to say to her. She just knew she wasn't the same girl she had been before those men had arrived on their doorstep, armed and dangerous. Her whole life had been like a dream until then, like a fairy tale, and it had been based on lies, built on quicksand. Everything she had ever believed in was without foundation, without substance. Even now, her father was out there, making sure that Billy's body was disposed of, taking care of business, and everyone acted as if it was the most natural thing in the world.

The truth was, she *didn't* care about Billy Thomas. She didn't care that he was dead. She had wanted to be found out from the start; she had never dreamt that she could get away with her behaviour for so long. But she had, and it was only because her parents had always thought the best of her. They should have known that something was wrong with her, but none of them had noticed anything amiss. That wasn't right; she resented them for assuming she would just pick herself up and carry on as normal. It had shown her that she was really no more than an outsider, that her mum and dad didn't really give her more than a passing thought. All they needed was each other.

'I can't answer that question, Mum. To be honest, he meant nothing to me. I wish I had realised that before. But what I do know is you and Dad don't need me – you never did, Mum. I feel like you and Dad built this big lie, and it was all for my benefit. You never leave the house now unless you have to. I don't feel like this is my home any more. Overnight I went from convent girl, with a perfect life, to no one. Everything I had ever believed in was stripped away, was destroyed. Dad even attacked Uncle Declan and put him in hospital. In a matter of days, I was thrust into *your* world, your vicious, violent world. I'm fifteen years old, Mum.'

Josephine Flynn was heart-sorry for her daughter, she understood what she was saying. But it was too late now, she should have said all this a long time ago.

'I'm sorry to hear you say that, Jessie. You were always everything to me and your dad. I tried to be honest with you.' Josephine finished her glass of wine and poured herself another. 'When I was a kid, Jessie, my dad was put away for a long time. I spent the best part of my youth visiting him in Parkhurst. I didn't like it, but I got on with it. My mum and me made his time bearable. We wrote, we visited. I had so many Christmases, so many birthdays without him, just me and her. We struggled without him, but we just got on with it. I didn't rail at the world, but I missed him, God how I missed him. He was my dad. I remember the Filth coming round our house, tearing it apart, searching for evidence, being dragged out of my bed. They even slit open my mattress with a huge knife, in case he had hidden anything inside it. I can still remember the court case, my mum coming back from the Old Bailey every night, and pretending everything was all right. My heart was broken, but I knew, even then, as young as I was, that my mum needed me to be strong for her. So I was. But I know in my heart that you knew about your dad, Jessie. You acting like it was all a fucking big surprise doesn't wash with me. All your mates know about us and, even though that doesn't make it right, it still makes me question why you would use it as an excuse to whore yourself out.'

Jessie pulled a chair out from under the table, and sat down beside her mother. 'I was scared out of my life, Mum. I can't believe you don't understand how much that affected me.'

Josephine looked at her lovely daughter and, getting up slowly, she went to the nearest cupboard and brought another wine glass to the table. She poured her daughter a small glass of red wine, pushing the glass towards her roughly.

'I *do* understand. I was there as well, remember? I protected us as best I could until your father arrived. You could have come to me at any time afterwards, but you didn't. I trusted you, as I had always trusted you, and I was wrong. I know that now. Drink your wine. From what I understand you aren't averse to alcohol.'

Jessie didn't want any wine. She pushed the glass away from her.

Josephine watched her daughter carefully, before saying sadly, 'Good girl. I knew you wouldn't drink that now you're sober. You're pregnant, aren't you?'

Jessie didn't answer her.

'Do you know whose it is?'

Jessie's usual arrogance came to the fore as she said haughtily, 'What difference does that make now? I don't want it. I'm only fifteen.'

Josephine sighed heavily. 'A word to the wise, Jessie love; your father is capable of a lot of things, as you know, but he would *never* be party to an abortion. You're carrying a life inside of you, girl, and we are Catholics. We celebrate a child. I think you need to remember that for the future. As the Bible says: as you sow, so shall you reap. The damage is done now, darling.'

Josephine opened up her arms and, as she hugged her young daughter tightly to her breast, she wondered at a God who could heap so much hurt on one household.

Book Four

Be not deceived, God is not mocked:
for whatsoever a man soweth, that shall he also reap

Galatians 6:7

For the wages of sin is death

Romans 6:23

Chapter Ninety-Two

2012

As Jessie Flynn walked out of a pub in Soho, the cold night air hit her. She staggered slightly in her high-heeled shoes, and leant back against the wall for a few seconds to steady herself. She was out of her nut, as per usual, and she was also bored – bored of the company she was in, bored of her life in general. Her father didn't seem bothered any more about her or her antics, something she was having trouble accepting. Even her mother was losing interest in her these days. After years of trying to buy her back into their life, controlling her with their cash, and attempting to make her take an interest in her son, her parents had suddenly stopped. She had a feeling she had won, but what she had actually won, she wasn't sure. In fact, she now felt much more like she was the one who had *lost* something important.

There was no more pretending from her father, no more acting like everything was OK between them. He wasn't rude as such, but he was clearly ashamed of her and the life she lived. That's exactly what she had always wanted; she had been determined to beat him, prove to him that she didn't care about anything, especially not him, or his precious reputation. Strangely, her dad turning away from her didn't make her feel as good as she had thought it would. In fact, her dad's attitude the last few times she had seen him had made her feel like *she* was the one in the wrong, that she was the bad bastard.

She sighed. She was too out of it to think about anything rationally. She rummaged through her handbag for a pack of cigarettes, and lit a Marlboro Light, toking on it deeply before blowing the smoke out into the night slowly. She was tired, but that wasn't anything new to her – she was always fucking tired lately. She spent more time out of her flat than she did inside it. She loved being in company, enjoying herself. Life was too short – her own father had shown her the truth of that. She had learnt at a young age the value of a human life. She was far too young to settle down anyway.

She was also far too young for the man she was with tonight. He was boring the arse off her – all he talked about was himself. She heard the door open and knew that it was Jonny Parsons looking for her. He was so sure of himself, it wouldn't occur to him that she was with him for no other reason than he was a lowlife piece of shit. She didn't have the patience for him now, he was getting on her nerves big time. The idiot. He looked baffled and sorry for himself. She could see the wrinkles around his eyes and the flakiness of his skin – he was a real prize. Lately, she'd noticed that the more out of it she got, the more she seemed to see the truth of her situation and the life she lived. She was feeling more and more disgruntled by the day.

'What's going on, babe? For fuck's sake, I turned around and you were gone.'

Jessie rolled her eyes in annoyance. He was a real prick. Why hadn't she admitted that to herself before now? He was on the wrong side of forty, he was overweight, he dressed like a fucking extra from *The Sopranos* and he talked like a fucking special guest on *The Jeremy Kyle Show*. He was a complete fucking embarrassment. She stepped away from him quickly, hating that he was too stupid to take the hint that she didn't want to associate with him any more. She had sussed out that her main attraction for him was her father – all he wanted from her was an in.

'I'm not your fucking *babe*, or anyone else's, you fucking moron. Who says "babe" in this day and age, for fuck's sake? Have you heard yourself? You sound like a reject from the eighties. Fuck off and leave me alone.'

Jonny Parsons was really drunk *and* stoned, although he wasn't capable of any kind of lucid conversation at the best of times. Jessie Flynn was starting to get on his tits. He had invested time and money in this arrogant little bitch, and she had the nerve to talk to him like he was a fucking corner boy? She was without any kind of reputation, she had fucked over more people than a high-street bank, and she had nothing going for her other than her name. Who the fuck did she think she was? She had a bad attitude and she talked to people like they were fucking idiots. She didn't seem to understand that she wasn't exactly a fucking prize herself. She was a whore – that was all she was and all she would ever be.

'Fuck *you*, Jessie Flynn. Just who the fuck do you think you are? I've fucking bankrolled you, lady, and don't you ever forget that. I won't be made a cunt of, especially not by a fucking no-mark like you.'

Jessie sighed dramatically; she was actually enjoying herself immensely. 'I think you and I both know the truth of this situation. We both know that I am far better than you, Jonny. That's what is bothering you.'

She could see her words hit home; she wasn't going to let him get the better of her without a fight. Well, that suited her fine. She liked a good fight, she liked to get a reaction. It just proved to her that she was right – all men were bastards and not worth her time or effort.

'If you really want to know the truth, Jonny, I think you're what is commonly known as a fucking moronic imbecile. I've had better conversations at bus stops with glue sniffers. So do me a favour and fuck off, will you?'

Jonny Parsons was not a man to take anything off a woman. A coward by nature, he didn't think twice about raising his hand to a female. Jessie Flynn's words were like a red rag to a bull – he was never going to let her treat him like a mug. Grabbing Jessie by her throat, he forced her up against the wall and, taking his fist back ready to use it, he said angrily, 'Don't you talk to me like that, you fucking whore. I don't take that shit off anyone, especially not from a fucking tramp like you.'

Jessie was laughing at him now, enjoying the drama and violence no end. 'Go on then, Jonny, I fucking *dare* you. Hit me. Go on, big man. Give it your best shot.'

Jonny Parsons could see the need in her face; she wanted a fight, she wanted a scene, and suddenly he wasn't sure he wanted to be a part of that. As drunk as he was, he knew this could only bring him untold aggravation. She was a Flynn, after all – Michael's daughter – and that fact alone was enough to sober him up, and remind him of why he had sought her out in the first place. She was even more fucked up than he had believed and, from what he had heard, she was a real fucking headcase. But she wasn't worth dying for.

He threw her away from him angrily, aware that she wanted him to hurt her. She would always insist on being the star of her own show. It was pathetic. She was a good-looking young woman, but she was dangerous and vindictive. A deadly combination.

'You destructive fucking bitch, you *want* me to hit you, don't you? You want me to hurt you, stoop down to your level. But I wouldn't give you the satisfaction. You're not worth a fucking slap – you're not worth the aggravation.'

He walked away from her unsteadily, and Jessie watched him warily. She had asked for that, she had pushed him too far. It was what she did. She pushed everyone to the limit. She loathed people like him, who saw her as nothing more than a stepping stone into her father's life, who thought that, by fucking her, they would somehow get Michael Flynn into the bargain. It grieved her, knowing that her only real value as a person was her name. She leant back against the wall once more and, closing her eyes tightly, she breathed in the cold night air for a few minutes, steadying her heartbeat, and trying to calm her nerves.

If only they knew the truth – that she was the kiss of death where her father was concerned. He loathed the men that she attracted; he saw them for the pieces of shit they really were. She did too, if she was really honest with herself. Not that she let that stop her, of course. She went out of her way to humiliate her father – he deserved everything he got.

She looked at her watch, a gold Rolex that had been a birthday present from her *loving* parents. If anything, it had been a bribe. Her mum and dad had tried to make her feel they loved her and cared about her, but it was a crock of shit. As long as her son was in her mum and dad's care, she could do what she liked and, in return for her son, her old man would happily bankroll her and her lifestyle. Jake was her parents' second chance at parenthood. He was the son they could never have, the golden boy, the heir apparent. Her dad had forced her to have her baby. The big Catholic, who saw abortion as tantamount to murder – and who would know more about that than her dad? But what they couldn't do was make her settle down, embrace her role as mother and pretend that she had learnt her lesson.

She closed her eyes tightly; she mustn't think about any of that now. It was pointless. She didn't want to look after her little lad anyway, so why did she let it bother her so much? She had handed him over to them willingly, glad to have someone else take the responsibility for her. It had been a fair exchange.

It was just after eleven, and she wasn't going to waste the rest of the night thinking about things she couldn't change. Flagging down a black cab, she climbed inside its warmth eagerly, making herself comfortable on the leather seat as she travelled back to East London, glad that the cab driver wasn't the usual fucking chatterbox. There was nothing worse than a cab driver with a loose mouth and too many stories to tell. It was irritating, especially when they tried to tell her how they knew all the Faces in London, particularly her dad. She saw the way they watched her in the mirror and knew they couldn't understand for the life of them how her father could let her live the way she did.

She jumped out of the cab at a pub she frequented in Upney, pleased that she had made it there in such good time. All she wanted to do was score and, if nothing interesting was going on, she would go home and sleep.

Her father had presented her with a lovely flat in Canary Wharf; it was the envy of everyone she knew. It *was* gorgeous – it had fabulous views across the river, and it was furnished to the highest standards; she would have expected nothing less from her dad. Like everything else in his life, he thought that if it cost a fortune then it must be good. She hated the place. It was another reminder of her father's hold over her. It wasn't in her name so she was no more than a lodger. It was hers only so he would know where she was living, just like he paid her a weekly wage so he could keep her within his orbit. Everything her parents did had an ulterior motive.

She slipped inside the public house, breathing in the familiar smell of sweat and stale beer. She saw the dealer she was looking for standing at the bar, and she made her way over to him quickly. It was late, and the place was nearly empty.

Georgie Burns smiled at her, displaying his gold teeth. It had been a slow night, and Jessie Flynn was always a good spender. She bought in bulk and paid cash, and that guaranteed her a very warm welcome. With his gold teeth and expensive dreads, Georgie looked every inch the bad man. In the real world, he had a degree in Sociology and his parents were both teachers. He had grown up in a nice house in North London with two sisters and an overweight Labrador called Bubbles. Now he was a dealer because it was the only way he could earn himself a decent living, pay his mortgage, and cover his two daughters' school fees. His wife was a woman who needed a good wage coming in; she liked the finer things in life. She was also more than willing to turn a blind eye to her husband's activities.

'Hello, Jessie. You looking for me, girl?'

Jessie smiled. She genuinely liked Georgie – he was a nice bloke and one of the few men in her life who had never tried to take advantage of her.

'Of course I am, Georgie. I wouldn't come inside this shithole otherwise, would I?'

They laughed together, and Georgie motioned to the barmaid for drinks. 'Agreed. So, what you after tonight?'

'Just the usual.' She glanced around her. 'It's empty in here tonight. I'm amazed you're still here.'

Georgie shrugged with irritation. 'Nothing going on anywhere, girl. I was just on my way home.' He passed her a large JD and Coke, and she swallowed it down quickly.

'Soho is the same. Dead as a fucking doornail.'

Georgie laughed at her delightedly. 'You should have gone clubbing. It's a week night, for fuck's sake.'

Jessie grinned. 'I know. But I didn't feel like it tonight. How much do I owe you?'

Ten minutes later she left the pub, and made her way towards Upney station. It was a few minutes' walk. There were usually plenty of minicabs outside the station, and she climbed into the back seat of the first taxi as usual, pleased that she knew the cab driver a little. He had driven her home before, so they chatted amiably together until they arrived at her apartment building.

She paid him, and then walked quickly towards her home. As she was about to unlock the main door that led into the lift area of the flats, she heard someone calling her name. Turning towards the sound of the voice, she expected to see someone she knew, someone like her who was always on the lookout for company, but the man she saw was a complete stranger. Before she could say another word, she felt something come into contact with her skull.

It was all over in seconds.

Chapter Ninety-Three

'Do you know what, Michael Flynn? If I didn't know any better I would think you were trying to annoy me now.' Josephine was joking, but the underlying question in her voice was clear.

Michael sighed. He hated all this ducking and diving, but it was a necessary evil – there was no other way to handle his wife. These days Josephine couldn't cope with the truth. She was quite happy living in her little dream world. Sometimes it could be very wearing. *He* had to live in the real world – it was how he earned his living.

'I just want to know if you think I should warn this Jonny bloke off, Josephine. I know that Jessie has been seeing him and, from what I can gather, he's another complete fucking waster.'

Josephine sat down on her bed. She wasn't sure what she should say – as much as Jessie's lifestyle disappointed her, she wasn't going to do anything that would alienate her daughter completely. She didn't want to be the bad guy – that was Michael's job.

She didn't look at her husband as she said quietly, 'What have you heard about this bloke, then?'

Michael snorted in derision. This was always the way – Josephine left him to find out everything of relevance where their daughter was concerned, then acted as if she was not expecting to hear what he told her.

'Well, for starters, he's forty-odd, has a wife and four kids and he's a druggie. A cokehead to be exact and a small-time dealer, who thinks he's a fucking big villain. And our Jessie is bankrolling him.'

Josephine put her head into her hands; she wasn't shocked at her husband's words, she was just disappointed in her daughter's choice of man. Why she felt so dismayed she didn't know – it was the same old story time and time again.

'Oh, let her get on with it, Michael. Don't interfere. She's promised to come and have tea with little Jake on Sunday. I'll see how she is then.'

The subject was closed and Michael knew it. 'Well, I'll be seeing her tomorrow anyway, Josephine. It's pay day.'

Josephine didn't answer. She knew that Michael detested paying his daughter just to keep his eye on her. If it was left to *him* she wasn't so sure he would still bother. It was all for her, to keep Jessie as close as she could.

Michael put his arm around his wife's shoulders and hugged her to him. His daughter had broken his heart, but she had given him her son, he had salvaged that much.

'How is the little man, anyway? Did he enjoy his school trip? Where did they go? To a farm, wasn't it?' Michael's grandson was his life; he adored the child.

'Yeah, he loved it, Michael. He was full of it when he got home. He's clever, you know, a real shrewdie. Six years old and he can already read anything. His teacher reckons he's well ahead of the other kids in his year.'

Michael was pleased. He knew his grandson was a one-off, now it seemed that the school was of the same opinion. Jake was a right little character.

'I said that, didn't I? He is a real fucking brainiac. He's always been ahead of the other kids. Look at how early he was with his counting and reciting things.'

Josephine basked in her husband's joy. Jake had always been quick off the mark. She was pleased he was showing such talent. 'Well, the school thinks he has real potential, so we need to make sure that he gets all the encouragement he needs.'

'A done deal, darling, you know that. Why don't you come downstairs with me and have a glass of wine? I could do with something to mellow me out a bit. I'm tired, but I'm not sleepy, if that makes sense?'

But Josephine was already shaking her head at his words, and Michael swallowed down his annoyance. Josephine rarely left her rooms these days. She went to the kitchen to cook occasionally, or to see Jessie, if she deigned to visit, but that was about it. She spent most of her life inside her bedroom and she had not ventured outside the house for years. Even the garden was off limits to her these days.

'Bring the bottle of wine up here, Michael. I need to get myself sorted out.'

She looked around her, as if she had important things to do. It was her usual reaction, and Michael wasn't going to say anything to challenge her. He got up from the bed slowly, pretending, as always, that he didn't notice the clutter everywhere, the boxes of rubbish that she surrounded herself with. Smiling easily at his wife, he said gently, 'I fancy a nice glass of red. You OK with that, darling?'

Josephine smiled back, grateful that her husband was always so kind to her, so very understanding. She saw how hard it was for him. 'That sounds good to me, Michael. I love a nice red.' As he opened the bedroom door, she had a sudden urge to say something else. 'I'm so sorry, Michael. I wish more than anything that I could make everything all right for us. You do know that, don't you?'

He turned back towards his wife and saw the sorrow on her lovely face. She was still a real beauty, still the only woman he had ever wanted. ''*Course* I know that. You're the love of my life, Josephine, always will be. Now, let me go and get the wine. I feel like spending some quality time with my lovely wife.' He winked at her saucily, then he left the room.

She watched him go and sighed. She had never wanted anyone else since the first time she had clapped eyes on him. She had always put him before everyone else in her life, even her daughter, and she always would. He was everything to her, and that would never change.

Michael came back with the wine and two Waterford crystal glasses. She followed him obediently out to her balcony; she knew he liked to see her in the fresh air. She sat down at the wrought-iron table, and took a large sip of the wine her husband had poured for her.

'It's chilly out here tonight, girl.'

'I know. I was out here earlier on. It's always cold in the evenings.' Josephine looked at her husband; he was still a very handsome man. 'Will you do me a favour, Michael? Will you ask our Jessie if she is really going to come on Sunday? Only Jake is expecting her, and I don't want him to be disappointed. Waiting all day and then she doesn't bother to show up.'

Michael nodded. He knew only too well what his daughter was capable of. 'I'll ask, but you know what she's like. She's so fucking unreliable. The only time I can guarantee her presence is when she picks up her money. Funny how she never sleeps in on a Thursday, isn't it?'

Josephine didn't respond to that; she knew how angry Michael could get over Jessie.

Michael sipped his wine, savouring the taste. He was looking over the gardens; he had turned the outside lights on earlier, and he was enjoying the view. So much had gone into making the gardens look beautiful, but his wife didn't seem to notice them any more. It was so sad. She took no pleasure in anything these days. How could she? All she did was sit out the days – and that was *all* she was capable of doing. She was unable to sleep at night, unable to enjoy her life in any meaningful way. His lovely bride, his Josephine, had gradually lost the knack for living life, and she didn't seem to want to find it again.

Josephine sighed; she missed her daughter so much, but there was no way Jessie was coming home again. She avoided them all like the plague, especially little Jake. Josephine blamed herself for her daughter's actions. Jessie had needed her, and she had not been there for her daughter – she had put her husband first and done what *he* wanted.

'Do you think we were wrong to make her have little

Jake? She was so young, Michael.' She watched her husband as he shook his head in swift and angry denial.

'How can you even think like that, Josephine? He is a lovely little lad. If we had let her have her way he wouldn't even fucking *be* here. For all her fucking antics, and her fucking determination to act like he doesn't exist, the day will come when she will realise that she did the right thing by having her baby, and that *we* did the right thing by making sure she gave the child a chance at life. She needed to understand the seriousness of what had happened to her. She needed to learn that having a child isn't a fucking game. As a Catholic, she had only one choice open to her. There would be no abortions in this fucking house, I made that perfectly clear to her.'

He was getting angry, so he drank some of his wine, and willed himself to calm down. His daughter's treatment of her son still rankled with him. 'The worst thing is, Josephine, I actually thought it might make her grow up, you know? I thought it might make her realise that eventually everything has to be paid for. But I was wrong. All it did was drive her further away.'

Josephine busied herself lighting a cigarette, even though she knew that Michael hated her smoking. She didn't know how to react to her husband's words. Michael was always so sure of everything, but she wasn't as sure as he was about her daughter. She leant forward in her chair and, looking directly at her husband, she said seriously, 'Do you know what I think, Michael? I think the night the Cornels came here ruined her. It was such a big trauma for all of us, but she never seemed to get over it, did she? She just went off the rails afterwards, and then with the baby on top of everything else, it was all too much for her. She was a mother at sixteen years old, that's a really big event for anyone, Michael, let alone a young girl like Jessie.'

Michael laughed sarcastically. He had no intention of making excuses for his daughter. She was the one who had got herself pregnant, and it wasn't even as if she had known who the culprit was. It could have been anyone. Josephine's problems had been made worse by her daughter's actions, and young Jessie was the main reason that Josephine couldn't bring herself to leave her home any more. There was no way he was going to sit here tonight and pretend anything different. He had seen first-hand the toll his daughter's lifestyle had had on his wife. Tonight he wasn't in the mood to overlook it.

'You listen to me, Josephine. I don't care what anyone says – she might have had a fright that night, and I get that – but that wasn't any reason to carry on the way she fucking did. She had never, *ever* in her life had anything other than love and care from us. There are kids in this world who are living in war zones, who have seen their families murdered, and they get over it. Our Jessie's fucking problem is that she let one fucking night cancel out all the years of love we had given her beforehand. I tell you now, and I'm being honest with you, I think she would have gone to the bad anyway. Look at how she's living now! How she's been living for years. Drink, drugs, fucking men. That is a *lifestyle*, Josephine, a fucking choice she's made. I was talking to Tommy Ambrose the other week, six kids he has, and one of his sons is a fucking heroin addict. It's breaking his heart but, as he said, there's nothing he can do about it. The kid's a fucking waste of space, end of. Tommy said a very true thing to me; he reckons it's a kink in the boy's nature. Nothing could have prevented it from happening. The boy was destined to be a fucking junkie. I think that applies to our Jessie. She would have found her level, eventually, I honestly believe that. She looked like a fucking paraffin lamp last week, when she came to get her money. I was so ashamed of her. Her breath was so bad, I could smell it from six feet away. Her clothes were dirty – she had obviously slept in them – her legs were scabbed over, and covered in fresh bruises, so I knew she had fallen over at some point. Then she had the fucking nerve to snatch the money out of my hand as if she was doing *me* a favour by taking it. I tell you now, Josephine, it took all of my willpower to stop myself from telling her to fuck off, and aiming her out the door on the end of my fucking boot.'

Josephine had never once heard her husband talk like that about their daughter, and she knew, then and there, that he had been thinking like that for a long time.

'Oh, Michael, I'm so sorry to hear you talking like that about our Jessie. But I do know what you're saying and, as much as it pains me to say this, I think you're right.'

Michael laughed in derision at his wife's words; he was angrier than he had realised. Without thinking, he found himself shouting with temper, 'Have a fucking day off, will you, Josephine? For Christ's sake! She's a fucking walking nightmare. If it wasn't for you, I would have cut her off years ago.'

Josephine started to cry real tears then, her whole body

shaking with her sobs. Michael was out of his seat and kneeling before his wife in seconds. Holding her to him tightly, he held her as she cried bitterly, knowing that this was something she should have done a long time ago. He hated himself for saying what he had. He knew that his Josephine didn't want to hear the truth, but sometimes he really felt that she *needed* to hear it, needed to be dragged back into the real world, no matter how much that might hurt her.

Chapter Ninety-Four

Declan Costello was laughing loudly; he liked a good joke, and he also liked a drink in the afternoon. The new barmaid was a real comedienne. She could make a cat laugh. Shame she looked like a fucking Russian athlete – if she had the looks he would have been on her in nanoseconds. He was getting older now, and was still overweight but that didn't bother him too much, he had never been what anyone would ever call a looker. Many girls had tried to tie him down, but he had never let himself get caught. After a few weeks they bored him, even the really good-looking ones. He didn't want a life partner, never had.

He was waiting for Michael. It was Thursday, and that meant Michael would meet him in the private club they owned in East London by one o'clock at the latest. It was something they had done for years. Michael always liked to hear everything that was going on first-hand, and Declan was more than happy to oblige. He always gave Michael the lowdown on everything and everyone he dealt with. After Michael had nearly murdered him all those years ago, no one had been more amazed than him when Michael had brought him back into the fold, treating him as if nothing untoward had happened between them. It had been a real learning curve for him, and he had never forgotten it. Michael had only ever mentioned their contretemps once, on the day he had come round to his house just after he had finally left the hospital. After enquiring about his health, Michael had looked at him sadly, before saying, 'I never want us to fall out again, Declan. All I want is for *you* to keep your eye on the ball in the future. You were supposed to have my back, you were supposed to be making my life easier.'

Declan had been so grateful to be given another chance, he had sworn to prove himself worthy of Michael's kindness. He had never once forgotten his role, and he relished his position, realising how easily it could be taken from him if he ever fucked up again. His laziness, combined with his refusal to think for himself, had nearly cost him not just his livelihood, but also his life. It was a mistake he wouldn't make a second time.

He took a deep gulp of his beer, enjoying the icy coldness as it slipped down his throat. He was a very happy man, and that was something that he really valued these days. He had lived through the humiliation of Michael's attack, and that had been very hard for him; without Michael Flynn he was basically worth nothing.

He held up his empty glass to the barmaid, and she took it quickly, filling it up once more for him. The bar was empty; they had just had the whole place decorated, and it was odd to see it so clean-looking. But it still had the old-fashioned vibe to it; the men who frequented this place would not be comfortable otherwise.

He glanced towards the stairs. He had heard the door

opening, and he watched Michael Flynn walking down the stairway slowly. He was still a very handsome man. Michael had never put on any weight, he still had a good body on him. He would get better looking as he got older, the jammy fucker; some men were lucky like that.

'All right, Michael.' It was a greeting, not a question.

Michael smiled. 'All right, Declan. You're looking good, mate.'

Declan grinned with pleasure. 'I feel fine anyway. That's the main thing. Drink?'

The barmaid took the order, and Declan was amazed to see Michael Flynn drinking a large whisky so early in the day. '*Are* you all right, Michael?'

Declan's voice was genuinely worried, and Michael swallowed his drink down in one before answering him. 'It's my Jessie. She didn't turn up for her money. I know it's silly to worry, but she's never missed a Thursday before.'

He motioned to the barmaid for another drink, and she took his glass from him without a word. She refilled it and placed it on the bar in front of him. He smiled his thanks, noticing she wasn't the usual eyeful they employed.

'I don't know, Declan. It's not like her. I'm worried.'

Declan knew how fragile Michael's situation was regarding his only daughter. He suspected that young Jessie was probably shacked up with some piece of shit lowlife somewhere, but he knew better than to say that. Instead he took a drink of his beer, before saying easily, 'I'm sure she will turn up. You haven't got anything to worry about there, mate. She probably had a late night.'

Michael looked at his old friend. Declan was ageing before

his eyes. It didn't help that he dressed like a fucking Nigerian refugee. He always looked like he had got dressed in the dark. 'I suppose so. But Josephine wanted me to report back to her, and how can I do that now? I've sent someone round to her gaff. She won't like it, but who gives a fuck? I need to know she's OK.'

Declan didn't say anything. Jessie Flynn was notorious in their world. Her name was a byword for whoring. She had used up all her brownie points with her uncle Declan years ago. She disgusted him now. If she was *his* daughter he would have crippled her many moons ago, put a stop to her gallop then and there. She had slept with everyone they knew.

'Daughters, eh, Declan? A breed apart!'

Declan laughed gently. 'I wouldn't know, Michael. I never wanted kids, or a wife, come to that. You know me, mate. I never felt the urge to reproduce.'

Michael was laughing despite himself. 'I can't say I fucking blame you for that. Anyway, what's the score? I heard about the aggro in the lap-dancing club.'

Declan groaned theatrically, pleased to be changing the subject. 'If you had seen the bloke who caused it, you'd freak out. He was as old as the hills for a start, and the girl was all of nineteen. He had made the fatal mistake they make, of course – assumed that because he had been giving her money all night he owned her. Then, when her shift was over and she tried to leave, he kicked off. Typical city type, thinks the whole world owes him allegiance. Well, he got a fucking slap in the end – there was no talking to him. He's barred now, the wrinkled up old ponce.' Declan motioned for more drinks before saying craftily, 'I had to laugh, though, he was two grand down, and drunk as a coot, but he was a game old fucker, I'll give him that.'

Michael was laughing with him now. 'It always amazes me that they just don't get it.'

Declan picked up his fresh pint, drinking deeply, enjoying it. ''Course they don't get it, Michael. If they did we wouldn't earn a fucking bean!'

Chapter Ninety-Five

Hannah Flynn was listening to her arch-enemy with interest. Lana wasn't her favourite person, but she did oftentimes have a good insight into her daughter's life.

'I tell you, Hannah, my Josephine is getting worse. If it wasn't for that little boy I don't know what she would do.'

Hannah nodded slowly in agreement. Her daughter-in-law was not a bad girl; as the years had gone on, she had become quite attached to her. Josephine was weak, that was her problem. She had no backbone. Jessie's antics had been the last straw really. Her pregnancy had knocked them all for six, but it had broken Josephine. She had never recovered.

She had made her way round to Lana's because, for the first time ever, Jessie hadn't turned up at her house for a late lunch. She always came to her on a Thursday. Jessie saw her dad first, picked up her cash, and then she came straight to her nana's. Hannah made them lunch, and they chatted together. It was the highlight of her week. But today she hadn't shown up; that wasn't right. Jessie never missed their lunch together. She had tried her mobile over and over again, and nothing – it had just rung. She had come round to Lana's house in the end, hoping to find out something about her granddaughter. But it was obvious Lana knew even less than she did.

'Has anyone seen Jessie today?'

Lana shrugged. 'Not that I know of, Hannah. When does anyone ever see the mardy bitch? I could smack her face at times.'

Hannah sipped at her tea. She was aware that Jessie didn't really bother with her mum's family, and that pleased her usually. Nevertheless she still felt uncomfortable about Jessie being a no-show. As unreliable as Jessie could be, she always came round to her house on a Thursday. It was their little secret.

Chapter Ninety-Six

Jake was so boisterous and loud, Josephine could hear him even through the tightly shut French doors in her bedroom. He was tearing around the gardens as usual and, smiling to herself, she made her way out on to her balcony to watch him. His nanny, Dana, was chasing him, and he was easily getting away from her. She could see the glee on his face as he laughed loudly. Jake had such a lust for life. She saw him standing on the lawn, his hands on his hips. He looked so much like her Michael, she felt the sting of tears in her eyes. She thanked God every day that her grandson didn't look like whoever had fathered him. It would have been very hard to look at the child if he had nothing of his family in him.

Josephine sat down on the nearest chair and wiped a hand across her mouth. She hated to think like that, but she couldn't help herself. Jake meant the world to her and, even though she couldn't bring herself to do much with him, she made sure that inside the house he spent quality time with her. He was already questioning her lifestyle, asking her why she never took him to school, or went for a walk with him. He was always asking about his mum; he knew she should be around more, that his friends' mums were always there. He didn't have his mum, and he didn't have his nana there for him either. She couldn't be there for him – she couldn't leave the house, not even for her grandson. Jake was getting to an age where he was noticing these things.

She saw Dana pick her grandson up and swing him around. The girl was so good with him. She genuinely did care for the child.

Josephine could feel the erratic beating of her heart and the shortness of breath that heralded a panic attack. She was sweating profusely, unable to prevent it happening. Closing her eyes tightly, she concentrated on her breathing, taking deep breaths slowly and evenly, like the doctor had taught her. She felt the panic subsiding, and the terror left her body as quickly as it had arrived. Then she heard her name being called and, standing up, she saw that Jake was now down below her, on the patio, looking up at her balcony, his handsome face cross. He had his hands on his hips; she had been away with the fairies, and had not heard him calling her name.

'Really, Nana, it's not good enough, you know! I've been calling up to you for ages!'

As he stormed off, Dana looked up at her and shrugged, before following him into the house.

Josephine closed her eyes in distress. This was happening to her more and more lately; she seemed to be losing all sense of time and place. She saw her pack of cigarettes on the table, and she lit one quickly, drawing on it deeply. Then she smoked it slowly until the trembling in her body subsided once again.

Chapter Ninety-Seven

'So you're sure she wasn't there?'

Daniel Carter nodded. 'I let meself in, Michael, as you told me to. I'm telling you, there wasn't a soul in that flat. I searched everywhere. Jessie had definitely left the building.'

Michael expected as much; his big fear had been that she would be in there, but dead as a doornail. With her lifestyle, that wasn't exactly unheard of. 'OK. Thanks, Daniel. I appreciate it.'

Daniel Carter was heart-sorry that he couldn't put the man's mind at rest. 'I can ask about if you want, Michael? See where she is?'

Michael laughed bitterly. 'I've already done that. Thanks anyway, mate.' He watched Daniel leave the room and, sitting down behind his desk, he sighed heavily.

No one seemed to have clapped eyes on Jessie since last night. She had scored in Upney, then cabbed it back to her flat. After that, no one had seen or, more to the point, heard from her. Her mobile was permanently attached to her lughole, yet she hadn't used it in the hours since. The piece of shit she had been hanging about with was shitting bricks now. He had been dragged from his bed, and questioned by three very large men. But he had been telling the truth – he had gone on to a club, which had been verified. Michael knew she hadn't been nicked or he would have heard about it by now. He owned the local Filth, and they always contacted him immediately whenever she was arrested. Nevertheless he insisted that they check. But nothing. Jessie had disappeared off the face of the earth.

He tried her mobile again, but it just rang and rang. Where else could he look for his daughter? Jessie didn't know that her whereabouts were always reported to him; if she turned up somewhere, he knew about it. It was his way of looking out for her and checking out the men she socialised with. It was so fucking hard having to pretend to everyone around him that he didn't care about her life choices, knowing that if he interfered she would turn away from her mother completely and could cause problems for them and her little boy. She had him by the nuts.

Chapter Ninety-Eight

Josephine was listening to Jake as he chattered away to her. He was dressed for school, and she looked at him with pride; he was such a handsome boy.

'Dana's promised to take me to the park after school. I wish you would come with us, Nana. It's such fun. I like the swings best. But Dana says that's because I am such a fidget bucket!' He laughed with delight. 'I promise you, Nana, I will be a very good boy. I won't make too much noise.'

Josephine hugged him tightly and kissed his forehead. 'I think you and Dana will have a good time, Jake. You know your nana has lots of work to do. But I will see you when you get home, and you can tell me all about it.'

Jake looked at his nana intently for long moments, and Josephine could tell that he didn't believe her about having to work.

'OK, then. But I wish you would try to come with us sometimes.'

'I will, Jake. Now get along or you'll be late.'

He kissed her on the cheek, and she could hear him talking and fussing as he made his way down the stairs. She heard the front door slam, and sighed sadly; the house was so empty when he wasn't in it. It had always been far too big really. Michael loved it and, in her own way, so did she. It was a home fit for a large family; as Michael used to joke, many years ago, the Von Trapps would get lost in it. That was back when they had thought they would be banging out babies as and when they desired them, before the pain of disappointment had settled over them. That was a long time ago.

She stood up slowly, and made herself cross the large landing to the bedroom she had once shared with her husband. As she walked into the room, she was pleased to see that he was already wide awake. He was sitting up in bed, watching the news on TV. He had a large mug of black coffee in his hands, so she knew he had already been up and about for a while.

'I didn't hear you come in last night, Michael.'

She sat on the bed beside him, and he leant over to kiss her lightly on the lips. 'I was late in, Josephine. I didn't want to wake you up, darling.'

'Did you talk to Jessie? She hasn't called since Tuesday morning. How did she seem yesterday? Did you ask her about Sunday?'

Michael Flynn looked at his lovely wife, who he loved more than anything else in the world. She was already in full make-up as always, and dressed in a very fetching cream-coloured silk dressing gown. It was expensive, he could see that, and it looked wonderful on her. Lana must have picked it out for her. She had always taken such good care of herself; the last few years, it was all she ever did. It was surreal, seeing her fully made-up night or day, her hair and her make-up perfect, as if she was going somewhere. His life was fraught with so many problems; sometimes, like now, he resented her for that. But he wouldn't say anything. It was too late.

'I didn't see her, love. I had a lot on yesterday, and I didn't hang about too long. To be honest, I wasn't in the mood for her anyway.'

Josephine smiled at her husband gently. 'I was hoping you'd seen her. But you know Jessie – she'll turn up at some point.'

Michael nodded his agreement. 'Like a fucking bad penny, she is. Anyway, we shouldn't let her bother us. She knows where we are.'

Josephine didn't like her husband's attitude but she didn't comment. 'I wish she'd call me though, Michael. We talk regularly, you know that.'

He grabbed his wife's hand, and squeezed it tightly. She had such small hands and feet, she was so fragile.

'Don't worry, Josephine. Knowing our Jessie, she's probably shacked up with some lowlife she met last night. It wouldn't be the first time, would it?'

Josephine didn't reply; this was upsetting her now. She didn't need her husband to remind her of her daughter's failings. She pulled her hand roughly away from Michael's, and he knew he had hurt her feelings. But he couldn't tell her the truth, that Jessie had dropped off the radar and no one seemed to know where she was.

'I better get myself back, Michael, I have a few things I need to sort out today.'

Michael felt his anger rising at Josephine's words, but he swallowed it down as always. All his wife actually did, day in and day out, was repair her make-up, paint her nails and re-arrange her boxes of crap. For the first time in years, he felt he needed her, wanted her to be like she was in the old days, when he could tell her anything, and she would advise him, listen to him. He didn't like having to admit to himself that his lovely wife Josephine was like a stranger to him these days. She would choose her old crap over him, over Jake, over Jessie, if she had to. He had done his best to see his wife happy; now he wasn't so sure he had done the right thing by her. All he had accomplished was to allow Josephine to live a life without any meaning. He had stood back and let it happen. The doctors had given her pills, but no one challenged her or told her that her life was odd, that *she* was odd. The psychiatrist talked to her for hours in her rooms; he paid the fucker a small fortune, but Josephine just got worse. Looking at her now, he wondered how he could have let it happen. When she had first started bulk-buying food, he should have put his foot down then. They rarely made love any more, and they talked only in generalities of things that were of no real importance. All they had in common was Jake.

He could see Josephine watching him warily, and he wanted to grab hold of her, drag her into bed with him, and give her a serious seeing to, like in the old days. But he didn't feel he could do that to her any more. She wasn't the old Josephine, the woman he had married – this was a woman who lived inside herself, whose every waking moment was lived in a vacuum.

'Are you happy, Josephine? I mean *really* happy?'

He could see the confusion on her face at his question,

and he wanted to slap her, wanted to make her react to him without thinking it through first. 'Answer me! It's not a hard question, is it? It's a simple yes or no.'

Josephine looked down at her hands, unable to look her husband in the face. 'Of course I'm happy, Michael. What a thing to ask.'

Michael put his finger under her chin, and he made her look him in the eyes, before he said seriously, 'I don't think you are, Josephine. I don't think you have been happy for a long time. Not really.'

Josephine looked at her husband, saw the sadness in his expression, and the way he was waiting expectantly for her answer. 'I am happy, Michael.'

She meant it. He smiled because he knew she was telling him the truth – as she saw it. 'Good. That's all I wanted to know.'

Chapter Ninety-Nine

Jessie was frightened and cold. She was also starving, which amazed her because she didn't think food would be high up on her priority list. But it was. She didn't eat that regularly anyway but, for the first time in years, her stomach felt empty; the hunger like a gnawing pain inside her. Her arms and legs were tied, and it was so painful; every time she tried to move her body, a burning pain shot through her limbs.

She was terrified. It was so very dark. She felt tears running down her face, and she forced herself to stop them. She wasn't going to cry, that wasn't sensible; she couldn't afford to let her emotions get the better of her. She was going to keep her wits about her, and try and work out what the situation actually was. If this was a kidnapping, which she doubted, whoever had organised it had better take the money and run as fast as possible. Her dad wouldn't let something like this go unpunished – he would take it very personally, see it as an act of treason against him, and all he stood for.

The pain was shooting through her skull again, and it was so acute she closed her eyes and bit down on her bottom lip, trying to ride it out. It was a losing battle – the pain was too intense. She felt herself losing consciousness again, and she didn't try to fight it this time. Her head was aching so badly, but at least it had stopped bleeding.

She embraced the sleep that washed over her; she was glad of it, even though she knew it wasn't natural.

Chapter One Hundred

'I have already got people out there searching for her, the Old Bill included, useless fuckers that they are. But I swear on my fucking eyesight, when I find out what's gone down, I will fucking kill the bastards responsible with my bare hands. How dare they! How dare anyone think they could touch my daughter and live to tell the fucking tale!'

Michael was stalking around the office of the nightclub in Ilford. He was so angry he couldn't even breathe properly. There was no doubt in his mind now; his Jessie was missing. It was over three days, and that wasn't normal, even for her. She was a fucking nuisance, living her life like a fucking hippy but, as much as she thought she was some kind of enigma, she was actually very predictable. Not that he would ever explain that to her, the dozy little mare. It suited him for her to think she was a fucking maverick, a fucking independent woman. As if. Without him and his protection she would have gone under a long time ago. She had more problems than the euro and, in real life, if she had to sort things out for herself, she would be seriously fucked. But she was still his baby, and he couldn't turn his back on her.

Declan Costello watched Michael as he stalked around the

small office; it was unusual to see him so flustered. He always kept his cool, no matter what happened. But this was different, Declan understood that; this was about his kid.

Declan sat back in his chair, heart-sorry for his friend. 'It can't be a kidnapping, Michael – you'd have heard from them by now. It's fucking mental! No one can just disappear like that.'

Michael sighed heavily. 'That's just it though, Declan – they can.'

Declan knew what Michael was trying to say, and he shook his huge head violently in denial. Who would bother to kill Jessie? People disappeared, that was a given, but there was always a reason.

'Fuck off, Michael! Will you listen to yourself? Why on earth would anyone want to kill young Jessie? It's ludicrous.'

Michael Flynn stood in front of his old friend, and he said honestly, 'Think about it, Declan. You know what she's like. I want to kill her myself half the time. She's got a fresh mouth on her, she talks to people like they're shit. I warned her time and again that, one day, if she wasn't careful, her big mouth would get her into real trouble. She pushes everything, pushes everyone.'

Declan laughed. 'Can you hear yourself, Michael? Ninety-nine per cent of the population couldn't kill a fucking earwig unless they had to. It's why people like us can do what we do. But you have to remember that there is no one on this planet who would dare to touch a hair on your daughter's head. She knows that herself – why do you think she acts like she does? For all her fucking arrogance, she knows that without your name she wouldn't last five minutes.'

Declan could see the real fear in Michael's face, could almost feel the worry the man had for his only child. It wasn't fair. He didn't deserve any of this. Michael Flynn, for all his faults, was basically a decent man, a good man where it counted. Even *he* acknowledged that, and he had been on the receiving end of the man's temper.

'You haven't even had a stand-off with anyone for years, Michael, so this can't be about payback, can it?'

Michael could see that Declan was speaking sense, but it didn't take the fear out of his chest. He had traced her calls, and there had been nothing for days to or from her number. Her 'friends' – and he used the word loosely – had been as baffled as he was about her whereabouts.

The office door opened, and Michael smiled nastily as Jonny Parsons was pushed into the room roughly. He tripped over his own feet, and just about stopped himself from falling flat on his face. He was absolutely terrified; that was more than evident to both the other men in the small room. The man looked what he was: a cheap imitation, a wannabe gangster, a fucking thug.

Jonny looked at Michael Flynn's hard face, and his heart stopped in his chest. He hadn't realised the power that the man radiated, the menace that surrounded him. This was what he had wanted: a meeting with Michael Flynn. It was why he had romanced Jessie, but he had not understood until now exactly what that entailed.

Michael Flynn towered over him and, in the confines of the room, the man looked almost demonic. It was easy to see why people were so wary of crossing him, why he had accumulated so much power over the years, why he was so respected by everyone around him. He was the main man throughout Europe, the boss of everyone around him, and that was not an easy task.

He could see Declan Costello sitting behind the desk like a big, overweight leprechaun, all smiles and expectation. Declan was watching him closely, waiting to see what was going to happen and, by the looks of him, he was going to enjoy it.

Jonny Parsons felt trapped. He just stood there like a fool, unable to talk or move.

Michael was looking at the man who had slept with his young daughter, his only child. He wasn't impressed with what he was seeing; in fact, he was disgusted. Jonny Parsons was forty if he was a day, his hair was cut like a teenager's, he was dressed in cheap knock-offs – even the man's Rolex was a cheap imitation.

Worst of all was that Jonny Parsons was without any kind of decency. The man was a complete and utter coward. Yet his daughter had taken this man into her bed. It galled him that she could lower herself to this level.

He poked his finger hard into the man's chest, making him lose his balance once more. He could feel the terror coming off him in waves, and he was glad. At least he had reason to let the man know what he truly thought of him.

'I'm looking for my daughter, Jessie Flynn. I assume you remember her? Do you know where she is?'

Jonny Parsons' mouth was so dry he wasn't sure if he could actually form any words.

Michael was enjoying every second of Jonny's discomfort, and he bellowed into his face suddenly, 'Are you fucking deaf? You useless cunt! I just asked you a fucking question.'

Jonny Parsons was shaking his head in denial, wondering how he had ever thought that, by using Jessie Flynn as a stepping stone, he could have somehow gained an entry into this man's world. He must have been off his head to have even contemplated it.

'No, Mr Flynn, I swear to you. I haven't heard from her.'

Michael sighed. The man was a fucking complete imbecile. What the fuck was Jessie thinking about? Didn't she even *look* at the men she slept with?

'You haven't spoken to her or called her – I already fucking know that. I just want to know if you've seen her, or spoken to anyone who has?'

Jonny Parsons was shaking his head vehemently. 'No. Nothing. Not a word. I ain't heard anything about her from anyone either.'

Michael turned around, and looked at Declan in abject disbelief. 'What a fucking Casanova this cunt is, Declan. He fucks them and leaves them by the sounds of it.'

Jonny was in deep trouble, and he didn't know what he could do to help himself. If he had any information about Jessie he would happily tell her father.

Michael shook his head sadly, and Declan knew what was coming next. The first punch lifted Jonny Parsons off his feet, and opened up a large gash in his right eyebrow. Michael watched the man go down. He collapsed on to the floor and, curling himself up into a tight ball, he tried to protect his head with his arms. Michael looked at the man for a few seconds, then used his feet and, as he kicked his daughter's bedmate over and over again, he was glad to be able to vent some of his anger. He had sussed Jonny Parsons out, knew the man had bragged about his relationship with his daughter, had seen her as his passport into the big time. He wasn't the first idiot to think that and, unfortunately, he probably wouldn't be the last. But it felt good hurting him, reminding the man of who he was dealing with.

Declan watched everything with his usual calm. He had been on the other end of Michael's anger himself, and he knew how violent it could be. Michael needed to vent his spleen – it would do him the world of good.

Declan waited until Michael's anger was spent before he stepped in. Jonny Parsons was a bloody mess and, pulling Michael away from the man firmly, he sat him down behind the desk. Then, going to the office door, he opened it and called in a couple of the bouncers. They knew the score as soon as they stepped into the room, and they picked up Jonny Parsons without any words needing to be spoken.

Declan shut the door behind them and, turning to Michael, he said carefully, 'Feeling better, are we? Now, we need to think about this logically, Michael.'

Michael sat forward in the old typist's chair and, holding his head in his hands, he said brokenly, near to tears, 'That's just it, there's *no* fucking logic to it, Declan. That's the problem. I know in my guts that this is fucking serious. This is fucking personal. This is not about my Jessie. How can it be? You said it yourself. Who would fucking dare to touch my daughter?'

Declan could see the man's point, but he still wasn't convinced. Michael Flynn had the Colombians behind him; there wasn't anyone who had the guts to take him on. He was too protected, too respected. He ran his empire fairly and squarely, and he made sure that everyone he was involved with earned so much they were loyal to him. Michael Flynn entertained some of the most dangerous men in the world. It was terrible to see him like this, so vulnerable, so worried.

'Look, Michael, what if she's shacked up somewhere, oblivious to all that's going on? You know what she's like.'

Michael looked at his old friend, and he sighed heavily. 'I hope you're right, Declan, I really do. But something is telling me, inside, that's not the case. She's in trouble. I just know it.'

Chapter One Hundred and One

Jake was all smiles, his happiness contagious. Josephine was watching him drawing pictures and, as he finished each one, he showed them to her with a flourish.

'That's you and Granddad eating your dinner!'

Josephine couldn't help but laugh – he had captured them perfectly. She looked at the drawing and saw herself and her husband sitting on her bed together, with plates on their laps. Then she saw that Jake had drawn himself on a chair all alone, watching them. He wasn't smiling. He looked sad.

'Why do you look so sad, Jake?'

He shrugged nonchalantly. 'I'm waiting for my mummy, of course. But she didn't come.'

Josephine felt so sorry for her little lad. 'I told you, Jake. Your mummy has to work a lot.'

He carried on drawing, but he didn't answer her. She could slap her daughter sometimes for the worry she caused. And now she was missing, and it was worrying them all. She had heard nothing from her daughter for nearly four days and, like Michael, Josephine was beginning to be seriously concerned.

Dana came into the room beaming, and when Josephine

saw the way that Jake reacted to her, she felt a stab of jealousy.

'Come on, you. It's your bath time, mister.'

Jake got up from the floor, abandoning his drawing without a thought. 'Can I play with my toys?'

Dana picked him up effortlessly. He was a big child for his age, but Dana didn't seem to notice that; she still treated him like a baby. ''Course you can! They are all there waiting for you!'

'See you later, Nana!'

Josephine waved to him, and watched as they left the room together. She knelt down on the rug, and busied herself tidying his paper and pencils away. Then she carefully picked up his sweet wrappers – fun-size Snickers and a Milky Way – and folded both of them neatly, before placing them into one of the boxes scattered around the room.

Glancing at herself in the mirror of her dressing table, she checked over her appearance. She looked perfect, which pleased her. She picked up her lipstick from the dressing table, and ran it over her lips quickly. The action alone calmed her, made her feel better in herself. She gained a lot of comfort from doing familiar things. Her doctor said it was about control, but she couldn't see that herself. She just liked the feeling of ease it gave her; there was a lot to be said for order, having a routine. She couldn't cope without it.

She sat down in her chair once more and glanced around, mentally counting the boxes in her room, and running through their contents in her head.

She picked up her glass of red wine from the small antique table beside her chair and sipped it, savouring its warmth.

She didn't see clutter around her or chaos – what she saw was her possessions, things she loved and needed. Today she needed the comfort more than ever. But no matter how hard she tried to calm herself and tell herself that Michael was right, she didn't need to worry, her daughter's disappearance *did* worry her – greatly. She knew that Jessie wouldn't do this to her mother without good reason.

Chapter One Hundred and Two

DI Timothy Branch was annoyed. He had been told in no uncertain terms to use every resource at his disposal to locate Michael Flynn's daughter. Easier said than done – the girl had been around the turf more times than a Grand National winner.

He had put the word out, but she was nowhere to be found. He wasn't relishing telling that to Michael Flynn – the man seemed to think he could somehow conjure the girl up from thin air. If only it was that easy. He now had the unenviable task of admitting to the man who had been paying him shedloads of money for a lot of years, that he couldn't help him. Jessie Flynn was, without doubt, a missing person.

Michael Flynn's minions had already questioned everyone in his daughter's orbit – and not in a nice way. Branch's men had been called out to disturbances by concerned citizens many times over the last few days. He had been expected to ensure that the people concerned didn't have to deal with the police on top of everything else. Not that any of the victims were willing to press charges, but it was still very stressful. It had been a hard few days for him in particular.

He had been forced to show his hand as a bent copper. He hadn't meant it to be common knowledge. But what could he do about it? As Michael Flynn had so forcefully pointed out to him, this was what he had been paid so handsomely for – even he couldn't argue with that.

Chapter One Hundred and Three

When Jessie opened her eyes again, she knew immediately that there was someone else in the room with her. She tried to steady her breathing which was so loud in the darkness. Then she realised that her hands were free, she wasn't tied up any more. She tried to sit up, but she couldn't manage that immediately. Her legs were still shackled and she was tied to the bed. As she became more aware of her circumstances she felt relief that she had been given at least a modicum of freedom. It took her a few minutes to finally drag herself into a sitting position; she was in a lot of pain – her arms and back felt like they had been broken.

'Who's there? I know you're there.' She could hear the tremor in her voice and she hated herself for her weakness. 'You fucking coward! Talk to me! I can't go anywhere, can I? I can't hurt you, can I?'

She listened intently, trying to penetrate the darkness. 'My dad will kill you for this. You know that, don't you?'

She could hear the person breathing near to her, they were only a few feet away. It was a man, she knew that much, and he clearly wasn't bothered by her words. She could feel that he was totally in control of the situation and of her. She was scared, but she couldn't bow down, she couldn't admit to her fears.

'I know you're there. I know you're near me. I can hear you, for fuck's sake.' Her voice was strong, and that pleased her, even as she braced herself for an attack. But it didn't come. She wasn't sure what she was supposed to do, what she was supposed to say. She lowered her voice, and said huskily, 'I'm starving and I'm thirsty. I had one bottle of water and that's gone.'

She was straining to hear something, but there wasn't anything except the quiet breathing. She lay back down; she was weak, and she was wasting her time trying to get a reaction. She hoped she wasn't going to be starved to death, just left alone to die in the darkness, that was such a terrifying thought. This couldn't be it for her, surely? She huddled into the mattress and, as she curled up, she heard the clinking of the chains around her ankles, felt the weight of them and, for the first time in the whole of her life, she felt completely alone.

'You really are your father's fucking daughter.'

The voice was low, it had a cockney twang to it. It was the voice of an older man. But this person, whoever he was, was a complete stranger to her.

'Why am I here? What did I ever do to you?'

She could hear his footsteps as he walked away from her slowly, heard the heaviness of the door as he pulled it open and, as it shut behind him, she started to cry.

Chapter One Hundred and Four

'I can't believe that no one knows where she is, Michael. It's just not possible. You're wrong. You need to start sorting this out properly.'

Michael looked at his wife, at her perfectly made-up face, and her expensive designer clothes that she wore indoors like other people wore pyjamas. It was the middle of the night and she was fully dressed, acting as if it was the most natural thing in the world to be dressed like a fucking supermodel at three a.m., when it was anything but. And, to top it all, she had the nerve to question him. To challenge him about his missing daughter, as if he wasn't even bothering to try and locate her. This from the mother who didn't care enough to leave her home and help him with his search. He was tired, worried, and now he was also fucking annoyed. How dare she question him, when she hadn't done anything at all to help?

'Do you know what, Josephine? You've got a brass neck on you. I have been searching high and low for Jessie, I've mobilised the whole of the London police force, every fucker on my payroll, and I have made sure that every person our Jessie ever knew has been routed. What have you done?

Other than repair your make-up, and reset your fucking hair? Oh, and let little Jake have a few minutes of your *precious* time with you? Playing the devoted nana, and keeping everything he touches as if it means anything to anyone else in the real world! Come on then – tell me, Josephine. I'm so fucking *interested*. You haven't left this house for years. You hide in here like a fucking Nazi war criminal. We pretend it's normal, you living in two rooms in a home that's big enough to house a fucking army, but it's *not*, Josephine, it's not *normal* at all. Then you have the nerve to tell me that I'm not doing enough to find Jessie. Where the *fuck* do you get off?'

Josephine was white-faced at this attack on her, and she wasn't able to answer her husband. His anger was so painful and raw. She had never seen him like this before. Somewhere in her head, she recognised he was telling her the truth, but it didn't make it any easier to hear.

Pulling herself upright in her chair and, squaring her shoulders, she gathered her pride. Looking at the man she had married, and who she still loved with all her heart, she said coldly, 'I don't need you or anyone else to tell me about my life, Michael. *I* am the one who has to live it, and I live it to the best of my ability.'

For the first time ever her words didn't have any effect on him; he didn't care about her problems or her needs. 'Oh, blow it out your arse, Josephine. It's not about you for once, is it? It's about Jessie, and where the fuck she might be. Because I don't think this is her usual old fanny. I think this time she might really be in serious trouble.'

Chapter One Hundred and Five

Jessie woke up to find a stone-cold McDonald's and a large bottle of water on the end of her bed. She was relieved there was finally some light, albeit not that bright, but at least she could peruse her surroundings. There wasn't much to see. As she gobbled down the food left for her, she didn't notice anything of use; the walls were concrete, badly rendered, and there was no furniture in the room other than the bed she was tied to. The smell of her urine was disgusting, but there wasn't anything she could do about that. She just hoped *that* would work in her favour – whoever this man was, he wouldn't want to rape her. She stank like a fucking polecat. But he'd already had his chance for that.

She finished her food and drank a deep gulp of the water; she had never been so hungry in her life. She had a feeling the man was sedating her with the water he allowed her, but she had no choice – she had to drink it. It was better to be asleep, if truth be told. She wasn't going anywhere anytime soon. Her arms were aching from being bound for days and, as she tried to flex her legs to get some feeling back into them, she saw a bundle of clothing on the floor beside her bed.

Grabbing the clothes eagerly, she noticed that he had left her a cheap wraparound skirt that was suitable for the beach and a tracksuit top; it was an ugly grey colour, but at least it looked warm. As she stripped off her clothes, she was ashamed to see just how soiled and dilapidated she had become.

She slipped off the end of the bed, and stood up unsteadily. In the dim light she could make out two thick metal plates fixed into the floor, and these were what held her captive. The chains themselves were tight, and they were very heavy. She couldn't remove them without a weapon of some kind, or the keys to her ankle chains, of course. It was a terrible feeling, being held captive like this, left to lie in her own stench, her own urine, like a fucking animal. But she wasn't going to let this man know how much that affected her. He'd not harmed her since that first night, when he had knocked her unconscious, but she could still feel the pain from where he had hit her. If he had hit her like that once, he wouldn't care about having to do it again.

She dressed herself quickly in the fresh clothes, pulling the skirt she'd been wearing over her head. Her underwear was filthy but she couldn't remove it with the chains. At least the clean clothes gave her a feeling of power and reminded her of how strong she could be if necessary. She could not allow herself to think otherwise; if she gave in to her fears, this man would beat her, and she was determined that she would never give up without a fucking fight. She had fought her father, the big dangerous villain, tooth and nail, so she was fucked if she was going to let anyone else get the better of her now. She forced herself to concentrate on the predicament that she was in, reminding herself that, no matter what might have passed between her and her father, he was the only chance she had to survive; if anyone was capable of finding her, and rescuing her, it was her dad.

She saw how stained the mattress was with her own bodily functions and, using all her strength, she finally managed to turn it over. It was difficult and exhausting, but it was something she needed to do. This was about her refusing to let the man who was holding her captive demoralise her completely. She climbed back on to the bed, pleased at what she had achieved for herself.

She still felt filthy, though. She could smell her own urine and body odour. Her breath was rank, her skin felt greasy, oily and grubby. She could feel the large scab on her scalp – from where the man had beaten her unconscious – which had bled quite badly. She still felt pain whenever she moved her head around.

She pulled the blankets from the floor and, even though they were dirty, she used them to cover herself. She felt the sting of tears again and for all her certainty that her father would come for her, she began to wonder if he was even looking for her yet. Why hadn't he found her already? He was the hardest man in fucking Europe! Why had she been taken? This couldn't be a kidnapping – if it was, surely she would have been forced to make a tape of the kidnapper's demands? Or talk to her father to prove she was still alive? Her father would insist on that. He wouldn't pay a penny until he was assured she was still in one piece. So what the fuck was this about? She still had her very expensive Rolex, and it gave her the time and the date. It was five days since she had been abducted, and the man who was keeping her chained up didn't seem to be bothered about anything. There was no urgency about him, or his movements – in fact, he was a bit *too* laid back. The food, the light and the clean clothes, though, made her think that maybe he wasn't going to leave her to starve to death. Maybe he did have a hidden agenda. But what that might be, she couldn't even hazard a guess.

Chapter One Hundred and Six

Dana O'Carroll was in her late thirties and she knew she wasn't a beauty. She was a heavyset woman with a flat face, heavy lips, and deep brown eyes. She had worked for the Flynns since three months before Jake had been born, employed to look after the child and also Josephine. She was a state-registered nurse, and she had taken this place knowing that she would stay for the duration – the lure of a newborn baby had been too much for her to resist. Jake Flynn was the child she would never have. She absolutely adored him.

Although Dana had ostensibly been brought in to look after Jake, she had known within the first five minutes that Josephine Flynn was seriously in need of psychiatric help. Dana thought the world of Josephine, but there was no getting away from the fact that she was becoming odder by the day, and that was why she was paid so much. She had to watch her like a hawk.

Dana gave Jake everything he needed, and he loved her with all his little heart. As he was getting older, he was starting to question his world and the people in it. His mother Jessie was an anomaly to him; she drifted in and out of his life and didn't know how to treat him when they *were* together. But what would she know about love and caring? It wasn't as though she had learnt it at home. Dana saw that Josephine would always put her husband Michael above anyone, even Jake, if it came to it. How was Jessie supposed to live with that knowledge? Now that Michael had given Josephine a much-needed reality check, forcing her to acknowledge the truth of her life for once, it seemed that Josephine had suddenly forgotten she had a small grandson who needed her. Josephine had locked herself away in her room, broken-hearted and full of self-pity. She had refused to see her little grandson, saying she was too upset. It was shocking and cruel to ignore the little boy like that, but what could she do about it?

Michael Flynn came into the kitchen and, sitting down beside his grandson, he kissed him on his cheek heartily, grabbing the boy out of his chair. Jake laughed loudly with happiness; he loved to be noticed.

'I hear a certain young man is going to Mass this morning with his school. He's learning about his Holy Communion.'

Jake grinned at his granddad. 'I am. That's me! How did you know?'

Michael shrugged theatrically. 'I heard about it, and I wanted to give him a hug before he went! It's a sacrament you know, Jake, Holy Communion, like a deal you make with God. It's very important. It's a big thing for anyone. Remember that. You'll make your First Confession, and then, when you've been absolved of all your sins, you can finally make your First Holy Communion. It's a big event in your life, mate.'

Jake was hanging on his granddad's every word.

'Never forget that you are a very special person, who is going to do a very special thing, and that being a Catholic is very important, OK?'

Jake nodded solemnly. 'Will my mummy be there?'

Michael hugged his grandson tightly. ''Course she will be there, Jake, she wouldn't miss something as important as this!'

As he said the words, he hoped he wouldn't be proved a liar. For all he knew, his daughter was already dead.

Chapter One Hundred and Seven

Declan Costello had spoken to all his workmen, and they said the same thing: Jessie Flynn was on the missing list. It was a fucking joke. Declan had honestly thought that Jessie, true to form, would be discovered tucked up in bed with some piece of shit, and everyone could then sigh with well-deserved relief. Now, he was starting to think that Michael might have a point – that there was something much more serious going on. But what the fuck could it be? And what was the reason behind it? He couldn't think of one person who would even dream of hurting Michael Flynn through his family. There was no logic to it – the fact they had even tried to involve his family would be tantamount to a death warrant. Michael would never swallow anything like that.

He waited patiently for Michael to arrive for the meeting as arranged. This time, though, he would be agreeing with his friend. There was something very off about this whole thing, he could see that now.

Chapter One Hundred and Eight

Josephine was heartbroken that her Michael could have spoken to her like that, lost his temper and insulted her with such viciousness. Especially now, knowing how worried she was, how scared she was for their daughter. He had shouted at her like *she* was the one in the wrong. He knew exactly the willpower it took for her to live even the limited life that she did, yet he had spoken to her with such anger that she had realised what he really thought about her deep down. It had hurt. Every single day was a challenge to her, every moment was so fucking hard, and he had always acted like he understood her pain. That had been a lie. She could feel the ache in her breast, the pain of betrayal. She would never forget what he had said to her. Even when he tried to grovel and apologise – as he would – she would never forget what he had said to her or how he had said it.

She looked at her reflection in the dressing table; she was perfectly made-up, and that was for her husband's benefit. She kept herself looking good for him, so he would appreciate her, remember how much they had meant to each other. She had put her husband before everyone, and she had thought that he had felt the same way about her. As Michael's world got bigger her world got smaller. Now she was trapped, reduced to living in a few rooms, and the outside world was terrifying to her. She had believed that Michael had understood her fears, as irrational as they might be, had accepted them as part of their life as husband and wife. But that wasn't the case.

She had heard him talking to Jake, laughing and joking with him, and she had also heard him leave the house, without even seeing how she was or asking after her. Her Michael had always made a point of saying goodbye to her, of making her feel like she was the centre of his life.

She wouldn't let herself cry; she had no intention of ruining her make-up, not for anyone. She would be here for him, as she had always been. He knew that he was all she had ever really cared about. She had placed him above everyone else and, as far as she was concerned, that alone should guarantee her his loyalty.

Chapter One Hundred and Nine

'How can there be no news, Declan? It's a fucking joke.'

Declan didn't say a word. What could he say? It was the truth. 'I think you might be right, Michael. There's a definite bad smell here.'

Michael laughed, but there was no mirth there. They were in the offices at Canary Wharf.

'At last! You can finally sec what I've been fucking saying all along. *Five* days, Declan, and not a fucking dicky-bird. My daughter hates my fucking guts, she flaunts every fucking thing she does in my face, so why not this time? If this was about her, she would make sure I knew about it.'

Declan got up from his seat and poured them both a coffee. The underlying worry in Michael's voice was clear. Giving Michael his mug, Declan said honestly, 'I really don't know, Michael, I can't answer that. All I do know is, I think you're right. I think you sussed this out before anyone else.'

Michael sipped at his coffee, glad to finally have someone agree with him. He had known from the off that this was suspect.

'I want to put the reward up to fifty grand cash. That will guarantee a good fucking shakedown, get the word out there. If anyone's information leads me to my daughter – even if it's to her dead body – I will put the money in their pocket myself. I've got to find her, Declan. I need to know what's going down. I know this is trouble, I can feel it.'

Declan nodded. 'I'll do it, Michael, but remember that *you* were the one who said dead or alive. Not me.'

It had crossed Declan's mind that she might be dead somewhere; considering the life she had insisted on living that wouldn't be unlikely.

'I just need to know what's going on, Declan, either way.'

Declan could understand that; he would feel the same if it was him.

Chapter One Hundred and Ten

Josephine heard the knocking on her door, and she guessed it was Dana – no one else bothered to knock. She plastered a smile on her face, and tried to look relaxed, but she knew that Dana had heard everything that had been said between her and Michael. Dana slipped into the room, and Josephine saw that she was holding a letter.

'This was in the post box outside the gates, Josephine. It's handwritten and addressed to you. I thought I should give it to you straight away. You know, just in case . . .'

Josephine took the letter from her warily. 'Thank you.'

Dana waited a few seconds, expecting Josephine to open it, but she didn't. Instead, she placed it carefully on the table beside her chair.

Dana smiled easily. 'Don't you think you should open it, Josephine? It might be important, with what's going on at the moment.'

Josephine smiled right back at her. 'I'll open it later, if it's all the same to you. How did Jake get on today?'

Dana shrugged. 'He had a good day, he's a good kid. He enjoyed the Mass, he hasn't stopped going on about it.'

'Good. Bring him up to me after his tea.'

Dana nodded. 'Of course. I'd best get on, then.'

She left the room as fast as decently possible. She cared about Josephine very much, but sometimes she could be very creepy.

Dana went back down to the kitchen. Bringing up a tray of tea and biscuits a few hours later, she didn't ask Josephine if she had finally opened the letter. It was still lying on the table, unopened.

Dana had a feeling that it might be important. She rang Michael, telling him everything she knew and, as she had expected, he was back home within the hour.

Chapter One Hundred and Eleven

'I can't fucking believe you sometimes, Josephine! Why haven't you even opened the fucking thing?' Michael snatched the letter off the table.

His annoyance bothered Josephine. He was looking at her as if she had done something wrong. Who the hell did he think he was?

He ripped open the envelope. It had one sheet of paper inside, folded up perfectly. He opened it up slowly, and Josephine realised that, just like her, he was frightened of what it might contain. She watched him as he read the contents.

'Well? Come on then, what does it say, Michael?'

He bent down, until he was level with his wife's face. 'Not fucking too much, Josephine. It just has a number that we were *supposed* to ring at three thirty this afternoon. Bit late for that now, though, don't you think? You silly bitch!'

Josephine was stricken with guilt, Michael could see that, but he didn't care. His wife wouldn't open a letter if you paid her a million pounds – she couldn't. She hadn't opened a letter for years; it was another one of her foibles. He had always accepted her eccentricities, tried his hardest to be supportive, because he loved her so much. Now he wasn't so sure he had done the right thing. All his support seemed to have achieved was to allow his wife to become more and more reclusive. He had enabled her to give in to her fears.

'Why didn't you fucking ring me, Josephine? Or get Dana to? Didn't it occur to you that this letter might be about your daughter? I mean, when was the last time anyone sent you a fucking letter? I can't believe that you didn't care enough about your own child to open it or at least ask someone else to do it for you. Now we've missed the chance to talk to whoever might be holding her. Can't you see how fucking wrong this is? How fucking dangerous you are? Because you still can't bring yourself to do something as normal as opening a fucking letter!' He was bellowing at her now, shouting at her with all his might, venting all the anger and frustration that had been brewing inside him for such a long time.

'For years I have pretended that there is nothing wrong with you. I loved you so fucking much I went along with everything – your fucking hoarding, your fucking refusal to accept reality. I even swallowed you becoming a recluse. I've paid out fortunes for the best doctors available. I've done everything in my power to help you. But do you know what? I wish I'd fucking known then what I know now. I think you *like* being a recluse, you *like* living in these two rooms, surrounded by your boxes of old fucking *crap*. It gives you the excuse you need to justify your life. Even Jake doesn't matter any more, does he? Like me and Jessie, he can't compete with the world you've created for yourself. No one can. How could they? Because it's all about you, isn't it?'

Michael opened his arms out wide. 'Look around you, Josephine. This is *it*, darling. This is your crowning achievement. Two rooms and a poxy little bathroom. I hope you think it was worth it.'

Josephine was unable to retaliate. As Michael looked at her he felt guilty. The colour had drained from her facc; even with her make-up she looked awful. His words had finally hit home. He had needed to say what he really wanted to, just once. His anger at her utter selfishness was so voracious, he just couldn't stop himself. He had been a good husband to her, no matter what she might think. He had gone along with whatever she wanted, *always*. Anything to make Josephine happy. And what had it got them in the long run? Nothing, that's what. Sweet fuck-all. She had left the real world behind, and he had let her do it, even though he had known it was wrong. Now he would never forgive her.

Chapter One Hundred and Twelve

Jessie felt ill. She had eaten the food left for her so quickly, she now had chronic indigestion. She didn't eat that much normally, but now she felt she should eat whatever she got, to keep her strength up, thereby making sure that, if it ever came to it, she could fight her own end. The man appeared to be immune to her charms and, as she had always used her feminine wiles to get what she wanted, she didn't know how to deal with him. He wouldn't talk to her for a start; in fact, he ignored her with such disdain it was an insult in itself. When he did look at her it was carefully, almost as if he was trying to get inside her head.

He was very nondescript, not very tall, and he looked to be well into his fifties. Although it was hard to tell in the dimness of the basement.

Even though she was still scared, she didn't think the man was capable of harming her without provocation. She had lived around violent men all her life, and this bloke didn't have the same feel to him as her father or her uncle Declan. They both had an air about them that warned you that these were men who would be capable of extreme violence, if the circumstances warranted it. Her nana Hannah, her father's own mother, had happily told her everything she wanted to know about her father and, unlike everyone else in her world, she had not tried to sanitise any of it. She had listened to her nana Hannah's stories. Even though she spent a lot of time with her, she had never really liked her; her nana Hannah was a vicious old bitch. But Jessie had needed her to tell her everything.

She looked at the man now and shouted angrily, 'Talk to me! Don't just fucking stand there staring at me.'

The man grinned at her for a few moments. Then he walked away, and she heard him leave the room, shutting the door behind him.

Jessie felt the fear building inside her chest again. How the hell had she ended up like this? How the fuck had this happened to her?

Chapter One Hundred and Thirteen

'I tried the number over and over, Declan, but no one answered. I could fucking lamp Josephine one. Why the fuck didn't she open the fucking letter? It's not fucking rocket science, is it? Her daughter's missing, and a letter arrives. Two and two springs to mind! But that's her all over, isn't it? Can't open a fucking letter, can't use the fucking stairs, can't leave the fucking house. The list of things that she can't do any more is fucking endless! I lived with her problems, you know I did. But today her fucking refusal to think about her daughter's welfare tipped me over the edge. I've seen her for the selfish cunt she really is.'

Declan didn't say anything, but Michael didn't expect an answer from him anyway. He already knew Declan's opinion of Josephine and her so-called 'problems'. Declan had never said anything outright, but his silence over the years had spoken volumes. His less-than-complimentary opinion of Josephine had always been there between them.

Michael was so worried about his daughter and what might be happening to her. 'I have more than most people could ever even dream of. I deal in millions of pounds. I single-handedly changed the whole infrastructure of British crime. Yet do you know something, Declan? I've really got fuck-all. My daughter treats me like a fucking leper, and my wife lives on her own fucking planet. Did you know that Josephine won't use the stairs nowadays? She lives in two rooms. The size of that fucking house, and she lives in less space than if she lived in a council flat. How insulting is that?'

Michael was more distressed than Declan had ever seen him. Michael Flynn was always in complete control of his emotions; seeing his friend so vulnerable was a first for Declan Costello. But these were difficult times, and he could understand Michael allowing his hard-man persona to slip.

Declan had poured them a large Scotch each and, as he handed Michael his drink, he wished there was something he could think of to say that might ease the man's plight.

'I love my daughter, Declan. For all our problems, I never stopped loving her. Now she's on the missing list, and I can't help her.'

'You should give the letter to the Old Bill, Michael, they might find a fingerprint or something.'

Michael looked at his old friend as if he had never seen him before. 'Oh, stop it, Declan. This isn't *CSI*, for fuck's sake. Gil Grissom isn't going to miraculously find the cunt's name out before the sixty minutes is up. You and I both know that's a fucking big stretch for anyone's imagination. Most people's fingerprints aren't on any database, unless you've been nicked, and DNA takes weeks to process. Even then they can only match it with a name if they happen to have the fucker's DNA there to start with. Can't see that, can you?'

'I just think you should use whatever you can, Michael.'

Michael shook his head sadly. 'All I can do now is wait until the bastard contacts me again.'

Chapter One Hundred and Fourteen

Michael had rung the number from the letter over and over again. Nothing. It was a waste of his time, but he couldn't stop himself. The phone didn't even fucking ring; it was probably a cheap throwaway. He couldn't understand why the person involved didn't seem bothered about making contact with him. If this had been a shakedown, a call for cash, then he would have heard something long before now. Michael felt sick with apprehension. There wasn't anyone he could think of with the guts to do something like this to him; he was too big, too respected for anyone to think they could dare get away with something like this. But he couldn't find out a fucking thing – even the police were stumped. He just sat in his home, waiting for a call, for another letter to be delivered, anything at all that might lead him to his daughter.

Jake bowled into the room, all smiley-faced. He smelt clean, and his sturdy little body looked bigger than ever. Michael ruffled his hair, pleased to see him, proud of the boy.

'Hello, Granddad! I've been learning my seven times table.'

Michael laughed at his grandson's complete enjoyment of his little life.

'Have you now! Very important, you know, learning your times tables.'

Jake nodded in absolute agreement. 'I know that, Granddad! Dana reckons it's what sorts the men from the boys!'

Dana laughed at his words. She was already making Jake's breakfast, and Michael laughed with her.

'Well, Dana knows about these things, Jake, so listen to her.'

Jake was pleased to hear his granddad sound happy. Jake hated the tension in the house. His nana was very sad, she didn't seem like her usual self. His nana had fallen out with his granddad, he had heard them shouting at each other. It was very worrying – other than Dana they were all he had in the world. He hadn't seen his mum for a long time and he was feeling very anxious about her too.

Dana placed his porridge on the table before him, and he started to eat it slowly. He liked it with honey and sugar, and Dana always made it perfectly for him.

Dana was leaning against the fridge, drinking a cup of coffee. She looked at Michael and, raising her eyebrows, she asked carefully, 'Any news?'

Michael shook his head sadly. 'No. Nothing. Not a dicky-bird.'

Jake listened to the talk between them, and he knew that they were talking about his mummy. He had heard enough to work out that she was in some kind of trouble. But then his mummy was always having some kind of problem. It wasn't anything unusual for her. Her whole life was one problem after another. His nana always seemed to think that was the case anyway. She always said to Dana, that her Jessie attracted trouble like other people contracted a rash. It was there before you knew it and it itched until it was scratched raw.

'You get yourself off to school, Jake. Have a good day, son.'

Jake liked it when his granddad called him 'son'. He finished his porridge quickly.

'I've got to take my drawing in, Granddad. It's a picture of me, you, Dana and Nana. We had to draw our family. It's going on the wall for our Communion. I drew us all in the garden. Even Nana!' He laughed, and Michael laughed with him, even though he was sad to think that the child knew, as young as he was, that his nana didn't use the garden, and also sad to think he had left his mother out of the equation.

'That sounds lovely. Nana would be pleased to know you've drawn a picture of her.'

Jake shrugged, a childish shrug that was as honest as it was natural. 'I suppose so, Granddad. But she won't see me, you know. Even though I've been a good boy.'

Michael was sorry to the heart for his grandson's predicament. Josephine forgot that her lifestyle affected everyone around her, little Jake especially. Her living in a fucking bubble when her daughter was missing just proved to him how selfish she really was.

'Your nana is not very well, Jake.'

Jake got off his chair slowly, and smiling at his granddad, he said with false gaiety, 'Dana told me already. I know that she's not well. Nana's never well.'

Chapter One Hundred and Fifteen

Jessie could feel the eyes of her captor on her. He watched her sometimes while she slept, and she hated knowing that he did that. It was creepy. She was feeling so sore, her ankles were bleeding as the cuffs were rubbing away her skin every time she moved. It was agony.

She sat up on the bed and shouted, 'I'm hungry, you know! Fucking starving! I need a real meal. I need a bath. I need to use a proper toilet. *Please* let me use a proper toilet!' She hated the whine in her voice, but she couldn't help herself. 'I'm bleeding, for fuck's sake. My ankles are rubbed raw. At least give me something to ease the pain.'

She was crying now, even as she was determined not to show him any weakness. She didn't want him to know that he had beaten her. But he had. No matter how much she tried to act tough, he had her shackled to a bed in a filthy basement. He had won from the moment she had woken up tied and bound and unable to free herself.

She was crying noisily now. She was hurting, bleeding and so frightened. Her resolve was breaking down by the second. Strong or weak, it made no difference to him. He just sat and watched as she screamed at him. Her fears and her worries had finally overwhelmed her; she was broken. Gut-wrenching sobs broke from her uncontrollably.

Her captor continued to watch her, only now she saw through her tears that he was smiling.

Chapter One Hundred and Sixteen

Detective Inspector Timothy Branch was nervous. He had never been to Michael Flynn's scrapyard before, but he knew that many people *had* gone there and never been seen again. That was the power of a crushing machine – an errant body placed in the boot of a car didn't really stand much chance of being located. Once the car was put into the crusher, it was reduced to a two-foot-by-two-foot cube of metal.

He drove into the yard slowly. The gates were already open for him, and he saw the men who had waved him inside so cheerfully closing the gates behind him.

He regretted taking Flynn's money for so many years. Now he was asking him for a favour and he couldn't deliver, and that wasn't sitting well with him. He had a feeling it wasn't sitting well with Michael Flynn either.

He pulled up outside the Portakabins and, as he stepped out of his car, he noticed that there were a few men scattered around. They were all watching him as he walked up the rickety stairs that led into the offices.

He looked at Michael and, nodding politely towards him, he said quietly and respectfully, 'I'm sorry, Michael. Still nothing. I've had my blokes out there again. They've pulled in everyone who knows Jessie, and they all say the same thing. They haven't seen her, she hadn't fallen out with anyone, and she isn't holed up anywhere. It's a fucking mystery. No one can just disappear overnight.'

Michael Flynn could see that Branch was genuinely disappointed.

'I even pulled the CCTV from the general area around Jessie's flats. Fuck-all again. The cameras that should show the outside of her flats had been disabled. According to the company who should be monitoring them, they only noticed the next morning. Well, I put a fucking rocket up their arses, but there's nothing we can do about it now, is there?'

Declan Costello got up from his chair reluctantly; he was comfortable. He pulled out a typist's chair from behind the desk, and offered it to Timothy Branch.

'Sit there. I'll get us all a drink. Same again, Michael?'

Michael gave him his empty glass. Declan busied himself pouring out the whiskies.

Timothy Branch took his drink gratefully, and he gulped at it, enjoying the taste.

Michael sipped his drink slowly.

'I wish I could tell you different, Michael, I really do. But I hear your blokes are getting the same reaction as mine.'

Michael nodded. 'You're right. No one seems to know sweet fuck-all. But I want to ask you something, Timothy, and I want you to tell me the truth. If this was a real police matter, if a girl went missing like my Jessie, how long before you would assume she was dead?'

Declan Costello had never thought he would feel sorry for DI Timothy Branch; the man was a fucking arsehole. But he did now. The man didn't know what to say for the best.

'The thing is, Michael, every case is different. I mean, there's no way I can answer that.'

Sighing with annoyance, Michael said quietly, 'Don't fucking mug me off, I'm not an idiot. I am asking you: if a girl was abducted, like my Jessie, how long would you give her before you assumed she was fucking *dead*?' He bellowed out the last word.

Timothy Branch shrugged, saying honestly, 'A couple of days. The fact that no one can explain her disappearance is not a good sign, to be honest. But, saying that, you know she is being held by someone. Your wife had that letter, it was hand-delivered. So that's a good thing, Michael.'

Michael Flynn shook his handsome head in a gesture of denial. 'But that's just it, though. Anyone could have her, couldn't they?'

Chapter One Hundred and Seventeen

Jessie woke to see the man standing over her. Up close he looked decidedly odd; there was no emotion on his face, nothing to say he even registered her presence. It was unnerving. He had pale grey eyes, and his skin was a dirty yellow. His mouth was partly open, and she could see his teeth – which were rotten – and smell his awful breath. She felt her stomach heaving; he actually made her feel physically sick. The stench was overpowering, a sickly sweetness of old food and long-neglected cavities. It was putrid.

He had not given her any food for over thirty-six hours, all he had given her was a bottle of water, which she still suspected was drugged. She hadn't seen him this close to her before and she was frightened of him. He looked crazy, like people you saw on the streets and knew at a glance were dangerous so you avoided eye contact and passed as fast as possible.

She just wanted to go home, get away from him, from here. She wanted to see her mum, her little boy – for the first time in years, she wanted her family around her.

The man licked his lips slowly, deliberately. Jessie knew he was taking some kind of chemical, because he looked stoned. His eyes didn't focus properly and over the course of the last few days he had seemed to be unravelling more and more. He smiled at her suddenly and as he laughed he started to cough, and the stench from his breath hit her directly in her face, spraying her skin with droplets of his saliva. It took all her willpower not to vomit everywhere.

He looked at her for long moments, before saying flatly, 'You must be starving. Are you starving?'

She nodded, wondering what this was leading to. She didn't shout at him or demand anything from him – she was too weak, too scared of him. He knew that – she had felt the change in him the last few days. It seemed the weaker she became, the stronger he felt. She had expected her father to have rescued her by now, but he hadn't. She was so worried that he wasn't bothered about her, had left her to her own devices. Or, worse still, that her parents had heard nothing from this man, and just assumed she was on the missing list. It wouldn't be the first time she had disappeared without telling anyone her whereabouts.

The man told her nothing. He rarely even spoke to her. He just watched her.

He stepped away from her and, taking out a packet of cigarettes, he lit one for himself. Then, almost as an after-thought, he offered the packet to her.

She took the pack of Lambert & Butler from him, pleased to have a distraction. Taking one out, she pulled herself upright on the mattress, and then he lit her cigarette with his lighter. His actions were very old-fashioned; he even cupped the lighter in his hand to ensure it didn't go out.

She pulled on the cigarette deeply and felt light-headed – it was the first cigarette she'd had in ages.

'Thank you. I appreciate this.'

He bowed, and she knew he was mocking her. She took another few puffs on the cigarette, feeling the nicotine as it hit her brain, enjoying it because it seemed to wake her up, break through the malaise that she was feeling constantly.

'My father, does he know you've got me? He will pay you a lot of money if you ask him to. Have you asked him for anything? What does he know?'

The man didn't answer; he just stared at her, as if he couldn't hear her. It was a very nerve-racking experience.

He dropped his cigarette on to the floor and put it out, slowly grinding it under his foot into the concrete floor. Then he shook his head, smiling at her as if it was a great joke. 'No, of course I haven't contacted him. Why on earth would I do that?'

His voice was almost conversational as though he expected her to have an answer for him. He was even looking at her quizzically. She felt the cold hand of fear clutching at her heart. None of this made any sense. Why had this man taken her?

'But surely money is what this is about? My father will pay for me, my mum will see to that. I mean, why else would you even bring me here in the first place? It doesn't make any fucking sense.'

He lit another cigarette, drawing on it noisily, but he didn't bother to answer her. Jessie threw her cigarette butt on to the floor at his feet, getting more worked up.

'Do you even know *who* my father is? Don't you *realise* exactly *who* you are dealing with? My father is not a man to try and have over in any way. He is very dangerous if he's crossed. He will be searching everywhere for me. You better understand that, and stop this before it goes too far.' She sounded petulant even to her own ears, but she was still reeling from his words. If he hadn't been in touch with anyone, how was she ever to escape? How could anyone find her? If this wasn't about money, about shaking down her old man, then what the hell did this fucking nutbag want with her?

The man settled himself on the end of the bed and, shrugging gently, he looked at her frightened face, and he said seriously, 'This isn't about *you*, Jessie. It never was. This is about your father. Michael Flynn. This is about payback. This is about reminding him that the past is always there, no matter how much he might have tried to forget about it. I certainly haven't. When I finally decide to deliver you to your parents, young lady, you will be as dead as a fucking doornail. That was always the plan.'

'But why? What have I ever done to you?' Jessie was sobbing now.

He laughed again, as if she was amusing him. 'You? You've never done anything to me, you silly girl. Like I said, this is not about you.' He stood up abruptly. 'By the way, I'm not going to be bringing you food any more. I think it's only fair to tell you that. You deserve that much from me, Jessie. You deserve to be treated decently. It's all in the Bible. John chapter eight, verse thirty-two: then you will know the truth, and the truth will set you free. Never forget that, Jessie

Flynn – it's a statement of fact. The truth is important, the *truth* is worth dying for.'

Jessie shouted angrily, 'But I don't want to fucking die! I have a little boy. He needs me.'

The man smiled once again. 'You see? You're lying again. It's the truth you need to hang on to, Jessie. You're just a fucking trollop. Your little boy is being brought up by your mum and dad. *Everyone* knows what a fucking piece of shit you are. I've done my homework, Jessie Flynn.'

Jessie was unable to answer the man; he was without reason. There was nothing she could do to make him listen to her.

The man looked at her sadly. 'I wasn't going to tell you this, but I think you need to know the truth, Jessie. I sent your mother a number to ring me on – that was last week. I was going to torture her, to be honest. I had no intention of ever letting you leave here. But do you know something? She didn't even call me. Three thirty that day, there I was, ready and waiting, and nothing – not a fucking peep. That is a truth you need to acknowledge. I gave her that one chance, a chance to contact *you*. Your mother didn't even bother herself. Now your dad, on the other hand, from what I can gather, has been looking for you all over. There's even a fifty-grand reward for information about your whereabouts. See what I'm saying? The truth will set you free, Jessie.'

She watched him as he walked away from her, and she knew that she was without hope. She was bloodied and bleeding and this man didn't care. She was nothing to him, her suffering meant nothing to him. She heard the door slam, and the scraping noise as he pulled the bolts into place, and she wondered if this was it for her. Was this how she was going to die, alone and frightened, starved to death, and without ever having the chance to tell her little son how much she had really loved him?

Chapter One Hundred and Eighteen

'With respect, Josephine, do you really believe for a fucking moment that I haven't been searching high and low for Jessie? No one knows a fucking thing. Not the Filth, not our workers. It's fucking outrageous.'

Josephine felt awful. 'I didn't mean it how it came out, Michael, but I'm so worried about her. You need to get out there again and retrace her steps, there has to be someone who knows something.'

Michael interrupted his wife. He was still furious with her for losing them the only lead they'd had with the letter. How could she kid herself like this? 'Are you having a fucking laugh? I've been out there looking for her since she first went AWOL. Unlike *you*, of course, Josephine, who still can't bring yourself to leave your fucking bedroom. Who has sat here on your arse the whole time, drinking wine and watching your DVDs to take your mind off it all, and couldn't even open a fucking letter! It's a joke, Josephine. Your whole *life* is a fucking joke. This is your fault. *Your life* is what helped our Jessie to go off the rails. You always pretended everything was all right, but it wasn't, Josephine. How dare you even try to tell me what I should be doing, when you have done fuck-all! You really can't see how hard it's been for me, can you? Watching you waste your life away up here like a fucking character from a storybook. It's a fucking excuse of a life, Josephine, it has been for years. And it's cost us our daughter.'

The pain Michael had caused his wife with his words was evident. She was white-faced, her eyes so big and wide she looked like a bushbaby. He had hurt her badly, but he didn't care. His daughter, for all she might be, was missing and could be dead, and he couldn't play this game with his wife any more. He was sick of pretending that everything was normal. He couldn't protect her from the truth any more – he didn't want to. Josephine needed a reality check, and it had been a long time coming.

As she dropped her eyes from his, and turned away from him – acting like she was the only one of them who was hurting – he felt his anger building up inside his chest once more. She really knew how to play the victim.

'Do you know what, Josephine? I can see what you're doing, acting the innocent, as always. Poor old Josephine, who can't be expected to do anything useful, not with all her problems, eh? Well, do you know what? You can go and fuck yourself because, unlike *you*, I've done everything in my power to locate Jessie. I know that and, more to the fucking point, *you* know that.'

Josephine Flynn was aware that she had finally used up all the goodwill that her husband had always shown to her. She was feeling thoroughly ashamed of herself. She had always known that Michael had given her more love than she had ever deserved from him. He had been losing patience with her for a while now, and she didn't know how to make it better, how to make him understand that she couldn't help herself, that she hated herself for her weakness.

'Please, Michael . . .'

He turned away from her, waving his arms in dismissal. 'I can't listen to you, Josephine. I'm sorry, but I've got to go.'

Chapter One Hundred and Nineteen

Declan wasn't sure if he was doing the right thing, but he couldn't, in all good conscience, ignore the woman's request for a meeting any longer. Nor could Michael either – he was already on his way to the meet.

She had contacted him personally, and she had waited a long time to be heard, refusing to discuss her business with anyone but Michael. She had been ringing his offices for over a week, but hadn't explained why. Declan had finally called her back, and realised from her tone she might have important information.

He smiled at the woman sitting opposite him, sipping her cup of tea, and she smiled back at him, a serene smile, that made him feel better about everything. No matter what the outcome might be, she was at least being genuine. What more could anyone ask for?

Michael arrived at the address he had been given by Declan, and he parked his Range Rover carefully outside the house in question. This was his old stomping ground; he had grown up round the corner from this street, and he was pleased to see the change in it. East London was now a desirable place to reside. The houses that were once barely one step above slums, were now changing hands for exorbitant amounts of money. It was a fucking joke – everyone else dreamt of getting away from the area; now it seemed certain people were determined to buy a property there. Wonders would never cease.

He was already feeling guilty about turning on Josephine, even though he knew she had been asking for it for a long time. But he did love her, and he felt as much to blame for the way she lived as she was, because he had never once challenged her about her lifestyle. Until now.

Michael got out of his Range Rover, and locked it behind him. He walked up the short pathway to the front door of the house, and rang the doorbell. The front door was opened by Declan Costello, and Michael was ushered inside the tiny house.

This was what used to be called a parlour-type house, and Michael knew the layout off by heart. He followed Declan down the narrow passageway into the front room. Mrs Singh, as he had always known her, was waiting for him patiently. She was sitting on a small two-seater sofa in a deep burgundy colour, and the two armchairs that matched it sat either side of the fireplace. There was a light wood cabinet against the party wall, and a matching coffee table in front of the fireplace. The carpet was expensive, a good Axminster, and where the only real money had been spent. The sole ornaments in the room were photographs of her family, and these were plentifully scattered round.

Michael took the woman's hand gently in his. 'It's very

good to see you again, Mrs Singh. It's a long time since I've been in here.'

She stood up to greet him. She was as tiny as he remembered, under five feet tall, as thin as a rake, her thick dark hair streaked with grey now, but she still had the power to make him feel like a kid again.

'Sit down, Michael, it's lovely to welcome you here once again.'

Michael and Declan both settled themselves into the armchairs by the fireplace. Mrs Singh poured Michael a cup of tea, and he took it from her carefully.

'I appreciated you coming to my husband's funeral, Michael, it would have pleased him so much. He always thought a lot of you. I'll never forget that, you know, never forget that you remembered the people from your childhood.'

Michael sipped his tea, embarrassed now. 'You and your husband were always very good to me. He was a good man, a decent man.'

She nodded in agreement. 'He was. I was very lucky.' She smiled widely. 'I always knew, Michael, that it was you who stopped the trouble we were experiencing at the shop. The threats and the hate all stopped overnight. Mr Singh always said that it could only be you. We were aware of how you had got on in life, and we were pleased for you.'

Declan Costello sat back in his armchair and relaxed; this was a woman Michael obviously respected, who he was happy to listen to.

'I did nothing really, Mrs Singh, I just put out a few feelers, explained that you were dear friends of mine. But if it helped you both then I am very pleased about that.'

She looked at him kindly with her deep brown eyes; she was a shrewd woman, that much was evident.

She was wearing a deep green sari, and she looked to Declan as if she had dressed for the occasion. She looked well-to-do, like a woman of substance, her jewellery was gold, very heavy, and well made. She had diamonds in her ears, and in the rings on her fingers.

'I have been trying to contact you for a while now, Michael. I heard about your Jessie going missing, and I heard you were looking for information about her.'

Michael immediately sat forward in his armchair, he knew this woman wouldn't have asked him here without good reason.

'Go on. I'm listening.' Michael's voice was quiet, interested.

'I must explain, Michael, I don't even know if this is anything of relevance. All I can say is, *I* found it odd and, considering what's been going on, I just thought I should let you know about it.'

Declan butted in quickly, 'There's also a fifty-grand reward for any information that leads to Jessie.'

Michael Flynn's head snapped sideways, looking at Declan with complete and utter disgust.

Mrs Singh shook her head slowly in denial. Holding her hand over her heart she said with real meaning, 'I can assure you, *Mr* Costello, that means very little to me.' That she was deeply offended by what Declan had said to her was more than obvious.

Michael Flynn was out of the armchair he was sitting in within nanoseconds and, kneeling down on the carpet in front of his old friend, he grabbed Mrs Singh's hands in his. Squeezing them tightly, he said, 'Ignore him, Mrs Singh, he's fucking ignorant at times. Just tell me what you know.'

She grasped Michael's hands, pulled them to her chest, knowing that he would listen to what she had to say.

'I was in the shop a few weeks ago. I rarely spend that much time there these days, but I still pop round once or twice a week. My eldest son Davinda and his wife took it over after my husband died, as you know. Anyway, I saw a man in there, and I could see he wasn't right, that he was, you know, what the cockneys always called "radio rental"? A bit mental? Remember how Mr Singh always loved the rhyming slang? But I knew this person. You know when you see someone and you can't place them? That is how I felt. He bought forty Lambert and Butlers, and a bottle of cheap vodka. My son Davinda served him and, as the man was leaving, he looked directly at me, and he smiled. It was a strange smile, Michael. I can't explain it. Anyway, it took me a day or two, but then I remembered who he was.'

She pushed Michael gently away from her, and she sat back on the settee. Michael could see the turmoil in her face, knew that she was worried about what she was going to say to him. 'It's so many years ago but I'm sure that it was Steven Golding.'

Declan Costello was quietly watching everything that was happening, and he saw the way that Mrs Singh looked at Michael as she told him who she thought she had seen. He also saw Michael Flynn's face drain of all its colour.

'I hope I was wrong, Michael, but I really don't think I was. Then I heard that your Jessie was missing.' She sighed heavily. 'I really don't know if any of this is related. I just thought that you should know.' She looked at Michael steadily, saying quietly, 'I always wondered about it, Michael.'

Michael was shaking his head slowly. Declan could see he had been thrown by the woman's revelations. It was absolutely amazing to witness this first-hand.

'I never planned it, I *swear*. It should never have happened.'

Mrs Singh opened her arms wide, she was crying now. 'I always knew that, Michael, I never doubted you.'

Michael enveloped the tiny woman in his arms, hugging her to him tightly, and she hugged him back. Declan watched with disbelief. He knew one thing, though – he should have brought these two together at the start, when she first rang them, asking for Michael Flynn, instead of fobbing her off. He had a terrible feeling that this might be too late now.

Chapter One Hundred and Twenty

Declan opened the door to his penthouse, and stood aside to allow Michael to enter before him. Once inside he shut the door and locked it. He followed Michael into the lounge, turning on the lights as he went.

Michael was standing by the patio doors that led out on to a large terrace. He was looking over London, and Declan left him to it for a while, going into his kitchen – a large airy room, twenty feet by sixteen – and pouring them each a large drink. The kitchen was state of the art; the cooker alone wouldn't have looked out of place in an expensive restaurant. Not that he had ever used it, of course, just like the American-style fridge or the two dishwashers. He made instant coffee and a slice of toast at a push. The black granite work surfaces he used as a bar. He didn't care to use the gadgets, but he liked to own them; they gave the place class.

He brought the drinks into the lounge, and he passed one to Michael. 'So, Mrs Singh? Nice lady.'

Michael tossed his drink back in one. 'How long was she trying to get hold of me, Declan?'

Declan tossed his own drink back then; he needed it. 'Since last week, I think. But be fair, Michael, we had no idea who she was or what she wanted. It was only because she was so persistent that I called her myself. And then came to you. I realise the error of my ways now, we should have been on top of it. But it wasn't deliberate, you know that.'

Michael held his empty glass out, and followed Declan out to the kitchen, where he waited for him to pour them both more Scotch.

'She *is* a nice lady, Mrs Singh.'

Declan nodded his agreement. 'I could see that, Michael. I could also see that you really think a lot of her, and her husband as well.'

Michael Flynn took out his cigarettes and lit one. 'She was very good to me, both her and her husband were. I went to school with Davinda, their oldest son, we were good mates. They are Sikhs and, years ago, the Sikhs and the Muslims sent their kids to a faith school – in other words, a Catholic school. So we all grew up together. It was nice. Davinda – Dave, as we called him – was a real fucking brainiac. He went on to university – that was Mr Singh's dream, you know? Education. He saw it as the jewel in the crown of the United Kingdom. He used to say, "Remember, boys, this country has the best education system in the world, and it's *free*." I didn't appreciate that until it was too late. But I used to spend a lot of time round there when I was a kid. Mrs Singh looked after me when my mum was working.'

Declan listened to his friend without interrupting. He knew he had to let him say what he needed to in his own time.

'When I went to work for your brother, I lost contact

with the Singhs and a lot of the people I had gone to school with. That was deliberate on my part. I wanted to pursue my own agenda but, to be absolutely honest, I also didn't want Davinda or anyone to get dragged into any of my shit, if it all went tits up.'

Declan shrugged. 'I can understand that, Michael. There're people we don't bring into our working lives. That's par for the course. But I have to ask you, who the fuck is Steven Golding?'

Michael Flynn looked Declan Costello straight in the eyes, and Declan knew that whatever had happened with this Steven Golding, Michael had buried a long time ago.

Michael lit another cigarette, and he drew on it deeply. He needed to calm himself down, needed to remind himself that he had come a long way since those days. He was at the top of his game, and there was no one with the strength to challenge his position.

'Steven Golding was one of the first jobs that your brother ever gave to me. Well not him, but his father. His father was Daniel Golding. Ringing any bells now, is it?'

Declan nodded; it had all just slipped into place. 'That was you? Fucking hell. I knew Patrick had something to do with it, but you'd only just come onboard. I never thought you'd be involved.'

Michael nodded. 'Patrick told me to go to an address in South London and burn the house down. It was about a debt he was owed. He said that if the house was torched, the insurance would pay out and everything would be hunky-dory. I did what he asked of me. I never knew there was anyone in there – I had been told it was an empty property.

But, as I found out afterwards, it wasn't empty. Daniel Golding, his wife, and his two young daughters were in there. Steven survived because he was staying the night at a friend's. I only realised later that Patrick had known all along that the house wasn't empty – he had planned for it to go down that way.'

Declan Costello was looking at Michael as if he was a stranger, as if he was someone who had gatecrashed his way into his home.

'I never knew. I never even dreamt that it might have anything to do with you. Everyone was up in arms about it – those girls were only twelve and fourteen years old. And it was *you*? *You* who poured the petrol through the letter box and burned them to death in their beds?'

Declan was outraged, absolutely disgusted. He was remembering the shock waves the deaths had sent through their community. Daniel Golding had owed money to everyone – like any compulsive gambler he had no real care about borrowing from all and sundry; he believed he could win anything he borrowed back. But no one he owed money to would have taken it out on his family, that just wasn't done. Daniel deserved whatever he might get, but his kids and wife were sacrosanct.

Michael Flynn grabbed hold of Declan's shirt front, dragging him roughly towards him and, looking into his face, Michael said furiously, 'I did what your fucking brother told me to do! I thought the house was fucking empty. Patrick had assured me of that. Afterwards, do you know what he said? He said, "Typical fucking Danny Golding. Always in the wrong place at the wrong time."'

Declan pulled himself away from Michael's grip. 'I'm sorry, Michael, I know that my brother was a fucking looney. Why do you think I stepped back after we took Patrick out? I loved him as my brother, but I knew that he needed to be culled, like a fucking wild animal. Now you've told me, I can see it perfectly. You were a young lad, taking his word at face value, and that would have appealed to him. The knowledge that you were unaware of the truth would have appealed to him.'

Michael laughed nastily. 'I swallowed it, I really believed that it was an accident at first, and I put it out of my mind. I convinced myself that it wasn't my fault. And do you know what, Declan? It *wasn't* my fault. I did what Patrick told me to do. When it went fucking pear-shaped, he stood by me and I appreciated that. But, years later, when I really knew him, I realised he was too shrewd not to have known that the house wouldn't be empty.'

Declan Costello poured them both more whisky. Michael took his drink gratefully.

'That was my brother Patrick all over, Michael. I know what he was capable of. That night, when we took him out, deep down I didn't feel guilty about it. I was relieved – so relieved to know that he was gone at last, and that I didn't have to police him any more. But, that aside, why would this Mrs Singh warn you about Steven Golding?'

Michael Flynn looked at Declan warily. He had just told this man the biggest secret of his life. The biggest shame of his life. But he trusted him.

'Mrs Singh saw me that night. I bumped into her husband outside their shop, and she came out to talk to me. She knew by then that I was working for your brother – she even tried to warn me off! She told me that night to get home and have a bath because I stank of petrol. Of course she didn't know *why* then but, as the Golding family only lived a few streets away, it wasn't long before she did the sums. I knew I could trust her. I never told Patrick about her – I knew that he would have seen her as a threat to him, to his world. It never occurred to him that some people might just be naturally loyal.'

Declan laughed then. 'My brother never trusted the concept of loyalty, Michael, that was his problem.'

Michael sighed heavily. 'I told you all this because you needed to know. But I can only tell myself that I did what I was told to do.'

Declan felt so sorry for Michael; he knew first-hand just how manipulative his brother had been.

'Look, Michael, what we need to do now is forget this shit, and hunt down Steven Golding. Mrs Singh is a fucking shrewd old bird. I'll get on to the Old Bill now, see what they can find out. About time they earned their fucking keep anyway. Then we can work from there.'

Michael Flynn nodded in agreement. 'I just want to know Jessie's all right.'

Declan patted his friend's shoulder gently. 'Of course you do, Michael, she's your daughter!'

Chapter One Hundred and Twenty-One

DI Timothy Branch was relieved to finally be able to give Michael Flynn some useful information. In fact, he'd excelled himself. He drove into the scrapyard and parked his BMW neatly, walking into the Portakabin like a conquering hero.

Michael and Declan were already there as he had expected. He bowled into the room all smiles and smugness until he registered that both Michael Flynn and Declan Costello looked tired and angry. It occurred to him that Michael's daughter was still missing, so he removed his smile, and settled his face into what he saw as serious work mode.

'I got here as soon as I could. I think you will be pleased with the information I've gathered.'

He waited to be offered a seat. Michael obliged, sweeping his arm out towards the old typist's chair, saying tightly, 'Sit and talk. It's about fucking time you earned your keep.'

Timothy sat down as requested, but his earlier euphoria was gone. Michael Flynn was a very scary man, there was no doubt about that. Declan and Michael were both watching him warily, waiting to hear what he had to say to them.

Timothy Branch knew that this was his only chance to

redeem himself. He opened up the file he had on Steven Golding which he had brought with him, and cleared his throat noisily, feeling very nervous once again.

'First of all, from what I have found out, Steven Golding has been under psychiatric care for many years. When he was fifteen, his mother, father, and two young sisters were all killed in a fire. It was an arson attack – deliberate. He had stayed overnight at a friend's so he survived. But he has never fully recovered; he has been in and out of psychiatric facilities for the best part of the last thirty-odd years. He was released again, four months ago, having accrued a large amount of money over the years from his benefits, et cetera. It came to over twelve thousand pounds in total. It seems he removed that from the bank in cash, and no one has seen him since. He hasn't turned up for any of his outpatient appointments, and he hasn't been near the flat he was allocated by the housing trust. He is unknown to the police – never been arrested for anything. According to his doctor, he suffers from delusions, and he is often unable to differentiate between fantasy and reality. But they have assured me that he is *not* violent. He is on quite heavy medication, Dolmatil and – ' Timothy Branch stared down at the page, unable to read his own writing – 'I can't read that, I'm afraid. But I assume it's an anti-psychotic drug of some description. Steven Golding has a very high IQ and is an avid reader – he can read a book in a day. He was last seen three weeks ago when he withdrew all his money out of the bank.'

Michael Flynn opened his arms out in a gesture of supplication. 'Is that it, then?'

Timothy Branch nodded. 'That is everything I could find

out. I've got my people watching out for him.' He quickly pulled out a picture from his file, and handed it to Michael. 'This is a recent photo of him.'

Michael Flynn looked at it. Steven Golding appeared older than he actually was – he was as grey as a badger and his eyes were the same dull grey; he looked almost lifeless. He was looking directly into the camera, his mouth was hanging open, his teeth were black, rotten, and his skin looked thick, like orange peel. He was not a man anyone would stop to talk to, that much was obvious.

Timothy Branch took a deep breath, and then said seriously, 'From what I can gather, if he doesn't take his medication he can become paranoid and quite aggressive. But I must stress that, according to his doctor, he is not a violent man – when he is taking his meds, of course.'

Michael handed the photograph to Declan. 'So, Timothy, let me see if I've got this right. Basically, he left the nuthouse three weeks ago, he cleared his bank account, and he is now on the missing list with twelve grand and, to add insult to injury, without his meds, he has a seriously bad fucking attitude?'

Timothy Branch didn't know what he could say to that. He was hoping that someone spied the fucker somewhere, so he could help Michael to track him down.

Declan passed the photograph back to Michael. 'Fuck me, Michael, what a smooth-looking bastard he is! Mouth full of dog-ends, and a face like a bag of fucking hammers. At least he won't be hard to pick out in a crowd!'

Michael Flynn smiled; Declan could make him laugh even at a time like this.

'If he's got my Jessie, he has had to rent somewhere for cash. We need to get our blokes out there asking around. Like you say, Declan, it's not like they wouldn't fucking remember him, is it? He isn't exactly the answer to a maiden's prayer.'

Timothy Branch stood up, a bundle of nerves once more. 'I will get all my people out there. I will let you know if I hear anything.'

Michael Flynn didn't even bother to answer. This man was useless in every way.

When Branch had left, Declan said with incredulity, 'How the fuck can these people just be allowed out of the nut farms? No one is monitoring them, looking out for them – they just let them go out into the community without a fucking thought. It's outrageous.'

Michael Flynn agreed with his friend. 'I tell you this much, Declan – if anything bad happens to my Jessie, whoever signed that cunt out of the funny farm had better be a fucking good runner, because I will hunt them into the ground. I will make sure they never have that kind of responsibility again.'

Declan grinned. 'You're preaching to the converted, Michael. I will be right beside you, mate. But, remember, now we know what he looks like.'

Chapter One Hundred and Twenty-Two

The pavement was alight with rumours. Jessie Flynn was missing and there was a fifty-grand reward up for grabs, so it was in everyone's best interests to keep an eye out. Now they were being shown a photograph of a right strange-looking cove. It wasn't as if it would be hard to pick *him* out of a line-up. The word was out.

Michael Flynn had everyone on his payroll asking questions, and insisting on answers. His house was like Fort Knox – there were people watching it twenty-four/seven. There was no doubt in anyone's mind that this was the real deal. The fifty grand was an incentive, for everyone concerned. It was not just a big chunk of change, it was also proof of how serious Michael Flynn was about finding his daughter and, more to the point, punishing the person who had caused him so much aggro.

Michael Flynn was a legend in his own lunchtime; no one in their right mind would take him on. After seeing the photo of the man he was looking for, it was obvious that he was a fucking nutbag – he had to be.

A few of the people had heard the name Golding, and put two and two together. He had lost his whole family – of course he was a fucking nutter. But why had he singled out Michael Flynn's only daughter? The gossip was Michael Flynn had refused to pay a ransom for her, and that seemed feasible; after all, Jessie Flynn wasn't the most lovable of people. She hated her dad as well, everyone knew that. She talked about him like he was a piece of dirt – she had always enjoyed the shock and awe she had caused when people heard her cunt her father into the ground.

That was shocking enough, but what was more so was the way that Michael Flynn ignored it. It had to be hard for him, knowing that his only daughter talked about him as if he was nothing. If anyone else had dared to say what his Jessie had said, they would have been dead within twenty-four hours.

So people were willing to believe that he wouldn't pay the ransom asked for his daughter, and a big majority of those people didn't blame him. They thought that the fifty-grand reward was so he could locate the fucker responsible – and if Jessie was there then that was just an added bonus.

The whole underbelly of the British Isles was looking for Steven Golding. His photo was being shown everywhere. He was famous, but for all the wrong reasons.

Chapter One Hundred and Twenty-Three

Josephine was listening to her grandson as he chattered away to her about school. Dana had brought him in to her, along with a tray of drinks and cake, and she tried her hardest to concentrate on what he was telling her.

Michael had been so right – she *didn't* have any true interest in her grandson. She loved him, but she didn't want to be bothered with the day-to-day care that was required. Dana saw to that. Josephine was always nervous that he would somehow interfere with her belongings.

Ever since Michael had let rip at her, she was deeply worried that they were never going to be able to recover. She had not seen him since – he had not even called her. She wondered if this was the end of the line for them. She didn't even encourage sex any more – she didn't want it. If she *did* succumb to him, she didn't take an active part, she just lay there and waited for it to be over. Michael wouldn't force her into something she didn't want – he was too decent, too kind to ever make her do anything she didn't want to. But now she wondered if she had inadvertently shot herself in the foot. He was still a handsome, vibrant man, and he could easily find a young woman to fulfil his needs. She had always believed that his love for her had been enough, but now she wasn't so sure. She always looked perfect, but that wasn't enough.

'Will you answer me, Nana!' Jake was cross, and his strident voice had broken into her reverie.

Josephine smiled at him. 'I'm sorry, my little darling. What were you saying?'

But Jake didn't answer her, he was feeling very cross. It was hard trying to talk to his nana when she was so obviously not listening to him. She *never* listened to him!

'Please, Jake, I'm *so* sorry. I didn't hear you. Nana has a lot on her mind today.'

Jake stood up, he had been sitting at her feet as usual, but he wasn't in the mood for his nana's strangeness today. 'I'm going, Nana. If you won't talk to me then I want to be in the garden.'

Josephine was mortified. Jake looked so cross with her. He really was Michael's double – he even had her husband's expressions, especially now as he stood before her with folded arms, his handsome face dark with anger.

'I'm going to ask Dana to play with me outside and when Granddad comes home, I'm going to ask him when my mummy will be back.'

He stormed out of the room, and Josephine didn't stop him. She sat back in her chair, aware that she should have chased after him, made him feel wanted. But how could she do that when, in all honesty, she didn't really want to?

She leant down and picked up his sweet wrappers; he had

eaten a Kit Kat and a miniature Mars Bar. She folded both of the wrappers up neatly and carefully and placed them in the box beside her chair.

She started to tremble all over. She was having trouble breathing, and she closed her eyes and concentrated on taking deep, long breaths. It was an awful feeling. Her doctor said the panic attacks came on when she was feeling stressed. Well, of course she was stressed! Her daughter was missing and her grandson was cross with her. Coupled with her husband's angry shouting, it was inevitable.

She forced back the tears that were threatening and, going to her dressing table, she repaired her make-up carefully. It didn't make her feel better as it usually did. She sat back down in her chair and wondered if her husband was going to ring her, and put her mind at rest. She poured herself out another large glass of red wine and, as she sipped it, she decided that she would put on one of her favourite DVDs.

Chapter One Hundred and Twenty-Four

'Look, Lana, I am doing all I can to locate my daughter. If I was *you*, I'd try and fucking sort out your *own* daughter – my *wife*! In case it's escaped your notice, she hasn't left her fucking bedroom since the old King died! Now fuck off and stop ringing me. If I have any news, you will be one of the first to hear it.'

Michael slammed down the phone. He was so angry. Who did she think she was? Lana was like Josephine and his mother – they expected him to miraculously sort everything out for them. And he did, most of the time, but the only thing he wanted to concentrate on now was finding Jessie, and chasing down that fucker Golding. The last thing he needed was to spend time on the phone with people he would happily avoid if he wasn't related to them!

Declan Costello laughed. 'Well, that fucking told her, anyway!'

Michael looked at Declan; he was such a good friend to him, despite everything that had happened in the past. 'Fucking Lana! She's a pain in the arse. Josephine takes after her. She thinks that everything in the world revolves around her and fuck everybody else. Do you know something, Declan? Josephine hasn't left the house for years. That mad cunt who's got my Jessie sent her a letter with a number to call, and she didn't even fucking ring me to tell me! She now can't even make a phone call apparently! The fucking mad bitch. But she can take a call. You tell me where the logic is in that?'

Declan sighed. 'I know, Michael, you told me this before, mate. We all know your Josephine is a bit eccentric. But don't say anything you'll regret tomorrow, eh?'

Michael had always played down Josephine's oddities. Personally, Declan thought she was fucking barking. But then he wasn't married to her, thank fuck.

Michael snorted with derision. '*Eccentric?* Is that what you really think? She is a fucking card-carrying, bona fide head banger. I just wish I'd admitted it to myself ages ago. My mother, another fucking so-called "strong" woman, warned me about her from the off. She said she was a bit fucking doolally tap. But I had to have her. I loved Josephine so much, like she was a fucking terminal disease I'd contracted. I let her get away with murder. No matter how fucking nutty she got, I just kept pretending that it was perfectly normal. But it's not, Declan. She doesn't give a fuck about Jessie, not really, or little Jake – or even me for that matter. All she cares about is herself, and her fucking problems. I am so fucking sick of it.'

The phone rang and Declan picked it up quickly, glad to shut off Michael's conversation. It was not like him to say anything derogatory about his Josephine.

Michael watched closely as Declan listened to whoever was on the other end of the phone.

'Are you a hundred per cent sure?'

Declan was once again the listener, and Michael was watching his every nuance. 'Good man. Fucking result. Tell them to bring it here. Canary Wharf.'

Declan replaced the receiver and, looking at Michael, he said quickly, 'It appears our Mr Golding has been spotted. That was Jack. It seems that one of his blokes is visiting his old mum in Essex – she lives in Canewdon, near Rochford – and he thinks he saw him coming out of the local SPAR there. By the time the geezer had got parked – and we all know what Essex is like for parking – he'd lost sight of him. But he's purchased the CCTV from the shop, and it's being brought to us now. So at least this is something, Michael. If it is him, we have a location.'

Michael Flynn felt tearful; the relief he felt was so potent, and overwhelming. Never before, in the whole of his life, had he felt so useless. He was the main man, everyone came to him for their earn, he dealt with the Colombians, he basically held Europe in the palm of his hand and yet, for all that, he still couldn't locate his own daughter. The irony.

Chapter One Hundred and Twenty-Five

The CCTV footage wasn't exactly HD, but it was good enough for what Michael needed. 'That's him, Declan! It's fucking him! At long last.'

Declan could feel Michael's euphoria. It was over two weeks since Jessie had gone missing, and not a soul had seen or heard anything of her since. That is, except her own mother, and she had kept the information to herself. What the fuck was that about? Everyone knew that Josephine was running on fucking fumes. She was a strange fucker at the best of times, but when Michael told him she had been contacted about her daughter and she hadn't bothered to follow it up, it proved how much of a fucking nut she really was. It was the only opportunity they had been given to find out the girl's location and Josephine Flynn had put her own fucking mentalness above her only child's welfare. That was harsh, by anyone's standards.

But now, *finally*, Michael had something to work with, something tangible he could use. He deserved every second of his relief; it had been a long time coming.

Michael was writing everything down in a notebook. 'He bought Lambert and Butler cigarettes, and a bottle of the cheapest vodka, just like he did at Mrs Singh's. We know that he has never passed his driving test, but that doesn't mean he hasn't got a vehicle. It just means it's not insured. But why isn't he buying food?'

Declan shrugged. He had wondered that himself, but he didn't want to say it and worry Michael.

'The Filth are combing everywhere, and so are our lads. If he has rented a place we will know about it. He can't fucking hide out for ever, Michael. It's not feasible. No one can drop off the radar these days.'

Michael grinned. This was the best he had felt since this nightmare had started.

The phone rang and Michael picked it up, hoping it was someone with the man's location, or something else he could use to find his daughter.

Declan was watching Michael with a wide grin on his face, expecting to hear that the man had been found, and they could finally do something constructive – like kill the fucker, torture him at their leisure, and wipe him off the face of the earth.

'You've got to be fucking kidding me!'

Declan could hear the disappointment in Michael's voice; whoever was calling them didn't have good news.

'OK, OK. We will wait for it – just get it here quickly.' Michael put the phone down slowly.

Declan held his breath as he waited for Michael to tell him the latest news.

Michael lit a cigarette and, after drawing on it a few times, he said helplessly, 'You're not going to fucking believe this, Declan. That was John Freed of all people. It seems there is another CCTV on its way here. This time Golding was spied in a Tesco Express in Kent. He bought the same things – forty Lambert and Butler and a bottle of cheap vodka. He was recognised by the woman working the till. She rang John, and he's looked at the CCTV for himself. He reckons it is definitely Golding.'

Declan was silent; this was getting a bit too creepy now. It was as if the man was goading them, deliberately sending them on different trails. It was a good tactic, but it was guaranteed to make Michael Flynn angry and vicious.

'He's fucking laughing at us, Declan! This mentally retarded fucking headcase is laughing at us, for fuck's sake! He is telling me that he has the upper hand. I get that – it's standard procedure to keep the enemy guessing. But what is happening to my Jessie while this is going on? Is he hurting her? Has he already fucking murdered her?'

Declan waved his hands in despair. 'You mustn't think like that, Michael. For fuck's sake, if he hurt Jessie, he wouldn't have a bargaining chip any more, would he? Think about it. Plus, from what we know about him, he isn't a violent person. He's a fucking nutbag granted, but there's no history of violent behaviour.'

Michael jumped up out of his chair. He was feeling so angry and so impotent. How was it possible this fucking Golding could operate under his radar? It was a nightmare. This man couldn't be underestimated, he knew that much – he was far more intelligent than anyone was giving him credit for.

'Declan, have a fucking day off, will you! Read the papers! Every other day some fucking headbanger kills somebody for no fucking reason. They stab them or attack them in a shopping centre in full view of everyone around them. And, the worst thing of all is, these people – these nutters – are only roaming the streets because some fucking shrink decides that they are not a danger to anyone. But they are. This cunt is a fucking Grade A looney. I don't care what the doctors in the nut-house might have said about him – he had the nous to fucking take my baby. He has a very high IQ, remember? And he reads a lot. Well, when I finally get my hands on him – Mr Fucking *Intellectual* – I will personally remove his brain from his skull and I will then cheerfully force-feed it to the useless cunt who decided he was fit enough to rejoin society. I can't believe this ponce is actually getting the better of *me*. That is the hardest part of all, Declan – this fucking no-mark, this mentally challenged fucker, is actually getting one over on me.'

Declan agreed with Michael wholeheartedly; this ponce was either very clever or very lucky; Declan had a feeling it was a combination of the two. But that wasn't what Michael needed to hear at this precise moment in time.

'That is fucking mental, Michael. Listen to yourself! He is a nut – granted – but that is his weakness, not his strength. He doesn't even want a ransom, for fuck's sake. That alone should tell you something.'

'It does, Declan. It tells me this isn't about money, this is fucking personal, and we both know why that is, don't we?'

Declan didn't answer.

'Patrick knew what he was asking of me. He *knew* the

house wasn't empty. He was using me to vent his fucking spleen. It was one of his biggest failings – his narrow-mindedness. He could hold a grudge for the tiniest of reasons, an imagined slight, or a small loan that was overdue – something he should have been big enough to overlook. But he couldn't. When he got that bee in his fucking bonnet . . .' He trailed off. His anger was threatening to take over, and he knew he had to calm himself down, think logically, not let his heart rule his head. 'You know what I am saying as well as I do, Declan.'

Michael Flynn looked out of his window. Today he wasn't enjoying the view he'd always loved. Today he was wondering how a man like Steven Golding could get the better of him. That was something Michael Flynn couldn't live with, something he would never be able to overcome. The man was on a fucking death wish, and Michael was going to make sure he got *exactly* what he was asking for.

Chapter One Hundred and Twenty-Six

Jessie woke up to see the man taking photos of her. She didn't even try to hide herself from him, she was too tired, too sore to move. Her ankles were so painful, the shackles had rubbed most of her skin away, and she could actually see her ankle bones poking through now. It was so disgusting to look at. The metal rings that held her in place were covered with dried blood and hardened lumps of her skin, a constant reminder of her predicament.

The man was laughing to himself, as if he was party to some private joke. Jessie had lost most of her fight – it was pointless trying to convince him of anything. He had already told her the worst – that he was going to let her die. She believed him. He was too fucking unbalanced to lie to her. He was on a mission, that much was evident; he lived on another planet, on another wavelength.

Now she was starving and in such agony she might welcome death at some point in the near future; anything had to be better than living like this. He had even taken the bucket from her, so she couldn't even open her bowels or have a pee with ease. She had been reduced to using the concrete floor. But what else could she do? She was limited by the shackles and, as her dad used to say, even a dog doesn't shit in its own basket. The less food her body got, the more she seemed to need to evacuate her bowels. It was like water, just diarrhoea, but it was very painful for her. And humiliating.

She wasn't sure how long it would be before it would be too difficult for her to move. Then she would have no choice but to lay in her own filth.

She wanted to cry again, but she didn't think she had any tears left. She opened the bottle of water – he still made sure she had that at least – and she drank it straight down, welcoming the oblivion of the drugged liquid. The sores on her ankles were infected, and she could smell her own rotting flesh. It was so disgusting, it even overshadowed her body odour, though the smell of faeces was overpowering.

The man himself didn't seem to notice anything was amiss; he didn't wrinkle his nose, or register the stench surrounding her. Jessie decided that he just wasn't interested enough to care. Like he kept telling her, this wasn't about her. It was as if he didn't even see her most of the time.

The man stepped closer to her, smiling inanely.

'Do you remember that quiz show that was on years ago? When people had to guess the price of things? It was a really good show.'

Jessie shook her head. 'No, I don't remember it. Probably before my time.'

The man grinned. 'Oh, you would have liked it. I did, I loved it. The man who asked the questions was very clever. I remember now, it was called *Sale of the Century*. I like quiz shows. I like questions. I always liked questions.'

Jessie forced herself to smile at him. 'Really? Can I ask you a question, then?'

He smiled at her, positively beaming with pleasure. 'Of course you can, silly! Ask me anything you like, anything at all. I bet I can answer it.'

Jessie pulled herself up on to her elbows and, looking the man straight in the eyes, she asked quietly, 'Why are you doing this to me? What have I ever done to you?'

He turned away from her, but when he turned back to face her, he was laughing again. 'I told you before, Jessie, this isn't about *you*! You are the weapon I need, Jessie, to bring your father to his knees. When I finally deliver you to him, starved, shackled and, of course, *dead*, he will finally understand the meaning of despair. Complete and utter despair. It's a pain that is unique. You see, one thing I have learnt, Jessie, is the worst pain of all is not your *own* suffering, but knowing about the suffering of the people you really care about. That's a far worse pain, worse than any physical harm you might have to endure yourself.'

He was smiling at her again, as if he had just given her the secret of eternal happiness. Then he said matter-of-factly, 'Think about your little boy Jake. Imagine if I starved him to death. That would be a far worse pain to you, than what you're experiencing now, wouldn't it? Do you see what I mean? Understand what I'm getting at?'

Jessie didn't answer him; she felt sick at what he had said to her. This was surreal, unbelievable, and yet it was really happening.

Chapter One Hundred and Twenty-Seven

'There are people searching Kent as well as Essex, Michael. He can't fucking evade us for ever. I have mobilised everyone that we work with throughout the British Isles, and they are all on the hunt as well. The fifty grand is a big incentive but, also, I think this cunt has really put a lot of backs up.'

Michael didn't reply. He was so tired, but he just couldn't sleep. He was still holed up in the offices at Canary Wharf with Declan. It was where everyone knew to contact them.

Michael didn't want to go home; he talked to little Jake on the phone, but there was no way he wanted to go back there and face Josephine. She was the last person he wanted to see. Every time he thought about her keeping that letter to herself, putting her own needs before her daughter's, he felt angry enough to strangle her with his bare hands. If she had told him, this might have been resolved by now. If this bloke was as big a nut as they all reckoned, maybe not phoning had sent him over the edge; after all, no one had heard a fucking word from him since.

'How the fuck can this ponce evade not just the police,

but every fucking Face in the country? It's fucking impossible, surely?'

Declan shrugged casually. 'Well, look at that Bin Laden bloke. He'd been on the trot for years when they caught him.'

Michael ran his hands through his hair; sometimes Declan didn't have a clue. He just opened his mouth before he put his brain in gear.

'Oh, by the way, Michael, I spoke to Jack earlier on, while you were in the shower. He has tracked down Golding's medical records. It cost him an arm and a leg, but he has all the addresses where he's ever lived – everything about him. Who knows – he might have a place he goes to regularly. It's worth a chance.'

Michael snorted with derision. 'I suppose so. It's amazing what you can fucking buy, isn't it?'

Declan laughed at Michael's sarcasm. Money could get literally anything usually.

Michael went on: 'If I could only know for certain that she was alive, Declan, I would feel so much better. I can't bear to think that she might be frightened, you know? Scared and alone somewhere, and wondering why I haven't rescued her.'

Declan was very blasé as he said honestly, 'I'm sorry, Michael, but it would take a lot to scare your Jessie. She isn't what anyone would call a shrinking violet, is she? Jessie Flynn is a woman who lives her own life. Fuck me – if *you* can't control her, how the fuck could anyone else?'

Michael didn't laugh with Declan this time; he appreciated his friend was just trying to allay his fears, but no one could do that now.

'I'm not so sure about that, Declan. She isn't as hard-faced as she acts. There is a softness there that few people ever see. She would ring her mum almost every day, because she knew that she worries about her. She also asks about Jake, of course. She loves that little boy, I know that for a fact.'

Declan wasn't so sure Jessie was this sweet young thing her father was describing, but if that was what Michael wanted to believe, he was happy to go along with it. In his opinion, Jessie Flynn was a selfish little fucker, who never had the sense to see how fucking lucky she was, and who had never appreciated just how loved and adored she was. She was a user, and she had used everyone around her. But Declan was shrewd enough to keep his own counsel; there were some things you couldn't tell people – they just didn't want to hear them.

'Well, Michael, you know her better than anyone, mate.'

Michael's phone vibrated and he picked it up, opening the text message. He was shocked to see a picture of his Jessie. She was shackled to a bed, looking ill and very frightened.

'Oh, my God.'

He passed the phone to Declan, who looked at the picture with abject horror. Jessie looked terrified, and she also looked like she was starving. He could see her ribcage in startling detail. He zoomed in so he could see the picture better, and he could see that her ankles were rubbed raw from the iron shackles. It looked as if the bones were exposed, and there were faeces on the floor around the bed. It was a wicked, vicious picture sent to cause the maximum of hurt.

It was her eyes, though, that really bothered him. They were looking right into the camera, and there was no life in them. They were already dead. He was so shocked, he couldn't speak for a few minutes.

Michael had crossed his arms over his chest and he was hugging himself. As he rocked himself to and fro, Declan was shocked to realise that the man was openly crying. Michael Flynn was sobbing like a baby; it was terrible to see him brought so low.

Declan forced himself into action. He picked up his phone and he rang a man called Arthur Hellmann. He was a technological wizard, and he had worked for everyone who was anyone. He also had a serious gambling habit, and he had owed money all over the Smoke. It had been Michael's idea to pay his debts off and get him into the firm. Now Declan hoped the man could use his expertise to track down the mobile phone Golding was using. It was clutching at straws, but it was all they had. Michael Flynn needed to feel like he was doing something, now more than ever. That image of young Jessie had achieved its goal; it was further proof that they didn't have any control over this situation whatsoever.

When he came off the phone, he looked at Michael sadly. 'I'm going to up the security at your house, Michael. I think this proves we can't take any chances.'

Michael nodded. 'Put them inside the house. I'll ring Dana, make sure that she doesn't even take Jake to school. Until this is over, we daren't chance anything.' Michael looked at the photo of his daughter again. 'She's fucking terrified, you can see it in her eyes. How in *fuck's* name has this happened? How the fuck has this mad cunt managed to get this far?'

Declan shrugged; he was genuinely disturbed himself now. This was well outside their usual remit. Until now, he would have bet his last penny that a situation like this would have been an impossibility. They were too big, too well known. But Declan knew, from bitter experience, that the greatest of threats nearly always came from the people you least expected.

Chapter One Hundred and Twenty-Eight

Hannah Flynn couldn't understand why Michael had not been around to see her for days. It wasn't like him – he always made a point of dropping in to see her. She was particularly worried after what Josephine had told her. If her Michael had lost his temper with his wife then there was something serious going on. Josephine had never been able to do any wrong in Michael's eyes. Now, it seemed, he had finally lost his patience, and she had found herself actually feeling sorry for Josephine. That alone had been a shock. The woman had been completely devastated by her husband's attack on her. But Christ Himself knew – she blessed herself automatically at the use of the Lord's name in vain – Josephine Flynn was one of the most selfish fuckers that had ever been put on this earth. Hannah sat down at her kitchen table. She was a bundle of nerves lately, she couldn't seem to settle. What had happened to Jessie was playing on her mind. The girl always kept in touch with her nana Hannah.

She poured herself out a glass of good Irish whiskey, and took a large gulp to steady herself. Then she poured herself another. She heard her doorbell, and sighed with annoyance.

Few people sought her company, and that suited her. She had never suffered fools gladly. But, as she walked to her front door, she hoped against hope that it was someone with news about her Jessie.

She opened the front door, expecting to see someone she knew. Instead she saw a skinny, grey-haired man, with sallow skin and a twisted smile. She detected a sour odour coming off him. She went to ask him what the hell he wanted, but before she could say a word, he lunged at her. As she tried to step back from him, she felt a sharp pain in her chest. Looking down, she saw the handle of a knife sticking out of her breast. It occurred to her that its blade was obviously buried deep inside her chest. It had all happened so quickly. The man was still smiling at her and, as she sank to her knees, he stepped away from her casually, and began taking photos of her on his phone. All she could do was watch him. She was trying to call out, get help, but there was nothing she could do. Her mouth was slowly filling up with blood, and it made her want to vomit. It tasted disgusting, it was so thick and it was suddenly dribbling out of her mouth. She could feel its warmth as it ran down her chin. She was lying on her back now, and she knew she would eventually choke on her own blood. She could feel her heartbeat getting slower by the second, and she could hear herself wheezing as she tried to breathe. She could feel the light-headedness as she gradually started to lose consciousness, and she welcomed the oblivion. Anything was better than this battle to take a single breath.

Chapter One Hundred and Twenty-Nine

Arthur Hellmann was a strange-looking man. He was tall, very thin, and he had deep brown eyes and white-blond hair. It was a startling combination. Whereas on some people, it would have given them striking good looks, on Arthur it just seemed to add to his general air of strangeness. He was a man who found it very difficult to socialise with other people, and who much preferred the anonymity of cyberspace.

As he walked into the office, Michael and Declan didn't even bother to greet him, and that suited him. He liked that Michael Flynn didn't feel the need to engage him in conversation unless it was of some relevance. Too many people talked for the sake of it, and they rarely had anything of interest to say.

He sat at the desk, and set up his laptop, before saying to no one in particular, 'I can access most phones. As long as this one's turned on, I can get a location on it. I can also work out where any calls were made – the area, that is.'

Michael Flynn passed his BlackBerry to him, and Arthur glanced at the photograph. It was shocking.

'I got that about three hours ago, Arthur. I need you to try and find the sender.'

Arthur nodded. He was aware that time was obviously of the essence. 'Well, there is one thing I can tell you straight off, this isn't the usual cheap throwaway phone. This picture has a lot of detail, which tells me the phone used was a fairly decent model.'

Michael Flynn wasn't even listening to the man. 'Just try and track the fucker down.'

The phone vibrated once more. Arthur Hellmann automatically opened the text. After a quick glance at the contents, he passed the phone to Michael Flynn without a word.

Michael looked at the photo of his mother lying in her hallway, a knife poking out of her right breast, and he shook his head slowly in disbelief. For the first time in his life he felt vulnerable, frightened. His mother was dying before his eyes, his daughter was dying somewhere, tied up like a fucking animal and obviously in extreme pain, and he couldn't do a thing. This man was taunting him. The phone in the office started ringing, and Michael Flynn knew exactly what the call would be about.

Chapter One Hundred and Thirty

Josephine sat on her balcony with a glass of red wine, looking out over the gardens and wondering if the man who had her daughter and who had murdered her mother-in-law was coming for her and Jake.

It felt unreal knowing that Hannah was dead. Stabbed in her own home, by some mad fucker who had evaded capture. Now her home was overrun with armed men, sent by Michael to protect them. Little Jake was loving the company, bless him, unaware of the danger they were in.

She had a twelve-gauge shotgun by her side, and a Glock 22 handgun lying on the table in front of her. If anyone was coming here, she was more than ready to fight her end. It was odd, but she had always found handling guns very easy from the time Michael taught her to use one. She liked the feel of them, the knowledge that they were capable of so much destruction. It was the secret of guns: the weakest person in the world could protect themselves from the biggest of enemies, because a gun was relatively lightweight, and had the power over life and death.

Even though Michael had seen fit to *drown* their home with his armed men, she felt much safer knowing that she was armed too. Hannah had been taken out on her doorstep, stabbed like a fucking animal, and whoever had done that also had her daughter in his clutches. If only she had been capable of passing his message on to Michael, this might have been avoided. She had been hoping that he would come to see her and, if he had, then she would have been able to show him the letter.

It was a learning curve, she supposed – she was unable to justify her actions any longer. It didn't mean she was going to be able to change overnight; this wasn't a fucking film, where everything was resolved in an hour and a half, this was her real fucking *life*. But she could at least make a conscious decision this time to get the help that she so desperately needed. Surely that was a start?

Jake came running into her room, hyper with excitement.

'Nana, one of Granddad's friends said he would teach me to play poker! Can I learn it, please?'

Josephine was grateful Jake was distracted. ''Course you can! It's a very tricky game, though, so make sure you listen to what the man tells you carefully.'

Jake Flynn was dressed in his favourite Peppa Pig pyjamas – he was obsessed with Peppa, and would happily wear these until they fell apart. He was holding his favourite book which he had tucked under his arm – he adored *The Gruffalo* and he had read it over and over again. He looked very handsome and so vulnerable, that Josephine felt almost tearful as she looked at him. He deserved much more than she had ever given to him. She had lost out on so much of his little life.

'I like playing cards. I told the man that and he laughed! He said I was Granddad's double, and I think that's a good thing, Nana, don't you? Dana is going to learn with me, so that we can play poker together.'

Josephine hugged him to her tightly. She kissed his thick, dark hair, drinking in the smell of Matey bubble bath and jojoba shampoo.

He hugged her back with one arm, before pulling away from her. Then he noticed the gun on the table in front of her. He said solemnly, 'Nana, you better be very careful with that.'

Josephine could hear the underlying fear in his voice. He was six years old and already he knew that guns were dangerous. One day, of course, he would have to understand that, in the world his granddad lived in, guns were a necessity – a part of their everyday life. The charmed life that they lived came at a price, and that price was often higher than anyone realised. It was a dangerous life, and that was more apparent now than ever before.

'I will, darling. I will be very careful. Now, you go and learn how to play poker. Don't worry about anything. No one will ever let anything bad happen to you, I promise.'

As he ran back down to the kitchen, she wondered if she could keep that promise. She remembered the night that the Cornel brothers had arrived at her door, remembered Jessie's shock and horror at the night's events. She could see herself telling her daughter to lock herself in her bedroom, and not to be frightened of anything. She had found an inner strength that night to protect her home, her sanctuary, from the threat of the outside world. Jessie had seen her with the gun that night, and it had terrified her. Jessie had understood the danger they were in. It had changed her daughter – she had been forced to grow up that night.

Now her only child was being held captive, and that was harder for Josephine to comprehend than anything else in her life so far. That her daughter's dire predicament had still not been enough to make her use a telephone, was something she was finding very hard to forgive herself for. But it was actually her Michael's reaction that she was really worried about. She feared he wouldn't be forgiving her any time soon.

A part of her hoped that this unknown man would come here and give her the chance to take him out. It might be her only opportunity to redeem herself.

Chapter One Hundred and Thirty-One

Timothy Branch was watching Michael Flynn as the man tried to take in the news of his mother's death; the woman had been slaughtered on her doorstep. It was unbelievable – no one could have predicted anything like this. Who would have thought that a man like Michael Flynn could ever have been game-played by a fucking toerag like Steven Golding? Golding was a fucking no-mark. But, somehow, he had managed to get the better of Michael Flynn. He had not only taken the man's daughter, he had also stabbed the man's mother to death in her own home.

It was Steven Golding's complete disregard for the consequences of his actions that truly bothered Timothy Branch. His was the mindset of a terrorist, someone whose only aim in life was to carry out the duty required of them, regardless of their own safety. It was only about the endgame. This man Golding didn't seem to have an agenda that any of them could understand – there wasn't room for bargaining; he honestly didn't seem to want anything of value from any of them. He was only interested in hitting Michael Flynn where it hurt. All he seemed to want was revenge. That was the only thing this could be about – not that Michael Flynn had been very forthcoming about his dealings with the man in the past. But he had read the man's medical reports, knew that his family had been wiped out in a fire – a fire that had been started deliberately. It didn't take an Albert fucking Einstein to work out that Michael Flynn had been involved in that shit somewhere along the line. Branch had been around long enough to suss out what was *really* going on, but it wasn't in his interests to pursue this train of thought – he knew when to leave well alone.

'I've had your mother's body taken to the morgue, and I have hushed it up for the moment, but you have to understand, Michael, I can't sit on this for too long. None of the neighbours saw anything – it was very fast. And, from what I can gather, your mum wasn't a woman who encouraged her neighbours' friendships, if you get my drift.'

Michael laughed wryly. 'You got that right. My mother was the female equivalent of Jack the Giant Killer. She saw most people in her orbit as completely fucking useless ponces. She wasn't known for her sparkling personality.'

Declan Costello could detect the catch in Michael's voice underneath his bravado. He had loved his mother, in spite of everything. She wasn't a woman who encouraged displays of affection, but she had loved her son too.

Timothy Branch was aware of Hannah Flynn's reputation as a woman of limited patience; it was well known she had a tongue in her head and she used it to her advantage. He sighed. 'Look, Michael, the bottom line is, this bloke is either very fucking clever, or very fucking lucky. In all my years on the force I have never seen anything like it. He's obviously watched you for a while and he's aware of your daily routine. How else could he know so much? One thing I do know, though, is he's not that far away. I'd say that he's operating from within an hour's journey of your house. He has to be. It stands to reason.'

Declan and Michael exchanged glances; at last the man was making sense. It was about time he earned his fucking keep! Branch was like all bent Filth – he wasn't liked or trusted by the people who paid his extra-curricular wages, *or* the people he had to work with in his capacity as an Old Bill. They would all know that he wasn't kosher or to be completely trusted. Word travelled fast, and that was something no one could prevent. It was a double-edged sword. He was paid a good wage to ensure that he was on their side if it ever went pear-shaped, but he was automatically suspect because he was selling out his own. Treachery wasn't looked on lightly in either of the circles Timothy Branch moved in.

Declan poured Michael another drink; he needed it – the man was in absolute shock. 'Come on, Michael, sit down and drink this. You've had a shock to your system.'

Michael allowed himself to be seated and took the drink offered to him. He had never felt so useless in his whole life. He kept seeing Jessie, the fear on her face, and the picture of his mother, dying in front of his eyes. No one seemed to be able to give him any information of use. He had a very large workforce, and not one of them could find out even the simplest thing about Steven Golding.

Timothy Branch cleared his throat noisily. 'I've had my blokes comb through his medical records, and there's nothing of value, Michael. They have been to every address where he's been registered, checked with his doctors, and not a fucking whisper.'

Michael Flynn started to laugh loudly, but it was an unnatural sound, too high pitched and too heartbreaking to be normal.

Declan and Timothy watched Michael laughing, warily.

Arthur Hellmann looked up from his computer in the corner of the room and he said triumphantly, 'I've got him. I think I've found the fucker.'

Declan knelt down in front of Michael and, grabbing the man's shoulders, he shook him roughly. 'Stop it, Michael! Will you just stop laughing. Listen to me! This isn't over yet.'

Eventually Michael began to quieten down, and then he seemed to pull himself together. Pushing Declan away, he picked up the glass of brandy from the table, and swallowed it in one gulp. He looked into Declan's eyes, saw the worry there and the genuine concern for his wellbeing. Michael wiped his hand across his mouth roughly; he had no choice left but to face this.

'It's OK, Declan. I'm fine. I'm OK.'

Declan was still kneeling on the floor, shocked by Michael's reaction. It wasn't like him to lose the plot. The man had every reason to – it just wasn't something he had expected. Michael Flynn was a hard man, harder than anyone Declan had ever known.

'Fucking hell, Michael, you can't lose it now. We're so close. You need to pull yourself together, get a fucking grip.'

Michael took a deep breath and expelled it slowly. He was

aware that he needed to keep himself on an even keel. 'I'm all right now, Declan. It's over.'

Arthur Hellmann was embarrassed at such a naked display of emotion, especially from a man like Michael Flynn. It was unseemly, humiliating – the man was almost hysterical.

Declan turned to him and said angrily, 'Well, come on then, Arthur. Where is the fucker?'

Chapter One Hundred and Thirty-Two

Jessie woke up as the man shook her. She felt so drained, so ill. She didn't even know where she was for a few moments; it was a while before she remembered the truth. Then it all came rushing back, and she closed her eyes in distress. She blinked back tears, looking at the man's filthy smile which was as familiar to her now as her mother's beautiful one, and she wondered if it would be the last thing she ever saw in this life. It was such a frightening thought. She hoped not. She hoped she would just go to sleep and slip away, that she could at least take away some of his power and die without him witnessing it. He was looking at her intently, and she couldn't turn away from his gaze. Her legs were swollen, and they felt like they were burning. Her toes were black, and she knew she had a serious infection. She had a temperature and she was burning up, sweating like a pig. Her hair was stuck to her head, and she couldn't concentrate any more. She just wanted it to be over.

The man was smiling at her as he said conversationally, 'You look awful, Jessie. Really bad.'

She didn't answer him; he didn't expect one anyway.

'I must tell you this.' He was giggling like a girl, and she could see the euphoria he was experiencing – it was almost tangible. He was sitting on the bed, with his hands underneath his behind, like a teenage girl who had just found out a juicy piece of gossip about her worst enemy.

'I want to show you a photograph. I know you will understand the importance of it. You're a very intelligent girl. I must be honest with you, it wasn't something I expected.'

He held his phone out to her, and she looked at the picture he showed her, as she knew he wanted her to. She didn't have a choice – her fight was gone. She saw her nana Hannah dead or dying. There was blood everywhere. It was sickening. Her nana had died violently, for no reason other than because this weirdo had decided it was her time. Seeing her nana stripped of her dignity and left to die was so very wrong. Hannah Flynn was a woman who had brought up her child alone, who had worked every hour God sent, to give her son the best that she could. It was an awful way to die, and worse at the hands of someone like this. Jessie felt a spark of hatred threaten to erupt, but made sure that she kept her face neutral.

'That's my nana. I assume she's dead?' She was pleased with how nonchalant her voice sounded, pleased that she had taken away some of his glory. He wanted a reaction from her, and she would give him one – just not the reaction he was expecting.

The man sat upright; he was so stiff it was like he had a board up his jumper.

Jessie sighed. 'No one liked her anyway. You did us all a

favour. I bet my dad would shake your hand if he knew.'

The man was sitting on the bed, staring at her, but she knew he wasn't seeing her – he was once more on his own private planet. What kind of person was he to kill an old lady, and show the pictures to her grandchild? Her fear of him was gone. She was dying – it was only a matter of time now. But she would die without giving this fucker another inch – she was not going to give him the satisfaction of knowing she was frightened of him any more. Seeing her nana Hannah like that, so brutally murdered, was the last straw. As tired and as ill as she felt, she wasn't going to let him think that he had broken her completely. Her nana Hannah deserved that much from her, surely?

She made herself laugh then, a low, deep-throated chuckle. 'God, I bet she was surprised to see you, eh? Hannah Flynn, the hardest woman in the East End, murdered on her doorstep. It's so ironic. You're lucky she didn't stab you first.'

She could sense the man was annoyed with her. He didn't like what she was saying, and that suited her – she hoped he would do the kind thing and finish her off as well. It wasn't as if she was ever going to leave this place alive. He had already made that abundantly clear to her.

'Me and my dad have had more fights than Michael Tyson. We *loathe* each other. My mum hasn't left the house for fucking years, she lives in two rooms and she's a hoarder. I bet you didn't know that, did you? She keeps everything, every scrap of paper, every fucking thing that someone she loves has touched. It's mental, I tell you. She still has sweet wrappers from when I was a toddler. And I can tell you now, mister, the minute I went on the missing list my dad would have made sure my mum had more bodyguards than fucking Whitney Houston. He *adores* her – she's his reason for living. When you deliver my body, as you promised, he will hunt you down like a dog, but not because of what you've done to me – he won't give a flying fuck about that. He will come after you, because you took something he owned. It's all about face with my dad, about front.' She laughed again, much harder this time. She could see the bafflement on his face and was enjoying his discomfort, and the knowledge that she had royally pissed all over his fireworks. If nothing else, she was going to make sure he didn't have the last laugh.

The man stood up abruptly, and she looked him right in the eyes. Then he punched her hard in her face. She didn't react, she let him hit her, and even as she felt her eye begin to swell, she still didn't say anything.

Suddenly, he was shouting at her, a deafening roar that was as unexpected as it was potent. 'I will *not* allow you to laugh at me. I will *not* let you do that.'

He hit her again, this time on her jaw. It was an uppercut, and she felt the blow snap her head back with its power. The next punch hit her straight in the mouth; he was so much stronger than she would have believed possible. Her lip split open and it started to bleed profusely. She could taste her own blood, feel it as it dripped down her face. She instinctively braced herself for the next onslaught, but it didn't come. She heard him walking away from her, leaving her all alone once more.

She didn't move. She waited until she heard the door

clang shut, and then she opened her eyes, glad to be by herself again. She couldn't help feeling like she had won something. It was a small victory, but it was a victory nonetheless. She spat the blood out of her mouth. She could feel the throb of her eye as it started to close, and the stinging from the cut on her lip. She tried to pull herself up into a sitting position, but she couldn't manage it. She welcomed the pain from her face; the fresh hurt took her mind off her other ills. She lay there, unable to move her body any more, praying to God for sleep to take her. While she was asleep she couldn't feel pain, she wasn't reminded of the state she was in, or the fact she was going to die chained to a bed. She couldn't think about how she had neglected her little son, or how she had wasted her young life, and all because she had seen the dark side of her parents' lives. Jake had been a constant reminder of her mistakes – she had always seen him as a symbol of her stupidity. Now, after this, she would give anything to turn back the clock, and do everything right – do what her father had urged her to do from the very beginning: stand up and face her responsibilities. She had fought him every step of the way and now it seemed so fucking futile. She had lain here and thought it over in depth, and accepted that she had not hurt anyone except herself.

She looked up at the ceiling. Her tears were rolling down her face – she could feel them dripping into her ears, and she didn't even wipe them away.

Chapter One Hundred and Thirty-Three

'Right then, people.' Arthur Hellmann was oblivious to most of what had been going on around him; that was his biggest failing as a human being, and his biggest asset as a computer whiz. 'From what I can work out, the person you're looking for is located within a one-quarter mile radius. He is in Essex, within two miles of Romford. The phone itself is registered to someone called Malcolm Briers, whose address, believe it or not, is within two miles of Romford. The address is White Farm on the Rainham Road. It was a clever fucking scam, I tell you. If I didn't have access to every fucking mobile number on the planet, we would never have located the fucker. He was well hidden. And if he had not left his phone on, I would never have found the bastard.'

Michael was listening to the man with absolute amazement. After all this time, this fucking weirdo had actually managed to track the bastard down, when even the police couldn't manage to do it. Michael was almost beside himself with euphoria – at last he had a fucking lead.

Arthur looked at the men around him warily. 'Look, it

doesn't mean he's *there*. It just means that is where it's all registered. But the phone *was* used within that area recently.'

Michael hugged the man to him. 'You fucking *diamond*! Whatever happens, mate, you get your wedge. At least you have given us a place to start. I could fucking kiss you!'

Declan was laughing now. He felt the same euphoria as Michael; this was a real fucking result.

Timothy Branch watched the two men as they bowled out of the room together. He felt he had failed; and of course he had – miserably. Turning to Arthur Hellmann, who was one weird-looking fucker, he said arrogantly, 'What you just did is illegal, you do know that?'

Hellmann laughed in his face. He couldn't give a toss what this man thought of him or his methods. If he worked within the law he would never have found out anything! No one would. Their hands were tied, Freedom of Information Acts, etc., etc. It was laughable. This was why he earned the big bucks – this man had to know that better than anybody.

Poking a finger into Branch's face, he said sarcastically, 'So fucking arrest me then! I *dare* you.' Hellmann hoped that he was fifty grand up on this deal – that was the asking price for locating Michael Flynn's daughter. He had followed the phone, followed the trail, he just hoped that he had done enough.

Chapter One Hundred and Thirty-Four

Michael was buzzing as they drove out of East London – *finally* he was actually doing something constructive. It had been a long time coming; this mad fucker was so elusive, he was beginning to think he would never find him. It was the first time in his life that he had been unable to meet a problem head on. He had been at the top of his game for so long, it was unbelievable to think that anyone could have got the better of him. It galled him, it *unnerved* him, if he was honest.

'I am going to kill this cunt with my bare hands, Declan. How *dare* he bring this to my door? Whatever might have happened in the past, his fucking beef was with *me*, not my family. I'm the one who fucked up.' He laughed sarcastically. 'Or, more to the point, *Patrick* was the one who fucked up. He knew what he was asking me to do. But what I can't get my head round is that, of all the people I have taken out for whatever fucking reason, the only time it's come back to bite me on the arse, is the one time I never intended to hurt a fucking soul. I would never have done that for anyone.

Taking out women and children? That's a fucking no-brainer. I would never have agreed to that.'

Declan sighed. He could understand Michael's feelings. He kept his voice neutral as he said calmly, 'It's all relative. That's in the past, Michael. All you can do now is sort out this shit as best you can.'

They were sitting in traffic at the Lodge Avenue roundabout in Barking. It was so frustrating. Michael was grasping the steering wheel with both hands, he was sweating all over, his fury and impatience intense now. He had no other choice – he had to sit there patiently until the traffic moved. There was nothing else he could do.

Declan could feel the man's tension – it was understandable, but it was also threatening to get out of control. He lit them both cigarettes, and he passed one to Michael. Then they were on the move. Michael manoeuvred his Mercedes through the traffic skilfully and, as they edged towards Dagenham, he said with obvious relief, 'Another five minutes in that traffic and I would have run fucking riot through Barking.'

Declan laughed with him; he felt the same way. It was dark now, and the sky was heavily laden with rain clouds. It was close, stormy, and it added to the feeling of urgency. As it started to spit, Michael put on the windscreen wipers. He was already relaxing as they passed the Ford Motor Works along the A13, and slipped into Rainham. After all this time, he finally had a fucking goal to head for.

'Every time I think of that picture of my Jessie I feel like screaming. And my mum's dead, Declan – I know it's true, but I just can't take it in. She was struck down in her own home, on her own fucking doorstep. How the fuck can this have happened to *me*? It's like a fucking living nightmare.' He wanted to cry again. The absolute power of his emotions amazed him. 'My old mum, for all her attitude, was always fucking good to me, Declan. She worked every hour God sent when I was a kid, and I never wanted for anything. She would have given me the food out of her mouth, I know that. I've always known that.'

Michael drove past Rainham Clocktower, and out towards the country lanes. They were nearly there now, and he could feel the adrenaline starting to kick in.

'My mum always said that Josephine was a selfish cunt, and she was right. I wouldn't listen to her. When Josephine first started hoarding food, all those years ago, my mum said I needed to nip it in the bud. But I didn't listen to her – I treated her like she was the fucking enemy. I just pretended that it wasn't happening. But she was proved right. If I had put my foot down from the off, I know that all this shit with Josephine would never have got this far. I stood by as my wife gradually retired from real life. All that money I have shelled out on psychiatrists for her, and they say the same thing – it takes *time.* She is mentally ill! Well, fuck me, Declan, I don't know about them, but I had already fucking worked that one out for myself. Hardly rocket science, is it? If it wasn't for Dana, Jake would never leave the house. That great, big, expensive *fucking* house, situated in its *own* grounds, with its thirty-grand kitchen, and its two full-time gardeners, and my wife lives in two rooms and, it seems, can't bring herself to make a phone call that might save her only daughter's life. All that money I have weighed out to get her help, and she is still unable to open a letter or dial a fucking telephone. How fucking messed up is that? This new bloke she's got on her case now – a right fucking arrogant cunt he is and all – is giving *me* lists of books I should be reading to acquaint myself with my wife's condition. Well, I pointed out to him, in the nicest possible way, that I was paying him good money to do all of that *for* me, and there was an old saying: why have a fucking dog and bark your fucking self. I was very angry at the time, and I think he noticed that. Suffice to say, Declan, he soon got with the fucking project.'

He slowed the car down. They were on the Rainham road, and he parked in a layby. 'We're here. The farm entrance is down the end of this lane.'

Michael got out of the car. It was raining hard now. Opening up the boot, he took out a large handgun, and passed it to Declan. He took out a Glock 22 for himself. It was his weapon of choice – lightweight, and easy to use; it was also easy to dispose of. It could be stripped down to nothing.

'I am so looking forward to meeting Mr Steven Golding, and blowing his fucking head right off.'

He shut the car boot carefully. He turned towards his old friend, and said gravely, 'I will never forget how good you've been to me, Declan, through all of this. I really have appreciated how you've stood by me through everything. I know that you have talked me down on more than one occasion, and stopped me from screwing this up completely. I appreciate just how good a friend you are, Declan.'

Declan was moved by Michael's words; he knew how hard

it was for him to even say them. 'Look, Michael, you know that I will always have your back.'

Michael grinned sadly. 'Do you know the worst thing about this for me? The one thing that I've learnt from this shit is that it all means *nothing*. Everything that we've worked for, everything that we've achieved, all the fucking stunts we've pulled to get what we wanted from life, all that planning, and forward thinking, all those fucking years we put into it and it turned out that it was for sweet F A, sweet fuck-all. We chased the fucking dollar day and night, living the so-called dream! The leaders of everyone around us, responsible for every fucking earn, as well as the people who we allow to gather up said earn for us. And it was a fucking waste of time. We have squandered so much of our lives accumulating money, power, *things* and, in reality, neither of us has a single thing of use to show for any of it. How fucking sad is that?'

Declan shrugged theatrically, and he said with a laugh, 'Well, when you put it like that, Michael . . .'

Michael was amazed to hear himself laughing, but he was. If anyone had said that he could have found any amusement in this situation he would have thought them mad. But Declan Costello had made him laugh, and that was something good. It felt so good to laugh, to really laugh, to find some humour at last.

They looked at each other for a few moments and then they walked side by side towards White Farm.

Chapter One Hundred and Thirty-Five

White Farm was a smallholding, and it had been a rental property for over two years. There were no animals there any more, but the barns and the outbuildings were still in a very good state of repair. The old couple who had lived there since before the war had died within a few days of each other. Their only son, a grammar-school boy they had both doted on, had emigrated to Canada in the early sixties. His education had eventually alienated him from the people who had happily bankrolled him through university, and who had eventually paid his fare out to Toronto. They had never seen him again – or met his wife, or his children, or their great-grandchildren – but they had been very proud of him, and they had cherished the Christmas cards and photos he had sent to them sporadically. When they died he had arranged his parents' burials, and he had then arranged for the farm he had grown up on to be rented out until property prices started to rise in the UK once again. It had all been done over the phone, and, like all absentee landlords, he had no idea of who might be occupying his old homestead. The rental agents had even less interest and, for someone like

Steven Golding, that was a situation he could exploit without fear of anyone ever bothering to chase him up, or even having to meet with anyone face to face. As long as the rent was paid promptly and, in his case, three months in advance, no one could give the proverbial flying fuck.

He had found all the old couple's belongings stored in the attic; their whole lives were packed into a few boxes. A life of occasional letters and greetings cards, the haphazard affection of a son who had left them both behind as soon as he could. He had hated the son who had walked away from parents who had loved him dearly.

Steven Golding sat at the kitchen table, a big scrubbed-pine monstrosity, that was very old and very scarred. It had seen a lot of use over its lifetime, that was evident. There were people who would pay a lot of money for it, he knew that. People who had to buy other people's lives, other people's possessions, because they didn't have anything of such value in their own families. It was a sad fact, but it was true.

The rain had stopped, but the wind was gathering momentum. It was early October, and autumn was already settling in. Steven Golding stood up quickly, and glanced around him, pleased that the kitchen looked so clean and tidy. He looked at his watch – it was after eight, and he made his way down into the cellar, locking the heavy door behind him carefully. No one was ever getting past that door, it was like Fort Knox. The smell assailed his nostrils, and he smiled at the discomfort he knew it must be causing Jessie Flynn. He stepped carefully down the stairs, and walked to where she was still lying on her bed.

She looked terrible. Her legs were swollen and they looked so painful. Her face was porcelain white, the skin tight on her skull, and her eyes had sunk back into their sockets. She was dying, and she knew that as well as he did. Her breathing was laboured – every breath she took was a long and drawn-out wheeze, loud in the quiet of the basement.

'Jessie, Jessie, wake up, lovely.' He was shaking her roughly and, as she opened her eyes, he bent over her. 'I need to talk to you, Jessie. You're dying, but I think you've worked that out for yourself, haven't you? Your dad should have been here by now. I really thought he would have found you a lot quicker than this.'

She didn't say anything; she was still trying to focus on him, trying to pull herself into the real world.

Steven Golding could see that Jessie Flynn was too far gone for him to have any kind of meaningful conversation with her; she had deteriorated rapidly in the last twelve hours. Her condition shocked him – he had thought she was a much stronger person, and thought she would have fought much harder than she had done. In the beginning she had been so cocky, so arrogant, threatening him with her dad. She had been convinced that he would help her. She had assumed this was about money – money was all people like the Flynns understood. When she had finally realised that it wasn't about him getting a ransom, that she was *never* going to be rescued, never going to leave this basement, she seemed to have succumbed to the inevitable. It was not what he had expected – he was not pleased about this turn of events.

He walked over to the tap by the stairs, and filled a bucket with cold water. Walking back over to her, he threw the contents into her face, drenching her. But, other than trying to catch her breath, which was a natural reaction, the shock of the cold water did nothing to revive her. He could see her trying to focus on him, on her surroundings, and he felt a sudden, fleeting moment of sorrow for her. He had quite liked her, and that wasn't something he had been prepared for – had certainly never expected.

He looked down at her; she was clearly unable to understand what was happening around her. It occurred to him that the infection from her ankles had probably entered her bloodstream, and she was likely suffering from blood poisoning. Even with the stench of faeces in the room, he could still detect the underlying odour of her rotting flesh. It was a sour smell, a heavy, cloying stench that seemed to rise up from her skin, and envelop the very air around her body. It was sharp in the nostrils, made your eyes water, and it smelt like imminent death.

He grabbed her hand, and held it gently between his palms. She was in a sorry state all right. But what could he do? This was what he had intended to happen. He had been left with nobody, all because Patrick Costello had held a grudge against his father. Costello had a perfect alibi for that night, and Steven had finally worked out that Michael Flynn, Costello's up-and-coming young wannabe, had done the dirty deed in his name. He had poured the petrol through the letterbox, and he had wiped out a whole family to better *himself*. All that so he could become Patrick Costello's blue-eyed boy. Well, as the Bible said, be sure your sins will find you out.

Chapter One Hundred and Thirty-Six

Michael and Declan had made their way around the property, carefully and quietly creeping towards the back of the house. It wasn't a large property – a pre-war, two-storey, red-brick house, with no aesthetic value. It was still in possession of its old-style Crittall windows – there was nothing of any beauty to give the house its own identity. It was very well built, but it needed a lot of work on it if anyone was going to live there for any length of time. It had been neglected, and that showed.

Michael looked through the kitchen window; other than this room, the house was in utter darkness. There were no outside lights either, and that was something both Michael and Declan were glad about. It made their life much easier. The kitchen was fairly large, and it looked like something from the Discovery Channel. It had faded yellow linoleum and hand-made wooden cupboards, the cooker was an old gas model, with an eye-level grill pan, and only three burners. The oven didn't look large enough to cook anything bigger than a family-sized chicken. Other than a modern electric kettle, the place could have been a museum.

Michael Flynn looked inside, and whispered to his friend, 'Fucking hell, Declan, this place is like something from fucking *Z Cars*!'

He moved quickly to the back door and, turning the handle slowly, he was relieved to find that it wasn't even locked. This fucker obviously didn't think anyone was going to find him. Stepping into the room, he held his breath, and listened carefully. The place smelt of neglect and poverty.

Declan followed him in, and he shut the door carefully behind him. The place felt totally empty, as if it hadn't been occupied for a long time.

Michael whispered huskily, 'Listen, Declan, can you hear that?'

Declan Costello listened to the house, straining his ears for any sound whatsoever. He shook his head slowly. 'No.'

Michael rolled his eyes in annoyance. He walked slowly across the kitchen. There was a door that was open which led into the hallway and, to the side of it, there was another door. Michael guessed that it led to a cellar. These old places were built to last, and they were also built with farmers in mind – a cellar was essential, an important storage facility, especially in the winter months.

Suddenly the two men heard music. It was very loud, and out of place in the grand scheme of things. It threw them both for a few seconds. Michael recognised the melody – it was 'Almaz' by Randy Crawford. The whole thing was getting more bizarre by the second and, when they heard the basement door being unbolted, they both slipped into the darkness of the hallway.

Michael could feel the thrumming of his heart as he

waited for the man to emerge from the basement. He was holding his breath, frightened to even breathe in case he gave himself away. All he wanted was to find his Jessie, his baby, and to finally prove to her that he loved her no matter what. Then he wanted to destroy this cunt, this man who had somehow snuck past him, had somehow got the better of him, had threatened his family, his life.

The door opened slowly. It was obviously a very heavy door, and it wasn't easy to negotiate. Declan and Michael waited with bated breath for Steven Golding to come into the kitchen, and to finally enter their orbit.

He did so slowly and, as he turned to face the men he knew would be waiting for him, he grinned amiably, saying cheerfully, 'I've been waiting for you, and so has Jessie.'

Chapter One Hundred and Thirty-Seven

Steven Golding looked so much smaller than Michael had expected. He was almost puny. It was hard to believe that this was the man who had caused him so much grief, who had been so fucking elusive. It was a joke, surely?

Golding laughed. 'You're too late, Mr Flynn. We waited for you, but you never came. Now your little Jessie is dying, I'm afraid.'

Michael stepped towards the man, intent on murder, and Declan grabbed him. 'Stop it, Michael. That's what he wants. Let's find Jessie first. I wouldn't believe a word this slippery fucker says.'

Michael knew that Declan was right, he couldn't do anything until he had found his daughter.

Steven Golding shrugged. 'Be my guest, she's down there.' He gestured towards the basement door. 'She's been down there since day one.'

Declan grabbed the man by his throat, and dragged him unceremoniously down the basement stairs behind Michael. The music was much louder inside the room, and it added to the surreal feeling that was enveloping them.

Declan was unsure for a few moments if he was actually seeing what was before his eyes. The stench alone was bad enough, but Jessie, if that really *was* Jessie, was like something from a horror film.

She was so bloated, and her feet, her lovely little feet, were almost devoid of skin. He looked at Michael; he could see the man's disbelief at what he was witnessing. He too was wondering if this was some kind of joke, even though they both knew that wasn't possible.

The photo Michael had been sent had been bad enough but, in the hours since then, it was obvious that Jessie had deteriorated. She looked dead already.

Declan went to the CD player and, kicking it with all his might, he watched as it rose up into the air, and then hit the wall. The ensuing silence was almost deafening.

Michael looked at his daughter, at the condition she was in. It was like a fucking nightmare, beyond anything he could ever have imagined. This was his baby girl – no matter what had happened in the past, she was his only child, and he loved her with a passion.

'Oh my fucking God. Oh dear God. Please don't do this to me . . .' Michael was trying to pick his daughter up in his arms, trying to comfort her. But she was unresponsive, her eyes were closed. Michael was openly crying, sobbing in despair.

Declan punched Golding in the side of his head, and he watched as the man skidded through the shit that was everywhere, and sprawled on the floor. Then grabbing him back up, he bellowed into his face, 'Where's the fucking keys, you fucking piece of shit!'

He was already pulling the man's jacket off him, and searching his trouser pockets. He finally found a set of keys in the man's jacket and, calling out Michael's name, he threw them to him.

As he did so, Jessie let out a long slow breath and opened her eyes. She tried to follow the sound of her father's voice, as he shouted loudly, 'Jessie darling, Jessie, it's me, your dad. Stay with me, love. Please . . .'

Declan screamed at his friend with annoyance, 'Will you unlock her, Michael? For fuck's sake! We need to phone a fucking ambulance! Get her some help! Pull yourself together, man. She needs you!'

Michael seemed suddenly to understand what was needed from him. He was visibly shaking as he picked up the keys from the floor and, taking out his mobile phone, he called for an ambulance. He was as coherent as possible, and he gave the address of White Farm, quickly and succinctly. He also explained the seriousness of his daughter's condition. Then he turned to Declan. 'It's not a key we need. He's fucking screwed these fuckers into place. We need a spanner.'

He turned on Steven Golding then, and, after kicking and punching him to the floor, he grabbed him by his prematurely grey hair and, pulling him back on to his feet, he pushed his face into his and demanded, 'You shackled her, so you can fucking get her loose.'

Both Michael and Declan watched as Golding dropped to the floor. He then crawled through the filth and, pulling himself up with difficulty, he took a spanner from the windowsill, and he held it out to the men like an offering.

'It's too tight, I can't undo it. Her blood has dried all over it. Now it's like fucking glue.'

He was still taunting them. Declan moved quickly to stop Michael from attacking him once more. 'This is like suicide by cop, Michael, but the ambulance will be here soon, remember? Get her free, get her help, and I will keep this cunt on ice, OK? I'll take him to the scrapyard. You've got Branch to smooth your path with the hospital et cetera. He will make sure this doesn't bite anyone's arse. All you need to do is get her help, OK?'

Declan watched as Michael did as he was told and, leaving him to it, he dragged Steven Golding out of the basement, walked him down the lane, and forced him into the boot of Michael's Mercedes.

He sat in the car and waited until the ambulance had arrived before he drove sedately though the London traffic to the scrapyard. Declan guessed that the nutcase wanted Michael to kill him. He had done what he had set out to do, and now he wanted to die. It was all so fucking mental. His punishment could be arranged, only at a later date. He wasn't getting away with this that easily, not by a long chalk.

Chapter One Hundred and Thirty-Eight

Timothy Branch arrived at the hospital, aware that he would be expected to smooth everything over for Michael Flynn, and to make sure that Michael could get on with the business at hand with the minimum of fuss.

When he saw young Jessie Flynn he was, for the first time in his life, speechless. The girl was lying on a bed in intensive care, and Michael Flynn was standing beside her bed, holding her hand. *He* looked seriously ill too – his face was devoid of colour, even his lips were white.

But Jessie, young Jessie, was a terrifying sight.

'Fucking hell, Michael, I'm so sorry. I'm so very sorry.'

And he meant it. Michael could hear it in the man's voice.

'He fucking planned this, Timothy. He shackled her to a bed, and he left her there to rot. Her heart gave out. The infection in her blood weakened it. Twenty-two years old and she had a massive fucking coronary. I got there too late. I was too late to help her.'

Michael started to cry again.

Timothy Branch automatically put his arm around the man's shoulders; he couldn't even imagine the pain that he must be feeling. To lose a child was hard enough for anyone, but to know she had been murdered – had died a slow and painful death – had to be unendurable.

'Listen, Michael, I will sort this, don't worry. I swear to you.'

Michael nodded. He appreciated the man's promise – for the first time he actually felt that the man was trustworthy. But it was the way Jessie had died. Even a fucking no-mark like Branch couldn't help but be affected. Just looking at her broken body was hard enough.

'That bastard soaked her with cold water, he starved her, he fucking held her there with home-made manacles. You should see her poor legs. The fetters were so fucking tight they rubbed away every piece of her skin – they even scraped against her bones. She must have been in absolute agony, Timothy. My baby lived her last few weeks on this earth in excruciating pain, waiting for me to find her, to help her. But I was too late.'

Detective Inspector Timothy Branch would never have believed that he would feel any kind of pity for Michael Flynn, but he did. He felt the man's pain as if it was his own. No one should ever have to see a child like this. It was outrageous – it took a certain kind of hate to be capable of harming another person so wickedly. Child murderers, rapists, were capable of such viciousness, of such cowardice, because *they* were cowards. They bullied the weakest people in society, little children and anyone who was smaller or weaker than them. Now Jessie Flynn, whose father was the hardest man in Europe, let alone London or the UK, who was responsible for every earn available, was dead. Murdered.

If this could happen to Michael Flynn's child, what chance did anyone else have? This just proved that no one was immune to hatred. As a police officer, Timothy had always known that – he had seen so much mindless violence, so many pointless murders. But when something like this happened to a man like Michael Flynn, a man who was by all accounts at the pinnacle of his power, it was food for thought. Here he was, crushed and weeping as he looked at his daughter's bruised and broken body. It was an eye-opening situation.

Michael Flynn looked at Timothy Branch, and he smiled eerily. 'I've got him though, Timothy, I've got the fucker, and I will make him pay. Don't you worry about that.'

Timothy Branch didn't answer him. He just stood there, silently thanking the Good Lord that it wasn't *his* child lying there dead.

Chapter One Hundred and Thirty-Nine

As Josephine heard her husband running up the stairs, she checked her make-up in her dressing table mirror, pleased to see that she looked perfect.

She sat up straighter in her chair, and turned off her DVD player. She knew that Michael hated her films, especially that she watched the same ones over and over again.

As he came into her bedroom, she was ready for him, she had a half smile on her face, and she looked towards him quizzically. It was a look she had practised and perfected over the years. There was no way she would lower herself to ask him why he had not bothered to get in touch with her. She still had her pride.

He stood before her, like an avenging angel, and she could see that he wasn't his usual self. In fact, he looked terrible. His clothes were crumpled as if he had slept in them, and he was badly in need of a shave. She looked him up and down, very slowly, taking in his dishevelled appearance, and letting him know she had noticed it.

'I thought I heard you, Michael, but it's been a while so I wasn't holding out too much hope of seeing you.'

He didn't say anything to her, and she looked at him straight in the eyes.

'Is that all you've got to say to me, Josephine? My mother is dead. I assumed that even *you* might have worried about how I was coping with that! She was murdered, remember?'

Josephine could hear the antagonism in his voice, the sarcasm that was dripping from every word he spoke. She wasn't going to say anything that would give him reason to attack her again, as he had the last time she had seen him. She had not been willing to accept his conduct then, and she wasn't prepared to accept it now. Even if he did have a right to call her out about her behaviour, that didn't mean that he should do it. They were married and, no matter what had happened to them in the past, they had always loved each other.

'I'm sorry about your mum, Michael. Of course I am. How can you even say something like that to me?'

She sounded so offended, so insulted by him. It was crystal clear to him now just how devious she actually was – had always been. He gave a low, mocking laugh. He was seeing her with fresh eyes. She looked wonderful – why wouldn't she? Her whole life was taken up with her appearance, with repairing her make-up, making sure her eyebrows were plucked and shaped, that her lipstick was faultless. Her hair looked salon-perfect twenty-four/seven, and her nails were coloured, shaped and buffed with a diligence that had to be seen to be believed.

'You're a piece of work, Josephine, do you know that? In case you were wondering, your only daughter's dead. Jessie had a massive heart attack today. Twenty-two years old, and her heart gave out. The man who had taken her, who had contacted *you*, if you remember, that man who you ignored, basically *tortured* our Jessie to death. She died in fucking agony waiting for someone to find her. Now she is gone from us, Josephine, like my old mum.'

Josephine knew that Michael was telling her the truth, but it was hard to take it all in.

'I am waiting for some kind of reaction from you, Josephine. I just told you that your only child is dead, and nothing. Not a fucking word.'

He stood there, looming over her, and waited for her to say something – anything – to acknowledge her only child's demise. But she didn't say a word.

'Do you know what, Josephine? Patrick Costello said something to me many years ago, and I never understood the real meaning of it until recently. You were just at your hoarding stage, and I was really worried about you, about your mental health. He knew that, and we were out one night, and he said to me, "Always remember this, Michael – people only do to you what you let them." I didn't understand what he meant until recently. He was a wise fucking man in some ways – mad as a fucking Russian road map – but he had you sussed out right, lady.'

Josephine could not believe that her Jessie was dead. It wasn't something she had ever contemplated, but now a part of her was relieved. It meant that Jake would now be wholly hers – hers and Michael's. He was the son they had never had.

'I can't believe what you're telling me, Michael. My baby girl, my Jessie is dead. Poor Jake. He's an orphan. We are all he's got left.'

Michael shook his head angrily. 'Oh, save it for someone who cares! Jake will survive, I will see to that. But I'm warning you now, Josephine, you are going to the nut farm, and this time I'm not going to stop it. If you don't go, then I will turn my back on you completely. Do you hear me? I'm deadly serious this time. I will *never* forgive you, Josephine, for what happened to our Jessie – for not even *trying* to let me know immediately when you heard from that cunt who was holding her hostage. You put yourself first as always, and I know now that you always will. You're going to end up a lonely old woman because I'm finished with you. Any love I had for you – and I loved you with all my heart – has died. It's gone.'

Josephine jumped from her chair, and she tried to grab her husband's hands. She couldn't live without him, without her Michael. He was the only thing that she really cared about.

But he pushed her away from him, unwilling to even touch her. 'I'm arranging with your shrink that if you don't go into hospital voluntarily in the next five days, I will have you sectioned. I can do that, Josephine, and I fucking will if I have to. Don't bank on your latest shrink to get you out of it. I pay him, and he will do whatever I ask him to.'

She sat back in her chair, panic overwhelming her. He meant every word he was saying, and she didn't know how she could stop him. He turned away from her in disgust.

At the door, he turned back to look at her, and said sadly, 'Jessie is dead, and you don't even seem able to fucking take that onboard. She died a death I wouldn't wish on my worst enemy and you've not even asked me anything about her at all. I know that you won't even bother to go to your daughter's fucking funeral, but you *will* go to the nut-house this time, Josephine.'

She looked at her husband, her handsome husband, who had always stood by her no matter what, and suddenly she felt so very lonely and frightened. She had pushed him away for years. She had known that he would never have done the dirty on her – he was too decent, too nice a person. She had relied on that, she had relied on his love for her.

He was still standing there, in the doorway, watching her intently. 'By the way, I'm burying Jessie with my mum. They were close and I want them to be together. I can't stand the thought of our Jessie down there in the ground all alone.' He swallowed back the tears once more. 'There was a lot of my mum in Jessie. I realise that now.'

He walked out of the room, and she heard him walking away from her, his tread heavy as he went down the stairs. She could hear Jake's shrieks of excitement as he was picked up and thrown in the air by his granddad. But it meant nothing to her – all she cared about was that her husband was going to walk away from her. She was finally without his protection, and it terrified her. Every time one of her doctors had recommended that she needed serious treatment, needed to be hospitalised, she had made sure that Michael replaced them. He had always tried to do whatever she wanted him to do. He had always done everything in his power to make her happy.

She put her head in her hands. She had never felt such a feeling of despair before in her whole entire life. She wouldn't cry, though, even though she wanted to. She *couldn't*, she could *not* let *anything* interfere with her make-up. She stood up quickly and, pulling out the small padded stool from underneath the dressing table, she sank down on to it. She stared at her face for long moments in the mirror, automatically checking her make-up, and she sighed with relief as she saw that it was all still in place. It was her mask. It was the façade that she showed to the world. But, deep down inside, she knew that she had not faced the real world for years. She registered suddenly that her daughter was really gone. That her Jessie would never again ring her, or come to visit her son. Her Jessie, her baby girl, was dead.

She closed her eyes in distress. Michael was right. She honestly didn't care enough about anyone; all she was really bothered about was Michael's threat of putting her into a mental institution. She wasn't a fucking fool. If she went into one, she knew that it would be a long time before she would ever get out again.

Chapter One Hundred and Forty

Michael drove through the gates of the scrapyard slowly. The old boy who worked the night shift was a stickler for fucking social etiquette. Michael waved at him in a suitably friendly fashion, and he saw his gratified smile. He sighed in annoyance. He was a nice old geezer, a Face in his younger days, but that didn't warrant all this fucking babysitting and smiles every time he drove into the yard. Declan had always said, it takes two minutes of your life to recognise a good worker, and that recognition would guarantee their loyalty for twenty years. He was absolutely right, of course. But tonight Michael wasn't in the mood.

He parked his Range Rover next to his Mercedes and, as he got out and stood on the tarmac stretching, he was gratified to hear that whoever was in the boot of his Merc was making one hell of a racket.

Declan came out of the Portakabin doorway. He looked huge against the lights. Declan had gradually got bigger and bigger over the years, and it was only now that Michael was really noticing that.

'Drink first?' Declan was miming drinking a cup of tea with his little finger raised up like an old biddy.

Michael laughed despite himself. You couldn't not like Declan Costello – the man was a genuine diamond. Even at a time like this he could bring a smile to Michael's face.

'Pour me a large brandy, but first up, open this fucking boot.'

Declan took the Mercedes keys from his trouser pocket, and opened the boot quickly.

Steven Golding was lying there, and he blinked as his eyes adjusted to the sudden light. He trained his gaze on Michael warily.

Michael looked around him. He was aware that there was no way this man could escape from the scrapyard's premises. There was a very high brick wall surrounding the place for a start, and the barbed wire that had been placed on the top of it years before had always been a very good deterrent. The gates were electric, and they too were very high. The night-watchman had a large German Shepherd who wasn't that enamoured of new people. There were also three other large dogs – two Dobermans and a Rottweiler bitch, which roamed the grounds during the daytime. The people who owned them worked there. It suited everyone to let the animals run free. There were people who came in ostensibly to look for a specific part for a specific car, who were quite capable of going on the rob. The hounds made sure they didn't feel the urge to come back later, when it was dark.

He looked once more at Steven Golding; it was patently obvious that the man wasn't going to climb out of the boot by himself. Michael laughed again, this was a fucking joke.

'Do you know something, Steven? I never knew there was anyone in your house that night. I really believed it was empty. I wasn't happy about burning people's possessions, you know? But it was for Patrick Costello, and I wanted to prove myself to him. I wanted to make something of myself. I wanted to be able to give my mum a few quid, make her life that bit easier. She had brought me up all on her own since I was a baby. I never would have dreamt of harming anyone. It was Patrick Costello who wanted that. He could be a very petty man, a very vicious man.'

Steven Golding was still lying in the boot of Michael's Mercedes. It was a fucking big boot, and Steven Golding was more than comfortable it seemed.

'If you had just come to me, if you had fucking had the sense to call me out, confront me, I would have done anything to make amends – I swear that to you. I've never really got over it. Even now I still wake up sweating. But I did learn how to put it aside. If I hadn't managed to do that, I would have ended up as big a fucking headcase as you are.'

Steven Golding looked feral. The man had no saving graces at all, from his rotten teeth to his pock-marked and scarred skin. He was obviously a loner. Michael knew that the man was mentally ill, and that he had been in and out of different institutions for the best part of his life. That was sad. But Michael couldn't change anything that had happened, even if he had wanted to. Steven Golding looked exactly what he was – a broken-down, disillusioned fantasist, who had been deprived of his whole family as a teenage boy. He was quite obviously madder than a fucking bull with a red-hot poker up its arse, and had managed to infiltrate every aspect of Michael's life, eventually destroying not just his only daughter but his mother as well.

'Do you know what, Steven? Stay where you are.'

Michael shut the boot noisily. Then he walked leisurely to one of the outbuildings. It was a shed that had been constructed over twenty years before from a job-lot of corrugated iron, and it was where they kept most of the flammable liquids.

Michael went inside and he felt around for one of the petrol cans that he knew would be there. He felt the weight of it in his hand, and then he shook it gently, relishing the noise of the liquid as it moved around.

He walked back to his Mercedes, calling out to Declan, who he knew had been watching everything from the Portakabin window. When Declan appeared, he gestured to him to open the boot once more. Declan Costello, as always, was more than happy to oblige.

Steven Golding was still curled up. As Michael opened the petrol can and started to pour it all over him, Golding attempted to get up and tried to get out of the boot. Michael Flynn punched him back down. The stench of petrol fumes was heavy in the air.

Steven Golding was terrified, and Michael could see that. His eyes were bulging out of his head with the fear of being burned alive.

'Answer me one last thing – would you have harmed my grandson?'

Steven Golding shook his head. 'Of course not. I would have left him alone.'

Michael snorted with derision. 'Why didn't you just come after me? *I* was the culprit, for fuck's sake!'

Golding looked him in the eye as he said, 'Too easy. I

know you will suffer much more over your Jessie and your mum's death. Guilt is a very destructive force.'

Michael didn't answer him. After all, who could argue with the truth? He took a book of matches out of his pocket and, smiling slightly, he said steadily, 'The truth is, Steven, I'm actually going to enjoy this.'

Steven Golding tried to get out of the boot, and Michael Flynn hammered him over and over again until the man couldn't move. Michael felt the man's face collapse beneath his fists and he still didn't stop battering him. He carried on hitting the man until he was completely spent.

He picked the book of matches up from the ground and tore off a match. Lighting it, he used it to ignite the whole pack, which he threw casually on to the man's chest.

As the whole car went up in flames, Declan shouted, 'What the fuck are you doing, Michael? Your car! What about your fucking car?'

Michael Flynn stood watching the man responsible for the vicious murders of his mother and daughter squirming and screaming in pain without blinking. Then he looked at Declan Costello and, laughing loudly, he said, 'Relax, Declan, for Christ's sake! I reported this car stolen hours ago.'

Declan went back into the Portakabin and came back with two large drinks. He handed one to Michael, and he stood beside him as Steven Golding was burned beyond recognition.

When the car finally blew they were both sitting side by side on the steps of the offices.

'It's over, Michael.'

Michael sipped his brandy, savouring the taste. 'Do you

know the worst of it for me now, Declan? I wish that cunt had been in the house that night. I wish I had burned him to death with his sisters and his mum and dad. So what does that make me?'

Declan put his arm around his friend's shoulders and, sighing heavily, he said, '*Human*, Michael. Unfortunately, that's what it makes you – *human*.'

Epilogue

The house of the righteous contains great treasure,
but the income of the wicked brings them trouble

Proverbs 15:6

Chapter One Hundred and Forty-One

'Nana looks different.'

Michael laughed at his grandson's seriousness. 'I know she does. She's not well. But she's getting better, that's the main thing.'

Jake nodded, but he wasn't so sure about anything any more. He knew his real mum was dead. He had seen her grave and she was buried with his great-nana Hannah. His granddad went to visit them a lot, and he sometimes went with him. It was funny thinking his mum was dead, up in heaven, but one of the nuns at school had told him that sometimes Jesus missed people so much that he called them back up to heaven early. He liked to think that was true, but he wasn't sure if it was. His mum had been a bit of a cow – at least that is what his nana Josephine had used to say about her. Now his nana Josephine was in a hospital, and she acted very strangely. He could see her walking towards them, and Jake felt his heart sink inside his chest.

'Here she comes, Jake.'

Jake could hear the false gaiety in his granddad's voice.

Josephine walked across the grass towards her husband and her grandson slowly. The drugs were responsible for that; she couldn't bring herself to break into a sprint these days. She sat down at the picnic table opposite her husband. He still looked so good, so very handsome. He got better looking as he got older; it was unfair.

Michael smiled at her. 'You're looking well, Josephine.'

But she wasn't. She looked awful these days. She didn't bother with her appearance any more. It was a good thing, according to her doctor. He wasn't so sure himself.

She didn't answer him. Instead she looked at Jake and, holding her arms out, she said sadly, 'I could do with a hug, young man.'

Jake looked at his granddad and, when Michael nodded slightly, he went around the table, and allowed his nana to squeeze him to her tightly. When Jake finally managed to pull himself away from her, he went straight back to sit beside his granddad.

Josephine knew that she had been well and truly rejected by her grandson, but there was nothing she could do about it.

'Really, Josephine, you do look much better. The doctor told me that you were finding it much easier to go outside. It's wonderful to see you out here with us now.'

Josephine looked at her husband for long moments. He visited her twice, sometimes three times, a week and he seemed genuinely interested in her progress. But it was bullshit. She wasn't stupid. She knew him better than he knew himself. He was just doing his duty. That was his trouble, he didn't have a treacherous bone in his body. He was determined to divorce her, though, she knew that.

'How are you, Michael? Good?'

He smiled gently. 'Yeah, I'm fine. You know me, same old, same old.'

Josephine nodded in agreement. 'I hear you're having a right old time of it. Katherine Rourk, Danny's *daughter*. I bet she could be *your* daughter, eh? She's young enough.'

Michael didn't answer her; it wasn't any of her business.

She laughed nastily. 'I still hear everything, Michael. I'm not fucking dead yet.'

He smiled back at her but his voice was steely as he said, 'If you don't watch your fucking mouth, that could be arranged sooner than you think, Josephine.'

'Are you threatening me?'

He saw how she narrowed her eyes, and he wondered how he had let her rule him for so long. 'Why would I do that, Josephine? If I was threatening you, believe me, you'd know it. I come here to see how you arc and to bring your little grandson in to visit you. There's no hidden agenda.'

Then she said angrily, 'It's been nearly six months, Michael. I want to go home.'

Michael turned to Jake. 'You can go inside now, and spend the pound I gave you in the sweet shop. Wait in the reception and I'll be there in a minute, OK?'

Jake nodded.

'Say goodbye to Nana.'

Jake waved at her quickly and, running off, he called out 'Goodbye' over his shoulder.

Michael knew that the lad found Josephine a trial – as *he* did if he was honest. She was stranger than ever now, but it was all to the good, according to the doctors. Personally, he thought she was getting madder by the day.

'Look, Josephine, I can't control everything any more. This is a proper hospital – you can't just buy the doctors here, and choose your own fucking meds. Look how far that got you. You need to do whatever the doctors tell you to do. For once in your life, Josephine, you can't rely on me to bail you out. You were *sectioned*, for fuck's sake! You can't just fucking *choose* what you want to do any more. It's out of our hands. The doctors decide when you can go home and, when that day comes, I have purchased a lovely little cottage for you. You will love it.'

'I've already got a home.'

He sighed heavily; he was sick and tired of this. 'Not any more you haven't. Once we get the divorce, I will see you all right. But you will never come back to that house again. It's in Jake's name now anyway.'

Josephine grinned nastily. 'You're loving this, aren't you? You dumped me, and then you put me away. Katie Rourk must be a blinding fuck, Michael. Got you right where she fucking wants you!'

Michael stood up slowly. 'I'm not doing this, Josephine. I've told you before. It's over between us. I will *never* forgive you for what happened to our Jessie. I will take care of you up to a point – I owe you that much. But don't treat me like a fucking earhole, OK? I come here so you can see Jake, so I can see how you're getting on. After all, I *am* the one footing the *fucking* bill for this, aren't I? If I pull out, lady, you will end up in a local NHS nut ward somewhere, so don't bite the hand that feeds you.'

Josephine couldn't believe that her Michael couldn't find

it in his heart to forgive her; he had *always* forgiven her in the past, no matter what she had done. She grabbed his hands in hers, and she tried to pull him back into his seat, to make him sit down and talk with her.

'Please, Michael, I promise you I will do anything . . . But don't do this to me . . .'

He pulled away from her and, stepping back, he said gently, 'I've got to go, Josephine. But if you don't stop this I can't visit you any more. I've told you over and over again I will bankroll your treatment, and I will always look out for you. But our marriage is over.'

He walked away from her purposefully, aware that he didn't have even a small sliver of doubt about what he was doing. She had ceased to exist for him when he had seen that letter. It was like he had woken from a coma, and seen his wife for what she really was. It had been a revelation. He had suddenly seen how much she had manipulated him over the years and, the worst thing was, he knew that he had gone along with it all: her agoraphobia, her fear of telephones, her fear of fucking everything that didn't suit her. But she didn't have a fear of wine – she could neck that all day and night. He had swallowed it until he had seen that letter which resulted in his daughter dying in such pain and with such injuries. Knowing that if Josephine had just *once* put someone else first it might have all have been avoided wasn't something he could excuse.

He walked into the reception room. Jake was waiting for him – he looked so worried, bless him.

'Is Nana OK?'

Michael grinned. ''Course she is. Come on, let's get

home, shall we? Dana is cooking us a shepherd's pie! With real shepherds in!'

Jake smiled a real smile at last. 'That's my favourite dinner!'

'And mine too! What's the chances of that, eh?' He grasped his grandson's hand and walked him out to the car park. Jake stopped in front of the Mercedes, and Michael looked at him quizzically.

'What's wrong, Jake?'

The little boy suddenly looked vulnerable and frightened. Michael smiled at him gently. 'You can tell me anything, Jake, you know that.'

Jake started to cry, and Michael rushed over to him, and he swept him up into his arms, hugging the boy to his chest tightly.

'Nana scares me. I don't like coming here, Granddad.'

Michael knew then, without a shadow of a doubt, that he would never come back here again. 'Then we won't come here any more, Jake.'

Jake pulled himself away from his granddad's chest and looked into his face as he said seriously, 'Promise?'

Michael smiled at the little lad; he loved him so very much. 'Promise.'

Chapter One Hundred and Forty-Two

Declan was well on the way to getting drunk. He was on the borderline at the moment, but he was feeling good. He watched the doorway, expecting Michael. Declan thought it was good for Michael to get out more, he had spent so much of his life pussy-footing around Josephine, it was good for the man to finally just do whatever he wanted to. It had been a hard year for him, he had buried his mother and his daughter, and he had seen his wife, the love of his life, sectioned, and dragged out of his home kicking and screaming. He deserved a bit of R and R. He had been getting that with young Katie Rourk, by all accounts, and good luck to him. Michael had never been the unfaithful type. He was a one-woman man. If anyone else had married Josephine they would have been out on the nest in no time, but not Michael.

Declan looked around the bar. There was no doubt that, for a private drinking club, it had a very good feel to it. No one got in unless they were members, and Michael and he agreed the memberships! How fucking neat was that? He could come here knowing that he wouldn't have to deal with anyone that he didn't want to.

He gestured to the barmaid for another drink, and she did as he requested immediately. It was early evening and the place was nearly empty. It didn't really liven up till later, so he was enjoying the quiet. He picked up his Jack Daniel's and Coke and, raising his glass towards the barmaid, he took a long drink.

Michael came down the stairs a few seconds later, all smiles, which pleased Declan. The man was finally looking relaxed again.

The barmaid was tiny – under five feet tall, and she had the smallest hands and feet Declan had ever seen on a grown woman. Her hair, on the other hand, was *huge*. It was beautiful, her crowning glory, and she was always smiling. She had that kind of nature – she was a glass-half-full girl, as she had told Declan on more than one occasion. She automatically mixed Michael Flynn a large vodka and tonic.

He took it from her with a smile and, turning to Declan, he said happily, 'I needed this, Declan. It's been a fucking mad day.' He took a large gulp of his drink; it was strong, even for him.

'So? How was Josephine?'

Michael shrugged. 'Same old, same old!'

Declan laughed then. 'Hark at you! Who'd have thought it, eh?'

Michael lit a cigarette, and he pulled on it quickly. As he blew out the smoke, he said honestly, 'I never thought we would ever have broken up. But we have, and I'm glad.' Michael grinned suddenly. Then, leaning forward, he said quietly, 'I have some news for you, Declan – you're the first person to know.'

Declan laughed at his mate's cloak-and-dagger voice. 'Oh yeah? So what is it, then?'

Michael Flynn grinned happily. 'Katie's pregnant. It wasn't planned, but I've got to tell you, Declan, I'm over the fucking moon.'

Declan Costello was taken aback, but he recovered quickly. 'Congratulations, mate. How old is Katie anyway?'

Michael gestured to the barmaid to refill their glasses.

'She's twenty-six. Not as young as she looks. But still a lot younger than me! Josephine has already pointed that out today. But I don't give a toss, Declan. I really care about her, and I think she does me. And I want a child, I want a child of my own. I will marry her, Declan, and I will give her and my babies the world.'

Declan Costello was speechless.

Michael Flynn looked into his friend's stunned countenance and he said gaily, 'I'm the wrong side of fifty, and I have nothing left, other than Jake, of course. I want what I never had, Declan – a couple of kids, *nice* kids, and a woman who isn't a fucking walking headcase. Josephine's doctor told me that nothing I could have done would have changed her life. She has a personality disorder. I always thought it was my fault that she wasn't the full five quid. But it would have happened anyway, no matter what. Katie is fun, she makes me laugh. So much of my life was spent holding Josephine's hand, or living down my only daughter's antics, pretending that I didn't care, when I did care. I cared more than I could ever let on. But not any more. That's all over now. She's gone – my Jessie is dead and gone. Josephine and all her fucking problems are gone. This time around I want what everyone else takes for granted. I just want a normal fucking life.'

Declan Costello smiled. He raised his glass in a toast, and he said sincerely, 'To you, Michael, and the next generation of Flynns.'

Have you read all of Martina Cole's phenomenal bestsellers? Available now in paperback and ebook.

DANGEROUS LADY

No one thinks a seventeen-year-old girl can take on the hard men of London's gangland, but it's a mistake to underestimate Maura Ryan: she's tough, clever and beautiful – and one very dangerous lady . . .

THE LADYKILLER

George Markham has a nasty little hobby, which erupts into an orgy of vicious sexual depravity. In charge of the case, DI Kate Burrows fears she'll lose everything she's ever cared about to . . . the ladykiller.

THE RUNAWAY

Cathy Connor's miserable life as a prostitute's child changes forever when she is forced into care. When she crosses paths with ruthless Eamonn Docherty she's an equal match for him. And nothing's going to make her run away . . .

TWO WOMEN

Brutalised throughout her marriage, Sue Dalston smashes her husband's skull with a claw hammer in a final act of desperation. Celled up with murderess Matilda Enderby, their fates become inextricably linked. And no one could have predicted the consequences . . .

BROKEN

One by one, children are being abandoned. Thankfully, they're rescued from harm. Then one victim is not so lucky, and DI Kate Burrows knows she's in a race against time to save lives . . .

FACELESS

Eleven years ago Marie Carter was convicted of killing her two best friends. Now she's being released from prison. But some people out there are watching her – they know that Marie Carter wants retribution.

MAURA'S GAME

Maura Ryan was once the queen of the criminal underworld. But enemies from her past are closing in and they're about to learn that the dangerous lady is back and she's as lethal as ever . . .

THE KNOW

When her eleven-year-old daughter Kira disappears, Joanie Brewer's darkest fears are realised, and her obsession to uncover the truth threatens to destroy her entire family.

THE GRAFT

Nick Leary couldn't say what kept him awake that night. When he heard footsteps downstairs, his instinct was to fight. But what happened was the start of something he could not stop . . .

THE TAKE

Families should stick together, but behind closed doors, jealousy and betrayal fester until everyone's life is infected. For the Jacksons, loyalty cannot win out. In their world everyone is on the take.

CLOSE

Patrick Brodie and Lily Diamond are determined their children will have everything they didn't. But when the unthinkable happens, Lily is left on her own in a world where you can trust no one and where your sins will find you out . . .

FACES

Danny Cadogan's ruthlessness doesn't stop at his front door. He rules his wife Mary and his children with an iron will – and his fists. But for a Face at the top of his game, there's only one way to go. Down . . .

THE BUSINESS

When Mary Dooley's husband is killed, she has to watch her daughter Imelda's life spiral into a vicious, hate-fuelled cycle of drugs and prostitution, whilst her adored grandchildren fight for survival – against all the odds.

HARD GIRLS

When a prostitute's body is found lifeless, mutilated and brutally raped, DCI Annie Carr and retired DCI Kate Burrows are determined to put the killer behind bars. But whoever it is won't be easily caught. And they are just warming up . . .

THE FAMILY

Phillip Murphy worships his mum and loves his wife Christine with a vengeance. To Phillip, family is everything. But he has rules, and he expects loyalty. Once you're in the family, you're in it for life.

THE FAITHLESS

To the outside world, Cynthia Tailor is someone to envy. But behind closed doors, her family see her for the cruel woman she really is . . . and, for her children, the pain she causes them will stay with them forever.

THE LIFE

Gangster brothers Peter and Daniel Bailey rule London's East End and it seems that no one can touch them. Daniel's daughter Tania is shielded from the Life, but when a terrible tragedy occurs, she is forced to make an irrevocable choice about her future . . .